# Understanding Modern Economics

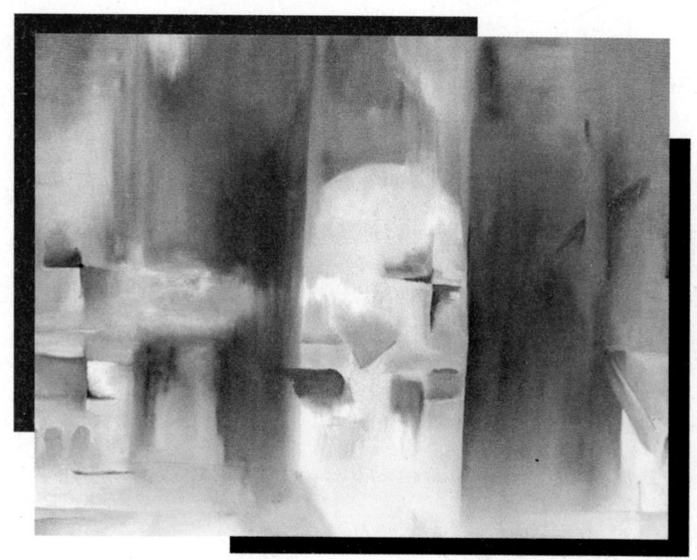

# The Addison-Wesley Series in Economics

**Abel/Bernanke**
*Macroeconomics*

**Bade/Parkin**
*Foundations of Economics*

**Bierman/Fernandez**
*Game Theory with Economic Applications*

**Binger/Hoffman**
*Microeconomics with Calculus*

**Boyer**
*Principles of Transportation Economics*

**Branson**
*Macroeconomic Theory and Policy*

**Bruce**
*Public Finance and the American Economy*

**Byrns/Stone**
*Economics*

**Carlton/Perloff**
*Modern Industrial Organization*

**Caves/Frankel/Jones**
*World Trade and Payments: An Introduction*

**Chapman**
*Environmental Economics: Theory, Application, and Policy*

**Cooter/Ulen**
*Law and Economics*

**Downs**
*An Economic Theory of Democracy*

**Ehrenberg/Smith**
*Modern Labor Economics*

**Ekelund/Tollison**
*Economics*

**Fusfeld**
*The Age of the Economist*

**Gerber**
*International Economics*

**Ghiara**
*Learning Economics*

**Gordon**
*Macroeconomics*

**Gregory**
*Essentials of Economics*

**Gregory/Stuart**
*Russian and Soviet Economic Performance and Structure*

**Hartwick/Olewiler**
*The Economics of Natural Resource Use*

**Hubbard**
*Money, the Financial System, and the Economy*

**Hughes/Cain**
*American Economic History*

**Husted/Melvin**
*International Economics*

**Jehle/Reny**
*Advanced Microeconomic Theory*

**Klein**
*Mathematical Methods for Economics*

**Krugman/Obstfeld**
*International Economics*

**Laidler**
*The Demand for Money*

**Leeds/von Allmen**
*The Economics of Sports*

**Lipsey/Courant/Ragan**
*Economics*

**Melvin**
*International Money and Finance*

**Miller**
*Economics Today*

**Miller**
*Understanding Modern Economics*

**Miller/Benjamin/North**
*The Economics of Public Issues*

**Miller/Benjamin**
*The Economics of Macro Issues*

**Mills/Hamilton**
*Urban Economics*

**Mishkin**
*The Economics of Money, Banking, and Financial Markets*

**Parkin**
*Economics*

**Perloff**
*Microeconomics*

**Phelps**
*Health Economics*

**Riddell/Shackelford/Stamos/Schneider**
*Economics: A Tool for Critically Understanding Society*

**Ritter/Silber/Udell**
*Principles of Money, Banking, and Financial Markets*

**Rohlf**
*Introduction to Economic Reasoning*

**Ruffin/Gregory**
*Principles of Economics*

**Sargent**
*Rational Expectations and Inflation*

**Scherer**
*Industry Structure, Strategy, and Public Policy*

**Schotter**
*Microeconomics*

**Stock/Watson**
*Introduction to Econometrics*

**Studenmund**
*Using Econometrics*

**Tietenberg**
*Environmental and Natural Resource Economics*

**Tietenberg**
*Environmental Economics and Policy*

**Todaro/Smith**
*Economic Development*

**Waldman**
*Microeconomics*

**Waldman/Jensen**
*Industrial Organization: Theory and Practice*

**Weil**
*Economic Growth*

**Williamson**
*Macroeconomics*

# Understanding Modern Economics

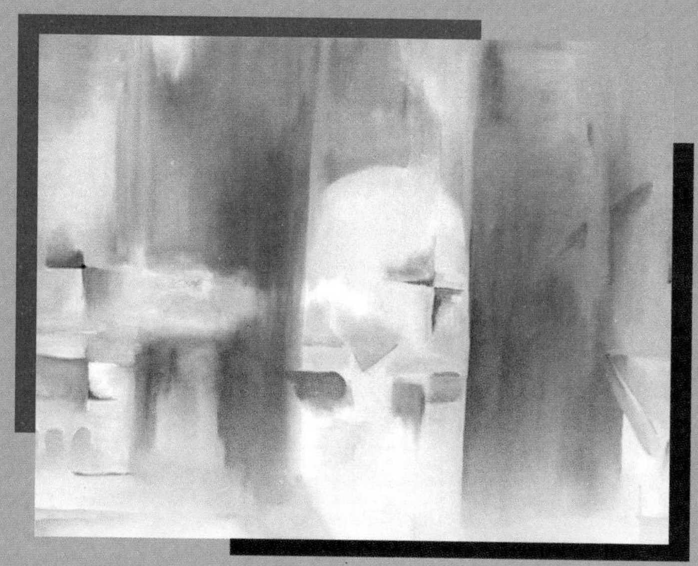

Roger LeRoy Miller

*Institute for University Studies, Arlington, Texas*

Boston San Francisco New York
London Toronto Sydney Tokyo Singapore Madrid
Mexico City Munich Paris Cape Town Hong Kong Montreal

**Cover Image: Original painting *Circulation, Place de l'Étoile,* by Francette Labatut**

Editor-in-Chief: *Denise Clinton*
Acquisitions Editor: *Adrienne D'Ambrosio*
Director of Development: *Sylvia Mallory*
Senior Development Editor: *Rebecca Ferris-Caruso*
Managing Editor: *James Rigney*
Senior Production Supervisor: *Katherine Watson*
Design Manager: *Regina Hagen Kolenda*
Executive Marketing Manager: *Stephen Frail*
Senior Media Producer: *Melissa Honig*
Cover Designer: *Regina Hagen Kolenda*
Digital Assets Manager: *Jason Miranda*
Senior Manufacturing Buyer: *Hugh Crawford*
Production House: *Orr Book Services*
Compositor: *Nesbitt Graphics, Inc.*

**Photo Credits:** *© AP Photo/Jerome Delay, 4; © Kevin M. Polowy/Evening Observer, 74; © Daly and Newton, 130; © Beth Anderson, 150; © AFP/Corbis, 239; © AP Photo/Misha Japaridze, 274; © Deborah Feingold/ Corbis, 316; © Beth Anderson, 340.*

Library of Congress Cataloging-in-Publication Data

Miller, Roger LeRoy.
Understanding modern economics / Roger LeRoy Miller
p. cm.
Includes bibliographical references and index.
ISBN 0-321-19753-4 (alk. paper)
1. Economics. I. Title

HB171.5.M64384 2005
330—dc22 2004000648

Copyright © 2005 by Pearson Education, Inc., publishing as Pearson Addison Wesley

All rights reserved. No part of this publication may be reproduced, stored in a retrieval system, or transmitted, in any form or by any means, electronic, mechanical, photocopying, recording, or otherwise, without the prior written permission of the publisher. Printed in the United States of America.

For information on obtaining permission for use of material in this work, please submit a written request to Pearson Education, Inc., Rights and Contract Department, 75 Arlington St., Suite 300, Boston, MA 02116 or fax your request to (617) 848-7047.

ISBN: 0-321-19753-4

3 4 5 6 7 8 9 10—VHP—08

# Brief Contents

# Detailed Contents

# Economics

## . . . a very wise investment in *every* student's future.

Economics instructors have long known what students will soon discover for themselves in this breakthrough book—that knowledge of the principles of economics is important to their lives every day . . . that the ability to analyze not only economic questions but those in politics, personal finance, and numerous other fields enriches their ability to function successfully throughout life.

But how can instructors best show students taking their first and perhaps only economics course how beneficial and practical knowledge of economics really is? I believe that many of the best ways are contained within the pages of *Understanding Modern Economics*, which I wrote specifically for the one-term survey course. This book—together with its interactive CD-ROM—presents economics with a judicious mix of theory and intriguing examples. There is just enough theory to allow students to fully understand economic reasoning and more than enough examples to drive this reasoning home.

**Essential theory . . . the practical tool of economic analysis.**
With this concise 460-page book to guide students, economic theory isn't intimidating. Rather, students learn to explore the practical value of economic analysis as it relates to economists' favorite topics—supply and demand, the theory of the firm, taxation, inflation, unemployment, national income determination, fiscal and monetary policy, economic growth, and international trade and finance.

**The right amount of theory . . . trade-offs in action.**
For the professional economist, there is so much great theory to teach that it's hard to decide what not to teach. Facing the trade-offs involved in deciding what to leave out and what to include in an economics textbook is never easy. This is especially true for a one-semester survey course. Therefore, I provide a guiding philosophy: Include that amount of theory that will allow students to understand the world around them.

Because one of the central goals of this book is to get the student reader to think like an economist, I include enough theory to provide the basic tools of how economists analyze virtually everything we observe, read about, see on television, or hear about in conversations. When instructors peruse this text, they will find about the same amount of theory they would teach in a two-semester course, but honed to its very essence and supported by numerous numbered real-world examples and more extensive application features.

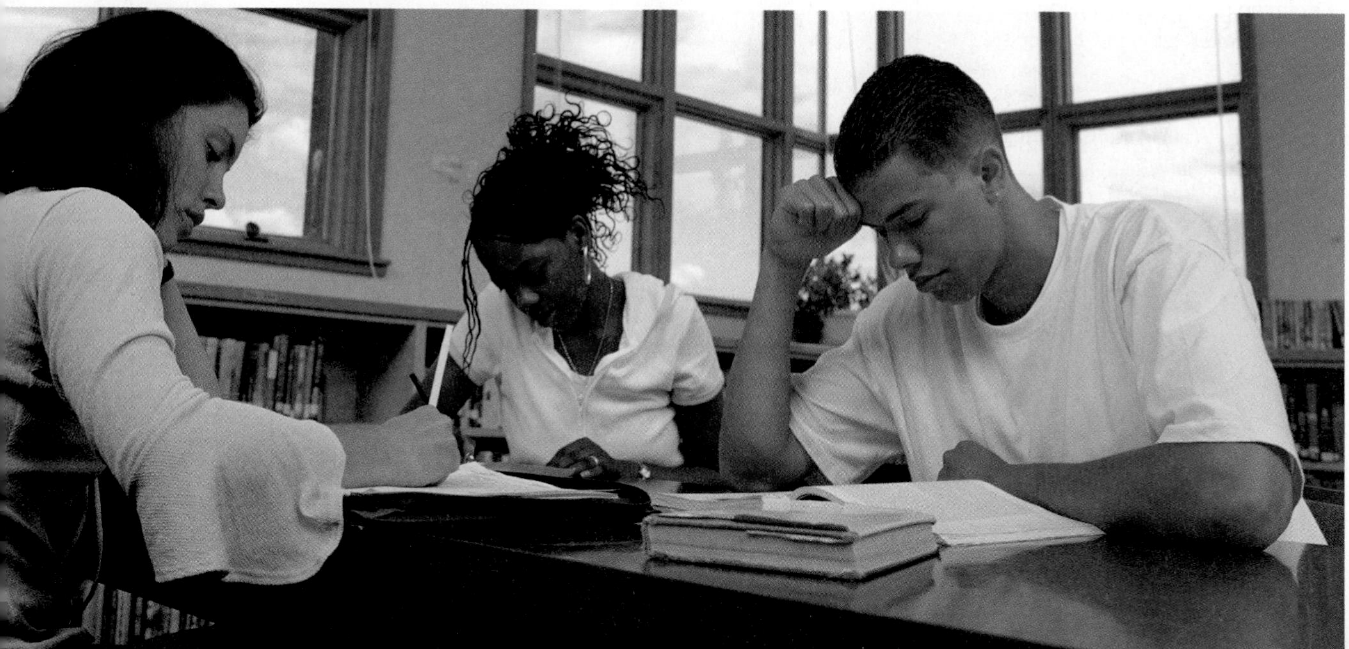

# Theory: The Practical Tool

## The Usual Suspects: Micro, Macro, and International

The flow of materials in this text follows what has become a familiar series of topics—microeconomics, macroeconomics, and finally, international economics. I explain the very essence of economics in Chapter 1—scarcity, opportunity cost, trade-offs, and production possibilities curves. I pay particular attention to the distinction between needs and wants. I also focus on our use of the rationality assumption. Chapter 2 includes an overview of the price system and resource classification, before giving a summary of the U.S. economy, especially as it relates to the world economy.

**Part II** consists of all the important microeconomic topics, including demand and supply (Chapter 3), consumer decision making plus elasticity calculation (Chapter 4), the theory of the firm (Chapter 5), the four standard classifications of market structures (Chapters 6 and 7), market and government failures (Chapter 8), and labor economics (Chapter 9).

**Part III** covers all major macroeconomics topics, including unemployment, inflation, and deflation (Chapter 10), the concepts of aggregate demand and supply with applications (Chapter 11), short-run stabilization via fiscal policy (Chapter 12) and via monetary policy (Chapter 14). Chapter 13 presents our banking system. Finally, I examine growth and development theories (and reality) in Chapter 15.

**Part IV** on international economics includes the real side in Chapter 16 and the financial side in Chapter 17.

CHAPTER 15

How Economies Grow

*Facing an Economic Problem:*
**Why Doesn't Foreign Aid Seem to Help Raise Living Standards?**

You have just been put in charge of distributing foreign aid from the United

**Learning Objectives:**

After reading this chapter, you should be able to:

CHAPTER 2

The United States Within the World Economy

*Facing an Economic Problem:*
**Just How Does Production Get Coordinated in This Country?**

When you go to your local supermarket, you see thousands of products from which you can choose. If you go to a full-range electronics store, such as Circuit City, you see an almost overwhelming array of TVs, home cinemas, and appliances. If you watch television for any length of time, you are bombarded with ads for yet hundreds of other products, ranging from luxury automobiles to slice-it-and-dice-it cooking tools.

How do all of these production decisions get made? Who decides how many different car types General Motors will produce and try to sell? Who determines the number of brands of cereal? Who picks the latest colors for spring fashion wear?

To answer these questions, you need to know about the U.S. economic system. But before examining that, let's first examine the U.S. economy in the context of the world economy.

**Learning Objectives**

After reading this chapter, you should be able to:

- **Explain how the price system answers the basic questions of what, how, and for whom to produce.**
- **List and explain the four main factors of production.**
- **Position the U.S. economy within the total world economy with respect to income, labor force, and global integration.**
- **Contrast GDP with per capita GDP and per capita real GDP.**
- **Compare the likely future population growth in the United States with that of Europe, China, and India.**

***Refer to the back of this chapter for a complete listing of multimedia learning materials available on the CD-ROM and the Web site.***

23

# Micro and Macro Economics

104 **Part 2** Microeconomics

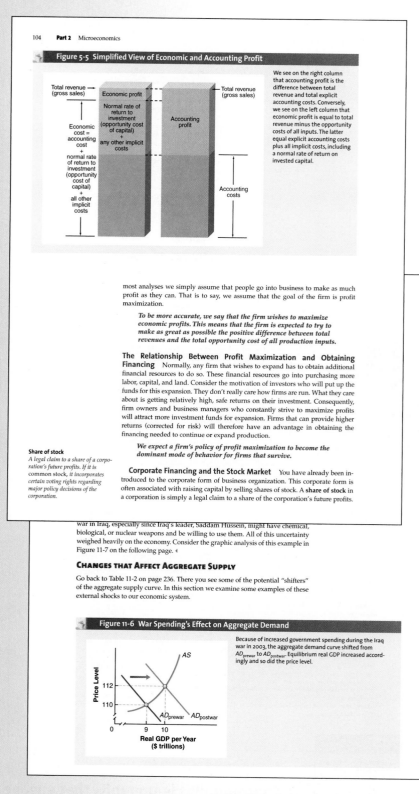

**Figure 5-5 Simplified View of Economic and Accounting Profit**

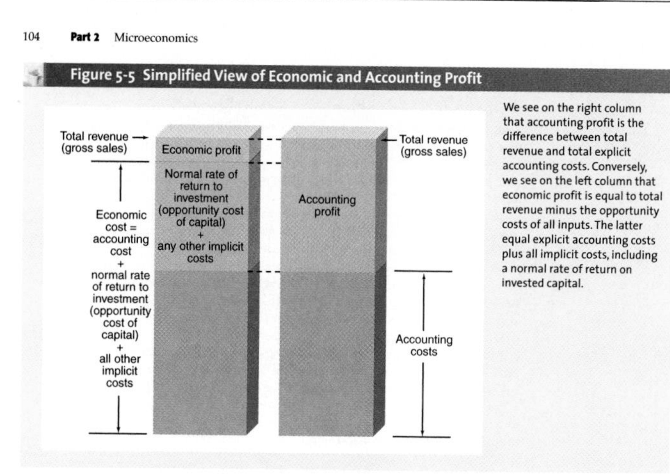


We see on the right column that accounting profit is the difference between total revenue and total explicit accounting costs. Conversely, we see on the left column that economic profit is equal to total revenue minus the opportunity costs of all inputs. The latter equal explicit accounting costs plus all implicit costs, including a normal rate of return on invested capital.

most analyses we simply assume that people go into business to make as much profit as they can. That is to say, we assume that the goal of the firm is profit maximization.

***To be more accurate, we say that the firm wishes to maximize economic profits. This means that the firm is expected to try to make as great as possible the positive difference between total revenues and the total opportunity cost of all production inputs.***

**The Relationship Between Profit Maximization and Obtaining Financing** Normally, any firm that wishes to expand has to obtain additional financial resources to do so. These financial resources go into purchasing more labor, capital, and land. Consider the motivation of investors who will put up the funds for this expansion. They don't really care how firms are run. What they care about is getting relatively high, safe returns on their investment. Consequently, firm owners and business managers who constantly strive to maximize profits will attract more investment funds for expansion. Firms that can provide higher returns (corrected for risk) will therefore have an advantage in obtaining the financing needed to continue or expand production.

***We expect a firm's policy of profit maximization to become the dominant mode of behavior for firms that survive.***

**Share of stock**
*A legal claim to a share of a corporation's future profits. If it is* common stock, *it incorporates certain voting rights regarding major policy decisions of the corporation.*

**Corporate Financing and the Stock Market** You have already been introduced to the corporate form of business organization. This corporate form is often associated with raising capital by selling shares of stock. A **share of stock** in a corporation is simply a legal claim to a share of the corporation's future profits.

war in Iraq, especially since Iraq's leader, Saddam Hussein, might have chemical, biological, or nuclear weapons and be willing to use them. All of this uncertainty weighed heavily on the economy. Consider the graphic analysis of this example in Figure 11-7 on the following page.

**CHANGES THAT AFFECT AGGREGATE SUPPLY**

Go back to Table 11-2 on page 236. There you see some of the potential "shifters" of the aggregate supply curve. In this section we examine some examples of these external shocks to our economic system.

**Figure 11-6 War Spending's Effect on Aggregate Demand**

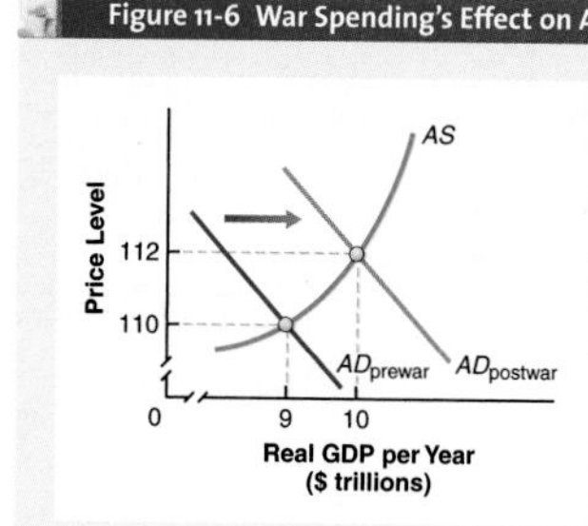


Because of increased government spending during the Iraq war in 2003, the aggregate demand curve shifted from $AD_{prewar}$ to $AD_{postwar}$. Equilibrium real GDP increased accordingly and so did the price level.

## A Few Important Theoretical Subtleties

**In the Micro Unit**—At the end of the supply and demand section, the student is exposed to alternative forms of rationing. During the discussion of elasticity of demand, the importance of the time period under study is emphasized. Because of its growing importance in the business world, I explain what a limited liability company is. In that same chapter (5), I present an explanation of why we should expect profit maximization to be the dominant mode of behavior. I carefully go over the concept of zero economic profits for pure competition and monopolistic competition alike. Advertising as signaling behavior is presented in Chapter 7, as is strategic and opportunistic behavior. Chapter 8 on government and market failures includes the principle of rival consumption when making the distinction between private and public goods. I also cover contestable markets and creative responses to regulation in that chapter. Chapter 9 includes human capital and discrimination as factors affecting income distribution.

**In the Macro Unit**—Chapter 10 covers the discouraged worker phenomenon, as well as the difference between anticipated and unanticipated inflation. Chapter 11 features numerous examples to demonstrate aggregate demand and supply, including recent tax cuts and the war in Iraq. The importance of how fiscal policy is financed, as well as time lags associated with its implementation, are key areas within Chapter 12. The potential for e-money, or digital cash, is examined in Chapter 13. The use of inflation targeting by some central banks is examined at the end of Chapter 14. I show how the legal structure of a nation can affect its long-run growth prospects in Chapter 15.

**In the International Unit**—In Chapter 16, I examine the reasoning behind the relationship between imports and exports, ultimately showing that in the long run, restrictions on imports lead to lower exports. Chapter 17 stresses the mirror-image nature of the current and capital accounts

# Examples and Applications

## ▸ Theory clarified . . . with hundreds of domestic and international examples

From the time I first discovered that my principles students learned theory better when I used more examples in my lectures, I have infused my textbooks with as many interest-grabbing examples as possible. *Understanding Modern Economics* is the first one, however, in which I explicitly number each example throughout chapters. In this way, instructors can refer directly to a specific example on which they might wish to expand the presentation. In addition, the examples are included within the flow of the text narrative, so it is clear to students that the examples are an integral part of the presentation. There are literally hundreds of domestic as well as international examples throughout the seventeen chapters of this text. They follow a key theoretical point and illustrate it. The result, I believe, is better comprehension by students.

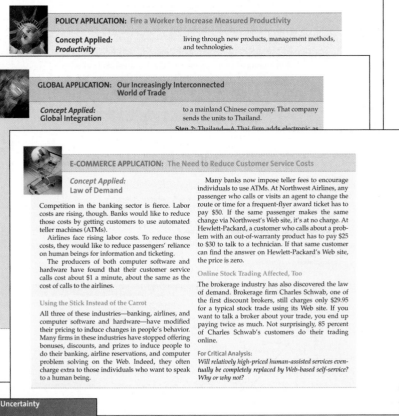

138 **Part 2** Microeconomics

**MONOPOLISTIC COMPETITION: COMPETITION AMONG THE MANY**

A large number of industries cannot be described as perfectly competitive, yet they cannot be described as pure monopolies either. A combination of consumers' desires for variety and competition among producers has led to similar, but at least slightly differentiated products in the marketplace. Differentiated goods or services are quite similar, but have variations in specific qualities or attributes that some consumers believe make them more valuable than other goods or services of the same kind. ▸ Example 7-1 Take retail sales. Think about the number of choices you have when you want to purchase a specific new MP3 player. You can go to your local drugstore; visit a large membership retail outlet, such as Costco; buy from literally thousands of firms on the Internet; visit a specialty electronic store in your mall; and so on. Retail sales is an industry with a tremendous amount of competitors. Each, though, offers a different shopping experience—a differentiated service as it were. ◂

A situation involving competition among many producers with differentiated products or services has been described as *monopolistic competition*, which is the subject of the first part of this chapter. In the second part of this chapter, we look at competition when there are only a few firms in an industry. This market structure is called *oligopoly* and was introduced at the beginning of Chapter 6 when we looked at the spectrum of market structures.

**CHARACTERISTICS OF MONOPOLISTIC COMPETITION**

**Monopolistic competition**
*A market situation in which a large number of sellers offer similar but slightly different products and in which each has some control over price.*

The most common form of market structure in the United States is **monopolistic competition,** in which a large number of sellers offer similar, but slightly different products. ▸ Example 7-2 The most obvious examples of monopolistically competitive industries are those that produce brand-name items such as toothpaste, cosmetics, and designer clothes. ◂

For an industry to be monopolistically competitive, five conditions must be met:

**POLICY APPLICATION:** Fire a Worker to Increase Measured Productivity

*Concept Applied:*
*Productivity*

living through new products, management methods, and technologies.

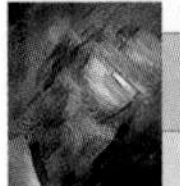

**GLOBAL APPLICATION:** Our Increasingly Interconnected World of Trade

*Concept Applied:*
Global Integration

to a mainland Chinese company. That company sends the units to Thailand.

**E-COMMERCE APPLICATION:** The Need to Reduce Customer Service Costs

*Concept Applied:*
Law of Demand

Competition in the banking sector is fierce. Labor costs are rising, though. Banks would like to reduce those costs by getting customers to use automated teller machines (ATMs).

Airlines face rising labor costs. To reduce those costs, they would like to reduce passengers' reliance on human beings for information and ticketing.

The producers of both computer software and hardware have found that their customer service calls cost about $1 a minute, about the same as the cost of calls to the airlines.

Using the Stick Instead of the Carrot

All three of these industries—banking, airlines, and computer software and hardware—have modified their pricing to induce changes in people's behavior. Many firms in these industries have stopped offering bonuses, discounts, and prizes to induce people to do their banking, airline reservations, and computer problem solving on the Web. Indeed, they often charge extra to those individuals who want to speak to a human being.

Many banks now impose teller fees to encourage individuals to use ATMs. At Northwest Airlines, any passenger who calls or visits an agent to change the route or time for a frequent-flyer award ticket has to pay $50. If the same passenger makes the same change via Northwest's Web site, it's at no charge. At Hewlett-Packard, a customer who calls about a problem with an out-of-warranty product has to pay $25 to $30 to talk to a technician. If that same customer can find the answer on Hewlett-Packard's Web site, the price is zero.

Online Stock Trading Affected, Too

The brokerage industry has also discovered the law of demand. Brokerage firm Charles Schwab, one of the first discount brokers, still charges only $29.95 for a typical stock trade using its Web site. If you want to talk a broker about your trade, you end up paying twice as much. Not surprisingly, 85 percent of Charles Schwab's customers do their trading online.

For Critical Analysis:
*Will relatively high-priced human-assisted services eventually be completely replaced by Web-based self-service? Why or why not?*

## ▸ Policy, Global, and E-Commerce Applications

To drive home the application of theory throughout each chapter, there are at least two separate features that take an in-depth look at specific policy, e-commerce, and global issues. Students will be exposed to domestic and international policy concerns, the impact of advances in information technology, and the interconnections of today's global economy. Each of these timely applications is followed by a critical-thinking question, the suggested answer to which can be found in the *Instructor's Manual*.

**Figure 11-7 The Negative Effect on Aggregate Demand of the Uncertainty Over War in Iraq**

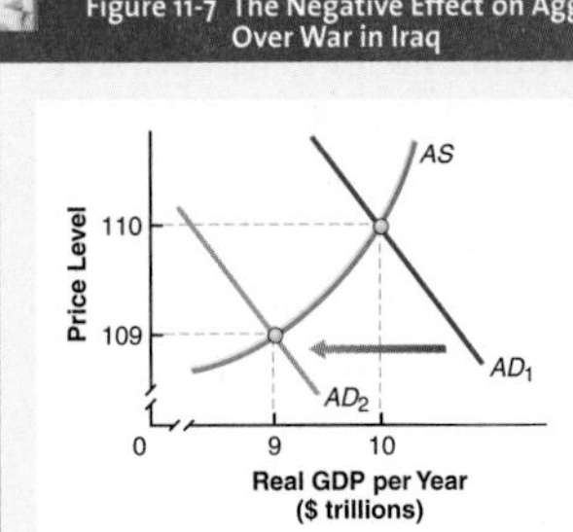


As uncertainty about the war in Iraq became prevalent, the aggregate demand curve shifted inward from $AD_1$ to $AD_2$. The equilibrium level of real GDP per year dropped from $10 trillion to $9 trillion.

## ◂ Conceptually clear graphs that engage

Because graphs are so important for student comprehension, this book's four-color graphs are bold and bright, and conceptually clear. My sense has always been that this type of graph presentation is less foreboding for beginning students.

# Real-World Problem Solving

### ▸ "Facing an Economic Problem" sections . . .

Found at the beginning of each chapter, the "Facing an Economic Problem" section poses an intriguing question—a real-life economic dilemma—and a brief discussion of facts and issues surrounding the problem. For example, Chapter 1's "Facing an Economic Problem," asks: "How much should society pay for an additional year of life for one individual?" And while students' first response might be "whatever it takes," I show how the economic answer is not always that obvious—explaining that they'll need to understand some basic economic concepts of scarcity and the use of our nation's resources, which are discussed in Chapter 1.

## Economics and the World of Scarcity

*Facing an Economic Problem:*
How Much Should Society Pay for an Additional Year of Life for One Individual?

If someone asked you how much an *extra* year of life is worth to you, your answer might be "whatever it takes." When society faces this question, in contrast, the answer is not so obvious. Consider the latest medical technologies. Gleevec, a new leukemia drug, costs about $12,000 a year to administer. It does not cure the disease, but it prolongs the lives of certain cancer-stricken individuals by a few years. Next, consider the latest artificial heart. The device itself costs over $100,000, and there is additional expense to implant and maintain it. Finally, full-body scans are available in major cities. They work especially well at detecting small tumors in current and former smokers. Does that mean that all current and former smokers should get full-body scans every year? To answer that question, you need to understand some basic economic concepts that revolve around *scarcity* and the use of our nation's *resources.*

**Learning Objectives**

After reading this chapter, you should be able to:

- **Explain the difference between needs and wants.**
- **Explain why scarcity exists.**
- **Determine how one measures opportunity cost.**
- **Show the relationship between opportunity cost, trade-offs, and the production possibilities curve.**
- **Show the relationship between the production possibilities curve and economic growth.**

***chapter for a complete arning materials available e Web site.***

*Solving the Economic Problem:*
How Much Should Society Pay for an Additional Year of Life for One Individual?

When deciding what medical services to offer U.S. residents, opportunity cost has to come into play. Body scans are indeed better than conventional X-rays at detecting tumors when they are small and easy to treat. There is a problem with body scans, though. They produce far more false-positive results, leading to unnecessary biopsies. Moreover, they cost about *ten* times more than an X-ray. A Johns Hopkins University team of researchers estimated that if current and former heavy smokers were all scanned once a year, for the next 20 years, there would be a 13 percent reduction in their deaths. (There would also be many more unnecessary biopsies.) Overall, such a screening program would cost the U.S. economy $2.3 million *per year* of life saved for former smokers. In other words, that is the opportunity cost to society. At least for the Johns Hopkins research team, that seemed too high a price to recommend this procedure on a yearly basis. Why? The economy would be giving up resources that could be better used to service others.

### ◂ . . . correlated with "Solving the Economic Problem" sections

These sections, located within each chapter, make use of the concepts presented in the chapter to provide some answers to the posed questions. In Chapter 1's "Solving the Economic Problem," students learn that when deciding on what medical services to offer U.S. residents, the principle of ***opportunity cost*** comes into play. I explain how a Johns Hopkins University team of researchers determined that although full body scans for every heavy smoker in the country could result in a 13 percent reduction in smoker-related deaths, the ***opportunity cost*** to society would be too high. Other "Facing" and "Solving Economic Problem" sections explore such issues and questions as:

- "Fighting the Rise in Cigarette Smuggling Worldwide"
- "Why Do Newspaper Vending Machines Let You Have Access to More Than One Copy?"
- "How to Fill Those Empty Airline Seats?"
- "Can We Make Sure That Everyone Earns at Least a 'Living' Wage?"
- "Why Doesn't Foreign Aid Seem to Help Raise Living Standards?"
- "Boycotting French Goods"

# Study, Comprehend–*Retain!*

## ▶ Step-by-step learning tools to ensure students' success.

When I first learned public speaking, I was told to "tell them what you're going to say; say it; and then tell them what you said." To some extent, this dictum is true for textbook writing, too. At the beginning of each chapter, there are **Learning Objectives** that focus students' attention on what they are about to learn. At the end of each major section, there is a feature called **Mastering Concepts,** which reviews the principal points they just learned. Finally, at the end of each chapter, there is a chapter summary in point-by-point form called **Summing It All Up.** I then present a list of key terms and concepts along with the page numbers where students can find explanations if they do not remember the meaning of a term.

**Learning Objectives**

After reading this chapter, you should be able to:

- Explain how the price system answers the basic questions of what, how, and for whom to produce.
- List and explain the four main factors of production.
- Position the U.S. economy within the total world economy with respect to income, labor force, and global integration.
- Contrast GDP with per capita GDP and per capita real GDP.
- Compare the likely future population growth in the United States with that of Europe, China, and India.

**Mastering Concepts:** Measuring Consumer Responsiveness—The Price Elasticity of Demand

- Price elasticity of demand shows how much consumers respond to a given change in the price of a particular good or service.
- When you respond greatly to a change in price, we say you have an elastic demand. When you respond very little to a change in price, you have an inelastic demand.
- If you don't respond at all to a change in price, you have a perfectly inelastic demand.

**SUMMING IT ALL UP**

- Prices signal to consumers the relative scarcity of goods and services. Consumers then determine whether they value those goods and services enough to buy them at current market prices.
- Prices signal to producers how much they should produce—rising prices signal that they should produce more, and falling prices that they should produce less.
- The price system via the demand for and the supply of different goods and services coordinates the decisions of consumers and producers.
- Competition and the lure of higher profits force producers to seek the least-cost combination of inputs.
- Who gets what is produced is normally determined by money income, plus inheritance and gifts.
- Factors of production include land, labor, capital, and entrepreneurship.
- There is physical capital, such as buildings, and human capital, which embodies individual workers' ability to produce because of education,

rall business activity, U.S. resi- increases in their living stan-

tivity of the economy by gross rrent market value of all final orders in a year.

**MASTERING ECONOMIC CONCEPTS**
**Questions and Problems**

**4-1.** Complete the following table by calculating the missing values for all columns:

| Slices of Pizza | | | Soft Drinks | | |
|---|---|---|---|---|---|
| Number of Slices | Total Utility | Marginal Utility | Number of Drinks | Total Utility | Marginal Utility |
| 0 | 0 | n/a | 0 | 0 | n/a |
| 1 | 40 | __ | 1 | __ | 30 |
| 2 | 55 | __ | 2 | 45 | __ |
| 3 | 65 | __ | 3 | 50 | __ |
| 4 | __ | 5 | 4 | 50 | __ |

**4-2.** Many amusement parks offer special discounts for return visits. The offers typically state that on the day of your visit to the park you may buy a discounted pass for a future visit to the park within a specified time period. Why do amusement parks provide such offers? How do these offers relate to the concept of diminishing marginal utility?

**4-3.** Typically, Earle purchases four DVDs and one PS2 video game each month. Each DVD costs $20, and the video game costs $50. Based on his current level of consumption of each good,

**4-5.** Classify each of the following goods as having relatively elastic or relatively inelastic demand and explain why.

a. heart surgery
b. Old Navy T-shirts
c. a DVD recorder
d. public transportation

**4-6.** Assume that the local Blockbuster store rents an average of 500 videos per day at a rental price of $4.25. If management decides to increase the rental price to $5.25 per video and the number of rentals decreases to 480 per day, what is the price elasticity of demand for these video rentals? Would this good be considered relatively elastic or relatively inelastic? Based on the results from this example, would you assume that this Blockbuster faces a large amount of competition or a small amount of competition?

**4-7.** If the price of new cars decreased by 5 percent and new-car purchases increased by 12.5 percent as a result, what is the price elasticity of demand? Is the demand for new cars relatively elastic or inelastic? Would this price reduction cause an increase in total revenues or a decrease? In other words, will this increase or decrease total consumer expenditures on new cars?

**4-8.** If the price of natural gas increased from $0.829

**THINKING CRITICALLY**

**4-1.** Who has a more inelastic demand for air travel—business travelers or vacation travelers? If airlines want to increase their revenues, which group of consumers should be charged a higher fare? How does vacation travelers' demand change during the holiday season? As a result, what happens to airfares during the holiday season?

**4-2.** The price of pay-per-view movies at home through most cable or satellite providers ranges from $4 to $5, but a typical "new release" pay-per-view movie in a hotel can cost as much as $12 to $15. Explain this price difference in terms of price elasticity of demand and its effect on total revenue. Explain why the price elasticity of demand for hotel guests could be different from that of customers in their own homes.

**4-3.** In 2002, New York City increased its cigarette tax to $1.50 per pack. This change, combined with a previous increase in the state tax, pushed the price of cigarettes up to approximately $7.50.

**HOMEWORK SET**

Go to the back of this book to find the Homework Problems for this chapter.

## ◀ Numerous opportunities to test comprehension

The end-of-chapter materials include two important sections called **Mastering Economic Concepts: Questions and Problems** and **Thinking Critically.** The selection of both questions and problems is plentiful. Answers for all odd-numbered questions and problems are provided at the back of the book.

In addition, **Homework Sets** at the end of the book, consisting of 10 additional problems per chapter, are included in each new textbook. At the end of each chapter, students are directed to the Homework Set for that particular chapter. Instructors can assign the perforated Homework Sets and have students hand them in for grading. To simplify the grading process, all suggested answers to the Homework Sets are found in the Instructor's Manual.

# Multimedia that Reinforces Chapter Concepts

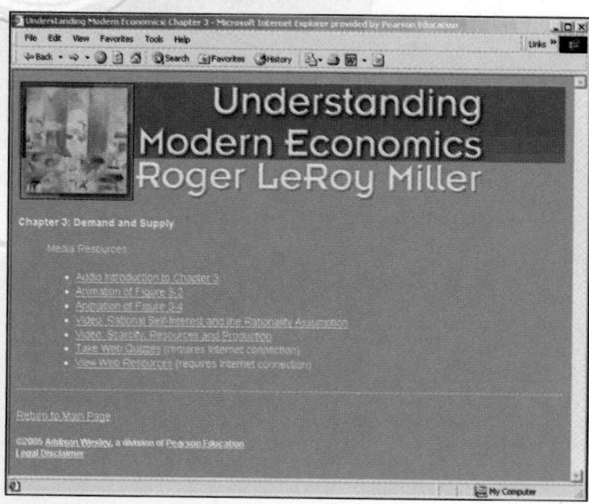


## Understanding Modern Economics CD-ROM

Working hand-in-hand with this book to bring economic concepts to life, the *Understanding Modern Economics CD-ROM* is packaged with each new textbook. The CD-ROM includes a variety of features designed specifically to enhance the student's learning experience.

Correlated chapter-by-chapter with the textbook, the CD-ROM contains the following resources for *each* chapter:

- **The author's audio introduction**—A lively overview of the chapter's topics where I focus student attention on critical concepts.
- **Numerous one- to three-minute video clips**—I address the chapter's key points and further clarify concepts that students find most difficult to grasp.
- **Animated graphs with full audio**—These ease apprehension about working with graphs by taking students step-by-step through the plotting of points, drawing of curves, and resulting curve shifts and intersection points.

# Integrated Online Resources

- **Media Resource Lists** located at the end of each chapter detail the specific animations, video clips, and audio clips that will sharpen students' overall mastery of economics and build their abilities to analyze graphs.
- **Logging On** sections at the end of every text chapter offer suggestions for Web research to help students build their economics research skills.
- **Using the Internet for Economic Analysis** sections each feature an extensive Internet problem that engages students in online research related to key chapter topics.

**MEDIA RESOURCE LIST**

The following media resources are available with this chapter:

- Load your CD-ROM to listen to the audio introduction to this chapter.
- Load your CD-ROM to access Graph Animations of Figure 4-1, *The Total and Marginal Utility of Watching DVDs*, and Figure 4-2, *Extreme Price*
- Load your CD-ROM to view the video on *The Determinants of the Price Elasticity of Demand.*
- Test your knowledge of chapter concepts with a quiz at www.miller-ume.com.
- Link to Web resources related to the text coverage at www.miller-ume.com.

**LOGGING ON**

1. To see the taxes that governments have placed on cigarettes in the United States and worldwide, go to http://www.drugs.indiana.edu/drug_stats/cigtax_burden.html.
2. For more information about the ways in which minors can evade regulations and taxes relating to cigarette consumption, go to http://www.unc.edu/courses/2003spring/law/357c/001/projects/akhill/Alcohol&Tobacco/Tobacco%20-%20Minors.htm.
3. To get more insight into how the price elasticity of demand relates to consumer expenditures, go to http://ingrimayne.saintjoe.edu/econ/elasticity/OverviewEl.html.

**USING THE INTERNET FOR ECONOMIC ANALYSIS**

Price Elasticity and Consumption of Illegal Drugs
Making the use of certain drugs illegal drives up their market prices, so the price elasticity of demand is a key factor affecting the use of illegal drugs. This application uses concepts from this chapter to analyze how price elasticity of demand affects drug consumption.

Title: The Demand for Illicit Drugs

Navigation: Go to http://ideas.repec.org/p/nbr/nberwo/5238.html.

Application Read the summary of the results of this study of price elasticities of participation in the use of illegal drugs, and answer the following questions.

1. Based on the results of the study, is the demand for cocaine more or less price elastic than the demand for heroin? For which drug, therefore, will quantity demanded fall by a greater percentage in response to a proportionate increase in price?
2. The study finds that decriminalizing currently illegal drugs would bring about sizable increases both in overall consumption of heroin and cocaine and in the price elasticity of demand for both drugs. Why do you suppose that the price elasticity of demand would rise? (Hint: At present, users of cocaine and heroin are restricted to only a few illegal sources of the drugs, but if the drugs could be legally produced and sold, there would be many more suppliers providing a variety of different types of both drugs.)

# Online Tools for Teaching and Learning

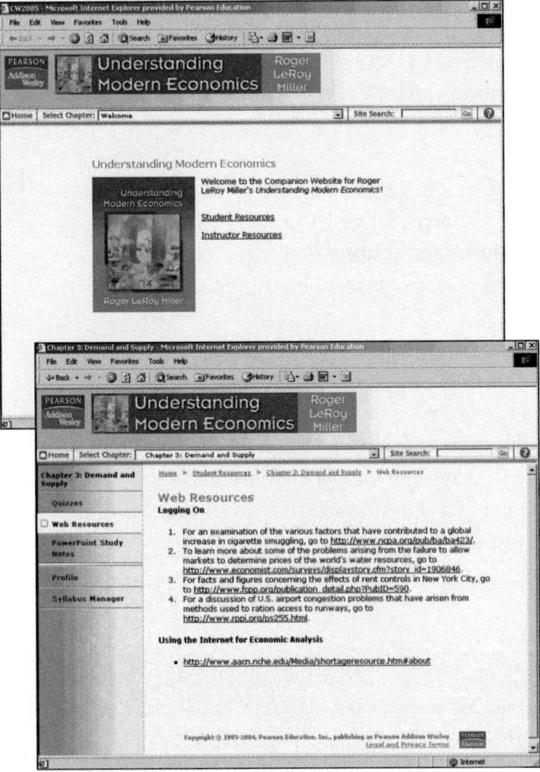


## The Companion Web Site

**www.miller-ume.com**

This robust site includes many resources to help students excel in their first economics course. **Quizzes**—four 10-question quizzes for every text chapter—offer many opportunities for self-testing. **Direct links** to the latest chapter-related information available online encourage students to explore chapter topics in greater depth. **PowerPoint® Study Notes** and **Glossary Flashcards** offer additional help in studying for exams. The latest micro-economic and macroeconomic **Current Events Articles** with discussion questions are posted weekly by Andrew J. Dane of Angelo State University. Also posted weekly is a five-question quiz to help students test their knowledge of current events. In addition, the Web site's **Syllabus Manager** gives instructors the tools to create a calendar of assignments for each class.

### Online Course Management

The Test Item File is also available in Blackboard format, which can be used with CourseCompass, Addison-Wesley's premier Blackboard-based course management system. For more information, contact your local Addison-Wesley sales representative.

# Innovative tools to lighten your teaching load

### Instructor's Resource Disk (IRD) with PowerPoint® Lecture Presentation

Compatible with Windows® and Macintosh® computers, this CD-ROM provides numerous resources. The PowerPoint Lecture Presentation was developed by Ethel Weeks of Nassau Community College. The IRD also includes Microsoft® Word files for the entire contents of the *Instructor's Manual* and computerized *Test Bank* files. The easy-to-use testing software (TestGen with QuizMaster for Windows and Macintosh) is a valuable test preparation tool that allows professors to view, edit, and add questions.

### Test Bank

### 175 questions per chapter

Authored by Debbie Mullin of the University of Colorado at Colorado Springs, the *Test Bank* provides 3,000 carefully prepared questions—*175 questions per chapter*—in multiple-choice, true-false, fill-in-the-blank, and short-answer format. The multiple-choice questions include an indicator of the level of difficulty and a reference to the topic the question is based on.

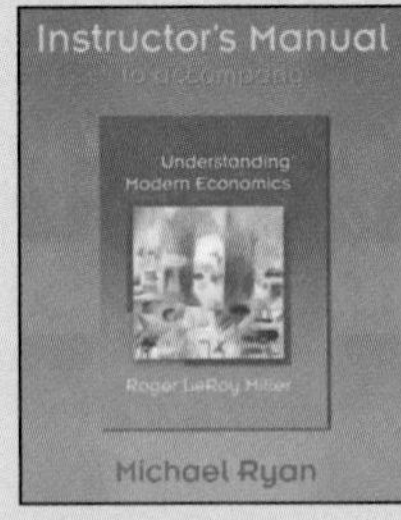


### Instructor's Manual

Authored by Michael Ryan of Gainesville College, this comprehensive manual pulls together a wide variety of teaching tools so that instructors can use the text easily and effectively. The *Instructor's Manual* includes the following materials:

- Chapter overviews, objectives, and outlines
- Media resource list
- Lecture tips for enlivening the classroom
- Answer key for the "Critical Thinking Questions" that appear in all of the Policy, Global, and E-Commerce Applications in the text
- Answer keys for "Mastering Economic Concepts Questions and Problems," "Exploring Critical Thinking" questions, and "Homework Sets"

# Resources That Guarantee Student Success

### Study Guide

The Study Guide was written by Lee J. Van Scyoc of the University of Wisconsin, Oshkosh. This valuable guide offers the practice and review students need to succeed in the course, including a review of the key concepts from each chapter, outline of the main points, tips on avoiding common errors, and self-test materials such as fill-in-the blank, true-false, and multiple-choice questions, as well as numerical- and graph-based questions.

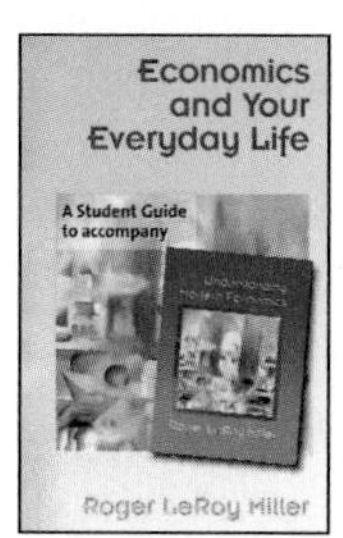


### Economics and Your Everyday Life . . . *FREE with every new copy of this book!*

Written by the text author, this booklet offers numerous applications of economics and guidance for analyzing economic news.

## Resources Available for Convenient Packaging with the Text:

### The Econ Tutor Center

Staffed by qualified, experienced college economics instructors, the Econ Tutor Center is open five days a week, seven hours a day. Tutors can be reached by phone, fax, and e-mail. The Econ Tutor Center hours are designed to meet your students' study schedules, with evening hours Sunday through Thursday. Students receive one-on-one tutoring on examples, related exercises, and problems. Please contact your Addison-Wesley representative for information on options for making this service available to your students.

### Economist.com Edition

The premier online source of economic news analysis, economist.com provides students with insight and opinion on current economic events. Through an agreement between Addison-Wesley and *The Economist*, your students can receive a low-cost subscription to this premium Web site for three months, including the complete text of the current issue of *The Economist* and access to *The Economist's* searchable archives. Other features include Web-only weekly articles, news feeds with current world and business news, and stock market and currency data. Professors who adopt this special edition will receive a complimentary one-year subscription to economist.com.

### *The Wall Street Journal* Edition

Addison-Wesley is also pleased to provide your students with access to *The Wall Street Journal,* the most respected and trusted daily source for information on business and economics. For a small additional charge, Addison-Wesley offers students a 10-week subscription to *The Wall Street Journal* print edition and *The Wall Street Journal Interactive Edition.* Adopting professors will receive a complimentary one-year subscription to both the print and interactive versions.

### *Financial Times* Edition

Featuring international news and analysis from journalists in more than 50 countries, the *Financial Times* will provide students with insights and perspectives on economic developments around the world. The *Financial Times* Edition provides your students with a 15-week subscription to one of the world's leading business publications. Adopting professors will receive a complimentary one-year subscription to the *Financial Times* as well as access to the Online Edition at FT.com.

# Acknowledgments

When I started this project several years ago, I had some pretty good ideas about what I should do to make the one-semester economics course more exciting while keeping the basic theory intact and obvious. As certain as I might have been, though, reviewers of the many drafts of the manuscript caused me to rethink different aspects of the project. The below-listed professors were kind enough to offer constructive comments on virtually all aspects of the text, including even the problems and homework assignments. I remain eternally in their debt.

Douglas Agbetsiafa, *Indiana University, South Bend*
Charles Anderson, *De Anza College*
Daniel Benjamin, *Clemson University*
Richard Bernstein, *Temple University*
Donald Boudreaux, *George Mason University*
Shawn Carter, *Jacksonville State University*
Rob Catlett, *Emporia State University*
Glenn Clayman, *Columbus State Community College*
Norman Cloutier, *University of Wisconsin, Parkside*
Michael Cohick, *Collin County Community College*
Carole Endres, *Wright State University*
Tommy Eshleman, *University of Nebraska, Kearney*
Rhona Free, *Eastern Connecticut University*
Robert Grafstein, *University of Georgia*
Abbas Grammy, *California State University, Bakersfield*
Peter Harman, *Rhode Island College*
James Hubert, *Seattle Central Community College*
Hussain Jafri, *Tarleton State University*
Louis Johnston, *College of Saint Benedict/Saint John's University*
Bentzil Kasper, *Broome Community College*
Marlene Kim, *University of Massachusetts, Boston*
Lea-Rachel Kosnik, *Montana State University*
Frances Lea, *Germanna Community College*
Loren Lee, *Palomar College*
Don Leet, *Fresno State University*
Herbert Meyer, *Scott Community College*
Thomas Meyer, *Patrick Henry Community College*
Hiranya Nath, *Sam Houston State University*
Z. Edward O'Relley, *North Dakota State University*
Michael Ryan, *Gainesville College*
Eric Schansberg, *Indiana University*
Mark Siegler, *California State University, Sacramento*
Garvin Smith, *Daytona Beach Community College*
Lee Van Scyoc, *University of Wisconsin, Oshkosh*
Bin Wang, *University of Wisconsin, Waukesha*
Ethel Weeks, *Nassau Community College*
William Wilkes, *Athens State University*

On a new project like *Understanding Modern Economics,* I expected some editorial help from Addison-Wesley. I was, in contrast, overwhelmed by the enormous amount of help, and from all departments in Addison Wesley. First, my editor, Adrienne D'Ambrosio, masterfully guided me to think about what the market really wanted in an entirely new one-semester economics text. Then, my developmental editor, Rebecca Ferris-Caruso, picked up the ball and relentlessly pursued reviewers, their criticisms, and the application of those criticisms to forcing me to rewrite and parse the various drafts of the manuscript. Rebecca also worked closely with the various professors who helped put together the numerous supplements. And, Rebecca stayed on board right up to just a few weeks before having her first baby. That's certainly going beyond the call of duty!

On the production side, Katy Watson made sure that every aspect of the project was done correctly and on time. Gina Hagen Kolenda created a beautiful and modern design for the entire text. She also conceived the cover design, using a painting that my wife, Francette Labatut-Miller, created. My long-time production editor, John Orr, working through his independent Orr Book Services, spent so many weekends and nights working on this project that I'm not sure when he ever slept or played with his kids.

On the multimedia side, the Web site and CD-ROM were expertly put together by Addison-Wesley's media department, and especially Melissa Honig. I am always in awe of what she and her co-workers can do when they put forward their best efforts to create multimedia materials that actually are useful and used by students.

To all of these people at Addison-Wesley and Orr Book Services and many others there, I thank you from deep inside me. You did a great job.

My former colleague and long-time friend Professor Dan Benjamin served as both critical reviewer and super proof reader. As always, he kept me honest. I thank you again, Dan, for all that you continue to do for me. Professor Mike Ryan served as both a reviewer and a provider of additional problems and homework assignments as well as the *Instructors' Manual*. Thanks for the hard work. I also thank the hard-working additional supplement preparers, Professor Ethel Weeks, Professor Debbie Mullin, and Professor Lee J. Van Scyoc. I am truly excited about the quality products you developed to help both students and instructors use my new book.

I again used the services of Sue Jasin of K & L Consulting for manuscript preparation. I think she probably memorized the book, given the large number of drafts she typed. As always, my appreciation goes out to her. Finally, super copyeditor and super proofer Pat Lewis did one of the most thorough jobs I've ever seen. You are wonderful, Pat. Make sure you are available for the next edition.

I expect to improve this book throughout the following 15 editions, so any of you who have comments, please send them to me via the publisher through the e-mail address on the book's Web site.

R.L.M

# PART 1

# An Introduction to Economics

# CHAPTER 1

# Economics and the World of Scarcity

## *Facing an Economic Problem:* How Much Should Society Pay for an Additional Year of Life for One Individual?

If someone asked you how much an *extra* year of life is worth to you, your answer might be "whatever it takes." When society faces this question, in contrast, the answer is not so obvious. Consider the latest medical technologies. Gleevec, a new leukemia drug, costs about $12,000 a year to administer. It does not cure the disease, but it prolongs the lives of certain cancer-stricken individuals by a few years. Next, consider the latest artificial heart. The device itself costs over $100,000, and there is additional expense to implant and maintain it. Finally, full-body scans are available in major cities. They work especially well at detecting small tumors in current and former smokers. Does that mean that all current and former smokers should get full-body scans every year? To answer that question, you need to understand some basic economic concepts that revolve around *scarcity* and the use of our nation's *resources.*

### Learning Objectives

After reading this chapter, you should be able to:

- **Explain the difference between needs and wants.**
- **Explain why scarcity exists.**
- **Determine how one measures opportunity cost.**
- **Show the relationship between opportunity cost, trade-offs, and the production possibilities curve.**
- **Show the relationship between the production possibilities curve and economic growth.**

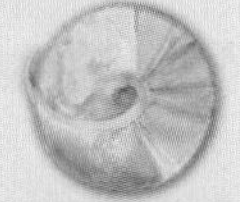

***Refer to the back of this chapter for a complete listing of multimedia learning materials available on the CD-ROM and the Web site.***

## WHY ECONOMICS?

"What, I have to take a course in economics?" Perhaps that was your first reaction to finding out that your college or university required you to take the course for which this book is the primary text. You may have already heard the study of economics referred to as "the dismal science." Don't despair, though. The study of economics is not dismal. In addition, economics is part of your life, day-in and day-out. ▸ Example 1-1 You have already used economics without knowing it. You chose to invest in more learning by taking this course. That means you gave up your highest valued alternative, such as getting a full-time job; spending a year traveling around the world; or going to a religious retreat to meditate. ◂

There are many ways to define economics. Economics is part of the social sciences and as such analyzes human behavior. We can define **economics** as the study of how people allocate their limited resources in an attempt to satisfy their unlimited wants.

**Economics**
*The study of how individuals and societies make choices about ways to use scarce resources.*

***Economics is the study of how people make choices.***

## LET'S GET ONE THING STRAIGHT—YOU DON'T *NEED* VERY MUCH

The way to benefit most by your study of economics is to eliminate one word from your vocabulary—*need*. It's tough to do so. All of us say, "I need a new shirt." "I need a new pair of shoes." "I need a vacation." Typically, we use the term *need* very casually. Usually, though, what people mean is that they want something that they do not currently have.

The word **needs** really only applies to the bare minimum physical necessities that allow you to survive. Therefore, anything above the bare minimum of basic food, shelter, and clothing is no longer a need.

**Needs**
*The bare minimum for subsistence.*

**Wants** include both those desires that we are able to pay for and those we are *unable* to pay for. Consequently, there is no end to the number of wants that you might have.

**Wants**
*What people would buy if their incomes were unlimited.*

***Wants are unlimited. There is always something else you might like to have, whether it is physical or spiritual.***

▸ Example 1-2 If you run out of physical items that you want, there are always nonphysical items, such as more love, affection, friendship, power, control, or companionship. Alternatively, your wants could be truly humanitarian and altruistic—more understanding among the peoples of the earth, less cause for war, and better living conditions for the poor. You could satisfy some of the latter wants by devoting your time to helping others. ◂

## UNLIMITED WANTS VERSUS REALITY

Have you ever been late for class? If you haven't, you are unusual. Most of us have been late for something. Being late means that we were doing something else instead of being on time for a particular activity, such as attending class. Obviously, there was an alternative use of your time that you thought was more valuable than getting to class on time. After all, there are only 24 hours in a day, and there are only so many days in your life.

The same is true for every other **resource**, defined as anything that has positive value that we want to consume or use to create the things we want to consume. Here is one fact of nature:

**Resources**
*Things used to produce other things to satisfy people's wants.*

***We live with unlimited wants in a world of limited resources.***

**Scarcity Is What It Is Called** A world in which there are unlimited wants and a limit to resources is a world of **scarcity.** We define scarcity as a situation in which nature does not provide us with all of the resources required to satisfy our unlimited wants. For many people, particularly very wealthy ones, the scarcest resource they face is time. That means that scarcity applies to everyone, even Bill Gates, founder of Microsoft and America's richest person. Economists did not invent scarcity any more than physicists invented gravity. Both are facts of life.

**Scarcity**
*The condition of not being able to have all of the goods and services one wants, because wants exceed what can be made from all available resources at any given time.*

Scarcity existed before men and women even thought about economic problems. ▸ **Example 1-3** You may think that air is not scarce. But if you consider *clean* air, you know that it is a scarce resource. All you have to do is walk around on a polluted day in Salt Lake City, Los Angeles, New York City, or Denver. You certainly cannot get all of the *clean* air you want for free! ◂

**Goods and "Bads"** Because our resources are limited, we use them to produce the things we wish to consume. Usually, we call those things **goods.** Sometimes we call them goods and services. Goods are defined as those items that give us satisfaction when we consume them.

**Goods**
*Objects that can satisfy people's wants.*

There are "bads," too. These are the by-products of production and consumption that we prefer to do without. They include pollution of any type. ▸ **Example 1-4** The smog that occurs in most major cities is a "bad." We would like to have much less of it. Oil tanker spills in the ocean create "bads" also, because they ruin fishing grounds, dirty beaches, and make swimming impossible. When too many drivers attempt to use the same road at the same time, they create a "bad" called congestion. ◂

You will read more about "bads" in Chapter 8 in the discussion of *market failure.*

**Mastering Concepts:** Why Economics?

- **Economics is the study of how people make choices.**
- **While basic needs are few, wants are unlimited.**
- **We live in a world of limited resources, even though our wants are unlimited.**
- **Scarcity exists because nature does not provide us with all of the resources necessary to satisfy our unlimited wants.**
- **Those things that we like to have and consume are called goods.**

## WHEN YOU CHOOSE, YOU GIVE UP AN OPPORTUNITY

Scarcity forces you to make choices. Clearly, because your time is scarce, you must decide how to use it. Even if you don't make an explicit decision, implicitly you are making a choice in the use of your time at every moment during your life.

### Opportunity Cost—The Only Game in Town

When you decide to do anything, you are implicitly deciding *against* doing something else. In other words, you are giving up an opportunity. That means that every action—whether it is the use of time, the purchase of a good or service, or even deciding on a marriage partner—involves a forgone opportunity. We call this the **opportunity cost** of every action.

**Opportunity cost**
*The value of the next-best alternative given up for the alternative that was chosen.*

The formal definition of opportunity cost is the value of the next-best alternative. ▸ **International Example 1-5** The United States made a commitment to spend billions of dollars in the reconstruction of Iraq after the 2003 war. Once that commitment was made, choices for the use of those resources had to be made.

*Many buildings in Iraq require complete reconstruction. Deciding which ones to rebuild is not easy. Why do such types of decisions involve economic reasoning?*

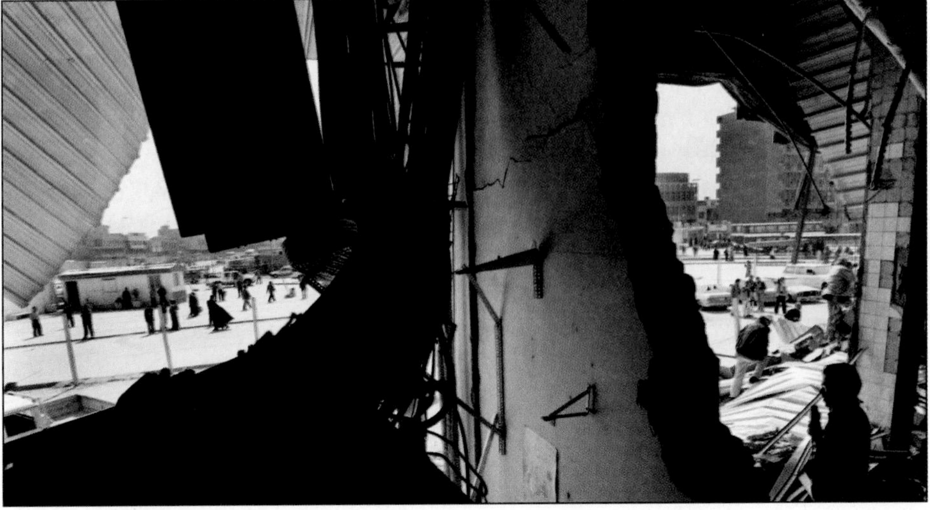

When a decision to spend $500,000 on repairing sanitation facilities in a particular town was made, an opportunity cost was incurred. There were thousands of alternative uses for those resources, but the true opportunity cost was the value of the *next-best* alternative. This might have been the creation of a new health center to inoculate children against communicable diseases. Obviously, the opportunity cost of the sanitation center would not be the value of building a cotton candy factory. Such a factory would be a rather frivolous use of resources in the reconstruction of war-torn Iraq. ◂

You now have the basic tools with which you can solve the economic problem posed at the beginning of this chapter.

## *Solving the Economic Problem:* How Much Should Society Pay for an Additional Year of Life for One Individual?

When deciding what medical services to offer U.S. residents, opportunity cost has to come into play. Body scans are indeed better than conventional X-rays at detecting tumors when they are small and easy to treat. There is a problem with body scans, though. They produce far more false-positive results, leading to unnecessary biopsies. Moreover, they cost about *ten* times more than an X-ray. A Johns Hopkins University team of researchers estimated that if current and former heavy smokers were all scanned once a year, for the next 20 years, there would be a 13 percent reduction in their deaths. (There would also be many more unnecessary biopsies.) Overall, such a screening program would cost the U.S. economy $2.3 million *per year* of life saved for former smokers. In other words, that is the opportunity cost to society. At least for the Johns Hopkins research team, that seemed too high a price to recommend this procedure on a yearly basis. Why? The economy would be giving up resources that could be better used to service others.

There is a basic notion about opportunity cost:

***Cost is always a forgone opportunity.***

Think of it this way: when you choose to do something, you lose something. What do you lose? The ability to engage in the next-highest-valued alternative. The cost of your choice is what you lose or sacrifice, which is by definition your next-highest-valued alternative. This is your opportunity cost. Apparently, some politicians do not quite understand this basic economic concept, particularly when it comes to deciding how we should obtain military personnel, as the following *Policy Application* describes.

## POLICY APPLICATION: Should We Bring the Draft Back?

### *Concept Applied:* Opportunity Cost

Until 1973, the federal government drafted men into the armed services for two years. In 1973, the United States abolished the draft, turning to an all-volunteer military. Nonetheless, during the military buildup in the early 2000s, some members of Congress argued in favor of bringing the draft back.

#### Revisiting the Arguments

Let's ignore the political aspects of bringing the draft back and concentrate on the economic analysis. Politicians and even some academics have stated that if the United States is going to be the world's global cop, it must lower the cost to the American public. What better way to lower the explicit cost than to require all men and women aged 18 to 26 to spend two years in military (or public) service? Indeed, the budget of the U.S. government would fall because the draftees would be paid much less than volunteer entry-level military personnel are paid today.

#### Opportunity Cost Rears Its Ugly Head

The true cost of any action, though, as you already know, is its opportunity cost. Although the U.S. government might pay only $100 a month to those individuals who are drafted, the cost to the U.S. economy would be the value of the next-best alternative uses of the draftees. If a draftee's best job opportunity was being an engineer at $4,000 per month, then the latter figure represents the true cost of using that draftee because the economy is losing that person's services, which are worth $4,000 per month. The $100 a month paid by the federal government to the draftee is the budgetary cost to the government. It does not represent the true cost to society.

**For Critical Analysis:**
*Why might a politician conveniently ignore the opportunity cost of bringing back the draft?*

**Mastering Concepts:** When You Choose, You Give Up an Opportunity

- **Whenever you do anything—buy something, work at something, spend time doing something else—you incur an opportunity cost.**
- **Out of the many alternative uses of your resources, the next-highest-valued alternative is your opportunity cost.**
- **Cost is always a forgone opportunity.**

## EVERY CHOICE INVOLVES A TRADE-OFF

Scarcity forces us to choose. When we choose, we give up something, and we call this its opportunity cost. Another way of stating this is that:

***Every choice involves a trade-off.***

**Trade-off**
*Sacrificing one good or service to obtain or produce another.*

The word **trade-off** is a commonly used expression. ▸ Example 1-6 The decision to use nicotine products involves a trade-off between current pleasure derived from their use and longer life expectancy. Even when you present long-term smokers with irrefutable evidence that they are injuring their health, most continue to smoke. They at least *implicitly* accept the trade-off. ◂

A more formal definition of trade-off is that it is the sacrifice of one good or service to acquire or produce another good or service. ▸ Example 1-7 We could build increasingly more fuel-efficient cars by making them lighter. The trade-off here, though, is between fuel efficiency and safety. Lighter cars are likely to contribute to more highway fatalities. Of course, we could then equip lighter, more fuel-efficient cars with more safety features. But then the price of cars would go up. Trade-offs exist all around us. ◂

## Trade-offs Involve Choosing Among Uses of Resources

A business has to decide how to use its resources—people and machines—to produce various goods that it knows it can sell. These are called production trade-offs. As it turns out, you face production trade-offs, too. ▸ Example 1-8 Say you devote a fixed number of hours a week to studying. The major resource you have at your disposal is your time. Let's say you are taking only two classes—economics and political science. With a fixed number of studying hours per week, every hour you spend studying economics means one less hour you spend studying political science. Presumably, the more you study one subject, the higher your grade in that subject. Therefore, you are looking at a trade-off between a higher grade in economics and a higher grade in political science and vice versa. ◂

✦ **Note!** *Everyone lives in a world of trade-offs.*

## Trade-offs Create Production Possibilities

Most businesses can produce different goods and services. When they produce more of one good, they therefore produce less of another, given a fixed amount of workers and machines and factory space, for example. Every nation faces similar types of production possibilities. ▸ Example 1-9 In any year, a nation can choose to use its resources to produce more sports equipment and less research equipment. Alternatively, the nation can choose to use its given resources to produce more medical services and fewer video game services. ◂

**Production possibilities curve**
*A graph showing the maximal combinations of goods and services that can be produced from a fixed amount of resources in a given period of time.*

### The Production Possibilities Curve

We can summarize production possibilities in what we call a **production possibilities curve (PPC)**. The production possibilities curve is a pictorial representation of the *maximum* combination of outputs that can be produced, *given* a fixed amount of resources.

The graphing of a production possibilities curve is straightforward. You put the annual quantities of one good or service on the horizontal axis and the annual quantities of a competing good or service on the vertical axis. Look at Figure 1-1. There you see the production possibilities curve for digital camcorders and DVD recorders. Hypothetically, if all the nation's resources went into building digital camcorders, it could produce 90 million per year. This is represented by point *A*. If all of the nation's resources went into building DVD recorders, it could produce 100 million of them per year. This is shown as point *E*. All the points *A*, *B*, *C*, *D*, and *E* are on the production possibilities curve. They are all possible.

The trade-offs are obvious. To increase production of DVD recorders from zero to, say, 60 million per year, you would have to move from zero to 60 million on the horizontal axis. This would give us point *C* on the production possibilities curve. Point *C* reflects the fact that the extra 60 million DVD recorders can be achieved only via a reduction of 30 million digital camcorders. In other words, in this example the opportunity cost of 60 million DVD recorders is 30 million digital camcorders.

**Being Inside the Production Possibilities Curve** Look at point Z in Figure 1-1. If the nation is at that point, it means that its resources are not being fully utilized. This occurs during periods of higher-than-normal unemployment. Any points inside the production possibilities curve, such as Z, are said to represent production situations that are not efficient.

**Efficiency** means many things to different people. Here we are talking about *productive efficiency*. This means that on the production possibilities curve, the economy is producing its maximum output with *given* technology and resources. Another way of thinking about efficiency is that we are getting the most out of what we have if we are at points *A* through *E* in Figure 1-1. If we are at point Z, we are certainly not getting the most out of what we have. We call point Z an **inefficient point.** Any point below the production possibilities curve is an inefficient point. Any point above the production possibilities curve, such as X, is impossible. Why? Because the production possibilities curve is defined as the *maximum* amount of output possible at any point in time.

**Efficiency**
*The case in which a given level of inputs is used to produce the maximum possible output. Alternatively, the situation in which a given output is produced at minimum cost.*

**Inefficient point**
*Any point below the production possibilities curve at which resources are being used inefficiently.*

Figure 1-1 is not just some fantasy you have to learn to pass the final exam. Rather, the United States faces an important production possibilities trade-off when it decides its military role in today's troubled world, as you will read in the next *Policy Application* on the next page.

▸ **Example 1-10** At the beginning of World War II, defense spending was only 1.7 percent of total national income. It reached almost 38 percent at the peak of the war. Before the war in Iraq, defense spending was 2.4 percent of total national income. It increased to 4.1 percent during the war in Iraq in 2003. ◂

**An Aside: Not Everyone Faces the Same Cost of Going to War** Although the United States as a whole clearly gives up civilian goods when it takes on the role of global cop, not everybody pays proportionately. It was estimated that the average U.S. family paid about $625 for the war in Iraq in 2003. The poorest 20 percent of U.S. families paid only $33 each. In contrast, families in the richest 5 percent paid on average $4,700 each. Families in the richest 1 percent paid $13,000 each.

**Figure 1-1: The Production Possibilities Curve for Digital Camcorders and DVD Recorders**

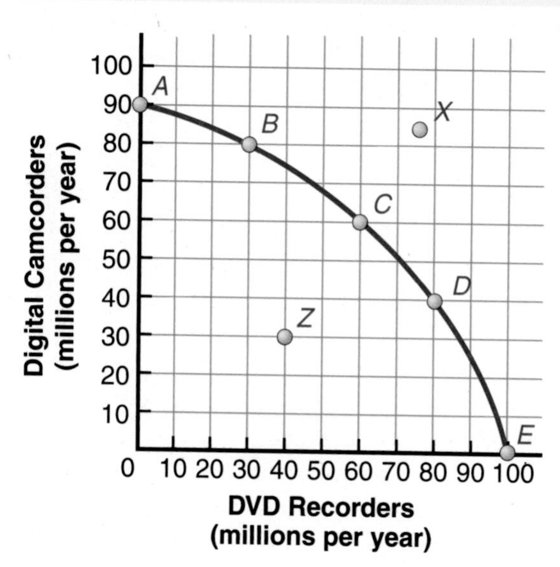


Assume that all the nation's resources go into building camcorders and DVD recorders. If only camcorders are produced, we can produce 90 million, shown as point *A*. If only DVD recorders are produced, we can produce 100 million, shown as point *E*. All of the points *A* through *E* are on the production possibilities curve, meaning that they are possible. Any movement from one combination to another always involves a trade-off. Point *Z* lies *inside* the production possibilities curve and therefore entails unemployment or underemployed resources. Point *X* is *outside* the production possibilities curve. It is impossible.

## POLICY APPLICATION: What Is the Cost to the United States of Being the World's Cop?

### *Concepts Applied:* Trade-offs, Production Possibilities Curve, Opportunity Cost

Since the beginning of the 2000s, politicians, economists, political scientists, and even the general public have asked an important question: Can the United States be the global cop? Let's ignore the political aspects of this question and focus only on the economics.

#### What It Means to Be the World's Cop

No one doubts that the United States is the world's only military superpower. No one doubts that the United States has the physical capability of fighting numerous conflicts, even simultaneously. The issue, though, is how much are U.S. residents willing to pay for the United States to be the global cop? Each global conflict that the United States enters costs us billions upon billions of dollars. We are still paying for the wars in Afghanistan and Iraq. That is because we are helping "reconstruct" those economies.

So, being the world's cop means not only ridding the world of supposedly dangerous dictators with weapons of mass destruction, but also helping rebuild war-torn economies, once the "dirty" work is done. Every $1 billion that goes into U.S. military activities implies an opportunity cost of $1 billion of nonmilitary goods and services. There is a trade-off in our use of resources between military goods and civilian goods.

#### Graphing the Military versus Civilian Trade-off

Look at Figure 1-2 below. Here you see the production possibilities curve between civilian goods and military goods. There is little question that as we move from point *A* to point *B*, we can indeed produce more military goods and continue to be the world's cop. But the trade-off is obvious, too. We lose out on the production of 30 billion units of health care, education, and other goods, because production of them must be reduced to 40 billion from its level of 70 billion.

**For Critical Analysis:**
*If Iraq started paying for its own reconstruction with oil revenues, how would this reduce the opportunity cost of such reconstruction to U.S. residents?*

## Figure 1-2: The Military versus Civilian Goods Trade-Off

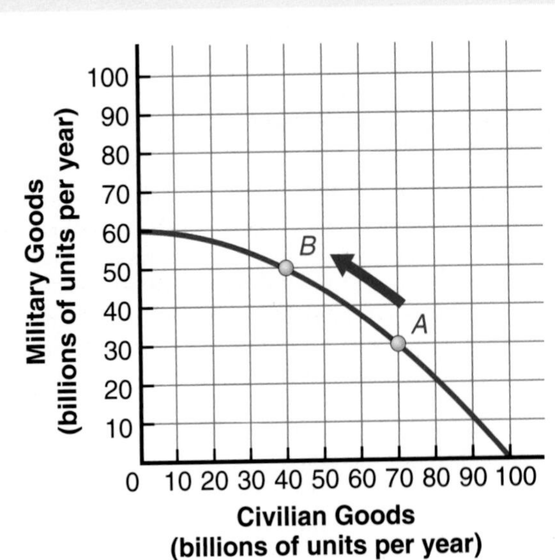


This figure is similar to Figure 1-1. Here, though, we show the trade-off between military goods and civilian goods. If we wish to be the global cop—moving from point *A* to point *B*—we are going to sacrifice civilian goods.

**Mastering Concepts:** Every Choice Involves a Trade-off

- **Because we live in a world of scarcity, choices must be made. Every choice involves a trade-off; that is, a cost must be incurred. With a given set of resources, this trade-off can be represented by a production possibilities curve (PPC).**
- **The production possibilities curve shows the maximum combination of outputs, given a fixed amount of resources.**

## ECONOMIC GROWTH DOESN'T ELIMINATE SCARCITY

One seeming way out of the production possibilities curve trade-off dilemma is for a nation to experiencje economic growth. **Economic growth** is defined as an increase in the production possibilities of a nation. We will have more to say about economic growth in a special chapter devoted just to that topic (Chapter 15). Here, we examine how to show economic growth using a production possibilities curve.

**Economic growth**
*Expansion of the economy, allowing it to produce more goods, jobs, and wealth.*

### GRAPHING ECONOMIC GROWTH

Look at Figure 1-3. There you see a set of three production possibilities curves, one labeled 2005, another labeled 2025, and another labeled 2045. In this example, we use pocket PCs and digital cameras as the two goods under study. We could have used civilian goods and military goods or any other combination of competing goods. In any event, the production possibilities curve moves out over time due to economic growth. Such growth may be caused by an increase in the number and productivity of workers or the amount of productive investment in equipment or by an increase in new inventions.

*Animated*

**Figure 1-3: The Effects of Economic Growth on the Production Possibilities Curve**

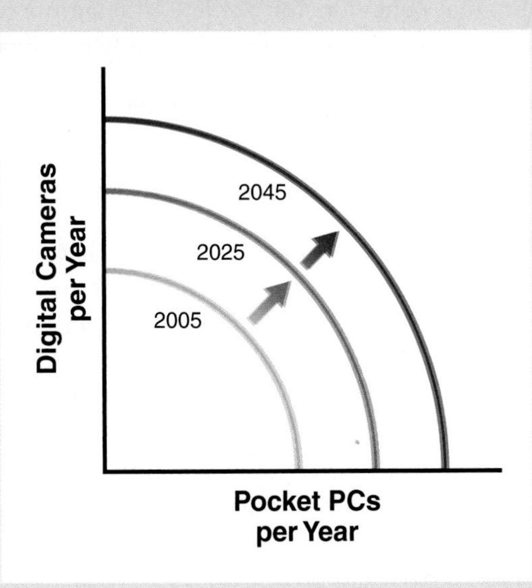


If a nation experiences economic growth, the production possibilities curve between digital cameras and pocket PCs will move out as shown here. In 2005, the nation is on the first curve. By 2045 it is on the third curve. The movement outward of the production possibilities curve graphically represents economic growth.

### SCARCITY STILL EXISTS

Do not get the impression that economic growth will eventually eliminate the problem of scarcity. It will not. No matter how much economic growth there is, at any future time we will always face some production possibilities curve. Therefore, we will always face trade-offs. The more we produce and consume of one thing, the less we will be able to have of others. ▸ **Example 1-11** If your income increased by 100 times, you would still face scarcity. You would not be able to buy all of the fine art that exists in the world, even with that high income. You would not be able to buy all of the private jets in the world, either. In other words, no matter how rich you are, you will still face trade-offs. ◂

**Mastering Concepts:** Economic Growth Doesn't Eliminate Scarcity

- **Economic growth can be depicted as an increase in the production possibilities of a nation. This is shown by an outward shifting of the production possibilities curve.**
- **Even with tremendous economic growth, scarcity still exists because at any point in time we will always face trade-offs.**

## LOOKING OUT FOR NUMBER ONE

**Rational self-interest**
*An assumption that we will never consciously choose an alternative that will make us worse off.*

Economics has not only been accused of being the dismal science, it has been accused of fostering selfishness. The reason is that as a science, it uses the assumption of **rational self-interest.** Some people have interpreted this assumption as supporting a "looking out for number one" view of the world. Nothing could be further from the truth.

### RATIONAL SELF-INTEREST IS JUST AN ASSUMPTION

Assumptions are the basis of hypotheses that allow us to analyze the world around us. All sciences use assumptions. So does economics. If you want to understand how the world around you works, you can't just say, "well, people do what they want to do and everybody has a different way of thinking." That is certainly true—we are all unique. But if you don't come up with some assumptions about human behavior, then you can never predict that behavior. You are left with simple cocktail-party conversation. Consider the following conversation I recently overheard:

***First person:*** ***"Gina is crazy. She rides her bike to work every day no matter how cold or rainy it is."***

***Second person:*** ***"Well, I guess she really likes biking."***

If we simply say that people do what they do because they like to act that way, we are really saying nothing. In the above conversation, the second person has added less than nothing. That person could have said the ubiquitous "Whatever" or "Really." There is no way to make any prediction about Gina's future behavior. If Gina stops biking, the second person can say, "I guess Gina no longer likes biking."

Most economists use the assumption that we can predict how humans act based on their perceived self-interest. Otherwise stated, we assume that individuals on average will rarely, if ever, consistently engage in behavior that makes them *worse off*.

**You Don't Have to Worry About How People "Really" Think** Often, critics of economics argue that people do not think rationally. You might say that you have a grandparent who never "thinks rationally." You might even say that, at times, you don't think rationally either and you do things that are against your self-interest. Not to worry—economics is not a science of human thought processes. Rather, it is a science that involves predicting how humans will act.

> ***When trying to predict how humans will react to changes in their economic environment,* just assume *that they act as if they were thinking about their own self-interest.***

## Defining Self-Interest

Self-interest does not always mean increasing one's wealth measured in dollars and cents. We assume that individuals seek many goals, not just increased wealth measured in monetary terms. Thus, the self-interest assumption includes goals relating to prestige, friendship, love, power, helping others, creating works of art, and many other matters. We can also think in terms of enlightened self-interest whereby individuals, in the pursuit of what makes them better off, also achieve the betterment of others around them.

✦ **Be Aware!** *Economics is* not *the study of thought processes.*

**Mastering Concepts:** Looking Out for Number One

- **Even though we use the assumption of rational self-interest to analyze human behavior, we do not imply that all individuals simply wish to increase their monetary wealth.**
- **Self-interest may involve helping the poor, working for world peace, or creating works of art.**

## SUMMING IT ALL UP

- Economics is the study of how people make choices.
- While basic needs are few, wants are unlimited.
- Scarcity exists because nature does not provide us with all of the resources necessary to satisfy our unlimited wants.
- Whenever you do anything—buy something, work at something, spend time doing something else—you incur an opportunity cost.
- Out of the many alternative uses of your resources, the next-highest-valued alternative is your opportunity cost.
- Because we live in a world of scarcity, choices must be made. Every choice involves a trade-off; that is, a cost must be incurred. With a given set of resources, this trade-off can be represented by a production possibilities curve (PPC).
- The production possibilities curve shows the maximum combination of two outputs, given a fixed amount of resources.
- Economic growth can be depicted as an increase in the production possibilities of a nation. This is shown by an outward shifting of the production possibilities curve.
- Even though we use the assumption of rational self-interest to analyze human behavior, we do not imply that all individuals simply wish to increase their monetary wealth.

## KEY TERMS AND CONCEPTS

economic growth 11
economics 4
efficiency 9
goods 5
inefficient point 9
needs 4
opportunity cost 5
production possibilities curve (PPC) 8
rational self-interest 12
resources 4
scarcity 5
trade-off 7
wants 4

## MASTERING ECONOMIC CONCEPTS
## Questions and Problems

**1-1.** Define economics. Explain briefly how economics—in terms of costs and benefits—relates to each of the following situations:

a. a student deciding to purchase a textbook for a particular class
b. a government increasing funding for mass transit
c. a municipality taxing hotel guests to obtain funding for a new stadium

**1-2.** Does the phrase "unlimited wants and limited resources" apply to both a low-income household and a middle-income household? Can the same phrase be applied to a very wealthy household?

**1-3.** Because some resources, such as labor, exist in every country, can we say that these resources are not scarce? Why or why not?

**1-4.** Rank the following items from most scarce to least scarce. Now rank these items from most expensive to least expensive. How do the two lists compare?

a. diamonds
b. water
c. oil
d. lumber
e. gold

**1-5.** Assume that you are a fan of the New York Yankees, a team whose chief rival is the Boston Red Sox. That being the case, would a Red Sox cap autographed by Red Sox pitcher Pedro Martinez be an economic good to you? Would your ability to transfer ownership of this cap by selling it on eBay affect your answer?

**1-6.** Define opportunity cost. What is your opportunity cost of attending an 11:00 A.M. class? How does it differ from your opportunity cost of attending an 8:00 A.M. class?

**1-7.** Assuming that Wendy's and Subway are my two favorite places to pick up lunch near campus, what would be my opportunity cost of buying lunch at Wendy's? How would your answer change if a Subway stand were located in the Student Union building, which is adjacent to my building?

**1-8.** If you receive a free ticket to a concert, what, if anything, is your opportunity cost? How does your opportunity cost change if there is a severe snowstorm in your town on the night of the concert?

**1-9.** Assume that you have two tests tomorrow—one in economics and one in accounting—but you have only two hours to study. Based on the following table, what is your opportunity cost of studying enough to earn an "A" on your economics test?

| Studying | Economics Grade | Accounting Grade |
|---|---|---|
| 2 hours on economics | A | D |
| 2 hours on accounting | B | B |

**1-10.** What is the opportunity cost of traveling by bus as opposed to traveling by plane? In general, what factors would account for different people having different opportunity costs for the same activity? In particular, how would the opportunity costs of traveling by bus differ for a busy executive as compared with a high school student on summer break?

**1-11.** Based on the production possibilities curve depicted below, what is the maximum amount of new homes that this country could produce in one month? What is the maximum amount of autos that this country could produce in one month?

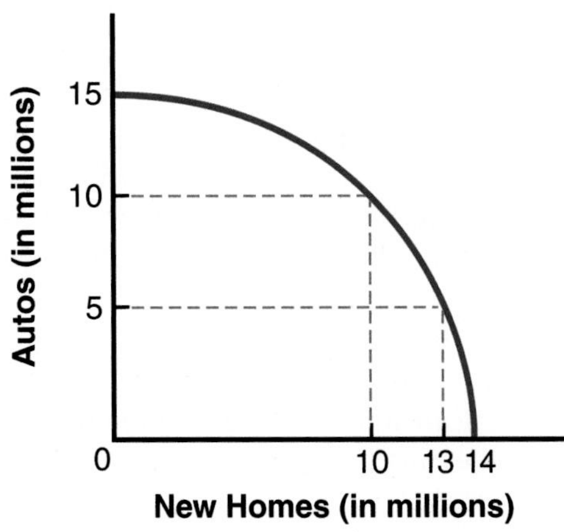


**1-12.** Based on the graph in 1-11 above, what is the maximum number of automobiles that the country could produce if it was also producing 10 million new homes? If it was also producing 13 million new homes? If it was also producing 14 million new homes?

**1-13.** Based on the graph in 1-11 above, what would be the opportunity cost to this country of increasing automobile production from zero to 5 million, from 5 million to 10 million, and from 10 million to 15 million? Explain why these opportunity costs could be different.

**1-14.** Based on the production possibilities curve depicted below, indicate whether each of these quantities would be a possible combination and, if so, whether that combination would be an efficient use of existing resources.

a. 50 units of wine and zero units of cheese
b. 28 units of wine and zero units of cheese
c. 46 units of wine and 60 units of cheese
d. 28 units of wine and 60 units of cheese

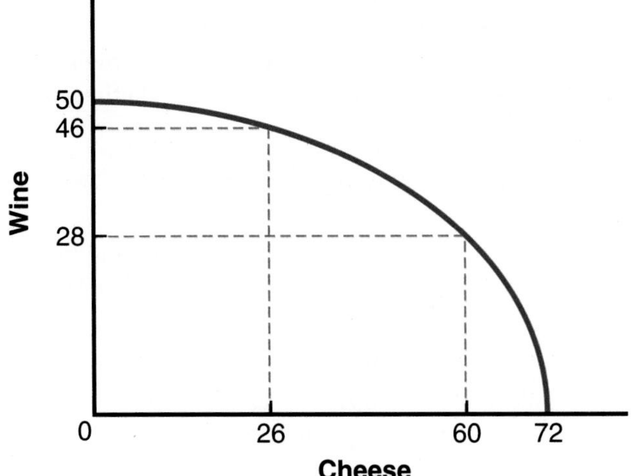


**1-15.** If the United States experienced economic growth, how would production possibilities curve A change? What factors could cause such growth and such a change?

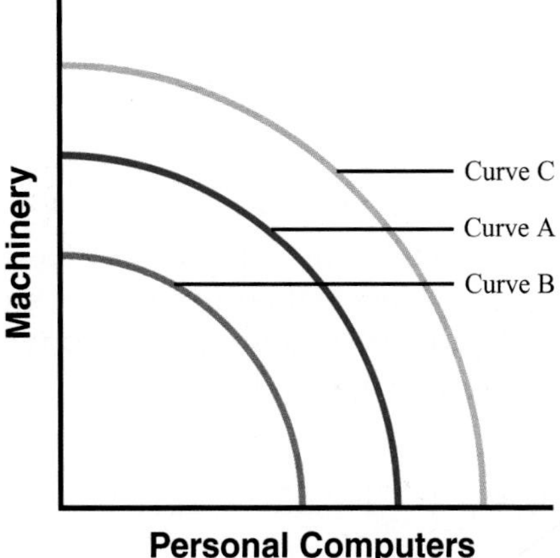


**1-16.** Shown below is the production possibilities curve for machinery and video games in the year 2005. What do all of the points *A, B,* and *C* have in common? Can we ever say that point *A* is preferable to point *B* or to point *C*? Do you think it would be possible to quickly move the economy from point *A* to point *C*? Why or why not?

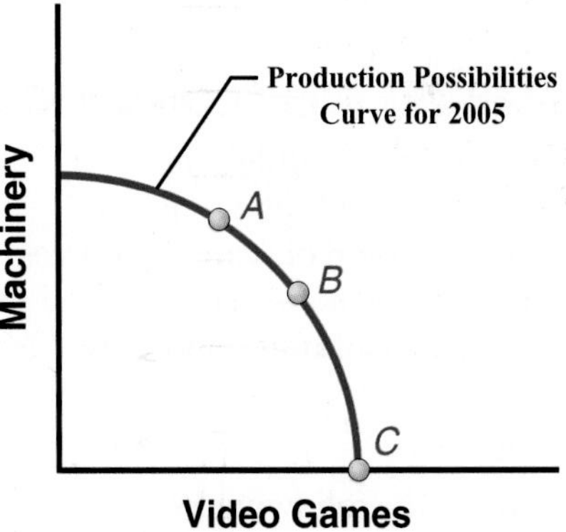


**1-17.** Consider the following events:

- In 2000 Mark Cuban purchased the NBA's Dallas Mavericks for $280 million even though the team traditionally lost more games than it won and reportedly was experiencing losses.
- In 1997 Ted Turner established a foundation to donate $1 billion to the United Nations.
- In 1994 an unnamed bidder purchased an antique Fabergé egg at auction for $5.5 million.

Based on your current situation, would you consider each of these to be a reasonable course of action for yourself? Would an economist conclude that each of these individuals had acted rationally? Why or why not?

## THINKING CRITICALLY

**1-1.** Is each of the following items a need, a want, or neither?

a. a cell phone
b. air pollution
c. a personal computer
d. water
e. an answering machine
f. a T-shirt from Abercrombie & Fitch

**1-2.** Over the past several years, developers have built many homes farther and farther away from the center of urban areas. As consumers, we have purchased many such homes. Discuss the various opportunity costs associated with this type of development.

**1-3.** Economists assume that individuals will act based on their own rational self-interest. Is it possible to reconcile the concept of rational self-interest with the following activities? In each case, why or why not?

a. sky diving, assuming some chance of injury or death
b. stealing an automobile, even though it is illegal
c. volunteering to work at a soup kitchen

## LOGGING ON

1. To learn about how scarcity of land is currently affecting housing markets in various U.S. locales, go to http://www.freerepublic.com/focus/f-news/893592/posts?page=7.
2. For a discussion of how economists think about dealing with a "bad" such as traffic congestion, go to http://stlouisfed.org/publications/re/pastissues/1997.html. Under "April," click on "Rush-Hour Horrors: How Economics Tackles Congestion."
3. To see how the concept of opportunity cost applies to the decision of how to finance the purchase of a new car, go to http://www.finance.cch.com/text/c10s10d060.asp.
4. For a discussion of arguments for and against a return to a military draft in the United States, go to http://www.cato.org/pubs/fpbriefs/fpb-006es.html.

## USING THE INTERNET FOR ECONOMIC ANALYSIS

**Children as a Scarce Resource** A couple's decision about whether to have a child is an economic choice involving the allocation of scarce resources. This application explores economic factors faced in choosing whether to have children—and how many children to have.

**Title:** To Bear or Not to Bear

**Navigation:** Go directly to the following Web site: http://stlouisfed.org/publications/re/2001/c/pages/economic-backgnd.html. If the link is broken, go to the home page of the Federal Reserve Bank of St. Louis at http://stlouisfed.org, click on "Economic Research, and under "Regional Economist," click on "Past Issues." Then click on "2001," and go to the July issue.

**Application** Read the article, and answer the following questions.

1. Why is there an opportunity cost associated with having a child?
2. How does an increase in a couple's income affect the trade-offs they face in choosing whether to bear a child?

## MEDIA RESOURCE LIST

The following media resources are available with this chapter:

- Load your CD-ROM to listen to the audio introduction to this chapter.
- Load your CD-ROM to access a Graph Animation of Figure 1-3, *The Effects of Economic Growth on the Production Possibilities Curve.*
- Load your CD-ROM to view the videos on *Scarcity and Resources* and *Rational Self-Interest.*
- Test your knowledge of chapter concepts with a quiz at www.miller-ume.com.
- Link to Web resources related to the text coverage at www.miller-ume.com.

## HOMEWORK SET

Go to the end of this book to find the Homework Problems for this chapter.

# Appendix A to Chapter 1: Using Graphs

A graph is a visual representation of the relationship between variables. In this appendix, we'll stick to just two variables: an *independent variable*, which can change in value freely, and a *dependent variable*, which changes only as a result of changes in the value of the independent variable. For example, if nothing else is changing in your life, your weight depends on the amount of food you eat. Food is the independent variable and weight, the dependent variable.

A table is a list of numerical values showing the relationship between two (or more) variables. Any table can be converted into a graph, which is a visual representation of that list. Once you understand how a table can be converted to a graph, you will understand what graphs are and how to construct and use them.

Consider a practical example. A conservationist may try to convince you that driving at lower highway speeds will help you conserve gas. Table A-1 shows the relationship between speed—the independent variable—and the distance you can go on a gallon of gas at that speed—the dependent variable. This table does show a pattern of sorts. As the data in the first column get larger in value, the data in the second column get smaller.

**Table A-1: Gas Mileage as a Function of Driving Speed**

| Miles per Hour | Miles per Gallon |
|---|---|
| 45 | 25 |
| 50 | 24 |
| 55 | 23 |
| 60 | 21 |
| 65 | 19 |
| 70 | 16 |
| 75 | 13 |

## GRAPHING NUMBERS IN A TABLE

Consider Table A-2 on the following page. Column 1 shows different prices for T-shirts, and column 2 gives the number of T-shirts purchased per week at these prices. Notice the pattern of these numbers. As the price of T-shirts falls, the number of T-shirts purchased per week increases. Therefore, an inverse relationship exists between these two variables, and as soon as we represent it on a graph, you will be able to see the relationship. We can graph this relationship using a coordinate number system—a vertical and horizontal number line for each of these two variables. Such a graph is shown in panel (b) of Figure A-1.

**Table A-2: T-Shirts Purchased**

| (1) Price of T-Shirts | (2) Number of T-Shirts Purchased per Week |
|---|---|
| $10 | 20 |
| 9 | 30 |
| 8 | 40 |
| 7 | 50 |
| 6 | 60 |
| 5 | 70 |

In economics, it is conventional to put dollar values on the $y$-axis. We therefore construct a vertical number line for price and a horizontal number line, the $x$-axis, for quantity of T-shirts purchased per week. The resulting coordinate system allows the plotting of each of the paired observation points; in panel (a), we repeat Table A-2, with an additional column expressing these points in paired-data $(x, y)$ form. For example, point $J$ is the paired observation (30, 9). It indicates that when the price of a T-shirt is $9, 30 will be purchased per week.

If it were possible to sell parts of a T-shirt ($\frac{1}{2}$ or $\frac{1}{20}$ of a shirt), we would have observations at every possible price. That is, we would be able to connect our paired observations, represented as lettered points. Let's assume that we can make T-shirts perfectly divisible so that the linear relationship shown in Figure A-1 also holds for fractions of dollars and T-shirts. We would then have a line that connects these points, as shown in the graph in Figure A-2.

In short, we have now represented the data from the table in the form of a graph. Note that an inverse relationship between two variables shows up on a graph as a line or curve that slopes *downward* from left to right. (You might as well get used to the idea that economists' data turn out to be curves, so they refer to everything represented graphically, even straight lines, as curves.)

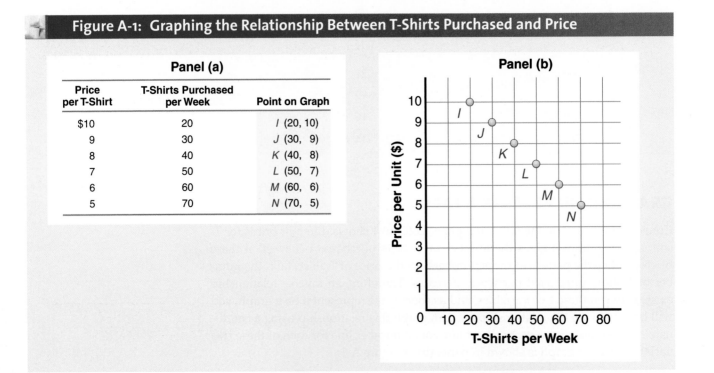

**Figure A-1: Graphing the Relationship Between T-Shirts Purchased and Price**

**Panel (a)**

| Price per T-Shirt | T-Shirts Purchased per Week | Point on Graph |
|---|---|---|
| $10 | 20 | *I* (20, 10) |
| 9 | 30 | *J* (30, 9) |
| 8 | 40 | *K* (40, 8) |
| 7 | 50 | *L* (50, 7) |
| 6 | 60 | *M* (60, 6) |
| 5 | 70 | *N* (70, 5) |

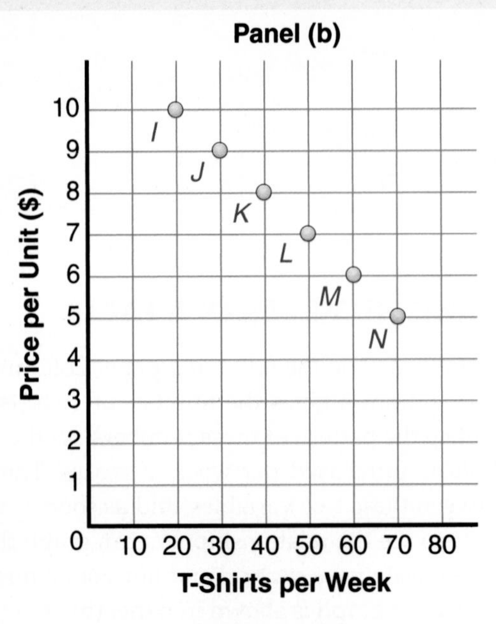

Figure A-2: Connecting the Observation Points

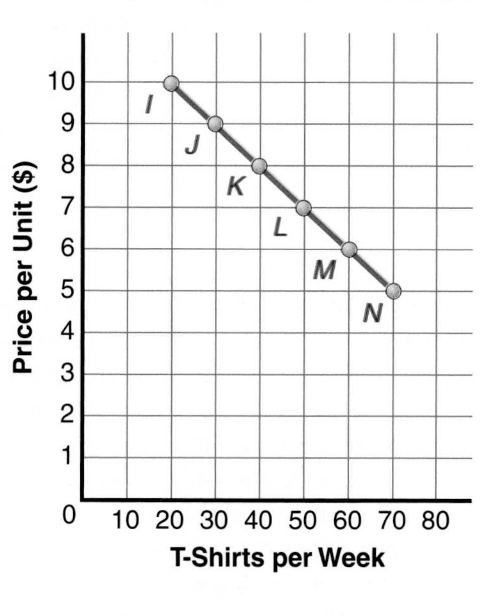


## THE SLOPE OF A LINE (A LINEAR CURVE)

An important property of a curve represented on a graph is its *slope*. Consider Figure A-3, which represents the quantities of shoes per week that a seller is willing to offer at different prices. Note that in panel (a) of Figure A-3, as in Figure A-1, we have expressed the coordinates of the points in parentheses in paired-data form.

Figure A-3: A Positively Sloped Curve

Panel (a)

| Price per Pair | Pairs of Shoes Offered per Week | Point on Graph |
|---|---|---|
| $100 | 400 | *A* (400,100) |
| 80 | 320 | *B* (320, 80) |
| 60 | 240 | *C* (240, 60) |
| 40 | 160 | *D* (160, 40) |
| 20 | 80 | *E* (80, 20) |

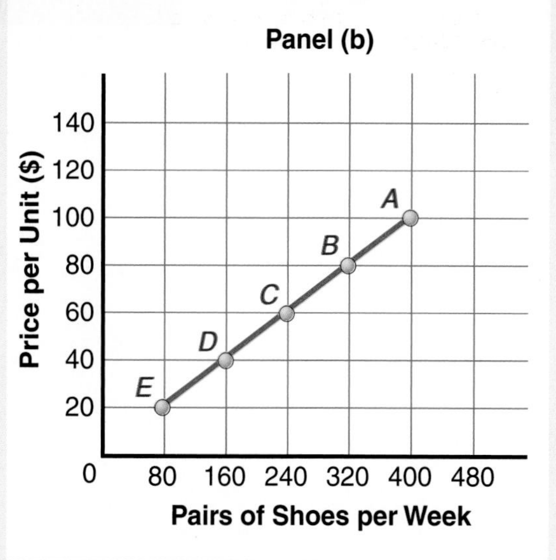

The *slope* of a line is defined as the change in the *y*-axis values divided by the corresponding change in the *x*-axis values as we move along the line. Let's move from point *E* to point *D* in panel (b) of Figure A-3 on the previous page. As we move, we note that the change in the *y* values, which is the change in price, is +$20, because we have moved from a price of $20 to a price of $40 per pair. As we move from *E* to *D*, the change in the *x* values is +80; the number of pairs of shoes willingly offered per week rises from 80 to 160 pairs. The slope calculated as a change in the *y* values divided by the change in the *x* values is therefore

$$\frac{20}{80} = \frac{1}{4}$$

It may be helpful for you to think of slope as a "rise" (movement in the vertical direction) over a "run" (movement in the horizontal direction). We show this abstractly in Figure A-4. The slope is measured by the amount of rise divided by the amount of run. In the example in Figure A-4, and, of course, in Figure A-3, the amount of rise is positive and so is the amount of run. That's because it's a direct relationship. We show an inverse relationship in Figure A-5. The slope is still equal to the rise divided by the run, but in this case the rise and the run have opposite signs because the curve slopes downward. That means that the slope will have to be negative and that we are dealing with an inverse relationship.

Now let's calculate the slope for a different part of the curve in panel (b) of Figure A-3 on page 17. We will find the slope as we move from point *B* to point *A*. Again, we note that the slope, or rise over run, from *B* to *A* equals

$$\frac{20}{80} = \frac{1}{4}$$

A specific property of a straight line is that its slope is the same between any two points; in other words, the slope is constant at all points on a straight line in a graph.

We conclude that for our example in Figure A-3, the relationship between the price of a pair of shoes and the number of pairs of shoes willingly offered per week is *linear*, which simply means "in a straight line," and our calculations indicate a constant slope. Moreover, we calculate a direct relationship between these

**Figure A-4: Figuring Positive Slope**

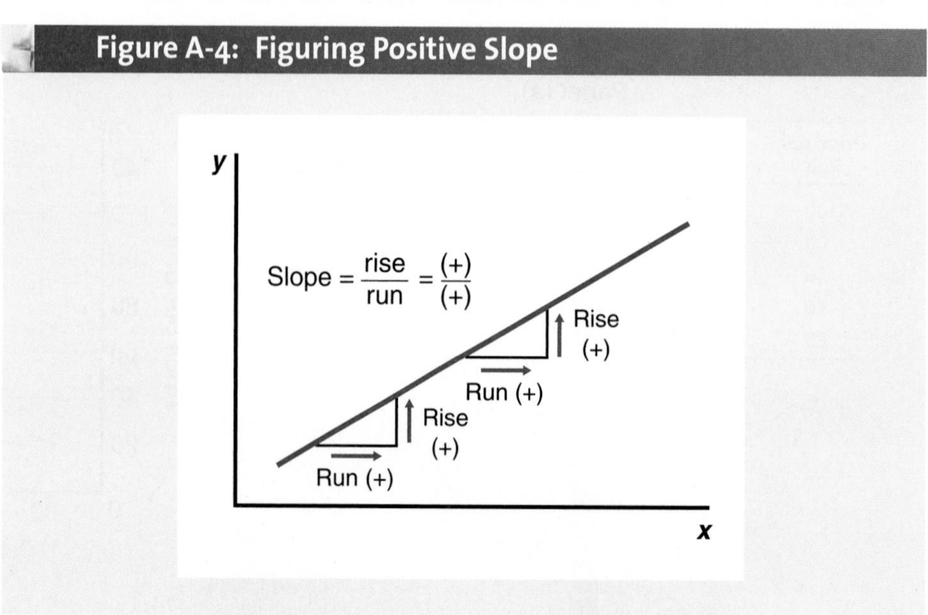

**Figure A-5: Figuring Negative Slope**

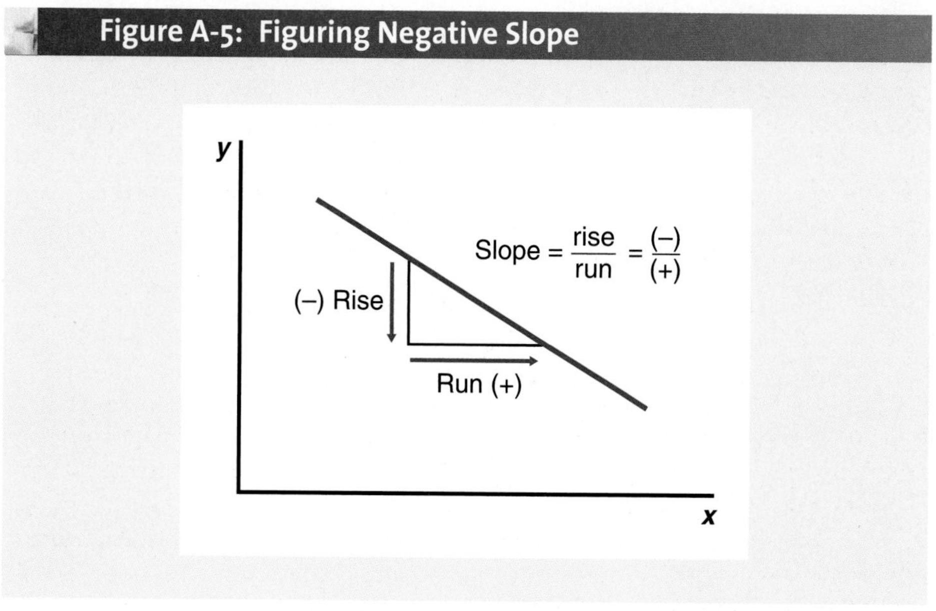


two variables, which turns out to be an upward-sloping (from left to right) curve. Upward-sloping curves have positive slopes—in this case, it is $+\frac{1}{4}$.

We know that an inverse relationship between two variables shows up as a downward-sloping curve—rise over run will be negative because the rise and run have opposite signs, as shown in Figure A-5. When we see a negative slope, we know that increases in one variable are associated with decreases in the other. Therefore, we say that downward-sloping curves have negative slopes. Can you verify that the slope of the graph representing the relationship between T-shirt prices and the quantity of T-shirts purchased per week in Figure A-2 is $-\frac{1}{10}$?

# CHAPTER 2

# The United States Within the World Economy

## *Facing an Economic Problem:* Just How Does Production Get Coordinated in This Country?

When you go to your local supermarket, you see thousands of products from which you can choose. If you go to a full-range electronics store, such as Circuit City, you see an almost overwhelming array of TVs, home cinemas, and appliances. If you watch television for any length of time, you are bombarded with ads for yet hundreds of other products, ranging from luxury automobiles to slice-it-and-dice-it cooking tools.

How do all of these production decisions get made? Who decides how many different car types General Motors will produce and try to sell? Who determines the number of brands of cereal? Who picks the latest colors for spring fashion wear?

To answer these questions, you need to know about the U.S. economic system. But before examining that, let's first examine the U.S. economy in the context of the world economy.

### Learning Objectives

After reading this chapter, you should be able to:

- **Explain how the price system answers the basic questions of what, how, and for whom to produce.**
- **List and explain the four main factors of production.**
- **Position the U.S. economy within the total world economy with respect to income, labor force, and global integration.**
- **Contrast GDP with per capita GDP and per capita real GDP.**
- **Compare the likely future population growth in the United States with that of Europe, China, and India.**

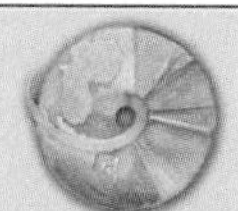

***Refer to the back of this chapter for a complete listing of multimedia learning materials available on the CD-ROM and the Web site.***

## ANSWERING SOME BASIC QUESTIONS—WHAT, HOW, AND FOR WHOM TO PRODUCE?

For over 200 years, the U.S. economy has been growing, thereby allowing most people to enjoy higher standards of living. But how does the U.S. economy actually operate? The economy produces millions of products and services each year, employing almost 145 million workers to do so. Some specialized goods and services are produced by one or two individuals working alone, whereas other goods are produced in huge factories with thousands of workers and numerous machines. At the end of the day, some people make enough income to buy just about everything they could possibly think of, whereas others make little or no income and rely on government for basic necessities. How does our **economic system**—the way we organize the use of our scarce resources—actually determine how things are produced and who gets what?

**Economic system**
*The way in which a nation organizes its resources to satisfy its residents' wants.*

### WHAT TO PRODUCE AND IN WHAT QUANTITIES?

As you learned in Chapter 1, we live in a world of scarcity and trade-offs. If more of a particular item is produced, then less of something else will be produced during the same period, with a given set of resources. ▸ Example 2-1 Even within government, if someone makes the decision to extend the interstate highway system to ten more medium-sized cities, then fewer resources will be available to upgrade our national parks. If your city decides to hire more police officers, fewer funds are going to be available to buy computers for the classroom. ◂

▸ Example 2-2 Even within one automobile company, there are trade-offs between using a given amount of machinery and labor to build SUVs, luxury vehicles, minivans, or pickup trucks. ◂

**Prices Provide Signals** Because we live in a world of scarcity, we cannot obtain all that we want for free. Goods and services in our economic system carry with them specific prices.

***Prices are the signals that tell the relative scarcity of a good or service.***

▸ Example 2-3 When you go to buy a watch, you find that the prices range from literally a few dollars to literally hundreds of thousands of dollars. The prices tell you the relative scarcity of each brand and model of those watches. You know that a $100,000 Frank Mueller watch is relatively more scarce than a $10 Casio. ◂

Another way of putting this discussion about prices is as follows: When a lot of people want something (the *demand* for that item) for which not much exists (the *supply*), prices tend to be relatively high and vice versa. In Chapter 3 you will look specifically at this analysis in terms of *demand* for and *supply* of goods and services.

It is normally the forces of demand and supply that determine the market prices for goods and services.

**Price system**
*An economic system in which relative prices are constantly changing to reflect changes in the supply of and demand for different commodities. The prices of those commodities are signals to everyone within the system as to what is relatively scarce and what is relatively abundant.*

**The Price System Comes to the Rescue** So, in the U.S. economy, for the most part, it is the interaction of the demand for and the supply of different goods and services that determines what and how much will be produced. This interaction is carried out via the **price system**. With a price system, when goods get scarcer, their prices go up. When they get less scarce, their prices go down.

▸ **Example 2-4** After a hurricane, many people are without electricity. Typically, the price of ice then goes up. When large quantities of strawberries come on the market during the summer, their prices plummet relative to other times in the year. ◂

Note, however, that if the highest price that consumers are willing to pay is less than the lowest cost at which a good or service can be produced, output will be zero. ▸ **Example 2-5** Space shuttles have existed for sometime now. Taxpayers, acting through the government, normally pay for them. For the moment, consumers do not purchase their own private space shuttles. The demand is not great enough in relation to the supply to create a market for private space shuttles. (But that may change sometime in the future when space shuttle production costs fall and U.S. residents become very rich.) ◂

## *Solving the Economic Problem:* How Does Production Get Coordinated in This Country?

In the United States, the price system tells producers whether they are producing the right or wrong types of goods. Whenever the price of a product yields **profits**, producers will produce more. Whenever the price of a product does not produce any profits, but rather causes producers to incur losses, they will produce less. Profits are measured as the difference between revenues received and costs incurred in producing a good or service.

Consumers compare prices with the value they place on goods and services. Whenever the price is less than the perceived value, consumers will buy more. Whenever the price is greater than the perceived value, consumers will buy less.

So, consumers need to know *nothing* about how producers decide what to do. Consumers simply need to know the price and how much they value different goods. Similarly, producers need to know *nothing* about consumers. They need to know the costs of producing and the price at which they can sell an item. Consequently, it is prices that guide consumers and producers and thus coordinate production in this country.

**Profits**
*The differences between total revenues and total costs.*

## How Should We Produce Our Goods and Services?

The price system indicates to producers what to produce. That is to say, if producers see that they can make profits by producing certain types of cars, breakfast cereals, and clothes, that is what they will produce. Once that decision is made, they must then decide how to produce these goods and services. Because a given amount of any good or service can be made in a variety of ways, producers of goods and services have numerous production choices.

Should more workers be hired? Should those workers be skilled or unskilled? Should a company invest in laborsaving automated machinery? Should a new plant be built? These are some of the decisions that every producer of goods and services faces. Each decision is based on the desire of firm owners and managers to make the highest profits possible. ▸ **Example 2-6** In the past, carpenters put together a roof using hammers and nails. Today, carpenters use nail guns to do the same job in much less time. In the past, banks hired numerous workers to type in the information found on checks. Today, optical scanning machines do the work of hundreds of such workers. ◂

**Competition Rears Its Head** Because of competition, producers of goods and services are forced to seek the least costly combinations of the inputs—described below—that are used in the production of a good or service.

***Because of competition and the desire to make the highest profits possible, producers must use the*** **least-cost *combination of inputs.***

Not only does doing this allow the producers to make the most profits, but in many cases it makes the difference between staying in business or failing. If they don't keep their costs down, they may go out of business. ▸ **Example 2-7** Every year thousands of firms in the United States declare bankruptcy, which means that their losses are so great that they cannot continue in business. Some of them successfully reorganize, but most eventually disappear. ◂

Seeking the lowest costs may mean that some U.S. suppliers outsource some of their work to firms in other countries. In any event, firms that choose the least-cost production techniques are able to produce a good or service at a lower price and still make a profit. This lower price induces consumers to shift purchases from competing higher-priced firms to the lower-priced firm. It is not surprising, consequently, that most firms are constantly seeking better and lower-cost production techniques. They relentlessly strive to reduce costs per unit of whatever they are producing and selling.

✦ **Note!** *While you might think that prices don't matter, as long as some consumers shop for the best deals, competition will force producers to seek ways to reduce prices while still making a profit.*

**Consumers Prefer Lower Prices** Clearly, if consumers did not care about prices, producers would not have to care about their costs. They could be inefficient and sloppy, charge higher prices to overcome their mistakes, and still sell enough to make a profit. But consumers do care about the prices they pay for goods and services. Some consumers will always seek out the best deals possible. ▸ **Example 2-8** In the early 2000s, the U.S. airline industry faced rising costs and falling demand. While virtually all airline companies were incurring huge losses, Southwest Airlines was making profits. Why? Because apparently it anticipated decreased demand early in the 2000s and made the appropriate adjustments. That is, Southwest figured out numerous ways to lower its costs. It was able to lower its prices accordingly and attract a larger share of airline customers. ◂

## For Whom Will Output Be Produced—Who Gets What?

After goods and services are produced, somehow there has to be a determination of who gets what. Who gets to buy all of those millions of new cars produced by General Motors and Ford? Who ends up renting that luxury apartment in the choice spot in the middle of the city overlooking a beautiful park? The answers to these questions are determined by the distribution of money income.

**Determination of Money Income** If you don't have the ability to pay for something that you want, you usually don't get it. Your ability to pay is based on the size of your money income. Your money income—apart from what you inherit or receive as gifts from your parents and the government—is usually determined chiefly by the value of your labor services to the outside world.

Ultimately, the size of your money income is determined by how well you are able to sell your labor services. It also depends on how well you have invested in the stock market, housing, and the like, but such investments are usually possible only because you have previously sold your labor for money income.

**Distribution of Goods** In the U.S. economic system, the distribution of finished products to consumers is based on different consumers' ability and willingness to pay the market prices for goods and services. There is no central governing body that decides which consumers will get which goods. ▸ **International Example 2-9** For over 70 years in the former Soviet Union (of which Russia was the most important part), the distribution of consumer goods was decided by government officials. The officials routinely miscalculated the demand for or the supply of a particular good, with disastrous results. Long lines were common, even for such basic consumer products as toilet paper and bread. ◂

**Mastering Concepts:** **Some Basic Questions—What, How, and for Whom to Produce?**

- **Prices signal to consumers the relative scarcity of goods and services. Consumers then determine whether they value those goods and services enough to buy them at those prices.**
- **Prices signal to producers how much they should produce—rising prices signal that they should produce more, and falling prices that they should produce less.**
- **The price system via the demand for and the supply of different goods and services coordinates the decisions of consumers and producers.**
- **Competition and the lure of higher profits force producers to seek the least-cost combination of inputs.**
- **Who gets what is produced is normally determined by money income, plus inheritance and gifts.**

## PRODUCING GOODS AND SERVICES REQUIRES RESOURCES

The U.S. economy produces millions upon millions of goods and services. Producing those goods and services each year requires resources. Typically, we call such resources **factors of production**, which are the resources required for final production of goods and services.

**Factors of production**
*The resources, or inputs, of land, labor, capital, and entrepreneurship that are used to produce goods and services.*

### Resource Classification

Traditionally, we classify productive resources in terms of land, labor, capital, and entrepreneurship.

1. **Land:** As an economic term, land refers not just to a place on which to stand or to build a house, but also to all natural resources present without human intervention. ▸ **Example 2-10** Land includes water, fish, animals, mineral deposits, surface land, timber, and other so-called gifts of nature. ◂
2. **Labor:** Labor is often called the human resource. It includes the services of anyone who works to produce goods and services. ▸ **Example 2-11** The services of steelworkers, farmers, physicians, and hairstylists are all included

**Land**
*Natural resources plus surface land and water.*

**Labor**
*Human effort directed toward producing goods and services.*

under the rubric labor. The taxi driver, the corporate executive, and the person who sweeps the floors are all part of labor.

**Capital**
*Previously manufactured goods used to make other goods and services.*

3. **Capital:** Typically, capital refers to the manufactured goods used to make other goods and services. ▸ Example 2-12 The machines, buildings, and tools used to assemble automobiles, skateboards, and computers are all capital goods. A good is not a capital good unless it is used in turn to produce other goods and services.

**Physical capital**
*Factories, equipment, and improvements to natural resources.*

**Human capital**
*The accumulated training and education of workers.*

Sometimes economists like to distinguish between **physical capital,** (factories, equipment, and improvements to natural resources) and human capital. **Human capital** is defined as the accumulated education and training of workers. To become more educated, individuals have to devote time and resources. When they do so, we say that they are adding to their human capital.

**Entrepreneurship**
*The ability of risk-taking individuals to develop new products and start new businesses in order to make profits.*

4. **Entrepreneurship:** The fourth factor of production is entrepreneurship. This refers to the ability of individuals to start new businesses, to introduce new products and processes, and to improve management techniques. Entrepreneurship involves initiative and willingness to take risks in order to reap profits.

Entrepreneurs are the ones who take risks. When they start and invest in new businesses, they know that the businesses may fail, as about half of new businesses do within ten years or less.

## Productivity Is the Result

You usually know when you are more productive. ▸ Example 2-13 If you work on an assembly line in an automobile factory, you can measure your productivity yourself. When you begin learning how to attach bumper assemblies to cars, perhaps you can do only two an hour. After a few weeks, you may be able to do three, and after a few months, maybe seven. You have become more productive.

**Productivity**
*The amount of output (goods and services) that results from a given level of inputs (land, labor, capital, and entrepreneurship); often measured in terms of how much output a given amount of labor input can produce.*

**Productivity** for an economy is linked to the amount of labor input required to produce one unit of output. If the labor input required to produce a unit of output falls, we say that productivity has increased.

Typically, productivity increases because of the increased use of capital, both physical and human.

In the beginning of the 2000s, measured productivity increased faster than expected. You'll read about why in the following *Policy Application.*

### POLICY APPLICATION: Fire a Worker to Increase Measured Productivity

**Concept Applied: *Productivity***

In 2002, measured labor productivity increased by almost 5 percent, the best performance since 1950. Economic commentators hailed this increased productivity as a sign that the U.S. economy was fundamentally sound. Others added that increased productivity ultimately leads to higher standards of living through new products, management methods, and technologies.

#### Firing May Raise Measured Productivity

Increased productivity in 2002 and other recent years may have been caused by layoffs. Shutting down the economy's least-efficient plants may also have contributed to increased productivity. Both actions may, and certainly did, increase measured productivity gains. McDonald's closed more than 700 of its poorest-performing franchises. Across the nation, consolidations in industries may lead to higher productivity, but with *fewer* employees in each industry. This actually happened during the depths of the Great Depression in the 1930s. Supermarkets wiped out small mom-and-pop grocery stores. Productivity soared in food marketing.

**Long-Run Increased Productivity Requires More**

Shutting down inefficient plants and laying off the least-productive workers may increase measured productivity in the short run. In the long run, though, productivity increases when managers hire workers with more human capital and develop production systems that are more efficient.

**For Critical Analysis:**
*Measured productivity can rise when inefficient plants are phased out. What are other ways for businesses to raise productivity?*

**Mastering Concepts:** Production Requires Resources

- **Factors of production include land, labor, capital, and entrepreneurship.**
- **There is physical capital, such as buildings, and human capital, which embodies individual workers' ability to produce because of education, training, and experience.**
- **Productivity can increase because of the increased use of physical and human capital.**

## PUTTING THE U.S. ECONOMY IN PERSPECTIVE

The economies of most European countries have been around for much longer than the U.S. economy. In fact, the United States was an undeveloped country, by world standards, until the latter part of the 1800s. Since then, it has grown to be a world powerhouse. Average living standards—measured by income per person or consumption per person—have increased many times just in the last century. Population has grown from a few million at the time the Constitution was ratified to close to 300 million today. Improvements in diet, working conditions, nutrition, hygiene, and medical care have all added to life expectancy. ▸ **Example 2-14** Life expectancy in the American colonies in the early 1700s was only 36 years. Today, life expectancy at birth is 77 years. By the year 2040, life expectancy will likely have increased to 85 years. ◂

### THE U.S. ECONOMY VIEWED BY ITSELF

Although there are 50 states, we typically look at the U.S. economy as one entity. A good reason why this is appropriate is that there is unrestricted trade among the states. The framers of the U.S. Constitution knew that the country would grow faster if individual states could be prevented from erecting barriers to trade in the form of taxes on out-of-state goods. Consequently, the Constitution prohibits almost all barriers to **interstate trade**.

**Interstate trade**
*Trade between and among states within the United States. (Trade within a single state is called* intrastate *trade.)*

**The U.S. Labor Force** Currently, almost 150 million U.S. residents are part of the **labor force,** defined as those over age 16 who are either working or seeking work. A hundred years ago, the labor force measured a mere 40 million. Given

**Labor force**
*All persons over 16 who are not in school or other institutions and are either working or actively looking for work.*

that the average percentage of the labor force without a job has stayed about the same over time, this means that the U.S. economy is capable of creating millions of jobs every year.

Today, the U.S. labor force is well schooled, well trained, and mobile. One in five families moves each year, usually for work-related reasons.

Look at Figure 2-1 to see the growth in the U.S. labor force.

### The Number and Quality of Goods That We Produce and Consume

For most of the early years of this country, we were an agrarian society. Over 90 percent of the population was engaged in farming until the mid-1800s. Incomes were low, and the products that we consumed were precious few and far between.

agarian = farmer

Today, the average U.S. resident can choose among dozens of car brands (not all manufactured in the United States, of course), dozens of brands and types of refrigerators, thousands of CDs, and millions of books. We are definitely a consumer-oriented society. ▸ **Example 2-15** To get an idea of how the number and quality of goods offered for sale have changed, consider the following: The 1909 Sears Roebuck catalog offered shoes, fancy chairs, and beds. You could buy a horse-drawn buggy as well as a gramophone. What was missing, compared to today? The automobile, light bulbs, radios, and TVs. Of course, there were no computers, MP3 players, CDs, or microwave ovens. ◂

**The Information Age** Perhaps one of the most startling changes in the U.S. economy has occurred in the area of information and communication. One of the reasons that we are such a "wired" society is the dramatic fall in the cost of computing power, as you can see in Figure 2-2.

▸ **Example 2-16** Cheaper and cheaper computing power and lower communication costs have led to an explosion in telecommuting and virtual offices. Whereas almost no workers worked for pay at home in 1980, the government estimates that currently almost 20 million workers telecommute. Many people run

**Figure 2-1 Rise in the U.S. Labor Force over Time**

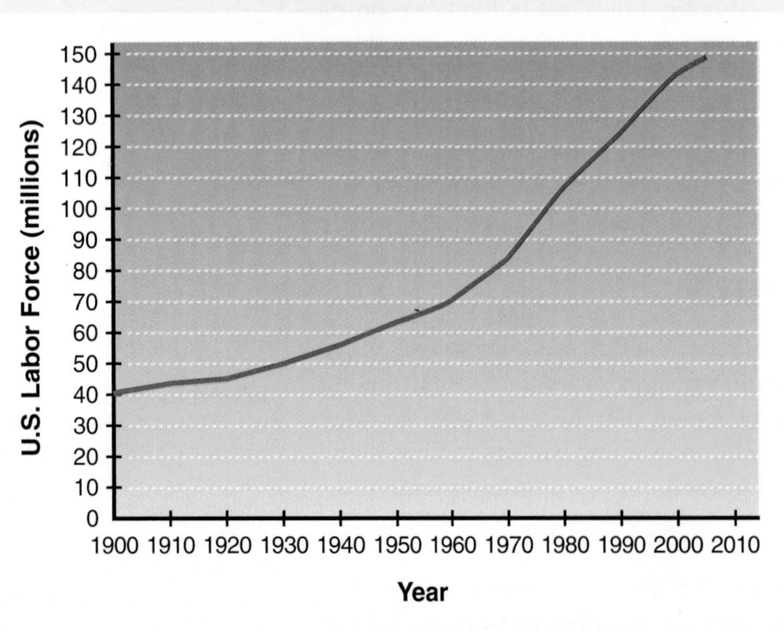


Since 1900, the U.S. labor force has increased from 40 million to almost 150 million.

**Figure 2-2 Evolution of the Cost per Unit of Speed for Microprocessor Chips**

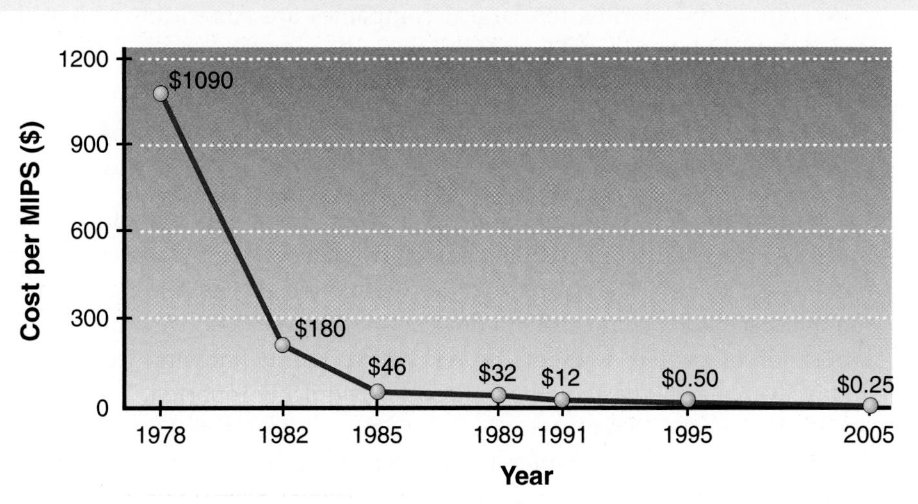


In less than three decades, the price per unit of speed (1 million instructions per second, or MIPS) has fallen from about $1,100 to 25 cents. Costs today are less than two-hundredths of one percent of what they were in 1978. (That's the same as a $50 item in 1978 costing only one penny today.)

companies from their homes, connected to employees, independent contractors, suppliers, and customers via phone, fax, and the Internet. ◂

**The Switch to a Service Economy** Obviously, when this nation started several hundred years ago, just about everybody worked in agriculture. Gradually, we became a more manufacturing-oriented economy. Workers moved from the farms to the cities to work in factories at higher wage rates. The heyday of the United States as an industrialized economy was probably during the first part of the twentieth century.

Oh, how times have changed. Today, less than 2 percent of the labor force is involved in agriculture. About 17 percent work in manufacturing and mining. The rest are involved in services—over 80 percent! Services include the obvious—health care, accounting, architecture, legal research, plumbing, electrical repair, and education. Services also include banking and finance, accounting, travel and vacation consulting, retailing, insurance, real estate, and providing restaurant meals.

## The United States' Place in the World Economy

Here are some data that allow you to place the U.S. economy in the context of the world economy:

- With 4.5 percent of the world population, the United States generates about 25 percent of total world industrial output.
- We consume 99 percent of what we produce and give the rest away to people in other nations.
- The U.S. economy has a total national income of over $11 trillion, compared to $30 trillion for the total world economy.
- Whereas annual energy use per capita worldwide is the equivalent of 9.5 barrels of oil, in the United States it is 60 barrels.
- Daily water use per capita worldwide is 465 gallons, compared to 1,512 gallons in the United States.

- The U.S. share of world energy consumption is 25 percent, down from 31 percent in 1970.
- Four of the world's ten largest companies are American, with Wal-Mart, General Motors, and ExxonMobil taking the top three spots.

## The United States Is Closely Intertwined with All Other Countries

We truly do live in a global economy. The information and communication revolution has caused the United States and its residents to be in closer contact with all parts of the planet. ▸ **Example 2-17** Before telegraphs, telephones, TVs, and the Internet, China could suffer a devastating earthquake or flood, killing tens of thousands of people, without the rest of the world knowing for a long time. Today, even a small earthquake in Ecuador is quickly reported. You know about events that affect different countries' economies almost in real time. ◂

As you will read in Chapter 16 on international trade, the United States depends greatly on other countries' purchases and sales of goods and services. The fact is that we are linked to every other country and every other country is linked to us, as you will read in the following *Global Application*.

### GLOBAL APPLICATION: Our Increasingly Interconnected World of Trade

***Concept Applied:***
**Global Integration**

American companies sell a stunning amount to the rest of the world. Dow-Corning makes over 10,000 deliveries a month to over 20,000 customers in 50 countries. Any disruption in trade routes can have immediate negative effects on Dow-Corning. Not surprisingly, before the war in Iraq in 2003, Dow-Corning's planners met on numerous occasions to create backup plans in case the war disrupted world trade movements. Of course, trade goes in both directions. Many goods are manufactured outside the United States and sold here. Such imported goods rely on global shipping.

#### Even the Lowly Car CD Player Relies on Total Global Transportation

Consider a South Korean car called the KIA. Its manufacturer has an elaborate supply system for every component, even the car's CD player. Look at Figure 2-3. There you see how many steps are required to get a CD player into a KIA automobile that will end up in an auto dealer's showroom in, say, Chicago.

**Step 1:** China—KIA subcontracts to Panasonic for the optical-pickup unit. Panasonic outsources it to a mainland Chinese company. That company sends the units to Thailand.

**Step 2:** Thailand—A Thai firm adds electronic as well as structural components to the CD player. These are shipped to another subcontractor, Matsushita, which has a plant in Mexico.

**Step 3:** Mexico—After the units are trucked from the port of entry to a Delco Electronics plant in Matamoros, they are added to the full audio system assembly.

**Step 4:** California—The complete audio systems are trucked to California. From there, they go to South Korea.

**Step 5:** South Korea—The CD players and audio systems are fitted into the KIA cars in the town of Hwaseong.

**Step 6:** United States—The KIAs, with their CD players, are shipped to the United States for distribution to various KIA auto dealers.

**For Critical Analysis:**
*After examining the many steps involved in just one part of a car sold in the United States, what do you conclude about the average cost of shipping?*

**Figure 2-3 All of This Just for a CD Player!**

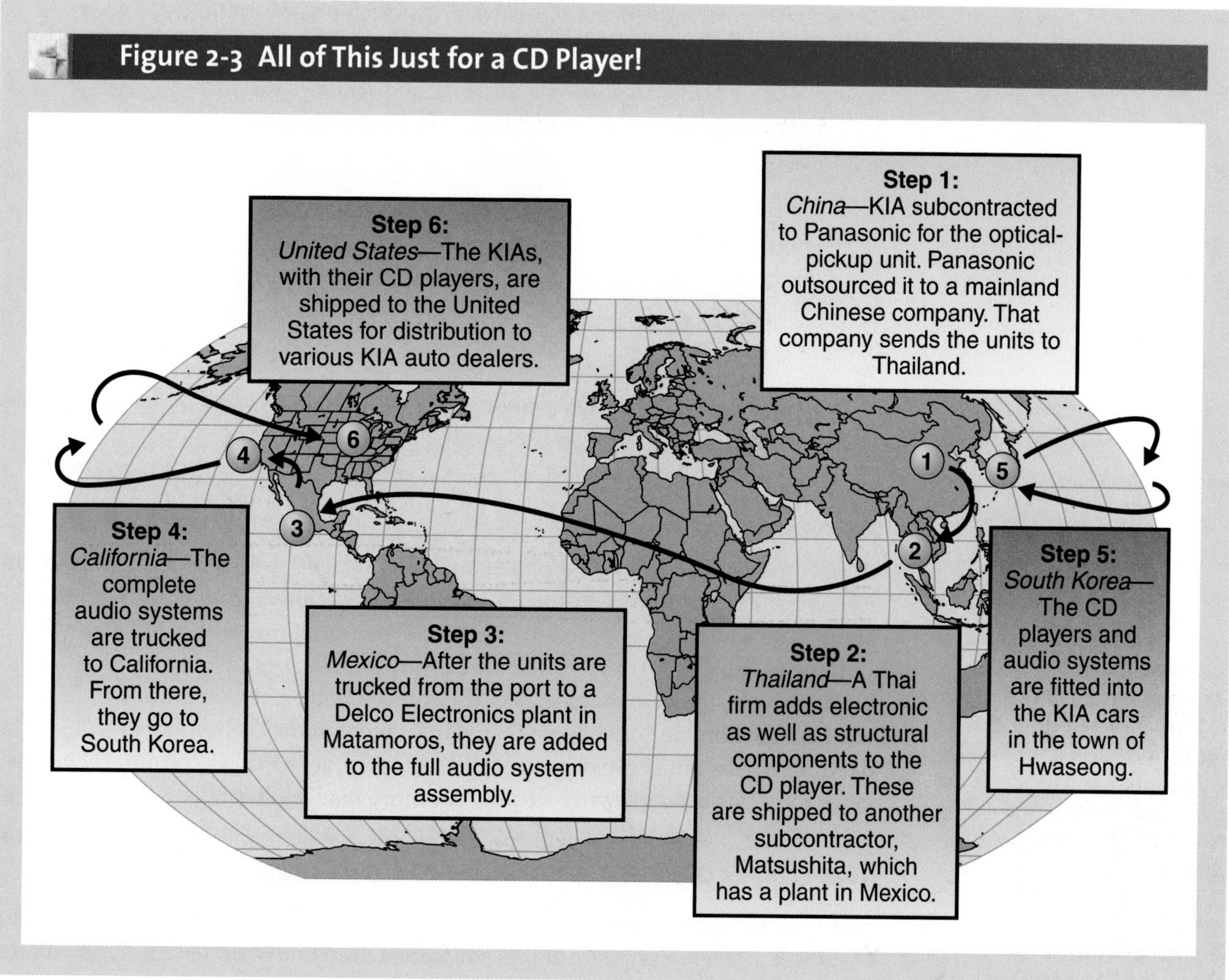
Step 1:
*China*—KIA subcontracted to Panasonic for the optical-pickup unit. Panasonic outsourced it to a mainland Chinese company. That company sends the units to Thailand.
Step 2:
*Thailand*—A Thai firm adds electronic as well as structural components to the CD player. These are shipped to another subcontractor, Matsushita, which has a plant in Mexico.
Step 3:
*Mexico*—After the units are trucked from the port to a Delco Electronics plant in Matamoros, they are added to the full audio system assembly.
Step 4:
*California*—The complete audio systems are trucked to California. From there, they go to South Korea.
Step 5:
*South Korea*—The CD players and audio systems are fitted into the KIA cars in the town of Hwaseong.
Step 6:
*United States*—The KIAs, with their CD players, are shipped to the United States for distribution to various KIA auto dealers.
1
2
3
4
5
6

With the benefits of increasing global integration also come some costs. The more dependent our businesses are on manufacturing in other countries, the more susceptible they are to crises caused by interruptions in their normal global supply routes. ▸ **Example 2-18** During the first Gulf War in Kuwait and Iraq in 1991, many companies were unprepared for the disruptions that occurred in their normal lines of supply for their parts. For example, Dow-Corning tried to handle the problems for its 10,000 deliveries a month in 50 countries by using faxes and phone calls. By the time the second Gulf War (the war in Iraq) occurred in 2003, Dow-Corning—and other companies as well—had already established alternative shipping routes to avoid delays. ◂

## The United States Draws on a Potential Global Labor Supply

A hundred years ago, most U.S. companies never thought about the possibility of using workers in distant lands. Of course, until relatively recently, communication was a problem. There were no faxes, FedEx, Internet, or e-mail then.

**Table 2-1 Estimated Number of Jobs Moving Offshore by 2015**

| | |
|---|---|
| Architecture | 185,000 |
| Business operations | 350,000 |
| Computer | 500,000 |
| Management | 300,000 |
| Office support | 1,700,000 |

*Source: Forrester Research, Inc.*

In the past several decades, U.S. companies have gone offshore to manufacture clothes, appliances, and home tools. Why? Lower costs, to be sure. In the past few years, this trend has expanded to many routine research and development and other high-tech jobs that do not require face-to-face coordination. ▸ **International Example 2-19** Computer-generated drawings for suburban homes, industrial parks, and industrial plants are being converted into blueprints by architects in Chile, Hungary, and the Philippines. An architect in the Philippines earns about $250 a month compared to over $3,000 per month in the United States. ◂

Look at Table 2-1. There you see the estimated number of jobs moving offshore by 2015. Note, though, that just because some U.S.-based companies will be using workers offshore does not mean that employment in the United States will fall. Indeed, new jobs are created in the millions every year in this country. The active labor force has been growing steadily for more than 200 years.

**Outsourcing**
*Assembling a product in a different country. With respect to services, the purchasing of services in another country that are then transferred back to the home country, often via the Internet.*

**Recession**
*A period of time during which the rate of growth of business activity is consistently less than its long-term trend. Another definition is when there is negative economic growth for at least two quarters (six months).*

## The U.S. Economy Is Huge and Growing

Just because we are **outsourcing** jobs in manufacturing offshore does not mean that the U.S. economy is shrinking. Far from it. You live in one of the most vibrant, resilient, and flexible economies in the world. It is an economy that has its difficulties, to be sure. When the economy is growing less rapidly than it has been on average over a long number of years, we say that there is a **recession**. The U.S.

SOURCE: WWW.CARTOONBANK.COM

*"Sorry boys, the production work is being shipped to the South Pole."*

economy has suffered recessions throughout its history and will continue to do so periodically.

On average, though, U.S. residents have experienced increases in their standards of living over most of this country's relatively short history. In addition, there has been growth in the number of jobs over the last 25 years. Our economy has created about 40 million new jobs during that period. ▸ **International Example 2-20** During the same 25-year period, some countries in Europe have created hardly any new jobs. Most of the jobs they have created have been in the government sector as opposed to the private sector. From 1980 to 2004, fewer than one million new private-sector jobs were created in France. In Germany, the number was not much more encouraging. ◂

Even though living standards in the United States have grown, not everybody has shared in the "American dream." Most people imagine that the dream also includes getting wealthier. **Wealth** can be thought of as the value of what you own minus the value of what you owe. As you will read in the following *Policy Application*, in the last 15 years, wealth disparity has increased at the same time that average wealth has risen sharply.

**Net worth**
*Usually defined as the difference between what you own and what you owe. Otherwise stated, the market value of stocks, bonds, houses, and the like minus all of your debts.*

**Incentive effect**
*The change in circumstances or a situation that causes humans to react by changing their behavior in response to the change in circumstances.*

**Wealth**
*Those things of value owned by a person, household, firm, or nation. Household wealth usually consists of a house, cars, stocks and bonds, bank accounts, and personal belongings.*

## POLICY APPLICATION: The Rich Get Richer and the Poor Do, Too (But Not Quite So Fast)

### *Concepts Applied:* Wealth, Wealth Inequality

The U.S. economy has been growing, but so too has the gap between the richest and the poorest. Now that does not mean that the rich have gotten richer and the poor have gotten poorer. Rather, in the last decade of the twentieth century, there was a consistent economic expansion—a rising tide that lifted all boats. The main beneficiaries were those who were already highly skilled and highly paid, but even less-skilled workers saw their earnings rise, too.

### Looking at Differences in Wealth

Normally, we measure wealth by looking at **net worth**—the value of stocks, bonds, houses, and other things that people own minus all of their debts. The average U.S. family has a net worth of close to $100,000. But the lowest 10 percent of U.S. households have a net worth of only $8,000, whereas the top 10 percent of households have an average net worth of over $800,000.

### More U.S. Residents Own Stocks—At All Levels of Income

Interestingly, from the richest to the poorest, a U.S. resident's net worth is likely to include shares of stock in U.S. corporations. Over 52 percent of U.S. families own stocks either directly or indirectly. In many European countries, this proportion is less than 5 percent. Not surprisingly, U.S. residents in general do not think negatively about U.S. corporations—after all, they own part of them!

### Is Inequality Necessarily Bad?

Some politicians and political commentators argue that wealth inequality in the United States is bad for the nation. They contend that it leads to a type of "class warfare" attitude. Furthermore, they say, wealth inequality could lead to even more inequality, because the children of the poor would have to work harder to succeed than do the children of the rich.

In contrast, others point out that the greater the disparity of wealth, the harder people may strive to become successful. Normally, the more that people strive to be successful, the more the nation's standard of living rises. This is exactly what has happened in the United States. This is one example of the **incentive effect**. In other words, if people, when they are young, observe that it is possible to make fabulously high incomes, more young people may spend the time, resources, and effort to try to break into the super rich group. In contrast, countries with much more wealth equality, such as France and Germany, tend to have higher unemployment and fewer increases in living

*Continued on next page*

standards. In 1980, the output per capita in the United States was about the same as in France and Germany. Since then, U.S. output per capita has increased over 50 percent while France and Germany have stagnated. Because of so much income and wealth equality in France and Germany, few young people believe (and rightly so) that it is possible to become very rich through hard work and long hours.

**For Critical Analysis:**
Forbes *magazine estimates that the number of billionaires in the United States has increased by almost 130 percent since 1990. During the same period, the number of billionaires in Germany increased by only 15 percent. Is the United States necessarily better off than Germany? Why or why not?*

**Mastering Concepts:** Putting the U. S. Economy in Perspective

- **Increased communication channels at lower and lower costs have led to companies manufacturing numerous items offshore where they can be produced at a lower cost.**
- **In spite of numerous down periods in overall business activity, U.S. residents have experienced large, sustained increases in their living standards over the last several hundred years.**
- **In the process, though, wealth inequality has increased in recent years.**

## MEASURING HOW MUCH WE PRODUCE

If someone asks you how much you make, you typically will *not* answer in terms of the number of restaurant meals, shoes, socks, CDs, or football games that you bought and consumed in one year. You will just say some dollar number for the year, such as $20,000, $30,000, or $100,000.

The same issue arises when determining what the nation produces in one year. We like to know this number for many reasons. At a minimum, we like to know how the nation's productive capacity is growing over time. This gives us an idea of whether the nation is getting richer. Second, we like to know if there are problems with economy-wide business activity. Policymakers need to know if things have slowed down so that they can institute appropriate policies to help the economy. Businesspeople also are interested in the health of the economy. They make investment decisions based on the strength (or weakness) of the economy and estimates of its future growth.

### It Is All in the Numbers—Gross Domestic Product, or GDP

**Gross domestic product (GDP)**
*The total dollar value of all* final *goods and services produced in a nation in a single year.*

The most frequently used statistic of economic performance is **gross domestic product (GDP),** which is the current value of all *final* goods and services produced in our nation each year. ▸ Example 2-21 GDP includes goods and services that consumers buy, such as haircuts, rewritable DVD burners, and take-out pizzas. It also includes business spending on such things as equipment and buildings, plus government spending on such things as highways, the salaries of our military personnel, and maintenance of national parks. ◂

**Assessing Money Values, Not Physical Units** GDP is usually expressed as so many trillions of dollars per year. That means that we obtain GDP by multiplying the *physical* units of final goods and services produced in a year by their individual prices. That gives us the total value of each good and service produced, which we add up to obtain gross GDP.

> ***GDP can be viewed as a summary measure of the market value of final U.S. output.***

Notice that the above definition stresses the word *final*. GDP is not the value of everything produced. Why not? Because many things are produced to be used to make other things. When a company makes car radiators, they are not used by themselves. They end up in the final product, which is a car. Thus, counting a radiator when it is produced and again when it adds value to an automobile would be double-counting.

**Adjusting for Population Changes—Per Capita GDP** If you found out that last year GDP was $12 trillion, but that 20 years earlier, it was only $6 trillion, could you draw any conclusions? You might say that the value of total production in the United States increased over those two decades. But what if the population had increased by 200 percent? GDP per person, or per capita, would have fallen. So, to get a better idea of what has been happening to the average person's standard of living, we typically have to divide by population to come up with **per capita GDP**. Per capita GDP does not tell us anything about the distribution of income, though; it just tells us its average level.

**Per capita GDP** *GDP divided by population.*

Look at Figure 2-4 where you see what has happened to per capita GDP in the United States over time (corrected for inflation—see below).

## Prices Do Rise—GDP Corrected for Inflation

In the last section, hypothetical GDP doubled. But what if the average of all prices doubled, too? The number of physical units of final output would not have

**Figure 2-4 Per Capita GDP in the United States over Time**

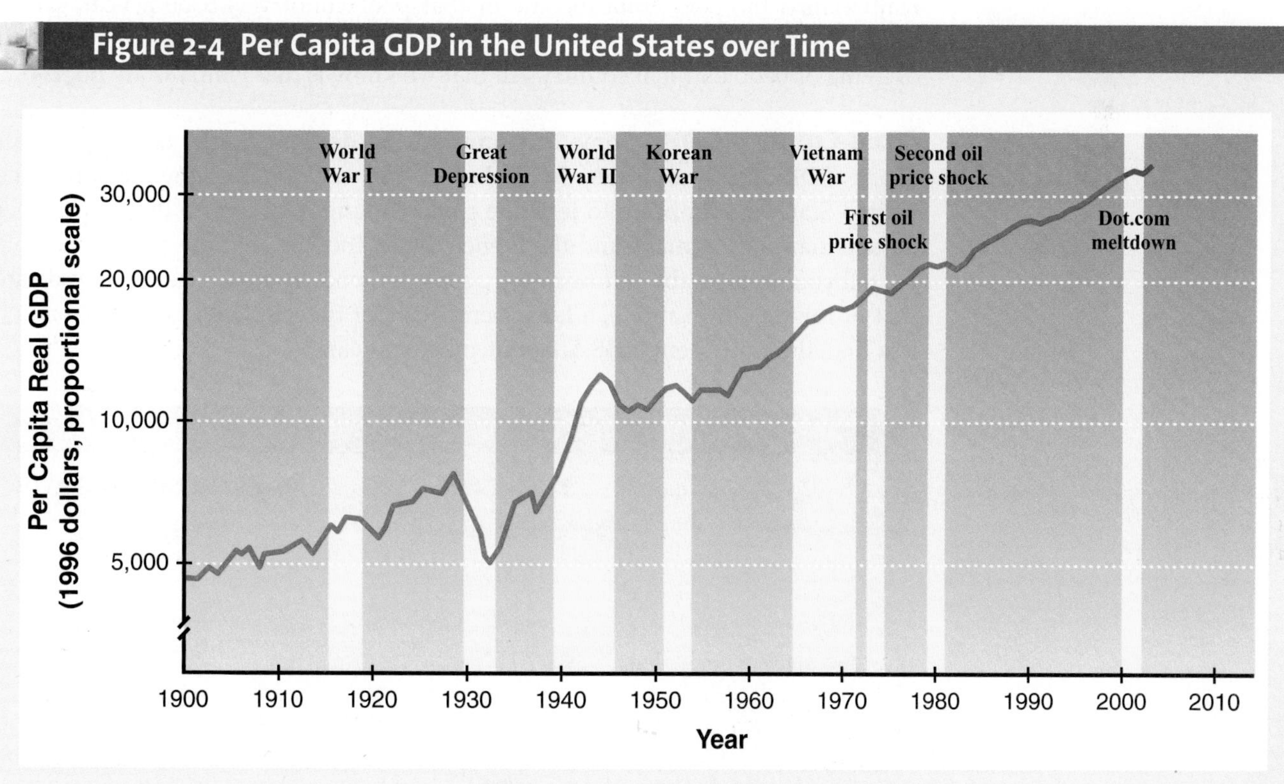

**Inflation**
*A sustained rise in the average of all prices over time.*

**Real GDP**
*GDP corrected for inflation, or changes in the average of all prices over time.*

increased. So, we must also take into account **inflation**, defined as a sustained rise in the average of all prices. When we adjust GDP for price-level changes, we end up with **real GDP**. The term *real* refers to the physical, or actual, quantities of goods and services produced.

Taking into account both inflation and population growth, we come up with the following concept:

> ***To compare living standards over time, we need to correct GDP for both inflation and population growth.***

**Per capita real GDP**
*Gross domestic product, corrected for inflation and then divided by the population for any given year.*

The result is called **per capita real GDP**.

## The U.S. Position in the World Economy?

Now that we have a way of measuring economic performance, we can place the United States within the world economy. The task is not as easy as it seems, though. The problems concern (1) the accuracy of GDP measurements in other countries and (2) the translation of values expressed in other countries' currencies.

**Good and Bad Statistics** The United States and many other developed countries have elaborate systems for estimating GDP each year. Some government statisticians work full-time doing so. In other countries, however particularly in the developing world, reliable GDP statistics are uncommon. In spite of known inaccuracies, world organizations such as the United Nations publish annual tables of how well all of the more than 200 countries are doing economically. It is probably safe to compare U.S. GDP with the GDPs of Japan, France, Germany, and the rest of Europe. Certainly, however, you would be less inclined to accept comparisons based on government figures from very poor countries, simply because those countries do not devote much effort to ensuring the accuracy of their statistics. ▶ **International Example 2-22** A government statistic from Haiti claims the per capita income of that poor country is $350 a year, which seems shocking. But such a statistic probably does not tell you the true standard of living of people in that country. All that we know is that Haitians are poor. ◀

**Cross-Country GDP** Some economists have devised a way to compare per capita GDP across countries. In Table 2-2, you see some of their results. The United States still appears to lead the pack, coming in at over a third richer per person than the Germans and the French. Note, though, that the figures in Table 2-2 tell you nothing about how many people are poor. Evidence seems to indicate that in Russia, for example, a large percentage of the residents experience much less than the equivalent of $8,410 of income per year.

**Table 2-2 Comparing Per Capita Incomes**

| Country | Yearly GDP (billions of dollars) | Yearly Per Capita GDP (dollars) |
|---|---|---|
| United States | 11,000 | 38,200 |
| Japan | 3,700 | 34,600 |
| Germany | 2,150 | 25,200 |
| France | 1,600 | 25,000 |
| Russia | 1,230 | 8,410 |
| Brazil | 1,300 | 7,370 |

**Mastering Concepts:** Measuring How Much We Produce

- **We measure the value of total economic activity of the economy by gross domestic product (GDP), which is the current market value of all *final* goods and services produced within U.S. borders in a year.**
- **When we adjust GDP for population growth and inflation, we get per capita real GDP. This is a figure we can compare through the years to determine if living standards are rising.**

## SUSTAINING U.S. POPULATION GROWTH

Population growth is important because labor is one of the most important factors of production. The United States has experienced steady population growth for more than 200 years. Right now, we expect that the U.S. population will grow by another 100 million individuals in the next 50 years. Some believe that such a number indicates a "population bomb," ready to explode into numerous economic and social problems. Others point out that a rising population in the United States means an increase in our labor force, with consequent increases in total production.

### Immigration Continues to Be the Key

U.S. residents have a **fertility rate** of about 2.1. That means that the number of children born per woman in the United States is a little over two. This magic number—2.1—is the total fertility rate necessary for a population to remain constant.

**Fertility rate**
*The average number of births per female of childbearing age in a given population.*

If the United States total fertility rate is 2.1, then how are we going to experience a population increase of 100 million over the next 50 years? The answer is immigration. In spite of the anti-immigration sentiments that increased sharply after September 11, 2001, the U.S. has not cracked down on immigration. Certainly, many argue that we should *not* make immigration more difficult. After all, the United States is a nation of immigrants. Whatever your stand on immigrants, recent studies show that many productivity increases in the last decade in this country were due to increased immigration.

### The U.S. Population Compared to the Rest of the World

While the U.S. population will increase by 100 million over the next 50 years, Europe will lose more than 100 million residents. At first blush, that might seem beneficial—less crowded cities, cheaper housing, and less pollution. Nonetheless, most European leaders are worried. When a country's population does not grow, its **median age** increases, and the percentage of individuals who are retired also increases. Retired individuals, particularly in Europe, receive large pensions financed by the government—that is, by other younger residents who are still working and paying taxes. The larger the percentage of the population that is retired, the greater the tax burden on those people who are still working—not a pleasant thought for young people in Europe today.

**Median age**
*In a given population, the age at which there is an equal number of people who are younger and older than that particular age. Also, the midpoint in the age distribution in a nation.*

In the next 50 years, the world population will likely increase from the current six billion to about nine billion. The greatest population growth will occur in developing nations, particularly in Asia.

In nations with positive population growth, there will be a continuing increase in the supply of labor. Additionally, a smaller percentage of tax revenues will have to go to pay pensions for retired people. In this sense, many countries will be economically better off than Europe and perhaps Japan.

## India and China—Future Economic Powers

While the U.S. population will stabilize at fewer than 400 million, both China and India already have populations exceeding one billion each. Most assuredly, their economic power and influence will increase during the decades to come.

✦ **Be Aware!** *As other nations, such as China, get richer, that does not mean that the U.S. will become poorer.*

At the same time, although the U.S. population will not be decreasing, many of our greatest allies in Europe will see population declines. That may mean a greater economic association between the United States and such nations as China and India. Our traditional economic ties with Europe may become less important. Already, our political and military ties with some European nations have weakened in the 2000s.

### Mastering Concepts: Sustaining U.S. Population Growth

- **Because the U.S. fertility rate is currently just that rate necessary to maintain a stable population, the only way that this country will add to its population is through immigration.**
- **The world population will almost surely rise over the next 50 years. Nonetheless, the population of Europe will decline. The greatest increases will be in the developing countries, especially in Asia.**

## SUMMING IT ALL UP

- Prices signal to consumers the relative scarcity of goods and services. Consumers then determine whether they value those goods and services enough to buy them at current market prices.
- Prices signal to producers how much they should produce—rising prices signal that they should produce more, and falling prices that they should produce less.
- The price system via the demand for and the supply of different goods and services coordinates the decisions of consumers and producers.
- Competition and the lure of higher profits force producers to seek the least-cost combination of inputs.
- Who gets what is produced is normally determined by money income, plus inheritance and gifts.
- Factors of production include land, labor, capital, and entrepreneurship.
- There is physical capital, such as buildings, and human capital, which embodies individual workers' ability to produce because of education, training, and experience.
- In spite of numerous down periods in overall business activity, U.S. residents have experienced large, sustained increases in their living standards over the last several hundred years.
- We measure the value of total economic activity of the economy by gross domestic product (GDP), which is the current market value of all final goods and services produced within U.S. borders in a year.

- When we adjust GDP for population growth and inflation, we get per capita real GDP. This is a figure we can compare through the years to determine if living standards are rising.
- Because the U.S. fertility rate is currently just that rate necessary to maintain a stable population, the only way that this country will add to its population is through immigration.
- The world population will almost surely rise over the next 50 years. Nonetheless, the population of Europe will decline. The greatest increases will be in the developing countries, especially in Asia.

## KEY TERMS AND CONCEPTS



## MASTERING ECONOMIC CONCEPTS
## Questions and Problems

**2-1.** In the U.S. economy, which is essentially a market economy, how do producers and consumers answer the following three economic questions: What items will be produced? How will these items be produced? For whom will these items be produced?

**2-2.** In a market economy, if there is an item that I want very much, am I entitled to that item? Suppose that I need the item in order to survive. Does this change your answer?

**2-3.** In addition to land, labor, and capital, what other type of resources exists to aid in the production process? Elaborate on this additional category of resources by listing a few examples.

**2-4.** If we adjust GDP to account for changes in the price level and the population, does this measurement account for changes in the quantity of the goods produced, the quality of the goods produced, or both?

**2-5.** In many instances U.S. policymakers and labor leaders argue in favor of utilizing only goods produced and sold in the United States. If their proposals were accepted, what would be the likely impact on the prices of goods purchased by U.S. consumers? Why?

**2-6.** Assume that Earle is very creative and has the ability to design interesting Web pages and video games. In this instance should his creative abilities be considered a resource? What type of firm could possibly utilize him as a resource?

**2-7.** Indicate whether each of the following would be included in U.S. GDP and explain why or why not.

a. a CD player purchased by General Motors to be installed in a new Chevy Malibu
b. lawn-care service that I provide for free to my brother while visiting him
c. a watch made in Switzerland and sold in New York City
d. a 1998 Cadillac sold to a retired U.S. steelworker in 2004

**2-8.** Why does the average age in a country increase if the country's population neither increases nor decreases? (Hint: Think life expectancy.)

**2-9.** Why is the fertility rate of approximately 2.1 considered to be "the magic number" in terms of population growth?

**2-10.** If per capita GDP increases by 9 percent and the price level increases by 3 percent, what would be the approximate impact on per capita real GDP?

**2-11.** When DaimlerChrysler introduced the PT Cruiser in 2000, the price of the car in the market began to increase significantly. At that time, what did that price increase indicate to the automaker?

**2-12.** Which of the following would be considered a resource?

a. shrimp in a fishery
b. a pair of rollerblades
c. an airline pilot
d. education

**2-13.** Assume that you purchase 100 shares of stock in Staples, Inc., at a price of $23.50 per share. As a result of your $2,350 transaction, your online brokerage service charges you a commission of $30. What amount or amounts are added to U.S. GDP and why?

**2-14.** Although ticket scalping is illegal in most of the United States, prices charged by ticket scalpers do provide information about the market. Using the concept of relative scarcity, explain how and why the ticket prices offered by scalpers might go up or down in each of the following situations.

a. Very few tickets are available for an event because it is held in a small arena.
b. The event is particularly popular like the Super Bowl.
c. The event will begin in just a few minutes.

**2-15.** If real GDP increased from $5 trillion to $6 trillion over a certain time period and the population increased from 200 million to 230 million over the same time period, did per capita real GDP increase or decrease? Indicate why or why not.

**2-16.** If nominal GDP increased 5 percent and real GDP increased 2 percent, what must have happened to the overall price level?

## THINKING CRITICALLY

**2-1.** In 2003, various safety groups initiated a campaign to induce U.S. automakers to alter electric window controls in U.S. autos so that small children could not accidentally activate the controls and injure themselves. These groups believe strongly that U.S. automakers should change their production processes and have pursued legal measures to require the automakers to do so. How effective is such legal action likely to be? In economic terms, how could these groups, as well as U.S. consumers, convey the importance of this issue to the automakers?

**2-2.** According to the U.S. Census Bureau, in the early 2000s, the official income for the wealthiest 20 percent of all U.S. households represented 50.1 percent of all U.S. income. In contrast, the income for the poorest 20 percent of all U.S. households represented only 3.5 percent of all U.S. income. If we were able to completely eliminate income inequality, what percentage of total income would be earned by the wealthiest 20 percent of all households? What percentage would be earned by the poorest 20 percent? What impact might the complete elimination of income inequality have on the incentive system within the U.S. economy? What impact would this have on economic growth?

**2-3.** Gross domestic product is defined as the total dollar value of all *final* goods and services produced in a nation in a single year. Consider a situation in which a parent stays home to care for a two-year-old child. How does the fact that this individual is not at work raise or lower officially measured GDP? How does the fact that this individual is providing child care raise or lower GDP? Based on your answers to the previous questions, how effective is GDP in accounting for the production of goods or services within the home?

## LOGGING ON

1. To consider why not everyone of working age chooses to be in the U.S. labor force, go to http://www.census.gov/hhes/www/laborfor.html.
2. For the latest statistics about U.S. trade with other nations, go to http://www.bea.doc.gov/bea/di/home/trade.htm.

3. To find out the latest figures on current GDP and real GDP in the United States, go to http://www.bea.doc.gov/bea/dn/home/gdp.htm.
4. For the latest available trends in the overall growth of productivity of U.S. factors of production, go to http://stats.bls.gov/news.release/prod3.toc.htm and click on "Multifactor Productivity Trends" for the most recent year.

## USING THE INTERNET FOR ECONOMIC ANALYSIS

**Global Per Capita Output Comparisons** The value of per capita income, which can be measured using either gross domestic product (GDP) or an alternative output measure called gross national product (GNP), varies considerably across nations. This application contrasts GDP and GNP and provides information about rankings of per capita income levels across countries.

**Title:** World Bank Competitiveness Indicators Database

**Navigation:** Go to the home page of the Indicators Database at http://wbln0018.worldbank.org/psd/compete.nsf. Read the introduction, and then click on "Go to Competitiveness Indicators Database." Next, click on "View the list of all indicators and their rankings by countries," and then click on "Overall Performance." Click on "Gross National Product (GNP) per Capita."

**Application** Read this page, and answer the following questions.

1. What is the difference between gross national product and gross domestic product?
2. In what types of countries might GNP per capita differ considerably from GDP per capita? (Hint: What characteristics of a nation's economy would tend to enlarge the difference between GNP and GDP?)
3. About how many times greater is per capita GNP in the United States than in the nation that ranks thirtieth in per capita GNP?

## MEDIA RESOURCE LIST

The following media resources are available with this chapter:

- Load your CD-ROM to listen to the audio introduction to this chapter.
- Test your knowledge of chapter concepts with a quiz at www.miller-ume.com.
- Link to Web resources related to the text coverage at www.miller-ume.com.

## HOMEWORK SET

Go to the end of this book to find the Homework Problems for this chapter.

# PART 2

# Microeconomics

# CHAPTER 3

# Demand and Supply

## *Facing an Economic Problem:* Fighting the Rise in Cigarette Smuggling Worldwide

Smuggling is as old as commerce. People smuggle to avoid taxes on smuggled items or to avoid outright bans on the shipment, production, and consumption of smuggled items. During Prohibition in the 1930s, there was a tremendous amount of smuggling of alcoholic beverages from Canada to the United States. Today, cigarette smuggling is on the rise worldwide. Of the trillion cigarettes exported from producing nations in any one year, smugglers sell an estimated 300 billion. Fifteen years ago, the number of smuggled cigarettes was only 100 billion. Why has the world seen such a rise in cigarette smuggling? You will find out the answer in this chapter as you learn demand and supply analysis.

### Learning Objectives

After reading this chapter, you should be able to:

- **Describe the relationship between price and quantity demanded and distinguish between changes in demand and changes in quantity demanded.**
- **Describe the relationship between price and quantity supplied and distinguish between changes in supply and changes in quantity supplied.**
- **Outline the forces that cause supply and demand to lead to an equilibrium price.**
- **List the different methods of rationing in addition to the price system.**

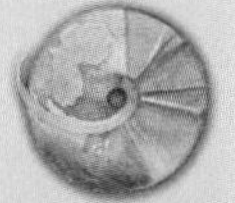

***Refer to the back of this chapter for a complete listing of multimedia learning materials available on the CD-ROM and the Web site.***

## DEMAND—A MAJOR ROLE PLAYER IN THE MARKET ECONOMY

**Demand**
*The amount of a good or service that consumers are able and willing to buy at various possible prices during a specified time period.*

Somehow, your unlimited wants have to be translated into what you actually purchase. In a market economy, individual desires do not mean anything until individuals are ready to "put their money where their mouths are." Stated in more polite terms, your **demand** for any good or service is how much you are willing to purchase at various prices. If the price is right, you will make an exchange—you will give up funds in exchange for the good or service that somebody is willing to sell you.

### THE LAW OF DEMAND—IT'S FAMOUS FOR A REASON

**Law of demand**
*An economic rule stating that the quantity demanded and price move in opposite directions.*

The heart of our analysis is the **law of demand:**

> ***At higher prices, consumers tend to purchase less of any good or service than at lower prices, all other things remaining the same. At lower prices, consumers tend to purchase more of any good or service, other things remaining the same.***

Many companies are now relying on the law of demand to induce customers to use the Internet, as you can see in the following *E-Commerce Application.*

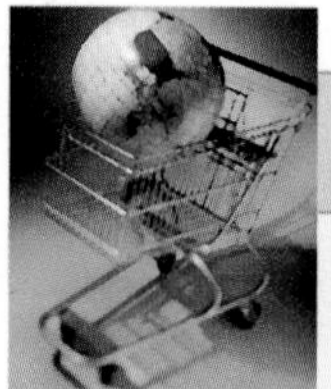

### E-COMMERCE APPLICATION: The Need to Reduce Customer Service Costs

**Concept Applied:**
**Law of Demand**

Competition in the banking sector is fierce. Labor costs are rising, though. Banks would like to reduce those costs by getting customers to use automated teller machines (ATMs).

Airlines face rising labor costs. To reduce those costs, they would like to reduce passengers' reliance on human beings for information and ticketing.

The producers of both computer software and hardware have found that their customer service calls cost about $1 a minute, about the same as the cost of calls to the airlines.

#### Using the Stick Instead of the Carrot

All three of these industries—banking, airlines, and computer software and hardware—have modified their pricing to induce changes in people's behavior. Many firms in these industries have stopped offering bonuses, discounts, and prizes to induce people to do their banking, airline reservations, and computer problem solving on the Web. Indeed, they often charge extra to those individuals who want to speak to a human being.

Many banks now impose teller fees to encourage individuals to use ATMs. At Northwest Airlines, any passenger who calls or visits an agent to change the route or time for a frequent-flyer award ticket has to pay $50. If the same passenger makes the same change via Northwest's Web site, it's at no charge. At Hewlett-Packard, a customer who calls about a problem with an out-of-warranty product has to pay $25 to $30 to talk to a technician. If that same customer can find the answer on Hewlett-Packard's Web site, the price is zero.

#### Online Stock Trading Affected, Too

The brokerage industry has also discovered the law of demand. Brokerage firm Charles Schwab, one of the first discount brokers, still charges only $29.95 for a typical stock trade using its Web site. If you want to talk a broker about your trade, you end up paying twice as much. Not surprisingly, 85 percent of Charles Schwab's customers do their trading online.

**For Critical Analysis:**
*Will relatively high-priced human-assisted services eventually be completely replaced by Web-based self-service? Why or why not?*

There is some basic reasoning behind the law of demand. This reasoning has to do with two effects that occur when prices change.

## Why the Law of Demand—The Real Income and Substitution Effects

There are two basic reasons why the quantity demanded is inversely related to the price of a good or service. One has to do with how price changes affect your *ability* to buy goods and service, and the other has to do with your *desire* to substitute among goods and services.

### The Real Income Effect

Even the richest person on earth cannot buy everything she or he might possibly want. People's incomes limit the amount they are able to spend. If the price of a good goes up, individuals cannot keep buying the same quantity of everything else if their income stays the same. This concept is known as the **real income effect**. Simply stated:

**Real income effect** The change in people's purchasing power that occurs when, other things being constant, the price of one good that they purchase changes. When that price goes up, real income, or purchasing power, falls, and when that price goes down, real income increases.

> ***If the price of a good or service that you normally buy goes up, your ability to buy the same quantities of everything you are buying has been reduced. Your real income has fallen. You therefore normally buy less of the higher-priced good.***

▸ **Example 3-1** Let's say that you are purchasing 30 gallons of gas a month and the price is $1.50 per gallon. That means that you are spending $45 a month on gas. If the price of gas goes up to $2 a gallon, you will be spending $60 a month, or $15 more. In a one-year period, if you purchase the same 30 gallons per month, you will spend $180 more than you used to. Clearly, with the same income, you will be unable to purchase everything else you normally do and still buy the same amount of gas. You will have to cut back somewhere, and one of these places will likely be your gas purchases. ◂

### The Substitution Effect

It happens all the time. If the price of one item goes up, you look for similar items that have not had price increases. In other words, when the price of one item goes up, you attempt to substitute another item that yields about the same satisfaction but has a lower price. This is called the **substitution effect:**

**Substitution effect** The tendency of people to substitute cheaper commodities for more expensive commodities.

> ***When the price of one item goes up, and the price of other items in your budget does not, you generally attempt to substitute away from the more expensive item in favor of the less expensive items. This is the essence of the substitution effect.***

▸ **International Example 3-2** For travel within Europe, high-speed trains are a close substitute with airline travel. For example, a high-speed train ride under the English Channel from London to Paris takes about 2.5 hours. Compare this to taking a plane. If you count travel time to and from the two cities' airports (which are outside the cities), plus check-in time, the high-speed train is either just as fast or sometimes even faster. The company running that train route has aggressively lowered its prices in the last few years. The Eurostar train now has 65 percent of the London–Paris market and 45 percent of the London–Brussels market. ◂

### It's Relative Prices That Count

As you probably know, in general, prices have been rising for most of your life. Of course, not all prices rise even when the

**Relative price**
*The price of one commodity divided by the price of another commodity; the number of units of one commodity that must be sacrificed to purchase one unit of another commodity.*

**Money price**
*The price that we observe today, expressed in today's dollars. Also called the* absolute *or* nominal *price.*

average of all prices rises. ▸ Example 3-3 The price of computing power has dropped consistently over the last several decades. Today, the price of a given amount of computing power has dropped by about 99 percent relative to what it was 30 years ago. ◂

The **relative price** of any good or service is its price in terms of the prices of other goods and services. In contrast, the price that you pay in dollars and cents today for any good or service is called its **money price**. Money prices are sometimes referred to as **nominal prices**.

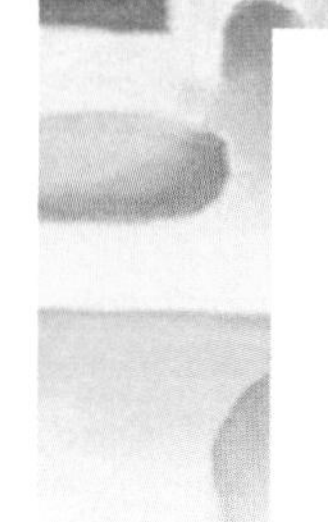

## *Solving the Economic Problem:* Fighting the Rise in Cigarette Smuggling Worldwide

There would be very little, if any, cigarette smuggling throughout the world if there were no taxes or if tax rates were low in every country. But tax rates vary widely across countries and even within the 50 U.S. states. In states and countries with very low taxes per pack of cigarettes, virtually none of the cigarettes consumed are smuggled in. In contrast, in locales where cigarette taxes are high, such as Hong Kong, Spain, certain Canadian provinces, and states, such as New York, California, and Michigan, smuggled cigarettes account for a relatively high percentage of cigarettes consumed. In Hong Kong alone, it is estimated that 40 percent of all cigarettes consumed are smuggled in from elsewhere.

Relative prices matter. If smugglers can offer the same pack of cigarettes at a much lower price—because they pay little or no taxes—cigarette consumers will respond by purchasing a greater quantity from smugglers.

**Nominal price**
*The same as the money price of a good or service; the price you pay for anything in today's dollars.*

The average of all prices has gone up so much over the years that any comparison between the money price of, say, a car today and a car 50 years ago is meaningless. In between, there has been inflation, or a rise in the general price level as you learned in Chapter 2. Thus, when comparing the price of a good now with its price in the past, don't make the mistake of comparing dollar (or nominal) prices. Instead, compare *relative* prices: How many other goods must be given up for the item now, compared to the past?

**Correct for Quality Changes, Too** When you compare prices over time, you must also take account of any quality changes. ▸ Example 3-4 The quality of a car today is not the same as it was 50 years ago. Today's cars are safer. You don't have to have the car tuned or the oil changed so often. Cars rarely break down today. So, you can't simply compare the price of cars today with the prices of cars 50 years ago. ◂ When you correct for quality changes, you implicitly are measuring goods and services in **constant-quality units**.

**Constant-quality units**
*Items whose quality has been adjusted to make them comparable to one another.*

***The only correct way to measure the change in the price of anything over time is to look at that item's price per constant-quality unit.***

*"I did have a house at that price but I sold it back in 1978."*

## Graphing Individual Demand

As an individual, you have a demand for numerous goods and services that you buy or might buy. We know from the law of demand that the quantities that you purchase are inversely related to the prices that you pay. Consider your demand for rewritable CDs.

**The Demand Schedule** Consider a hypothetical **demand schedule** showing the quantities of rewritable CDs that you wish to purchase per year versus the price of rewritable CDs. Look at panel (a) of Figure 3-1 on page 52. At a price of $5 per rewritable CD, you purchase only 10 per year, but at a price of only $1 per CD, you would purchase 50 per year. Notice that in panel (a) we talk in terms of quantities of constant-quality rewritable CDs. That means that they are all of the same quality.

**Demand schedule**
*A table showing the quantities demanded at different possible prices.*

**Plotting the Schedules on a Graph—The Demand Curve** If you put together a simple graph with the number of rewritable CDs per year on the bottom and the price of rewritable CDs on the left side, you end up with panel (b) in Figure 3-1 on page 52. There you see combinations of prices and quantities demanded of rewritable CDs from combination *A* through combination *E*. This is the **demand curve**. It is downward sloping, showing the inverse relationship between quantity demanded and price.

**Demand curve**
*A downward-sloping line that graphically shows the quantities demanded at each possible price.*

If a good had an *upward*-sloping demand curve, a producer could keep charging more and more and people would keep buying larger and larger quantities. Although you might think that this is possible, remember the income and substitution effects that we discussed earlier. Then you might think twice about such a possibility.

## Many Individuals Make Up the Market

To go from an individual demand curve to a demand curve for the entire market, we have to add together all the demands of individual buyers. When we refer to

**Figure 3-1 The Individual Demand Schedule and the Individual Demand Curve**

In panel (a), we show combinations *A* through *E* of the quantities of rewritable CDs demanded, measured in constant-quality units at prices ranging from $5 down to $1 per CD. In panel (b), we plot combinations *A* through *E* on a grid. The result is the individual demand curve for rewritable CDs.

Panel (a)

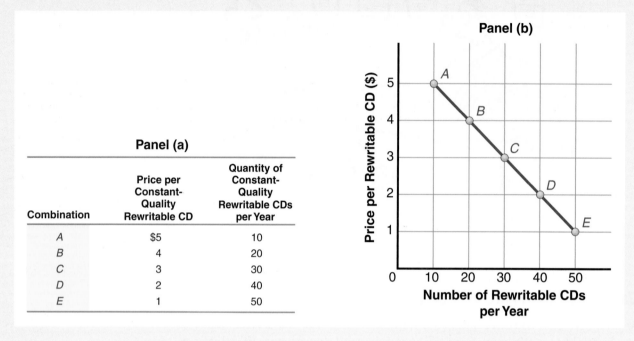

| Combination | Price per Constant-Quality Rewritable CD | Quantity of Constant-Quality Rewritable CDs per Year |
|---|---|---|
| *A* | $5 | 10 |
| *B* | 4 | 20 |
| *C* | 3 | 30 |
| *D* | 2 | 40 |
| *E* | 1 | 50 |

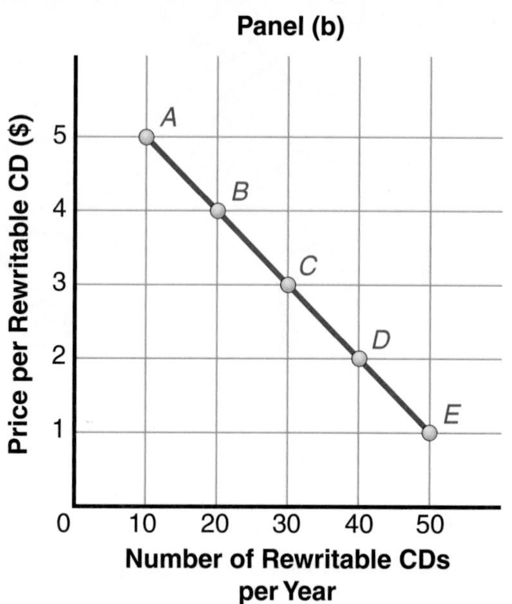


the entire market, we are looking at all actual and potential buyers of a particular good or service. We do this in Figure 3-2. In that figure, we horizontally add up the demand schedules for two buyers, the first one being you and the second one being someone else. This is shown in panels (b) and (c) of Figure 3-2. The result is the combined demand curve for two buyers, which you see in panel (d). To go from the combined demand curve for two buyers to the market demand curve for all buyers, you just horizontally add up all the individual demand curves for everybody buying rewritable CDs over a year period. The result might be something like Figure 3-3 on page 54.

▸ **International Example 3-5** Sometimes all consumers react dramatically to a price increase. The German government passed a law requiring consumers to pay a deposit on all carbonated soft drinks sold in cans or plastic bottles after January 1, 2003. The deposit ranged from 25 to 50 euro cents (about 29 to 59 U.S. cents) depending on the container size. The new deposit represented a dramatic increase in the price of soft drinks. The result followed the law of demand to the letter. Most soft drink manufacturers experienced decreases in sales of more than 30 percent in the first few months of 2003. The makers of cans and bottles reported 20 to 60 percent drops in sales. ◂

## Market Demand Can Change—Looking at the Causes

When we draw the demand curve for rewritable CDs, we assume that nothing changes, but the world does change. If every state government gave away free CD burners to students, the demand curve that we drew in Figure 3-3 on page 54

*Animated*

## Figure 3-2 The Horizontal Summation of Two Demand Schedules

Panel (a) shows how to sum the demand schedule for one buyer with that of another buyer. In column 2 is the quantity demanded by buyer 1, taken from panel (a) of Figure 3-1. Column 4 is the sum of columns 2 and 3. We plot the demand curve for buyer 1 in panel (b) and the demand curve for buyer 2 in panel (c). When we add those two demand curves horizontally, we get the combined demand curve for two buyers, shown in panel (d).

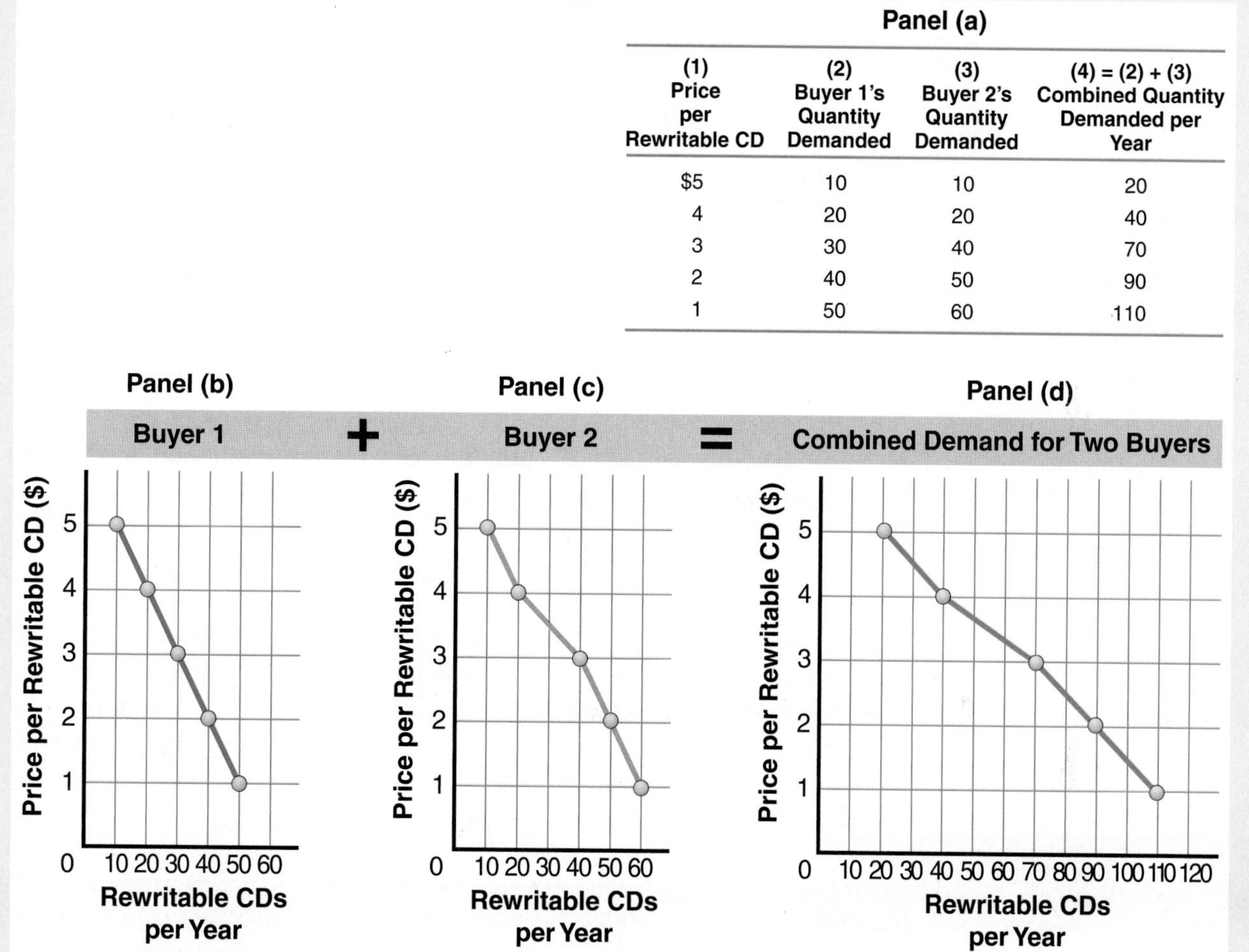

**Panel (a)**

| (1) Price per Rewritable CD | (2) Buyer 1's Quantity Demanded | (3) Buyer 2's Quantity Demanded | (4) = (2) + (3) Combined Quantity Demanded per Year |
|---|---|---|---|
| $5 | 10 | 10 | 20 |
| 4 | 20 | 20 | 40 |
| 3 | 30 | 40 | 70 |
| 2 | 40 | 50 | 90 |
| 1 | 50 | 60 | 110 |



certainly would not be valid. Rather, the demand curve would shift rightward. This would mean that at each and every price, the quantity demanded of rewritable CDs would increase. You can see this in Figure 3-4 on the following page.

If, in contrast, all the state governments passed a law prohibiting students from recording rewritable CDs, the demand for rewritable CDs would shift from $D_1$ in Figure 3-4 to $D_3$, which is to the left.

▸ **Example 3-6** U.S. residents are living longer, which is bad news for undertakers. The demand for undertaking services is, of course, a function of the number of deaths in the United States. With increased spending on medical services and technological advances, including better and more effective pharmaceuticals, the death rate in the United States is falling. In 2002, the number of deaths fell by 5.3 percent compared to the previous year. Not surprisingly, the leading

## Figure 3-3 The Market Demand Schedule for Rewritable CDs

In panel (a), we add up the existing demand schedules for rewritable CDs. In panel (b), we plot the quantities from panel (a) on a grid; connecting them produces the market demand curve for rewritable CDs.

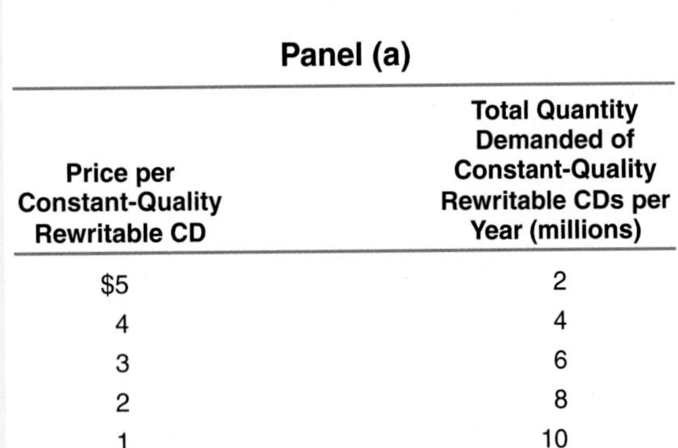

Panel (a)

| Price per Constant-Quality Rewritable CD | Total Quantity Demanded of Constant-Quality Rewritable CDs per Year (millions) |
|---|---|
| $5 | 2 |
| 4 | 4 |
| 3 | 6 |
| 2 | 8 |
| 1 | 10 |

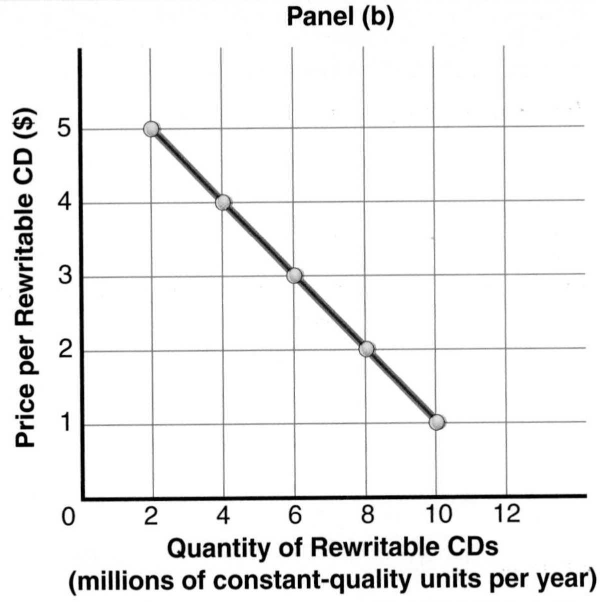


funeral business, Service Corporation International, experienced a sales revenue decrease of over 1 percent in 2002. The demand for undertaking services has definitely shifted inward to the left.

*Animated*

## Figure 3-4 A Shift in the Demand Curve

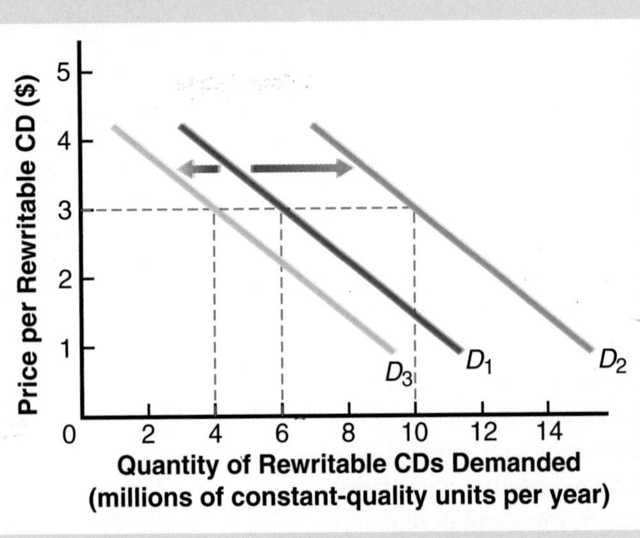


If some factor other than the current price changes, we show its effect by moving the entire demand curve, say, from $D_1$ to $D_2$. Consider the example of the state governments' giving a free CD burner to every registered college student. That means that at *all* prices, a larger number of rewritable CDs will be demanded than before, shown by a shift from $D_1$ to $D_2$. In contrast, curve $D_3$ represents reduced demand compared to curve $D_1$, caused by, say, a law prohibiting CD burners on campus.

**The Broad Categories of the Determinants of Demand** Of course, many things determine the demand for different goods and services. In fact, you might be able to come up with dozens, or even hundreds, if you wanted to delve into the psychology of each individual consumer, or even yourself. Nonetheless, we can specify some of the most important determinants of demand. Realize that any change in these determinants will change, or shift, the demand curve for the good or service in question.

1. **Tastes or Preferences:** Anytime tastes or preferences for a good or service change, the demand curve will change, too. ▸ Example 3-7 When styles change such that baggy pants that touch the ground are no longer in fashion, the demand curve for such pants will shift to the left, such as the movement from demand curve $D_1$ to demand curve $D_3$ in Figure 3-4. ◂
2. **Population:** The size of the market is important. As population increases, the demand for most goods and services increases, such as illustrated by a shift in the demand curve from $D_1$ to $D_2$ in Figure 3-4. ▸ International Example 3-8 The populations of Sweden, France, Italy, Japan, and a number of other developed countries have either stabilized or started to decline slightly. Over the next several decades, these and other developed countries will experience population decreases. Consequently, the demand for many goods and services in these developed countries will fall. ◂
3. **Income:** Typically, as incomes rise (corrected for inflation, of course), the demand for most goods and services increases. In other words, as a nation gets richer, the demand for desired goods and services typically rises. ▸ International Example 3-9 As developing nations get richer, their demand for meat and other sources of protein rises, sometimes dramatically. It is not surprising, then, that average heights in countries such as Japan have increased rather dramatically in the last 50 years. These developed countries' residents have added many more sources of protein to their diets as they got richer. ◂
4. **The Prices of Related Goods:** We already talked about the substitution effect. Here we are concerned with the price of **substitutes.** When the price of a substitute rises, the demand for the other good or service rises, too. ▸ Example 3-10 If the price of imported cars goes up, the demand for domestically produced cars increases. ◂

   Sometimes goods are used together with other goods. They are called **complements**. If the price of a complement goes up, the demand for the other good or service decreases. ▸ Example 3-11 As the price per constant-quality unit of MP3 players falls, the demand for fee-based music downloads will increase. ◂

**Substitutes**
*Two goods that can be used for consumption to satisfy a similar want—for example, coffee and tea. For substitutes, a change in the price of one causes a shift in demand for the other in the same direction as the price change.*

**Complements**
*Two goods that are used together for consumption or enjoyment—for example, coffee and cream. The more you buy of one, the more you buy of the other. For complements, a change in the price of one causes an opposite shift in the demand for the other.*

## Changes in Demand versus Changes in Quantity Demanded

We have made repeated references to demand and to quantity demanded. It is important to realize that there is a difference between a *change in demand* and a *change in quantity demanded.*

***Demand refers to a schedule of planned rates of purchase and depends on a great many nonprice determinants. Whenever there is a change in a nonprice determinant, there will be a change in demand—a shift in the entire demand curve to the right or to the left.***

Now consider quantity demanded.

> ***A quantity demanded is a specific quantity at a specific price, represented by a single point on a demand curve. When price changes, quantity demanded changes according to the law of demand, and there will be a movement from one point to another along the same demand curve.***

▸ **Example 3-12** A recent spate of newspaper and magazine articles stated roughly the following: "As the price of flat-panel displays falls, demand is expected to soar." Clearly, the writers of these articles have confused demand and quantity demanded. What they should have said was, "As the price of flat-panel displays falls, the *quantity demanded* is expected to soar." ◂

Look at Figure 3-5. At a price of $3 per rewritable CD, 6 million rewritable CDs per year are demanded. If the price falls to $1, quantity demanded increases to 10 million per year. This movement occurs because the current market price for the product changes. In Figure 3-5, you can see the arrow point down the given demand curve *D*.

When you think of demand, think of the entire curve. In contrast, a single point on the demand curve represents quantity demanded.

> ***A change or shift in demand refers to a movement of the entire curve. The only thing that can cause the entire curve to move is a change in a determinant other than its own price.***

In economic analysis, we cannot emphasize too much the following concept that must constantly be made:

> ***A change in a good's own price leads to a change in quantity demanded, for any given demand curve, other things held constant. This is a movement along the curve.***

**Figure 3-5 Movement Along a Given Demand Curve**

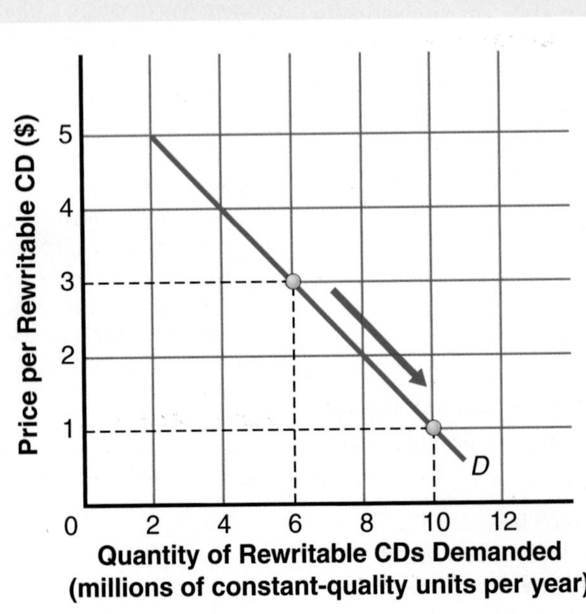


A change in price causes a change in the quantity of a good demanded. This can be represented as movement along a given demand schedule. If, in our example, the price of rewritable CDs falls from $3 to $1 apiece, the quantity demanded will increase from 6 million to 10 million units per year.

**Mastering Concepts:** Demand—A Major Role Player in the Market Economy

- **The law of demand states that at higher prices, less is purchased than at lower prices, all other things held constant.**
- **The law of demand occurs because of the real income effect as well as the substitution effect.**
- **To compare prices over time, you must first correct for inflation and then correct for quality changes to arrive at the relative (or real) price per constant-quality unit.**
- **The demand curve is always downward sloping, reflecting the inverse relationship between the quantity demanded and the price.**
- **The demand curve will shift if one of the following changes: (1) tastes or preferences, (2) population, (3) income, and (4) prices of related goods.**
- **Anytime the price of a good changes, there is a movement along the given demand curve. Anytime another determinant changes, the entire demand curve shifts in or out.**

## SUPPLY—THE OTHER SIDE OF THE PICTURE

To understand how markets work, you have to look at supply as well as demand.

### The Law of Supply: Almost as Famous as the Law of Demand

To understand how suppliers or producers of goods and services react to price changes, consider the **law of supply:**

> ***As the price goes up for a good or service, producers of that good or service generally provide larger quantities, all other things being constant.***

**Law of supply**
*An economic rule stating that price and quantity supplied move in the same direction.*

Otherwise stated, price and quantity supplied are typically positively related. That also means that when relative prices go down, the quantity supplied will go down, too. ▸ Example 3-13 How many hours per week would you be willing to work? You answer probably depends on the price per hour you would be paid—your wage rate. At $5 an hour, you might not be willing to work very much. In contrast, at $100 an hour you might be willing to work 50 or 60 hours per week, at least for a while. ◂

### The Supply Schedule

Look at panel (a) of Figure 3-6 on the next page. There you see various price and quantity combinations for the supply of rewritable CDs. This is called the **supply schedule**. You might ask why producers and sellers are willing to provide more at higher prices. The answer, at least at a theoretical level, is that producers seek the most gain possible from their activities. If the price of rewritable CDs goes up, producers earn higher profits if they can produce more rewritable CDs, so they then desire to hire more workers, pay overtime wages, and even utilize their machinery more intensively. In other words, rewritable CDs producers are willing to incur higher costs if the price they can fetch for their product goes up.

**Supply schedule**
*A table showing the quantities supplied at different possible prices.*

## THE SUPPLY CURVE

**Supply curve**
*A graphic representation of the supply schedule, showing the various quantities supplied associated with different prices.*

If you take the price-quantity combinations in panel (a) of Figure 3-6 and plot them on a graph, the result is panel (b). This is an upward-sloping **supply curve** showing the positive relationship between price and quantity supplied.

## THE DETERMINANTS OF SUPPLY

The position of the supply curve in Figure 3-6 will change if other things change. Otherwise stated:

> ***When things other than the product's own price change, the position of the supply curve will shift.***

Consider the following possible determinants of supply:

1. **Price of Inputs Used to Produce a Good or Service:** If one or more input prices fall, producers will produce more of a good or service. That is to say, if a production cost falls because an input price falls, shifting the supply curve to the right, more will be produced at each and every price of the final product.

   The converse is true, too. When input prices rise, shifting the supply curve to the left, suppliers will supply less at every given price of that product.
   ▸ **International Example 3-14** The major ingredient of chocolate is cocoa. During much of the early 2000s, a civil war raged in Africa's Ivory Coast, the world's largest cocoa producer. Not surprisingly, the price of cocoa rose—from $1,439 per metric ton in early 2002 to $2,293 in the middle of 2003. The price of chocolate started to rise in late 2003 as chocolate producers responded to the higher cocoa prices by cutting chocolate production. ◂

**Figure 3-6 The Market Supply Schedule and the Market Supply Curve for Rewritable CDs**

In panel (a), we show the summation of all the individual producers' supply schedules; in panel (b), we graph the resulting supply curve. It represents the market supply curve for rewritable CDs and is upward sloping.

Panel (a)

| Price per Constant-Quality Rewritable CD | Quantity of Rewritable CDs Supplied (millions of constant-quality units per year) |
|---|---|
| $5 | 10 |
| 4 | 8 |
| 3 | 6 |
| 2 | 4 |
| 1 | 2 |

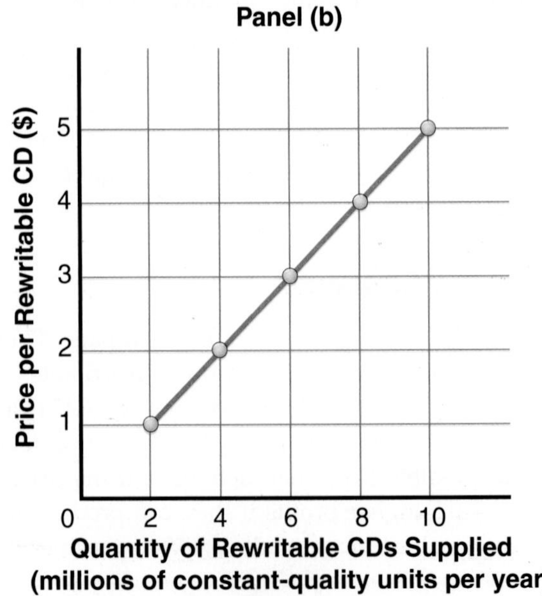

2. **Technology and Productivity:** Supply curves are drawn by assuming a given technology, or "state of the art." When available production techniques change, the supply curve will shift. In our continuing example, when a better production technique for rewritable CDs becomes available, the supply curve will shift to the right. A larger quantity will be forthcoming *at each and every* price because the cost of production is lowered by the improved technology.
3. **Taxes:** An increase in taxes on a particular item is effectively an increase in production cost. It will reduce the amount supplied at each and every price of the final product. A reverse tax, or a **subsidy**, does the opposite; that is, it will induce an increase in the supply of the subsidized good.
4. **Number of Firms in the Industry:** In the short run, when firms can change only the number of employees they use, the number of firms in the industry is constant. In the long run, the number of firms (or the plant size of some existing firms) may change. If the number of firms increases, the supply curve will shift outward to the right. If the number of firms decreases, it will shift inward to the left. ▸ Example 3-15 After the airlines suffered billions of dollars of losses in the early 2000s, some smaller firms went out of business. On routes that were left with fewer firms, the supply curve shifted inward to the left. ◂

**Subsidy**
*A negative tax; a payment to a producer from the government, usually in the form of a cash grant.*

## CHANGES IN SUPPLY VERSUS CHANGES IN QUANTITY SUPPLIED

We cannot overstress the importance of distinguishing between a movement along the supply curve, which occurs when the price changes for a particular good or service, and a shift in the supply curve, which occurs only with changes in other nonprice factors. A change in price *always* brings about a change in quantity supplied along a given supply curve. We move to a different coordinate (point) on the existing supply curve. This is specifically called a *change in quantity supplied.* When the price changes, quantity supplied changes, and there will be a movement from one point to another along the same supply curve.

When you think of *supply,* think of the entire curve.

> ***A change or shift in supply involves the entire curve moving. The only thing that can cause the entire curve to move is a change in a determinant* other than its own price.**

In contrast, a single point on the supply curve represents quantity supplied. Thus, we say that:

> ***A change in the price leads to a change in the quantity supplied, other things being constant. This is a movement* along *the curve.***

✦ **Compare!** *The logic is the same for contrasting movements along a curve and changes in the curve, whether we are discussing demand or supply.*

**Mastering Concepts:** Supply—The Other Side of the Picture

- **The law of supply tells us that as the price goes up, the quantity supplied will generally rise and as the price goes down, the quantity supplied will generally fall.**
- **Supply curves are generally upward sloping, reflecting the positive relationship between price and quantity supplied.**
- **The position of the supply curve will change when determinants of supply, other than its own price, change. They are (1) the cost of inputs, (2) technology and productivity, (3) taxes, and (4) the number of firms in the industry.**
- **Any change in price will cause a movement along the supply curve; any change in other determinants will cause a shift in the supply curve.**

## EQUILIBRIUM: PUTTING DEMAND AND SUPPLY TOGETHER

To find out why the prices of goods are what they are, we have to put demand and supply together. An interaction occurs between demand and supply that determines both price and quantity in the market. In this section, you will learn how they interact and how the interaction determines the prices that prevail in our market economy.

### COMBINING THE DEMAND AND SUPPLY SCHEDULES

In panel (a) of Figure 3-7, you see that we have combined the demand and supply schedules from Figures 3-3 and 3-6. We have also added two columns that you have not seen before. New column 4 presents the difference between the quantity supplied of, and the quantity demanded for, rewritable CDs per year. Whenever the price is high, the quantity supplied exceeds the quantity demanded. You see in new column 5 that this is called an excess quantity supplied, or a **surplus**. When prices are low, the quantity supplied is less than the quantity demanded, as you see in column 4 with the minus signs. In column 5 we label these conditions excess quantity demanded, or **shortages**.

**Surplus**
*The situation in which quantity supplied is greater than quantity demanded at a particular price above the market clearing price.*

**Shortage**
*The situation in which the quantity demanded is greater than the quantity supplied at a price below the market clearing price.*

### GRAPHING SUPPLY AND DEMAND TOGETHER

In panel (b) of Figure 3-7, we graph the demand curve and the supply curve. The supply curve slopes up, showing that at higher prices, producers of rewritable CDs are willing to supply more. The demand curve slopes down, showing that at higher prices, consumers will purchase fewer rewritable CDs.

### EQUILIBRIUM

Now, do you notice something special about the price of $3? At that price, both the quantity supplied and the quantity demanded per year are 6 million. The difference then is zero. There is neither excess quantity demanded (shortage) nor excess quantity supplied (surplus). Hence, the price of $3 is very special. It is called the **market clearing price**—it clears the market of all excess quantities demanded or supplied. There are no willing consumers who want to pay $3 per CD but are turned away by sellers. There are no willing suppliers who want to sell rewritable CDs at $3 but cannot sell all they wish at that price.

Another term for the market clearing price is the **equilibrium price**, the price at which there is no tendency for change. Consumers are able to get all they want at that price, and suppliers are able to sell the amount that they want at that price.

**Market clearing price**
*The price that clears the market, at which quantity demanded equals quantity supplied; the price where the demand curve intersects the supply curve.*

**Equilibrium price**
*The price at which the quantity producers are willing to supply is equal to the amount consumers are willing to buy.*

### THE WORLD OF SHORTAGES AND SURPLUSES

If the equilibrium price for a CD is $3, any price that is not $3 creates either a shortage or a surplus. At $4, there would be a surplus of 4 million rewritable CDs offered for sale per year that consumers do not wish to purchase at that price. Alternatively, at a price of $2, consumers would wish to buy 4 million more rewritable CDs than producers wish to produce and sell at that price.

In an unrestricted marketplace, whenever prices are different from equilibrium prices, there are forces that tend to push them toward an equilibrium, or market clearing, price. When prices are higher than equilibrium, producers end up with too much unsold product. Producers don't like to pay for storage costs, so they start offering to sell those goods at lower and lower prices until they do reach an equilibrium price.

## Figure 3-7 Putting Demand and Supply Together

In panel (a), we see that at the price of $3, the quantity supplied and the quantity demanded are equal, resulting in neither an excess in the quantity demanded nor an excess in the quantity supplied. We call this price the equilibrium, or market clearing, price. In panel (b), the intersection of the supply and demand curves is at *E*, at a price of $3 and a quantity of 6 million per year. At point *E*, there is neither an excess in the quantity demanded nor an excess in the quantity supplied. At a price of $1, the quantity supplied will be only 2 million per year, but the quantity demanded will be 10 million. The difference is excess quantity demanded at a price of $1. The price will rise, so we move up the supply curve from point *A* and up the demand curve from point *B* to point *E*. At the other extreme, $5 elicits a quantity supplied of 10 million but a quantity demanded of only 2 million. The difference is excess quantity supplied at a price of $5. The price will fall, so we move down the demand curve and the supply curve to the equilibrium price, $3 per rewritable CD.

**Panel (a)**

| (1) Price per Constant-Quality Rewritable CD | (2) Quantity Supplied (rewritable CDs per year) | (3) Quantity Demanded (rewritable CDs per year) | (4) Difference (2) – (3) (rewritable CDs per year) | (5) Condition |
|---|---|---|---|---|
| $5 | 10 million | 2 million | 8 million | Excess quantity supplied (surplus) |
| 4 | 8 million | 4 million | 4 million | Excess quantity supplied (surplus) |
| 3 | 6 million | 6 million | 0 | Market clearing price—equilibrium (no surplus, no shortage) |
| 2 | 4 million | 8 million | –4 million | Excess quantity demanded (shortage) |
| 1 | 2 million | 10 million | –8 million | Excess quantity demanded (shortage) |

**Panel (b)**

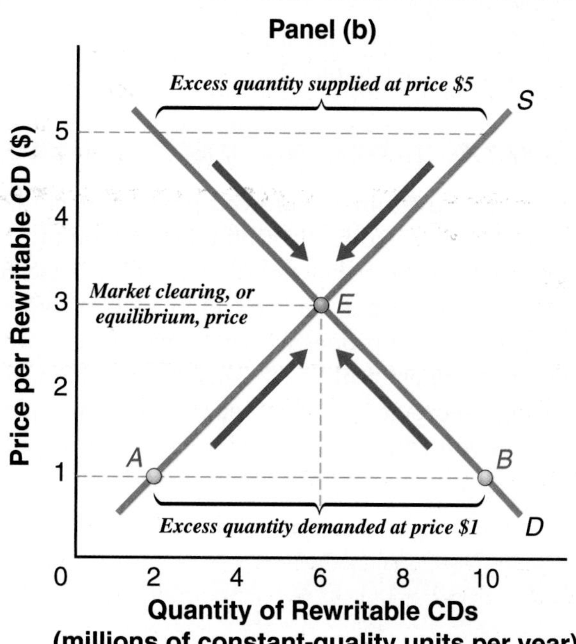

When prices are lower than equilibrium, consumers tend to bid up prices to avoid being prevented from consuming the good. ▸ **Example 3-16** Often, sports footwear manufacturers underestimate the popularity of a particular new shoe style. When consumers cannot purchase all that they want at the current price, they tend to bid up the price. This is true everywhere, but it is particularly obvious at Internet auction sites such as eBay. ◂

**Mastering Concepts:** Equilibrium—Putting Demand and Supply Together

- **Equilibrium occurs at the intersection of the demand and supply curves, where the market clearing price occurs. This is also called the equilibrium price.**
- **At prices above the market clearing price, there will be surpluses.**
- **At prices below the market clearing price, there will be shortages.**
- **At the equilibrium price, no one is frustrated in attempting to buy or sell.**

## THE RATIONING FUNCTION OF PRICES

A *shortage* creates a situation that forces the price to rise toward a market clearing, or equilibrium, level. A *surplus* brings into play forces that cause the price to fall toward its market clearing level. The synchronization of decisions by buyers and sellers that creates a situation of equilibrium is called the **rationing function of prices**.

**Rationing function of prices**
*Because both consumers and producers respond to price changes, when prices go up, consumers wish to buy less and producers wish to produce more. Prices reflect relative scarcity and thereby ration available goods and services in our market economy.*

***Prices are indicators of relative scarcity.***

An equilibrium price clears the market. The plans of buyers and sellers, given the price, are not frustrated. The free interaction of buyers and sellers sets the price that eventually clears the market. Price, in effect, rations a commodity to demanders who are willing and able to pay the highest price. (You were first introduced to this concept in Chapter 2.)

### WAYS THE RATIONING FUNCTION CAN BE FRUSTRATED

Sometimes government-enforced price ceilings that set prices below the market clearing level frustrate the rationing function of prices. The inevitable result is a prolonged shortage that cannot correct itself via the upward adjustment of the price. ▸ **Example 3-17** In New York City and elsewhere, there are maximum prices (rents) that property owners may charge prospective and actual tenants in certain apartment buildings. Consequently, New York City always suffers from a housing "shortage." ◂ Another common example of incorrect pricing concerns water, as you will read in the next *Policy Application*.

**POLICY APPLICATION:** Solving the World's Looming Water Crisis

***Concepts Applied:* Supply and Demand, Pricing**

The United Nations (U.N.) recently released a 600-page report assessing the state of the planet's most essential natural resource—water. The conclusion of this report: in just 20 years, the average supply of water per person worldwide will have dropped by one-third, affecting virtually every nation. In 50 years, four billion people in 60 countries will face water "shortages." In summary, within half a century, more than half of humanity will be living with water shortages.

The U.N. argues that mismanagement and population growth have caused a crisis. The organization further contends that fresh water must be recognized as a common resource heritage for all peoples.

### A Little Economic Analysis Goes a Long Way

Water is a resource. Like any resource, water is subject to the laws of supply and demand. The world can never "run out" of water. At a high enough price, we would obtain our water from desalination plants (which is, in fact, already being done in some locations).

It is not enough to say that water is becoming increasingly scarce. All resources, by definition, are scarce, or we would not be studying them, at least not in an economics course. It is not enough to talk about water "needs." As you learned in Chapter 1, we have difficulty defining what a true need is, once we have attained a bare minimum for survival.

The way to analyze water problems is to look at how water is priced. Although other issues also affect water—who owns it, for example—here we will look at just the pricing issue.

### Incorrect Pricing

Wherever and whenever there is a water "shortage," we typically find that whoever controls the water supply has not priced it properly. Look at Figure 3-8. There you see the demand for and supply of water in a particular region with quantities measured in acre-feet (a common measure). At a price of, say, $300 per acre-foot, there would be no talk of water shortages. Whenever there is talk of water shortages, whoever controls the water—a municipality, a national government, or usually some other government entity—is pricing the water well below the market clearing price, say, at $150 per acre-foot. It is not surprising then that there is an excess quantity demanded at that "too" low a price.

At prices approaching market equilibrium, two things happen: (1) those who consume water, such as farmers, figure out ways to conserve it; and (2) those who supply water figure out more effective ways to obtain and sell it.

**For Critical Analysis:**
*Are there any circumstances under which the world could run out of a natural resource?*

## Figure 3-8 Water Shortages

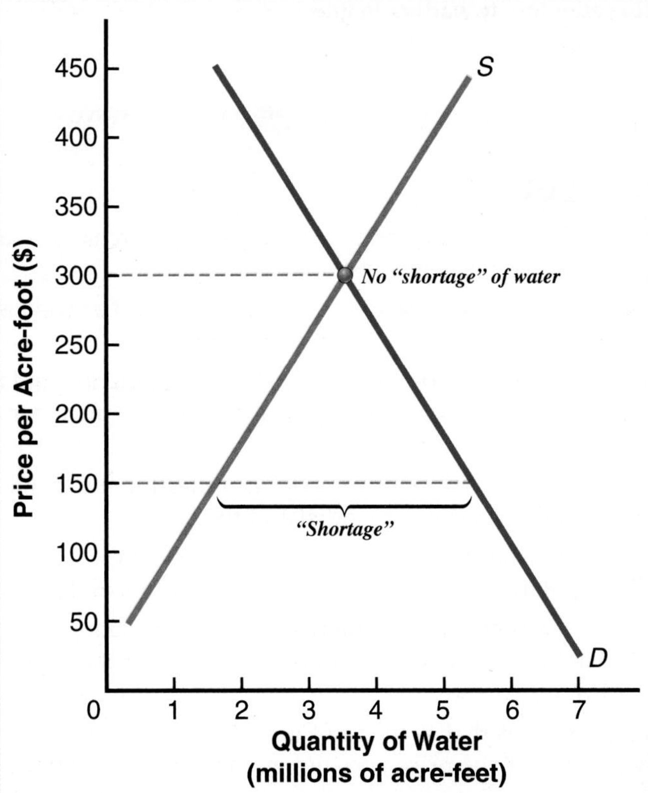


In a given region, if water is priced at $300 per acre-foot, there is no talk of shortages. At a price of $150 per acre-foot, there will be shortages.

## Other Forms of Rationing

In a world of scarcity, there is, by definition, competition for what is scarce. After all, any resources that are not scarce can be had by everyone at a zero price in as large a quantity as everyone wants, such as air to burn in internal combustion engines. Once scarcity arises, there has to be some method of rationing the available resources, goods, and services. The price system is one form of rationing, but there are other forms of rationing scarce goods and services. Here are just a few:

1. First come, first serve
2. Political power
3. Physical force
4. Lotteries
5. Rationing by coupons
6. Rationing by waiting in line

✦ **Be Aware!** *Whenever someones argues in favor of a system of rationing other than by the price system, some inefficiencies will result.*

Economists cannot say which system of rationing is best. They can, however, say that rationing via the price system leads to the most efficient use of available resources. This means that generally in a price system, further exchanges could not occur without making somebody worse off. In other words, in a freely functioning price system, all of the gains from mutually beneficial trade will be exhausted.

**Mastering Concepts:** The Rationing Function of Prices

- **Prices are indicators of relative scarcity, and as such, they tell consumers the value to society of goods and services.**
- **Alternative ways of rationing, other than the price system, are (1) first come, first serve; (2) political power; (3) physical force; (4) lotteries; (5) rationing by coupons; and (6) rationing by waiting in line.**

## SUMMING IT ALL UP

- The law of demand states that at higher prices, less is purchased than at lower prices, all other things held constant.
- The law of demand occurs because of the real income effect as well as the substitution effect.
- To compare prices over time, you must first correct for inflation and then correct for quality changes to arrive at the relative (or real) price per constant-quality unit.
- The demand curve is always downward sloping, reflecting the inverse relationship between the quantity demanded and the price.
- The demand curve will shift if one of the following changes: (1) tastes or preferences, (2) population, (3) income, and (4) prices of related goods.
- Anytime the price of a good changes, there is a movement along the given demand curve. Anytime another determinant changes, the entire demand curve shifts in or out.
- The law of supply tells us that as the price goes up, the quantity supplied will generally rise and as the price goes down, the quantity supplied will generally fall.

- Supply curves are generally upward sloping, reflecting the positive relationship between price and quantity supplied.
- The position of the supply curve will change when determinants of supply, other than its own price, change. They are (1) the cost of inputs, (2) technology and productivity, (3) taxes, and (4) the number of firms in the industry.
- Any change in price will cause a movement along the supply curve; any change in other determinants will cause a shift in the supply curve.
- Equilibrium occurs at the intersection of the demand and supply curves, where the market clearing price occurs. This is also called the equilibrium price.
- At the equilibrium price, no one is frustrated in attempting to buy or sell.
- Prices are indicators of relative scarcity, and as such, they tell consumers the value to society of goods and services.

## KEY TERMS AND CONCEPTS

complements 55
constant-quality units 50
demand 48
demand curve 51
demand schedule 51
equilibrium price 60
law of demand 48
law of supply 57
market clearing price 60
money price 50
nominal prices 50
rationing function of prices 62
real income effect 49
relative price 50
shortages 60
subsidy 59
substitutes 55
substitution effect 49
supply schedule 57
supply curve 58
surplus 60

## MASTERING ECONOMIC CONCEPTS
## Questions and Problems

**3-1.** Would each of the following cause an increase, a decrease, or no change in the demand for cell phones?

a. a decrease in the price of monthly cellular service
b. a decrease in the cost of the inputs used to make cell phones
c. an increase in income levels across the population
d. a decrease in the price of personal pagers

**3-2.** Determine if each of the following statements is true or false and indicate why.

a. Lower price leads to an increase in demand.
b. An increase in the quantity supplied leads to an increase in price.
c. Any price above the equilibrium price will cause a shortage.
d. A decrease in consumer income will cause a decrease in supply.

**3-3.** How do changes in a retailer's inventory serve as a signaling mechanism? What would excessive inventory levels indicate that a retailer should do to its prices?

**3-4.** Recently, the price of travel on cruise ships has decreased notably. Which curve do you think has shifted to create this decrease in price, and why did the curve shift?

**3-5.** If the equilibrium price of a good decreased while the equilibrium quantity increased, which curve—supply or demand—must have moved in which direction?

**3-6.** If income levels decrease across the country, what impact will this have on the new-auto market? Detail your answer by indicating which curve or curves will shift, in what direction(s), and how the price and quantity of cars sold in the market will change.

**3-7.** What role does the income effect play in consumer spending if the price of electricity increases? If electricity becomes more expensive, what types of goods for the home might consumers choose to substitute over others?

**3-8.** Based on the demand schedule for hamburgers from Sidelines Grill below, how many hamburgers will be demanded if the price is \$6.95? How many will be demanded if the price is \$8.95? How much will the quantity of hamburgers demanded change if the price decreases from \$5.95 to \$4.95?

**Demand Schedule—Hamburgers at Sidelines**

| Price | Quantity |
|---|---|
| \$8.95 | 8 |
| 7.95 | 20 |
| 6.95 | 34 |
| 5.95 | 52 |
| 4.95 | 74 |

**3-9.** Based on the following individual monthly demand schedules for CDs, construct a market demand schedule. Assume that these are the only consumers in this market.

| John | | Paul | | George | |
|---|---|---|---|---|---|
| Price | Quantity | Price | Quantity | Price | Quantity |
| \$10 | 4 | \$10 | 9 | \$10 | 7 |
| 15 | 2 | 15 | 5 | 15 | 3 |
| 20 | 0 | 20 | 2 | 20 | 1 |

**3-10.** Based on the graph below, what quantity will be demanded at a price of \$5.00? What quantity will be supplied at a price of \$5.00? Will a shortage or a surplus take place at \$5.00, and what will be the size of the shortage or surplus?

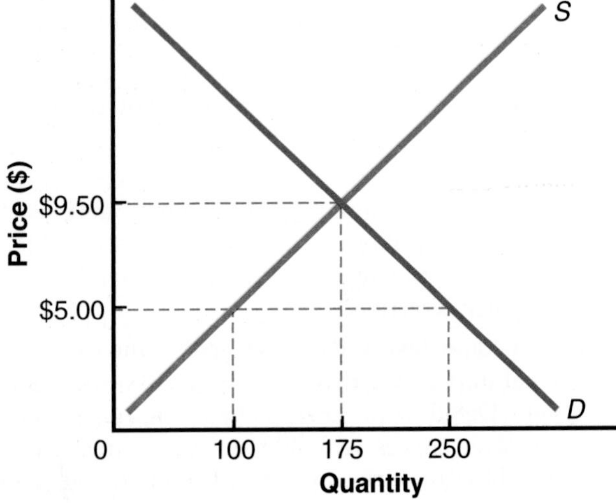


**3-11.** Complete the table in the next column by computing the shortage or surplus at each price for paperback books. If no shortage or surplus exists at a price, indicate that price as the equilibrium price.

| Price | Quantity Demanded | Quantity Supplied | Condition |
|---|---|---|---|
| \$10 | 50 | 250 | _____ |
| 9 | 100 | 200 | _____ |
| 8 | 150 | 150 | _____ |
| 7 | 200 | 100 | _____ |
| 6 | 250 | 50 | _____ |
| 5 | 300 | 0 | _____ |

**3-12.** Define the law of demand and the law of supply and indicate whether each law illustrates a direct relationship or an inverse relationship between price and quantity.

**3-13.** Would each of the following cause an increase, a decrease, or no change in the supply of new autos?

a. a decrease in the interest rates for auto loans
b. a decrease in taxes on automakers
c. a decrease in the number of businesses making new cars
d. a decrease in the price of aluminum and steel used in auto production

**3-14.** If the price of sweaters decreases, what will happen to the quantity of sweaters that consumers wish to purchase? Would this be a change in quantity demanded or a change in demand?

**3-15.** What impact will a decrease in supply have on equilibrium price and equilibrium quantity?

**3-16.** Assume that the cost of aluminum used by soft drink companies increases. Which of the following statements would accurately describe the situation in the market for soft drinks? (More than one statement may be correct.)

a. The demand for canned soft drinks will decrease.
b. The quantity of canned soft drinks demanded will decrease.
c. The supply of canned soft drinks will decrease.
d. The quantity of canned soft drinks supplied will decrease.

**3-17.** If the price of processor chips used to make personal computers decreases, what will happen to the equilibrium price and the equilibrium quantity in the market for personal computers? Draw a graph to illustrate your conclusions.

**3-18.** If both the equilibrium price and the equilibrium quantity of a good decreased, which curve must have moved? In which direction did it move?

**3-19.** Based on the supply curves depicted below for the two ice cream stands in the area, draw the market supply curve for ice cream in this area.

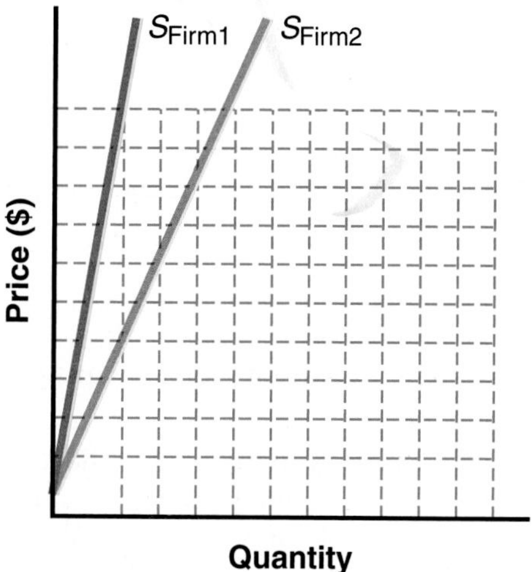


**3-20.** If the population in a certain area increases, what impact will this have on the equilibrium price and quantity for retail goods in the area? If the number of retail establishments in a certain area increases, what impact will this have on the equilibrium price and quantity for retail goods in the area? If both of the above events take place during the same time period, what will be the impact on the equilibrium price and the equilibrium quantity?

## THINKING CRITICALLY

**3-1.** The lease for my apartment uses the term "market rate." The lease estimates the "market rate" for a two-bedroom apartment at $1,050 per month, but the apartment complex rents such apartments for $950 per month. Based on this information, is $1,050 actually the equilibrium price in this market? If 20 percent of the apartments in this apartment complex are vacant at this time, does this suggest that the equilibrium rental rate is actually higher or lower than $950? If the apartment complex also offers move-in specials, in which new tenants receive one month's free rent, what does this imply about the actual market rate?

**3-2.** The NCAA distributes tickets to the general public for the Final Four through a lottery. In a typical year, the NCAA will provide about 9,000 tickets to the general public and receive about 85,000 requests for tickets. To request a ticket, you must pay the ticket price of $240. If you do not win tickets in the lottery, the NCAA returns your money to you. Does this situation indicate a shortage or a surplus of tickets at the current price level? Based on the number of requests in relation to the number of tickets, how does the equilibrium price compare to the price charged by the NCAA? Why might the NCAA want to charge a price other than the equilibrium price? In what market could we look to see a more accurate indication of the true equilibrium price for these tickets? (HINT: Look again at problem 2-14.)

**3-3.** In the 1970s, an international group of oil-exporting countries did a very effective job of significantly raising the price of crude oil, which resulted in a substantial increase in the price of gasoline. With higher gasoline prices, how did consumers likely react in terms of the income effect and their purchases across all markets? How did consumers likely react in terms of the substitution effect in the automobile market? Based on the current popularity of large SUVs, what do you think has happened to the relative price of gasoline from the 1970s to the present?

**3-4.** During 2003, interest rates on residential mortgages fell to record low levels. What impact did the low interest rates have on the market for homes with respect to supply, demand, price, and quantity? How are the two goods—mortgages and homes—related to each other? By the end of August 2003, many consumers and lenders observed that the interest rates on mortgages were beginning to increase again. What impact did this belief have on the market for mortgages and homes?

## LOGGING ON

1. For an examination of the various factors that have contributed to a global increase in cigarette smuggling, go to http://www.ncpa.org/pub/ba/ba423/.
2. To learn more about some of the problems arising from the failure to allow markets to determine prices of the world's water resources, go to http://www.economist.com/surveys/displaystory.cfm?story_id=1906846.
3. For facts and figures concerning the effects of rent controls in New York City, go to http://www.fcpp.org/publication_detail.php?PubID=590.
4. For a discussion of U.S. airport congestion problems that have arisen from methods used to ration access to runways, go to http://www.rppi.org/ps255.html.

## USING THE INTERNET FOR ECONOMIC ANALYSIS

**The U.S. Nursing Shortage** For some years media stories have discussed a shortage of qualified nurses in the United States. This application explores some of the factors that have caused the quantity of newly trained nurses demanded to tend to exceed the quantity of newly trained nurses supplied.

**Title:** Nursing Shortage Resource Web Link

**Navigation:** Go to the Nursing Shortage Resource Web Link at http://www.aacn.nche.edu/Media/shortageresource.htm#about, and click on "Enrollment Increase Insufficient to Meet the Projected Increase in Demand for New Nurses."

**Application** Read the discussion, and answer the following questions.

1. Since 1995, what has happened to the demand for new nurses in the United States? What has happened to the supply of new nurses? Why has the result been a shortage?
2. If there is a free market for the skills of new nurses, what can you predict is likely to happen to the wage rate earned by individuals who have just completed their nursing training?

## MEDIA RESOURCE LIST

The following media resources are available with this chapter:

- Load your CD-ROM to listen to the audio introduction to this chapter.
- Load your CD-ROM to access Graph Animations to Figure 3-2, *The Horizontal Summation of Two Demand Schedules*, and Figure 3-4, *A Shift in the Demand Curve*.
- Load your CD-ROM to view the videos on *A Change in Demand Is Not the Same as a Change in Quantity Demanded, A Change in Supply Is Not the Same as a Change in Quantity Supplied,* and *The Rationing function of Prices*.
- Test your knowledge of chapter concepts with a quiz at www.miller-ume.com.
- Link to Web resources related to the text coverage at www.miller-ume.com.

## HOMEWORK SET

Go to back of this book to find the Homework Problems for this chapter.

# CHAPTER 4

# Consumer Decision Making and Consumer Reaction to Price Changes

## *Facing an Economic Problem:* Why Do Newspaper Vending Machines Let You Have Access to More Than One Paper?

Have you ever noticed that newspaper vending machines on street corners and in airports seem to rely an awful lot on your honesty? If you put in the required amount of money, you get to open the machine and take a newspaper or, for that matter, all the remaining papers.

If you go to a soft drink or a candy vending machine, in contrast, your honesty seems to be questioned. Food and drink vending machines are much more complicated; designed to be tamper-proof, they grudgingly spit out only one item at a time. Does this mean that food and drink purchasers are less honest than newspaper purchasers? You will find out that the answer is "no," as you study the concept of diminishing marginal utility in this chapter.

## Learning Objectives

After reading this chapter, you should be able to:

- **Distinguish between total and marginal utility.**
- **Distinguish between elastic and inelastic demand.**
- **Define the price elasticity of demand and state the formula for measuring it.**
- **List and describe three determinants of the price elasticity of demand.**
- **Explain the relationship between price elasticity of demand and consumer expenditures.**

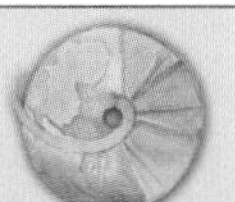

***Refer to the back of this chapter for a complete listing of multimedia learning materials available on the CD-ROM, and the Web site.***

## IF IT DOESN'T HAVE UTILITY, YOU WON'T BUY IT

All of the discussion about the demand for goods and services in Chapter 3 implicitly assumed something important: the goods and services under study are desired by you and by other consumers.

So, everything for which you have a demand must generate satisfaction. Another way of describing satisfaction is **utility**, defined as want-satisfying power. Obviously, all *desired* goods and services have utility, even if you don't know exactly how to measure it. The concept of utility, after all, is purely subjective.

**Utility**
*The ability of any good or service to satisfy consumer wants; the amount of satisfaction one gets from a good or service.*

▸ Example 4-1 "Ugh. How can you eat those snails and raw oysters?" As an old Latin saying puts it, roughly translated, there is no accounting for taste. In other words, the utility that an aficionado of snails or raw oysters receives from eating those delicacies does not mean that everyone else will receive utility from doing the same. Utility is purely subjective and very personal. ◂

### It's Hard to Predict What Others Will Like

Common statements about rich people always involve how much they can "afford." Even if a person has lots and lots of income, that does not tell you much about the utility that that rich person might receive from consuming any particular good or service. Otherwise stated, it is literally impossible to compare the utilities that different people experience from consuming the same good or service. ▸ Example 4-2 Some of the richest people on earth buy and drive low-priced cars. The late founder of Wal-Mart, Sam Walton, drove around in an old pickup truck much of his life. We cannot say that he was "irrational" or "silly." We cannot compare the utility he received from driving his pickup to the utility that you and I might receive from driving a much more expensive car. ◂

### Measuring Utility

Of course, there is no way to really measure utility. That is just too personal a notion for economists to get a true handle on it. Nonetheless, to help us understand utility better, we arbitrarily define units of utility as **utils**. A util is simply an abstract concept that is defined as a representative unit by which utility is measured. ▸ Example 4-3 We might hypothesize that the first game of video blackjack yields you four utils and that the first game of The Legends of Zelda yields you nine utils of satisfaction. But there is never any way that we can truly measure utility. We do this only as a way to analyze consumer behavior. ◂

**Utils**
*A hypothetical representative unit by which utility might be measured, even though we know that it cannot be measured. Thus, a util is an analytical construct only.*

### Of Total and Additional Utility

By definition, everything that you consume gives you some amount of satisfaction, or utility. If you watch ten movies a month, you get a certain amount of total utility from that activity over the month.

But what about the *additional* utility you receive when you see another movie? You know it has to be positive, or you would not watch the movie. We call this additional utility **marginal utility**, where the word *marginal* means "additional" or "incremental." ▸ Example 4-4 If you have already rented and watched five DVDs from Netflix.com, the marginal utility you receive from watching the next rental during a fixed time period, say, a week, might be six utils. ◂

**Marginal utility**
*An additional amount of satisfaction.*

**Figuring Out Marginal Utility** The way you figure out marginal utility is by looking at *changes* in total utility as you increase your consumption rate. Assume your total utility from consuming two units of a given item is 16 utils. Also, assume your total utility for consuming three of that same item is 19 utils. Then, obviously, the marginal utility of consuming the *third* unit is 19 minus 16, or 3 utils.

**Looking at Total and Marginal Utility with a Graph** Look at Figure 4-1 on the next page. There you see three separate panels. In panel (a) we calculate the marginal utilities of watching DVDs each week. In panel (b) we simply plot the total utility taken from columns 1 and 2 in panel (a). In panel (c) we plot the marginal utility taken from columns 1 and 3 in panel (a).

## Marginal Utility Falls As You Consume More Units

Look again at panel (c) in Figure 4-1. There you see that marginal utility falls as more DVDs are watched per week. This should not surprise you. After all, in almost all cases, the first of anything you consume seems to be the best. As you consume more of anything, you have to admit that the additional satisfaction—marginal utility—that you receive falls. That is exactly what you see in panel (c).

Look at what happens after you watch four DVDs per week. You see in panel (c) of Figure 4-1 that the marginal utility actually becomes *negative*. ▸ Example 4-5 A very rich friend takes you to a sporting event and offers you all of the hot dogs you want at no charge to you. Certainly, the first hot dog will bring you a certain amount of satisfaction. If you are hungry and have a great appetite, the second will still bring you some satisfaction, but your marginal utility will fall. If you are offered a third hot dog, you might actually be worried about getting sick. So, even through there's no charge to you, you politely refuse the third hot dog. ◂

## Diminishing Marginal Utility

All the previous discussion comes down to something very fundamental about human behavior. Marginal utility continuously declines for just about any good or service you consume. This property has been called the **principle of diminishing marginal utility**. We cannot prove that diminishing marginal utility exists. Most economists and laypersons alike, nonetheless, believe so strongly in this principle that they sometimes call it the law of diminishing marginal utility. This is a subjective, or psychological, concept.

**Principle of diminishing marginal utility**
*A principle, law, or rule that asserts that as consumers consume more of any given good or service, at a point in time, the additional (marginal) utility of even more units will continue to decline.*

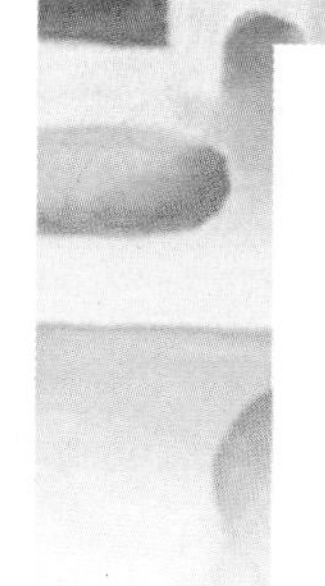

### *Solving the Economic Problem:*
### Why Do Newspaper Vending Machines Let You Have Access to More Than One Paper?

Now that you have learned about diminishing marginal utility, you can probably solve the chapter-opening economic problem yourself. What is the marginal utility to you of "stealing" one, two, three, or four extra newspapers when you buy one from a vending machine? Probably zero, if not negative, because you have to carry them around. You get a certain amount of utility from reading a newspaper, but certainly not from reading the same newspaper twice.

*Continued on next page*

In contrast, even though marginal utility is diminishing for candy and soft drinks, you nevertheless get positive marginal utility from extra units of these goods. Therefore, you would still benefit if you took two from the vending machine instead of just the one that you paid for. Moreover, you can store candy and soft drinks for later use.

So, it is not because newspaper purchasers are more honest than food and beverage purchasers. Rather, the marginal utility of the second newspaper on the same day is effectively zero or negative. Not so for candy and cold beverages

*Animated*

## Figure 4-1 The Total and Marginal Utility of Watching DVDs

**Panel (a)**

| (1) Number of DVDs Watched per Week | (2) Total Utility (utils per week) | (3) Marginal Utility (utils per week) |
|---|---|---|
| 0 | 0 | |
| | | 10 (10 – 0) |
| 1 | 10 | |
| | | 6 (16 – 10) |
| 2 | 16 | |
| | | 3 (19 – 16) |
| 3 | 19 | |
| | | 1 (20 – 19) |
| 4 | 20 | |
| | | 0 (20 – 20) |
| 5 | 20 | |
| | | –2 (18 – 20) |
| 6 | 18 | |

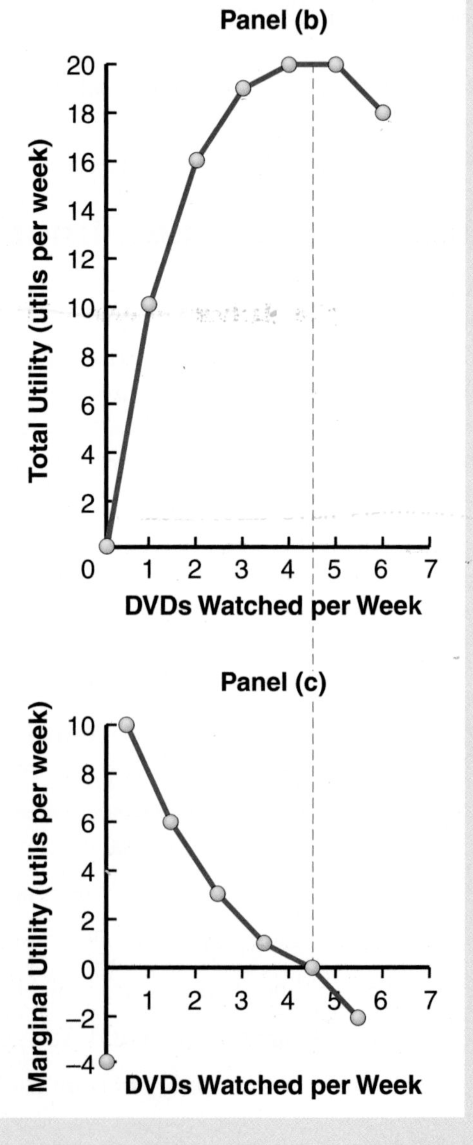


If we were able to assign specific values to the utility derived from watching DVDs each week, we could obtain a marginal utility schedule similar in pattern to the one shown in panel (a). In column 1 is the number of DVDs watched per week; in column 2, the total utility derived from each quantity; and in column 3, the marginal utility derived from each additional quantity, which is defined as the change in total utility due to a change of one unit of watching DVDs per week. Total utility from panel (a) is plotted in panel (b). Marginal utility is plotted in panel (c), where you see that it reaches zero at between 4 and 5 units, where total utility hits its maximum.

**Mastering Concepts:** If It Doesn't Have Utility, You Won't Buy It

- **Utility means the want-satisfying power of the good or service.**
- **Marginal utility is derived by comparing total utility for a given rate of consumption to total utility when you consume one more unit of a good or service.**
- **Even at no charge to you, there are many items that you will stop consuming because marginal utility eventually becomes negative.**
- **The law of diminishing marginal utility tells you that after you consume a good or service, the marginal utility you receive for yet more of that same good or service will start falling.**

## MEASURING CONSUMER RESPONSIVENESS—THE PRICE ELASTICITY OF DEMAND

You certainly know that for some items, even a large percentage reduction in price is not going to cause you to change your consumption very much. But you also know that for other items, even a small percentage change in price will markedly affect your desired rate of consumption. ▸ **Example 4-6** If the price of salt goes down 50 percent, how much more would you purchase in a year? Probably not very much. In other words, your salt consumption is not going to be very responsive to a change in the price of salt. In contrast, if you normally buy fast-food dinners once a week, and the price of fast food were to drop by 50 percent, you would probably increase the number of fast-food dinners you buy quite a bit. You would be very price responsive then. ◂

The official term for consumer responsiveness to price changes is **elasticity**. Hence, the **price elasticity of demand** is a measure of how much consumers respond to a given change in price.

**Elasticity**
*A measure of how much consumers respond to a given change in the price of a particular good or service.*

**Price elasticity of demand**
*The degree to which consumers respond to a given change in the price of a particular good or service; measured in terms of the relative change in quantity demanded compared to the relative in price.*

> ***If consumers react a lot to a given percentage change in price, we say they have an* elastic demand. *If they do not react very much, we say they have an* inelastic demand.**

Economists have discovered that teenagers do respond to price changes for tobacco products. Therefore, many policymakers have used this fact as an argument to raise cigarette taxes. As you will read in the next *Policy Application*, though, the Internet may frustrate policymakers' attempts to curb teen smoking.

### POLICY APPLICATION: A Crack in the Wall Against Teenage Smoking

***Concept Applied:***
**Price Elasticity of Demand**

Numerous studies show that the probability of becoming an adult nicotine addict is ten times greater if one starts smoking as a teenager. Consequently, governments at the federal, state, and local levels have made a concerted effort to crack down on teenage smoking. A favorite approach has been to increase cigarette taxes. Indeed, evidence shows that a 10 percent increase in the price of a pack of cigarettes reduces teenage smoking by 6 percent. The Internet, however, is proving to be a significant alternative to high cigarette taxes, which might otherwise have discouraged youths from smoking.

*Continued on next page*

### Internet Sales of Tobacco Products Are on the Rise

At the beginning of the 2000s, Internet sales of cigarettes amounted to $1.2 billion per year. The estimate for 2005 is $5 billion per year. Internet sales of cigarettes have increased because of the dramatic increase in state-levied cigarette taxes. A carton of Marlboro Kings from DirtCheapCigs.com costs about $35, including shipping. In New York City, state and city taxes alone would be $30, yielding a retail price of $50 or more for that same carton. You can easily see the incentive for cigarette smokers to buy over the Internet. New York and other states have passed laws to bar Internet and mail-order sales of cigarettes to their residents. They argue that Internet sales encourage teenage smoking because Internet companies have no way of confirming purchasers' ages.

### Most Online Tobacco Sellers Are on American Indian Reservations

At least 80 percent of all online tobacco sellers are located on American Indian reservations. Why? Because Indian reservations are exempt from state sales taxes. Thus, most Indian reservations have thriving on-site cigarette businesses. Smokers who live nearby simply drive onto the reservations to make their purchases.

### Regulation and Enforcement on the Internet Are Difficult

No matter what laws are passed to prevent Internet sellers from offering cigarettes to teenage smokers, enforcement will be difficult. States that attempt to crack down on tobacco Web sites find that the Web sites simply disappears only to come up in some other form the next day. Regulating the sale of cigarettes online is not easy either. California has a law that requires online sellers to verify the age of the purchaser by matching his or her name and address with dates of birth on government records. Although online cigarette sellers pay lip service to this regulation, most do not spend the resources necessary to perform the checks.

**For Critical Analysis:**
*What similarity do you see between regulating the sale of cigarettes online and regulating the illegal downloading of copyrighted songs?*

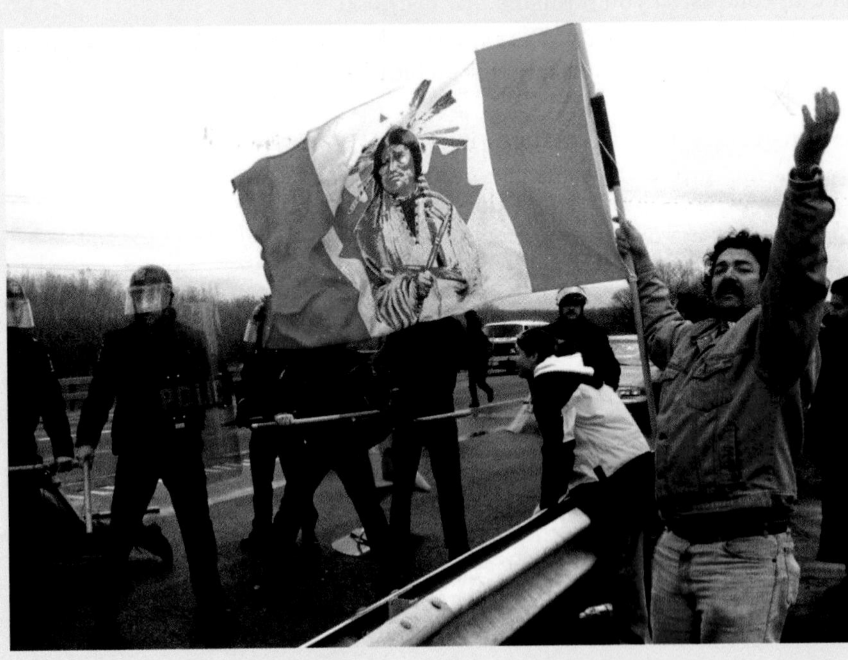

*This Native American protester is from the Cattaraugus Indian Reservation in upstate New York. He and others protested that state's attempt to force them to collect sales taxes on cigarettes (and other items) from non-Indians at their reservation stores.*

## Elastic versus Inelastic Demand

We typically divide people's demands into those that involve a more-than-proportionate response to price changes and those that involve a less-than-proportionate response.

**Elastic Demand** For some goods, a rise or fall in price greatly affects the amount people are willing to buy. The demand for these goods is said to be *elastic*—consumers can be flexible when buying and not buying these items. We say that such goods have elastic demands. Many business opportunities have to do with services that have elastic demands, as you will read about in the next *Policy Application*.

## POLICY APPLICATION: Seeking New Businesses by Examining Price Elasticities

***Concept Applied:***
**Price Elasticity**

There is a man out there whose name is Stelios Haji-Ioannou. He has a vision—compete against high-priced services throughout Europe. He is the one who started EasyJet, EasyCar Rentals, EasyInternet Cafes, and EasyCinemas.

### A Rather Simple Business Formula

Stelios has a relatively simple business formula: Scout out services in Europe that have high price elasticities of demand.

First, he discovered that some airline travelers have high price elasticities of demand. Many consumers are willing to take an airplane if the price is dropped relative to rivals' prices. Therefore, Stelios created EasyJet with one class of cheap service and no frills. His EasyCar Rentals operation rents only one class of car, and the customer must return the car, already cleaned, to the same location.

### Changing Prices All of the Time

Stelios's business model also looks at shifts in demand during each day. He wants to have all of his airplane seats, Internet terminals, and cars in use all of the time. When you call up to rent from EasyCar, you can pay as low as $15 and as high as $80 per day, depending on how many cars are booked for the same period. As a result, on any given day EasyCar rents 90 percent of its available vehicles.

**For Critical Analysis:**
*During what periods do you think EasyCar charges the highest prices per day? Why?*

Certainly, when there are many choices, demand is going to be more elastic than when there are few choices. ▸ **Example 4-7** Carbonated soft drinks represent a very competitive market. There are numerous choices. Consequently, if only one particular brand and style of carbonated beverage goes up in price, consumers' reactions will probably be quite obvious—they will reduce their consumption of that brand more than in proportion to the percentage increase in price. ◂

**Inelastic Demand** For other goods and services, price changes seem to have less effect on people's purchase decisions. Goods for which this is true are said to have inelastic demands. ▸ **Example 4-8** We often characterize drug addicts as those who "must" have their fix of their drug of choice. Indeed, most studies show that the price elasticity of demand of illegal drugs is relatively low—that is, inelastic. It takes a considerable increase in the price of an illegal drug to get addicts to reduce their consumption by very much. ◂

## THE EXTREMES IN PRICE ELASTICITY

There are two extreme types of elasticity of demand.

**Perfectly Inelastic Demand** If you have to have something, no matter what the price, we say that you have a *perfectly* inelastic demand for that good or service. Look at panel (a) in Figure 4-2 on page 76. There you see that the demand is a vertical curve. No matter what the price, the quantity demanded will be the same. In the real world, though, for the market for any good looked at as a whole, there cannot be perfectly inelastic demand. Why? Because individuals have

*Animated*

**Figure 4-2 Extreme Price Elasticities**

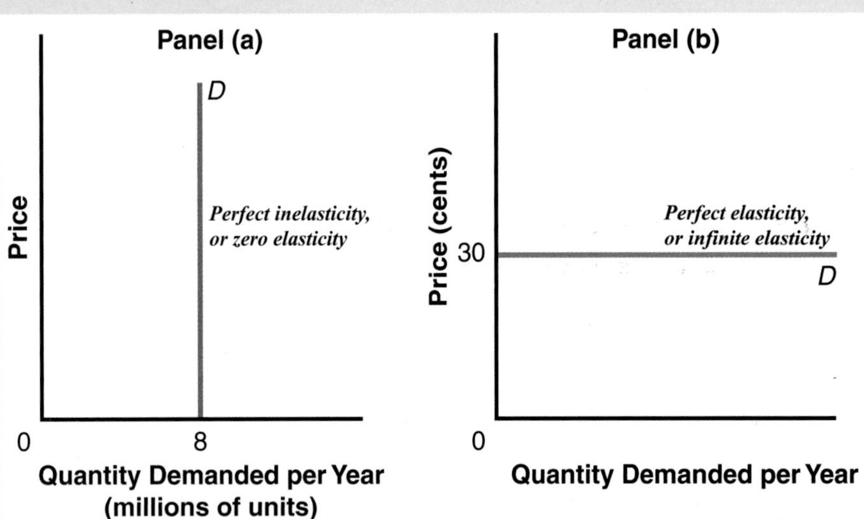

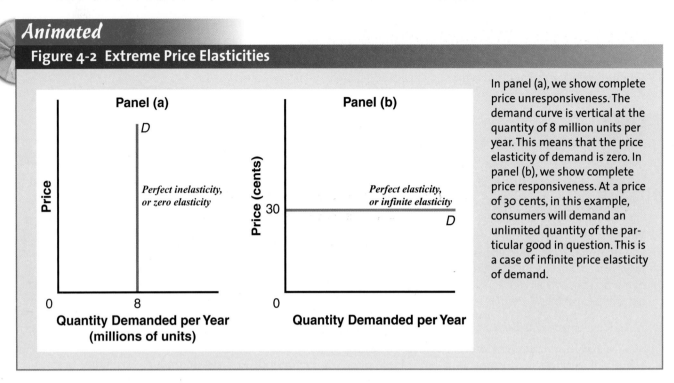

In panel (a), we show complete price unresponsiveness. The demand curve is vertical at the quantity of 8 million units per year. This means that the price elasticity of demand is zero. In panel (b), we show complete price responsiveness. At a price of 30 cents, in this example, consumers will demand an unlimited quantity of the particular good in question. This is a case of infinite price elasticity of demand.

limited incomes. At high enough prices, there would be no income left over to buy anything else.

### Perfectly Elastic Demand

The opposite of a perfectly inelastic demand is, of course, a perfectly elastic demand. With a perfectly elastic demand, consumers demand virtually an unlimited quantity of a particular good at a particular price. You can see this in panel (b) of Figure 4-2. There you see that at a price of 30 cents, the quantity demanded goes from a very small amount to a very large amount. ▸ **Example 4-9** In a market in which all producers produce a similar good and there are lots of buyers and sellers, the individual seller faces a demand curve similar to that in panel (b) of Figure 4-2. An individual producer and seller of wheat can sell all that she wants at the market price. If that person tries to raise the price by even a cent, she will experience zero sales. Why? Because there are so many alternative sellers of wheat at the market price, no one will buy from her at a higher price. Conversely, if she cuts price even a penny, she will be able to sell quantities far in excess of her capacity to produce. Why? Because customers all throughout the market will be trying to take advantage of her (lower) price. ◂

**Mastering Concepts:** Measuring Consumer Responsiveness—The Price Elasticity of Demand

- **Price elasticity of demand shows how much consumers respond to a given change in the price of a particular good or service.**
- **When you respond greatly to a change in price, we say you have an elastic demand. When you respond very little to a change in price, you have an inelastic demand.**
- **If you don't respond at all to a change in price, you have a perfectly inelastic demand.**

## ON DOING ELASTICITY CALCULATIONS

A commonsense way to come up with a measure of the price elasticity of demand is to compare the percentage change in quantity demanded with the percentage change in price.

### A FEW FORMULAS FIRST

That is exactly what we do with this simple formula:

$$\textbf{Price elasticity of demand} = \frac{\textbf{percentage change in quantity demanded}}{\textbf{percentage change in price}}$$

What will price elasticity of demand tell us? It will tell us the *relative* amount by which the quantity demanded would change in response to a change in the price of a particular good.

Assume that a 10 percent rise in the price of oil leads to a reduction in quantity demanded of only 1 percent. Putting these numbers into the above formula, we find that the price elasticity of demand for oil in this case equals the percentage change in quantity demanded divided by the percentage change in price, or

$$\textbf{Price elasticity of demand} = \frac{-\ 1\%}{+\ 10\%} = -0.1$$

An elasticity of –0.1 means that a 1 percent *increase* in the price would lead to a mere 0.1 percent *decrease* in the quantity demanded. If you were now told, in contrast, that the price elasticity of demand for oil was –1, you would know that a 1 percent increase in the price of oil would lead to a 1 percent decrease in the quantity demanded.

◂ **International Example 4-10** When the owner of the British daily newspaper *Today* reduced prices by about 85 percent, unit sales increased by a little over 56 percent. So, the price elasticity of demand was about 0.66 (= 56/85). ◂

**Relative Quantities Only** Notice that in our elasticity formula, we say *percentage* change in quantity demanded divided by *percentage* change in price. We are therefore not interested in the absolute changes, only in relative amounts. This means that it doesn't matter if we measure price changes in cents, dollars, or hundreds of dollars. It also doesn't matter whether we measure quantity changes in ounces, grams, or pounds. The percentage change will be independent of the units chosen.

**Always Negative** The law of demand states that quantity demanded is *inversely* related to the relative price. An *increase* in the relative price of a good leads to a *decrease* in the quantity demanded. If a *decrease* in the relative price of a good should occur, the quantity demanded would *increase* by a certain percentage. The point is that price elasticity of demand will always be negative. By convention, however, *we will ignore the minus sign in our discussion from this point on.*

Basically, the greater the *absolute* price elasticity of demand (disregarding sign), the greater the demand responsiveness to relative price changes—a small change in price has a great impact on quantity demanded. Conversely, the smaller the absolute price elasticity of demand, the smaller the demand responsiveness to relative price changes—a large change in price has little effect on quantity demanded.

▸ **Example 4-11** Current estimates indicate that a 1 percent increase in the price of heroin induces a 0.7 percent decrease in adult consumption of this addictive drug. A 1 percent increase in the price of cocaine reduces the quantity demanded by adults by only 0.5 percent. Among teenagers, however, a 1 percent increase in the price of either of these drugs causes the quantity demanded to fall by 1.0 to 1.5 percent. The quantity of addictive drugs demanded by teenagers, therefore, is more responsive to an increase in the market price than the quantity demanded by adults. ◂

## HOW WE ACTUALLY CALCULATE ELASTICITY IN THE REAL WORLD

To calculate the price elasticity of demand, we have to compute percentage changes in quantity demanded and in relative price. To obtain the percentage change in quantity demanded, we might divide the change in the quantity demanded by the original quantity demanded:

$$\frac{\textbf{Change in quantity demanded}}{\textbf{Original quantity demanded}}$$

To find the percentage change in price, we divide the change in price by the original price:

$$\frac{\textbf{Change in price}}{\textbf{Original price}}$$

**An Arithmetic Problem** There is an arithmetic problem, though, when we calculate percentage changes in this manner. The percentage change, say, from 2 to 3—50 percent—is not the same as the percentage change from 3 to 2—$33\frac{1}{3}$ percent. In other words, it makes a difference where you start. One way out of this dilemma is simply to use average values.

**Using Average Formulas** To compute the price elasticity of demand, we take the average of the two prices and the two quantities over the range we are considering and compare the change with these *averages*. The formula for computing the price elasticity of demand then becomes

$$\textbf{Price elasticity of demand} = \frac{\textbf{change in quantity}}{\textbf{sum of quantities/2}} \div \frac{\textbf{change in price}}{\textbf{sum of prices/2}}$$

We can rewrite this more simply if we do two things: (1) We can let $Q_1$ and $Q_2$ equal the two different quantities demanded before and after the price change and let $P_1$ and $P_2$ equal the two different prices. (2) Because we will be dividing a percentage by a percentage, we simply use the ratio, or the decimal form, of the percentages. Therefore,

$$\textbf{Price elasticity of demand} = \frac{\textbf{change in } Q}{(Q_1 + Q_2)/2} \div \frac{\textbf{change in } P}{(P_1 + P_2)/2}$$

## PRICE ELASTICITY RANGES

**Elastic demand**
*If a given change in price elicits a more-than-proportionate change in quantity demanded, demand is said to be elastic.*

There are two ranges of elasticity:

1. Whenever the price elasticity of demand is numerically *greater* than 1, we say that there is **elastic demand**. In other words, any given percentage change in

price will lead to a *more*-than-proportionate change in quantity demanded—obviously, in the opposite direction because of the law of demand.

2. If the price elasticity of demand is numerically *less* than 1, we say that we are dealing with **inelastic demand**. Otherwise stated, any given percentage change in the price of the good or service under study will lead to a *less*-than-proportionate change in the quantity demanded—in the opposite direction, of course.

**Inelastic demand**
*If a given change in price elicits a less-than-proportionate change in quantity demanded, demand is said to be inelastic.*

When the price elasticity of demand is neither elastic nor inelastic, it is said to be **unit-elastic demand**. In other words, a 1 percent change in price will lead to an exactly 1 percent change in quantity demanded, in the opposite direction.

**Unit-elastic demand**
*If a given change in price leads to an exactly proportionate change in quantity demanded, this represents unit-elastic demand.*

## What Determines the Price Elasticity of Demand?

Why do some goods have an elastic demand and others an inelastic demand? There are at least three factors that determine the price elasticity of demand for a particular item:

1. **The Existence of Substitutes:** The more and better substitutes that exist for a product, the more responsive consumers will be to a change in the price of that good. We already gave the example of carbonated soft drinks. ▸ Example 4-12 Someone who is diabetic needs insulin, which has virtually no substitutes. We therefore predict that the price elasticity of demand for insulin is very low—highly inelastic. ◂
2. **The Percentage of a Person's Total Budget Devoted to the Purchase of That Good:** If you spend a small percentage of your budget on a particular item, changes in the price of that item will not affect your *real* income (purchasing power) very much. In contrast, if you spend a large percentage of your budget on a particular item, even small price changes will affect your real income noticeably. Remember that we talked about the *real income effect* in Chapter 3. There we pointed out that if the price of one good changes and nothing else changes, your purchasing power must change in the opposite direction. Here purchasing power is another way to describe real income. We predict that the larger the share of your budget devoted to an item, the more price elastic will be its demand. ▸ Example 4-13 Most people spend anywhere from 20 to 50 percent of their total income on housing services. Consequently, the demand for housing services is relatively elastic. ◂
3. **The Time Allowed for Adjustment:** The longer the time allowed for adjustment to a price change, the more that consumers will react. First of all, it usually takes time to *learn* about price changes. The faster this learning occurs, the more difficult or costly it is. Secondly, it is costly to change how you purchase and use different items in your budget. The faster you try to do so, the more costly it becomes. ▸ Example 4-14 If the price of electricity goes up by 50 percent, you can react immediately by turning off lights more often, using your electric air conditioning less, and so on. In the longer run, though, you can do even more. The next time you buy a major electric appliance, you may search out one that is much more energy efficient. You may also decide to have your attic insulated to keep your house cooler in the summer to avoid the need for more air conditioning. ◂

Look at Figure 4-3 on page 80. There you see how quantity demanded changes over time for any given change in the price. We can state the following:

## Figure 4-3 Short-Run and Long-Run Price Elasticity of Demand

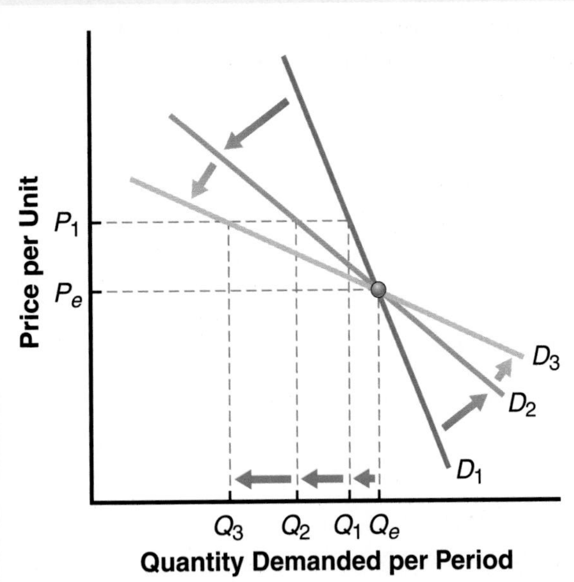


Consider a situation in which the market price is $P_e$ and the quantity demanded is $Q_e$. Then there is a price increase to $P_1$. In the short run, as evidenced by the demand curve $D_1$ we move from quantity demanded $Q_e$ to $Q_1$. After more time is allowed for adjustment, the demand curve rotates at original price $P_e$ to $D_2$. Quantity demanded falls again, now to $Q_2$. After even more time is allowed for adjustment, the demand curve rotates at price $P_e$ to $D_3$. At the higher price $P_1$ in the long run, the quantity demanded fails all the way to $Q_3$.

***The longer any price change persists, the greater the elasticity of demand, other things held constant. Elasticity of demand is greater in the long run than in the short run.***

## Economists' Research in the Real World—Estimated Price Elasticities of Demand

For decades economists have measured both short-run and long-run price elasticities of demand. Remember from the discussion above that the longer the time allowed for adjustment, the greater the price elasticity of demand. Consequently, it should not surprise you that estimated long-run price elasticities of demand are often two to three times greater than estimated short-run price elasticities of demand.

Take a look at Table 4-1. There you see a sampling of real-world estimated price elasticities of demand.

**Mastering Concepts:** On Doing Elasticity Calculations

- **We measure price elasticity of demand by dividing the percentage change in quantity demanded by the percentage change in price.**
- **Price elasticity of demand is calculated in terms of percentage changes in quantity demanded and in price. Therefore, the units used for either quantity demanded or prices do not matter.**
- **The price elasticity of demand depends on (1) the existence and suitability of substitutes, (2) the proportion of a person's budget devoted to that good, and (3) the time allowed for adjustment.**

**Table 4-1 Selected Estimated Short- and Long-Run Price Elasticities of Demand**

Here are estimated price elasticities of demand for selected goods. All of them are negative, although the minus sign is omitted. The long run is associated with the time necessary for consumers to adjust fully to any given price change.

| Category | Estimated Elasticity | |
|---|---|---|
| | Short Run | Long Run |
| Air travel (business) | 0.4 | 1.2 |
| Air travel (vacation) | 1.1 | 2.7 |
| Electricity | 0.1 | 1.7 |
| Gasoline | 0.2 | 0.5 |
| Hospital services | 0.1 | 0.7 |
| Intercity bus service | 0.6 | 2.2 |
| Physician services | 0.1 | 0.6 |
| Private education | 1.1 | 1.9 |
| Tires | 0.9 | 1.2 |

## THE RELATIONSHIP BETWEEN PRICE ELASTICITY OF DEMAND AND CONSUMER EXPENDITURES

Suppose that you are in charge of the pricing decision for a cellular telephone service company. How would you know whether it is better to raise prices or not to raise prices? The answer depends in part on the effect of your pricing decision on consumer expenditures—which become your total revenues or receipts—on your service. It is commonly thought that the way to increase total receipts is to increase price per unit. But is this always the case? Is it possible that a rise in price per unit could lead to a decrease in consumer expenditures on your service? The answers to these questions depend on the price elasticity of demand.

### ELASTIC DEMAND

As it turns out, when demand is elastic, a *negative* relationship exists between changes in price and changes in total consumer expenditures. That is to say, with elastic demand, if price is lowered, consumer expenditures on that item will, in fact, rise. Conversely, when a firm that faces elastic demand raises its price, total consumer expenditures on that item will fall.

▸ Example 4-15 If the price of Diet Coke were raised by 25 percent and the prices of all other diet drinks remained constant, the quantity demanded of Diet Coke would probably fall dramatically. The decrease in quantity demanded due to the increase in the price of Diet Coke would lead in this example to a reduction in total consumer expenditures on Diet Coke and hence reduce the total revenues of the Coca-Cola Company. We see here then, that if demand is elastic, price and consumer expenditures will move in *opposite* directions. ◂

### UNIT-ELASTIC DEMAND

When facing unit-elastic demand, any small changes in price will not change consumer expenditures. Why? Because the percentage change in price will lead to an equal opposite percentage change in quantity demanded. When a firm that is facing unit-elastic demand increases its price, consumer expenditures will not change; if it decreases its price, consumer expenditures will not change either.

## INELASTIC DEMAND

When demand is inelastic, a *positive* relationship exists between changes in price and total consumer expenditures. When a firm that is facing inelastic demand raises its price, consumer expenditures will go up; if it lowers its price, consumer expenditures will fall.

▸ **Example 4-16** You have just invented a cure for the common cold that has been approved by the Food and Drug Administration for sale to the public. You are not sure what price you should charge, so you start out with a price of $1 per pill. You sell 20 million pills at that price over a year. The next year, you decide to raise the price by 25 percent, to $1.25. The number of pills you sell drops to 18 million per year. The price increase of 25 percent has led to a 10 percent decrease in quantity demanded (ignoring the average formula on page 78). Total consumer expenditures on your new product, however, will rise to $22.5 million because of the price increase. We therefore conclude that if demand is inelastic, price and total consumer expenditures on your new product move in the *same* direction. ◂

## SUMMARIZING THE ELASTICITY–CONSUMER EXPENDITURES RELATIONSHIP

The relationship between price elasticity of demand and consumer expenditures brings together some important economic concepts. Consumer expenditures are the product of price per unit times the number of units sold. As you learned in Chapter 3, the law of demand states that along a given demand curve, price and quantity demanded will move in opposite directions. Consequently, what happens when price is multiplied by quantity demanded depends on which of the opposing changes exerts a greater force on consumer expenditures. But this is just what price elasticity of demand is designed to measure—responsiveness of quantity demanded to a change in price. The relationship between price elasticity of demand and consumer expenditures is summarized in Table 4-2.

**Mastering Concepts:** The Relationship Between Price Elasticity of Demand and Consumer Expenditures

- **Total consumer expenditures are related to price elasticity of demand.**
- **When demand is *elastic*, a change in price elicits a change in consumer expenditures in the direction opposite that of the price change.**
- **When demand is *unit-elastic*, a change in price elicits no change in consumer expenditures.**
- **When demand is *inelastic*, a change in price elicits a change in consumer expenditures in the same direction as the price change.**

**Table 4-2 Relationship Between Price Elasticity of Demand and Total Consumer Expenditures**

| Price Elasticity of Demand | | Effect of Price Change on Consumer Expenditures (CE) | |
|---|---|---|---|
| | | Price Decrease | Price Increase |
| Inelastic | (<1) | CE ↓ | CE ↑ |
| Unit-elastic | (=1) | No change in CE | No change in CE |
| Elastic | (>1) | CE ↑ | CE ↓ |

## SUMMING IT ALL UP

- Utility means the want-satisfying power of the good or service.
- Marginal utility is derived by comparing total utility for a given rate of consumption to total utility when you consume one more unit of a good or service.
- Even at no charge to you, there are many items that you will stop consuming because marginal utility eventually becomes negative.
- The law of diminishing marginal utility tells you that after you consume a good or service, the marginal utility you receive for yet more of that same good or service will start falling.
- Price elasticity of demand shows how much consumers respond to a given change in the price of a particular good or service.
- When you respond greatly to a change in price, we say you have an elastic demand. When you respond very little to a change in price, you have an inelastic demand.
- If you don't respond at all to a change in price, you have a perfectly inelastic demand.
- We measure price elasticity of demand by dividing the percentage change in quantity demanded by the percentage change in price.
- The price elasticity of demand depends on (1) the existence and suitability of substitutes, (2) the proportion of a person's budget devoted to that good, and (3) the time allowed for adjustment.
- Total consumer expenditures are related to price elasticity of demand.
- When demand is *elastic*, a change in price elicits a change in consumer expenditures in the direction opposite that of the price change.
- When demand is *unit-elastic*, a change in price elicits no change in consumer expenditures.
- When demand is *inelastic*, a change in price elicits a change in consumer expenditures in the same direction as the price change.

## KEY TERMS AND CONCEPTS



## MASTERING ECONOMIC CONCEPTS Questions and Problems

**4-1.** Complete the following table by calculating the missing values for all columns:

| Slices of Pizza | | | Soft Drinks | | |
|---|---|---|---|---|---|
| **Number of Slices** | **Total Utility** | **Marginal Utility** | **Number of Drinks** | **Total Utility** | **Marginal Utility** |
| 0 | 0 | n/a | 0 | 0 | n/a |
| 1 | 40 | __ | 1 | __ | 30 |
| 2 | 55 | __ | 2 | 45 | __ |
| 3 | 65 | __ | 3 | 50 | __ |
| 4 | __ | 5 | 4 | 50 | __ |

**4-2.** Many amusement parks offer special discounts for return visits. The offers typically state that on the day of your visit to the park you may buy a discounted pass for a future visit to the park within a specified time period. Why do amusement parks provide such offers? How do these offers relate to the concept of diminishing marginal utility?

**4-3.** Typically, Earle purchases four DVDs and one PS2 video game each month. Each DVD costs $20, and the video game costs $50. Based on his current level of consumption of each good, Earle's marginal utility for one more DVD is 10, and his marginal utility for one more video game is 30. Based on this information, would you suggest that Earle buy another DVD or another video game? Why?

**4-4.** Assuming that Brad consumes more and more cookies, determine whether each of the following statements is accurate. If a statement is not accurate, indicate why not.

a. His total utility will be positive.
b. The change in his total utility will be positive.
c. His marginal utility will be negative due to diminishing marginal utility.

**4-5.** Classify each of the following goods as having relatively elastic or relatively inelastic demand and explain why.

a. heart surgery
b. Old Navy T-shirts
c. a DVD recorder
d. public transportation

**4-6.** Assume that the local Blockbuster store rents an average of 500 videos per day at a rental price of $4.25. If management decides to increase the rental price to $5.25 per video and the number of rentals decreases to 480 per day, what is the price elasticity of demand for these video rentals? Would this good be considered relatively elastic or relatively inelastic? Based on the results from this example, would you assume that this Blockbuster faces a large amount of competition or a small amount of competition?

**4-7.** If the price of new cars decreased by 5 percent and new-car purchases increased by 12.5 percent as a result, what is the price elasticity of demand? Is the demand for new cars relatively elastic or inelastic? Would this price reduction cause an increase in total revenues or a decrease? In other words, will this increase or decrease total consumer expenditures on new cars?

**4-8.** If the price of natural gas increased from $0.829 per therm to $1.129 per therm and the quantity consumed in one metropolitan area decreased from 1.8 billion therms to 1.7 billion therms, what is the price elasticity of demand for natural gas in this area? Based on your numerical answer is demand for natural gas relatively elastic or relatively inelastic? How would the elasticity of demand differ in the winter as compared to the summer across the majority of the United States?

**4-9.** If the price elasticity of demand for dinner at Kool Beans café is –3.2 and the owner decides to increase menu prices, will total revenues at the restaurant increase or decrease? Why?

**4-10.** Assume that the price of Intel's stock is currently $26.75 and that 58 million shares are traded every day. If so, how many shares could you sell immediately at a price of $30.00? At $27.00? Why might these answers be similar? If you offered to sell all of the shares that you owned at a price of $26.00, how many shares would people want to buy from you? What type of elasticity of demand do these answers suggest?

**4-11.** The demand for gasoline is generally assumed to be fairly inelastic in the short run. Why is this true? How would the elasticity of demand for gasoline change if consumers were given more time to change their travel patterns? What changes could you make over the next five years if the price of gasoline permanently doubled in your area?

**4-12.** Put the following graphs of demand in order from most elastic to least elastic (at the price $P_1$ in all panels).

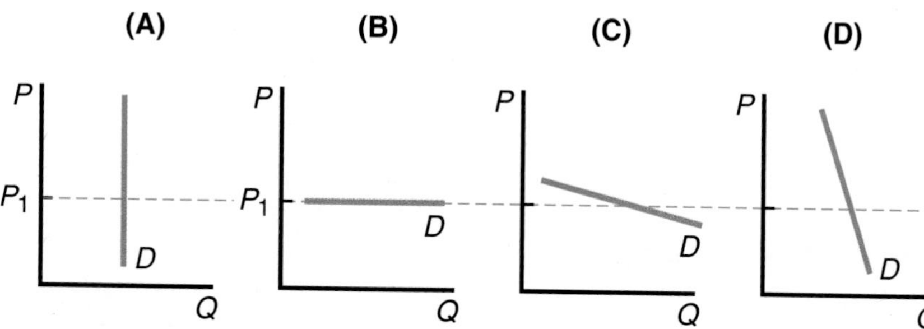


**4-13.** If the price of an item increased by 15 percent and the total revenues generated by the sale of this product increased by 5 percent, is the demand for this item elastic or inelastic?

**4-14.** At Turner Field, the site for Atlanta Braves home games, a deluxe hot dog costs $7.50. Assume that the concession stands at the stadium sell approximately 1,000 hot dogs at each home game. If lowering the price to $5.00 per hot dog increases sales to 1,100 hot dogs, what is the numerical measure of price elasticity over this price range? Is demand for these hot dogs elastic or inelastic? What factors likely contribute to this result?

**4-15.** If a 5 percent price decrease leads to a 5 percent increase in quantity demanded, what is the numerical value of the price elasticity of demand for this good? What term would you use to describe the elasticity of demand for this good? What would be the impact of the change in price on consumer expenditures or total revenues for this good?

**4-16.** If a watchmaker increases the price of gold watches by 12 percent and the price elasticity of demand is –2.0, by what percentage will the quantity of watches sold decrease?

**4-17.** If the price of candy bars in the campus vending machines increased from $0.60 to $1.00 and the quantity of candy bars purchased across campus decreased from 300 to 100 each day, what is the price elasticity of demand?

## THINKING CRITICALLY

**4-1.** Who has a more inelastic demand for air travel—business travelers or vacation travelers? If airlines want to increase their revenues, which group of consumers should be charged a higher fare? How does vacation travelers' demand change during the holiday season? As a result, what happens to airfares during the holiday season?

**4-2.** The price of pay-per-view movies at home through most cable or satellite providers ranges from $4 to $5, but a typical "new release" pay-per-view movie in a hotel can cost as much as $12 to $15. Explain this price difference in terms of price elasticity of demand and its effect on total revenue. Explain why the price elasticity of demand for hotel guests could be different from that of customers in their own homes.

**4-3.** In 2002, New York City increased its cigarette tax to $1.50 per pack. This change, combined with a previous increase in the state tax, pushed the price of cigarettes up to approximately $7.50.

Which smokers are likely to decrease their consumption based on this change—those who have been smoking for several years or those who have just begun smoking? Based on income levels, who is more likely to decrease consumption—teenagers or middle-aged individuals?

**4-4.** Patrick is fond of consuming several beers at a time. The enjoyment that he obtains by drinking responsibly creates a utility for him as an individual. If he consumes too many beers, however, he sometimes feels very ill, and the quality of his work the next day will typically suffer. Discuss this situation in the context of marginal utility and specifically the principle of diminishing marginal utility. In such a situation, is it ever possible for a good to actually provide negative marginal utility if more is consumed?

## LOGGING ON

1. To see the taxes that governments have placed on cigarettes in the United States and worldwide, go to http://www.drugs.indiana.edu/drug_stats/cigtax_burden.html.
2. For more information about the ways in which minors can evade regulations and taxes relating to cigarette consumption, go to http://www.unc.edu/courses/2003spring/law/357c/001/projects/akhill/Alcohol&Tobacco/Tobacco%20-%20Minors.htm.
3. To get more insight into how the price elasticity of demand relates to consumer expenditures, go to http://ingrimayne.saintjoe.edu/econ/elasticity/OverviewEl.html.

## USING THE INTERNET FOR ECONOMIC ANALYSIS

**Price Elasticity and Consumption of Illegal Drugs** Making the use of certain drugs illegal drives up their market prices, so the price elasticity of demand is a key factor affecting the use of illegal drugs. This application uses concepts from this chapter to analyze how price elasticity of demand affects drug consumption.

**Title:** The Demand for Illicit Drugs

**Navigation:** Go to http://ideas.repec.org/p/nbr/nberwo/5238.html.

**Application** Read the summary of the results of this study of price elasticities of participation in the use of illegal drugs, and answer the following questions.

1. Based on the results of the study, is the demand for cocaine more or less price elastic than the demand for heroin? For which drug, therefore, will quantity demanded fall by a greater percentage in response to a proportionate increase in price?
2. The study finds that decriminalizing currently illegal drugs would bring about sizable increases both in overall consumption of heroin and cocaine and in the price elasticity of demand for both drugs. Why do you suppose that the price elasticity of demand would rise? (Hint: At present, users of cocaine and heroin are restricted to only a few illegal sources of the drugs, but if the drugs could be legally produced and sold, there would be many more suppliers providing a variety of different types of both drugs.)

## MEDIA RESOURCE LIST

The following media resources are available with this chapter:

- Load your CD-ROM to listen to the audio introduction to this chapter.
- Load your CD-ROM to access Graph Animations of Figure 4-1, *The Total and Marginal Utility of Watching DVDs,* and Figure 4-2, *Extreme Price Elasticities.*
- Load your CD-ROM to view the video on *The Determinants of the Price Elasticity of Demand.*
- Test your knowledge of chapter concepts with a quiz at www.miller-ume.com.
- Link to Web resources related to the text coverage at www.miller-ume.com.

## HOMEWORK SET

Go to the end of this book to find the Homework Problems for this chapter.

# CHAPTER 5

# The Firm: Production and Cost

## *Facing an Economic Problem:* What Kind of Business Organization Is Right?

During any one year in the United States, hundreds of thousands of new businesses are formed. Indeed, the rate of new-business creation in the United States is the highest on earth. One of the reasons is that our legal system encourages new-business formation by putting up almost no roadblocks to doing so. Moreover, the legal costs of setting up a new business are, for the most part, very small.

Nonetheless, when you or anyone else decides to start a new business, you face an economic (and legal) problem—what is the appropriate legal structure of the new business? Today, you have a wider variety of types of business organizations from which to choose than ever before. So, should you incorporate? Should you form a partnership? Should you just set up shop as a sole proprietor? Are there other options? As you will see shortly, there are many options, one of which might be most appropriate for you.

## Learning Objectives

After reading this chapter, you should be able to:

- **List the advantages and disadvantages of the sole proprietorship, partnership, and corporation.**
- **Distinguish between average and marginal product and relate this distinction to the law of diminishing returns.**
- **Define and distinguish between fixed and variable costs and explain why marginal costs are the most important guide to decisions.**
- **Explain how to calculate economic profits and why they differ from accounting profits.**

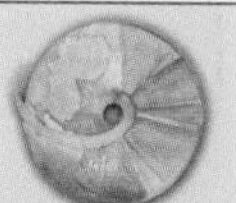

***Refer to the back of this chapter for a complete listing of multimedia learning materials available on the CD-ROM and the Web site.***

## TYPES OF BUSINESS ORGANIZATIONS

The three main types of business organizations in the United States are (1) the sole proprietorship, (2) the partnership, and (3) the corporation. There are also certain hybrid forms of these types of business organizations, which have become more popular in recent years.

### SOLE PROPRIETORSHIPS

**Sole proprietorship**
*A noncorporate business owned and operated by one person.*

The most basic and simplest type of business organization is a **sole proprietorship**. This is a business owned by one person. It is the most common type of business organization, as you can see from Table 5-1. Most sole proprietorships are small. They are the easiest and least expensive to start and to run, at least in terms of legal and accounting expenses.

**Unlimited liability**
*The requirement that an owner is personally and fully responsible for all losses and debts of a business.*

The biggest advantage of a sole proprietorship is that the proprietor answers to no one else when making decisions about how to run the business. In addition, the owner receives all of the profits. The biggest disadvantage is that the owner has **unlimited liability**, meaning that he or she has complete legal responsibility for all debts and damages arising from doing business. ▸ **Example 5-1** You can start and operate a sole proprietorship in virtually any service business. You could, with very little expense, purchase a server and some data storage devices in order to host Web pages for others. You could do this for friends, relatives, and neighbors and spend very little on advertising. At the end of the year, you would have to figure out all of your income and expenses. You would report them on your federal income tax returns and maybe on state tax returns. Any net profits would be taxable as current income. Any losses would be deductible from other taxable income. ◂

### PARTNERSHIPS

**Partnership**
*A noncorporate form of business owned and operated by two or more individuals.*

A **partnership** is a business that two or more individuals own and operate. Normally, you sign a partnership agreement that lays out the rules under which your partnership will be run.

The advantages of a partnership are that more than one person is available for specialized management. In addition, partners can pool their financial capital in order to have a larger business base. The disadvantage is that partners have unlimited liability for debts incurred while in business. That means that if one partner cannot pay her or his share of a debt, the other partner or partners have to ante up the rest. ▸ **Example 5-2** You've been running a landscaping partnership with your cousin for several years. Recently, you both signed a loan to buy a new tractor and hauling trailer. Two months later, your cousin moves to Europe

**Table 5-1 Forms of Business Organization**

| Type of Firm | Percentage of U.S. Firms | Average Size (annual sales in dollars) | Percentage of Total Business Revenues |
|---|---|---|---|
| Proprietorship | 72.2 | 53,000 | 4.8 |
| Partnership | 7.7 | 827,000 | 8.1 |
| Corporation | 20.1 | 3,412,000 | 87.1 |

without a forwarding address. You are stuck with having to pay off his part of the loan. ◂

Another disadvantage of a partnership is that when a partner decides to leave the partnership or dies, the partnership normally ends. It must be reorganized.

## CORPORATIONS

A **corporation** is a legal entity that may conduct business in its own name just as an individual does. The owners of a corporation are called *shareholders* because they own shares of the profits earned by the firm.

> ***By law, shareholders enjoy* limited liability, *so if the corporation incurs debts that it cannot pay, the shareholders' personal property is protected from claims by the firm's creditors.***

As shown in Table 5-1, corporations are far less numerous than partnerships and sole proprietorships, but because of their large size, they are responsible for almost 90 percent of all business revenues in the United States.

The corporation dates back to the mid-1800s in England, as you can read about in the following *Global Application*.

**Corporation**
*A type of business organization owned by many people but treated by law as though it were a person; it can own property, pay taxes, make contracts, and so on.*

**Limited liability**
*Limitation of an owner's responsibility for a company's debts to the size of the owner's investment in the firm.*

### GLOBAL APPLICATION: The Birth of a Corporation—Merry Old England

***Concept Applied:* Limited Liability**

Because of the limited liability of modern corporations, large amounts of capital can be raised. That is the essence of corporate America. Some argue that without the corporate form of business, this country and virtually all the developed countries in the world would be much poorer. Perhaps surprisingly, the concept of limited liability did not generally exist until the mid-1800s in England.

**The Father of the Modern Company**

Robert Lowe was the vice-chairman of London's Board of Trade in the mid-1800s. He came up with the concept that gave birth to the modern corporation. He put this concept into the Joint Stock Companies Act of 1856. Specifically, Lowe instituted in this act a measure that limited each shareholder's liability to his or her own stake, or investment. That is why corporations in England often have the word *limited (Ltd.)* at the end of their names. Between 1856 and 1867, 25,000 limited liability companies were incorporated. Millions more followed throughout the world in the years to come.

**For Critical Analysis:**

*State in your own words why limited liability is such an important aspect of modern-day corporations.*

**Advantages of Corporations** Perhaps the greatest advantage of corporations is that their owners (the shareholders) enjoy *limited liability*, as just mentioned. The liability of shareholders is limited to the value of their shares. The second advantage is that, legally, the corporation *continues to exist* even if one or more owners cease to be owners. A third advantage of the corporation stems from the first two: corporations are well positioned to *raise large sums of financial capital.* People buy ownership shares or lend funds to the corporation knowing that their liability is limited to the amount they invested. These corporate investors are also confident that the corporation's existence does not depend on the life of any one of the firm's owners.

**Double taxation**
*Occurs with corporate profits because they are first taxed at the corporate level and then, if dividends are distributed to shareholders, taxed again at the shareholder level.*

**Dividends**
*The portion of a corporation's profits paid to its stockholders.*

**Disadvantages of Corporations** The chief disadvantage of the corporation is that corporate income is subject to **double taxation**. The profits of the corporation are subject first to corporate taxes. Then, if any of the after-tax profits are distributed to shareholders as **dividends**, such payments are treated as personal income to the shareholders and subject to personal taxation. Due to this double taxation, owners of corporations pay as much in taxes on corporate income as they do on other forms of income. ▸ Example 5-3 In 2003, the Bush administration attempted to eliminate the double taxation of dividends. The best it could do was to reduce their tax rate from a possible maximum of 39 percent to 15 percent. ◂ A second disadvantage of the corporation is that corporations are potentially subject to problems associated with the *separation of ownership and control.* The owners and managers of a corporation are typically different persons and may have different incentives. There are many problems that can result.

## S Corporations and Limited Liability Companies

There are several ways to avoid the double taxation associated with the corporate form of business organization. They are legally available for most business ventures.

**S corporation**
*A corporation in which the profits and losses pass directly through to the individual owners, who then pay federal personal income taxes on any profits. Similar to a corporation because of limited liability and to a partnership because only the individual pays the income taxes rather than the business entity.*

**Limited liability company (LLC)**
*A hybrid form of business enterprise that offers the limited liability of the corporation but the tax advantages of a partnership.*

**S Corporations** One can choose the **S corporation** form, which has a special feature. It is a true corporation—a legal entity—but all of the net profits are passed through to the individual owner or owners. That means that the owner or owners pay personal income taxes only. Several million S corporations exist in the United States.

**Limited Liability Companies, or LLCs** The **limited liability company,** or **LLC,** is a hybrid form of business enterprise that offers the limited liability of a corporation and the tax advantages of a partnership (or S corporation). LLCs first started in 1977 in Wyoming. Increasingly, LLCs are becoming an organizational form of choice among businesspeople.

The federal government automatically taxes one-member LLCs as sole proprietorships unless they indicate that they wish to be taxed as corporations. There are a few disadvantages to an LLC. One of those disadvantages is that the state laws governing LLCs are not uniform. Until all of the states have adopted a uniform law, an LLC in one state has to check the rules in the other states in which the firm does business to ensure that it retains its limited liability. Additionally, both LLCs and S corporations cannot become publicly held and publicly traded companies. In other words, to be listed on any of the regional over-the-counter or national stock exchanges, companies have to use the regular corporate form of business organization.

### *Solving the Economic Problem:* What Kind of Business Organization Is Right?

As you have just seen, advantages are associated with each form of business organization in the United States. The simplest form—the sole proprietorship—may be best for your business concept because it costs virtually nothing to start and you don't have to deal with associates. You do face unlimited liability,

*Continued on next page*

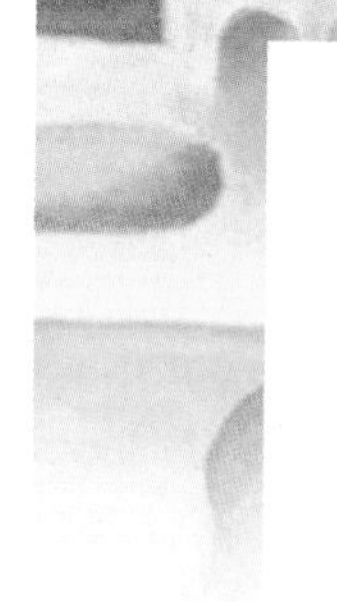

though. At the other end of the spectrum is the corporation. While corporations are associated with the "big guys," such as Microsoft, Costco, and General Motors, there are many one-person corporations, too. Typically, these are S corporations that are restricted to no more than 75 shareholders, none of whom can be a nonresident alien. Perhaps the best of all worlds for many new businesses is the limited liability company (LLC). You get the benefits of limited liability and at the same time enjoy the tax benefits of sole proprietorships, partnerships, and S corporations. In the years ahead, you will see LLC tacked onto the names of more and more companies in the United States.

Many new "virtual" companies use the LLC form of business organization, as you can see in the *E-Commerce Application* below.

## E-COMMERCE APPLICATION: This Kid Is All Right

### *Concepts Applied:* Partnership, Limited Liability Company

Starting a business in the United States has always been easy, at least from a legal point of view. A sole proprietorship requires virtually no paperwork, a partnership some, and a corporation not much more. Additionally, partners in partnerships today can live and work across state lines because of easy communications—cheap long-distance telephone service, virtually free e-mail, and instant messaging systems, such as MSN Messenger. One of the latest beneficiaries of this business environment is Max Oshman, the author of *Macro Media/Super Samurai,* a book about how to use a 3-D graphics program.

### Creating Web Sites with a Virtual Company

Max's first big project after his book was creating a corporate Web site for SeanJohn.com. SeanJohn is a clothing label of rap singer P. Diddy. Max had help on the $500,000 Web design project. He and 11 other programmers put the Web site together at breakneck speed without ever meeting each other. They live all over the world—Britain, Sweden, Croatia, Texas, Amsterdam, New York, and California among other places. The name of their company is pLotdev Multimedia Development, LLC. It specializes in the entertainment industry. The shared objective of the programmers is to create upbeat designs with lots of user interaction. These individuals chose the limited liability company form of business organization to avoid double taxation and to obtain, obviously, limited liability.

### Something Else You Might Want to Know

While the description of Max Oshman's virtual company may sound commonplace today, there is an interesting tidbit to this story about e-commerce. Max wrote his first book, mentioned above, at age 15. At 17, he earned almost $100,000 for creating the SeanJohn.com Web site—while still living with his parents.

### For Critical Analysis:

*What might be some of the downsides to a virtual company?*

## Mastering Concepts: Types of Business Organizations

- **Sole proprietorships are the easiest business organization to create, but carry unlimited liability for owners.**
- **Partnerships allow for a broader management and financing, but still carry unlimited liability for owners.**

- **Corporations have the benefit of limited liability, but have the disadvantage of facing the double taxation of corporate income.**
- **While an S corporation avoids double taxation, a limited liability company (LLC) avoids such double taxation, too.**

## BUSINESSES COMBINE FACTORS OF PRODUCTION

A business firm has a goal—profits. To make profits, business firms combine land, labor, capital, and entrepreneurship. A combination of these factors of production constitutes the inputs into the production process. When they are used in different ways, the firm ends up creating different outputs. This process is the subject of this section.

### RELATING THE FACTORS OF PRODUCTION AND OUTPUT—THE PRODUCTION FUNCTION

**Production function**
*The relationship between inputs and maximum physical output.*

A business takes all of its inputs and combines them to end up with an output. We say that output is some function of—depends on—inputs. For the moment, to make the analysis simple, we assume that all inputs are fixed except the labor input. Therefore, there is a **production function** that relates output per some specific time period to the amount of labor input used.

▸ International Example 5-4 The United States has a higher output per person than does the European Union (EU). You would think, then, that the United States would be adding more capital for production than the EU. Since 1970, however, the reverse has been occurring. EU countries have dramatically increased the amount of capital relative to the amount of labor in the production process. Labor laws are much stricter in Europe than in the United States, leading to very high costs for hiring and especially firing workers. Not surprisingly, European managers constantly seek ways to automate—buy more automated systems—because machines don't go on strike. In contrast, U.S. firms are not afraid to hire more workers. ◂

### RELATING OUTPUT TO INPUT—A NUMERICAL EXAMPLE

You can see the relationship between labor input, measured in worker-weeks, and total output of computer printers per week for a typical firm in panel (b) of Figure 5-1. Panel (b) comes from the numbers in panel (a), columns 1 and 2. Not surprisingly, as the firm continues to add workers, total production rises, at least through the addition of the seventh worker.

**Average physical product**
*Total product (output) divided by the number of units of the variable input.*

**Marginal physical product**
*The change in output resulting from the addition of one more worker. The marginal physical product of the worker equals the change in total output accounted for by hiring the worker, holding all other factors of production constant.*

**Physical Product** The physical output of each worker is called *physical product*.

**Average Physical Product** If you divide the total output by the total number of workers, you come up with **average physical product**. That is what you see in column 3, panel (a) of Figure 5-1. In economics, though, average numbers are less interesting than what happens on the margin.

**Marginal Physical Product** Remember from Chapter 4 that the word *marginal* means a *small change in* something. Here the **marginal physical product**

*Animated*

## Figure 5-1 The Production Function and Marginal Physical Product

Marginal physical product is the addition to the total product that results when one additional worker is hired. Thus, in panel (a), the marginal physical product of the fourth worker is eight computer printers. With four workers, 44 printers are produced, but with three workers, only 36 are produced; the difference is 8. In panel (b), we plot the numbers from columns 1 and 2 of panel (a). In panel (c), we plot the numbers from columns 1 and 4 of panel (a). When we go from 0 to 1, marginal product is 10. When we go from one worker to two workers, marginal product increases to 16. After two workers, marginal product declines, but it is still positive. Total product (output) reaches its peak at seven workers, so after seven workers, marginal physical product is negative. When we move from seven to eight workers, marginal physical product becomes −1 printer.

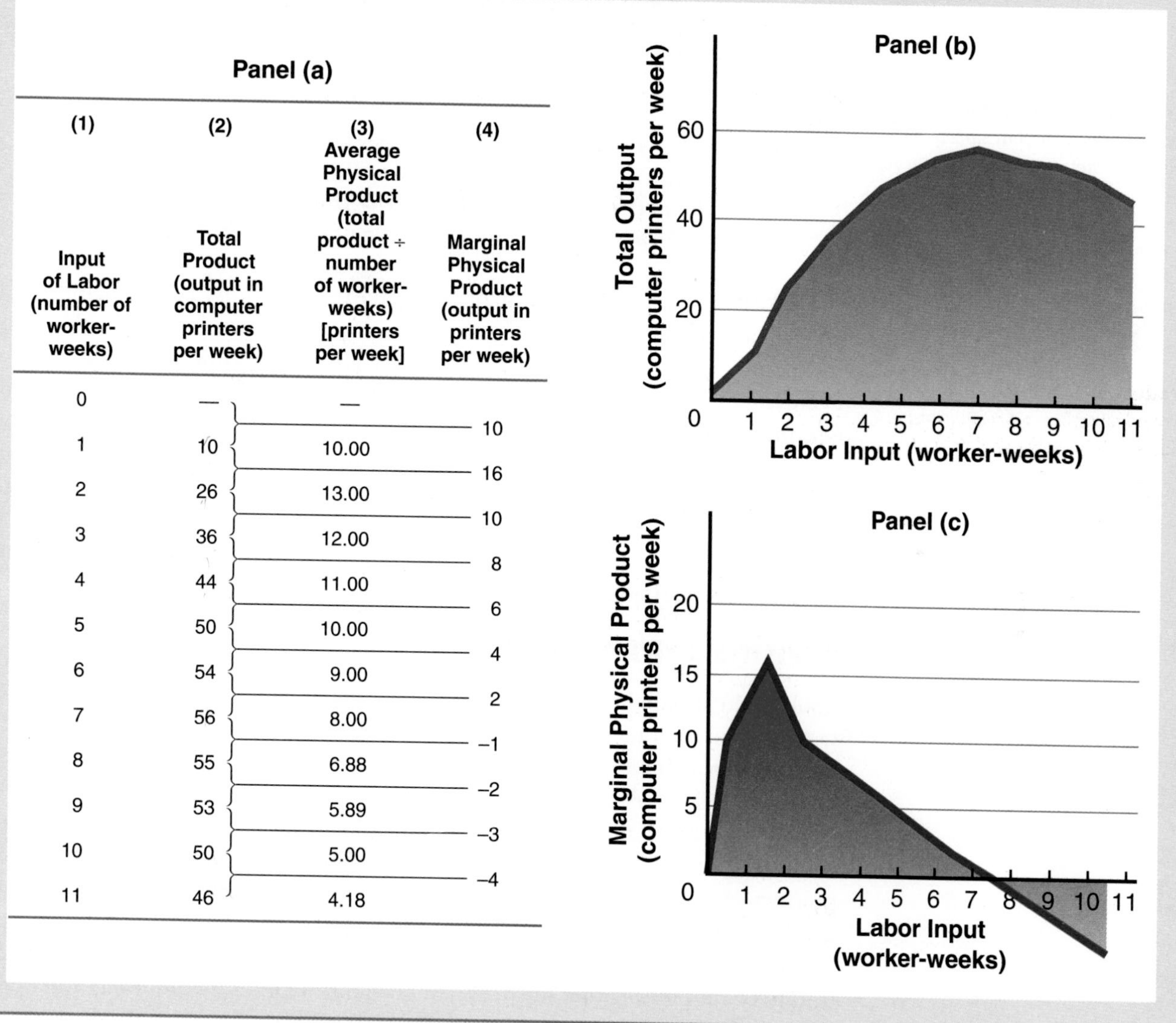

Panel (a)

| (1) Input of Labor (number of worker-weeks) | (2) Total Product (output in computer printers per week) | (3) Average Physical Product (total product ÷ number of worker-weeks) [printers per week] | (4) Marginal Physical Product (output in printers per week) |
|---|---|---|---|
| 0 | — | — | |
| 1 | 10 | 10.00 | 10 |
| 2 | 26 | 13.00 | 16 |
| 3 | 36 | 12.00 | 10 |
| 4 | 44 | 11.00 | 8 |
| 5 | 50 | 10.00 | 6 |
| 6 | 54 | 9.00 | 4 |
| 7 | 56 | 8.00 | 2 |
| 8 | 55 | 6.88 | −1 |
| 9 | 53 | 5.89 | −2 |
| 10 | 50 | 5.00 | −3 |
| 11 | 46 | 4.18 | −4 |



of labor is the change in total output that occurs when a worker joins an existing production process. You can see marginal physical product in column 4, panel (a) of Figure 5-1. These numbers are plotted in the figure in panel (c).

As you can observe, marginal physical product first rises, then falls, then eventually becomes negative after the seventh worker is hired. ▸ **Example 5-5** You have a thriving computer software business. The space in which you are operating, though, is small. You have room for only ten workstations. When you hire the eleventh programmer, that person will have to share a workstation. When you hire the twelfth, thirteenth, or fourteenth worker, at some point the additional programmer will actually cause total output to fall because he or she will get in everybody else's way and reduce everyone else's productivity. ◂

## Diminishing Marginal Returns

If you look again at panel (c) on the previous page, you will see that when the second worker is hired, that worker's contribution to total output is less than the previous worker's. The contribution of workers hired thereafter falls even more rapidly. What we observe here is that the marginal physical product diminishes for most of the workers hired. Indeed, it will always be true that beyond some point, *diminishing returns* to hiring more workers must set in—*not* because new workers are less qualified, but because each successive worker has less capital with which to work. (Remember, we hold all inputs fixed—including capital—except labor in our example.)

**Law of diminishing returns**
*An economic rule that says as more units of a factor of production (such as labor) are added to a given amount of other factors of production (such as equipment), total output continues to increase but at a diminishing rate.*

We come up with the **law of diminishing returns:**

> ***As successive equal increases in a variable factor of production are added to fixed factors of production, there will be a point beyond which the extra, or marginal, product that can be attributed to each additional unit of the variable factor of production will decline.***

▸ Example 5-6 Production of computer printers provides an example of the law of diminishing returns. With a fixed amount of factory space, assembly equipment, and quality-control diagnostic software, the addition of more workers eventually yields smaller increases in output. After a while, when all the assembly equipment and quality-control diagnostic software are being used, additional workers will have to start assembling and troubleshooting quality problems manually. They obviously won't be as productive as the first workers who had access to other productive inputs. The marginal physical product of an additional worker, given a specified amount of capital, must eventually be less than that of the previous workers. ◂

## Revisiting the Numbers

Look again at panel (a) of Figure 5-1 on the previous page. Notice that when one worker is hired, total output goes from 0 to 10. Thus, marginal physical product is 10 computer printers per week. When the second worker is hired, total product goes from 10 to 26 printers per week. Marginal physical product therefore increases to 16 printers per week. When a third worker is hired, total product again increases, from 26 to 36 printers per week. This represents a marginal physical product of only 10 printers per week. Therefore, the point of diminishing marginal returns occurs after two workers are hired.

Note that after seven workers per week, marginal physical product becomes negative. That means that the hiring of an eighth worker would *reduce* total product. Sometimes this is called the *point of saturation,* indicating that given the amount of fixed inputs, there is no further positive use for more of the variable input. We have entered the region of *negative* marginal returns.

**Mastering Concepts:** Businesses Combine Factors of Production.

- **The production function relates output to the different factors of production used to create that output during a specified time period.**
- **After some point, when a variable factor of production, such as labor, is increased, the additional output obtained from each additional unit of that input starts to diminish. This is called the law of diminishing returns.**

## THE FIRM FACES ITS COSTS

Labor costs, of course, are not all of the costs involved in production. A firm also faces the cost of renting space, the cost of electricity, insurance costs, and the like. Businesses need to understand what their costs are in order to determine whether they are producing the way they should and even whether they should stay in business. All firms have costs. To analyze costs correctly, we must look at the different types of costs that each firm encounters.

### FIXED VERSUS VARIABLE COSTS

Some costs are fixed in the short run. Others are variable. Labor costs normally are **variable costs.** Businesses can hire and fire without too much trouble. They can also have workers increase hours or decrease hours.

**Fixed costs** are those costs that by definition cannot change. In other words, fixed costs do not vary with the rate of output. ▸ **Example 5-7** You operate a small publishing company. You have to pay rent on your office space each month. It doesn't matter whether you produce one book a month or 20 books: Your rent will remain the same. It is a fixed cost. ◂

When you add up all fixed costs and all variable costs, you end up with **total costs.**

**Variable costs**
*Costs that vary with the rate of production. They include wages paid to workers and purchases of materials.*

**Fixed costs**
*Costs that do not vary with output.*

**Total costs**
*The sum of total fixed costs and total variable costs.*

### GRAPHING TOTAL COSTS

It is pretty easy to graph total costs, total variable costs, and total fixed costs. You simply put total costs in dollars on the vertical axis and output on the horizontal axis. That is what we do in Figure 5-2. The example we use is for recordable DVDs. The firm's total fixed costs will equal the cost of insurance it has to pay plus rent on its equipment, for example. Assume that this is $10 per day. That is what we show in Figure 5-2.

Notice that the horizontal line labeled total fixed costs in Figure 5-2 is at $10. No matter how many recordable DVDs are produced per day, fixed costs will remain at $10 per day.

**Figure 5-2 Graphing Total Costs**

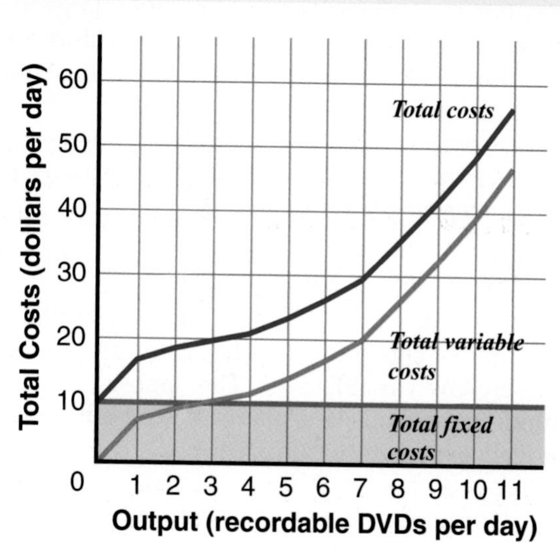


In this example, you see the total cost of producing recordable DVDs. Total costs consist of total variable costs and total fixed costs. Total fixed costs are assumed to be $10 per day.

## AVERAGE COSTS

**Average total costs**
*Total costs divided by the number of units produced.*

**Average variable costs**
*Total variable costs divided by the number of units produced.*

Businesses sometimes want to know what their per-unit cost, or **average total costs**, is in order to make certain per-unit profit calculations. That is relatively easy to find out. Just divide total costs by the number of units of output.

You can find **average variable costs** by using variable rather than total costs. Divide total variable costs by the number of units of output produced.

▸ Example 5-8 Sometimes companies spend tens or even hundreds of millions of dollars to develop systems that reduce average variable costs by a small amount. This makes sense if the number of transactions is high. FedEx did just that when it put $150 million into developing a wireless PowerPad, a new handheld wireless device used by 50,000 FedEx couriers. When the courier picks up a package, the PowerPad communicates with a device on the courier's waist belt to create a bar-coded shipping label. Customs and tracking information is then transmitted instantly to FedEx's main office. The time savings per transaction? Only ten seconds. The cost savings over a year to FedEx? Over $20 million. ◂

**Average fixed costs**
*Total fixed costs divided by the number of units produced.*

Finally, you can obtain **average fixed costs** by dividing total fixed costs by output. We can put average total costs, average variable costs, and average fixed costs in simple formulas, as follows:

$$\textbf{Average total costs (ATC)} = \frac{\textbf{total costs (TC)}}{\textbf{output}}$$

$$\textbf{Average variable costs (AVC)} = \frac{\textbf{total variable costs (TVC)}}{\textbf{output}}$$

$$\textbf{Average fixed costs (AFC)} = \frac{\textbf{total fixed costs (TFC)}}{\textbf{output}}$$

A comparison of fixed versus variable costs helps some businesses decide which production process to use, as you will discover in the following *Policy Application*.

### POLICY APPLICATION: Electric Utilities Must Decide When to Use Expensive Natural Gas

***Concepts Applied:***
**Fixed Costs, Variable Costs**

U.S. residents and domestic companies consume 6 billion megawatts of electricity each year. Aside from a few large companies that generate their own electricity, everybody else buys electricity from electric utility companies. These utilities have a variety of sources for the electricity that they generate.

#### Coal, Oil, Nuclear, and Hydro Plants—Assessing Their Relative Fixed Costs

In one way or another, large spinning turbines create electricity, but something must power them. Hydroelectric power comes from dams—building a dam is an expensive initial project, meaning large fixed costs. Nuclear power requires another large fixed cost to get things moving. The use of coal as a fuel also requires a high initial expense. In contrast, natural gas and oil-fired electricity-generating plants are the least expensive to put in place. In other words, they have the lowest fixed costs of all possible electricity-generating sources.

#### Now Take a Look at Variable Costs

Once coal, nuclear, and hydro plants are built, they are relatively cheap to run. That is to say, they have relatively low variable costs. The opposite is true for natural gas and oil-fired plants. Once built, they are relatively expensive to run.

*Continued on next page*

What to Do?

So, how do managers of electric utilities decide which energy source they should choose to make those large turbines turn? Essentially, they have chosen to build coal, nuclear, and hydro plants to satisfy basic, around-the-clock usage of electricity. This is called their *base-load demand*. They have chosen to use natural gas and oil-fired plants to provide for *reserve capacity* when peak demand occurs, such as during very cold winters or very hot summers. On average, U.S.-based electrical utilities use natural gas and oil-fired power for 15 percent of their total electricity-generating capacity while keeping another 10 percent as a reserve against unexpected outages; the other 75 percent of capacity is composed of coal, nuclear, and hydro plants.

**For Critical Analysis:**
*How could electric utilities reduce their peak demand requirements? (HINT: Go back to Chapter 3.)*

## Marginal Costs Are What Matters

We have stated before that:

***The basis of decision making is always on the margin—choices are always determined at the margin.***

This dictum is just as true within the firm. Firms, according to the analysis we use to predict their behavior, are very interested in their **marginal costs.** Because the term *marginal* means "additional" or "incremental" (or "decremental," too) here, marginal costs refer to costs that result from a one-unit change in the production rate. ▸ Example 5-9 You are producing hand calculators. If the production of 1,000 calculators per day costs you $500, but the production of 1,001 calculators cost you $500.45, than the marginal cost of the last hand calculator is $0.45. ◂

**Marginal costs**
*The change in total costs due to a one-unit change in the production rate.*

Marginal cost is defined as:

$$\textbf{Marginal cost} = \frac{\textbf{change in total cost}}{\textbf{change in output}}$$

Typically, marginal costs of production fall as output increases up to a certain point; then marginal cost starts to rise.

## Graphing Average Costs

Just as we were able to graph total costs in Figure 5-2 for recordable DVD production, we can do the same for average and marginal costs. We first have to come up with some numbers, which we do in Table 5-2 on page 100.

You can see that average total costs are derived by dividing the rate of output into total costs. Look at Figure 5-3 (p. 100). There you see average total costs graphed. The ATC line starts relatively high at $15 and continues to drop until it reaches a minimum at about seven units per day of output. Then it starts to rise again.

## Graphing Marginal Costs

Remember that we defined marginal costs as the change in total costs divided by the change in output. To create this graph, we look at how total costs change as output changes. This is done first in Table 5-3 on page 101.

You can see that in Table 5-3 marginal cost drops from $5 to $1 as output increases from zero to four per day. Thereafter, marginal cost increases from $1 to $8. You can see this graphed in Figure 5-4 on the same page.

✦ **Remember!** *Because marginal means "small change in" it can actually be positive or negative.*

### Table 5-2 Average Total Costs of Producing Recordable DVDs

| (1) Total Output per Day | (2) Total Fixed Costs (TFC) | + | (3) Total Variable Costs (TVC) | = | (4) Total Costs (TC) | (5) Average Total Costs (ATC) |
|---|---|---|---|---|---|---|
| 0 | $10 | | $ 0 | | $10 | — |
| 1 | 10 | | 5 | | 15 | $15.00 |
| 2 | 10 | | 8 | | 18 | 9.00 |
| 3 | 10 | | 10 | | 20 | 6.67 |
| 4 | 10 | | 11 | | 21 | 5.25 |
| 5 | 10 | | 13 | | 23 | 4.60 |
| 6 | 10 | | 16 | | 26 | 4.33 |
| 7 | 10 | | 20 | | 30 | 4.28 |
| 8 | 10 | | 25 | | 35 | 4.38 |
| 9 | 10 | | 31 | | 41 | 4.56 |
| 10 | 10 | | 38 | | 48 | 4.80 |
| 11 | 10 | | 46 | | 56 | 5.09 |

**The Relationship Between Diminishing Marginal Product and Marginal Cost** You can see in Figure 5-4 that at lower levels of output, marginal cost declines. The reasoning is that as marginal physical product increases with each addition of output, the marginal cost of this last unit of output must fall. But,

### Figure 5-3 Graphing Average Total Costs

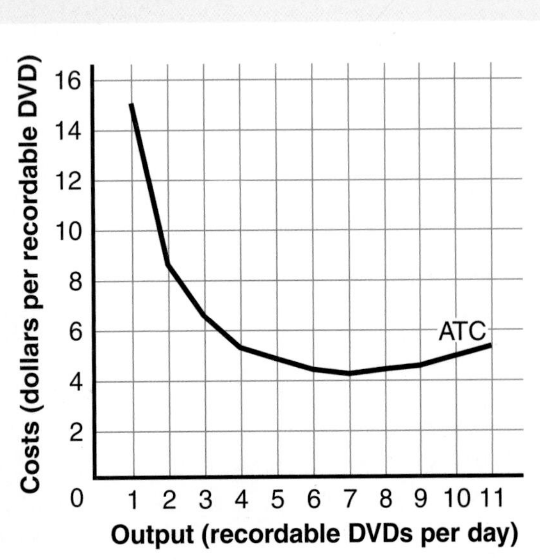


You can see that the ATC curve falls until an output of about seven recordable DVDs per day. Then it starts to rise.

## Table 5-3 Marginal Cost of Producing Recordable DVDs

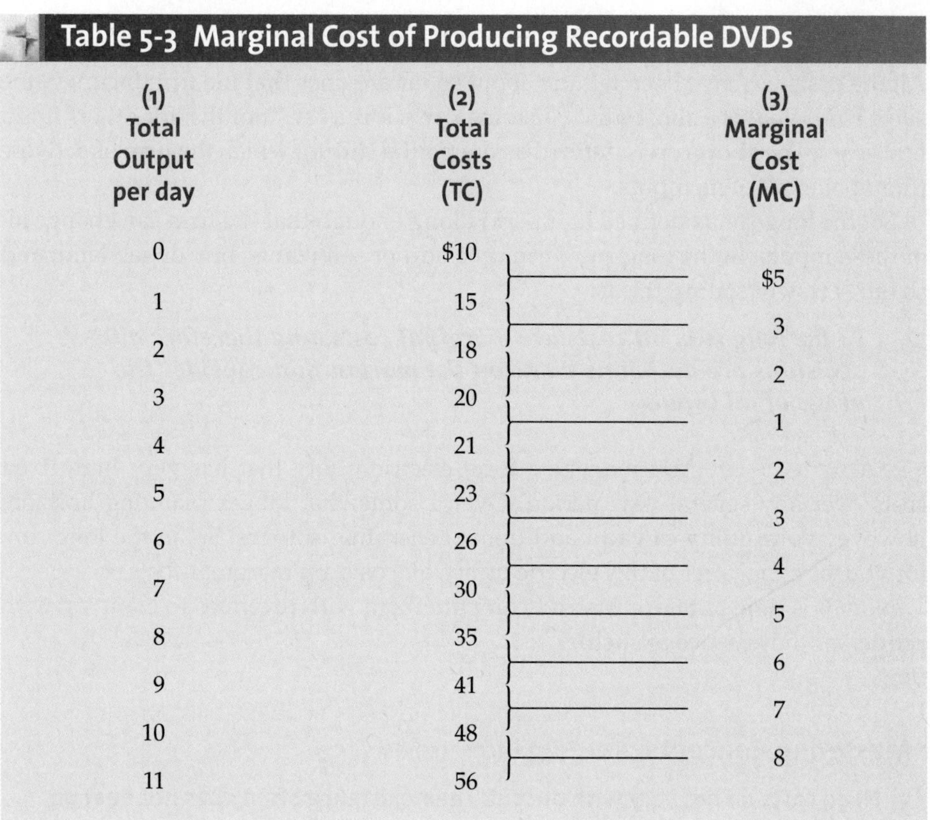

| (1) Total Output per day | (2) Total Costs (TC) | (3) Marginal Cost (MC) |
|---|---|---|
| 0 | $10 | |
| | | $5 |
| 1 | 15 | |
| | | 3 |
| 2 | 18 | |
| | | 2 |
| 3 | 20 | |
| | | 1 |
| 4 | 21 | |
| | | 2 |
| 5 | 23 | |
| | | 3 |
| 6 | 26 | |
| | | 4 |
| 7 | 30 | |
| | | 5 |
| 8 | 35 | |
| | | 6 |
| 9 | 41 | |
| | | 7 |
| 10 | 48 | |
| | | 8 |
| 11 | 56 | |

when diminishing marginal returns set in, marginal physical product decreases. Marginal cost must rise when marginal product begins its decline. That is exactly what you see in Figure 5-4.

## Figure 5-4 The Marginal Cost Curve

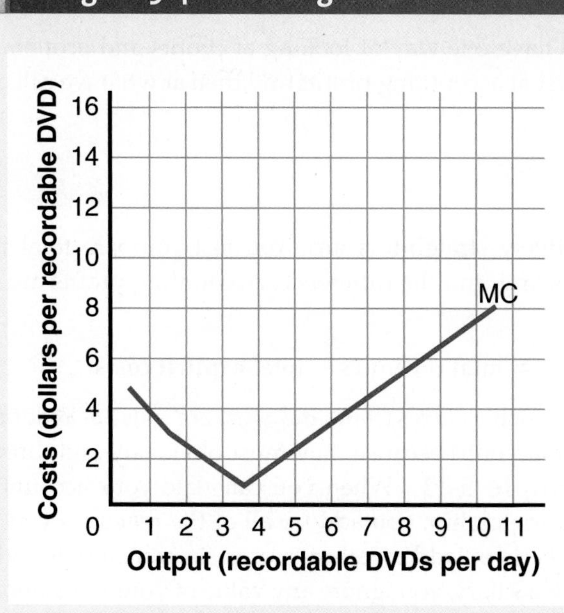


Marginal cost falls until about 3.5 units of output. Thereafter, it rises.

## In the Long Run, There Are No Fixed Costs

**Short run**
*The time period when at least one input, such as plant size, cannot be changed.*

All the costs we have been talking about so far are ones that the firm incurs in the short run. What is a short run? For some firms it is a few months; for others it is a few years. The **short run** is defined as the period during which the firm effectively cannot alter all of its inputs.

So, the long run is defined as a period long enough that the firm can change all of these inputs. In the long run, firms can add or sell plants, buy or sell land, and so on. A way of stating this is:

> ***In the long run, all costs are marginal costs, and therefore all decisions are decisions made on the margin that consider the usage of all inputs.***

▸ Example 5-10 You manage a local electric utility that has very high fixed costs over any several-year period. Over a somewhat longer planning horizon, however, your utility can add additional generating sources. So, in the long run, for you, as a manager of this electric utility, all costs are marginal costs. ◂

Now it is time to take costs and compare them with revenues to come up with profits (or the absence of such).

**Mastering Concepts:** The Firm Faces Its Costs

- **Fixed costs do not vary with output. Their existence often does not bear on future decision making.**
- **Average total, variable, and fixed costs are obtained by dividing total costs, variable costs, and fixed costs by output, respectively.**
- **Marginal costs are a key decision variable and are defined as the change in total costs associated with a one-unit change in output.**

# PROFITS: ACCOUNTANTS VERSUS ECONOMISTS

It turns out that accountants have one way of looking at profits and economists another way. We shall look first at accounting profits and then at what we call economic profits.

## Accounting Profits

**Accounting profits**
*Total revenues minus total explicit costs.*

**Accounting profits** are relatively straightforward. You just compare total revenues with total *explicit* costs and find the difference. Accounting profits are defined as follows:

**Accounting profits = total revenues − total explicit costs**

**Explicit costs**
*Costs that business managers must take account of because they must overtly be paid; examples are wages, taxes, and rent.*

**Explicit costs** are expenses such as taxes, rent, and workers' salaries that business managers must take into account because they must obviously and directly be paid by the firm. ▸ Example 5-11 When you calculate your accounting profits for your own sole proprietorship, you add up all of the revenues you obtained throughout the year. Then you add together your costs of materials and so on. If you did not pay yourself a salary, you ignore any value of your own labor in this calculation. Accounting profits will be the profit figure obtained when you subtract one total from the other. Typically, you will have to pay federal and state taxes on such measured profits (assuming they are positive, of course). ◂

## Economic Profits

Remember from Chapter 1 the critical concept of opportunity costs:

> ***For accurate analysis of just about anything, the costs that matter are opportunity costs.***

Not surprisingly, the way economists view profits is by taking into account *all* opportunity costs. That is to say, you have to look at the opportunity cost of every input into the production process.

Here is the definition of **economic profits:**

**Economic profits** *Total revenues minus total opportunity costs of all inputs used, or the total of all implicit and explicit costs. Economic profits can also be viewed as the difference between total revenues and the opportunity cost of all factors of production.*

**Economic profits = total revenues − total opportunity cost of all inputs used**

▸ Example 5-12 You run an Internet medical research site. For a fee, you will research on the Web any difficult-to-analyze illnesses. Occasionally, you hire outside experts to help you. At the end of the year, here are the numbers that you give to your accountant:

| | Revenues | Expenses |
|---|---|---|
| Revenues | $100,000 | |
| Outside consultants | | $20,000 |
| High-speed Internet access | | 1,000 |
| Computer lease payments | | 1,000 |
| Insurance | | 1,000 |
| TOTAL | **$100,000** | **$23,000** |

Your accountant comes back and tells you that your profits are $77,000, because your revenue is $100,000 and your explicit costs are $23,000. If you want to know your economic profits, though, you have to include the opportunity cost of your time. In fact, you were offered a job recently paying $80,000 a year, implying that your opportunity cost is $23,000 + $80,000 = $103,000. So what are your true economic profits? Minus $3,000. You are in fact making an economic loss! ◂

**The Opportunity Cost of Capital Is Important, Too** In Example 5-12, the opportunity cost of the labor input was highlighted. The opportunity cost of capital is important, too, when calculating economic profits.

▸ Example 5-13 You just inherited a working farm from a distant relative. You examine the books carefully and discover that accounting profits are $100,000 per year. The full opportunity cost of all the labor going into producing the farm products is included. In contrast, no explicit costs for the land and the buildings on it are included. To get an idea of economic profits for the inherited farm, you have to estimate the opportunity cost of the land and buildings and equipment. You could do this by estimating how much you could get if you leased the farm—with all its buildings and equipment—to some other farmer. When you do that, you discover that the lease payments would be $75,000 per year. Hence, your estimated economic profits are only $25,000. ◂

We can graphically show the relationship between economic and accounting profits by using the discussion about the opportunity cost of all resources. Look at Figure 5-5 on the following page. There you see this relationship.

✦ **Note!** *There is a good reason why accountants determine profits the way that they do: For federal and state tax calculations, they have no choice.*

## Profits Are What Matters

The reason that people are so interested in costs versus revenues is that most people do not go into business unless they think they can make a profit. Indeed, for

## Figure 5-5 Simplified View of Economic and Accounting Profit

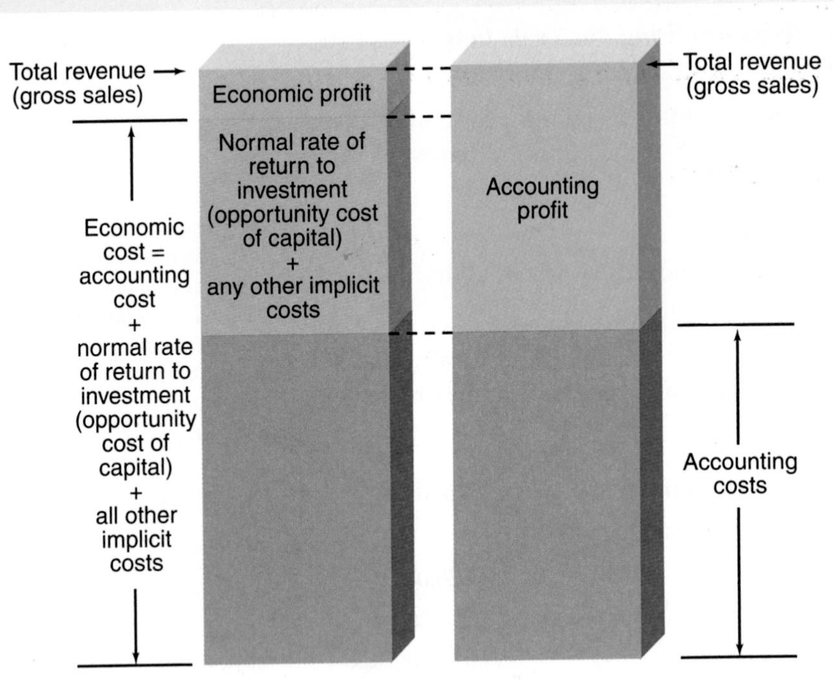


We see on the right column that accounting profit is the difference between total revenue and total explicit accounting costs. Conversely, we see on the left column that economic profit is equal to total revenue minus the opportunity costs of all inputs. The latter equal explicit accounting costs plus all implicit costs, including a normal rate of return on invested capital.

most analyses we simply assume that people go into business to make as much profit as they can. That is to say, we assume that the goal of the firm is profit maximization.

***To be more accurate, we say that the firm wishes to maximize economic profits. This means that the firm is expected to try to make as great as possible the positive difference between total revenues and the total opportunity cost of all production inputs.***

**The Relationship Between Profit Maximization and Obtaining Financing** Normally, any firm that wishes to expand has to obtain additional financial resources to do so. These financial resources go into purchasing more labor, capital, and land. Consider the motivation of investors who will put up the funds for this expansion. They don't really care how firms are run. What they care about is getting relatively high, safe returns on their investment. Consequently, firm owners and business managers who constantly strive to maximize profits will attract more investment funds for expansion. Firms that can provide higher returns (corrected for risk) will therefore have an advantage in obtaining the financing needed to continue or expand production.

***We expect a firm's policy of profit maximization to become the dominant mode of behavior for firms that survive.***

**Share of stock**
*A legal claim to a share of a corporation's future profits. If it is* common stock, *it incorporates certain voting rights regarding major policy decisions of the corporation.*

**Corporate Financing and the Stock Market** You have already been introduced to the corporate form of business organization. This corporate form is often associated with raising capital by selling shares of stock. A **share of stock** in a corporation is simply a legal claim to a share of the corporation's future profits.

▸ **Example 5-14** If there are 100,000 shares of stock in a company and you own 1,000 of them, you own the right to 1 percent of that company's future profits. If the stock you own is *common stock*, you also have the right to vote on major policy decisions affecting the company, such as the selection of the corporation's board of directors. Your 1,000 shares would entitle you to cast 1 percent of the votes on such issues. ◂

Many corporate stocks are traded on organized exchanges, such as the New York Stock Exchange (NYSE). More than 2,500 companies' stocks are traded on the NYSE. The other major U.S. stock exchange is the National Association of Security Dealers Automated Quotation (NASDAQ) system. The NASDAQ is home to nearly 5,500 companies' stocks, including Microsoft, Intel, and Cisco.

**Reading Stock Quotes** Every business day the financial press publishes stock quotations from which you can find out lots of valuable information if you

© Roz Chast. Reprinted by permission of the New Yorker.

### Table 5-4 Reading Stock Quotes

| YTD % CHG | 52-WEEK HI | 52-WEEK LO | STOCK | (SYM) | DIV. | YLD % | PE | VOL 100s | CLOSE | NET CHG |
|---|---|---|---|---|---|---|---|---|---|---|
| –17.8 | 111.18 | 64.20 | GenDynam | GD | 1.20 | 1.8 | 14 | 50907 | 65.25 | 0.40 |
| –1.6 | 41.84 | 21.40 | GenElec | GE | 0.76 | 3.2 | 16 | 217850 | 23.95 | 0.40 |
| –5.6 | 52.29 | 40.20 | GenGrthProp | GGP | 2.88 | 5.9 | na | 1466 | 49.09 | 0.04 |
| 19.5 | 14.20 | 4.78 | GenMaritime | GMR | 4.78 | na | na | 657 | 8.90 | 0.10 |

The summary of stock market information presented on the financial pages of many newspapers reveals the following:

**YTD%CHG** The percentage change in the stock price since the beginning of the year.
**52 Weeks HI/Lo:** The highest and lowest prices, in dollars per share, of the stock during the previous 52 weeks
**STOCK:** The name of the company (frequently abbreviated)
**(SYM):** Highly abbreviated name of the company, as it appears on the stock exchange ticker tape
**DIV:** Dividend paid, in dollars per share
**YLD%:** Yield in percent per year; the dividend divided by the price of the stock
**PE:** Price-earnings ratio; the price of the stock divided by the earnings (profits) per share of the company
**VOL 100s:** Number of shares traded during the day, in hundreds of shares
**CLOSE:** Last price at which the stock traded that day
**NET CHG:** Net change in the stock's price from the previous day's closing price

are considering investing in the stock market. Look at Table 5-4. There you see information about the stocks of four companies.

**Company Name and Symbol, Highest and Lowest Bids** Under the heading "Stock" we find the name of the company—in the second row, for example, is General Electric. The first column gives the calendar year-to-date percentage change in the price of the company's stock. The next two columns to the left of the company's name show the highest and lowest prices at which shares of that company's stock traded during the past 52 weeks.

Immediately to the right of the company's name you will find the company's *symbol* (SYM) on the NYSE. This symbol (omitted by some newspapers) is simply the unique identifier used by the exchange when it reports information about the stock. For example, the designation GE is used by the exchange as the unique identifier for the firm General Electric.

**Behavior of Stock's Price** The last two columns of information for each firm summarize the behavior of the firm's stock price on the latest trading day. On this particular day, the last (or closing) price at which it traded was $23.95 per share. The *net change* in the price of General Electric stock was $0.40, which means that it *closed* the day at a price about $0.40 per share above the price at which it closed the day before.

**Dividends (If Any)** The dividend column, headed "DIV," shows the annual dividend (in dollars and cents) that the company has paid over the preceding year on each share of its stock. In General Electric's case, this amounts to $0.76 a share. If the dividend is divided by the closing price of the stock ($0.76 ÷ $23.95), the result is 3.2 percent, which is shown in the yield percentage ("YLD %") column for General Electric. In a sense, the company is paying interest on the stock at a rate of about 3.2 percent.

**Price-Earnings Ratio and Volume of Trading** The column heading "PE" stands for *price-earnings ratio.* To obtain the entries for this column, the firm's total earnings (profits) for the year are divided by the number of the firm's shares in existence to give the earnings per share. When the price of the stock is divided by the earnings per share, the result is the price-earning ratio.

The column to the right of the PE ratio shows the total *volume* of the shares of the stock traded that day, measured in hundreds of shares.

**Mastering Concepts:** Profits: Accountants versus Economists

- **Whereas accounting profits equal total revenues minus total explicit costs, economic profits equal total revenues minus all opportunity costs.**
- **In determining all costs, one must consider the full opportunity cost of capital and labor.**
- **We assume that businesspeople are in business to maximize profits.**
- **Businesses that attempt to maximize profits find that obtaining financial capital is easier than if they were maximizing something else, such as goodwill in the community.**
- **Some corporations obtain financing by selling shares of stock. Larger corporations may have their shares of stock listed on national exchanges, such as the New York Stock Exchange, or regional stock exchanges.**

## SUMMING IT ALL UP

- Sole proprietorships are the easiest business organization to create, but carry unlimited liability for owners.
- Partnerships allow for a broader management and financing, but still carry unlimited liability for owners.
- Corporations have the benefit of limited liability, but have the disadvantage of facing the double taxation of corporate income.
- While an S corporation avoids double taxation, a limited liability company (LLC) avoids such double taxation, too.
- The production function relates output to the different factors of production used to create that output during a specified time period.
- After some point, when a variable factor of production, such as labor, is increased, the additional output obtained from each additional unit of that input starts to diminish. This is called the law of diminishing returns.
- Fixed cost do not vary with output.
- Average total, variable, and fixed costs are obtained by dividing total costs, variable costs, and fixed costs by output, respectively.
- Marginal costs are a key decision variable and are defined as the change in total cost associated with a one-unit change in output.
- Whereas accounting profits equal total revenues minus total explicit costs, economic profits equal total revenues minus all opportunity costs.
- In determining all costs, one must consider the full opportunity cost of capital and labor.

- We assume that businesspeople are in business to maximize profits.
- Businesses that attempt to maximize profits find that obtaining financial capital is easier than if they were maximizing something else, such as goodwill in the community.

## KEY TERMS AND CONCEPTS

accounting profits **102**
average fixed costs **98**
average physical product **94**
average total cost **98**
average variable costs **98**
corporation **91**
dividends **92**
double taxation **92**
economic profits **103**
explicit costs **102**
fixed costs **97**
law of diminishing returns **96**
limited liability **91**
limited liability company (LLC) **92**
marginal costs **99**
marginal physical product **94**
partnership **90**
production function **94**
S corporations **92**
share of stock **104**
short run **102**
sole proprietorship **90**
total costs **97**
unlimited liability **90**
variable costs **97**

## MASTERING ECONOMIC CONCEPTS
## Questions and Problems

**5-1.** Compare the advantages of a corporation as a form of business organization with those of a sole proprietorship. What are the disadvantages of each form of business organization?

**5-2.** What special feature of an S corporation distinguishes it from a standard corporation?

**5-3.** Complete the following table by calculating average physical product and marginal physical product.

| Machines | Total Output | Average Physical Product | Marginal Physical Product |
|---|---|---|---|
| 3 | 300 | ____ | |
| 4 | 425 | ____ | ____ |
| 5 | 575 | ____ | ____ |
| 6 | 700 | ____ | ____ |
| 7 | 750 | ____ | ____ |

**5-4.** Based on the following table, at what worker does diminishing marginal product begin to appear?

| Workers | Output |
|---|---|
| 10 | 100 |
| 11 | 115 |
| 12 | 135 |
| 13 | 156 |
| 14 | 176 |
| 15 | 190 |

**5-5.** Assume that you spent $1,200 on a PC four years ago and now the computer is obsolete (with zero resale value) and no longer suitable for your purposes. If you must decide whether to purchase a new PC that costs $1,000 for a business venture you are considering, what role should the $1,200 cost of the original PC play in your decision-making process? Would the $1,200 be considered a sunk cost?

**5-6.** Is each of the following more likely to be a fixed cost or a variable cost in the short run?

a. employees' salaries
b. raw materials
c. rent
d. electricity

**5-7.** Based on the information in the table below, compute total costs, average fixed costs, average variable costs, and average total costs at each level of output.

| Quantity | Fixed Costs | Variable Costs | Total Costs | Average Fixed Costs | Average Variable Costs | Average Total Costs |
|---|---|---|---|---|---|---|
| 13 | $400 | $100 | $____ | $____ | $____ | $____ |
| 14 | 400 | 105 | ____ | ____ | ____ | ____ |
| 15 | 400 | 109 | ____ | ____ | ____ | ____ |
| 16 | 400 | 112 | ____ | ____ | ____ | ____ |
| 17 | 400 | 117 | ____ | ____ | ____ | ____ |

**5-8.** Assume that Earle's company makes picture frames and his total fixed costs are $3,000 each month. If his variable costs are $1,000 at 100 units of output, what is his average total cost at this level of output?

**5-9.** Assume that the total fixed costs for the Subway location near campus are $200 each day. If the variable costs per sub are $2, what is the average total cost if the store sells 150 subs each day?

**5-10.** Complete the following table by calculating the missing values for all columns.

| Output | Total Cost | Marginal Cost |
|---|---|---|
| 1 | $450 | |
| 2 | 475 | $____ |
| 3 | 495 | ____ |
| 4 | 510 | ____ |
| 5 | | 10 |
| 6 | | 15 |

**5-11.** The four curves below represent average total costs, average variable costs, average fixed costs, and marginal costs. Which of the curves depicted is the average total cost curve?

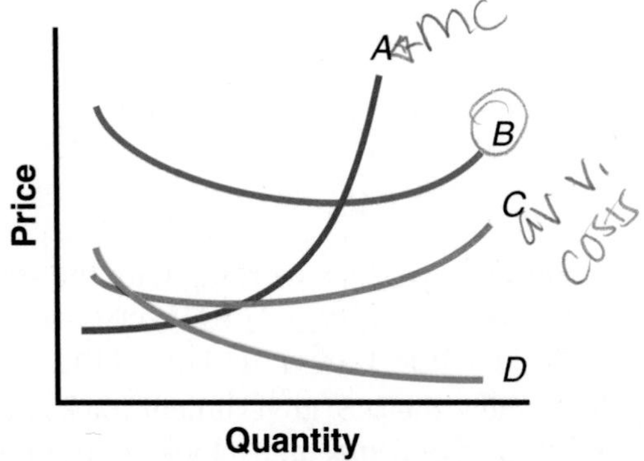


**5-12.** Is it possible for accounting profit to be less than economic profit? Why or why not?

**5-13.** Assume that Brad starts his own business doing construction and home improvement work for customers in the Philadelphia area. He spends $10,000 on supplies and $15,000 on pay for workers who help him on bigger jobs. As a result, he earns a total of $100,000 for a one-year period. By working for himself, however, he is forced to give up his job with IBM, which paid $65,000 per year. Excluding any tax effect, what are Brad's economic profits for this year?

**5-14.** Draw a marginal cost curve based on the numbers in the following table.

| Output | Fixed Costs | Variable Costs |
|---|---|---|
| 1 | $1,000 | $ 80 |
| 2 | 1,000 | 140 |
| 3 | 1,000 | 190 |
| 4 | 1,000 | 235 |
| 5 | 1,000 | 285 |
| 6 | 1,000 | 355 |

**5-15.** Based on the graph below, what does marginal cost equal at a quantity of 90 units? At a quantity of 82 units, what does average total cost equal? At a quantity of 60 units, what does average variable cost equal?

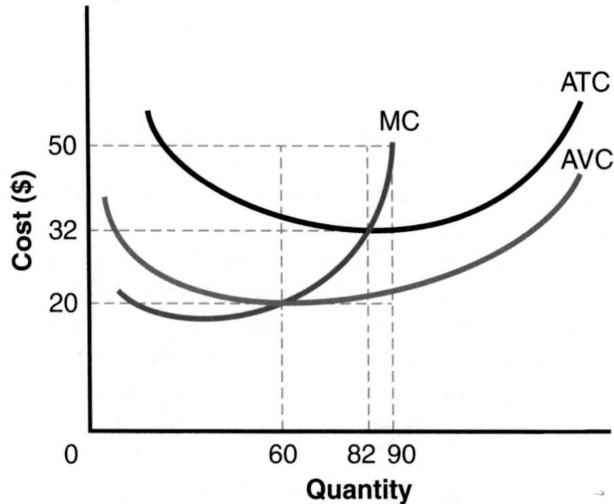


**5-16.** Based on the graph below, what is the marginal cost of the second unit produced? What is the marginal cost of the tenth unit produced?

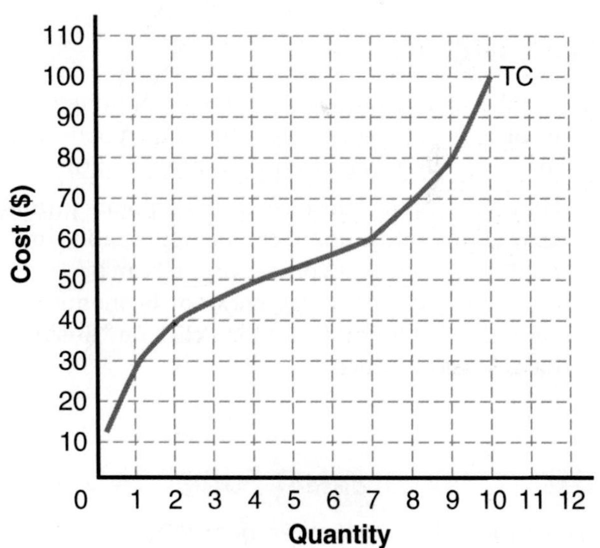


**5-17.** Assume total fixed costs are $12,000 and total variable costs are $4,000 at an output level of 2,000 units. Compute average fixed costs, average variable costs, and average total costs.

## THINKING CRITICALLY

**5-1.** Delta Airlines recently advertised a special on air travel from Miami to Denver. The price for a round-trip ticket was $178. If the average total cost to fly passengers to and from Denver is $250, how does this offer provide any benefit to Delta? How does Delta's opportunity cost of an empty seat change as the date of the flight approaches?

**5-2.** If you start your own business after graduating from college and your business generates $225,000 in revenues annually and incurs $100,000 in explicit costs, what are your accounting profits? Assume that you invested $200,000 in this business, that you could have earned a $10,000 return on this amount each year, and that your education would allow you to hold a position with another company earning $75,000 per year. Based on these figures, what would be the measure of your economic profit? Which of these figures—accounting profit or economic profit—should you use to decide if having your own business was a wise move? Use this figure to argue in favor of this business or against it.

**5-3.** Use the table below to compute marginal product, marginal cost, and average total cost. Based on this table at what level of output does diminishing marginal product begin to set in? How does this correspond to the changes in marginal cost?

| Labor | Daily Output | Marginal Product | Total Cost | Marginal Cost | Average Total Cost |
|---|---|---|---|---|---|
| 1 | 50 | | $1,100 | | $____ |
| | | ____ | | $____ | |
| 2 | 125 | | 1,200 | | ____ |
| | | ____ | | ____ | |
| 3 | 225 | | 1,300 | | ____ |
| | | ____ | | ____ | |
| 4 | 350 | | 1,400 | | ____ |
| | | ____ | | ____ | |
| 5 | 450 | | 1,500 | | ____ |
| | | ____ | | ____ | |
| 6 | 525 | | 1,600 | | ____ |
| | | ____ | | ____ | |
| 7 | 575 | | 1,700 | | ____ |
| | | ____ | | ____ | |
| 8 | 600 | | 1,800 | | ____ |

## LOGGING ON

1. For the latest information on the accounting profits of sole proprietorships in the United States, go to http://bizstats.com/spprofitscurrent.htm.
2. For a view of the latest trends in corporate profits, after taking into account capital depreciation, go to http://www.newyorkfed.org/research/directors_charts/us.html, click on "Economic Growth and Output," and then click on "Business Income and Finance."
3. To get more practice working with the production function, go to http://ingrimayne.saintjoe.edu/econ/TheFirm/ProductionFunct.html.
4. To see how the U.S. government tracks industry inputs and outputs, take a look at "Input-Output (I-O) Accounts" at http://www.bea.doc.gov/bea/dn2.htm.

## USING THE INTERNET FOR ECONOMIC ANALYSIS

**Cost Considerations for Sole Proprietorships** As you learned in this chapter, both advantages and disadvantages are associated with forming a sole proprietorship. This application emphasizes the real-world relevance of this issue for costs incurred by small businesses.

**Title:** Sole Proprietorships: Simple, But Not Very Flexible

**Navigation:** Go to http://www.bcentral.com/articles/anthony/107.asp.

**Application** Read the article, and answer the following questions.

1. Is the process of keeping tax records and the annual task of filing taxes a fixed cost or a variable cost?
2. The article recommends forming a limited liability company whenever a small business hires employees. Based on the discussion, are fixed costs, variable costs, or both fixed and variable costs more likely to increase when a sole proprietorship takes on employees?

## MEDIA RESOURCE LIST

The following media resources are available with this chapter:

- Load your CD-ROM to listen to the audio introduction to this chapter.
- Load your CD-ROM to access a Graph Animation of Figure 5-1, *The Production Function and Marginal Physical Product*.
- Load your CD-ROM to view the video on *Profit Maximization.*
- Test your knowledge of chapter concepts with a quiz at www.miller-ume.com.
- Link to Web resources related to the text coverage at www.miller-ume.com.

## HOMEWORK SET

Go to the back of the book to find the Homework Problems for this chapter.

# CHAPTER 6

# The Two Extremes: Perfect Competition and Pure Monopoly

## *Facing an Economic Problem:* Should You Shut Down Your Business?

For generations, your family has been involved in manufacturing high-end wooden furniture. Recently, you made a major investment in automated, computer-controlled, wood-finishing machines. Then, a slowdown in business occurred for two reasons: (1) a worldwide recession and (2) ferocious competition from Indonesian furniture makers. You have done the calculations. You know that your prices are not even covering average per-unit costs. Should you shut down? To answer this question, you need to know how firms determine how much to produce and when to stop producing.

### Learning Objectives

After reading this chapter, you should be able to:

- **List the four characteristics of a perfectly competitive market.**
- **Describe how a perfect competitor makes the decision to stay in business or to go out of business.**
- **List the characteristics of monopoly.**
- **List and describe three types of monopolies.**
- **Explain the difference between marginal revenue for a perfect competitor and marginal revenue for a pure monopolist.**

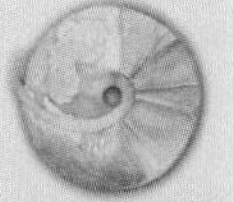

***Refer to the back of this chapter for a complete listing of multimedia learning materials available on the CD-ROM and the Web site.***

## THE SPECTRUM OF MARKET STRUCTURES

**Market structure**
*The number, size, and interaction of firms in a given industry, or market.*

You have probably heard the words *competition* and *monopoly*. As it turns out, these terms are loosely used in casual conversation, but they have a more specific meaning in the way we describe market structures. **Market structure** relates to the number, size, and interaction of firms in a particular market.

### THE EXTREMES

**Perfect competition**
*A market situation in which there are numerous buyers and sellers, and no single buyer or seller can affect price.*

**Pure monopoly**
*A market situation in which there is only one seller of a good or service with no close substitutes.*

**Imperfect competition**
*Any form of market structure in which the sellers have some control over price.*

One extreme of market structure occurs when there are literally thousands upon thousands of sellers. We call this a situation of **perfect competition**. At the other extreme is **pure monopoly,** when there is only one seller of a given good or service for which there are no close substitutes. In between, of course, there are varying degrees of what is called **imperfect competition**. Look at Figure 6-1. There you see the spectrum of market structures that are possible.

In this chapter, you will learn about the two extremes in market structures—perfect competition and pure monopoly.

### IMPERFECT COMPETITION

Imperfect competition, the subject of Chapter 7, can take on at least three forms, if not more. They are:

**Duopoly**
*Two sellers in a single market for a good or service for which there is no close substitute.*

**Oligopoly**
*A market situation in which there are very few sellers. Each seller knows that the other sellers will react to its changes in prices and quantities.*

**Monopolistic competition**
*A market situation in which a large number of firms produce similar but not identical products. Entry into the industry is relatively easy.*

1. **Duopoly:** Two firms supply a particular good or service for which there are no close substitutes.
2. **Oligopoly:** Several firms supply a very large percentage of a market for a particular good or service.
3. **Monopolistic Competition:** Numerous firms provide a slightly different versions of the same product.

**Mastering Concepts:** The Spectrum of Market Structures

- **Market structure refers to the number, size, and potential interactions among firms in a particular industry.**
- **The extremes of market structure are perfect competition, in which there are thousands of sellers of the same product, and pure monopoly, in which there is only one seller.**

Figure 6-1 Different Market Structures

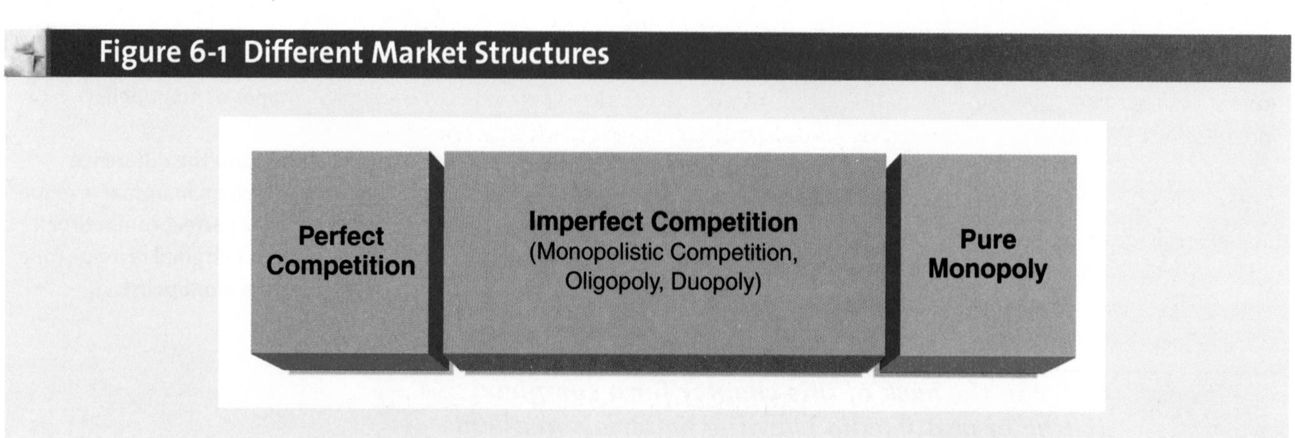

## LOTS OF FIRMS + ONE SIMILAR PRODUCT = PERFECT COMPETITION

In the chapter-opening economic problem, the product was high-end wooden furniture. While there are many competitors in this market—especially from Southeast Asia—the product is certainly not **homogeneous.** That is to say, wooden furniture is not like bushels of wheat, which can be treated as all the same for analytical purposes. Perfect competition is, of course, a theoretical construct. That is to say, there are *not* a lot of industries in which the product is exactly identical and there are tens of thousands of sellers. But there are enough industries that are close to being perfectly competitive that studying this market structure is important. Whenever an individual seller cannot control the price at which his or her product is sold, we are in the realm of perfect competition. Perfect competitors are **price takers.** They simply accept the market price as given.

**Homogeneous**
*Uniform in structure or composition throughout; of the same or similar nature or kind.*

**Price taker**
*A competitive firm that must take the price of its product as given because the firm cannot influence its price.*

### DEFINING A PERFECT COMPETITOR

There is certainly a lot of competition among firms in many industries in the United States. ▸ Example 6-1 Today, there are tens of thousands of instant copy and print shops. There are thousands of desktop publishing firms. There are thousands of Web site designers. There are thousands of Internet service providers (ISPs). Every participant in each one of these industries faces fierce competition from its rivals. ◂

We need to go from this general notion of competition and rivalry to a narrower market structure, one that we briefly defined above as perfect competition.

**Defining Perfect Competition** Here is a more complete view of what perfect competition means:

- There are a very large number of buyers and sellers, all of which are relatively small.
- The product sold by each seller is substantially identical to the product sold by other sellers.
- Firms can easily enter or exit the industry.
- Everybody involved has good information about price and product qualities.

▸ Example 6-2 The market for wheat, corn, and many other farm commodities is as close to an example of perfect competition as we can get, provided that the government does not intervene in the marketplace. Number 2 winter wheat in one silo is substantially identical to number 2 winter wheat in another silo. A bushel of corn for feeding cattle in one part of the country is essentially identical to a bushel in another part. There are literally hundreds of thousands of buyers of farm products and, worldwide, hundreds of thousands of wholesalers and retailers. Information about prices and quantities can be readily obtained. ◂

**Remember, These Are a Set of Assumptions** Even though agricultural commodities provide an example of a very competitive industry, not very many industries out there satisfy *all* of the requirements for perfect competition. Nonetheless, we can still use this model—and that is what it is—to make statements about how competitive firms will react, for example, to changes in taxes or changes in competition from abroad.

At least one new industry fits many of the requirements of perfect competition, as you will read in the next *E-Commerce Application* on the next page.

## E-COMMERCE APPLICATION: The Expanding World of Spammers

### Concept Applied: *Perfect Competition*

Anybody who uses e-mail knows about spam—unrequested commercial advertising messages. The spamming industry is one that is highly, if not perfectly, competitive.

#### Costs of Entry and Exit Are Low

What do you need to do to become a spammer? Not much. You can buy a low-cost server for under $500. You can purchase various bulk e-mail address lists for less than $100 each. You can advertise your services to those who want to use spam to advertise by—you guessed it—spamming, which costs very little, not even a penny a name. If things don't work out very well, you can readily sell your server and just go out of business.

#### Marginal Costs Are Small

What is the cost of sending an additional spam? Probably close to zero. After all, lines of communication through the Internet are virtually free. This is certainly true in the United States where local calls can be made at zero cost. Once you have paid for a bulk e-mail mailing list and the creative aspect of your electronic bulk mail advertisement, the cost of reaching one million more potential customers is virtually zero.

#### Spamming Is International

Because many Internet service providers do not allow spamming, spammers often have to use international-based servers to do their "dirty work." Not surprisingly, hundreds of spamming companies are based outside the United States. This fierce international competition has lowered the price of spamming dramatically over the last five years.

**For Critical Analysis:**
*Legislatures continue to pass laws prohibiting spamming. Why do you think it is so difficult to prevent spamming?*

## What Kind of Demand Curve Does a Perfect Competitor Face?

If you are a willing participant in a perfectly competitive industry, it is not hard to find out what type of demand curve you are facing. If the going price in your market is $5.00 per unit, try to charge $5.10 per unit. How much business do you think you will get? The answer, of course, is probably zero. Additionally, if everyone else were charging $5.00 per unit, you would be foolish to charge less than $5.00. The fact is, you can sell all that you want at $5.00 per unit. You essentially have no control over the price you charge for your product. We say, then, that a perfect competitor is a *price taker.* She or he simply takes the price as given—determined by market forces outside the control of the individual perfect competitor.

Look at Figure 6-2. In panel (a) you see the industry demand and supply curve represented by *D* and *S*. In the recordable DVD industry, the going price is $5 per unit. To find out the demand curve facing the individual firm, simply project that $5 over to the right to panel (b) and you get the individual demand curve. It is labeled *d*. Notice that the demand curve facing the individual firm is perfectly elastic. This means that customers will buy all that any one individual firm might want to produce at the going market price and none at a higher price.

## Okay, You Know the Price, but How Much Should You Produce?

Though a perfect competitor has no control over price—it is determined by market supply and market demand—he or she does have control over how much to produce. In fact, that is the major decision that the perfect competitor faces.

**Figure 6-2 The Demand Curve Facing the Perfect Competitor**

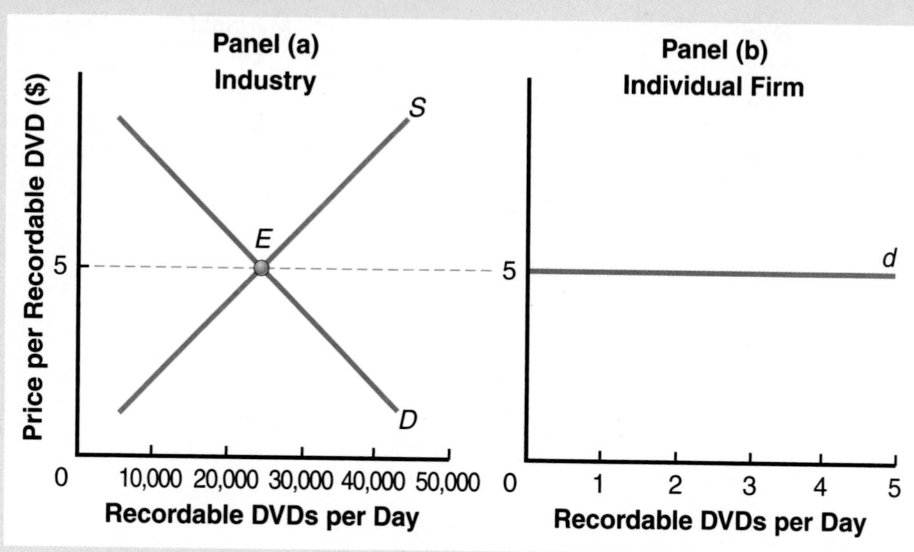

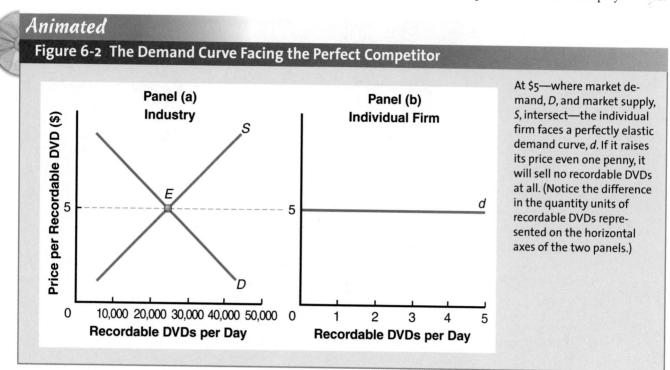

At $5—where market demand, *D*, and market supply, *S*, intersect—the individual firm faces a perfectly elastic demand curve, *d*. If it raises its price even one penny, it will sell no recordable DVDs at all. (Notice the difference in the quantity units of recordable DVDs represented on the horizontal axes of the two panels.)

**Marginal Benefit and Marginal Cost** The decision of how much to produce is similar to all decisions in economics (and in life). Never do anything past the point at which **marginal benefit** equals marginal cost. So, a perfect competitor will look at marginal benefit—the price of each unit that can be sold—and compare it with marginal cost:

> ***A perfect competitor produces up to the point at which marginal benefit equals marginal cost or, otherwise stated, the point at which the price per unit equals marginal cost.***

**Marginal benefit**
*Additional benefit resulting from doing a small incremental amount of an activity, i.e., the extra revenue a firm gets when it sells one more unit of output.*

**Profit Maximization** This decision-making process is really one in which the perfect competitor *maximizes profits,* a behavior we discussed in Chapter 5. If the perfect competitor produced a larger quantity, marginal costs would exceed the price per unit. There is never a reason to do that, because the firm would then be making losses on the last units produced. Conversely, if the firm stops producing before marginal benefit equals marginal cost, then it is forgoing potential profits on additional units of output.

You were already introduced to the marginal cost curve in Chapter 5. Now what is marginal benefit for the perfect competitor? Marginal benefit here is the firm's **marginal revenue,** defined as the change in total revenues when there is a one-unit change in production and sales. In other words

**Marginal revenue**
*The change in total revenues due to a one-unit change in output or sales.*

$$\textbf{Marginal revenue} = \frac{\textbf{change in total revenues}}{\textbf{change in output}}$$

Because a perfect competitor can sell all it wants at the going market price, marginal revenue is equal to unit price at all rates of output. Look at Table 6-1 on the following page where you see marginal cost and marginal revenue for a recordable DVD producer.

Now look at Figure 6-3 on page 118. There we have plotted the individual firm demand curve from panel (b) of Figure 6-2. We have added the marginal cost curve from Table 6-1. It is simply a plot of columns 1 and 4 in that table. The demand curve for the perfect competitor, *d*, is also its marginal revenue curve.

### Table 6-1 Marginal Cost and Marginal Revenue for Producing Recordable DVDs

| (1) Total Output and Sales per day (*Q*) | (2) Total Costs (TC) | (3) Market Price (*P*) | (4) Marginal Cost (MC) (4) = Change in (2) / Change in (1) | (5) Marginal Revenue (MR) (5) = Change in (3) / Change in (1) |
|---|---|---|---|---|
| 0 | $10 | $5 | | |
| | | | $5 | $5 |
| 1 | 15 | 5 | | |
| | | | 3 | 5 |
| 2 | 18 | 5 | | |
| | | | 2 | 5 |
| 3 | 20 | 5 | | |
| | | | 1 | 5 |
| 4 | 21 | 5 | | |
| | | | 2 | 5 |
| 5 | 23 | 5 | | |
| | | | 3 | 5 |
| 6 | 26 | 5 | | |
| | | | 4 | 5 |
| 7 | 30 | 5 | | |
| | | | 5 | 5 |
| 8 | 35 | 5 | | |
| | | | 6 | 5 |
| 9 | 41 | 5 | | |
| | | | 7 | 5 |
| 10 | 48 | 5 | | |
| | | | 8 | 5 |
| 11 | 56 | 5 | | |

**Maximizing Profits** In Figure 6-3, the marginal cost curve intersects the marginal revenue curve somewhere between seven and eight recordable DVDs per day. The firm has an incentive to produce and sell until the amount of additional revenue received from selling one more recordable DVD just equals the additional costs incurred for producing and selling that DVD.

But how much should it produce? It should produce at point *E*, where the marginal cost curve intersects the marginal revenue curve. The firm should continue production until the cost of increasing output by one more unit is just equal to the revenues obtainable from the extra unit. This is a fundamental rule in economics:

### Figure 6-3 The Perfect Competitor Determines How Much to Produce

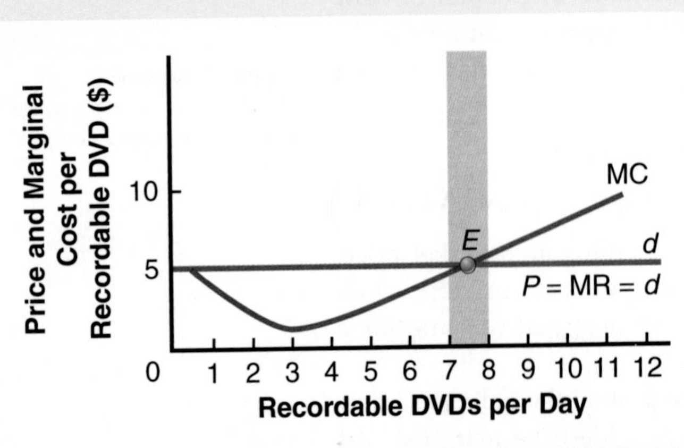


The perfect competitor faces a perfectly elastic demand curve at a price of $5 per unit. The demand curve facing the individual firm is represented by *d*. The perfect competitor's marginal cost curve is MC. The intersection, *E*, is the profit-maximizing rate of output at somewhere between seven and eight units per day.

***Profit maximization occurs at the rate of output at which marginal revenue equals marginal cost.***

For a perfectly competitive firm, this is at the intersection of the demand schedule, *d*, and the marginal cost curve, MC. When MR exceeds MC, each additional unit of output adds more to total revenues than to total costs, so the firm can earn higher profits if it expands output. When MC is greater than MR, each unit produced adds more to total costs than to total revenues, causing profits to decrease or losses to increase. Therefore, profit maximization occurs when MC equals MR. In our particular example, our profit-maximizing, perfectly competitive producer of recordable DVDs will produce at a rate of either seven or eight DVDs a day. (If we were dealing with a very large rate of output, we would come up with an exact profit-maximizing rate.)

## Measuring Short-Run Profits

It is possible for a perfect competitor to make profits in the short run, but not in the long run. To show what these profits might look like, we need to add the average total cost curve to Figure 6-3. This becomes Figure 6-4.

In Figure 6-4, the lower boundary of the rectangle labeled "Profits" is determined by the intersection of the profit-maximizing quantity line represented by vertical dashes and the average total cost curve. Why? Because the ATC curve gives us the cost per unit, whereas the price ($5), represented by *d*, gives us the revenue per unit. The difference is profit per unit. So, the height of the rectangular box representing profits equals profit per unit, and the length equals the amount

**Figure 6-4 Showing Short-Run Economic Profits**

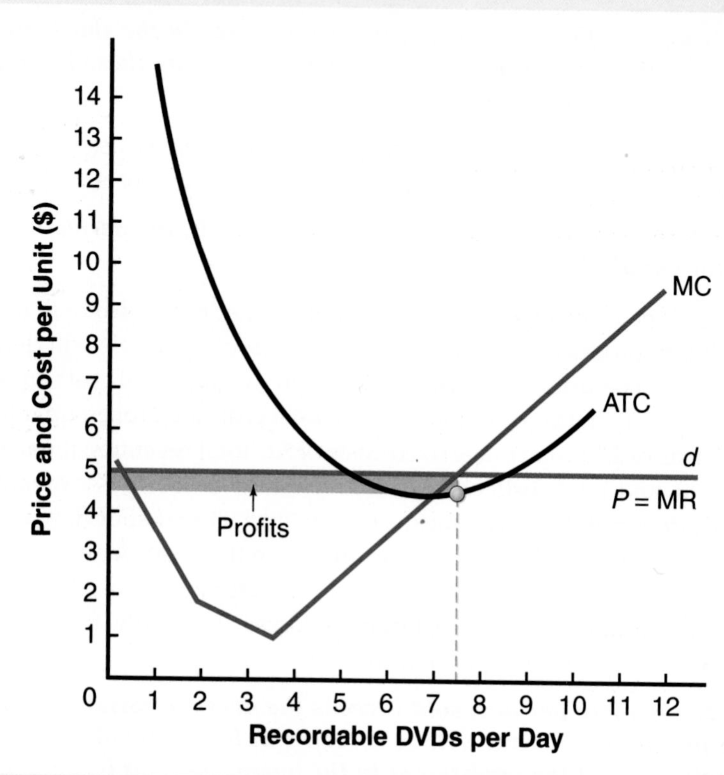


Profits are represented by the shaded area. The height of the profit rectangle is given by the difference between average total costs and price ($5), because price is also equal to marginal revenue. This is found by the vertical difference between the ATC curve and the price, or average revenue, line *d*, at the profit-maximizing rate of output of between seven and eight recordable DVDs per day.

of units produced. When we multiply these two quantities, we get total profits. Note that, as pointed out earlier, we are talking about *economic profits* because a normal rate of return on investment is included in the average total cost curve, ATC.

**Mastering Concepts:** Lots of Firms + One Similar Product = Perfect Competition

- **A perfectly competitive industry is one in which (1) there are a very large number of buyers and sellers; (2) products are identical; (3) firms can easily enter and exit the industry; and (4) good information is available about prices and product qualities.**
- **The perfect competitor faces a perfectly elastic horizontal demand curve.**
- **The perfect competitor produces up to the point at which marginal revenue equals marginal cost, or the point at which the price per unit equals marginal cost per unit.**

## DECIDING WHEN TO CALL IT A DAY

Given the number of businesses that fail, the prospect of failure is a reality. Each individual competitor knows that someday she or he may have to make the decision to shut down.

### WHEN SHOULD A PERFECT COMPETITOR SHUT DOWN?

Whenever a perfect competitor's price is below its average total cost, it will be incurring economic losses. That does not mean that the firm should necessarily shut down. Rather, the firm's managers must address the decision in the following way:

> ***Whenever a perfect competitor is sustaining losses in the short run, it must compare the cost of producing, while incurring these losses, with the cost of shutting down.***

Another way of looking at this is by looking at total variable costs. The cost of continuing to produce in the short run is given by total variable costs.

> ***Whenever total revenues exceed total variable costs, the perfect competitor should keep production going.***

As long as price exceeds average variable costs, the owner of the firm will be better off continuing to produce. ▸ Example 6-3 A simple example will demonstrate this situation. The price of a product is \$8, and average total costs equal \$9 at an output rate of 100. In this example, average total costs are broken up into average variable costs of \$7 and average fixed costs of \$2. Total revenues, then, equal \$8 × 100, or \$800, and total costs equal \$9 × 100, or \$900. Total losses therefore equal \$100. This does not, however, mean that the firm should shut down. After all, if it does shut down, it still has fixed costs to pay. In this case, because average fixed costs equal \$2 at an output of 100, the fixed costs are \$200. Thus, the firm has losses of \$100 if it continues to produce, but it has losses of \$200 (the fixed costs) if it shuts down. ◂ The logic is straightforward:

> ***As long as the price per unit sold exceeds the average variable cost per unit produced, the firm will be covering at least part of the opportunity cost of the investment in the business—that is, part of its fixed costs.***

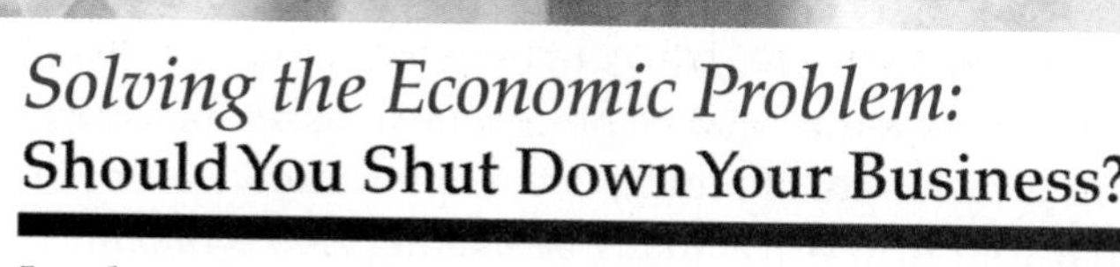

## *Solving the Economic Problem:* Should You Shut Down Your Business?

Just because your average revenues are not covering your average costs, this does not necessarily mean you should shut down your high-end wooden furniture business. The investment you made in new machinery, as outlined at the beginning of the chapter, is a sunk cost. Assuming that you cannot easily resell this specialized equipment, your best bet is to estimate whether you can cover at least part of the investment. You do this by looking at your average variable costs. Do your average revenues exceed your average variable costs? If they do, even though you are not covering average total costs, you are covering variable costs plus something to pay down the investment in the new machines.

If you find out, however, that you are not even covering average variable costs, then you should call a family meeting and argue that your furniture manufacturing plant should close its doors.

## Perfect Competitors Generally Make Zero Economic Profits

In the short run, even in a perfectly competitive industry, an individual firm might make positive economic profits. These profits tend to disappear in the long run. That is to say, in the long run, because of so much competition, those who remain in a perfectly competitive industry end up making zero economic profits. In other words, they are just breaking even.

You might now ask the question, why would a firm continue to produce when it is making no profits whatsoever?

### Distinguishing Between Accounting and Economic Profits—Yet Again

To understand the previous statement, you once again have to make the distinction between accounting profits and economic profits. When a perfectly competitive firm is making *zero economic* profits, it will be making *positive accounting* profits. After all, accounting profits are total revenues minus total *explicit* costs. What is often ignored is the reward offered to investors—the opportunity cost of capital—plus any other implicit costs that do not show up on the books.

**Average Costs Include the Opportunity Cost of All Factors of Production** In economic analysis, all of the average unit costs or average total costs that we consider include the full opportunity cost of capital. Thus, when we say a perfect competitor normally is at the break-even point, economic profits are by definition zero. But accounting profits remain positive—in order to pay investors, for example. ▸ Example 6-4 You and nine friends each put in $10,000 to start manufacturing tennis rackets. At the end of the year, those of you who work in the company have paid yourself a competitive salary, that is, an amount equal to what you could earn elsewhere. In addition, you find that after you subtract all explicit costs from total revenues, you end up earning $10,000. Your rate of return on the total investment of $100,000 is 10 percent a year. Assume that this turns out to be the same rate of return that all other tennis racket manufacturers make. That $10,000, or 10 percent rate of return, is the opportunity cost of invested capital in your industry. Your firm will actually be making zero economic profits. ◀

So, competitive firms (or any firm for that matter) will continue to operate in the long run with zero economic profits because of the following:

> ***Zero economic profits provide for a normal rate of return to the entrepreneur's time and capital, and that is the best one can do in a perfectly competitive market in the long run.***

**Mastering Concepts:** Deciding When to Call It a Day

- **As long as total revenues exceed total variable costs, the firm should stay in business.**
- **Included in any firm's average costs is an implicit rate of return to invested capital.**
- **Otherwise stated, as long as price exceeds average variable cost, the opportunity cost of staying in business will be covered.**
- **Even though perfect competitors tend toward making zero *economic* profits, they make positive accounting profits.**

## THE OTHER END OF THE SPECTRUM—PURE MONOPOLY

While a perfect competitor faces many other competitors, a pure monopoly faces none. The definition of *pure monopoly* is straightforward—a producer of a specific good or service for which there are no close substitutes and, to be sure, no competitors. Therefore, a pure monopolist faces the entire industry's demand curve. Why? Because, by definition, the pure monopolist is the entire industry.

### THERE ARE DIFFERENT TYPES OF MONOPOLIES

For analytical purposes, we often lump all types of monopolies together and just call them monopolies. Nonetheless, there are different types of monopolies:

1. **Natural Monopoly:** In the past, it was thought to be more efficient, or natural, to have just one company providing a widespread good or service, such as electricity. This belief led the government to grant exclusive rights to supposed *natural monopolies*—providers of such things as electric and natural gas utilities, bus services, and cable TV. The large size, or scale, of most natural monopolies seemed to give them **economies of scale**, meaning that they could produce a larger amount at the lowest cost. Today, government is making moves to open up these industries to competition.
2. **Technological Monopoly:** Someone who invents something that allows for the creation of a unique product often has a technological monopoly. Normally, the government provides a **patent** that gives the creator of the technological invention the exclusive right to manufacture, rent, or sell that invention, usually for 20 years. ▶ **Example 6-5** For several decades, Polaroid held a patent on instant developing photos. During that time it enjoyed a technological monopoly (created by the government-granted patent). ◀

**Natural monopoly**
*A monopoly that arises from the peculiar production characteristics in an industry. It usually arises when there are large economies of scale relative to the industry's demand, such that one firm can produce at a lower average cost than can be achieved by multiple firms.*

**Economies of scale**
*Decreases in long-run average costs of producing that result from the large scale of output.*

**Technological monopoly**
*A monopoly that usually arises from an invention that has been patented.*

**Patent**
*Government protection that gives an inventor the exclusive right to make, use, or sell an invention for a specified number of years.*

3. **Government Monopoly:** Governments—federal, state, and local—often create their own monopolies. That is, they decide that only they, and no one else, may lawfully provide a good or service. ▸ **International Example 6-6** In France, for many decades the provision of telephone and electric services has been a government monopoly. Not surprisingly, the relative price of telephone services and electricity has been higher than it would have been with competition. Recently, though, the European Union (EU) has forced France to open up some of its telephone and electricity markets to competition. ◂

**Government monopoly**
*A monopoly created and enforced by the government. In some countries, governments provide postal service and electricity and do not allow others to compete in those services.*

In the real world, there are not many examples of monopolies in manufacturing where there is unfettered entry and exit into industries. Most of the examples of monopolies that you read about in newspapers and magazines have received special privileges from the government. ▸ Example 6-7 You cannot compete with the U.S. Postal Service to deliver first class mail—that would be illegal. You cannot start your own local telephone service. Usually, your city permits one garbage collection company, and you do not have a choice. Most of the time only one cable TV option is available in a particular area. All of these examples exist because government has restricted entry. ◂

## Barriers to Entry

For any amount of monopoly power to continue to exist in the long run, the market must be closed to entry in some way. Either legal means or certain aspects of the industry's technical or cost structure may prevent entry. We will discuss two of the **barriers to entry** that have allowed firms to reap monopoly profits in the long run (even if they are not pure monopolists in the technical sense).

**Barriers to entry**
*Obstacles to competition that prevent others from entering a market.*

**Ownership of Resources Without Close Substitutes** Preventing a newcomer from entering an industry is often difficult. Indeed, some economists contend that no monopoly acting without government support has been able to prevent entry into the industry unless that monopoly has controlled some essential natural resource.

Consider the possibility of one firm owning the entire supply of a raw material input that is essential to the production of a particular commodity. The exclusive ownership of such a vital resource serves as a barrier to entry until an alternative source of the raw material input is found or an alternative technology not requiring the raw material in question is developed. ▸ Example 6-8 The Aluminum Company of America (Alcoa) originally had control of a vital input. Prior to World War II, Alcoa controlled the world's bauxite, the essential raw material in the production of aluminum. Consequently, it could charge monopoly prices for its products. ◂

**Regulations** During much of the 1900s and early 2000s, government regulation of the U.S. economy increased, especially along the dimensions of safety and quality. ▸ Example 6-9 Pharmaceutical quality-control regulations enforced by the Food and Drug Administration may require each pharmaceutical company to install a $200 million computerized testing machine that necessitates elaborate monitoring and maintenance. This large fixed cost can be spread over a larger number of units of output by larger firms than by smaller firms, thereby putting the smaller firms at a competitive disadvantage. Such a regulation also deters entry to the extent that the scale of operation of a potential entrant must be sufficiently large to cover the average fixed costs of the required equipment. ◂

## International Cartels

"Being the only game in town" is desirable because such a monopoly position normally allows the monopolist to charge higher prices and make greater profits. Not surprisingly, manufacturers and sellers have at times attempted to form an organization that acts like a single firm with no competitors. This is called a **cartel.**

**Cartel**
*An arrangement among groups of industrial businesses, often in different countries, to reduce international competition. This reduction in competition permits increased control over price, production, and distribution of goods.*

Cartels represent an attempt by their members to earn higher-than-competitive profits. Cartels set common prices and output quotas for their members. The key to success for a cartel lies in keeping one member from competing against other members by expanding production and thereby lowering price. ▸ International Example 6-10 One of the most successful international cartels ever is the Organization of Petroleum Exporting Countries (OPEC), an association of the world's largest oil-producing countries, including Saudi Arabia, which at times has accounted for a significant percentage of the world's crude oil output. OPEC effectively organized a significant cutback on the production of crude oil in the wake of the so-called Yom Kippur War in the Middle East in 1973. Within one year, the price of crude oil jumped from $2.12 to $7.61 per barrel on the world market. By the early 1980s, the price had risen to over $30. ◂

The most common cartels have been in internationally sold commodities, as you will learn in the following *Global Application.*

### GLOBAL APPLICATION: Those International Cartels Just Keep Trying

***Concepts Applied:* Cartel, Competition**

International cartels often claim that they are not trying to raise prices. They say that their goal is simply to keep markets "stable." The reality is that the cartel members are seeking higher prices and profits. Because demand curves always slope downward (see Chapter 3), the only way to keep prices up is to restrict supply. International cartel members must agree to reduce production to less than it would be otherwise. That is to say, cartel members have to withhold production from the marketplace. Otherwise, the cartel will fail.

#### International Cartels Are Widespread for Commodities

Commodities seem to be the area in which international cartels have functioned most extensively. For example, the International Coffee Organization lasted over 30 years until the United States pulled out. As another example, cocoa has the International Cocoa Association. There is even an ostrich cartel called the Little Karoo Agricultural Cooperative. Outside the commodity area, the diamond cartel is a good example of a very successful one. Between 1986 and 1998, the De Beers diamond cartel controlled world diamond prices. It did so by restricting diamond sales through a marketing subsidiary.

#### Even the U.S. Government Helps International Cartels

The U.S. government has at times sanctioned the equivalent of a cartel. A few years ago, a meeting was held in Washington, D.C. On one side of the table were executives from a dozen global aluminum producers. On the other side were government officials from the European Union, the United States, and four other nations. The two groups ultimately reached an agreement to reduce aluminum production. All reductions were voluntary except for Russia. Russia received the promise of $250 million of U.S. taxpayers' money in exchange for cutting primary aluminum production by 500,000 tons over a two-year period. Nonetheless, U.S. government officials claimed, "The markets are still open."

**For Critical Analysis:**

*How could the U.S. government justify sending so much of U.S. taxpayers' funds to Russia?*

**Mastering Concepts:** The Other End of the Spectrum—Pure Monopoly

- **There are natural, technological, and government monopolies.**
- **Barriers to entry include (1) ownership of a resource without close substitutes and (2) government regulations.**
- **International cartels are usually found in commodities such as coffee or oil. They attempt to restrict production by their members, thereby raising prices.**

## THE MONOPOLIST GETS TO DECIDE WHAT PRICE TO CHARGE

At the beginning of the chapter, you learned that a perfect competitor has no control over price. The perfect competitor accepts the going price: he or she is a *price taker*. By definition, a pure monopolist is in the opposite situation. A pure monopolist is in fact a **price setter**. This is because a monopolist no longer faces a perfectly elastic demand curve as shown in panel (b) of Figure 6-2 on page 117.

**Price setter**
*A firm, other than a perfectly competitive one, that can control the price at which it sells its product. Price setters face downward-sloping demand curves.*

***Even though the monopolist decides what price to charge, consumers get to decide how many units to buy.***

### WHAT KIND OF DEMAND CURVE DOES THE MONOPOLIST FACE?

The definition of a pure monopolist is the sole supplier of one product, good, or service. Consequently, a pure monopolist faces a demand curve that is the industry demand curve for the entire market.

***The monopolist faces the industry demand curve because a monopolist is the* entire *industry.***

**Comparing Two Different Demand Curves** Look at Figure 6-5 on the following page. There you see in panel (a) the demand curve facing the perfect competitor, reproduced from panel (b) in Figure 6-2. Next to it in panel (b) you see the pure monopolist's demand curve. It is labeled $d = D$ because it is the demand curve facing both the individual firm and the industry—they are one and the same.

***For a monopolist, selling more units requires lowering the price.***

If you look even casually at the downward-sloping demand curve in panel (b) of Figure 6-5, you see the results of the law of demand. To sell larger quantities, the monopolist has to offer the product or service at a lower price. But something special happens here. The monopolist cannot simply offer to sell *just* the *last* unit at a slightly lower price than the previous unit sold. After all, if a monopolist tried to sell some units at a lower price than other consumers pay, those getting the lower price would be able to resell those units. Most monopolists do not have the ability to prevent resales of this nature. Consequently,

✦ **Be Aware!** *Every monopolist would love to charge each customer a different price. The trouble is that it's hard to prevent those who pay a low price from reselling to those who would be charged a high price by the monopolist.*

***In order to sell more units, the monopolist has to lower the price on* all *units.***

## Figure 6-5 Demand Curves for the Perfect Competitor and the Monopolist

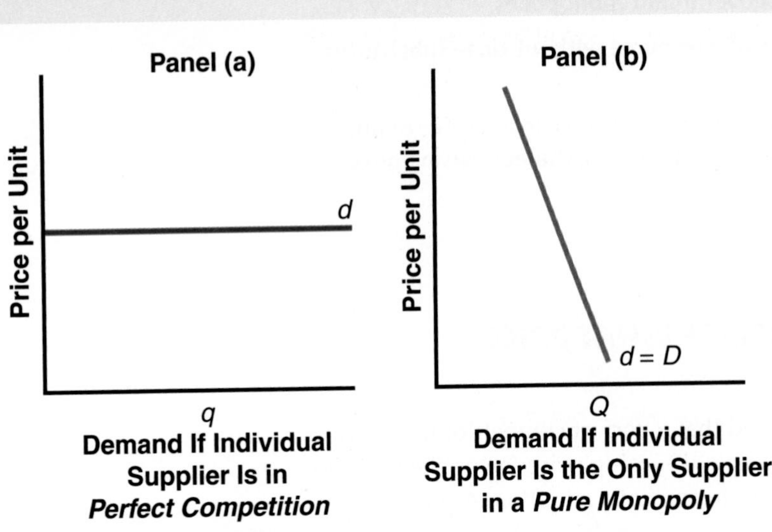


The perfect competitor in panel (a) faces a perfectly elastic demand curve, *d*. The monopolist in panel (b) faces the entire industry demand curve, which slopes downward.

**Marginal Revenue for the Monopolist** Remember that the word *marginal* means "change in."

> ***Marginal revenue equals the change in total revenue due to a one-unit change in the quantity produced and sold.***

Remember from earlier in the chapter that a perfect competitor can sell all she or he wants at the going market price. That means that marginal revenue for a perfect competitor is always equal to the unit price of the product. Not so for a monopolist. Because the monopolist is the industry and faces the industry demand curve, in order to sell more, the monopolist has to lower price not only on the last unit sold, but also on all previous units.

▸ **Example 6-11** Put yourself in the shoes of a monopoly ferryboat owner. You have a government-bestowed franchise, and no one can compete with you. Your ferryboat goes between two islands. If you are charging $1 per crossing, a certain quantity of your services will be demanded. Let's say that you are ferrying 100 people a day each way at that price. If you would like to ferry more individuals, you must lower your price to all individuals—you must move *down* the existing demand curve for ferrying services. To calculate the marginal revenue of your change in price, you must first calculate the total revenues you received at $1 per passenger per crossing and then calculate the total revenues you could receive at, say, 90 cents per passenger per crossing. ◂

We can state a basic fact of life for the pure monopolist:

> ***Because a pure monopolist faces the industry downward-sloping demand curve, it can sell more only by charging less for all units sold. Consequently, for a pure monopolist, marginal revenue is always less than price.***

## Showing Graphically Why Marginal Revenue Is Always Less Than Price for the Monopolist

An essential point is that for the monopolist, marginal revenue is always less than price. To understand why, look at Figure 6-6, which shows a unit increase in output sold due to a reduction in the price of electricity from $P_1$ to $P_2$. After all, the only way that the firm can sell more output, given a downward-sloping demand curve, is for the price to fall. Price $P_2$ is the price received for the last unit. Thus, price $P_2$ times the last unit sold represents the revenue received for the last unit sold. That is equal to the vertical column, which is area A. Area A is one unit wide by $P_2$ high.

But price times the last unit sold is *not* the addition to *total* revenues received from selling that last unit. Why? Because price had to be reduced on all previous units sold $(Q)$ in order to sell the larger quantity $Q + 1$. The reduction in price is represented by the vertical distance from $P_1$ to $P_2$ on the vertical axis. Because the price cut applies to all $Q$ units, the loss in revenues formerly being earned is equal to $Q$ multiplied by the price change. This is shown by area B. Area B is $Q$ units wide by the difference between $P_1$ and $P_2$. We must therefore subtract area B from area A to come up with the *net change* in total revenues due to a one-unit increase in sales.

Clearly, the change in total revenues—that is, marginal revenue—must be less than price because marginal revenue is always the difference between areas A and B in Figure 6-6. For example, if the initial price is \$8 and quantity demanded is 3, to increase quantity to 4 units, it is necessary to decrease price to \$7, not just for the fourth unit, but on all three previous units as well. Thus, at a price of \$7, marginal revenue is \$7 – \$3 = \$4 because there is a \$1-per-unit price reduction on three previous units. Hence, marginal revenue, \$4, is less than price, \$7.

**Figure 6-6 Marginal Revenue: Always Less Than Price**

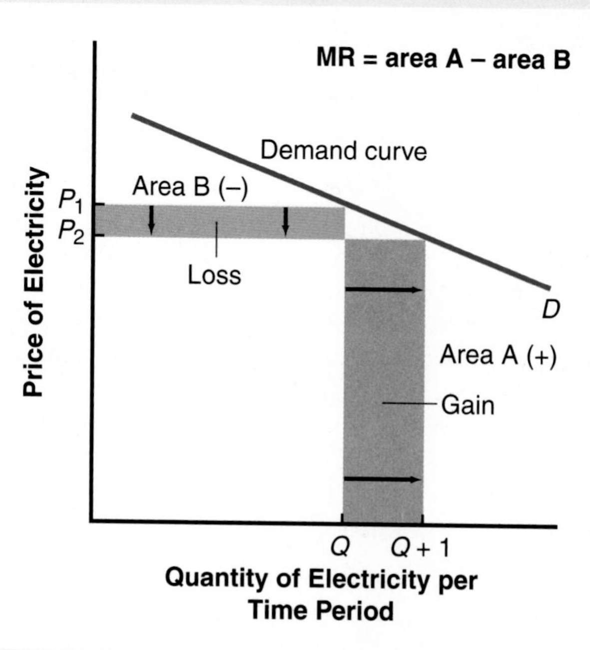


The price received for the last unit sold is equal to $P_2$. The revenues received from selling this last unit are equal to $P_2$ times one unit, or the area of the vertical column. Because a single price is being charged for all units, however, total revenues do not go up by the amount of the area represented by the column. The price had to be reduced on all the previous $Q$ units that were being sold at price $P_1$. Thus, we must subtract area B—the rectangle between $P_1$ and $P_2$ from the origin to $Q$—from area A in order to derive marginal revenue. Marginal revenue is therefore always less than price.

## A Numerical Example—Marginal Revenue for the Monopolist

Let's put together a simplified set of numbers that shows the relationship between the marginal revenue curve and the demand curve of a monopolist. First, we look at Table 6-2. In column 1 you see the output. Column 2 is the price, column 3 is total revenues, and column 4 is marginal revenue.

One thing that you can see right away from Table 6-2 is that after the first unit, the price per unit is always greater than marginal revenue. That means that marginal revenue is less than price.

**Graphing the Marginal Revenue Curve** Look at Figure 6-7. There you see the demand curve, which you can derive from columns 1 and 2 in Table 6-2. The marginal revenue curve is taken from output in column 1 and marginal revenue in column 4, which is simply the difference between total revenues when there is a one-unit change in output. Notice that the marginal revenue curve slopes down, too.

**Mastering Concepts:** The Monopolist Gets to Decide What Price to Charge

- **A monopolist faces the entire industry demand curve.**
- **To increase the quantity sold, a monopolist must lower the price on not only the last unit, but on all previous units.**
- **For a monopolist, marginal revenue is always less than price.**

**Table 6-2 Total Revenues and Marginal Revenue for a Monopolist**

| (1) Output (units) | (2) Price per Unit | (3) Total Revenues (TR) | (4) Marginal Revenue (MR) |
|---|---|---|---|
| 0 | $8.00 | $ .00 | |
| 1 | 7.80 | 7.80 | $7.80 |
| 2 | 7.60 | 15.20 | 7.40 |
| 3 | 7.40 | 22.20 | 7.00 |
| 4 | 7.20 | 28.80 | 6.60 |
| 5 | 7.00 | 35.00 | 6.20 |
| 6 | 6.80 | 40.80 | 5.80 |
| 7 | 6.60 | 46.20 | 5.40 |
| 8 | 6.40 | 51.20 | 5.00 |
| 9 | 6.20 | 55.80 | 4.60 |
| 10 | 6.00 | 60.00 | 4.20 |
| 11 | 5.80 | 63.80 | 3.80 |
| 12 | 5.60 | 67.20 | 3.40 |

**Figure 6-7 Marginal Revenue for a Monopolist**

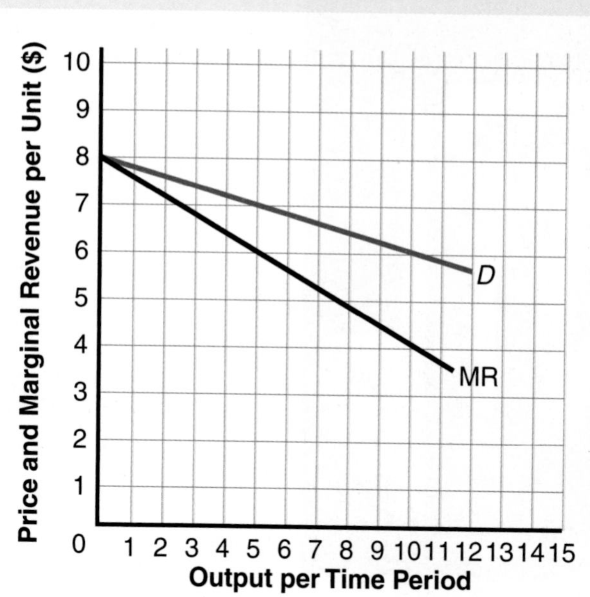


Here you see the monopolist's demand curve, which slopes down throughout its entire range. The marginal revenue curve is always below the downward-sloping demand curve.

## HOW THE MONOPOLIST MAXIMIZES PROFITS

As you saw earlier in this chapter, a perfectly competitive firm does not decide price. Rather, it decides its rate of production. It does this by comparing marginal benefit (which equals marginal revenue, which equals price) to marginal cost.

> ***A perfect competitor always produces at that rate at which marginal revenue (here, price) equals marginal cost.***

The monopolist maximizes profits in the same way. The difference is that:

> ***For the monopolist, marginal revenue is always less than price.***

### HAVING A MONOPOLY DOES NOT GUARANTEE PROFITS

Just because you have a pure monopoly does not mean that you are guaranteed high profits or any profits at all, for that matter.

The term *monopoly* conjures up the notion of a greedy firm ripping off the public and making exorbitant profits. In many monopoly situations, though, that is not the case. There may be *no* price-output combination at which you, as a monopolist, can sell your product and cover average total costs. In other words, the price you are able to charge may not be high enough to justify staying in existence, even though you have a monopoly. ▸ **Example 6-12** A clear government monopoly is New York City's massive public transit system. Just because New York City has a monopoly, though, does not mean that it makes profits. Indeed, for every mass transit passenger who boards a bus or a subway in New York City, the city loses $2. Moreover, New York City's mass transit system was once private, and it operated profitably at a fare of less than $1 expressed in today's dollars. ◂

*New York City subway commuters often endure a cramped ride to their various destinations. The municipal government has a monopoly in providing subway services. Although we often associate a monopoly with high profits, such is not the case for this monopolist. Indeed, in spite of the millions of tickets sold, the city still incurs losses every year. What might cause such losses?*

## Why Monopolies Are Considered "Bad"

Competition is "good" and monopoly is "bad." This is the impression you get from casually reading the press. Actually, there is an economic justification for such opinions.

Competition leads to lower prices. That is what competition is all about. Monopoly, in contrast, implies no competition. The result, then, is that monopolists tend to charge higher prices than competitors would charge, if they existed. To understand this fact of life, consider the following *Global Application*.

### GLOBAL APPLICATION: Mexico Keeps Those Phone Rates High

***Concept Applied:* Monopoly**

The phone company in Mexico is called Telmex. Until a decade ago, it was a state-owned company. Even though the government claimed that it would end Telmex's monopoly, it remains a monopoly to this day.

#### How to Keep Your Telephone Monopoly

The government has allowed Telmex to prevent potential competitors in the Mexican phone market from connecting through its switching equipment. The result has been extremely high connection charges and virtually no new connections. That's one way to keep a monopoly without letting everyone know that you still have one.

#### A Monopoly Leads to High Prices

Mexico has only 10 telephones per 100 inhabitants compared to 111 in the United States. Even Poland has twice as many of telephones per 100 inhabitants as Mexico. The phone service in Mexico is, to say the least, poor. Most outrageous, though, are the long-distance prices charged to Mexican telephone customers. In the United States, five phone calls of four minutes each to Britain would cost about $5.40. In Mexico those same calls would cost over $25!

**For Critical Analysis:**

*Who benefits from the Mexican telephone monopoly?*

Economists generally consider monopolies undesirable not only because they keep prices high, but also because they lead to an inefficient use of society's resources. After all, in perfect competition, the price you pay is equal to the marginal cost that the producer incurs. We saw that for a monopoly, the price always exceeds marginal cost. That means that you are paying more than the value of the resources that society is giving up to produce the product that the monopoly provides.

**Mastering Concepts:** How the Monopolist Maximizes Profits

- **While a perfect competitor produces at the point at which price equals marginal cost, the monopolist produces at the point at which marginal revenue (which is less than price) is equal to marginal cost.**
- **If a monopolist cannot find the price-output combination that allows it to cover average total costs, it will not make profits or even stay in business.**

## SUMMING IT ALL UP

- Market structure refers to the number, size, and potential interactions among firms in a particular industry.
- A perfectly competitive industry is one in which (1) there are a very large number of buyers and sellers; (2) products are substantially identical; (3) firms can easily enter and exit the industry; and (4) good information is available about prices and product qualities.
- The perfect competitor faces a perfectly elastic horizontal demand curve.
- The perfect competitor produces up to the point at which marginal revenue equals marginal cost, or the point at which the price per unit equals marginal cost per unit.
- Even though perfect competitors tend toward making zero *economic* profits, they make positive accounting profits.
- Barriers to entry include (1) ownership of a resource without close substitutes and (2) government regulations.
- A monopolist faces the entire industry demand curve.
- To increase the quantity sold, a monopolist must lower the price on not only the last unit, but on all previous units.
- For a monopolist, marginal revenue is always less than price.
- While a perfect competitor produces at the point at which price equals marginal cost, the monopolist produces at the point at which marginal revenue (which is less than price) is equal to marginal cost.

## KEY TERMS AND CONCEPTS

barriers to entry **123**
cartel **124**
duopoly **114**
economies of scale **122**
government monopoly **123**
homogeneous **115**
imperfect competition **114**
marginal benefit **117**
marginal revenue **117**
market structure **114**
monopolistic competition **114**
natural monopoly **122**
oligopoly **114**
patent **122**
perfect competition **114**
price setter **125**
price taker **115**
pure monopoly **114**
technological monopoly **122**

## MASTERING ECONOMIC CONCEPTS
## Questions and Problems

**6-1.** Is each of the following likely to be an example of perfect competition, monopoly, or neither?

a. soybean production
b. the stock market
c. natural gas suppliers
d. airline industry

**6-2.** Determine whether each of the following statements describes a perfectly competitive market.

a. There are a large number of buyers and sellers.
b. Each producer sells a unique product or service.
c. There are large barriers to entry or exit.
d. Each firm is small in relation to the market.

**6-3.** Assume that wheat farming is a perfectly competitive industry and the market price of wheat is $3.30 per bushel. For a wheat farmer, what would be the marginal revenue of the first bushel sold? What would be the marginal revenue of the second bushel sold? What would be the marginal revenue of the 50th bushel sold? If this farmer decided to sell wheat at a price of $4.00 per bushel, what would happen to the number of bushels sold?

**6-4.** Assume that you operate a firm in a perfectly competitive industry and the market price for the good you are selling is $10. Using the information in the table below, compute total revenue, marginal revenue, and marginal cost. Which quantity of output would produce the highest amount of profit?

| Quantity | Total Revenue | Total Cost | Marginal Revenue | Marginal Cost |
|---|---|---|---|---|
| 1 | $___ | $ 8 | $___ | $___ |
| 2 | ___ | 14 | ___ | ___ |
| 3 | ___ | 18 | ___ | ___ |
| 4 | ___ | 24 | ___ | ___ |
| 5 | ___ | 32 | ___ | ___ |
| 6 | ___ | 42 | ___ | ___ |
| 7 | ___ | 54 | ___ | ___ |
| 8 | ___ | 68 | ___ | ___ |
| 9 | ___ | 84 | ___ | |

**6-5.** Assume that Earle runs a hot dog stand in a perfectly competitive environment. If the equilibrium price for hot dogs is $1.50, how many hot dogs should he produce in order to maximize profits? What would his total profits equal at this quantity of output? (See numbers below.)

| Quantity | TR | TC | MR | MC | Profit |
|---|---|---|---|---|---|
| 20 | $___ | $10.00 | $___ | $___ | $___ |
| 21 | ___ | 10.40 | ___ | ___ | ___ |
| 22 | ___ | 11.00 | ___ | ___ | ___ |
| 23 | ___ | 11.90 | ___ | ___ | ___ |
| 24 | ___ | 13.20 | ___ | ___ | ___ |
| 25 | ___ | 15.80 | | | ___ |

**6-6.** Use the graph below to determine total revenues and profits for this perfectly competitive firm, assuming that the firm operates at the profit-maximizing level of output.

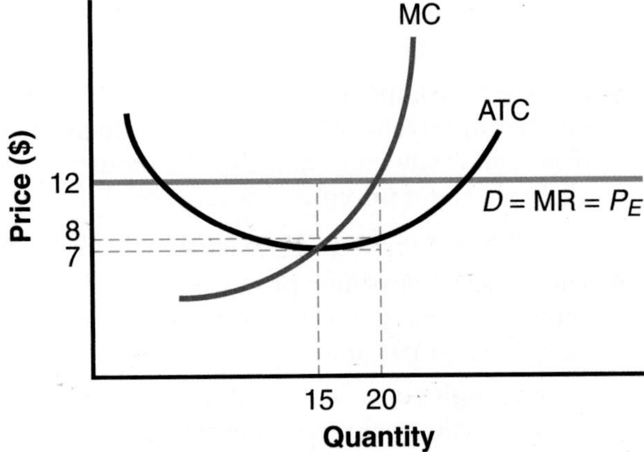


**6-7.** Based on the following graph, which quantity would produce the highest level of profits? What price would this firm charge to generate these profits?

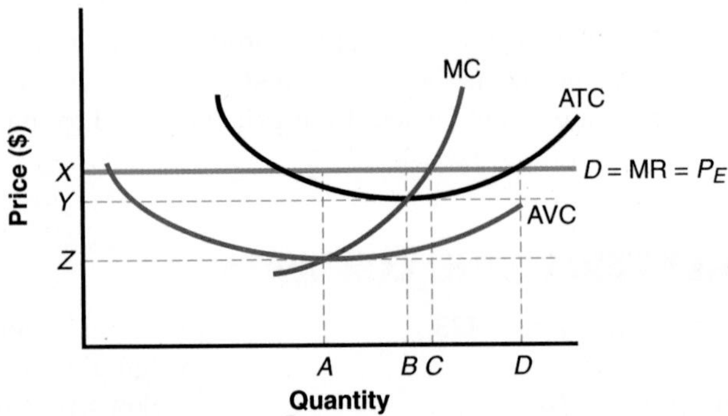


**6-8.** Use the following graph to determine the price and quantity this firm must use to maximize its profits. What profit or loss would result?

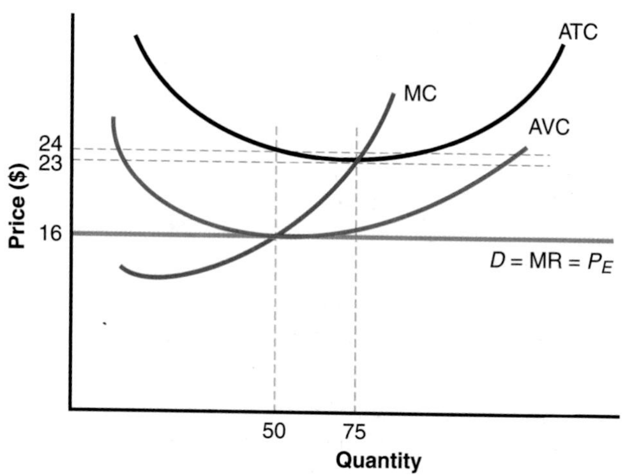


**6-9.** Assume that you run a music store and your total fixed costs are $2,000 per week. If your total variable costs are $3,500 per week and your revenues are $3,300 per week, should you shut down immediately or remain in business for the short run? Why?

**6-10.** If marginal revenues are greater than marginal costs at the current quantity, should a firm increase or decrease production? Why?

**6-11.** Determine whether each of the following statements is true or false. If a statement is false, explain why.

a. A monopolistic firm faces a demand curve that is identical to the industry demand curve.
b. For a monopolistic firm, marginal revenue will always be greater than price.
c. A perfectly competitive firm faces a demand curve that is less elastic than that of a monopolistic firm.

**6-12.** Classify each of the following monopolies by determining what type or types of barriers to entry are likely to exist for each.

a. water and sewer service
b. Viagra production
c. diamond production

**6-13.** Use the following demand schedule for cable services to compute total revenue and marginal revenue at each level of output.

| Quantity | Price | TR | MR |
|---|---|---|---|
| 100 | $45 | $____ | |
| | | | $____ |
| 101 | 44 | ____ | |
| | | | ____ |
| 102 | 43 | ____ | |
| | | | ____ |
| 103 | 42 | ____ | |
| | | | ____ |
| 104 | 41 | ____ | |
| | | | ____ |
| 105 | 40 | ____ | |

**6-14.** Use the following table to compute total revenue, marginal revenue, and marginal cost at each level of output. Which level of output would generate the highest profit level? What would the maximum profit be?

| Quantity | Price | TR | TC | MR | MC | Total Profit |
|---|---|---|---|---|---|---|
| 10 | $20 | $____ | $150 | | | $____ |
| | | | | $____ | $____ | |
| 11 | 19 | ____ | 156 | | | ____ |
| | | | | ____ | ____ | |
| 12 | 18 | ____ | 160 | | | ____ |
| | | | | ____ | ____ | |
| 13 | 17 | ____ | 166 | | | ____ |
| | | | | ____ | ____ | |
| 14 | 16 | ____ | 174 | | | ____ |
| | | | | ____ | ____ | |
| 15 | 15 | ____ | 184 | | | ____ |

**6-15.** Based on the following table including marginal revenue and marginal cost only, determine the profit-maximizing level of output for this firm and explain why.

| Quantity | MR | MC |
|---|---|---|
| A | $35 | $24 |
| B | 33 | 26 |
| C | 31 | 28 |
| D | 29 | 30 |
| E | 27 | 32 |

**6-16.** Does the information in the table below depict a firm that will be able to generate a profit? Why? Does this table depict a perfectly competitive firm or a monopolistic firm? Why?

| Quantity | TR | TC |
|---|---|---|
| 50 | $1,150 | $900 |
| 51 | 1,173 | 915 |
| 52 | 1,196 | 935 |
| 53 | 1,219 | 960 |
| 54 | 1,242 | 990 |
| 55 | 1,265 | 1,025 |

**6-17.** In the long run in a perfectly competitive market would economists expect each firm to generate an economic profit, an economic loss, or an economic breakeven? Is this result considered good, bad, or satisfactory from the firm's perspective? Why?

**6-18.** Based on the graph for a perfectly competitive industry on page 134, what price will each firm in this industry receive? Will the marginal revenue of each unit sold be more than this price, less than this price, or neither?

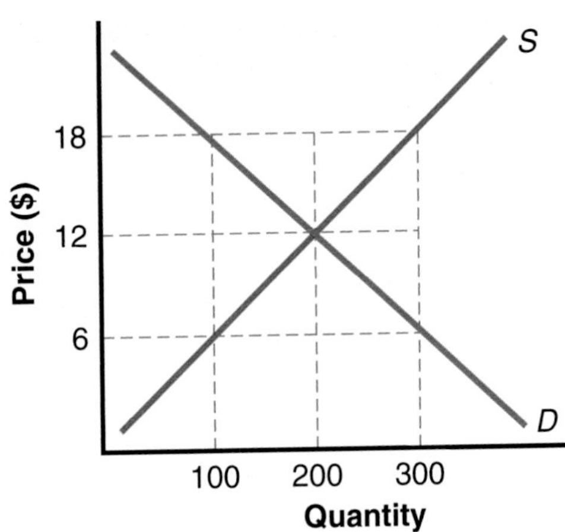


**6-19.** Assume that Danny owns a company providing lawn care services in a perfectly competitive industry. On average, he mows six lawns each day, charges $40 per lawn, and works six days a week. Calculate his weekly total revenue, average revenue, and marginal revenue. Explain the relationship between your results for average revenue and marginal revenue.

**6-20.** If George operates the perfectly competitive firm depicted in the next column, what quantity should he elect to produce in order to maximize profits if the market price for his good is $25? At this quantity, what will his profit or loss equal?

| Quantity | Total Cost |
|---|---|
| 5 | $200 |
| 6 | 210 |
| 7 | 230 |
| 8 | 260 |
| 9 | 300 |

**6-21.** The graph below depicts the operations of a perfectly competitive firm at long-run equilibrium. If a technological advance allowed firms to decrease the costs that they face, in the short run would each of these firms generate an economic profit, loss, or breakeven? Based on this result, in the long run would new firms be likely to enter this industry, would existing firms be likely to exit, or neither?

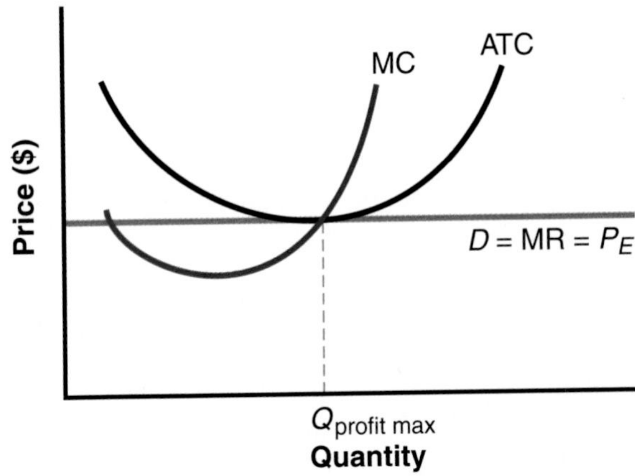


## THINKING CRITICALLY

**6-1.** Assume that you are a sugar farmer and you employ 10 laborers. For the purposes of this problem, mortgage and loan payments of $10,000 per month are your only fixed costs, and salaries of $11,000 per month are your only variable costs. If your monthly revenues are $17,000, are you better off remaining in business in the short run or discontinuing farming operations immediately? From a long-run perspective, assuming that you have a chance to sell your property, are you better off remaining in business or selling your property and discontinuing operations? If other farmers faced the same situation, what would be the impact of your decision as a group on the price of sugar in the area?

**6-2.** Although cocaine production is illegal throughout much of the world, it is an industry that functions like many other industries from an economic perspective. The Cali cartel that operated in Colombia organized producers in order to increase profits for the industry through collusion. Obviously, this cartel would have preferred to increase price, but from an economic perspective would you assume that they preferred to increase or decrease the quantity of cocaine produced? Why? How would the development of other cocaine producers and traffickers affect the industry with respect to the price and quantity of cocaine sold? Based on what you have read or seen, how would existing producers respond to additional competition in this market?

**6-3.** Many people assume that Ticketmaster produces tickets to concerts and sporting events, but Ticketmaster itself does not actually produce concerts or sporting events. Rather it provides a service. What service does it provide? How would the value of Ticketmaster's service to you change if you lived 120 miles from the site of the next event featuring your favorite band or sports team? Ticketmaster maintains exclusive agreements with large arenas in most cities. How do these agreements fit into the characteristics of a monopolistic industry? Based on your experience, does the "convenience charge" for Ticketmaster's service lead you to believe that the company is a monopoly?

## LOGGING ON

1. For a discussion of the economics of spam, go to http://www.eprivacygroup.com/article/articlestatic/58/1/6.
2. To learn more about competition in the market for bank automated-teller-machine services, go to http://www.cbo.gov and click on "Publications." Next, click on "Financial Institutions," and then click on "Competition in ATM Markets: Are ATMs Money Machines?"
3. For more information about how the U.S. government awards patents, go to http://www.uspto.gov/, and click on "Patents."
4. To see how OPEC's share of sales in the world oil market has fluctuated over the years, go to http://www.wtrg.com/opecshare.html.

## USING THE INTERNET FOR ECONOMIC ANALYSIS

**Trying to Control Diamond Prices** This chapter emphasizes that setting monopoly prices requires a firm or cartel to control virtually all production of a good or service. This application relates the concepts of cartels and monopoly pricing to the market for primary diamonds.

**Title:** Sorting and Distributing Diamonds—From the Mine to the Diamond Dealer

**Navigation:** Go to the American Museum of Natural History's discussion of the mechanism of diamond distribution at http://www.amnh.org/exhibitions/diamonds/sorting.html.

**Application** Read the article, and answer the following questions.

1. Based on what you learned in this chapter, how do you suppose that the Central Selling Organization for distribution of primary diamonds could "stabilize" diamond prices?
2. The American Museum of Natural History is a little behind the times, because in the early 2000s the De Beers diamond firm gave up trying to control primary diamond prices through the Central Selling Organization. How do suppose that major diamond discoveries in Russia and other nations in the 1980s and 1990s helped contribute to De Beers's decision to abandon its diamond cartel?

## MEDIA RESOURCE LIST

The following media resources are available with this chapter:

- Load your CD-ROM to listen to the audio introduction to this chapter.
- Load your CD-ROM to access a Graph Animation of Figure 6-2, *The Demand Curve Facing the Perfect Competitor.*
- Load your CD-ROM to view the video on the *Short-Run Shutdown Price.*
- Load your CD-ROM to view the video on the *Meaning of Making Zero Economic Profits.*
- Load your CD-ROM to view the video on *Barriers to Entry.*
- Test your knowledge of chapter concepts with a quiz at www.miller-ume.com.
- Link to Web resources related to the text coverage at www.miller-ume.com.

## HOMEWORK SET

Go to the end of this book to find the Homework Problems for this chapter.

# CHAPTER 7

# In Between the Extremes: Imperfect Competition

## *Facing an Economic Problem:* How to Fill Those Empty Airplane Seats?

Airline companies face an interesting economic problem. When their airplanes take off with empty seats, the airlines have given up the opportunity not only to earn additional revenues, but also probably to make higher profits (or, for the last few years, reduce their losses). An airline incurs high fixed costs to get a plane airborne. Whether the airplane is carrying 200 passengers or 201 passengers does not change the number of flight attendants on board and certainly not the number of people running the plane in the cockpit. In addition, the cost of the landing slot at the airport remains the same whether or not that extra, or marginal, passenger is on board.

So, how to fill those empty seats? To answer this economic problem, you need to learn about situations of imperfect competition. In the case of airlines, there are certainly fewer competitors than in perfect competition. Also, no one single airline company dominates the industry.

***Refer to the back of this chapter for a complete listing of multimedia learning materials available on the CD-ROM and the Web site.***

### Learning Objectives:

After reading this chapter, you should be able to:

- **List the five conditions that must be met for the existence of monopolistic competition.**
- **Describe the methods that firms can use to signal to consumers that their products are of high quality.**
- **List the four characteristics of oligopoly.**
- **Explain opportunistic behavior and why most firms (and consumers) do not engage in it consistently.**
- **Describe one form of tacit collusion among firms in an oligopolistic industry.**

## MONOPOLISTIC COMPETITION: COMPETITION AMONG THE MANY

A large number of industries cannot be described as perfectly competitive, yet they cannot be described as pure monopolies either. A combination of consumers' desires for variety and competition among producers has led to similar, but at least slightly differentiated products in the marketplace. Differentiated goods or services are quite similar, but have variations in specific qualities or attributes that some consumers believe make them more valuable than other goods or services of the same kind. ▸ Example 7-1 Take retail sales. Think about the number of choices you have when you want to purchase a specific new MP3 player. You can go to your local drugstore; visit a large membership retail outlet, such as Costco; buy from literally thousands of firms on the Internet; visit a specialty electronic store in your mall; and so on. Retail sales is an industry with a tremendous amount of competitors. Each, though, offers a different shopping experience—a differentiated service as it were. ◂

A situation involving competition among many producers with differentiated products or services has been described as *monopolistic competition*, which is the subject of the first part of this chapter. In the second part of this chapter, we look at competition when there are only a few firms in an industry. This market structure is called *oligopoly* and was introduced at the beginning of Chapter 6 when we looked at the spectrum of market structures.

### CHARACTERISTICS OF MONOPOLISTIC COMPETITION

**Monopolistic competition**
*A market situation in which a large number of sellers offer similar but slightly different products and in which each has some control over price.*

The most common form of market structure in the United States is **monopolistic competition,** in which a large number of sellers offer similar, but slightly different products. ▸ Example 7-2 The most obvious examples of monopolistically competitive industries are those that produce brand-name items such as toothpaste, cosmetics, and designer clothes. ◂

For an industry to be monopolistically competitive, five conditions must be met:

1. **Numerous Sellers:** No single seller or small group dominates the market.
2. **Relatively Easy Entry:** Entry into the market is easier than in a monopoly or in an industry with just a few dominant firms.
3. **Differentiated Products:** Each supplier sells a slightly different product to attract customers.
4. **Nonprice Competition:** Businesses compete, at least in part, by using product differentiation and by advertising.
5. **Some Control over Price:** By building a loyal customer base through product differentiation, each firm has some control over the price it charges. ▸ International Example 7-3 Very famous wines from France, Australia, New Zealand, and Italy have many competitors. Nonetheless, there are clients who remain loyal to their preferred high-end winemaker. Consequently, Chateau Petrus in the Bordeaux region of France, for example, could raise prices considerably in any given year and still sell all of its output. ◂

### COMPARING DEMAND CURVES FOR PERFECT COMPETITORS, PURE MONOPOLISTS, AND MONOPOLISTICALLY COMPETITIVE FIRMS

Remember from Chapter 6 that the demand curve facing a perfect competitor is perfectly elastic. Remember further that the demand curve facing a pure monopolist is the entire industry's demand curve, so it is downward sloping.

**The Monopolistically Competitor's Demand Curve Is Somewhere in Between** What about the demand curve facing a firm in a monopolistically competitive industry? Well, right away you know that since there are fewer competitors than in perfect competition, this firm's demand curve will *not* be perfectly elastic. You also know that there are still quite a few competitors within a monopolistically competitive industry so the firm's demand curve will *not* be the entire industry's demand curve. Hence, it is somewhere in between the two extremes.

**Graphing the Demand Curves** Look at Figure 7-1. There you see the perfect competitor's demand curve labeled $d_1$, and it is perfectly elastic. The pure monopolist's demand curve is the industry's demand curve. It is labeled *D*. The firm within a monopolistically competitive industry has the demand curve labeled $d_2$. Assume that the market price for a perfect competitor is $5 per unit. The perfect competitor's demand curve, $d_1$, is perfectly elastic at that price. The pure monopolist's demand curve, *D*, is much less elastic at price $5. At that same price, the monopolistically competitive firm faces demand curve $d_2$, which is somewhere in between.

## Times Are Tough: Zero Economic Profits in the Long Run

In Chapter 6, we discovered that one of the key characteristics of a perfectly competitive industry is that most of the players end up making zero *economic profits* in the long run. In other words, they end up making a normal rate of return on their investment even though they show this as *positive accounting profits*. In contrast, the benefit of being a pure monopoly is, of course, the possibility of making monopoly profits, even in the long run (note that the lack of competition in a monopoly does not guarantee such profits, but at least they are possible).

In a monopolistically competitive industry, you would think that at least a little bit of monopoly profits would be possible. Although that may be true in the short run, it is not true in the long run.

**Figure 7-1 Comparing Demand Curves for Three Types of Industry Structures**

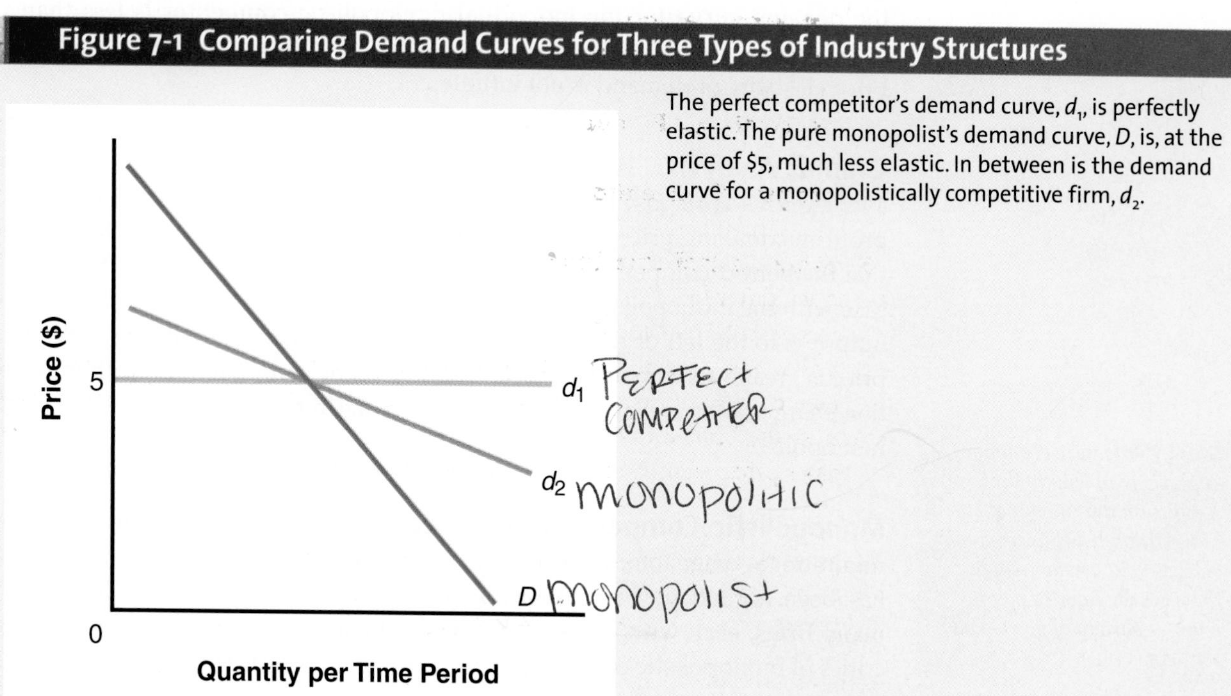


The perfect competitor's demand curve, $d_1$, is perfectly elastic. The pure monopolist's demand curve, *D*, is, at the price of $5, much less elastic. In between is the demand curve for a monopolistically competitive firm, $d_2$.

**The Long Run: Zero Economic Profits** The long run is where the similarity between perfect competition and monopolistic competition becomes most obvious.

> ***In the long run, in a monopolistically competitive industry, because so many firms produce substitutes for the product in question, any economic profits will disappear through competition.***

Economic profits will be reduced to zero either through entry of new firms seeing a chance to make a higher rate of return than elsewhere or by changes in product quality and advertising outlays by existing firms in the industry, as they imitate profitable products.

The flip side is that although economic losses are possible in the short run, they will disappear in the long run because the firms that suffer them will leave the industry. These firms will go into another business where the expected rate of return is at least normal.

> ***In the long run, the price that the monopolistically competitive firm can charge will just equal its average total cost. It will be making a normal rate of return and zero economic profits.***

**A Word of Warning** You should be aware of something about the analysis just presented: it is an idealized, long-run equilibrium situation for each firm in the industry. We live in a dynamic world in which we may temporarily observe positive or negative profits. All we are saying is that if this model is correct, the rate of return will *tend toward* normal—economic profits will *tend toward* zero.

**Comparing Perfect Competition with Monopolistic Competition** If both the monopolistic competitor and the perfect competitor make zero economic profits in the long run, how are they different? The answer lies in the fact that the demand curve for the individual perfect competitor is perfectly elastic, whereas the demand curve for the individual monopolistic competitor is less than perfectly elastic. Hence, the monopolistic competitor has some control over price. Price elasticity of demand is not infinite.

**Graphic Analysis** We see the two situations in Figure 7-2. Both panels show average total costs just touching the respective demand curves at the particular profit-maximizing price at which the firm is selling the product. Notice, however, that the perfect competitor's average total costs are at a minimum. This is not the case with the monopolistic competitor. The profit-maximizing equilibrium rate of output is to the left of the minimum point on the average total cost curve where price is greater than marginal cost. A monopolistic competitor at profit maximization charges a price that exceeds marginal cost. (In this respect, it is similar to the monopolist.)

> ✦ **Note!** *While pure economic analysis may lead to the conclusion that monopolistic competition leads to economic waste, such "waste" may be the price we have to pay for a larger variety of goods and services.*

**Monopolistic Competition May Lead to Waste** Consequently, because minimum average total costs are not achieved and price exceeds marginal cost, it has been argued that monopolistic competition involves waste. There are too many firms, each with excess capacity, producing too little output. According to critics of monopolistic competition, society's resources are being wasted.

Animated

**Figure 7-2 Comparison of the Perfect Competitor with the Monopolistic Competitor**

In panel (a), the perfectly competitive firm has zero economic profits in the long run. The price is equal to marginal cost, and the price is $P_1$. The firm's demand curve just touches the minimum point on its average total cost curve. The monopolistically competitive firm in panel (b) also earns zero economic profits in the long run. Because its price is greater than marginal cost, however, the monopolistically competitive firm does not find itself at the minimum point on its ATC curve. It is operating at a rate of output to the left of the minimum point on the ATC curve.

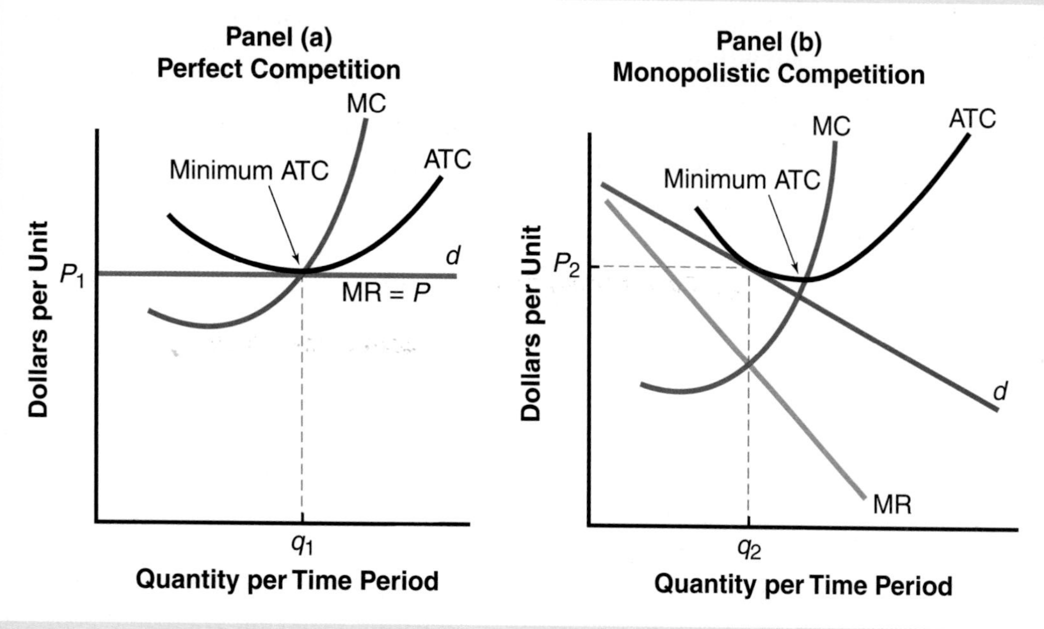


**Mastering Concepts:** Monopolistic Competition: Competition Among the Many

- **In a monopolistically competitive industry, there are (1) numerous sellers, (2) relatively easy entry, (3) differentiated products, (4) nonprice competition, and (5) some control by firms over price.**
- **Even though monopolistically competitive firms face downward-sloping demand curves, they ultimately earn zero economic profits in the long run because of competition.**
- **In the long run, the prices charged by monopolistically competitive firms will just equal their average total costs.**

## ADVERTISING COMES TO THE FORE

Advertising was not part of our discussion of perfect competition in Chapter 6. Why not? Because the individual perfect competitor took the going market price as given and could sell all she or he wanted at that price. Thus, there was no reason to advertise. In contrast, once a firm faces a downward-sloping demand curve, there may be a good business reason to advertise.

## Sales Promotion and Advertising

Monopolistic competition differs from perfect competition in that no individual firm in a perfectly competitive market will advertise. A perfectly competitive firm, by definition, can sell all that it wants to sell at the going market price anyway. Why, then, would it spend even one penny on advertising? Furthermore, by definition, the perfect competitor is selling a product that is identical to the product that all other firms in the industry are selling. Any advertisement that induces consumers to buy more of that product will, in effect, be helping all the competitors, too. Therefore, an individual perfect competitor cannot be expected to incur any advertising costs.

But, because the monopolistic competitor has at least *some* monopoly power, advertising may result in increased profits.

> ***Advertising is used to increase demand and to differentiate one's product.***

How much advertising should be undertaken? It should be carried to the point at which the additional revenue resulting from one more dollar of advertising just equals one dollar.

## Advertising as Signaling Behavior

**Signal**
*A compact method of conveying to economic decision makers information needed to make decisions. A true signal not only conveys information but also provides the incentive to react appropriately. Economic profits and economic losses are such signals.*

**Signaling behavior**
*Behavior that either implicitly or explicitly gives a signal to a third party about the intentions of the entity doing the signaling. Companies that invest large amounts in advertising give signals to consumers that the product and the company will be around for a long time.*

**Brand name**
*A word, picture, or logo on a product that helps consumers distinguish it from similar products. Brand names are used to create a reputation for products and services.*

**Trademark**
*A distinctive mark or motto that a manufacturer stamps, prints, or otherwise affixes to the goods it produces so that they may be identified on the market and their origins made known. Once a trademark is established, the owner is entitled to its exclusive use.*

**Signals** are compact actions that convey information. High profits in an industry are signals that resources should flow into that industry. Losses in an industry are signals that resources should flow out of it.

**Individual Companies Engage in Signaling Behavior** Individual companies can explicitly engage in **signaling behavior**. They do this by establishing a **brand name** or **trademark** and then promoting it heavily. This is a signal to prospective consumers that the company plans to stay in business. ▸ Example 7-4 Before the modern age of advertising, U.S. banks needed a way to signal their financial soundness. Were they going to stay in business, or were they fly-by-night fraudulent operations? To show that they were not the latter, financially strong banks chose to construct bank buildings that were large, imposing, and usually made out of marble or granite. The heavy, expensive stone communicated permanence. The effect was to give the bank's customers confidence that they were *not* doing business with an unreliable operation. ◂

**Advertising Is Expensive** Much advertising requires relatively large expenditures to have any effect. Look at Figure 7-3. There you see estimated 2004 advertising expenditures in the United States.

> ***There is only one reason a monopolistically competitive firm will incur large outlays for advertising—as an attempt to make more profits in the short run.***

That means that at any point in time, the firm that advertises believes that by doing so it will increase revenues not only to pay for the additional sales promotion, but also to add to the bottom line. Companies invest millions in advertising their brand names because they want to establish themselves in a particular market. In particular, they want to obtain *repeat* customers. No business can live on new customers alone. ▸ Example 7-5 Dell Inc. advertises its brand name heavily. Its ads appear on television, in magazines, and in most newspapers. It incurs substantial costs—to the tune of $200 million per year—for its heavy adver-

**Figure 7-3 U.S. Advertising Expenditures—All Media***

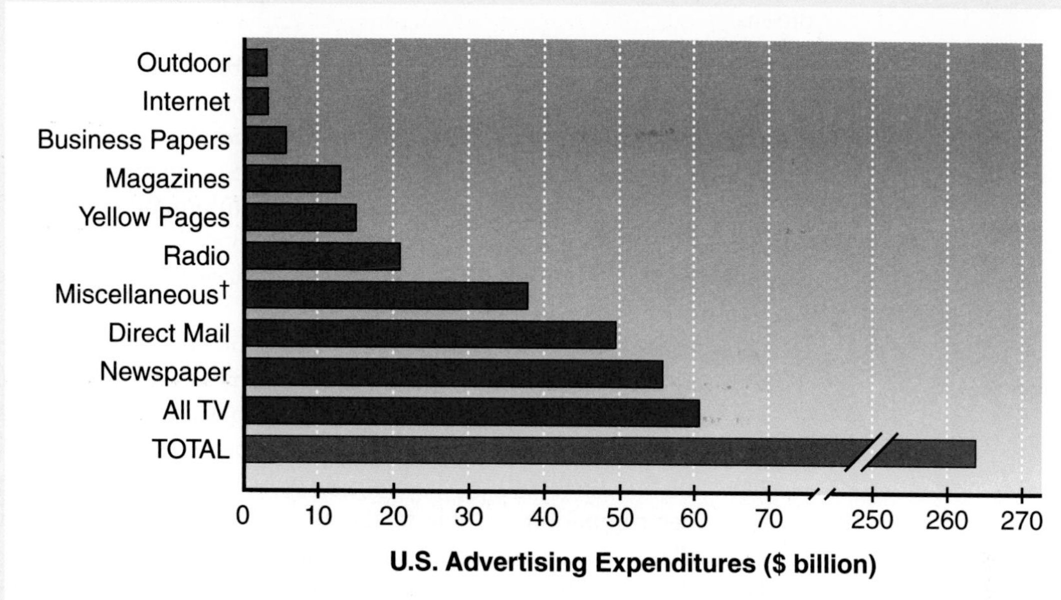


*2004 estimates from McCann-Erickson, Inc.
†Includes weeklies, shoppers, penny savers, and cinema advertising.

tising campaigns. The only way Dell can recoup those costs is by selling many Dell computers over a long period. Thus, heavy advertising of its brand name is a signal to personal computer buyers that Dell is interested in each customer's *repeat* business. ◂

We also see lots of advertising in another market structure, one that involves competition among only a few large firms. We study it next.

**Mastering Concepts:** Advertising Comes to the Fore

- **While it makes no sense to advertise in a perfectly competitive industry, in a less-than-perfectly competitive industry, advertising and sales promotion are used to increase demand and to differentiate products.**
- **Companies engage in signaling behavior to let customers know that they have high-quality products. They establish brand names or trademarks to do so.**

## OLIGOPOLY—COMPETITION AMONG THE FEW

There is another market structure that we have yet to discuss in detail, and it is an important one indeed. In this structure, a few large firms dominate an entire industry. They are not competitive in the sense that we have used the term; they are not even monopolistically competitive. And because there are several of them, a pure monopoly does not exist.

We call such a situation an **oligopoly**, which is an industry structure consisting of a small number of *inter*dependent sellers. Each firm in the industry knows that other firms will react to its changes in prices, quantities, and qualities. An oligopoly market structure can exist for either a homogeneous or a differentiated product.

**Oligopoly**
*A market structure in which the industry has a few sellers that supply a large percentage of the total output of the industry. Oligopolists have some control over price.*

## Characteristics of Oligopolistic Industry Structure

For a market structure to be labeled an oligopoly, it must meet the following conditions:

1. **Few Sellers:** Several large firms are responsible for 60 to 80 percent of the market.
2. **Identical or Slightly Different Products:** The goods and services provided by oligopolists are very similar. ▸ Example 7-6 The most obvious examples here are airline travel, domestically produced automobiles, and kitchen appliances. Within each industry, the product or service is very similar. ◂
3. **Nonprice Competition:** Advertising emphasizes minor differences and attempts to build customer loyalty.
4. **Interdependence:** Any change in competitive practices on the part of one firm will cause a reaction on the part of other firms in the oligopolistic industry. ▸ Example 7-7 Today, a majority of textbooks are sold by only three publishing firms—McGraw-Hill, Pearson (which owns Addison-Wesley, the publisher of this textbook), and Thomson (which owns South-Western, which publishes competitors to this textbook). The interdependence among these three oligopolists is often quite apparent. A while back, one firm—McGraw-Hill—started publishing new editions of important textbooks in the summer, thereby getting lots of new business for these new editions in the fall. Gradually, the other two firms started publishing their revisions of important titles in the summer, too. Then, a few titles started to be published in the spring, in order to pick up business in the summer and have larger sales in the fall. Gradually, the other publishers followed suit. Now, many books are brought out on January 2 with the following year's copyright! The oligopolistic world of textbook publishing is indeed interdependent. ◂

## Looking at Oligopoly via Industry Concentration

**Industry concentration ratio**
*The percentage of all sales contributed by the leading four firms in an industry; sometimes called the concentration ratio.*

There is no one way to determine whether an industry is oligopolistic. Nonetheless, economists have chosen to use **industry concentration ratio** statistics in order to talk about oligopolies. Imagine looking at an entire industry and finding out what percentage of total sales are accounted for by the top four firms. This is what we do in Figure 7-4. This figure shows a number of industries in which the four largest firms produce about 60 percent or more of the total industry output. Many economists would designate these industries as oligopolies.

✦ **Be Aware!** *An industry may be considered an oligopoly if we only look at domestic producers, but not so if we look at the world market. Just because there are only a few domestic carmakers means little, given the existence of Kia, Toyota, Honda, BMW, Volkswagen, and other competitors.*

**Are Oligopolies Harmful to Consumers?** Although oligopoly is not the dominant form of market structure in the United States, oligopolistic industries do exist. To the extent that oligopolists have *market power*—the ability to *individually* affect the *market* price for the industry's output—they lead to resource misallocations, just as monopolies do. Oligopolists charge prices that exceed marginal cost. But what about oligopolies that occur because of economies of scale? Consumers might actually end up paying lower prices than if the industry were composed of numerous smaller firms.

All in all, there is no definite evidence of serious resource misallocation in the United States because of oligopolies. In any event, the more competition U.S. firms face from the rest of the world, the less any existing oligopoly will be able to exercise significant market power.

## Figure 7-4 Selected Potential Oligopolies

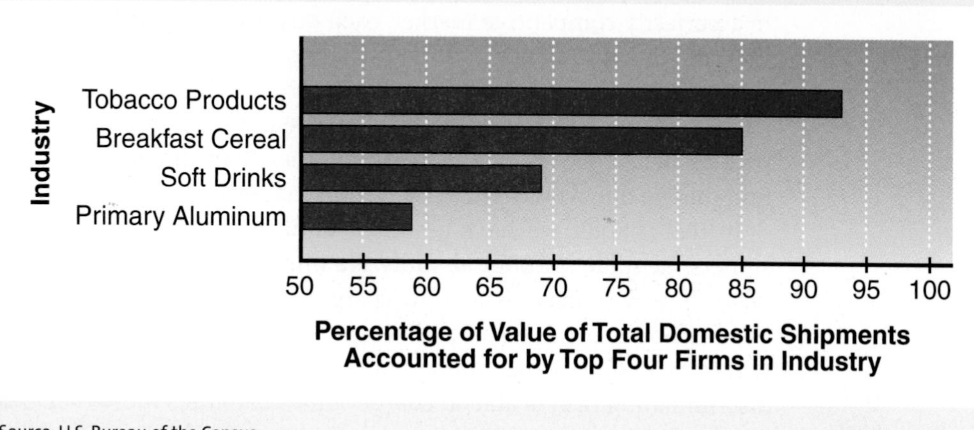


Source: U.S. Bureau of the Census

**The Extreme Oligopoly—A Duopoly** It is possible to have only two firms in one market. This is called a **duopoly**. There are very few duopoly markets in the world today. Nonetheless, when they exist, it is relatively easy for the two members of the duopoly to collude on prices and perhaps market share. You can read about one such duopoly in the art auction market in the following *Policy Application*.

**Duopoly**
*A market structure in which there are only two sellers of a particular good or service for which there is no close substitute.*

## POLICY APPLICATION: Art Auction Houses—Really Only Two Players

***Concepts Applied:***
**Price Fixing, Imperfect Competition, Duopoly**

The fine art world seems mysterious indeed. This was true until the early 2000s when the U.S. Department of Justice investigated the two major auction houses, Christie's and Sotheby's, for anticompetitive behavior. The Department of Justice discovered that these two companies had for years agreed to fix the price of their services. In other words, if a would-be seller of a large number of Old Masters paintings went to Christie's and was offered a deal that involved a 10 percent commission, that same seller would be offered exactly the same deal—namely, a 10 percent commission—by Sotheby's.

### A Party Crasher Appears

While Sotheby's and Christie's were under investigation, a small auction house called Phillips tried to crash the party. Backed by a French luxury goods company, Phillips started giving fine art sellers lavish guarantees with promises to purchase their art at pre-agreed prices if the bidding fell flat.

The so-called duopoly—two sellers—for auctioning fine art appeared to be cracking.

### It's Still a Duopoly, More or Less

As the economy weakened in the early 2000s, all auction houses suffered. The one that seemed to suffer the most, though, was Phillips. In 2003 it lost its financial backing from France and was forced to fire half its staff and close all but four of its auction departments. In that same year, Sotheby's and Christie's raised their commission rates. The duopoly remains intact.

**For Critical Analysis:**
*Do Sotheby's and Christie's have any control over the auction prices of the art that they agree to sell? Why or why not?*

## How to Make Higher Profits Through Price Discrimination

In a perfectly competitive market, each buyer is charged the same price for every unit of the particular commodity (corrected for differential transportation charges). Because the product is homogeneous and we also assume full knowledge on the part of the buyers, a difference in price cannot exist. Any seller of the product who tried to charge a price higher than the going market price would find that no one would purchase it from that seller.

In this chapter we have assumed until now that each firm charged all consumers the same price for all units. An imperfect competitor (including a monopolist), however, may be able to charge different people different prices. When there is not a cost difference, this strategy is called **price discrimination**. A firm will engage in price discrimination whenever feasible to increase profits. A price-discriminating firm is able to charge some customers more than other customers. Profitable price discrimination involves charging a higher price to customers who have a relatively low price elasticity of demand. At the same time, customers with high price elasticity of demand are charged lower prices.

**Price discrimination**
*Selling a given product at more than one price, with the price difference being unrelated to differences in cost.*

## *Solving the Economic Problem:* How to Fill Those Empty Airplane Seats?

The airline industry, with the help of cheaper high-intensity computing services, came up with a way to solve its pricing problem. The airlines receive information on changes in demand for particular flights to particular destinations virtually around the clock. They obtain this information from their computerized reservation services. A sophisticated program analyzes such data continually. The airlines change their prices according to anticipated demand for a particular flight at a particular time. In fact, some airlines change the price of round-trip tickets to the same location, from the same city, as often as seven times *per hour*. The goal of each airline is to fill every seat on every flight. After all, the marginal cost of taking on that extra passenger is extremely small. Therefore, selling even very cheap seats makes sense to a struggling airline. So, in contrast to a perfectly competitive industry structure, airlines do not charge the same price for the same service all of the time. Airlines price discriminate, often charging businesspeople who don't stay over on a Saturday night much more than those who purchase tickets way in advance and do stay over on a Saturday night. It is not unusual for different people in the same row on the same flight to have each paid a very different price for their tickets.

**Mastering Concepts:** Oligopoly—Competition Among the Few

- **The main characteristics of oligopoly are (1) few sellers, (2) identical or slightly different products, (3) nonprice competition, and (4) interdependence.**
- **One way to increase profits is to price discriminate by charging higher prices to those customers with less elastic demands.**

## INTERDEPENDENCE AND CHEATING IN AN OLIGOPOLISTIC INDUSTRY

The one thing that the perfect competitor and the pure monopolist have in common is that, by definition, they cannot or do not take account of competitors' actions or reactions. In the case of the perfect competitor, he or she cannot even worry about competitors because there are so many. In the case of a pure monopolist, there are no competitors by definition. Not so for the oligopolist.

### Interdependence and Strategic Dependence

All markets and all firms are, in a sense, interdependent. But only when a few large firms account for a majority of sales in an industry does the question of the **strategic dependence** of one firm on the others' actions arise. The firms must, and do, recognize that they are interdependent. Any action on the part of one firm with respect to output, price, quality, or product differentiation will cause a reaction on the part of the other firms. A model of such mutual interdependence is difficult to build, but examples of such behavior are not hard to find in the real world. ▸ Example 7-8 Oligopolists in the cigarette industry are constantly reacting to each other. When one oligopolist offers special promotional deals on its brands of cigarettes, the other oligopolists introduce promotional deals on their brands, too. ◂

**Strategic dependence**
*A situation in which one firm's actions with respect to price, quality, advertising, and the like may be strategically countered by the reactions of one or more other firms in the industry. Such dependence can exist only when there are a limited number of major firms in an industry.*

Recall that in the model of perfect competition, each firm ignores the behavior of other firms because each firm is able to sell all that it wants at the going market price. At the other extreme, the pure monopolist does not have to worry about the reaction of current rivals because it has none.

> ***In an oligopolistic market structure, the managers of firms are like generals in a war: They must attempt to predict the reaction of rival firms. This is a strategic game.***

▸ Example 7-9 In the automobile industry, when General Motors offers large rebates for the purchase of its new cars, Ford and Chrysler often follow suit. In that same industry, when one company offers zero percent financing, the other domestic rivals seem to do so, too. ◂

### Opportunistic Behavior and Cheating

Oligopolists prefer higher to lower profit, so you might think they would want to "cheat." In other words, they might try to fool their rivals.

Imagine two oligopolists trying to decide on a pricing strategy. Each can have either a high price or a low price. If both of these oligopolists choose high prices, they can make higher profits. But even if they have a "deal" to charge high prices, one may cheat.

**Opportunistic behavior**
*Actions that ignore the possible long-run benefits of cooperation and focus solely on short-run gains.*

In another context, oligopolists (or all firms, for that matter) could advertise a product with lots of features at a specific price, knowing that some of those features do not exist. This is called **opportunistic behavior**. You as an individual consumer could engage in opportunistic behavior, too. ▸ Example 7-10 You could write a check for a purchase knowing that it is going to bounce because you have just closed that bank account. As a worker or independent contractor, you could agree to perform a specific task for a specific pay rate and then perform the work in a substandard way. These are all examples of opportunistic behavior. ◂

### The Result of Everyone Engaging in Opportunistic Behavior

**Noncooperative behavior**
*Behavior among individuals or firms in which the parties attempt to maximize their own welfare at the expense of other parties. With noncooperative behavior, the parties neither negotiate nor cooperate in any way.*

If all of us, consumers and sellers alike, engaged in opportunistic behavior all of the time, the world would be a mess. We would constantly be engaged in what is called **noncooperative behavior**.

The reality is that this is not the world in which most of us live. Why not? Because most of engage in *repeat transactions*. Manufacturers want us to keep purchasing their products. Sellers want us to keep coming back to their stores. As sellers of labor services, we all want to keep our jobs, get promotions, be paid more, or be hired away by another firm at a higher price. So, even though opportunistic behavior is observed among a few firms and individuals, the vast majority avoid such actions because the value of repeat business is just too great.

**Mastering Concepts:** Interdependence and Cheating in an Oligopolistic Industry

- **Oligopolists have to take account of their rivals' reactions, just as generals must take account of their enemy's reactions.**
- **Opportunistic behavior is a type of cheating and can also be classified as noncooperative behavior. Firms and consumers do not consistently engage in such behavior because of their desire for repeat business.**

## PRICE LEADERSHIP AND PRICE WARS—THEY DO EXIST

**Collusion**
*A secret agreement among two or more parties to engage in some illegal activity, such as fixing prices or dividing up a specific market.*

Most oligopolists do not explicitly engage in **collusion**. That is to say, they don't have meetings where they split up the market (although you can read about one example in which they did in the *Global Application* below).

### GLOBAL APPLICATION: International Chemical Hauling—Boring, but Profitable for At Least Two Companies

***Concepts Applied: Oligopoly, Collusion***

Hauling liquid chemicals across the seas doesn't sound like much of a business. Nonetheless, chemicals, fats, and oils are the building blocks of life as we know it today. The computer you use has a plastic shell made from chemicals shipped by sea. Even shaving cream and salad dressing contain chemicals or oils that are shipped by sea. Consequently, when international chemical haulers raise their rates, you end up paying slightly higher prices for just about everything.

#### Two Major Players May Have Divided the Market

In the international chemical hauling business, two Norwegian chemical haulers—Stolt and Odfjell—

*Continued on next page*

have almost 25 percent of the entire $2.5 billion market. The question is, did they illegally collude to divide that market?

Some evidence suggests they did. At a meeting in 1998, Stolt managers were told by the vice president for tanker trading that Odfjell and Stolt had agreed on which customers belonged to whom. In effect, they had "carved up the world." When two big chemical companies merged, Odfjell and Stolt met again to decide in detail which company was going to ship what and for whom. A series of investigations by competition commissions in Europe found numerous memos referring to such discussions.

**Business Life Is Easier When Competition Is Reduced**

It is clear that the two major international chemical haulers wanted to make their lives easier. When they divided the market, they did not have to worry about competitive bidding for every project. Not surprisingly, some of the memos discovered by investigators showed that executives from the companies planned to bid higher prices for their contracts. They thought they could get away with it. But they didn't. In the fall of 2003, Odfjell pleaded guilty to price-fixing charges made by the U.S. Justice Department. The company agreed to pay a fine of $45.5 million. Several company executives pleaded guilty, too, and paid fines. One was sentenced to jail for four months.

**For Critical Analysis:**

*Examine the definition of oligopoly again. In what ways is the seagoing chemical hauling market an oligopoly?*

Oligopolists can, though, figure out ways implicitly to determine prices together. This is called **tacit collusion**. One example of this is the model of **price leadership**.

**Tacit collusion**
*Collusion among market participants—usually business firms—without those firms actually meeting and deciding on an explicit action such as fixing prices or dividing up a market.*

**Price leadership**
*A practice in many oligopolistic industries whereby the largest firm publishes its price list ahead of its competitors, which then match those announced prices.*

## Price Leadership

In the model of price leadership, the basic assumption is that there is one dominant firm, usually the biggest firm. It sets the price that it thinks is profit maximizing. Then it allows other firms to sell all they can at that price. The dominant firm sells the remainder.

In this model, the dominant firm always makes the first move. By definition, price leadership requires one firm to be the leader. ▸ Example 7-11 Some observers have argued that Harvard University was once the price leader among Ivy League schools. Indeed, the U.S. Justice Department investigated documents that circulated among Ivy League schools in the 1980s and early 1990s. These documents listed potential tuition increases by Harvard as well as some other Ivy League schools. Each time there was a tuition hike, all of the schools in the Ivy League ended up raising their tuitions to within one half of a percentage point of each other. ◂

## Price Wars

Price leadership may not always work. If the price leader ends up much better off than the other firms, those firms may not follow the prices set by the dominant firm. The result may be a **price war**. When this occurs, the dominant firm lowers its prices a little bit, but the other firms lower theirs even more. Price wars have occurred in many industries, including cigarettes and airlines. Price wars even occur in situations that can hardly be called oligopolistic, such as supermarkets. ▸ Example 7-12 Supermarkets within a given locale often engage in price wars, especially during holiday periods. One may offer turkeys at so much per pound on Wednesday; competing stores cut their price on turkeys on Thursday, so the first store cuts its price even more on Friday. Supermarkets that get into price wars over turkeys often end up selling them at cost. ◂

**Price war**
*A pricing campaign designed to capture additional market share by repeatedly cutting prices.*

*Just before Thanksgiving, supermarkets heavily promote low-priced turkeys. Indeed, sometimes there are local price wars over turkey prices. The result might even be prices at or below cost. Is there any difference between such marketing ploys and simply paying for more traditional forms of advertising?*

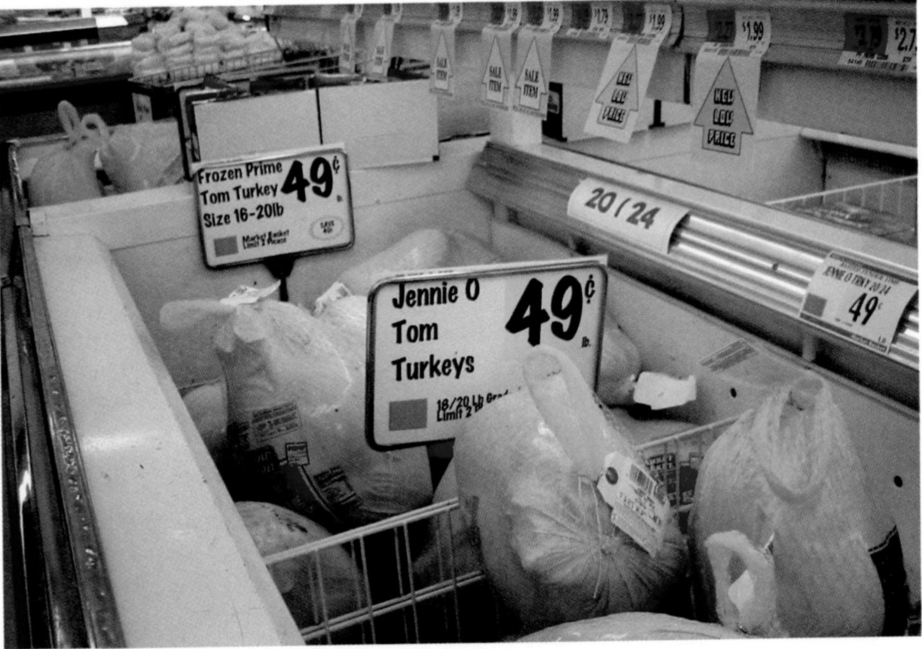


**Mastering Concepts:** Price Leadership and Price Wars—They Do Exist

- **One type of tacit collusion involves price leadership in which the dominant firm sets the price and all other firms follow with price changes accordingly.**
- **When price leadership does not work, price wars can ensue, in which the non-dominant firms cut their prices below the price set by the dominant firm.**

## SUMMING IT ALL UP

- In a monopolistically competitive industry, there are (1) numerous sellers, (2) relatively easy entry, (3) differentiated products, (4) nonprice competition, and (5) some control by firms over price.
- Even though monopolistically competitive firms face downward-sloping demand curves, they ultimately earn zero economic profits in the long run because of competition.
- While it makes no sense to advertise in a perfectly competitive industry, in a less-than-perfectly-competitive industry, advertising and sales promotion are used to increase demand and to differentiate products.
- Companies engage in signaling behavior to let customers know that they have high-quality products. They establish brand names or trademarks to do so.
- The main characteristics of oligopoly are (1) few sellers, (2) identical or slightly different products, (3) nonprice competition, and (4) interdependence.
- One way to increase profits is to price discriminate by charging higher prices to those customers with less elastic demands.
- Oligopolists have to take account of their rivals' reactions, just as generals must take account of their enemy's reactions.

- Opportunistic behavior is a type of cheating and can also be classified as noncooperative behavior. Firms and consumers do not consistently engage in such behavior because of their desire for repeat business.
- One type of tacit collusion involves price leadership in which the dominant firm sets the price and all other firms follow with price changes accordingly.

## KEY TERMS AND CONCEPTS

brand name **142**
collusion **148**
duopoly **145**
industry concentration ratio **144**
monopolistic competition **138**
noncooperative behavior **148**
oligopoly **143**
opportunistic behavior **148**
price discrimination **146**
price leadership **149**
price war **149**
signal **142**
signaling behavior **142**
strategic dependence **147**
tacit collusion **149**
trademark **142**

## MASTERING ECONOMIC CONCEPTS: Questions and Problems

**7-1.** Determine whether each of the following attributes is a characteristic of monopolistic competition.

a. a small number of buyers and sellers
b. each firm having no control over price in the market
c. identical products from each firm
d. limited barriers to entry
e. zero economic profits in the long run

**7-2.** Indicate whether each of the following is likely to be an example of an oligopoly.

a. oil production
b. manicures and pedicures
c. textbook publishing
d. breakfast cereals

**7-3.** Arrange the following industry models in order from most competitive to least competitive.

a. oligopoly
b. perfect competition
c. monopolistic competition
d. monopoly

**7-4.** For each of the following, indicate whether the statement is true with respect to perfect competition and/or with respect to monopolistic competition.

a. Economic profits will equal zero in the long run.
b. Accounting profits will equal zero in the long run.
c. If existing firms are generating economic losses, new firms are unlikely to enter.
d. In the long run, each firm produces at a quantity where ATC = *D*.
e. In the long run, each firm produces at the lowest possible average total cost.

**7-5.** Based on the graph below illustrating the operations of a monopolistically competitive firm, what quantity will this firm produce in order to maximize profits?

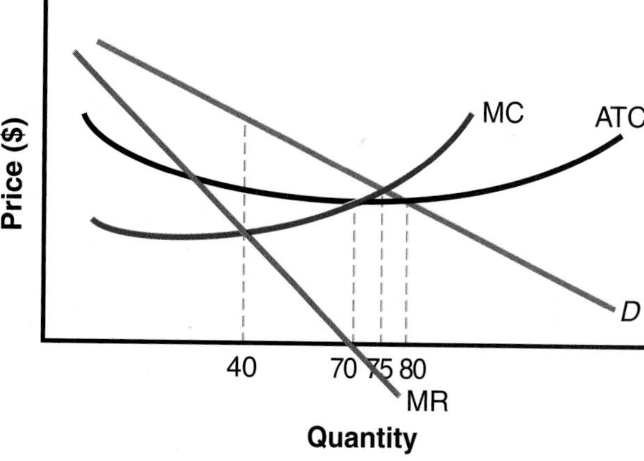


**7-6.** In the graph for problem 7-5, will the monopolistically competitive firm depicted generate an economic profit, loss, or breakeven? As such, does the graph depict the short-run or long-run operations of a monopolistically competitive firm?

**7-7.** GEICO provides auto insurance as well as other insurance services. Recently, this company advertised its services through a play on the words *GEICO* and *gecko*. By spending a substantial amount of money on this ad campaign and tying the company name to an identifiable lizard mascot, what was GEICO attempting to signal to consumers? Based on the apparent popularity of these ads, was the company successful in achieving its advertising goal?

**7-8.** Based on your experience, does the soft drink industry resemble a monopolistically competitive industry or an oligopolistic industry? Formulate an argument based on the characteristics of these two industry models.

**7-9.** Based on the following table for a monopolistically competitive firm, what quantity should this firm produce in order to maximize profits? Based on your result, would additional firms be likely to join this industry, or would existing firms be likely to exit?

| Output | Price | Total Costs |
|---|---|---|
| 100 | $4.00 | $500 |
| 120 | 3.90 | 535 |
| 140 | 3.80 | 575 |
| 160 | 3.70 | 620 |
| 180 | 3.60 | 680 |

**7-10.** Explain why each of the following is necessary in order for price discrimination to exist.

a. Each firm faces a downward-sloping demand curve.

b. There are at least two distinct groups of consumers with different elasticities.

c. Firms are able to prevent resale between consumers.

**7-11.** Delta Airlines accounts for nearly 80 percent of all passengers who travel through Atlanta's Hartsfield International Airport. How would you expect Delta to set the price for flights in and out of this airport? Holding everything else constant, would other airlines be likely to set their prices lower, higher, or the same as Delta's? Why?

**7-12.** If movie theaters charge different prices for admission based on age, is this price discrimination? If movie theaters charge different prices for admission based on the show time, is this price discrimination? Based on these examples and your own experience, what type of person or group receives a lower ticket price for movies? Would you describe this group's demand as more elastic or less elastic?

**7-13.** Draw a graph representing the long-run equilibrium for a monopolistically competitive firm.

**7-14.** Based on the following graph representing the demand curve for a monopolistic firm, draw in a second demand curve representing the demand curve for a monopolistically competitive firm.

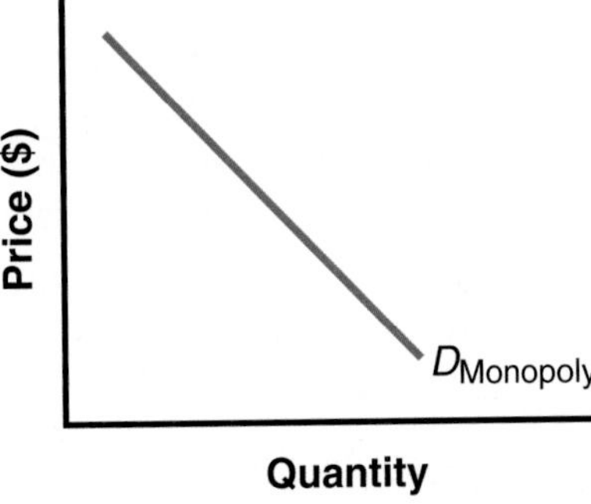


**7-15.** Economists consider advertising to be a signal of higher quality for any good. In many cases, however, particularly on the local level, we see television ads or hear radio spots for goods whose quality may seem questionable. Reconcile the existence of questionable ads with the economic theory involving signaling behavior.

## THINKING CRITICALLY

**7-1.** Assume that two of the large companies that produce potato chips are unveiling new products this year and they might advertise during the Super Bowl. A 30-second ad will cost $2 million in addition to the other costs involved with the ad campaign. Assume that both companies realize how good their products are. If one company has a superior product and the other company has an inferior product, which company is more likely to advertise during the Super Bowl? Why?

**7-2.** The Organization of Petroleum Exporting Countries (OPEC) is a cartel that was established to coordinate oil pricing for its member countries. If all the countries act under the unified direction of OPEC, what will happen to the price of oil, and what will happen to the quantity of oil produced? If these countries collude, will this market function more like perfect competition or more like a monopoly? If Venezuela, an OPEC member, decided to lower the price of oil it was producing while other countries' prices remained constant, what would happen to the quantity of oil sold by Venezuela? What would happen to the quantity of oil sold by the other OPEC countries? How would these countries respond?

**7-3.** Jenny is a golf enthusiast. She recently noticed two special offers on golf in her area. The first is a "twilight golf" offer available to anyone who begins a round of golf after 3:30 p.m. The other is a "play your age" offer that allows golfers to pay $10 plus their age for a round of golf. For each of these offers, determine if the offer actually implies price discrimination and explain why or why not.

## LOGGING ON

1. For links to interesting real-world applications of the concept of monopolistic competition, go to http://subscribe.wsj.com/microexamples/monopolisticcompetition.html.
2. To learn more about advertising techniques and examine case studies of how firms have engaged in Web advertising efforts, go to http://www.iab.net/ and click on "Resources and Research."
3. To see the latest available concentration ratios for U.S. industries, go to http://www.census.gov/epcd/www/concentration.html.
4. For links to interesting real-world applications of the concept of oligopoly, go to http://subscribe.wsj.com/microexamples/oligopoly.html.

## USING THE INTERNET FOR ECONOMIC ANALYSIS

**Legal Services on the Internet** A number of legal firms now offer services on the Internet, and in this application you contemplate features of the market for Web-based legal services.

**Title:** Nolo.com—Law for All

**Navigation:** Go to the Nolo.com site at http://www.nolo.com.

**Application**

1. In what respects does the market for legal services, such as those provided online by Nolo.com, have the characteristics of a monopolistically competitive industry?
2. How can providers of legal services differentiate their products? How does Nolo.com attempt to do this?

## MEDIA RESOURCE LIST

The following media resources are available with this chapter:

- Load your CD-ROM to listen to the audio introduction to this chapter.
- Load your CD-ROM to view the video on *Monopolistic Competition.*
- Load your CD-ROM to access a Graph Animation of Figure 7-2, *Comparison of the Perfect Competitor with the Monopolistic Competitor.*
- Load your CD-ROM to view the video on *Opportunistic Behavior.*
- Load your CD-ROM to view the video on *Price Leadership.*
- Test your knowledge of chapter concepts with a quiz at www.miller-ume.com.
- Link to Web resources related to the text coverage at www.miller-ume.com.

## HOMEWORK SET

Go to the end of this book to find the Homework Problems for this chapter.

# CHAPTER 8

# Market and Government Failures

## *Facing an Economic Problem:* Is There a Relationship Between Increased Cigarette Taxes and Increased Violence?

On July 3, 2002, New York's mayor Michael Bloomberg saw his long-sought cigarette tax increase put into effect. This was not just a few cents per pack, but rather a 19-fold increase in the city's levy. The result is that in New York City, combined state and local cigarette taxes are $3 a pack—the highest in the United States.

Bloomberg declared, "Increasing cigarette taxes saves lives." He was referring to reducing smoking, a known cause of premature death. Indeed, during the first four months after the tax hike, cigarette sales in New York City fell by 50 percent. At the same time, though, there was a marked increase in violent activities, including armed robbery, kidnapping, and murder.

Is there a relationship?

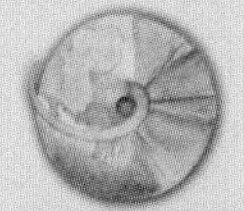

***Refer to the back of this chapter for a complete listing of multimedia learning materials available on the CD-ROM and the Web site.***

### Learning Objectives:

After reading this chapter, you should be able to:

- **Distinguish between private and social costs and explain their relationship to negative externalities.**
- **Identify the two characteristics of public goods.**
- **Contrast economic and social regulation and give examples of both.**
- **List three important antitrust acts.**
- **Compare and contrast proportional, progressive, and regressive taxation systems.**

## WHEN SOCIAL AND PRIVATE COSTS DIFFER—A POTENTIAL FAILURE OF OUR PRICING SYSTEM

After reading the first seven chapters of this text, you may have concluded that if individuals are left to their own devices, demand and supply can solve all problems. Otherwise stated, the pricing system as a way to allocate resources seems, at first glance, to be quite appealing. There are occasionally some problems, though, with letting the pricing system "do its thing."

Sometimes the price system does not generate the most beneficial results to society. Too few or too many resources may be going to specific activities. Such situations are called **market failures**.

**Market failures**
*Situations in which unrestrained market operations lead to either too few or too many resources going to a specific economic activity.*

***Market failures prevent the price system from obtaining economic efficiency. Market failure offers one of the strongest arguments in favor of government stepping in.***

Otherwise stated, market failure may occur when society is not using its available resources in an optimal manner. Remember back in Chapter 1 when we talked about the production possibilities curve? There we showed that any point inside the production possibilities curve was inefficient. We can link such inefficient points to market failures. They occur when the normal workings of the marketplace do not lead the economy to move to a point *on* the production possibilities curve.

▸ Example 8-1 If one company has a monopoly in the production and sale of a much needed good—think insulin—then that pure monopolist will charge a price that is higher than would prevail with competition. The price that people end up paying for this particular good will exceed the opportunity cost to society of producing it. In this sense, some economists call this a market failure. ◂

### Some Potential Sources of Market Failures

Although there may be numerous ways in which supply and demand do not lead to optimal resource use in our society, we will focus mainly on three sources:

1. Externalities
2. Public goods
3. Excessive market power

You will read about these sources and how we define them in the following sections.

### Knowing the True Opportunity Cost of One's Actions

It is difficult to know how to treat correctly economic resources if you do not know their true opportunity cost. ▸ Example 8-2 Your parents own a gas station. They let you fill up your car as often as you want without paying for it. For you, the opportunity cost of gasoline is zero. You act accordingly. You drive more than you would if you had to pay the full opportunity cost of gasoline. ◂

### Ignoring Externalities

When you drive a car, you take account of the cost of gas, maintenance, insurance, wear and tear, and the car's falling resale value. These are some of the **private costs** of driving. In contrast, when a cost is associated with your actions, but you do not have to consider that cost, we say that it is external to your decision-

**Private costs**
*Costs borne solely by the individuals who generate them; also called* internal costs.

making process. This cost that you do not consider in your decision making is an example of an **externality**.

**Externality**
*Economic side effects or by-products that affect an uninvolved third party; can be negative or positive.*

## Traffic Congestion and Negative Externalities

When a driver pulls onto a road, he or she normally does not have to worry about the external costs imposed on the thousands of other drivers who have to slow down just a tiny bit more. We say that each driver in a congested environment imposes **negative externalities** on all other drivers. Drivers also impose other negative externalities, such as pollution.

**Negative externalities**
*The results of a production or consumption activity that impose costs on third parties; for example, pollution from a factory and congestion from driving.*

At least one big city mayor decided to do something about these externalities. He attempted to bring the private cost of driving in line with the full social cost of driving. See the following *Global Application* to find out if this mayor succeeded in reducing congestion.

### GLOBAL APPLICATION: Overcoming Congestion the London Way

***Concepts Applied:***
**Social versus Private Costs**

Until relatively recently, London was no different than New York City, Tokyo, Mexico City, Paris, or Cairo. That is to say, rush hour meant extremely clogged streets with cars moving even slower than pedestrians. In 2002, Ken Livingston, the mayor of London, decided to change things.

#### You Have to Pay to Play

Anyone driving in the eight-square-mile area of the so-called congestion zone in London from Monday through Friday from 7:00 a.m. to 6:30 p.m. has to pay. How much? Five pounds a day, or about $8. You have a choice of paying by the day, the week, the month, or the year. You can pay through the Internet, by phone, or at gas stations or newsstands.

To make sure you are honest, the city installed more than 700 video cameras. Their job is to scan license plates and log them into a national database. In addition, the city has mobile cameras on the tops of roving vans.

If you are caught driving in the city without having paid for that privilege, you can be fined up to 120 pounds, or about $200.

#### The Results—As Predicted by Economists, at Least

Not surprisingly, a $2,000-a-year charge for driving in London caused a number of car owners to think twice about entering the city. Traffic in the eight-square-mile area dropped by a third and average speeds increased by 50 percent.

The toll has had some unintended consequences, though. To avoid it, many Londoners have taken to riding two-wheeled motorized vehicles. While two-wheeled vehicles constitute only one-tenth of the traffic, they are involved in one-third of the accidents. Apparently, many people are not as competent on a two-wheeled vehicle as they are inside a car.

**For Critical Analysis:**
*America's freeways are often packed bumper to bumper at rush hour. How might you apply London's experience to reducing rush-hour freeway congestion?*

**Examining External Costs in Graphical Form** Look at Figure 8-1 on the next page. The example concerns the production of steel. Steel mill owners look at only their private costs—land, labor, capital, and entrepreneurship. In fact, the price of steel charged by these steel mill owners reflects only those private costs.

The supply curve in panel (a) of Figure 8-1 is labeled $S_1$. It reflects those private costs just mentioned. The demand curve is $D$. The equilibrium is at $E$. The equilibrium price and quantity combination is $P_1$ and $Q_1$.

If the steel mill owners were required to take into account negative externalities, the situation would be different. These negative externalities definitely in-

*Animated*

## Figure 8-1 External Costs and Benefits

In panel (a), we show external costs that are at first ignored by steel producers, thus giving us supply curve $S_1$. The equilibrium price of steel is too low at $P_1$ because it does not reflect external costs of pollution. If those external costs are imposed on steel producers, the supply curve will shift to $S_2$. The price will rise to $P_2$ after the supply curve shifts the vertical distance from $A$ to $E_1$, which is equal to the marginal external costs of producing steel. In panel (b), we show the external benefits from inoculations against communicable diseases. The demand curve $D_1$ does not include these external benefits. The quantity demanded and supplied at $Q_1$ is too low. If everyone took account of external benefits, the demand curve would shift to $D_2$. The vertical shift would be equal to the marginal external benefits. The quantity demand and supplied would increase to $Q_2$, but at a higher price $P_2$.

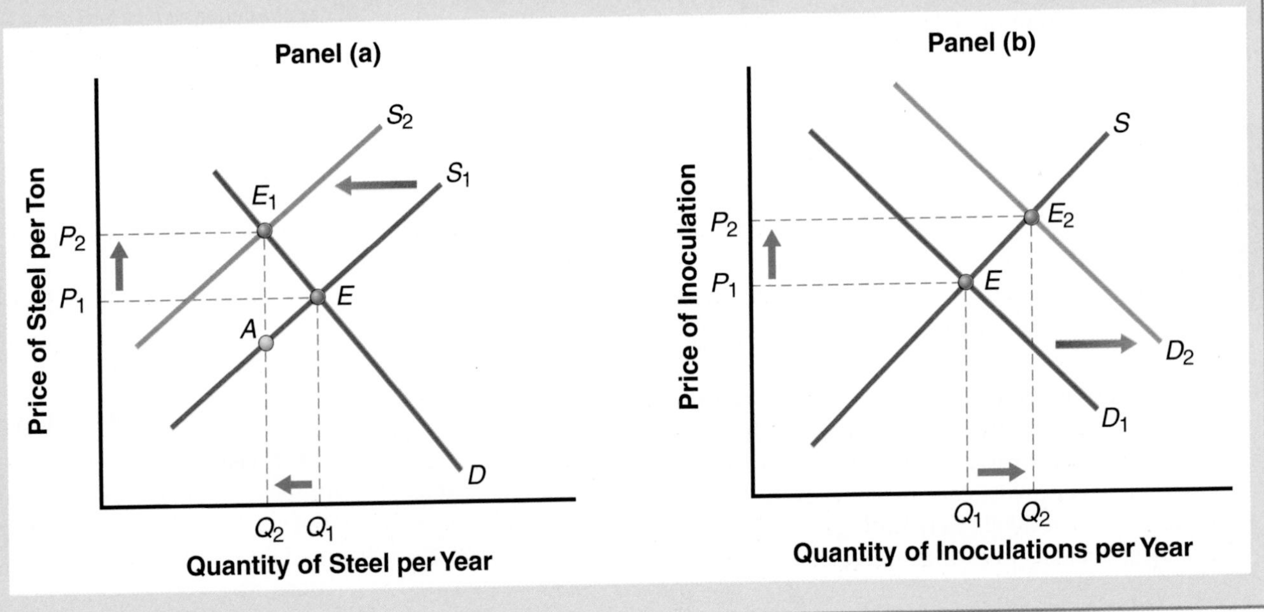


clude all of the health costs associated with increased pollution. They also include the cost of washing clothes more often, washing cars more often, and repainting houses more often. If the steel mill owners had to pay for these additional costs, the supply curve would shift the vertical distance from $A$ to $E_1$. In other words, the distance from $A$ to $E_1$ equals the marginal external costs of producing steel. In this situation, the supply curve would be $S_2$. The new equilibrium would be at $E_1$ with a new equilibrium price at $P_2$ and a lower quantity demanded and supplied at $Q_2$.

**How Could Government Take Account of Negative Externalities?** It is possible, and indeed actually happens, that governments charge companies for the amount of pollution they generate. ▸ **International Example 8-3** Manufacturing operations that dump wastewater into rivers in and around Glasgow, Scotland, must pay a fee to the government depending on the amount of pollutants in the wastewater. One such company, Fresh Baked Foods, which manufactures frozen sausages, had been paying hundreds of thousands of dollars a year in water waste fees. Finally, Fresh Baked installed its own on-site water treatment system using ultrafiltration. It ended up saving over $150,000 a year in wastewater charges. ◂ Alternatively, governments can simply seek to regulate the amount of pollution each company can generate.

## There Can Be Positive Externalities

It is also possible to generate positive benefits that you do not take into account when making decisions about the use of resources. ▸ Example 8-4 When you mow your lawn regularly, trim your shrubs, and plant numerous flowers for different seasons, others who live near you or pass by benefit. They enjoy a **positive externality**. They do not pay you, though, so in principle you might be spending too little from society's point of view to enhance the appearance of your grounds. ◂

**Positive externality**
*A benefit from a production or consumption activity that is bestowed on third parties without them having to pay for this benefit; for example, you spend time to maintain a flower bed bordering your property with the result that all passersby benefit from its beauty, but do not have to pay for your time and expenses.*

### Graphing Positive Externalities

Look at panel (b) of Figure 8-1. There you see a situation in which positive externalities exist.

Consider inoculations against communicable diseases. Those individuals who do not get inoculated obtain benefits because epidemics of communicable diseases will not occur when most people in a society are inoculated. Nonetheless, individuals tend to take account of only the benefit to themselves. The total demand curve is therefore $D_1$ in panel (b) of Figure 8-1. With the supply curve at $S$, the quantity of inoculations demanded per year will be $Q_1$. In contrast, if purchasers of inoculations take account of external benefits, the demand curve will shift to $D_2$. The equilibrium quantity of inoculations per year will increase to $Q_2$. The vertical difference between demand curve $D_1$ and demand curve $D_2$ is a measure of the marginal external benefits from inoculations.

### How the Government Might Correct Positive Externalities

There are several ways in which the government can correct positive externalities. Here, when we talk about correcting externalities, we mean causing society to allocate more resources to these activities. Of course, the government can finance such activities, or it can even produce them, as governments often do for inoculations. Alternatively, governments can subsidize the production or the consumption of a good or service. Finally, a government can regulate. ▸ Example 8-5 The government can require, and often does, that all school-age children be inoculated before entering public and private schools. ◂

**Mastering Concepts:** When Social and Private Costs Differ—A Potential Failure of Our Pricing System

- **When social costs exceed private costs, negative externalities may occur.**
- **When social benefits exceed private benefits, positive externalities may occur.**
- **The government can correct externalities in principle via regulation or taxes and subsidies.**

## WHEN YOU CAN'T STOP PEOPLE FROM CONSUMING—THE CASE OF PUBLIC GOODS

When we examine goods in the world today, we can classify them as either private goods or public goods.

**Private goods**
*Goods that can be consumed by only one individual at a time. Private goods are subject to the principle of rival consumption.*

**Principle of rival consumption**
*The recognition that individuals are rivals in consuming private goods because one person's consumption reduces the amount available for others to consume.*

## Private Goods

Up until now, we have implicitly been talking about **private goods**. With private goods, when I use them, you cannot and vice versa. This is called the **principle of rival consumption**. By definition, this principle applies to all private goods. ▸ Example 8-6 You like to study alone. You also like to listen to your favorite tunes on your MP3 player. While you are using your MP3 player, your roommate, who likes to study in the library, cannot use it. ◀

## The Opposite of Private Goods—Public Goods

**Public goods**
*Goods for which the principle of rival consumption does not apply; they can be jointly consumed by many individuals simultaneously at no additional cost and with no reduction in quality or quantity. Also, non-payers cannot be excluded.*

There is an entire class of goods that are not private goods. These are called **public goods**.

> ***A key characteristic of public goods is that many individuals can consume them simultaneously. When you partake in the use or benefit of a public good, you do not necessarily take away from anyone else's share of these goods.***

▶ Example 8-7 Our national defense system is a public good. Your benefiting from national defense does not reduce the benefits that anyone else in the United States receives. ◀

✦ **Note!** *Some services may have the two attributes of public goods but still be provided by the private sector. For example, satellite and cable TV transmissions require decoders, such that users must pay a monthly fee. Also, large outdoor concerts are usually fenced in order to prevent those who don't pay from sitting close enough to enjoy the music.*

**Characteristics of Public Goods** Public goods have two distinguishing characteristics that set them apart from all other private goods:

1. *Additional users of public goods do not deprive others of any of the services of the goods.* For the continental United States, when more people benefit from national defense, others do not receive less of it.
2. *It is difficult to design a collection system for a public good based on how much individuals use it.* Because everyone benefits from national defense, it would hard to figure out who benefits more and, therefore, who should be charged more.

**The Private Sector Has Trouble Providing Public Goods** Because it is difficult to exclude people from consuming public goods once they exist, the private sector sometimes has a difficult time providing them. After all, in the private sector, business owners have to make profits or they will not stay in business. If the production and sale of a purely public good do not yield profits in the private sector, the purely public good will not get produced. This is where government steps in to provide purely public goods, such as national defense.

**Mastering Concepts:** When You Can't Stop People from Consuming—The Case of Public Goods

- **The key characteristics of public goods are that (1) additional users do not take away from others' benefits and (2) it is hard to collect payments for a public good based on individual use.**
- **True public goods may represent a market failure because the private sector has trouble providing them.**

## REGULATION: THE GOVERNMENT STEPS IN

Consider the following occupations:

- Law
- Medicine
- Massage therapy
- Architecture
- Taxi services
- Plumbing
- Electrical repairs
- Astrology

What do these occupations have in common? All of them are regulated by government agencies, at least in some states. **Regulation** is a fact of life in the United States. The government—federal, state, and local—engages in economic and social regulation throughout the country. ▸ Example 8-8 Tennessee passed a law making it a crime to sell caskets without a funeral director's license. Obtaining a funeral director's license costs thousands of dollars and hundreds of hours of effort. The result of the law was higher prices for burials. When casket makers sued the state of Tennessee, the courts agreed with them, throwing out the licensing requirement. The judge stated that the Tennessee licensing law was a "naked attempt" to raise "a fortress protecting . . . funeral directors [from competition]." ◂

**Regulation**
*A way in which government at all levels—federal, state, and local—imposes rules on business activities. These rules may take the form of economic regulation, in which prices or profits are regulated, or social regulation, in which the method of production or the way workers are treated is delineated by government.*

## Economic Regulation

When government regulatory agencies determine prices, acceptable levels of profits, and/or rates of output in a particular industry, we say that the government is engaged in **economic regulation.** The goal of economic regulation has been, at least in principle, to prevent certain firms from making monopoly profits and other firms from engaging in too-aggressive forms of competition, sometimes called *cutthroat competition.*

**Economic regulation**
*Rules imposed by state and federal governments on the way businesses price their products, the way they market their goods and services, and how much they earn in profits.*

▸ Example 8-9 For years, the federal government regulated telephone rates. Additionally, the federal government prevented any type of serious competition. Though unknown to the younger generation, there was a period in U.S. history when you could not legally buy your own telephone equipment. Instead, you had to lease it directly from the only telephone company in the country—AT&T. ◂

## Social Regulation

When the government regulates for the benefit of public welfare—health, safety, and environment—across all industries, this is called **social regulation.** Social regulation at both the federal and state levels involves imposing occupational, health, and safety rules on a wide variety of employers.

**Social regulation**
*Any method of government regulation that imposes rules on how a productive activity is undertaken; for example, environmental and worker safety regulations.*

Social regulations focus on the impact of production on the environment and society, the working conditions under which goods and services are produced, and sometime the physical attributes of goods. ▸ Example 8-10 The Food and Drug Administration (FDA) attempts to protect against impure and unsafe foods, drugs, cosmetics, and other potentially hazardous products. Look at Table 8-1 on the following page. There you see a listing of some of the other major federal regulatory agencies and their areas of concern. ◂

## Reactions to Regulation—The World of Creative Response

Regulated firms commonly try to avoid the effects of regulation whenever they can. In other words, regulated firms engage in **creative response.** They conform to the letter of the law, but undermine its spirit. ▸ Example 8-11 Consider laws that require equal pay for men and women. Employers that pay the same wage to men and women are not in violation of the law. Yet wages are only one component of total employee compensation. Another component is fringe benefits, such as on-the-job training. Employers can—and sometimes do—offer less on-the-job training to one gender than to the other and still not be in technical violation of the equal pay regulation. ◂

**Creative response**
*Behavior on the part of a firm that allows it to comply with the letter of the law but violate its spirit, significantly lessening the law's effect.*

Individuals also have a type of creative response to regulation. It has been labeled a **feedback effect.**

**Feedback effect**
*The reaction of firms to government regulations; also the reaction of consumers to government regulations.*

***Regulation may alter individuals' behavior after the regulation has been put into effect.***

**Table 8-1 Some Federal Regulatory Agencies**

| Agency | Jurisdiction | Date Formed | Major Regulatory Functions |
|---|---|---|---|
| Federal Trade Commission (FTC) | Product markets | 1914 | Is responsible for preventing businesses from engaging in unfair trade practices and monopolistic actions, as well as for protecting consumer rights. |
| Federal Communications Commission (FCC) | Product markets | 1934 | Regulates broadcasting, telephone, and other communication services. |
| Securities and Exchange Commission (SEC) | Financial markets | 1934 | Regulates all public securities markets to promote full disclosure. |
| Equal Employment Opportunity Commission (EEOC) | Labor markets | 1964 | Investigates complaints of discrimination based on race, religion, gender, or age in hiring, promotion, firing, wages, testing, and all other conditions of employment. |
| Environmental Protection Agency (EPA) | Environment | 1970 | Develops and enforces environmental standards for air, water, toxic waste, and noise. |
| Occupational Safety and Health Administration (OSHA) | Health and safety | 1970 | Regulates workplace safety and health conditions. |

▸ **Example 8-12** If regulation requires fluoridated water, then parents know that their children's teeth will receive significant protection against tooth decay. Consequently, the feedback effect on parents' behavior is that they may be less concerned about how many sweets their children eat. Some argue that the rise in obesity among children may be partly due to this feedback effect. ◂

## Contestable Markets, or Why All the Worry?

Part of the reason for economic regulation is the fear that there is not enough competition in certain industries, which may result in a market failure. The results as you learned in Chapter 6 might be monopoly profits. Consumers can be harmed while monopolists benefit.

Does a relatively small number of firms necessarily mean a tendency toward noncompetitive prices and profits? No, according to some economists. They argue that competitive prices can prevail even though there are only a few firms. The model they use is called the **theory of contestable markets.** According to this theory,

**Theory of contestable markets**
*A hypothesis concerning pricing behavior that holds that even though there are only a few firms in an industry, they are forced to price their products more or less competitively because of the ease of entry by outsiders. The key aspect of a contestable market is relatively cheap entry into and exit from the industry.*

> ***Under certain circumstances, a few firms may still produce the output at which price equals marginal cost in both the short run and the long run. These firms will receive zero economic profits in the long run, just as perfect competitors do.***

Contestable markets can occur assuming two conditions.

1. **Unconstrained Ease of Entry and Exit:** For a market to be perfectly contestable, firms must be able to enter or leave the industry easily. In other words, there has to be freedom of entry and exit. The government cannot prevent firms from entering or from exiting the industry. ▸ **International**

**Example 8-13** In numerous European countries, once you enter an industry, the government may decide that you cannot leave it even though you want to shift production of your product to a lower-cost country. Therefore, such industries cannot be perfectly contestable. ◂

2. **Relatively Cheap Entry and Exit:** There must be an absence of important fixed costs for perfectly contestable markets to exist. In other words, a firm need buy no specific durable inputs in order to enter. Alternatively, if it does, it must be able to sell those durable inputs upon exit from the industry without significant losses. The issue is whether a *potential* entrant can easily get his or her investment out at any time in the future.

▸ **Example 8-14** Some economists argue that the market for regional airlines represents a contestable market. They point out that start-up regionals can lease airplanes relatively easily. Further, it is not too costly to back out of those leases if a particular regional market proves to be unprofitable. ◂

**Mastering Concepts:** Regulation: The Government Steps In

- **Economic regulation involves regulating prices, profits, and rates of output.**
- **Social regulation involves regulating for the public welfare by imposing occupational, health, and safety rules, for example.**
- **Firms and individuals react to regulations with creative responses that generate feedback effects, some of which may not be beneficial to society.**
- **Contestable markets occur when there is unconstrained ease of entry and exit and when it is relatively cheap to enter and exit the industry.**

## STRIKING BEFORE THINGS GET MESSY—THE RATIONALE OF ANTITRUST LAWS

While competition generally benefits consumers, producers and sellers certainly would prefer the easier life of monopoly. The federal government, though, decided a long time ago that monopolies and attempts to monopolize are not beneficial to the economy. Consequently, the federal government has passed a variety of **antitrust laws.** These laws aim to prevent new monopolies from forming and to break up those that already exist. The name *antitrust* is used because in the 1800s, numerous business **trusts** were created in which a number of businesses in the same industry allowed themselves to be part of a trust. In other words, a number of businesspeople in the same industry legally tied themselves together by transferring the ownership rights in their own companies to one or more persons, called trustees, who then managed all of the different firms' business affairs. Not surprisingly, the trust then acted as a monopolist, charging higher-than-competitive prices.

**Antitrust laws**
*Laws passed by federal and state governments to prevent new monopolies from forming and to break up those that already exist. Additionally, antitrust law attempts to prevent anticompetitive behavior, such as price fixing.*

**Trust**
*In the business context, an arrangement in which owners of firms in the same industry temporarily pass the ownership of their business to a trustee who then runs all of the businesses for the benefit of their owners, usually in a manner more consistent with monopoly than with competition.*

### ANTITRUST LEGISLATION

The industrial expansion after the Civil War fueled the rise of big businesses. John D. Rockefeller's Standard Oil Company was the most notorious for attempting to drive competitors out of business and pressuring customers not to deal with rival oil companies. He would also place members of Standard Oil's board of directors onto the board of a competing corporation. Because the same group of people, in effect, controlled both companies, it was less tempting for them to compete with one another. Rockefeller perfected this practice of creating **interlocking directorates**.

**Interlocking directorates**
*A board of directors, the majority of whose members also serve as the board of directors of a competing corporation.*

**Price-fixing agreement**
*An agreement between competitors to fix the prices of products or services at a certain level; prohibited by the Sherman Act.*

**Sherman Antitrust Act** Public pressure against Rockefeller's monopoly, or trust, over the oil business led Congress to pass the Sherman Antitrust Act in 1890. This law sought to protect trade and commerce against unlawful restraint—such as **price-fixing agreements**—and monopoly. ▸ Example 8-15 The first case prosecuted under the Sherman Act was *Standard Oil Company v. United States* in 1911. At that time Standard Oil of New Jersey consisted of 33 corporations bound together in a trust arrangement. The United States Supreme Court found that the trust combination controlled 90 percent of the business of producing, shipping, refining, and selling oil and was able to fix the price of crude and refined oil. Ruling that this was a blatant attempt to restrain and monopolize all interstate commerce in oil, the Court broke up the Standard Oil trust. ◂

Some economists believe that of all antitrust legislation the prohibition against price-fixing agreements has yielded the most positive benefits to the U.S. economy. Repeatedly, the United States Supreme Court has used the Sherman Act to hold illegal even implicit price-fixing agreements. The Court has never allowed any argument in favor of the "reasonableness" of a price-fixing agreement to be used as a defense. One famous justice, William O. Douglas (1898–1980), compared a freely functioning price system to the human body's central nervous system, condemning price-fixing agreements as threats to "the central nervous system of the economy."

**Clayton Act** Because the language in the Sherman Act was so vague, a new law was passed in 1914 to sharpen its antitrust provisions. The Clayton Act prohibited or limited a number of very specific business practices that lessened competition substantially. The Clayton Act, however, does not state what the term *substantially* means. As a result, it is up to the federal government to make a subjective decision as to whether the merging of two corporations would substantially lessen competition.

The Clayton Act also restricted price discrimination, or the practice of selling the same good to different buyers at different prices (see Chapter 7). In addition, the act prohibited sellers from requiring that a buyer not deal with a competitor. Finally, the act outlawed interlocking directorates.

### The Federal Trade Commission Act of 1914 and Its 1938 Amendment

The Federal Trade Commission Act was designed to stipulate acceptable competitive behavior. In particular, it was supposed to prevent cutthroat pricing—so-called excessively aggressive competition that would tend to eliminate too many competitors.

Among other things, the act created the Federal Trade Commission (FTC), which is charged with the power to investigate unfair competitive practices. The FTC can do this on its own or at the request of firms that feel they have been wronged. If it discovers "unfair methods of competition in commerce," it can issue cease and desist orders.

**Monopolization**
*The possession of monopoly power in the relevant market and the willful acquisition or maintenance of that power, as distinguished from growth or development as a consequence of a superior product, business acumen, or historical accident.*

## How Does the Government Enforce Antitrust Laws?

Most antitrust enforcement today is based on the Sherman Act. The Supreme Court has defined the offense of **monopolization** as involving the following elements:

1. The possession of monopoly power in the relevant market
2. The willful acquisition or maintenance of that power, as distinguished from growth or development as a consequence of a superior product, business acumen, or historical accident.

## Monopoly Power and the Relevant Market

The Sherman Act does not define monopoly. Monopoly clearly does not mean simply a single entity. Also, monopoly is not a function of size alone. ▸ **International Example 8-16** The top three corporations in the entire world are Wal-Mart Stores, General Motors, and ExxonMobil. Each firm's revenues per year exceed $180 billion. They operate in many countries in the world. Nonetheless, their gigantic size gives them virtually no monopoly power. Indeed, they are in some of the most competitive markets that exist—retail sales, automobiles, and gasoline. ◂

**The Market Share Test** It is difficult to define and measure market power precisely. As a workable proxy, courts often look to the firm's percentage share of the "relevant market." This is the so-called **market share test**. A firm is generally considered to have market power if its share of the relevant market is 70 percent or more. This is not an absolute pronouncement, however. It is only a loose rule of thumb; in some cases, the courts may hold that a smaller share constitutes monopoly power.

**Market share test**
*The percentage of a market that a particular firm supplies; used as the primary measure of market power.*

**What Is the Relevant Product Market?** The relevant market consists of two elements: a relevant product market and a relevant geographic market. What should the relevant product market include? It must include all products produced by different firms that have identical attributes, such as sugar. Yet products that are not identical may sometimes be substituted for one another. Coffee may be substituted for tea, for example.

In defining the relevant product market, the key issue is the degree of *interchangeability* between products. If one product is a sufficient substitute for another, the two products are considered to be part of the same product market. In the following *Policy Application,* you will read about the interchangeability of Internet browsers.

### POLICY APPLICATION: *United States v. Microsoft Corporation*

**Concepts Applied:**
***Market Power, Relevant Market, Interchangeability Between Products***

At the end of the 1990s and the beginning of the 2000s, the U.S. Department of Justice (as well as several state attorneys general) brought suit against Microsoft for monopolization in violation of Section II of the Sherman Act.

**Background of the Case**

In 1994, Netscape Communications Corporation began marketing Navigator, the first popular graphical Internet browser. Navigator worked with Java, a technology developed by Sun Microsystems, Inc. Java enabled applications to run on a variety of platforms, which meant that users did not need Microsoft's Windows. Perceiving a threat to its dominance of the operating-system market, Microsoft developed a competing browser, Internet Explorer

*Continued on next page*

(Explorer). Microsoft then began to require computer makers that wanted to install Windows also to install Explorer browser and exclude Navigator. Meanwhile, Microsoft commingled browser code and other code in Windows so that deleting files containing Explorer would cripple the operating system. Microsoft offered to promote and pay Internet service providers (ISPs) to distribute Explorer and exclude Navigator. Microsoft also developed its own Java code and deceived many independent software sellers into believing that this code would help in designing cross-platform applications when, in fact, it would run only on Windows.

### The Reasoning Behind the Court's Decision

The Court found that provisions in Microsoft's agreements licensing Windows to computer makers reduced the usage share of Netscape's browser and hence protected Microsoft's operating-system monopoly. In other words, Microsoft had acted to keep rival browsers from gaining sufficient users to attract software developers' attention away from Windows as the dominant platform for software development. The Court stated that "by insuring that the majority of all Internet service providers subscribers are offered [Microsoft's Internet Explorer] either as a default browser or as the only browser, Microsoft's deals with the Internet service providers clearly have a significant effect in preserving its monopoly."

### The Ultimate Agreement Between the Government and Microsoft

On November 1, 2002, a federal trial court judge approved a settlement between the government and Microsoft. Generally, the settlement gave customers more choices and allowed Microsoft's rivals more flexibility in offering competing software features on computers running Windows.

**For Critical Analysis:**
*Microsoft's operating system, Windows, is on about 90 percent of the world's personal computers. Does this fact alone necessarily indicate that Microsoft has obtained an illegal monopoly in computer operating systems? Why or why not?*

**What Are the Relative Geographic Boundaries** The second component of the relevant market is the *geographic boundaries* of the market. For products that are sold nationwide, the geographic boundaries of the market encompass the entire United States. If a producer and its competitors sell in only a limited area (one in which customers have no access to other sources of the product), the geographic market is limited to that area. A national firm may thus compete in several distinct areas and have monopoly power in one area but not in another. ▸ **International Example 8-17** Within the geographic boundaries of Mexico, the national cement company has monopoly power. Within the United States, in contrast, the same company competes with different companies. Consequently, the Mexican cement company does not have much, if any, monopoly power anywhere in this country. ◂

**Mastering Concepts:** Striking Before Things Get Messy—The Rationale of Antitrust Laws

- **The first national antitrust law was the Sherman Antitrust Act, passed in 1890, which made illegal every contract and combination in the form of a trust in restraint of trade.**
- **The Clayton Act made price discrimination and interlocking directorates illegal.**
- **The Federal Trade Commission Act of 1914 established the Federal Trade Commission.**
- **To enforce antitrust laws, the government must determine not only the relevant product market, but also the relevant geographic market.**

## GOVERNMENT: ITS FINANCING AND ITS FAILURES

As you have seen, government is involved in regulation, antitrust activities, national defense, and literally hundreds of thousands of other activities. Government is all around you. The first question we have to answer is how we pay for government. We do so, for the most part, via taxation.

### PAYING FOR THE PUBLIC SECTOR—TAXATION

Jean-Baptiste Colbert, the seventeenth-century French finance minister, said the art of taxation was in "plucking the goose so as to obtain the largest amount of feathers with the least possible amount of hissing." In the United States, governments have designed a variety of methods of plucking the private-sector goose. To analyze any tax system, we must first understand the distinction between marginal tax rates and average tax rates.

**Marginal and Average Tax Rates** If somebody says, "I pay 28 percent in taxes," you cannot really tell what that means unless you know whether the person is referring to average taxes paid or the tax rate on the last dollars earned. The latter concept refers to the **marginal tax rate.**

The marginal tax rate is expressed as follows:

$$\textbf{Marginal tax rate} = \frac{\textbf{change in taxes due}}{\textbf{change in taxable income}}$$

It is important to understand that the marginal tax rate applies only to the income in the highest **tax bracket** reached, where a tax bracket is defined as a specified level of taxable income to which a specific and unique marginal tax rate is applied.

The marginal tax rate is not the same as the **average tax rate,** which is defined as follows:

$$\textbf{Average tax rate} = \frac{\textbf{total taxes due}}{\textbf{total taxable income}}$$

**Marginal tax rate**
*The change in the tax payment divided by the change in income; the percentage of additional dollars that must be paid in taxes. The marginal tax rate is applied to the highest tax bracket of taxable income reached.*

**Tax bracket**
*A specified interval of income to which a specific and unique marginal tax rate is applied.*

**Average tax rate**
*The total tax payment divided by total income; the proportion of total income paid in taxes.*

▸ Example 8-18 Assume you are taxed 10 percent on the first $100 you make and 20 percent on the second $100 you make. In one week you earn $200. The government will take $10 of the first $100 you make and $20 of the second $100 you make. Your total taxes paid will be $30. So, your average tax rate will be $30 divided by $200, or 15 percent. But, because you were taxed 20 percent on the second $100, your marginal tax rate is 20 percent. ◂

**Taxation Systems** No matter how governments raise revenues—from income taxes, sales taxes, or other taxes—all taxes fit into one of three taxation systems, depending on the relationship between the tax rate paid and income: proportional, progressive, and regressive. To determine whether a tax system is proportional, progressive, or regressive, we simply ask, what is the relationship between the *average* tax rate and the *marginal* tax rate?

1. **Proportional Taxation: Proportional taxation** means that regardless of an individual's income, taxes comprise exactly the same proportion. In terms of marginal versus average tax rates, in a proportional taxation system, the marginal tax rate is always equal to the average tax rate. If every dollar is taxed at 20 percent, then the average tax rate is 20 percent, as is the marginal tax rate.
▸ Example 8-19 With a proportional tax rate of 20 percent, an individual

**Proportional taxation**
*A tax that takes the same percentage of all incomes. As income rises, the amount of tax paid also rises in proportion.*

with an income of $10,000 will pay $2,000 in taxes, while an individual making $100,000 will pay $20,000. The identical 20 percent rate is levied on both. ◀

**Progressive taxation**
*A tax that takes a larger percentage of higher incomes than lower incomes.*

2. **Progressive Taxation:** Under **progressive taxation**, as a person's taxable income increases, the percentage of income paid in taxes increases. In terms of marginal versus average tax rates, in a progressive system, the marginal tax rate is above the average tax rate. ▶ Example 8-20 If you are taxed 5 percent on the first $10,000 you make, 10 percent on the next $10,000 you make, and 30 percent on the last $10,000 you make, you face a progressive income tax system. Your marginal tax rate is always above your average tax rate. ◀

**Regressive taxation**
*A tax that takes a larger percentage of lower incomes than higher incomes.*

3. **Regressive Taxation:** With **regressive taxation**, a smaller percentage of taxable income is taken in taxes as taxable income increases. The marginal rate is *below* the average rate. As income increases, the marginal tax rate falls, and so does the average tax rate. ▶ Example 8-21 The U.S. Social Security tax is regressive. Once the maximum taxable wage base is reached, no further Social Security taxes are paid. Thus, after that maximum wage base, the *marginal* tax rate is zero and the more you earn, the lower is your *average* Social Security tax. ◀

## Government Failures

**Government failure**
*Any situation in which the government intervenes in the economy with a negative result; that is, a situation in which government intervention reduces, rather than improves, the welfare of society.*

When government engages in activities that reduce social welfare or economic efficiency, we call this situation one of **government failure**. This failure is akin to the concept of market failure. Just as with market failure, there are many possible types of government failures. To end this chapter, we will look at the following types of government failures:

1. Government actions that reduce competition, especially from abroad.
2. Improper pricing of health care, particularly through Medicare.
3. Inefficient methods of regulation.

**The Government Actually Stifles Some Competition** We live in a democracy in which citizens, including businesspeople, can lobby Congress to change or enact legislation. Not surprisingly, these lobbying efforts often, if not always, are aimed at benefiting small groups of individuals, usually in a specific industry. Whenever these lobbying efforts are successful, the interested small group benefits at the expense of the general public.

One of the most flagrant examples of government failure involves the imposition of specific taxes on imported goods or quotas on certain imported goods. In both cases, the benefits to the domestic industries that are protected are far outweighed by the costs to the rest of society. We treat such *protectionism* in more detail in Chapter 16. ▶ Example 8-22 In 2002, President George W. Bush fought for and obtained a 30 percent "special" tax on all steel imported into the United States. One of the effects was a doubling of the price of hot-rolled steel, a major industrial commodity. The higher price of steel cost U.S. jobs. The Consuming Industries Trade Action Coalition found that higher steel prices destroyed 200,000 U.S. jobs and cost $4 billion in lost wages for the period February to November 2002. Some of those lost jobs were in auto supply factories. ◀

In general, much federal government legislation in the area of foreign trade is carried out at the behest of special interest groups and paid for by the general public in the form of higher prices for imports and import-competing goods.

**Incorrectly Pricing Health Care Services** The U.S. health care industry is huge. The United States spends a larger percentage of gross domestic product

(GDP) on health care than any other country. Currently, as you can see in Figure 8-2, we are spending about 15 percent of GDP on health care.

Part of the reason that health care spending in the United States has increased so much is that the government—along with private insurance companies—gives the wrong signals to consumers of health care services. Specifically, the government through **Medicare** slowly but surely has driven the apparent price of medical care to zero for recipients and their families, inducing them to make choices that are wasteful by any criteria. ▸ Example 8-23 When Medicare started in the 1960s, the volume of government-reimbursed medical services increased almost immediately by more than 65 percent. Medicare is now the second-biggest domestic spending program in existence, and it is guaranteed to become the largest domestic spending program in the federal government's budget in the future. ◂

**Medicare**
*A federal government program designed to help those over 65 pay for health care services.*

**Inefficient Regulation Systems** We have already talked about economic and social regulation in this chapter. Such regulation has as its basis an attempt to rectify market failures. In fact, though, regulations are sometimes applied in a way that leads to government failures instead. Many of the regulations supposedly aimed at protecting consumers from unethical, unsavory, or incompetent professionals actually lead to a restriction in supply. One certainly cannot reasonably argue that astrologers should be licensed, yet they are in some states. ▸ Example 8-24 Many municipalities severely restrict the number of taxicab licenses. The city governments generally claim that they impose those restrictions so that passengers do not have to worry about incompetent or dishonest drivers. In fact, though, these restrictions simply restrict entry into that business. Additionally, the restrictions have prevented the development of alternative forms of transportation such as jitneys—taxis that follow a fixed route picking up and letting out customers along the way. ◂

✦ **Be Aware!** *The result of some government regulations is to restrict entry, thereby benefiting existing businesses.*

Many types of regulation designed to reduce the negative externalities from pollution are carried out in such a manner that they are inefficient. This may occur whenever government regulators impose a production process to reduce pollution

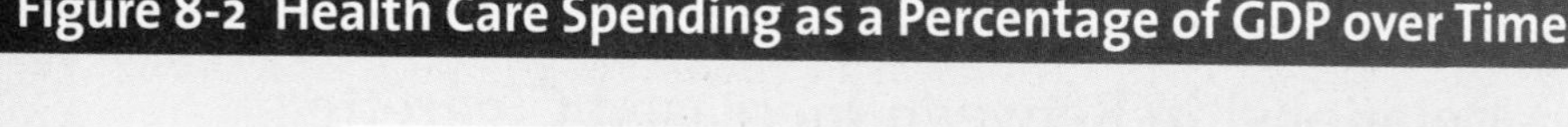

**Figure 8-2 Health Care Spending as a Percentage of GDP over Time**

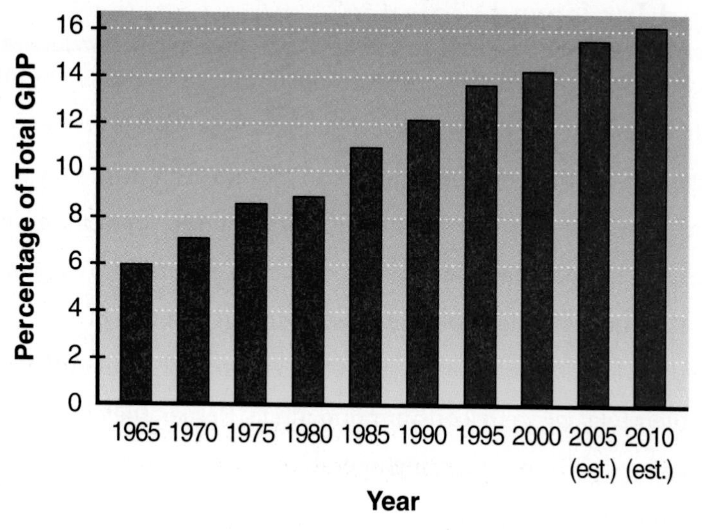

*"You're in luck, in a way. Now is the time to be sick—while Medicare still has some money."*

©J.B. Handelsman. Reprinted by permission of the New Yorker.

rather than setting a particular pollution reduction requirement and letting businesses figure out the most efficient ways to meet that standard. ▸ **Example 8-25** The government required that electric utilities install sulfur "scrubbers" rather than simply making the utilities meet an emissions standard. The effect is to keep inefficient West Virginia coal mines in business. Additionally, the air is actually dirtier, not cleaner, than it would be if electric utilities met emission requirements by buying cleaner western coal instead of eastern coal. ◂

## *Solving the Economic Problem:* Is There a Relationship Between Increased Cigarette Taxes and Increased Violence?

At $3 a pack for taxes, the lure of profits from smuggling relatively lightly taxed cigarettes from such states as North Carolina into New York is just too great. Several important rival gangs that operate in and around New York City are involved in large-scale cigarette smuggling. They want to protect their turf, so they "wipe out" competition. This competition can come from rival gangs, but more often than not, it comes from small-scale smugglers. When New York City residents reduced their purchases of cigarettes via normal retail outlets, they did not reduce their total cigarette consumption much. Rather, they began to purchase their cigarettes from smuggling operations, from retailers in border states, and through the Internet.

**Mastering Concepts:** Government: Its Financing and Its Failures

- **Whereas the average tax rate is simply the total amount of taxes due divided by total taxable income, the marginal tax rate is calculated by dividing the change in taxes due by the change in taxable income.**
- **In a proportional tax system, the marginal and average tax rates are the same, whereas in a progressive tax system, the marginal tax rate is greater than the average tax rate.**
- **With a regressive tax system, the marginal tax rate is below the average tax rate.**
- **Government failure occurs whenever government actions lead to lower overall welfare for the nation.**
- **Some areas of government failure involve stifling competition from abroad, incorrectly pricing health care services, and inefficiently applying regulations.**

## SUMMING IT ALL UP

- When social costs exceed private costs, negative externalities may occur.
- When social benefits exceed private benefits, positive externalities may occur.
- The government can correct externalities in principle via regulation or taxes and subsidies.
- The key characteristics of public goods are that (1) additional users do not take away from others' benefits and (2) it is hard to collect payments for a public good based on individual use.
- True public goods may represent a market failure because the private sector has trouble providing them.
- Economic regulation involves regulating prices, profits, and rates of output.
- Social regulation involves regulating for the public welfare by imposing occupational, health, and safety rules, for example.
- Firms and individuals react to regulations with creative responses that generate feedback effects, some of which may not be beneficial to society.
- Contestable markets occur when there is unconstrained ease of entry and exit and when it is relatively cheap to enter and exit the industry.
- The first national antitrust law was the Sherman Antitrust Act, passed in 1890, which made illegal every contract and combination in the form of a trust in restraint of trade.
- The Clayton Act made price discrimination and interlocking directorates illegal.
- The Federal Trade Commission Act of 1914 established the Federal Trade Commission.
- To enforce antitrust laws, the government must determine not only the relevant product market, but also the relevant geographic market.
- Whereas the average tax rate is simply the total amount of taxes due divided by total taxable income, the marginal tax rate is calculated by dividing the change in taxes due by the change in taxable income.

- In a proportional tax system, the marginal and average tax rates are the same, whereas in a progressive tax system, the marginal tax rate is greater than the average tax rate.
- With a regressive tax system, the marginal tax rate is below the average tax rate.
- Government failure occurs whenever government actions lead to lower overall welfare for the nation.

## KEY TERMS AND CONCEPTS

antitrust laws **163**
average tax rate **167**
creative response **161**
economic regulation **161**
externality **157**
feedback effect **161**
government failure **168**
interlocking directorates **164**
marginal tax rate **167**
market failures **156**
market share test **165**
Medicare **169**
monopolization **164**
negative externalities **157**
positive externality **159**
price-fixing agreements **164**
principle of rival consumption **159**
private costs **156**
private goods **159**
progressive taxation **168**
proportional taxation **167**
public goods **160**
regressive taxation **168**
regulation **161**
social regulation **161**
tax bracket **167**
theory of contestable markets **162**
trusts **163**

## MASTERING ECONOMIC CONCEPTS
## Questions and Problems

**8-1.** For a good like cigars that features an external cost, would an unregulated market produce too much of this good or too little? Would the market price the good too high or too low?

**8-2.** Based on the characteristics of public goods, are public tennis courts an example of a public good? Why or why not?

**8-3.** If Ana Maria earns $200,000 and pays income taxes of $40,000 each year and Luis earns $80,000 and pays income taxes of $16,000 each year, is their tax system progressive, proportional, or regressive?

**8-4.** Would the U.S. software industry and Microsoft's role in it constitute a contestable market based on the two conditions of contestable markets?

**8-5.** Which antitrust law prohibited overly competitive behavior with respect to pricing? In an economy that favors competition, why is it necessary to limit competitive behavior in any case?

**8-6.** During 2002, General Motors sold about 4.7 million vehicles in the U.S. Over the same time period, industry sales totaled 16.7 million units. Based on these figures alone, did General Motors represent a virtual monopoly based on the standard market share test?

**8-7.** Above an income level of $87,000, U.S. wage earners did not pay any Social Security tax in 2003. At any income level below $87,000, however, all wage earners paid 6.2 percent. Below the $87,000 income level is the Social Security tax progressive, proportional, or regressive?

**8-8.** In some situations, sales of items purchased over the Internet are not subject to sales tax. Make an argument as to whether this lack of sales tax on e-commerce is progressive or regressive.

**8-9.** Consider a fishery management program designed to prevent overfishing that could lead to near extinction of certain species. If this program limits the number of fishing vessels and the fishing season for a certain area, what creative response might we expect to see from commercial fishers?

**8-10.** In the United States, gasoline taxes range from 7.5¢ to 36¢ per gallon from state to state. As a result, the price that consumers pay at the pump is very different in each state. How could a gas tax be used as a means of dealing with the external cost of pollution associated with gas consumption? Would a higher gas tax be more progressive or regressive?

**8-11.** State highway departments have two general options for de-icing roadways—salt or calcium magnesium acetate (CMA). The cost of using salt for roadways across the United States is approximately $1 billion less than the cost of using CMA. According to the Environmental Protection Agency, however, using CMA would reduce environmental and property damage by approximately $1.9 billion. Based on these figures, which substance would you choose to use to de-ice roads? Does the fact that state highway departments use salt constitute government failure?

**8-12.** My friend Brad made the following statement: "Because the rich pay more dollars in taxes than the poor do, the U.S income tax system is progressive." Although the U.S. income tax system is progressive, there is an error in his statement. What is the error?

**8-13.** Why have some state and local governments elected to eliminate taxes on groceries? Would grocery taxes be progressive, proportional, or regressive? Why?

**8-14.** Consider the "market" for a visit to a doctor's office as depicted by the graph alongside. Assume that HMOs require only a $10 copay for any visit. Based on this graph, what quantity of visits would consumers demand at $10? What quantity would the doctors wish to supply at a price of $10? Does the difference between these quantities result in a change in the costs within the industry?

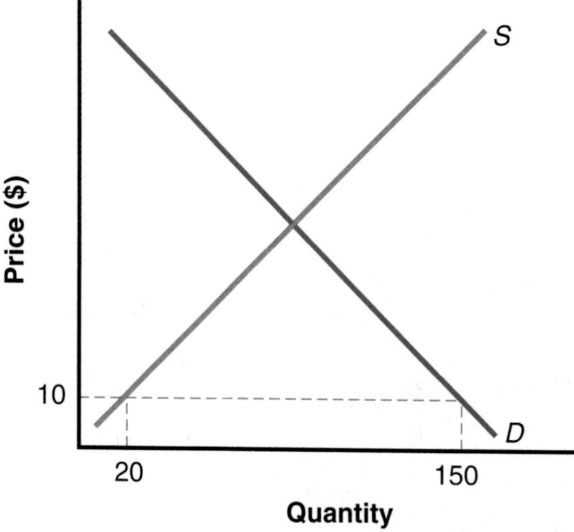


**8-15.** There are more than ten gas stations within 3 miles of my home, but there are only two gas stations near my work, which is 40 miles away. In terms of geographic boundaries, would these two areas be considered part of the same relevant product market? Why or why not?

## THINKING CRITICALLY

**8-1.** In Manhattan, the rental price for a one-bedroom apartment can easily exceed $3,000. As a result, the city has established a price ceiling on some apartments through its rent control policy. What would this price ceiling do to the quantity of apartments demanded? What would it do to the quantity of apartments supplied? Would this result in a surplus or a shortage? In terms of creative response, what might some landlords choose to do with respect to the quality of the apartment units or the apartment building itself? If you were renting out a furnished apartment, how could you attempt to get around the rent controls?

**8-2.** The 2003 U.S. income tax rate schedule for a single filer is listed alongside. Based on this table, an individual earning $80,000 in taxable income will pay $17,145.32 in income taxes to the U.S. government. What is the average tax rate for this individual? At an income level of $80,000, what is this individual's marginal tax rate? If this individual can earn another $10,000 in income by working harder, which rate should he or she use in determining if the extra work is worth the effort? How much of this additional $10,000 would the individual have to pay to the federal government in taxes?

| Taxable Income | Tax Rate |
|---|---|
| $0—$7,000 | 10% |
| $7,001—$28,400 | 15% |
| $28,401—$68,800 | 25% |
| $68,801—$143,500 | 28% |
| $143,501—$311,950 | 33% |

**8-3.** Various state and local governments have instituted policies aimed at promoting water conservation. Each of these policies has as its goal a reduction in water consumption. Evaluate the following policies to determine if each would be effective in reducing consumption; also point out any flaws or shortcomings of each policy.

a. Consumers are allowed to water their lawns or wash their cars only on even days of the month if their address ends in an even number and only on odd days if their address ends in an odd number.

b. Consumers are billed an extra $100 if their total household water consumption exceeds 25,000 gallons per month.

c. Consumers are billed $1.85 for every 1,000 gallons of water they use.

d. Consumers are billed $1.65 per 1,000 gallons for the first 20,000 gallons they use and $2.65 per 1,000 gallons thereafter.

## LOGGING ON

1. Learn about how the U.S. Environmental Protection Agency seeks to induce companies to comply with efforts to reduce the external costs of pollution by going to http://www.epa.gov/compliance/.
2. To see the various regulatory activities of just one U.S. government agency, the Federal Trade Commission, go to http://www.ftc.gov/.
3. Take a look at recent activities of the U.S. Justice Department's Antitrust Division at http://www.usdoj.gov/atr/.
4. To contrast European antitrust policies with the U.S. approach, go to http://europa.eu.int/comm/competition/index_en.html.

## USING THE INTERNET FOR ECONOMIC ANALYSIS

**Exploring U.S. Government Regulations** The chapter discusses the breadth of coverage of federal regulation of economic activities. This application allows you to get a feel for the pervasiveness of U.S. government regulations.

**Title:** Code of Federal Regulations

**Navigation:** Go to http://www.gpoaccess.gov/cfr/index.html.

**Application** Perform the indicated operations, and answer the following questions.

1. Under "Quick Search," type in the name of three products that come to mind, such as drugs, kitchen sinks, and textbooks. For each product, the following page records the number of "hits" in the *Code of Federal Regulations*. Scroll to the very end of the list, and next to "Query Report for this Search," click on "Text." How many times does the word appear in government regulatory documents? In how many documents does it appear? Why do you suppose the federal government regulates (or, in rare cases, does not regulate) the products you selected?
2. Go back to the main page, and under "Related Resources," click on "Federal Register," which is the main publication reporting U.S. government regulatory activities. Click on "Go" next to "Browse the Table of Contents from back issues" for the most recent full year, and then click on the last December issue of that year. Page numbers appear under each entry. About how many pages were in the *Federal Register* for this particular year? Why do you suppose that some economists use annual page counts from the *Federal Register* as a measure of the pervasiveness of U.S. government regulations?

## MEDIA RESOURCE LIST

The following media resources are available with this chapter:

- Load your CD-ROM to listen to the audio introduction to this chapter.
- Load your CD-ROM to access a Graph Animation of Figure 8-1, *External Costs and Benefits.*
- Load your CD-ROM to view the video on *Providing Public Goods.*
- Load your CD-ROM to view the video on *Results of Regulation—Creative Response.*
- Load your CD-ROM to view the video on *Contestable Markets.*
- Load your CD-ROM to view the video on *Enforcement of Antitrust Laws.*
- Load your CD-ROM to view the video on *Paying for the Public Sector.*
- Load your CD-ROM to view the video on *Medicare.*
- Test your knowledge of chapter concepts with a quiz at www.miller-ume.com.
- Link to Web resources related to the text coverage at www.miller-ume.com.

## HOMEWORK SET

Go to the back of this book to find the Homework Problems for this chapter.

# CHAPTER 9

# Labor Economics

## *Facing an Economic Problem:* Can We Make Sure That Everyone Earns at Least a "Living" Wage?

"Working for peanuts" is not something most people like to do. Nonetheless, many U.S. residents believe that that is exactly what they are being paid—peanuts. Indeed, more than 26 million workers in this country earn less than $8.25 an hour.

A number of cities have decided that they can solve this problem of low wages. They have passed so-called living wage laws, guaranteeing that those who work for city governments earn anywhere from $8 to $15 an hour. For example, a living wage in New York City is $9.60. In Cincinnati it is $8.70. In Fairfax, California, it is $14.75. Some cities impose such living wages on all employers within city limits.

Of course, at the federal level, Congress has legislated a type of living wage called the *minimum wage.* Under most circumstances, it is illegal to pay workers less than the minimum wage. The question remains, though, whether we can solve the problem of low wages by legislating so-called living wages. After you read the analysis of labor supply and demand in this chapter, you will better understand why it is difficult to solve the low-wage problem by legislating minimum wage rates.

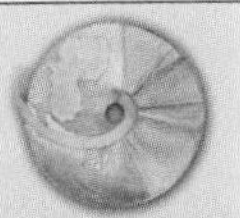

***Refer to the back of this chapter for a complete listing of multimedia learning materials available on the CD-ROM and the Web site.***

### Learning Objectives:

After reading this chapter, you should be able to:

- **Determine why the demand curve for labor slopes downward.**
- **List some of the reasons why the demand curve for labor will shift and why the supply curve for labor will shift.**
- **Explain why raising the federal minimum wage typically leads to higher unemployment among unskilled workers.**
- **State one of the major roles of a labor union.**
- **Describe the determinants of the differences in income.**

## THE SUPPLY OF LABOR

Starting in Chapter 3, you became used to analyzing many problems in terms of the supply of and the demand for a particular good or service. Analyzing the labor market in the United States requires the same use of demand and supply analysis. Though some social, political, and philosophical commentators would like to think otherwise, from an economic perspective, the labor market is the same as all other markets.

### WHAT DETERMINES THE TOTAL SUPPLY OF LABOR?

Think about what determines how many hours you would be willing to work. Obviously, how much you like the job counts. Working conditions, including the congeniality of your coworkers, count, too. In fact, numerous factors might enter into your decision about how many hours to work at a particular job.

**The Wage Rate Is the Most Important Determinant of How Much People Choose to Work** It turns out that the single most important determinant of your quantity of labor supplied is how much you are paid. The more you are paid per hour, in general the more hours you are willing to work—up to a certain point, obviously. You will never want to work 24 hours a day, seven days a week, or not even close to that, no matter how high a wage rate someone offers you.

**Labor-Leisure Choice** The choice you have is between working and not working. Not working, of course, is our leisure time. Ignore the time that you sleep and think about just the time that you are awake. The *opportunity cost* of working one more hour is the value that you place on an hour of leisure activities. These could include reading, listening to music, playing with your children (if you have them), spending time with relatives and other loved ones, and watching television.

*"It's a good thing this is a leisure-time activity, because you could't pay me to do it."*

© Barbara Smaller. Reprinted with permission of the New Yorker.

Another way of looking at it is in terms of the opportunity cost of one more hour of leisure. If you decide to work one hour less, what is your opportunity cost? It is your after-tax wage rate.

***The higher your after-tax wage rate, the higher the opportunity cost of an hour of leisure.***

As an individual, then, you would expect that the higher the opportunity cost of leisure, the lower would be your quantity demanded. What does that mean?

***The higher the after-tax wage rate you are offered, the more hours you will work.***

Economists call this the **substitution effect**. The substitution effect occurs as individuals change the quantity demanded due to the substitution of a relatively cheaper good for a relatively more expensive good (holding all other things constant). Here, the more expensive good is leisure, and so people substitute away from it as its opportunity cost goes up. You can see this in Figure 9-1.

**Substitution effect**
*The change in the quantity demanded due to the substitution of a relatively cheaper good for a relatively more expensive good.*

**The Income Effect—When Things Really Get Good** Assume that your wage rate just keeps going up and up and up. In other words, you are getting richer and richer. This means that every hour of leisure has a higher and higher opportunity cost. Does that necessarily mean you will want to keep working more and more hours because the alternative—leisure—has such a high opportunity cost? The answer is probably no, at least after a certain income level.

At some point the **income effect** takes over. That is to say, because you are getting richer, you decide that in spite of the high opportunity cost of leisure, you want to buy more. Otherwise stated, you will want to work less. At some point, for just about everybody, higher wage rates lead the individual worker to work less rather than more. ▸ **International Example 9-1** After Algeria became independent of France in the 1960s, U.S. companies came and offered Algerian

**Income effect**
*The change in the quantity demanded of a good due to a change in real income.*

**Figure 9-1 The Supply of Labor Curve for One Individual**

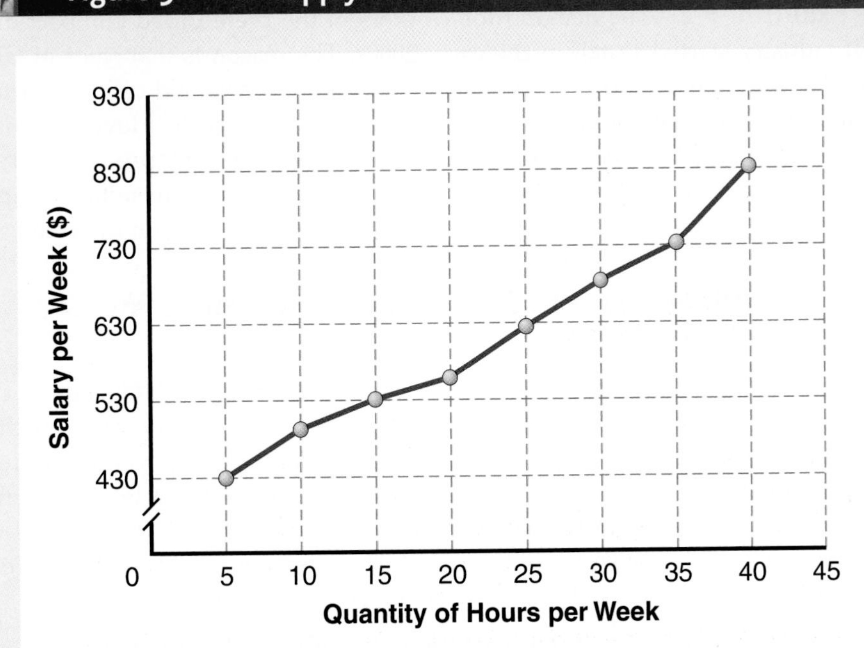


This individual, if offered $430 a week, is willing to work only 5 hours. At $630 a week, though, he or she would work 25 hours a week. At $830 a week, this person will work a full 40-hour week.

workers considerably higher wages than they had been receiving. Many of the workers worked for a few months and then quit. Why? Because, after a few months, they had already earned more than they were used to earning in an entire year. They decided to take the rest of the year off! ◂

**Mastering Concepts:** The Supply of Labor

- **Because the cost of leisure is its opportunity cost, the higher the after-tax wage rate, the larger the quantity of labor supplied, in general. This is called the substitution effect.**
- **As after-tax wages rise, eventually workers become so rich that they want to buy more of everything, including leisure, so the quantity supplied of labor actually starts to fall. This is called the income effect.**

## THE DEMAND FOR LABOR

As always, there is a flip side to the analysis. In this case, it is the demand for workers. The first thing that becomes obvious when we discuss the demand for labor is that it is not exactly the same as the demand for a good or service that you individually wish to purchase. After all, factories do not hire workers simply because the factory owners like to have workers around. Rather, workers are hired to produce a good or service.

### Labor Demand as a Derived Demand

**Derived demand**
*Demand for an input factor that is derived from the demand for the final product being produced.*

The demand for labor is a **derived demand**, derived from the demand for a final good or service.

***All other things held constant, the greater the demand for the final good or service being produced, the greater the demand for workers.***

▸ Example 9-2 The demand for workers in the prerecorded compact disc (CD) industry started to fall in the early 2000s. The reason is that sales of CDs started to fall as more people, especially those in high school and college, started file sharing over the Internet, thereby avoiding having to buy their favorite artists on CDs. (Not surprisingly, the music industry has attacked the problem in two ways: creating Web sites that sell individual songs and filing lawsuits for copyright infringement against those who aid and abet music sharing on the Web.) ◂

### The Demand for Labor Also Depends on How Much a Worker Can Produce

Because the demand for labor is a derived demand, labor demand depends on the demand for final output. Additionally, labor demand depends on how much a worker can produce. This is true whether we are talking about a worker producing automobiles or a worker producing the services involved in telemarketing, laser skin treatments, or software development.

Moreover, even if a worker can produce 1,000 horseshoes in one day, if there is not much demand for horseshoes, they are not going to be very valuable.

***The two factors that determine the value of a worker to an employer are how much product—goods or services—the worker can produce in a given time period and how much each unit of that product is worth.***

▸ Example 9-3 In many school districts, teachers who obtain additional advanced degrees are paid higher salaries. The reasoning is that they are able to provide their students with higher-quality teaching. In many businesses, managers who complete executive MBA programs receive raises. Presumably, the value of their services goes up after they obtain the additional education. ◂

## Deriving the Demand Curve for Labor

To derive a hypothetical demand curve for labor, we need to have some numbers. We will look at the industry that sells blank CDs. We assume that, even though the individual supply curve of labor slopes up as in Figure 9-1, any given employer in the blank CD industry can hire all the workers he or she wants at the going market wage rate. In other words, any one CD manufacturer faces a perfectly elastic supply of labor, which is shown in panel (b) in Figure 9-2 on page 182 as the curve *s*.

We know from the discussion above that employers need to look at the physical output workers can generate as well as the value of the product they generate. Let us look at those two elements of the demand for labor now.

**Marginal Physical Product** Look at panel (a) of Figure 9-2. In column 1, we show the number of workers per week that the firm can hire. In column 2, we show, the total *physical* production of packages of 10 CDs that different quantities of the labor input (in combination with a fixed amount of other inputs) will generate in a week's time. In column 3, we show the additional output gained when the CD manufacturing company adds workers to its existing manufacturing facility. This column, the **marginal physical product (MPP) of labor**, represents the extra (additional) output attributed to employing additional units of the variable input factor. If this firm employs seven workers rather then six, the MPP is 118.

**Marginal physical product (MPP) of labor**
*The change in output resulting from the addition of one more worker. The MPP of the worker equals the change in total output accounted for by hiring the worker, holding all other factors of production constant.*

The law of diminishing marginal returns predicts that additional units of a variable factor will, after some point, cause the MPP to decline, other things held constant.

**Why Marginal Physical Product Declines—Diminishing Marginal Returns Revisited** We are assuming that all other nonlabor factors of production are held constant. So if our CD manufacturing firm wants to add one more worker to its production line, it has to crowd all the existing workers a little closer together because it does not increase its capital stock (the production equipment). Therefore, as we add more workers, each one has a smaller and smaller fraction of the available capital stock with which to work. If one worker uses one machine, adding another worker usually won't double the output because the machine can run only so fast and for so many hours per day. In other words, MPP declines because of the law of diminishing marginal returns, which you learned about in Chapter 5.

**Marginal Revenue Product** We now need to translate into a dollar value the physical product that results from hiring an additional worker. Multiplying the marginal physical product by the marginal revenue of the firm does this. Because our CD firm is selling its product in a perfectly competitive market, marginal revenue is equal to the price of the product. If employing seven workers rather than six yields an MPP of 118 and the marginal revenue is $10 per package of 10 CDs, the **marginal revenue product (MRP)** is $1,180 (118 × $10). The MRP is shown in column 4 of panel (a) of Figure 9-2 on the next page.

**Marginal revenue product (MRP)**
*The marginal physical product (MPP) times marginal revenue. The MRP gives the additional revenue obtained from a one-unit change in labor input.*

***Marginal revenue product represents the incremental worker's contribution to the firm's total revenues.***

*Animated*

## Figure 9-2 Marginal Revenue Product

In panel (a), column 4 shows marginal revenue product (MRP), which is the amount of additional revenue the firm receives for the sale of that additional output. Marginal revenue product is simply the amount of revenues the additional worker brings in—the combination of that worker's contribution to production and the additional revenue that that production will bring to the firm. For this perfectly competitive firm, marginal revenue is equal to the price of the product, or $10 per unit. At a weekly wage of $830, the profit-maximizing employer will pay for only 12 workers because then the MRP is just equal to the wage rate or weekly salary.

**Panel (a)**

| (1) Labor Input (workers per week) | (2) Total Physical Product (TPP) (CD packages per week) | (3) Marginal Physical Product (MPP) (CD packages per week) | (4) Marginal Revenue (MR = *P* = $10 net) x MPP = Marginal Revenue Product (MRP) ($ per additional worker) | (5) Wage Rate ($ per week) = Marginal Factor Cost (MFC) = Change in Total Costs ÷ Change in Labor |
|---|---|---|---|---|
| 6 | 882 | | | |
| | | 118 | $1,180 | $830 |
| 7 | 1,000 | | | |
| | | 111 | 1,110 | 830 |
| 8 | 1,111 | | | |
| | | 104 | 1,040 | 830 |
| 9 | 1,215 | | | |
| | | 97 | 970 | 830 |
| 10 | 1,312 | | | |
| | | 90 | 900 | 830 |
| 11 | 1,402 | | | |
| | | 83 | 830 | 830 |
| 12 | 1,485 | | | |
| | | 76 | 760 | 830 |
| 13 | 1,561 | | | |

In panel (b), we find the number of workers the firm will want to hire by observing the wage rate that is established by the forces of supply and demand in the entire labor market. We show that this employer is hiring labor in a perfectly competitive labor market and therefore faces a perfectly elastic supply curve represented by *s* at $830 per week. As in other situations, we have a supply and demand model; in this example, the demand curve is represented by MRP, and the supply curve is *s*. Equilibrium occurs at their intersection.

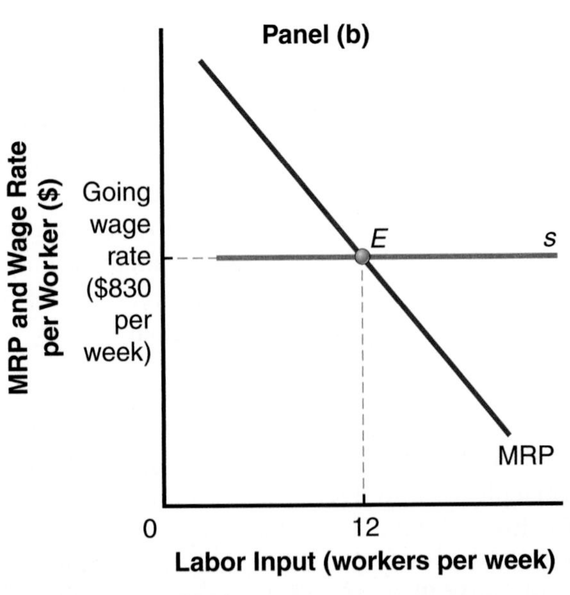

▸ **Example 9-4** Two economists, Daniel Hamermesh and Jeff Biddle, attempted to discover whether there was any relationship between people's looks and their marginal revenue product. Through their research, the economists discovered that "plain-looking" people earn 5 to 10 percent less than people having "average looks," who in turn earn 5 percent less than those who are considered "good looking." According to Hamermesh and Biddle, part of the wage differential may be created by the fact that attractiveness leads to higher MRP. More attractive individuals may have higher self-esteem, which in turn causes them to be more productive on the job. ◂

**Marginal Factor Cost** In column 5 of panel (a) of Figure 9-2, we show the wage rate, or *marginal factor cost*, of each worker. The marginal cost of workers is the extra cost incurred in employing an additional unit of that factor of production. We call that cost the **marginal factor cost (MFC)**. Otherwise stated,

**Marginal factor cost (MFC)**
*The cost of using an additional unit of an input. For example, if a firm can hire all the workers it wants at the going wage rate, the MFC of labor is the wage rate.*

$$\textbf{Marginal factor cost} = \frac{\textbf{change in total cost}}{\textbf{change in amount of resource used}}$$

Because each worker is paid the same competitively determined wage of $830 per week, the MFC is the same for all workers. And because the firm is buying labor in a perfectly competitive labor market, the wage rate of $830 per week really represents the supply curve of labor to the firm. That curve is perfectly elastic because the firm, as a minuscule part of the entire labor-purchasing market, can purchase all labor at the same wage rate. (Recall the definition of perfect competition.) We show this perfectly elastic supply curve as *s* in panel (b) of Figure 9-2.

**General Rule for Hiring** Virtually every optimizing rule in economics involves comparing marginal benefits with marginal cost. Because the benefit from added workers is extra output and consequently more revenues, a firm's hiring decision follows this general rule:

> ***The firm hires workers up to the point at which the additional cost associated with hiring the last worker is equal to the additional revenue generated by the worker.***

In a perfectly competitive market, this is the point at which the wage rate just equals the marginal revenue product (MRP). If the firm hired more workers, the additional wages would not be covered by additional increases in total revenues. If the firm, hired fewer workers, it would be forfeiting the contributions that those workers could make to total profits.

Therefore, referring to columns 4 and 5 in panel (a) of Figure 9-2, we see that this firm would certainly employ at least seven workers because the MRP is $1,180 while the MFC is only $830. The firm would continue to add workers up to the point at which MFC = MRP because as workers are added, they contribute more to revenue than to cost.

## The Demand for Labor Curve Is the Marginal Revenue Product Curve

We can also use panel (b) of Figure 9-2 to find out how many workers our firm should hire. First, we draw a line at the going wage rate, which is determined by demand and supply in the labor market. The line is labeled *s* to indicate that it is the supply curve of labor facing the *individual* firm purchasing labor in a perfectly competitive labor market. That firm can purchase all the labor it wants of equal quality at $830 per worker. This perfectly elastic supply curve, *s*, intersects the MRP curve at 12 workers per week.

✦ **Remember!** *All demand curves slope down, even for labor. Therefore, the higher the price of labor—the wage rate—the lower the quantity demanded, all other things held constant.*

At the intersection, *E*, the wage rate is equal to the marginal revenue product.

***Equilibrium for the firm is obtained when the firm's demand curve for labor, which turns out to be its MRP curve, intersects the firm's supply curve for labor, shown as* s.**

The firm in our example would not hire the thirteenth worker, who will add $830 to cost but only $760 to revenue. If the price of labor should fall to, say, $760 per worker per week, it would become profitable for the firm to hire an additional worker; there is an increase in the quantity of labor demanded as the wage decreases.

**Mastering Concepts:** The Demand for Labor

- **Because labor demand is a derived demand, the greater the demand for final output, the greater the demand for workers.**
- **The marginal physical product (MPP) of labor represents the additional output attributed to employing additional units of labor.**
- **The marginal revenue product (MRP) is the additional worker's contribution to the firm's total revenues.**
- **The wage rate in a perfectly competitive labor market is the marginal factor cost (MFC) for an employer.**
- **The MRP curve represents the demand curve for labor.**

## WHAT HAPPENS WHEN LABOR DEMAND OR SUPPLY CHANGES?

Just as we discussed shifts in the supply curve and the demand curve for various products in Chapter 3, we can discuss the effects of shifts in supply and demand in labor markets.

### REASONS FOR LABOR DEMAND CURVE SHIFTS

Many factors can cause the demand curve for labor to shift. We have already discussed a number of them.

***Because the demand for labor or any other variable input is a derived demand, the labor demand curve will shift if there is a shift in the demand for the final product.***

**Changes in Demand for Final Product** The demand for labor or any other variable input is derived from the demand for the final product. As you already learned, the marginal revenue product (MRP) is equal to marginal physical product times marginal revenue. For a perfectly competitive market, marginal revenue is equal to price (see Chapter 6). Therefore, any change in the price of the final product will change MRP. This applies to the market demand for labor. The general rule of thumb is as follows:

***A change in the demand for the final product that labor (or any other variable input) is producing will shift the market demand curve for labor in the same direction.***

There are two other important determinants of the position of the demand curve for labor: changes in labor's productivity and changes in the price of related factors of production (substitutes and complements).

**Changes in Labor Productivity** The second part of the MRP equation is marginal physical product, or MPP, which relates to **labor productivity**. We can surmise, then, that, other things being equal,

**Labor productivity**
*The amount of product that a worker can produce in a given time period.*

***A change in labor productivity will shift the market labor demand curve in the same direction.***

Labor productivity can increase because labor has more capital or land with which to work, because of technological improvements, or because labor's quality has improved. ▸ Example 9-5 Such considerations explain why the real standard of living of workers in the United States is higher than in most countries. American workers generally work with a larger capital stock, have more natural resources, are in better physical condition, and are better trained than workers in many other countries. Hence the demand for labor in the United States is greater, other things held constant. ◂

**Change in the Price of Substitute Factors** Labor is not the only resource used. Some resources are substitutes and some are complements. If we hold output constant, we have the following general rule:

***A change in the price of a substitute input will cause the demand for labor to change in the same direction.***

▸ Example 9-6 Telemarketing can be done in two ways. Either human beings or automated telemarketing machines can be used to make phone calls to try to convince people to purchase goods and services. If the price of telemarketing machines goes up, the demand for human telemarketers will go up. If the price of telemarketing machines goes down, the demand for telemarketers will go down, too. ◂

**Change in the Price of Complementary Inputs** Complements are inputs that must be used jointly. Assume now that capital and labor are complementary. In general, we predict the following:

***A change in the price of a complementary input will cause the demand for labor to change in the opposite direction.***

If the cost of machines goes up, but they must be used with labor, fewer machines will be purchased and therefore fewer workers will be used.

## Determinants of the Industry Supply of Labor

There are a number of reasons why labor supply curves will shift in a particular industry. The first concerns changes in wage rates across industries. ▸ Example 9-7 If wages for factory workers in the computer industry go up dramatically, the supply curve of factory workers in the CD industry will shift inward to the left as these workers move to the computer industry. ◂

Changes in working conditions in an industry can also affect its labor supply curve. ▸ Example 9-8 If employers in the CD industry discover a new production technique that makes working conditions much more pleasant, the supply curve of labor in the CD industry will shift outward to the right because more people will want jobs there. ◂

Job flexibility may also determine the position of the labor supply curve. ▸ Example 9-9 In an industry that allows workers more flexibility, such as the ability to work at home via computer, the workers are likely to work more hours. That is to say, their supply curve will shift outward to the right. ◂

The supply of labor can also increase if more foreign workers obtain visas, as you will read about in the next *Policy Application*.

## POLICY APPLICATION: Bringing in Foreign Information Technology Workers

### *Concept Applied:* Increasing Supply

More than 350,000 foreigners work in the United States under a visa program called the L-1. L-1 visas were originally designed only for transfers within multinational companies with offices in the United States. Many firms have presumably abused the L-1 visa program, however, in order to bring in low-wage foreign information technology workers who replace much higher paid U.S. workers.

#### Breaking the Rules

L-1 visas are supposed to apply only to executives, managers, and workers with "specialized knowledge." Nonetheless, foreign outsourcing companies use the L-1 visas to supply literally thousands of high-tech workers to U.S. companies at wage rates well below those paid to equivalently trained U.S. workers. Unlike other types of work-related visas, the L-1 visa does not prohibit displacing U.S. workers, nor does it require that the foreign workers be paid prevailing wages. Consider Bombay-based Tata, an Indian software-servicing company. Bank of America, General Electric, Dell, and Merrill Lynch all use Tata employees. Half of Tata's 5,000 workers who have been placed in U.S. companies are foreign.

#### Showing All of This on a Graph

Look at Figure 9-3 below. Here you see that before the use of the L-1 visa to supply high-tech workers, the supply curve and the demand curve yielded an equilibrium wage rate of $50 an hour. Adding the supply of foreign workers through the L-1 visa shifts the supply curve out to the right to $S_2$ from $S_1$. The equilibrium wage rate falls to $40 per hour.

**For Critical Analysis:**
*What motivates U.S. firms to hire software-servicing companies such as Tata?*

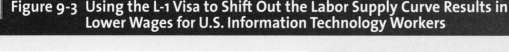

**Figure 9-3 Using the L-1 Visa to Shift Out the Labor Supply Curve Results in Lower Wages for U.S. Information Technology Workers**

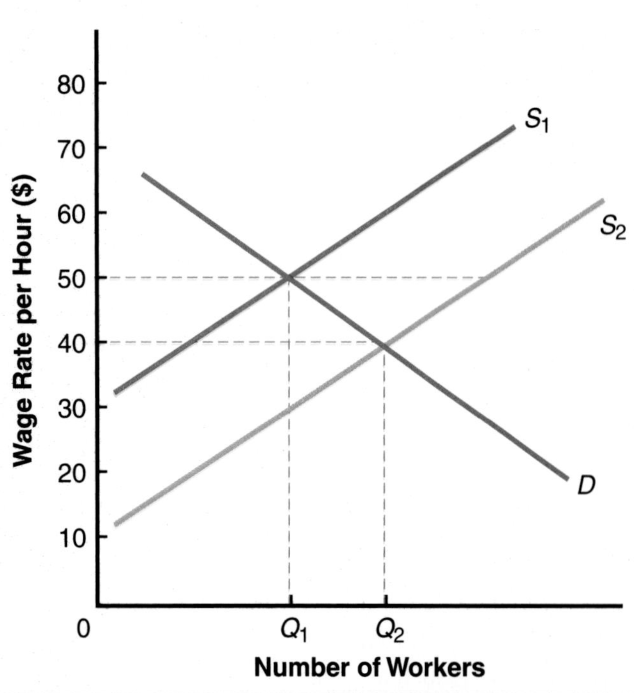


Prior to the use of the L-1 visa to increase the labor supply, the wage rate for high-tech workers is $50 per hour in equilibrium, and the quantity demanded and supplied is $Q_1$. When the L-1 visa is used, the supply curve for high-tech workers shifts from $S_1$ to $S_2$. The equilibrium wage rate falls to $40 per hour, and the quantity demanded and supplied is $Q_2$.

**Mastering Concepts:** What Happens When Labor Demand or Supply Changes?

- **Any shift in the demand for the final product will shift the demand for labor or any other variable input.**
- **Any change in labor productivity will shift the market labor demand curve in the same direction.**
- **When the price of a substitute input changes, the demand for labor will change in the same direction.**
- **In general, a change in the price of a complementary input will shift the demand for labor in the opposite direction.**
- **The position of the supply of labor curve depends on (1) working conditions, (2) job flexibility, and (3) wage rates in other employments.**

## PUTTING A FLOOR ON WAGES—THE MINIMUM WAGE

Not all labor markets are unrestricted. Nationwide, there is a federal **minimum wage,** which is the lowest legal hourly wage rate that may be paid to certain types of workers.

**Minimum wage**
*A wage floor, legislated by government, setting the lowest hourly rate that firms may legally pay workers.*

The federal minimum wage started at 25 cents per hour in 1938. At that time, 25 cents represented 40 percent of the average manufacturing wage. Since 1938, the federal minimum wage has stayed at about 40 to 50 percent of average manufacturing wages. In 1995, Congress increased it to $5.15. Undoubtedly, it will be increased regularly throughout your lifetime.

### EFFECTS ON THE QUANTITY OF LABOR SUPPLIED

As you might imagine, at higher wage rates, more people are willing to work, and those who work are willing to work longer hours. That is the meaning of the upward-sloping supply of labor curve that we showed in Figure 9-1. ▸ Example 9-10 Assume that 10 million unskilled and untrained workers are willing to work at $5 an hour. If the government imposes a legal minimum wage of $6 an hour, perhaps 12 million unskilled U.S. resident workers will offer their labor services. ◂

All this means is that:

> ***The higher the federal minimum wage, the greater the quantity of unskilled labor supplied.***

### HOW IS THE QUANTITY OF LABOR DEMANDED AFFECTED?

Remember that we said an employer is willing to hire workers up to the point at which the wage rate equals the value of that worker's marginal product (the worker's marginal revenue product). The reason that some workers earn so little is that the value of their marginal product is not very high for actual or prospective employers. Often this is because the workers have little schooling or training.

If the federal minimum wage goes up, employers will demand a lower quantity of unskilled workers. Why? Because at higher wage rates, some of these same workers do not have a value of marginal product that justifies their employment.

Otherwise stated:

> ***At higher federal minimum wages, a lower quantity of unskilled labor will be demanded.***

## The Result: A Surplus of Workers at the Minimum Wage Rate

If the federal government sets the minimum wage rate above the equilibrium wage rate shown in Figure 9-4, the inevitable will result: a surplus of workers at that relatively high wage rate. This surplus of workers represents higher unemployment. This increased unemployment occurs because of two interacting factors:

- ***A higher wage rate increases the quantity of workers supplied.***
- ***A higher wage rate reduces the quantity of labor demanded.***

▸ **Example 9-11** Typically, the individuals who have the lowest-valued marginal product (lowest marginal revenue product) are teenagers. They have had relatively little schooling and certainly relatively little experience and training. Not surprisingly, when there is a significant increase in the federal minimum wage rate, teenage unemployment rates usually rise. Also, teenage unemployment rates are usually three times the national unemployment rate, in part because of the minimum wage. In 2003, when the national rate of unemployment was 6.4 percent, among teenagers it was 19.3 percent. ◂

**Figure 9-4 The Results of Setting the Minimum Wage Above the Market Clearing Wage Rate**

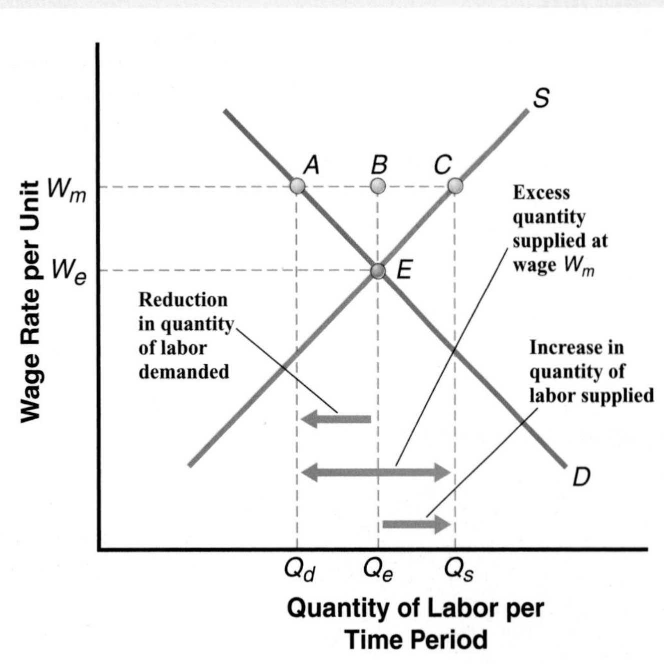


The market clearing wage rate is $W_e$. The market clearing quantity of employment is $Q_e$, determined by the intersection of supply and demand at point *E*. A minimum wage equal to $W_m$ is established. The quantity of labor demanded is reduced to $Q_d$; the reduction in employment from $Q_e$ to $Q_d$ is equal to the distance between *B* and *A*. Together, the rise in the quantity supplied and fall in quantity demanded yield the surplus at $W_m$. The distance between *B* and *C* is the increase in the quantity of labor supplied that results from the higher minimum wage rate.

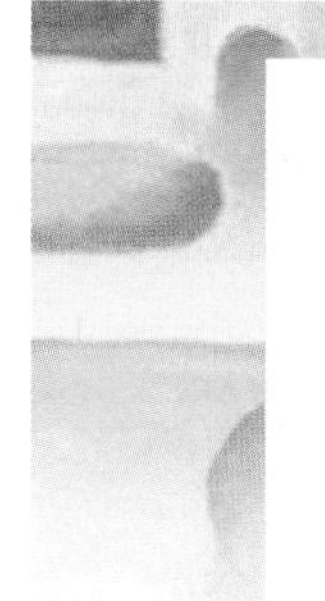

## *Solving the Economic Problem:* Can We Make Sure That Everyone Earns at Least a "Living" Wage?

All of the arguments about a "living" wage are really arguments about the need to increase the minimum wage rate. Governments, no matter how magnanimous they want to be, cannot avoid the consequences of the laws of supply and demand. Every city that imposes a "living" wage on employers within its boundaries will find increased unemployment among unskilled workers. This is because when a municipality imposes a relatively high "living" wage rate, the quantity of unskilled workers supplied will increase, while the quantity demanded falls.

**Mastering Concepts:** Putting a Floor on Wages—The Minimum Wage

- **The higher the minimum wage, the greater the quantity of labor supplied by those covered by the law.**
- **The higher the minimum wage, the lower the quantity of unskilled workers demanded.**

## ORGANIZED LABOR: ITS EFFECT ON LABOR SUPPLY AND WAGES

Our simplified supply and demand analysis of the labor market ignored the possibility of **labor unions**. Labor unions exist for many reasons, but analytically we will see that:

**Labor unions**
*Associations of workers organized to improve wages and working conditions for their members.*

> ***Labor unions usually help their members if in some way they can restrict supply in order to obtain higher-than-competitive wage rates and benefits—working conditions, job security, health insurance—for their members.***

### THE AMERICAN LABOR MOVEMENT

In the 1800s, workers began to form unions in an attempt to force employers to improve wages and working conditions, to shorten the workday, and to end child labor. Unionism met with strong resistance, however. In the 1800s, state legislatures passed laws against unions, and the courts upheld those laws.

For much of its history, organized labor in this country has been split into two groups: craft unions and industrial unions. A **craft union** is made up of workers in a specific trade like bricklaying. ▸ Example 9-12 The first national federation of labor unions was the American Federation of Labor (AFL) and was composed only of craft unions. Samuel Gompers served as its president from 1886 to 1924. ◂ Some craft unions in Europe have been around for over 800 years and are now causing problems, as you will see in the following *Global Application*.

**Craft union**
*A union made up of skilled workers in a specific trade or industry.*

## GLOBAL APPLICATION: Twelfth-Century German Labor Rules Now Under Attack

***Concepts Applied:***
**Craft Unions, Supply Restrictions**

About 800 years ago, Germany established craft unions to cover 94 professions. The avowed goal then, as it is now, was to preserve high-quality standards. Today, in a Germany suffering from perennial 11 percent unemployment, economists there argue that the strict rules governing these 94 professions hinder new businesses and job growth. Those arguments fall on deaf ears when it comes to enforcing the 800-year-old rules, however.

### Craft Union Regulators Are Serious

Thomas Melles worked for 13 years as a carpenter. Government detectives from a local craft union, though, learned that he did not have his master craftsman's diploma. So they followed his van and took videos of him at work. He soon got a letter in the mail saying that if he did not stop working as a carpenter, he would be sent to jail for two weeks or fined $2,000, or both.

### Craft Union Members Know What's Good for Them, at Least

Craft union members, of course, want to keep the system of master diplomas. Getting one demands a decade of training and thousands of euros in fees. Their argument is the same one used throughout the world whenever labor supply restrictions are imposed—to ensure high quality. For those who know a craft but cannot work, like Thomas Melles, such arguments smack of bold-faced entry restrictions.

**For Critical Analysis:**
*What "crafts" have restrictions on entry in the United States? (HINT: Are there any professions that you cannot enter without long years of schooling, at a minimum?)*

**Industrial union**
*A union made up of all the workers in an industry, regardless of job or skill level.*

In contrast to the craft union, there is an **industrial union**. It is made up of all of the workers in an industry, regardless of job or level of skills. ▸ Example 9-13 The first significant effort to unionize both skilled and semiskilled workers in one industry began with the formation of the Congress of Industrial Organizations (CIO) in 1938. (In 1955, the AFL and CIO merged to form the AFL–CIO.) ◂

## COLLECTIVE BARGAINING

**Collective bargaining**
*The process by which unions and employers negotiate the conditions of employment.*

**Collective bargaining** is the process by which unions and employers negotiate the conditions of employment and wages. At the center of the collective bargaining process is a compromise. Employers desire to keep wages and benefits low in order to have lower labor costs and thus remain competitive. Labor unions wish to increase wages and benefits for their workers.

During negotiations, labor and management spar over the following:

- Wages
- Working hours
- Fringe benefits
- Working conditions
- Job security
- Grievance procedures

**Strike**
*Deliberate work stoppage by workers to force an employer to give in to their demands.*

**Strikes** Most collective bargaining negotiations are successful. When negotiations break down, a **strike** results. ▸ Example 9-14 The last major strike in the United States occurred on January 14 through January 16, 2003, when 14,000 workers at General Electric Company plants nationwide went on strike to protest the company's shifting of health care costs to workers. The strike was the first nationwide strike against General Electric in 30 years. Strikers picketed 48 locations in 23 states. ◀ The actual number of strikes in the United States has fallen dramatically since the mid-1970s, as you can see in Figure 9-5.

Striking unions may use a **boycott** to exert more economic pressure against firms in an industry. In a boycott, a union urges the public not to purchase goods or services produced by the company it is striking.

**Boycott**
*Economic pressure exerted by unions urging the public not to purchase the goods or services produced by a company.*

**Management Fights Back—Lockouts** When faced with a strike, management has tactics of its own to use. One is a **lockout**, which occurs when management prevents workers from returning to work until they agree to a new contract. Alternatively, under certain circumstances employers may hire **strikebreakers** to take the place of striking workers.

**Lockout**
*A situation that occurs when management prevents workers from returning to work until they agree to a new contract.*

**Strikebreakers**
*Temporary or permanent workers hired by a company to replace union members who are striking.*

## The Goals of the Union

Remember that when we discussed minimum wages above, we stated that a minimum wage rate above the equilibrium market wage rate would lead to a surplus of workers at the minimum wage rate.

You can think of unions as setters of minimum wages. Whenever they set minimum wages above market clearing wages, there will be a surplus of workers willing to work at that wage rate. (Note that the wage rate is a shorthand term that encompasses *all* of the benefits that workers receive, including paid vacations, paid health insurance premiums, paid child care, and the like.)

Consequently, we can state the following:

> ***One of the major roles of a union that succeeds in establishing a wage rate* above *the market clearing wage rate is to ration available jobs among the surplus of workers who wish to work in unionized industries.***

**Figure 9-5 The Declining Number of Labor Strikes**

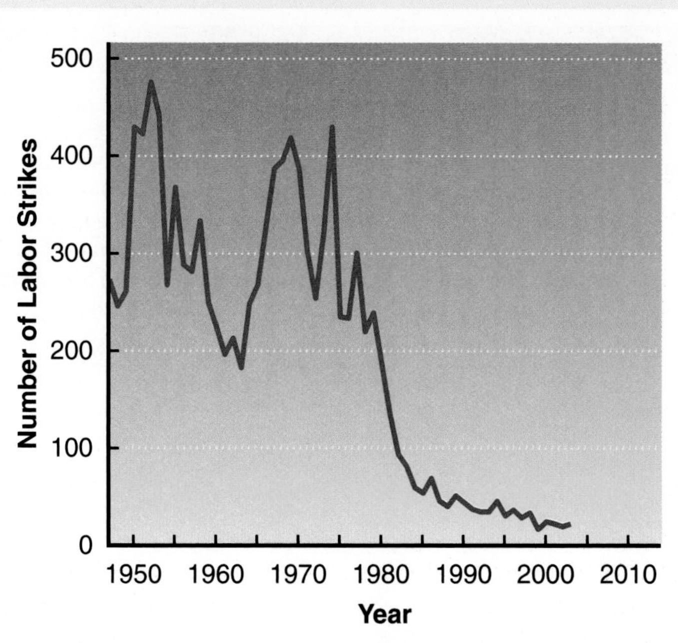


Since about 1974, the number of labor walkouts each year has declined steadily. The power of unions seems to be on the wane.

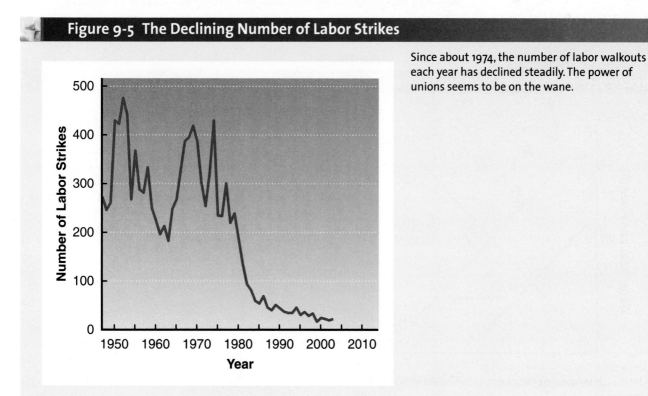

▸ **Example 9-15** Typical rationing techniques include lengthening the apprenticeship period to discourage *potential* members from joining. When the first videotape recorders were being used for editing in major TV studios, unions imposed a ten-year apprenticeship for those who wished to be full-fledged tape editors (so-called journeymen editors). ◂

## Restricting the Supply of Union Labor over Time

Sometimes unions become important at the very beginning of an industry. They may set wages at a certain wage rate, say, $19 per hour. Assume that this wage rate is the equilibrium wage rate. As the economy grows, though, the demand for labor in that unionized industry will grow in this developing business sector. This is shown as an increase in the demand for labor from $D_1$ to $D_2$ in Figure 9-6.

The union may simply not allow any more workers in. In this way, the supply curve no longer slopes upward. Rather, it becomes a vertical line at the original union membership. With the greater demand for labor, the obvious results—a gradual increase in union wage rates. In the hypothetical example we show in Figure 9-6, you see that the wage rate rises to $21 per hour instead of the $20 it would have risen to in the absence of the union.

**Mastering Concepts:** Organized Labor: Its Effect on Labor Supply and Wages

- **The main activity of labor unions is to implicitly or explicitly raise union members' wages.**
- **Unions can be craft or industrial.**
- **Unions engage in collective bargaining to determine wages, working hours, fringe benefits, working conditions, and other aspects of union jobs.**
- **Whenever unions raise wage rates above equilibrium levels, their major role becomes that of rationing available jobs among the surplus of workers.**

*Animated*

**Figure 9-6 Restricting Labor Supply over Time**

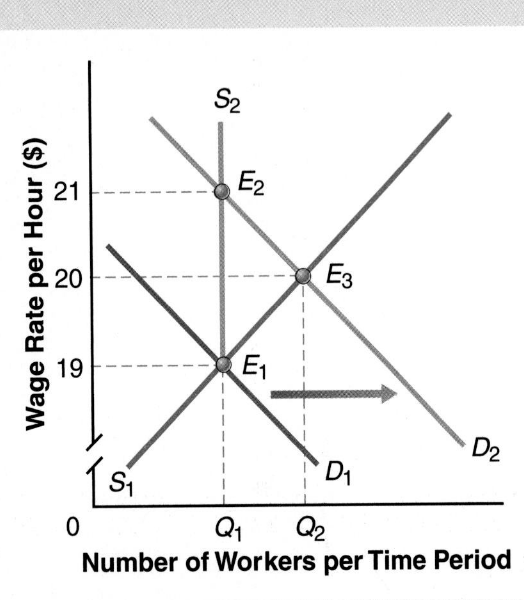


When the union was formed, it didn't affect wage rates or employment, which remained at $19 and $Q_1$ (the equilibrium wage rate and quantity). However, as demand increased—that is, as the demand schedule shifted outward to $D_2$ from $D_1$—the union restricted membership to its original level of $Q_1$. The new supply curve is $S_1S_2$, which intersects $D_2$ at $E_2$, or at a wage rate of $21. Without the union, equilibrium would be at $E_3$ with a wage rate of $20 and employment of $Q_2$.

## THE BENEFITS OF LABOR UNIONS

To now, we seem to have shown only the negative aspects of labor unions—they restrict supply. In contrast, some economists believe that labor unions bestow benefits not only on their members, but also on the economy as a whole. For example, some believe that labor unions can increase labor productivity through a variety of means. Harvard economists Richard B. Friedman and James L. Metoff have come up with a number of conclusions about labor unions.

### A POSITIVE VIEW OF LABOR UNIONS

According to Friedman and Metoff:

1. Unions may reduce wage inequality.
2. Unions in some cases reduce profits, thereby shifting wealth from shareholders to members of unions.
3. Even though unions may reduce employment in the unionized sector, their actions may lead to improved workplace practices that are valuable to workers.
4. In some settings, unions are associated with increased productivity.
5. Internally, unions provide a political voice for all workers.
6. Unions tend to increase the stability of the workforce by providing services, such as negotiation proceedings and grievance procedures.

### FOR ALL THAT UNIONS MAY DO, UNION MEMBERSHIP IS STILL ON THE DECLINE

As the United States has shifted from an agricultural and manufacturing economy to a service-oriented economy, the percentage of the labor force belonging to unions has dropped. Look at Figure 9-7. There you see that currently union

**Figure 9-7 Declining Union Membership**

Numerically, union membership in the United States is much higher than in the 1930s, but as a percentage of the labor force, union membership peaked around 1960 and has been falling ever since. Most recently, the absolute number of union members has also diminished.

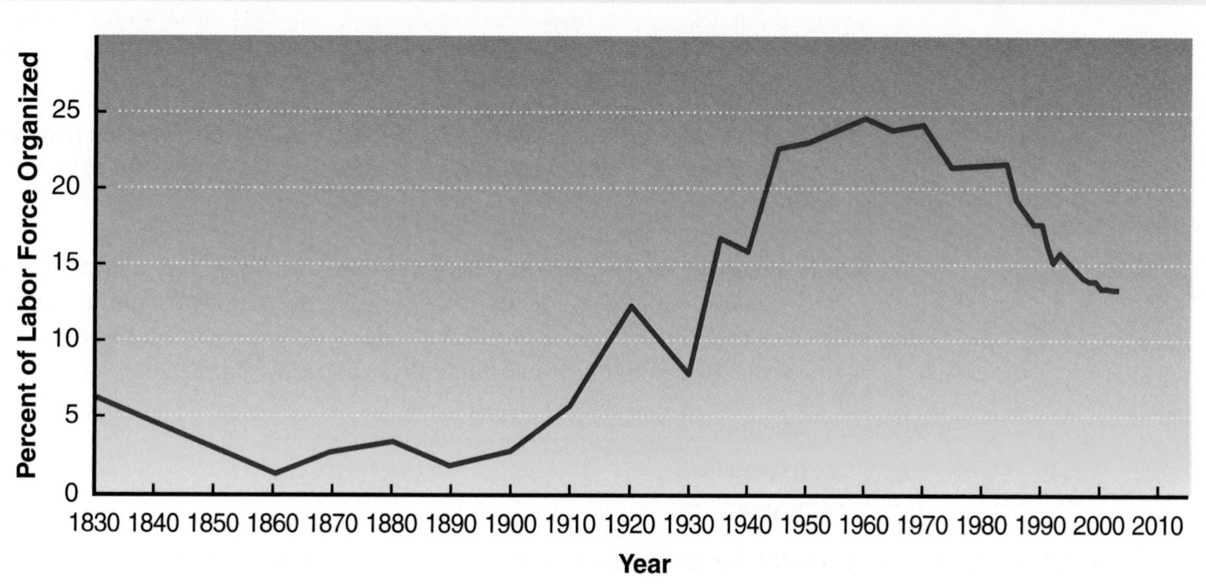

membership is just 13 percent of the entire labor force. The only area in which union membership has grown is among government employees. Thus, the evidence shows that in spite of the purported benefits of unions outlined on page 193, employees in the United States are shifting away from union membership.

**Mastering Concepts:** The Benefits of Labor Unions

- **Some economists believe that unions bestow some benefits on the economy as a whole. These include a reduction in wage inequality, a shift of wealth from shareholders to union members, greater job satisfaction, and an increase in the stability of the workforce.**
- **Despite the benefits of being a member of a union, the percentage of union members has steadily declined in the United States.**

## INCOME DISTRIBUTION—WHAT DETERMINES HOW MUCH YOU MAKE?

**Income distribution**
*The way in which income differences are distributed throughout society; for example, the percentage of "rich" versus the percentage of "poor" in a given economy.*

While a lot of people enjoy working, most would certainly be willing to accept higher wages. But higher wages don't just happen. Indeed, how much you earn is determined by numerous factors. We call these the determinants of income differences or **income distribution**. Although there are many reasons for income differences, the three main ones we will look at are marginal productivity, inheritance, and discrimination.

### Marginal Productivity

When trying to determine how many workers a firm would hire, we had to construct a marginal revenue product curve. We found that as more workers were hired, the marginal revenue product fell due to diminishing marginal returns. If the forces of demand and supply established a certain wage rate, workers would be hired until their marginal physical product times marginal revenue (which equals the market price under perfect competition) was equal to the going wage rate. Then the hiring would stop. This analysis suggests what workers can expect to be paid in the labor market:

> ***Workers can each expect to be paid their marginal revenue product (assuming that there are low-cost information flows and that the labor and product markets are competitive).***

**Determinants of Marginal Productivity** If we accept marginal revenue product theory, we have a way to find out how people can earn higher incomes. If they increase their marginal physical product, they can expect to be paid more. Some of the determinants of marginal physical product are:

- Talent
- Experience
- Training

Most of these are means by which marginal physical product can be increased. In addition, investing in oneself can raise one's marginal productivity.

**Investment in Human Capital** Investment in human capital (see Chapter 1) is just like investment in anything else. If you invest in yourself by going to college, rather than going to work after high school and earning more current income, you will presumably be rewarded in the future with a higher income or a more interesting job (or both). This is exactly the motivation that underlies the decision of many college-bound students to obtain a formal higher education.

> ✦ **Keep in Mind!** *People respond to changing incentives, such that when the rate of return to investing in human capital—by going to college or by obtaining more training—goes up, more people will be willing to invest in themselves.*

We do expect that the higher the rate of return on investing in ourselves, the more such investment there will be. ▸ Example 9-16 Government data demonstrate conclusively that, on average, high school graduates make more than grade school graduates and that college graduates make more than high school graduates. The estimated annual income of a full-time worker with four years of college in the early 2000s was about $51,000. That person's high school counterpart was estimated to earn a little less than $30,000, which gives a "college premium" of just over 70 percent. ◂

## Inheritance

It is not unusual to inherit cash, jewelry, stocks, bonds, homes, or other real estate. Yet only about 10 percent of income inequality in the United States can be traced to differences in wealth that was inherited. If for some reason the government confiscated all property that had been inherited, the distribution of income in the United States would undergo only a modest change.

## Discrimination

Economic discrimination occurs whenever workers with the same marginal revenue product receive unequal pay due to some noneconomic factor such as their race, gender, or age. Alternatively, it occurs when there is unequal access to labor markets. It is possible—and indeed quite obvious—that discrimination affects the distribution of income.

Certain groups in our society are paid wages at rates that are not comparable to those received by other groups, even when we correct for productivity. Differences in income remain between whites and nonwhites and between men and women. ▸ Example 9-17 The median income of black families is about 65 percent that of white families. The median wage rate of women is about 70 percent that of men. Some people argue that all of these differences are due to discrimination against nonwhites and against women. ◂

**Mastering Concepts:** Income Distribution—What Determines How Much You Make?

- **Marginal productivity is one determinant of income differences. Marginal productivity may be affected by talent, experience, and training.**
- **Investment in human capital—education—pays off, for each additional degree earned results in a markedly higher average income.**
- **Inheritance and discrimination may affect income differences, although inheritance accounts for only 10 percent of income inequality in the United States.**

## SUMMING IT ALL UP

- Because the cost of leisure is its opportunity cost, the higher the after-tax wage rate, the larger the quantity of labor supplied, in general. This is called the substitution effect.
- Because labor demand is a derived demand, the greater the demand for final output, the greater the demand for workers.
- The marginal physical product (MPP) of labor represents the additional output attributed to employing additional units of labor.
- The marginal revenue product (MRP) is the additional worker's contribution to the firm's total revenues.
- The MRP curve represents the demand curve for labor.
- Any shift in the demand for the final product will shift the demand for labor or any other variable input.
- When the price of a substitute input changes, the demand for labor will change in the same direction.
- In general, a change in the price of a complementary input will shift the demand for labor in the opposite direction.
- The position of the supply of labor curve depends on (1) working conditions, (2) job flexibility, and (3) wage rates in other employments.
- Whenever unions raise wage rates above equilibrium levels, their major role becomes that of rationing available jobs among the surplus of workers.
- Some economists believe that unions bestow some benefits on the economy as a whole. These include a reduction in wage inequality, a shift of wealth from shareholders to union members, greater job satisfaction, and an increase in the stability of the workforce.
- Marginal productivity is one determinant of income differences. Marginal productivity may be affected by talent, experience, and training.
- Investment in human capital—education—pays off, for each additional degree earned results in a markedly higher average income.

## KEY TERMS AND CONCEPTS



## MASTERING ECONOMIC CONCEPTS
## Questions and Problems

**9-1.** In terms of the labor market, what is your opportunity cost of spending the weekend watching television? How would your opportunity cost change if you needed funds in order to be able to go on spring break in Cancún later in the school year?

**9-2.** Based on the labor market depicted in the grid below, how many people will be willing to work if the wage is $8 per hour?

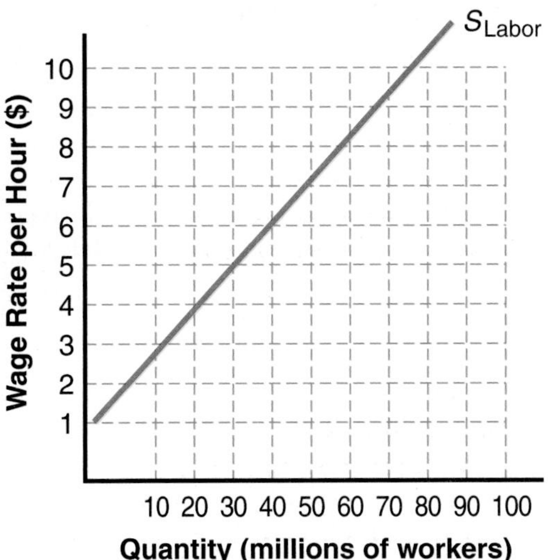


**9-3.** If the wage rate that you are offered decreases and you have no financial obligations, in which direction will you substitute—toward labor or leisure? If instead you need to pay your cell phone bill and make your car payment, how will the income effect of the lower wage change your decision as to the number of hours you work each week?

**9-4.** If there is an increase in the demand for new homes, what will happen to the demand for electricians needed to wire such homes? What term describes the relationship between the demand for new homes and the demand for electricians?

**9-5.** Use the weekly information provided in the table below to compute the marginal physical product for each worker. Assuming that this is a perfectly competitive market and that the market price of the good being sold is $12, compute marginal revenue for this table. If the wage rate for these workers is $950 per week, how many workers should this firm employ?

| Labor | Total Physical Product | Marginal Physical Product | Marginal Revenue |
|---|---|---|---|
| 2 | 100 | ____ | $____ |
| 3 | 200 | ____ | ____ |
| 4 | 350 | ____ | ____ |
| 5 | 450 | ____ | ____ |
| 6 | 525 | ____ | ____ |

**9-6.** The table below depicts a supply schedule for labor. Assume that your firm is hiring from this pool of labor. Compute the total labor cost per hour to your firm and the marginal factor cost for each level of employment, assuming that you must pay all of your workers the same hourly wage. Is this labor market perfectly competitive?

| Quantity of Labor Supplied | Hourly Wage |
|---|---|
| 8 | $6.00 |
| 9 | 6.25 |
| 10 | 6.50 |
| 11 | 6.75 |
| 12 | 7.00 |
| 13 | 7.25 |

**9-7.** If the marginal factor cost of labor is less than the marginal revenue product of labor, should a firm employ more workers, employ fewer workers, or maintain the same number of workers? Why?

**9-8.** What impact will an increase in the supply of labor have on the wage paid to employees and the quantity of employment?

**9-9.** Based on the graph below, which of the three wages would we wish to select as a minimum wage in order to increase compensation for these workers? Would this wage rate create a shortage or a surplus and in what amount?

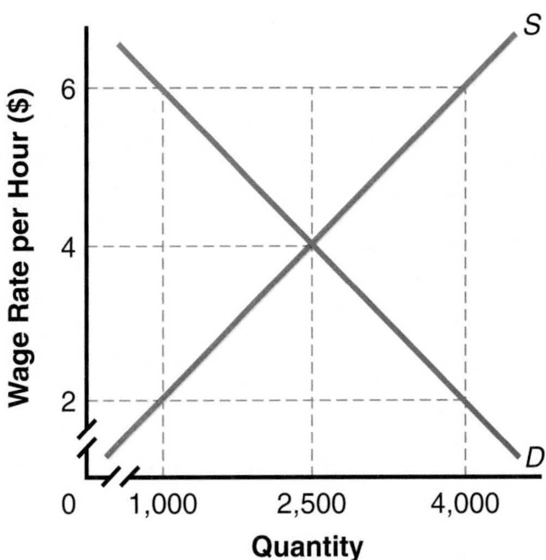


**9-10.** What is the difference between a craft union and an industrial union?

**9-11.** Although some criticize labor unions in some respects, others point out some potential benefits. List four potential benefits of labor unions.

**9-12.** Approximately what percentage of U.S. workers currently belong to labor unions? By comparison, approximately what percentage of U.S. workers belonged to labor unions in 1960?

**9-13.** Based on the following table, graph a supply curve for this labor market.

**Labor Supply Schedule**

| Wage | Hours of Work |
|---|---|
| $6 | 20 |
| 7 | 30 |
| 8 | 40 |
| 9 | 50 |

**9-14.** Determine whether each of the following factors will cause an increase, a decrease, or no change in the demand for labor.

a. a decrease in the price of automated robotics that could be used to replace workers
b. a decrease in the wage rate
c. a decrease in the productivity of labor

**9-15.** Indicate whether each of the following is true or false with respect to labor markets.

a. The income effect of a wage increase results in an increase in the quantity of labor supplied
b. The substitution effect of a wage increase results in an increase in the quantity of labor supplied.
c. A firm should lay off workers when marginal revenue product is greater than marginal factor cost.
d. The market demand for labor is derived from the marginal revenue product of labor.

## THINKING CRITICALLY

**9-1.** In 1994 the American Society of Anesthesiologists (ASA) commissioned a survey that essentially indicated that only 90 percent of the labor resources in the anesthesiology field were being utilized. At the same time, for various reasons the Clinton administration recommended limiting the number of residents in this field. In terms of supply and demand, what impact could these recommendations have had on this labor market? Through the 1990s, the number of people in the United States over age 65 increased by 11 percent. In terms of supply and demand, what impact would this demographic change have on this labor market? Based on your two previous answers, what do you think has happened to the wages paid to anesthesiologists since the 1990s? At present, the ASA is publicly suggesting that more new anesthesiologists are needed. What will this suggestion do to wages in the field? Why would the ASA make such a suggestion?

**9-2.** Based on the economic principle of a price floor, holding all else constant, what impact would economists expect a minimum wage to have on the level of unemployment? Two economists conducted a study of the fast-food industry in New Jersey and Pennsylvania, and their evidence suggested that an increase in the state minimum wage increased employment in this industry. Assuming that their methodology was sound, what other factors might account for this apparent contradiction? If a higher wage created a greater incentive for hard work, how would this change the marginal revenue product of these workers?

**9-3.** When the economy is sluggish, state tax revenues and budgets are affected significantly. As a result, many states decide to eliminate raises or even reduce wages for state employees, including educators at the primary, secondary, and postsecondary levels. Within the field of education, how many other employment options do educators have besides teaching within the public educational system? Are there other options rather than teaching? If the educators in a certain state or at a certain level were organized into a union, how would this affect the state government's attempt to limit wages or wage increases? Assuming that a state neither increases nor decreases wages for state employees, what would happen to the real wages of these individuals? Why?

## LOGGING ON

1. For an argument that the main beneficiaries of living wage laws are members of public employees unions, go to http://www.bcnys.org/whatsnew/2002/0410livwage.htm.
2. To learn about the wages earned in a variety of U.S. occupations, go to http://www.bls.gov/bls/blswage.htm.
3. For the latest information on employment levels in a variety of sectors of the U.S. economy, go to http://research.stlouisfed.org/fred2/categories/10.
4. To see how the minimum wage has varied over time when adjusted for inflation, go to http://oregonstate.edu/instruct/anth484/minwage.html.

## USING THE INTERNET FOR ECONOMIC ANALYSIS

**Evaluating Union Goals** As discussed in this chapter, unions can pursue a number of goals. The AFL–CIO's home page provides links to the Web sites of several unions, and reviewing these sites can help you to determine the objectives of these unions.

**Title:** American Federation of Labor–Congress of Industrial Organizations

**Navigation:** Go to http://www.aflcio.org.

**Application** Perform the indicated operations, and answer the following questions:

1. At the top of the page, click on "About the AFL–CIO." Next, click on "About Us," and then click on "Mission Statement." Does the AFL–CIO claim to represent the interests of all workers, or just workers in specific firms or industries? Can you discern what broad wage and employment strategy the AFL–CIO pursues?
2. Back up to the AFL–CIO's home page, and click on "All About Unions," and then click on "Unions of the AFL–CIO." Explore two or three of these Web sites. Do these unions appear to represent the interests of all workers, or just workers in specific firms or industries? What general wage and employment strategies do these unions appear to pursue?

## MEDIA RESOURCE LIST

The following media resources are available with this chapter:

- Load your CD-ROM to listen to the audio introduction to this chapter.
- Load your CD-ROM to access a Graph Animation of Figure 9-2, *Marginal Revenue Product.*
- Load your CD-ROM to view the video on *Shifts in Labor Supply and Demand.*
- Load your CD-ROM to view the video on *Price Floors in the Labor Market.*
- Load your CD-ROM to view the video on *Union Goals.*
- Load your CD-ROM to access a Graph Animation of Figure 9-6, *Restricting Labor Supply over Time.*
- Load your CD-ROM to view the video on *Benefits of Labor Unions.*
- Load your CD-ROM to view the video on *Determinants of Income Differences.*
- Test your knowledge of chapter concepts with a quiz at www.miller-ume.com.
- Link to Web resources related to the text coverage at www.miller-ume.com.

## HOMEWORK SET

Go to the back of this book to find the Homework Problems for this chapter.

# PART 3

# Macroeconomics

# Unemployment, Inflation, and the Business Cycle

## *Facing an Economic Problem:* Choosing a Fixed or Variable Rate Mortgage

The moment has finally arrived: you are going to buy your first house. Obviously, you do not have 100 percent of the purchase price readily available. Consequently, you must borrow much of the necessary funds. You have been comparing deals from local banks. The interest rates they offer depend on whether you agree to let them charge you a fixed interest rate for the next 20 years or a variable interest rate, one that depends on the average interest rate in the economy over time. The variable interest rate offered is considerably lower than the fixed interest rate. What should you do? To answer this question, you need to know about inflation and the relationship between interest rates and inflation. Before we tackle these subjects, we first look at unemployment in our economy.

### Learning Objectives:

After reading this chapter, you should be able to:

- **List and explain the four types of unemployment.**
- **Outline the steps involved in deriving the measured rate of unemployment.**
- **Contrast anticipated inflation with unanticipated inflation and relate those concepts to the nominal rate of interest.**
- **Compare deflation and inflation.**
- **List the three potential causes of business fluctuations.**

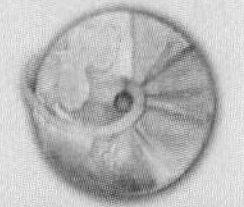

***Refer to the back of this chapter for a complete listing of multimedia learning materials available on the CD-ROM and the Web site.***

## THERE ARE DIFFERENT TYPES OF UNEMPLOYMENT

**Microeconomics**
*The study of decision making undertaken by individuals (or households) and by firms.*

**Macroeconomics**
*The study of economy-wide phenomena such as unemployment, inflation, interest rates, and government stabilization policies.*

In the first nine chapters, you learned about **microeconomics**, or the study of the behavior of individuals and businesses. The current chapter on unemployment, inflation, and the business cycle will serve as an introduction to what is usually considered macroeconomics. **Macroeconomics** is the study of economy-wide phenomena such as the topics in this chapter, plus the determination of interest rates, government attempts at stabilizing the economy, and so on. You have already been introduced to one important macroeconomic concept in Chapter 2—how to measure overall national economic activity. You learned that gross domestic product (GDP) is the measure of national economic activity that we normally use when talking about what is happening to the economy.

### LOOKING AT UNEMPLOYMENT

Now, in order to understand the phenomenon of unemployment, we first define it and then look at different types of unemployment. Finally, we examine how the federal government measures unemployment. Then we turn to the concept of inflation.

**Unemployment**
*The inability of those who are in the labor force to find a job; sometimes referred to as the total number of those in the labor force actively looking for a job, but unable to find one.*

Some psychologists say that unemployment is one of the most traumatizing events in a person's life. **Unemployment** is the inability of those who are in the labor force to find a job. (Remember from Chapter 2 that the labor force consists of those who are employed plus those looking for employment.) No matter how one examines unemployment, it costs the economy. ▸ **Example 10-1** When the unemployment rate was around 6 percent in 2003, factories were running at about 80 percent of their capacity. Some estimated that due to idle resources in that year, the economy lost about 3 percent of its potential output. That was equivalent to about $300 billion of houses, restaurant meals, automobiles, schools, and movies that *could have been produced*. ◂

There are several reasons why individuals become unemployed.

> ***Economists categorize unemployment into four basic types: frictional, structural, cyclical, and seasonal.***

### FRICTIONAL UNEMPLOYMENT

**Frictional unemployment**
*Unemployment due to the fact that workers must search for appropriate job offers. This takes time, and so they remain temporarily unemployed.*

We live in a dynamic economy. Some people enter the labor force and have to look for their first job. Some people reenter the labor force and have to look again. Some people are fired or laid off and have to look for a job. Others just want to change occupations. All of the ins and outs in the labor market result in **frictional unemployment,** defined as the continuous flow of individuals from job to job and in and out of employment.

> ***Until we live a world of free information in which people can look for a new job just as effectively whether they are working or not, there will always be some frictional unemployment.***

Otherwise stated, finding information about alternative job possibilities is a costly activity. This information may be acquired more cheaply when one is unemployed, thus leading to frictional unemployment.

Frictional unemployment includes people who are slow to realize that their skills are no longer needed in a particular occupation. Sometimes people take a while to become convinced that their human capital has a new, lower market

© Dan Rosandich. Reprinted with the permission of the New Yorker.

value. ▸ Example 10-2 Consider the high-tech bust, especially in the Internet industry. Many formerly high-paid "dot.com" whiz kids were out of a job in the early 2000s. It took them a while to realize that their skills no longer had the same value as during the dot.com boom years in the late 1990s. They remained unemployed while they readjusted their expectations. ◂

## Structural Unemployment

Structural changes in our economy cause some workers to become unemployed permanently or for very long periods because they cannot find jobs that use their particular skills. This is called **structural unemployment**.

> **Structural unemployment**
> *Unemployment resulting from a poor match of workers' abilities and skills with current requirements of employers.*

> ***Structural unemployment is not caused by general business fluctuations, although business fluctuations may affect it. Structural unemployment is often caused by institutional actions on the part of governments and unions, for example.***

Economists increasingly look at structural unemployment from the viewpoint of employers, many of whom face government orders to provide funds for social insurance programs for their employees, to announce plant closings months or even years in advance, and so on. There is now considerable evidence that government labor market policies influence how many job positions businesses wish to create, thereby affecting structural unemployment. ▸ Example 10-3 In the United States, many businesses appear to have adjusted to government policies by hiring more "temporary workers" or establishing short-term contracts with "private consultants." Such adjustments may have actually reduced the extent of U.S. structural unemployment in recent years. ◂

## Cyclical Unemployment

**Cyclical unemployment**
*Unemployment resulting from recessions; unemployment that is associated with business cycles—hence, the word* cyclical.

**Cyclical unemployment** is just that—it happens as business activity cycles through good times and bad times. Cyclical unemployment corresponds with the *business cycle,* a topic we discuss at the end of this chapter.

When overall economic activity slows down, there will be cyclical unemployment. Therefore, cyclical unemployment is not the same as frictional unemployment, which relates mainly to mobility between jobs. It is not the same as structural unemployment, much of which is caused by either the lack of specific skills required in today's labor force or government mandates that cause employers to reduce their demand for labor. ▸ **Example 10-4** During the last serious business slowdown in 2001–2003, the rate of unemployment increased from 4.0 to 6.5 percent. The most dramatic example of cyclical unemployment occurred during the Great Depression during the 1930s. Relatively high rates of unemployment—over 10 percent—persisted for more than ten years. ◂

One way to lessen cyclical unemployment is to reduce the intensity, duration, and frequency of the ups and downs of nationwide business activity. Indeed, economic policymakers, particularly at the federal level, are constantly attempting to reduce cyclical unemployment. That is the subject of Chapters 12 and 14.

## Seasonal Unemployment

**Seasonal unemployment**
*Unemployment resulting from the seasonal pattern of work in specific industries. It is usually due to seasonal fluctuations in demand or to changing weather conditions that render work difficult, if not impossible, as in the agricultural, construction, and tourist industries.*

**Seasonal unemployment** varies with the seasons of the year as the demand for particular jobs rises and falls. ▸ **Example 10-5** Summer resort workers can usually get jobs in such resorts only during the summer months. They become seasonally unemployed during the winter. The opposite is true for ski instructors. ◂

Businesses have an incentive to devise ways to continue in operation even in the face of difficult weather conditions, thereby reducing the amount of seasonal unemployment in their industries. ▸ **Example 10-6** In the past in intemperate climates in the northern United States, virtually all building construction came to a halt during the coldest winter months, particularly when it snowed. Today, provided that the foundation has been laid and the framing has been done on a house or other structure, work can continue throughout the winter. Why? Because through technology, builders have developed methods of enveloping their unfinished structures with thick plastic sheeting that keeps the inside free from snow and rain and warm enough for construction workers to continue working. ◂

✦ **Be Aware!** *Those who are affected by seasonal unemployment often find ways to minimize it. For example, ski instructors can learn to teach tennis in the summer or work in construction.*

Because of changes in employment due to the seasons, the official unemployment numbers released by the Bureau of Labor Statistics are typically "seasonally adjusted." This means that the government has adjusted the reported unemployment rate to remove the effects of variations in seasonal unemployment.

### Mastering Concepts: There Are Different Types of Unemployment

- **Because obtaining information about alternative jobs is costly, it is sometimes cheaper for participants in the labor force to become unemployed in order to look for other employment opportunities, thereby leading to frictional unemployment.**
- **The three other types of unemployment are structural, cyclical, and seasonal.**

## HOW WE MEASURE THE UNEMPLOYMENT RATE

We have been talking about unemployment and the unemployment rate, but we have not presented a formal explanation of how the federal government actually measures the rate of unemployment.

### WHO'S IN THE LABOR FORCE AND WHO'S OUT?

When you think about your relationship to the labor force, there are—excluding the military—three possibilities. The first situation is that you may not even be in the civilian labor force at all because you are a full-time student, under 16 years of age, a homemaker, or a retiree.

If you are in the labor force, then there are two possibilities—you are either employed or unemployed. Look at Table 10-1. There you see these three categories.

### MEASURING THE UNEMPLOYMENT RATE

To determine the rate of unemployment, the government first adds up the employed and the unemployed, to obtain the measured labor force. Then it divides the unemployed by that total. ▸ **Example 10-7** If the number of unemployed is 10 million and the number of employed is 140 million, then the labor force is 150 million. If we divide the 10 million unemployed by the 150 million in the labor force, we get 0.067, or 6.7 percent. This is the measured rate of unemployment. ◂

### THE LOGIC OF THE UNEMPLOYMENT RATE

Because there is a transition between employment and unemployment at any point in time—people are leaving jobs and others are finding jobs—there is a simple relationship between the employed and the unemployed, as can be seen in Figure 10-1 on the following page. People departing jobs are shown at the top of the diagram, and people taking new jobs are shown at the bottom. If job leavers and job finders are equal, the unemployment rate stays the same. If departures exceed new hires, the unemployment rate rises. If new hires exceed departures, the unemployment rate falls.

**Table 10-1 The Three Mutually Exclusive Categories of Employment Status**

The so-called civilian noninstitutional population measures about 222 million people in the United States. This population includes only individuals 16 years of age or older. Not included here are the approximately 1.2 million members of the U.S. armed services.

| | |
|---|---|
| Employed | About 138 million |
| Unemployed | About 9 million |
| Not in the labor force | About 75 million |

*Animated*

**Figure 10-1 The Logic of the Unemployment Rate**

On the bottom of the graph, job finders are leaving the unemployed and becoming part of the employed. On the top of the diagram are the job leavers who leave the employed to become part of the unemployed. When job finders equal job leavers, the unemployment rate remains stable.

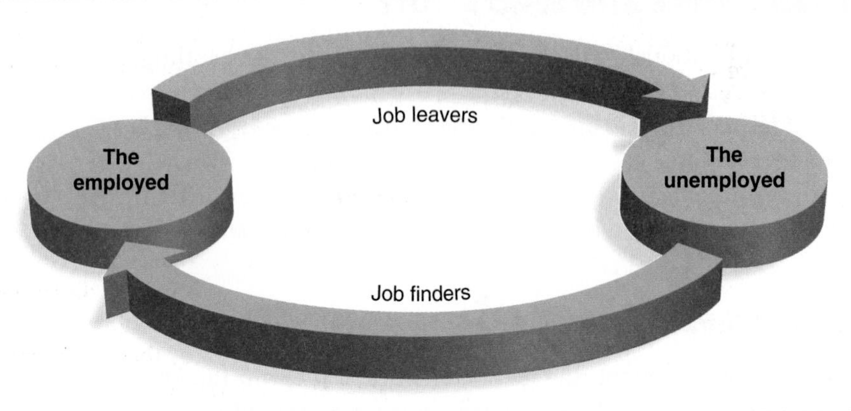


## The Discouraged Worker Phenomenon

**Discouraged workers**
*Individuals who have stopped looking for a job because they are convinced that they will not find a suitable one.*

Critics of the published unemployment rate calculated by the federal government believe that it fails to reflect the true numbers of **discouraged workers** and "hidden unemployed." Though there is no exact definition or way to measure discouraged workers, the Department of Labor defines them as people who have dropped out of the labor force and are no longer looking for a job because they believe that the job market has little to offer them.

To what extent do we want to include in the measured labor force individuals who voluntarily choose not to look for work or those who take only a few minutes a day to scan the want ads and then decide that there are no jobs?

Some economists argue that people who work part-time but are willing to work full-time should be classified as "semihidden" unemployed. Estimates range as high as 6 million workers at any one time. Offsetting this factor, though, is *overemployment*. An individual working 50 to 60 hours a week is still counted as only one full-time worker.

## Labor Force Participation

**Labor force participation rate**
*The percentage of noninstitutionalized working-age individuals who are employed or seeking employment.*

The way in which we define unemployment and membership in the labor force will affect what is known as the **labor force participation rate.** It is defined as the proportion (percentage) of working-age individuals who are employed or seeking employment.

Over the last 60 years, the labor force participation rate of females has risen, and the labor force participation rate of males has fallen. One reason the male labor force participation rate has fallen (and the female participation rate did not rise faster) may have to do with a particular government program. You can read about this in the following *Policy Application*.

## POLICY APPLICATION: Can Being Too Generous Lead to Lower Labor Participation Rates?

### *Concept Applied:* Labor Force Participation Rate

Whatever you might think about our federal government, it has become more generous over time. Consider just the part of the Social Security program that concerns **disability payments**.

#### Social Security Disability Insurance (SSDI)

Originally established in 1956 as a way to help disabled individuals under age 65, Social Security Disability Insurance (SSDI) has become the federal government's fastest-growing program. Each year Uncle Sam spends over $50 billion in SSDI payments.

#### A Program in Full Expansion

Since 1990, the number of people receiving disability payments from the Social Security Administration has more than doubled to over 5.5 million. This increase should not be surprising when you look at the economics underlying such payments. In the last 30 years, the value of the monthly benefits corrected for inflation has gone up over 50 percent. The federal government now spends more on disability payments than on food stamps or unemployment benefits.

#### The Incentive Creates an Effect—Lower Labor Participation Rates

The relatively generous disability payments under Social Security have resulted in the following: some of those who might have worked through chronic pain and temporary injuries—particularly those without extensive training and education—have sometimes chosen to receive a government disability payment instead. The average Social Security disability payment is over $800 a month, *tax-free*. For some, $800 a month tax-free is a tempting alternative to working. Consequently, those receiving disability payments make up the largest group of the 2 million or so who have left the labor force during and since the 2001 recession. As a result, the labor force participation rate is lower than it would otherwise have been if the government did not have such a generous disability program.

**For Critical Analysis:**
*If we did not correct the value of monthly disability payments for inflation, how would our view of what has happened to disability payments over the last three decades be distorted?*

**Disability payments**
*Government payments to individuals who satisfy a definition of being disabled.*

In Figure 10-2 on the following page you can see how the unemployment rate has changed over the last 115 years.

**Mastering Concepts:** How We Measure the Unemployment Rate

- **Individuals are either (1) not in the labor force, (2) unemployed, or (3) employed.**
- **The unemployment rate is defined as the number of unemployed divided by the labor force, expressed as a percentage.**
- **Many people leave the labor force because they become discouraged, and these discouraged workers may constitute a type of hidden unemployment.**

## INFLATION AND DEFLATION

**Inflation**
*A sustained rise in the general price level of goods and services.*

Some prices go up over time. Yet other prices fall. When we consider **inflation**, we are talking about adding up all of the different price changes in the economy and coming up with a measure of a rise in the *general* price level.

> ***We define inflation as a* sustained *upward movement in the average level of* all *prices.***

Some people prefer to discuss inflation in terms of reduced *purchasing power*.

## Figure 10-2 More Than a Century of Unemployment

Unemployment reached lows during World Wars I and II of less than 2 percent and a high during the Great Depression of more than 25 percent.

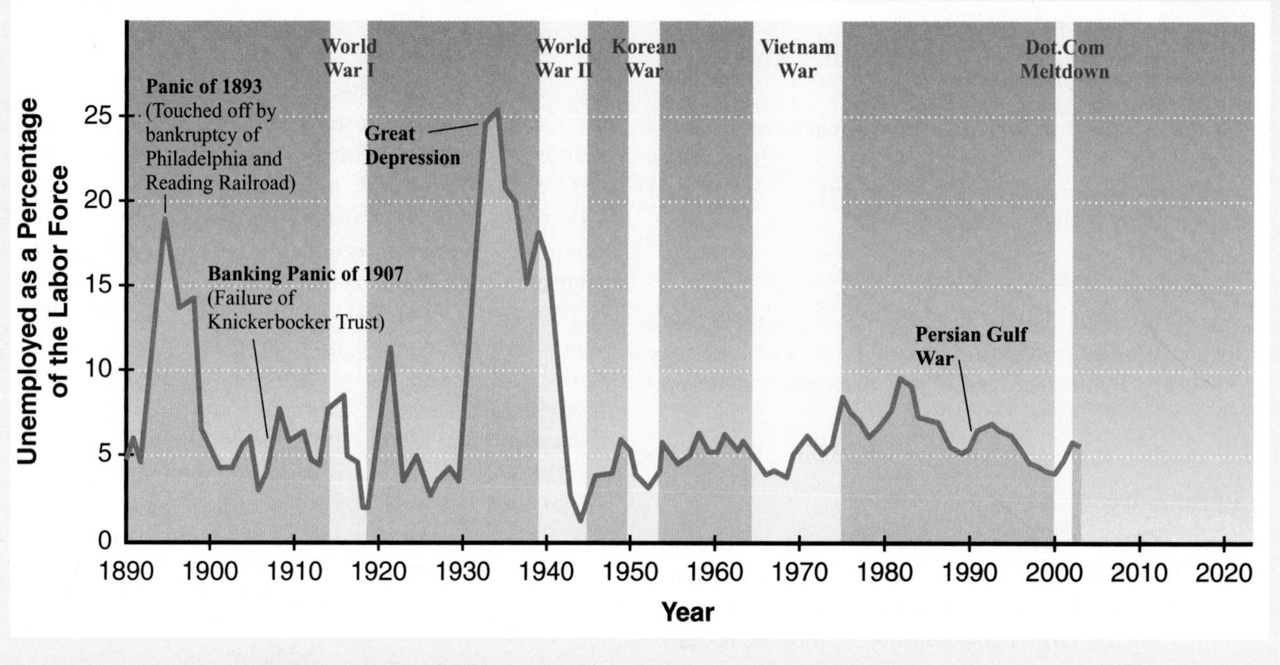


Source: U.S. Department of Labor, Bureau of Labor Statistics.

## How Much Purchasing Power Do You Have?

**Purchasing power**
*The value of money for buying goods and services. If your money income stays the same but the price of one good that you are buying goes up, your effective purchasing power falls, and vice versa.*

While a rose is a rose is a rose, a dollar is not always a dollar. The value of a dollar does not stay constant when there is inflation. The value of money is usually referred to in terms of its **purchasing power.**

***A dollar's purchasing power is the amount of real goods and services that it can buy. Consequently, another way of defining inflation is as a decline in the purchasing power of money over time.***

The faster the rate of inflation, the greater the rate of decline in the purchasing power of money. ▸ Example 10-8 The year is 1967. You have $100. You can buy clothes, food, movie tickets, and so on. Jump to 2004. You again have $100. Can you buy the same amount of real goods and services that you did with that $100 in 1967? Certainly not. In fact, you would be able to buy only about $18 worth of good and services from 1967 with $100 in 2004. In other words, the purchasing power of your money has fallen by over 80 percent from 1967 to 2004. ◂

Perhaps a better way of understanding purchasing power is to think in terms of how much income you make over time. In the above example, if you or your parents were making, say, $1,000 a month in 1967, today you or your parents would have to be making over five times that—in excess of $5,000 a month—to have the same purchasing power.

## How We Measure the Rate of Inflation

How can we measure the rate of inflation? This is a thorny problem for government statisticians. It is easy to determine how much the price of an individual commodity has increased: if last year a light bulb cost 50 cents and this year it costs 75 cents, there has been a 50 percent increase in the price of that light bulb over a one-year period.

We can express the change in the individual light bulb price in several ways: we can say compared to last year, the price has gone up 25 cents; the price is one and a half (1.5) times as high; or the price has increased by 50 percent. An *index number* of this price increase is simply the second way (1.5) multiplied by 100, meaning that the index today would stand at 150. We multiply by 100 to eliminate decimals because it is easier to think in terms of percentage changes using whole numbers. This is the standard convention adopted for convenience in dealing with index numbers or price levels.

**Computing a Price Index** The measurement problem becomes more complicated when it involves a large number of goods, and when some prices have increased faster than others and some have even decreased. What we have to do is pick a representative bundle, a so-called **market basket,** of goods and services and compare the cost of that market basket over time. When we do this, we obtain a **price index,** which is defined as the cost of a market basket of goods and services today, expressed as a percentage of the cost of that identical market basket of goods and services in some starting year, known as the **base year.** Here is what the formula looks like:

**Market basket**
*A representative group of goods and services used to compile the consumer price index.*

**Price index**
*The cost of today's market basket of goods and services expressed as a percentage of the cost of the same market basket during a base year.*

**Base year**
*The year used as a point of comparison for other years in a series of statistics.*

$$\textbf{Price index} = \frac{\textbf{cost today of market basket}}{\textbf{cost in base year of market basket}} \times 100$$

In the base year, the price index will always be 100 because the year in the numerator and in the denominator of the fraction is the same; therefore, the fraction equals 1, and when we multiply it by 100, we get 100. A simple numerical example is given in Table 10-2. In the table, there are only two goods in the market

**Table 10-2 Calculating a Price Index for a Two-Good Market Basket**

In this simplified example, there are only two goods—corn and computers. The quantities and base-year prices are given in columns 2 and 3. The cost of the 1995 market basket, calculated in column 4, comes to $1,400. The 2005 prices are given in column 5. The cost of the market basket in 2005, calculated in column 6, is $1,650. The price index for 2005 compared with 1995 is 117.86. This means that, on average, prices have risen 17.86 percent over this period.

| (1) Commodity Prices | (2) Market Basket Quantity | (3) 1995 Price per Unit | (4) Cost of Market Basket in 1995 | (5) 2005 Price per Unit | (6) Cost of Market Basket in 2005 |
|---|---|---|---|---|---|
| Corn | 100 bushels | $ 4 | $ 400 | $ 8 | $ 800 |
| Computers | 2 | 500 | 1,000 | 425 | 850 |
| **Totals** | | | **$1,400** | | **$1,650** |

$$\text{Price index} = \frac{\text{cost of market basket in 2005}}{\text{cost of market basket in base year 1995}} \times 100 = \frac{\$1{,}650}{\$1{,}400} \times 100 = 117.86$$

basket—corn and computers. The *quantities* in the basket remain the same between the base year, 1995, and the current year, 2005. Only the *prices* change. Such a *fixed-quantity* price index is the easiest to compute because the statistician need only look at the prices of goods and services sold every year rather than observing how much of these goods and services consumers actually purchase each year.

**Consumer price index (CPI)**
*A measure of the change in price over time of a specific group of goods and services used by the average household.*

**The CPI** The **consumer price index,** or **CPI,** attempts to measure changes in the level of prices of all goods and services purchased by all urban consumers. The Bureau of Labor Statistics (BLS) has the task of identifying a market basket of goods and services purchased by the typical consumer. Today, the BLS uses as its base the period 1982–1984. In contrast, its market basket of goods reflects consumer spending patterns for 1993–1995.

Look at Figure 10-3 where you can see changes in the CPI over the last 150 years.

**Figure 10-3 Changing Rates of Inflation, 1860 to the Present**

Since the Civil War, the United States has experienced alternating inflation and deflation. Here we show them as reflected by changes in the consumer price index. Since World War II, the periods of inflation have not been followed by periods of deflation; that is, even during peacetime, the price index has continued to rise. The vertical yellow areas represent wartime.

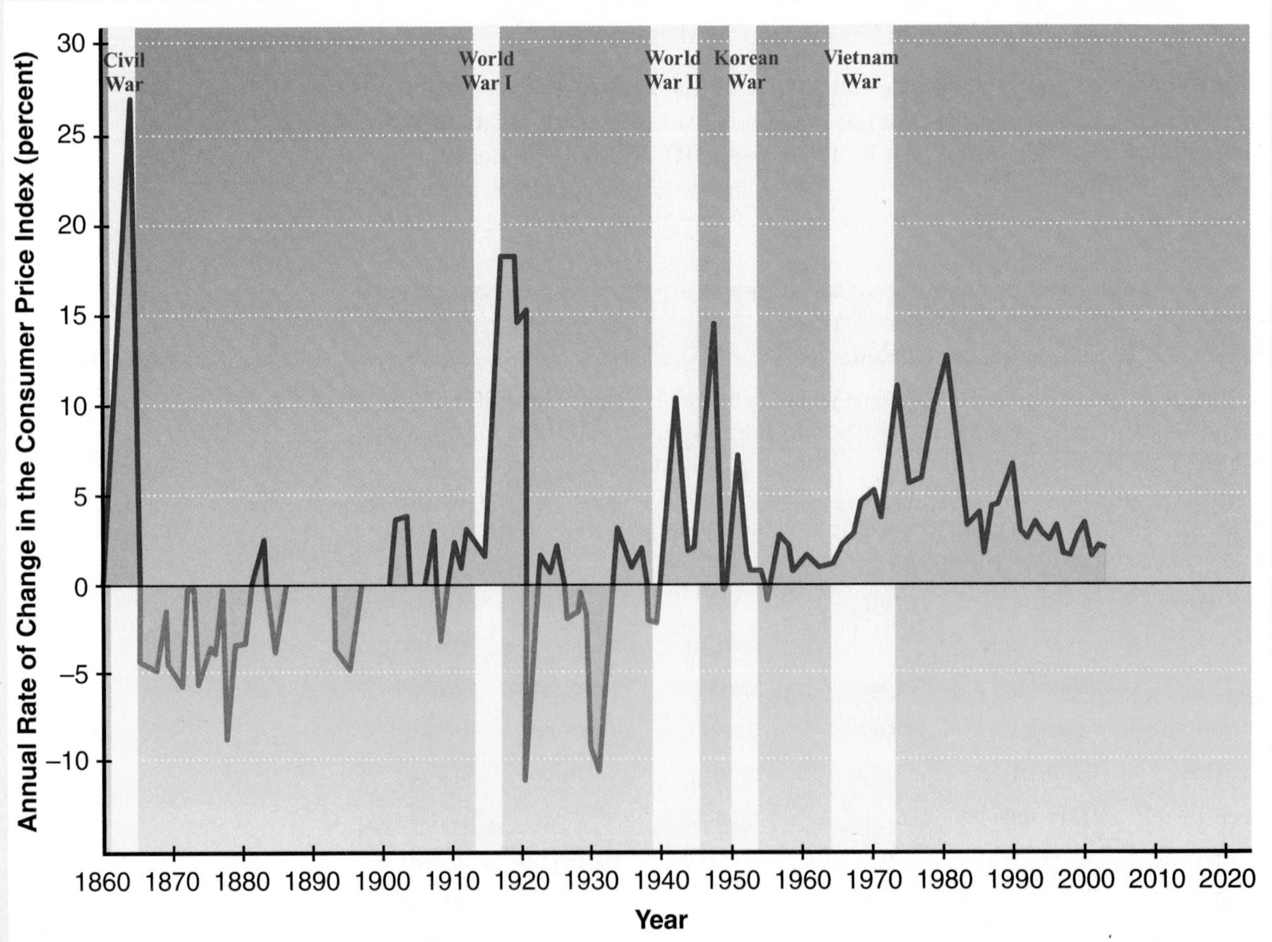


Source: U.S. Department of Labor, Bureau of Labor Statistics.

**Flaws in Measuring the CPI** Economists have known for years that the way the BLS measures changes in the consumer price index is flawed. Specifically, the BLS has been unable to account for the way consumers substitute less-expensive items for higher-priced items. The reason is that the CPI is a fixed-quantity price index, meaning that each month the BLS samples only prices, rather than relative quantities purchased by consumers.

In addition, until recently, the BLS has been unable to consider quality changes as they occur. Currently, though, the BLS is subtracting from certain list prices the estimated effects of qualitative improvements and adding to other list prices for deterioration in quality.

A remaining flaw is that the CPI usually ignores successful new products until long after they are introduced.

**The GDP Deflator** The broadest price index reported in the United States is called the **GDP deflator,** where GDP, of course, refers to gross domestic product, which you learned about in Chapter 2. Unlike the CPI, the GDP deflator is not based on a fixed market basket of goods and services. Rather, the basket is allowed to change with people's consumption and businesses' investment patterns. In this sense, the changes in the GDP deflator reflect both price changes and the public's market response to those price changes. Why? Because new expenditure patterns are allowed to show up in the GDP deflator as people respond to changing prices. Usually, the GDP price deflator is used to create measures of real GDP, which we first discussed in Chapter 2 and will use in the next chapter.

**GDP deflator**
*A price index that measures the changes in prices of all new goods and services produced in the economy.*

## Anticipated versus Unanticipated Inflation

**Anticipated inflation** is the rate of inflation that is generally expected by individuals in the economy. ▸ Example 10-9 If the rate of inflation this year turns out to be 10 percent, and that's about what most people thought it was going to be, we are in a situation of fully anticipated inflation. ◂

**Unanticipated inflation** is inflation that comes as a surprise to individuals in the economy. ▸ Example 10-10 If the inflation rate in a particular year turns out to be 10 percent when, on average, people thought it was going to be 5 percent, there will have been unanticipated inflation—in this case, inflation greater than expected. ◂

**Anticipated inflation**
*The inflation rate that we believe will occur; when it does, we are in a situation of fully anticipated inflation.*

**Unanticipated inflation**
*Inflation at a rate that comes as a surprise, either higher or lower than the rate anticipated.*

***Some of the issues caused by inflation arise when it is unanticipated. In contrast, when inflation is anticipated, many people are able to protect themselves from disadvantageous contracts, for example.***

Keeping the distinction between anticipated and unanticipated inflation in mind, we can analyze who is hurt by inflation.

## How Inflation Hurts

Most people think that inflation is bad. After all, inflation means higher prices, and when we have to pay higher prices, are we not necessarily worse off? The obvious answer, yes, is not quite the correct one, though. The truth is that inflation affects different people differently. Its effects also depend on whether it is anticipated or unanticipated.

**Unanticipated Inflation: Creditors Lose and Debtors Gain** In most situations, unanticipated inflation benefits borrowers because the interest rate they are being charged does not fully compensate for the inflation that actually occurred. In other words, the lender did not anticipate inflation correctly. Whenever inflation rates are underestimated for the life of a loan, creditors lose and debtors gain. ▸ Example 10-11 Periods of considerable unanticipated (higher-than-anticipated) inflation occurred in the late 1960s, the early 1970s, and the late 1970s. During those years, creditors lost and debtors gained. ◂

**Cost-of-living adjustments (COLAs)**
*Clauses in contracts that allow for increases in specified nominal values to take account of changes in the cost of living.*

**Protecting Against Inflation** Banks attempt to protect themselves against inflation by raising interest rates to reflect anticipated inflation. Adjustable-rate mortgages in fact do just that: the interest rate varies according to what happens to interest rates in the economy. Workers can protect themselves through **cost-of-living adjustments (COLAs),** which are automatic increases in wage rates to take account of increases in the price level.

▸ Example 10-12 To the extent that you hold non-interest-bearing cash, you will lose because of inflation. If you have put $100 in a mattress and the inflation rate is 10 percent for the year, you will have lost 10 percent of the purchasing power of that $100. If you have your funds in a non-interest-bearing checking account, you will suffer the same fate. Individuals attempt to reduce the cost of holding cash by putting it into interest-bearing accounts, a wide variety of which often pay rates of interest that reflect anticipated inflation. ◂

**The Resource Cost of Inflation** Some economists believe that the main cost of inflation is the opportunity cost of resources used to protect against inflation and the distortions introduced as firms attempt to plan for the long run. Individuals have to spend time and resources to figure out ways to cover themselves in case inflation is different from what it has been in the past. That may mean spending a longer time working out more complicated contracts for employment, for purchases of goods in the future, and for purchases of raw materials.

Another major problem with inflation is that it usually does not proceed perfectly evenly. Consequently, the rate of inflation is not exactly what people anticipate. When this is so, the purchasing power of money changes in unanticipated ways.

***Because money is what we use as the measuring rod of the value of transactions we undertake, we have a more difficult time figuring out what we have really paid for things during periods of inflation that proceed unevenly.***

As a result, in such situations, resources, such as labor and capital, tend to be misallocated because people have not really valued them accurately.

## Inflation and Interest Rates

Let's start this analysis in a hypothetical world in which there is no inflation and anticipated inflation is zero.

**Nominal rate of interest**
*The market rate of interest at any point in time.*

**The Nominal Rate of Interest** In that world, you may be able to borrow money—to buy a motorcycle or a car, for example—at a **nominal rate of interest** of, say, 10 percent. If you borrow the money to purchase a motorcycle or a car and your anticipation of inflation turns out to be accurate, neither you nor the lender will have been fooled. The dollars you pay back in the years to come will be just as valuable in terms of purchasing power as the dollars that you borrowed.

**Real rate of interest**
*The nominal rate of interest minus the anticipated rate of inflation.*

**The Real Rate of Interest** What you ordinarily need to know when you borrow funds is the *real rate of interest* that you will have to pay. The **real rate of interest** is defined as the nominal rate of interest minus the anticipated rate of inflation. If you are able to borrow money at 10 percent and you anticipate an inflation rate of 10 percent, your real rate of interest will be zero if the actual rate of inflation turns out to be 10 percent. Your real rate of interest will be negative if the actual rate of inflation turns out to be greater than 10 percent.

> ***The nominal rate of interest is equal to the real rate of interest plus an* inflationary premium *to take account of anticipated inflation. That inflationary premium covers the expected fall in the purchasing power of the dollars repaid by borrowers.***

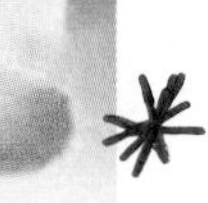

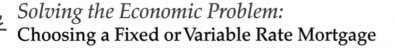

## *Solving the Economic Problem:* Choosing a Fixed or Variable Rate Mortgage

A variable rate mortgage means just that—the mortgage rate will vary over the life of the mortgage depending on what interest rates do in the economy as a whole. You are buying a new house. Your mortgage banker offers you two choices: a 20-year fixed rate mortgage at 6.5 percent or a variable rate mortgage at 4.2 percent for six months, after which the rate will adjust according to what has happened to interest rates in the economy. It will continue to adjust every six months for the remainder of the 20-year mortgage.

Remember that the nominal interest rate is equal to the real rate of interest plus the expected rate of inflation. If you expect the rate of inflation to fall in the future, you might be tempted to take the variable rate mortgage. Why? Because you expect to see *nominal* interest rates either stay the same or fall in the future. Therefore, you reason that the variable rate you will pay will not climb up to the alternative 6.5 percent fixed rate.

In contrast, if you anticipate higher rates of inflation in the future than in the past, you might wish to take the fixed rate mortgage. If your predictions turn out to be correct, nominal rates will rise over time, and future fixed mortgage rates will exceed 6.5 percent per year. You will end up paying a lower real rate of interest on your mortgage in the process.

## DEFLATION: FALLING PRICES

The opposite of inflation is **deflation,** defined as a sustained decrease in the average price level. We pointed out that during inflationary periods, some prices might go up, some prices may remain stable, and some may fall. We can say the same about periods of deflation. During deflation, some prices may fall, some may be stable, and some may even rise. The trick is figuring out whether the average of *all* prices is actually going down. ▸ **International Example 10-13** Japan has been mired in a recession for over a decade. Starting in 1999, the consumer price index in Japan started to fall. The rate of consumer price deflation

**Deflation**
*A sustained decline in the general price level of goods and services.*

since that year has been 0.7 percent a year. Contrast this with the last serious deflationary period in U.S. history, which occurred between November 25, 1929, and April 29, 1934. During that period, U.S. consumer prices fell 1.8 percent a year. ◂

If the price of one category of goods or services falls, that does not necessarily mean that the prices of all other goods and services will be falling, too. Otherwise stated, looking at certain prices, noticing that they are falling, and then concluding that there is deflation is not a good line of reasoning. You can see this in the following *Policy Application*.

## POLICY APPLICATION: Should the Government Be Worried About Deflation?

### *Concepts Applied:* Relative Prices, Deflation

During the early years of the 2000s, numerous industries were plagued by falling prices. Many articles were written about the coming or actual deflation in the United States and in parts of Europe. These articles had titles such as "A Sinking Feeling at the Register: Lower Prices Are Disrupting Many Industries" and "Clearance Sales, 99¢ Whoppers, and Falling Car Prices Are Some of the Signs of the Growing Threat of Deflation."

What does the evidence say? Look at Table 10-3. There you will see a list of some products that experienced declines in prices for the year 2000.

Within specific categories, certain brands had dramatic price drops. The price of a 50-inch Hitachi television dropped from $1,400 to $1,000 in one year. Twenty years ago, Burger King's Whopper sandwich cost $1.40; today, it costs $.99 (over the same period, hourly wages roughly doubled).

#### Does It All Add Up to Deflation?

Remember that deflation is defined as a sustained reduction in the average of *all* prices over time. Therefore, deflation would occur if some price index in the economy fell regularly year in and year out. In contrast, sighting numerous examples of prices of goods and services that have fallen over a specific period does not tell you very much about whether the economy is experiencing deflation.

Rather, the information about falling prices in Table 10-3 simply shows you that the relative prices of certain goods and services are falling. After all, during the same time period gasoline prices rose by 26 percent, outpatient hospital services rose by 13 percent, and college tuition and fees rose by 7 percent. Overall, the measured rate of inflation in the United States has consistently been between 2 and 4 percent per year over the last ten years. The rate of inflation flirted with the 1 percent per year level in 1998 and again at the beginning of 2002. Still that is not deflation.

#### So, Should the Government Be Worried?

Although individual industries may have been feeling the price pinch because of increased competition from abroad and a slowdown in general economic activity, that probably does not mean that the government should worry about deflation. The last time this nation saw a serious deflation was at the beginning of the 1920s and then again from the mid-1920s to the late 1930s. We are certainly not there yet.

**For Critical Analysis:**
*Consumers are rarely unhappy about paying lower prices. How might lower prices, nonetheless, create problems in a particular industry?*

**Table 10-3 Products Experiencing Price Declines in 2000**

| | |
|---|---|
| Personal computers | –22% |
| Butter | –19% |
| TVs | –11% |
| Toys | –9% |
| Long-distance telephone services | –6% |
| Used cars and trucks | –6% |
| Audio equipment | –4% |

**Mastering Concepts:** Inflation and Deflation

- **The rate of inflation is defined as the rate of change of some average of all prices; it can also be thought of as the rate of decrease in the purchasing power of a dollar.**
- **To compute a price index, we compare the cost today of a market basket of goods and services with the cost of that same market basket in a specified base year.**
- **The consumer price index measures changes in the prices of goods and services purchased by all urban consumers.**
- **The GDP deflator is the broadest measure of inflation and does not use a fixed basket of goods and services.**
- **Unanticipated inflation causes creditors to lose and debtors to gain.**
- **Some types of contracts, such as variable rate mortgages and labor contracts with cost-of-living adjustments, can avoid the cost of unanticipated inflation.**
- **The nominal rate of interest is the real rate of interest plus the anticipated rate of inflation.**
- **Deflation is defined as a sustained decline in the average of all prices.**

## BUSINESS FLUCTUATIONS AND BUSINESS CYCLES

Nationwide economic activity does not just go up at a steady pace every year. If it did, there would be no need to make predictions about the state of the economy. Nor would there be any need for government policymakers to worry about the state of the economy.

### EXPANSIONS AND CONTRACTIONS

During some years, unemployment goes up, and in other years, it goes down. During some years, there is a lot of inflation, and in other years there isn't. We have fluctuations in all aspects of our **macroeconomy.** The ups and downs in economy-wide economic activity are sometimes called **business fluctuations.**

When a business fluctuation is positive, it is called an **expansion**—a speedup in the pace of national economic activity. The opposite of an expansion is a **contraction**—a slowdown in the pace of national economic activity. The top of an expansion is usually called its *peak,* and the bottom of a contraction is usually called its *trough.*

Business fluctuations used to be called *business cycles,* but that term no longer seems appropriate because *cycle* implies regular or automatic recurrence, and we normally don't observe automatic recurrent fluctuations in general business and economic activity. What we have had are contractions and expansions that vary greatly in length. For example, nine post–World War II expansions averaged 48 months, but three of those exceeded 55 months, and two lasted less than 25 months.

**Macroeconomy**
*The economy as a whole.*

**Business fluctuations**
*Ups and downs in an economy.*

**Expansion**
*The part of the business cycle in which economic activity increases.*

**Contraction**
*The part of the business cycle during which economic activity is slowing down, leading to a trough.*

## Recessions and Depressions

**Recession**
*A part of the business cycle in which the nation's output (real GDP) does not grow for at least six months; usually associated with rising unemployment and slumping industrial production and manufacturing.*

**Depression**
*A major slowdown of economic activity during which millions are out of work, many businesses fail, and the economy operates at far below capacity.*

If the contractionary phase of business fluctuations becomes severe enough, we call it a **recession.** An extremely severe recession is called a **depression.** ▸ Example 10-14 The Great Depression lasted throughout most of the 1930s. By 1932, 13 million people were unemployed. By 1933, actual output was at least 35 percent below the nation's productive capacity. By 1932, the net income of farm operators was barely 20 percent of its 1929 level, even though total farm output had risen 3 percent in the interim. In those same three years, prices received by farmers had fallen to 40 percent of their already low 1929 level. Between 1929 and 1932, more than 5,000 banks, one out of every five, failed, and their customers' deposits vanished. ◂

## Typical Business Fluctuations

In Figure 10-4, you see the typical course of business fluctuations. The business fluctuations occur around a growth trend in overall national business activity. The straight upward-sloping line shows this growth trend. Starting out at a peak, the economy goes into a contraction (recession). Then an expansion starts that moves up to its peak, higher than the last one, and the sequence starts over again. That is where the term *cycle* comes from in business cycle.

## A Historical Picture of National Business Activity in the United States

Figure 10-5 traces changes in U.S. business activity from 1880 to the present. Note that the long-term upward trend line is shown as horizontal, so all changes in business activity focus around that trend line. Major changes in business activity in the United States occurred during the Great Depression and World War II. Note

Animated

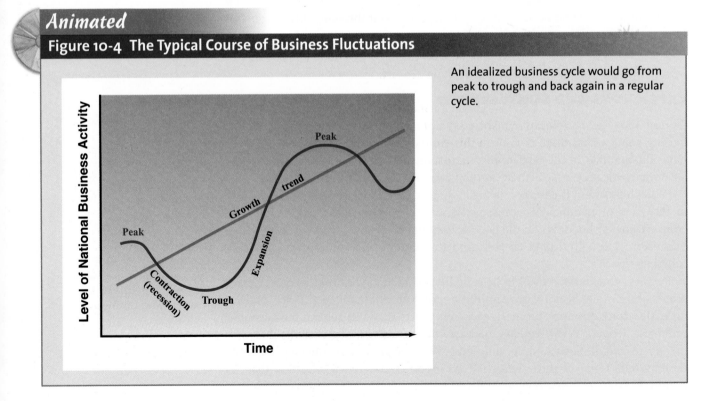

**Figure 10-4 The Typical Course of Business Fluctuations**

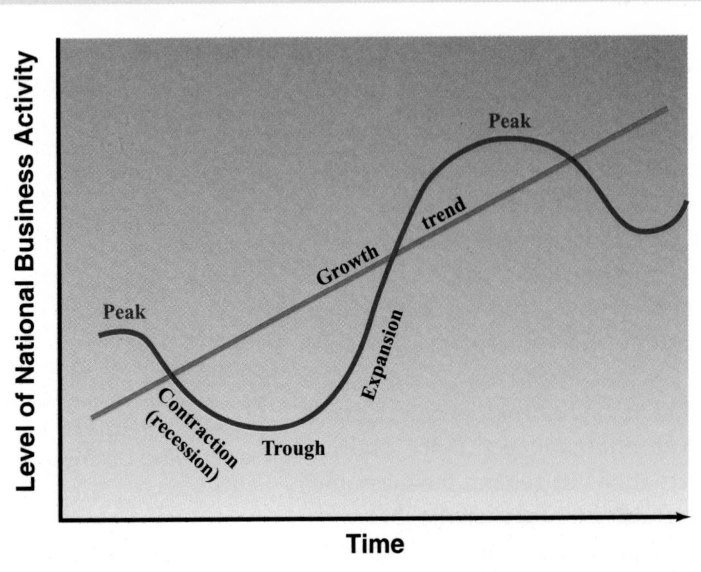


An idealized business cycle would go from peak to trough and back again in a regular cycle.

**Figure 10-5 National Business Activity, 1880 to the Present**

Variations around the trend of U.S. business activity have been frequent since 1880.

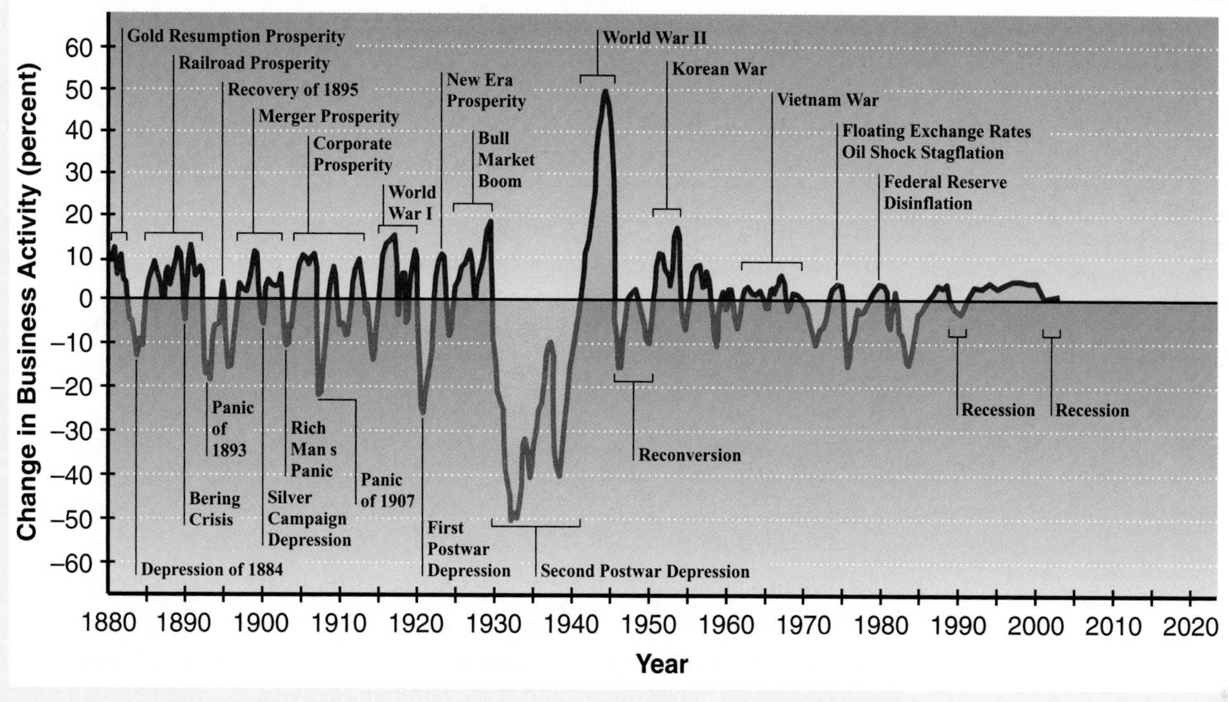


Sources: *American Business Activity from 1790 to Today*, 67th ed. (AmeriTrust Co., January 1996), plus author's projections.

that none of the business fluctuations that you see in Figure 10-5 exactly mirror the idealized typical course of a business fluctuation shown in Figure 10-4.

## Explaining Business Cycles

Today, economists tend to link business fluctuations to three main forces: external factors, business investment, and government activity.

**External Shocks** For years, one of the most obvious explanations has been external events that tend to disrupt the economy. ▸ Example 10-15 World War II turned out to be a critical point in this nation's economic history. A war is certainly an external shock—something that originates outside our economy. ◂

✦ **Compare!** *Internal shocks can come from hurricanes, floods, and massive labor strikes, whereas external shocks come from outside our borders.*

Other examples of external shocks, particularly for an agrarian nation, have to do with abrupt changes in the weather. When the majority of Americans worked on farms, long-term drought tended to create downturns in national business activity. Today, major droughts or floods usually affect specific regions of the U.S. economy. Even a hurricane or an earthquake that dramatically affects one area rarely causes a national economic downturn.

▸ Example 10-16 In the 1970s, due to actions on the part of certain countries in the Middle East, the United States received an "oil shock" in the form of a supply restriction. The price of oil increased dramatically then, and some economists argue that this had a major effect on national economic activity. ◂

**Business Investment** Some economists believe that business decisions are the key to business fluctuations. Suppose a firm believes that prospects for future sales are good. It will probably increase its capital investment: buy new machines, build new factories, expand old ones, and so on. This expansion will create new jobs and more income for consumer spending.

**Innovations**
*New products, systems, or processes that have wide-ranging effects.*

**Innovations**—inventions and new production techniques—can have a similar effect on the economy. When one firm begins to use an innovation, others must imitate the product or production method in order to remain competitive.

When businesses anticipate a downturn in the economy, they cut back on their capital investment and inventories. Producers, in turn, cut back on production to prevent a surplus. Enough inventory cutbacks could lead to a recession.

**Government Activity** A number of economists believe that the changing policies of the federal government are a major reason for business cycles. The government affects business activity in two ways: through its policies on taxing and spending, and through its control over the supply of money available in the economy. You'll learn more about these government actions in Chapters 12 and 14.

### Mastering Concepts: Business Fluctuations and Business Cycles

- **Business fluctuations consist of expansions and contractions. When a contraction lasts long enough, it is classified as a recession.**
- **When a recession lasts for a long time or becomes extremely severe, it is called a depression.**
- **Business fluctuations may be caused by changes in (1) external factors; (2) business investment, and (3) government activity.**

## SUMMING IT ALL UP

- Because obtaining information about alternative jobs is costly, it is sometimes cheaper for participants in the labor force to become unemployed in order to look for other employment opportunities, thereby leading to frictional unemployment.
- The three other types of unemployment are structural, cyclical, and seasonal.
- The unemployment rate is defined as the number of unemployed divided by the labor force, expressed as a percentage.
- The rate of inflation is defined as the rate of change of some average of all prices; it can also be thought of as the rate of decrease in the purchasing power of a dollar.
- To compute a price index, we compare the cost today of a market basket of goods and services with the cost of that same market basket in a specified base year.
- The consumer price index measures changes in the prices of goods and services purchased by all urban consumers.
- Some types of contracts, such as variable rate mortgages and labor contracts with cost-of-living adjustments, can avoid the costs of unanticipated inflation.
- The nominal rate of interest is the real rate of interest plus the anticipated rate of inflation.

- Deflation is defined as a sustained decline in the average of all prices.
- Business fluctuations may be caused by changes in (1) external factors, (2) business investment, and (3) government activity.

## KEY TERMS AND CONCEPTS

anticipated inflation **213**
base year **211**
business fluctuations **217**
consumer price index (CPI) **212**
contraction **217**
cost-of-living adjustments (COLAs) **214**
cyclical unemployment **206**
deflation **215**
depression **218**
disability payments **209**
discouraged workers **208**
expansion **217**
frictional unemployment **204**
GDP deflator **213**
inflation **209**
innovations **220**
labor force participation rate **208**
macroeconomics **204**
macroeconomy **217**
market basket **211**
microeconomics **204**
nominal rate of interest **214**
price index **211**
purchasing power **210**
real rate of interest **214**
recession **218**
seasonal unemployment **206**
structural unemployment **205**
unanticipated inflation **213**
unemployment **204**

## MASTERING ECONOMIC CONCEPTS
## Questions and Problems

**10-1.** If Brett is searching for a position as an architect but cannot find one that suits his interests in the field, what type of unemployment does this represent?

**10-2.** If the CPI increased from 107.8 in 1985 to 183.9 in 2003, by what percent did the average of all prices increase over this time period?

**10-3.** Classify each of the following as employed, unemployed, or not part of the labor force.

a. a full-time student taking an overload of seven classes this semester
b. an individual with an engineering degree working 10 hours each week as a waiter
c. a chemical researcher who is not able to find work and has given up looking
d. a house painter who cannot find work due to a downturn in the economy

**10-4.** In what year since 1900 did we see the lowest unemployment rate in the United States? Why was the unemployment rate particularly low at that time?

**10-5.** If the U.S. population was 200 million, the number employed was 150 million, and the number unemployed was 10 million, what would the unemployment rate equal?

**10-6.** In problem 10-5, there is a difference of 40 million between the number of people in the population and the combined total of the employed and unemployed. Who does this 40 million represent? Based on these figures, what is the labor force participation rate?

**10-7.** If the labor force is 100 million, the population is 120 million, and the unemployment rate is 4 percent, how many people are classified as unemployed?

**10-8.** Use the table below to compute a price index for a market basket consisting of these three goods in 1993 and in 2005. Based on these figures, by what percent did the price of these goods increase over this time period?

| Goods | Quantity in Market Basket | 1993 Price per Unit | 1993 Market Basket Cost | 2005 Price per Unit | 2005 Market Basket Cost |
|---|---|---|---|---|---|
| CDs | 20 | $14 | | $14.50 | |
| Mid-size auto | 0.5 | 20,000.00 | | 24,000.00 | |
| 2-liter soda | 50 | 1 | | 1.50 | |
| | | 1993 Total: | | 2005 Total: | |

**10-9.** Which year or years are the base years currently used for the CPI? Approximately what is the value of the CPI in these base years? What is the value of any price index in its base year? If the CPI had increased to 180.9 at the end of 2005, by what percent did prices increase between the base year or years and 2005?

**10-10.** When was the last year in which the United States recorded deflation?

**10-11.** How is the market basket used in computing the GDP deflator constructed differently from the market basket used in computing the CPI? Which of these price indices would overstate inflation by ignoring the substitution effect?

**10-12.** Assume that you loaned a trustworthy friend $100 for one year at an interest rate of 5 percent. If the rate of inflation was 2 percent during that year, what was your real interest rate? If you made the same loan the next year but the expected rate of inflation increased to 4 percent, what interest rate would you charge?

**10-13.** If you want to make sure that you earn a real interest rate of at least 6 percent and you expect that the rate of inflation next year will be 2 percent, what is the lowest nominal interest rate you should charge if you make a loan?

**10-14.** During an expansion in economic activity, which is more likely—an increase or decrease in GDP? Which is more likely—an increase or decrease in unemployment? Which is more likely—an increase or decrease in inflation?

**10-15.** Prior to the year 2000, when was the most recent recession experienced by the U.S economy?

**10-16.** Based on the data below, compute the unemployment rate and the labor force participation rate.

| | |
|---|---|
| Employed | 60 million |
| Unemployed | 2 million |
| Population | 70 million |

## THINKING CRITICALLY

**10-1.** Most of us hate to hear about an increase in inflation. In the late 1800s, however, during a period of significant price declines, farmers throughout the Midwest actually looked forward to inflation. Why would they possibly look upon inflation so favorably? Would you assume that most farmers at that time tended to borrow more money or lend more money? For any loans that exist, is the interest rate to which the parties explicitly agree a nominal interest rate or a real interest rate?

**10-2.** In the 1970s, various savings and loan associations (S&Ls) offered very competitive rates on fixed rate mortgages as well as deposits. How did the rate of inflation in the mid-1970s compare with the rate of inflation in the early 1980s? Based on your previous answer, what impact did the change in the inflation rate have on the real interest rate earned by these S&Ls? In most cases the S&Ls made long-term fixed rate loans and obtained funds through deposits that were more short term in nature. How would this fact make the situation even worse for the S&Ls? What does the term *adjustable rate mortgage* stand for in a financial context, and how does it relate to the S&L example?

**10-3.** Unemployment might appear to be never beneficial to the individual who is unemployed. Nonetheless, some types of unemployment are necessary to our economy. How is frictional unemployment necessary or even beneficial to the economy? How is structural unemployment necessary or even beneficial to the economy?

## LOGGING ON

1. To learn about the history of the growth of the U.S. labor force and to see projections of its future growth, go to http://www.bls.gov/opub/mlr/2002/05/art2exc.htm.
2. For an update on the current U.S. unemployment rate, go to http://www.bls.gov/cps/home.htm.
3. For a discussion of how Social Security has affected the labor force participation rates of older workers, go to http://www.ncpa.org/pd/economy/pd022699f.html.
4. To see the latest CPI inflation rate for the United States, go to http://www.bls.gov/cpi/home.htm.

## USING THE INTERNET FOR ECONOMIC ANALYSIS

**Official Dates of U.S. Business Cycles** In the United States, a nonprofit organization called the National Bureau of Economic Research (NBER) is responsible for determining the official starting and ending points of business expansions and contractions. This application gives you a chance to see the NBER's formal business cycle dates and learn more about business cycle trends.

**Title:** Business Cycle Expansions and Contractions

**Navigation:** Go to http://www.nber.org/cycles.html/.

**Application** Examine the NBER tabulation of dates when expansions and contractions have officially started and ended, and answer the following questions.

1. On average, have business contractions been longer or shorter in recent years? Has the average duration of business expansions been longer or shorter recently?
2. During the two most recent recessions, a number of politicians stated that the contractions were among the worst economic downturns in our nation's history. Were these statements factual?

## MEDIA RESOURCE LIST

The following media resources are available with this chapter:

- Load your CD-ROM to listen to the audio introduction to this chapter.
- Load your CD-ROM to view the video on *Major Types of Unemployment.*
- Load your CD-ROM to access a Graph Animation of Figure 10-1, *The Logic of the Unemployment Rate.*
- Load your CD-ROM to view the video on *Measuring the Rate of Inflation.*
- Load your CD-ROM to view the video on *Inflation and Interest Rates.*
- Load your CD-ROM to access a Graph Animation of Figure 10-4, *The Typical Course of Business Fluctuations.*
- Test your knowledge of chapter concepts with a quiz at www.miller-ume.com.
- Link to Web resources related to the text coverage at www.miller-ume.com.

## HOMEWORK SET

Go to the end of this book to find the Homework Problems for this chapter.

# CHAPTER 11

# Aggregate Demand and Supply

## *Facing an Economic Problem:* What Are the Hidden Costs of Terrorism?

After terrorists flew commercial jets into the World Trade Center towers and the Pentagon (and into the ground in Pennsylvania) in 2001, the war on terrorism began in earnest. At first blush, this war involved additional security measures that were obvious. They included more guards at airports, more use of the military to protect critical installations in addition to airports, more backup electrical systems for critical buildings, and so on. Indeed, the United States is still adding additional security measures at virtually all levels of government and private business.

The economic problem is the following: Many of the additional security measures undertaken since September 2001 to guard against terrorism have involved additional spending and employment. For example, security firms have seen the demand for their services skyrocket. Trucking firms have paid drivers to work overtime reparking trucks in plain view and under security lights. More engineers have been hired to figure out ways to make doors more secure to protect pilots from intrusion by would-be hijackers. Other engineers have been hired to develop antimissile systems to protect commercial aircraft. How, then, can it be that the war on terrorism has actually led to *lower* economic growth than would have occurred in its absence after September 11, 2001?

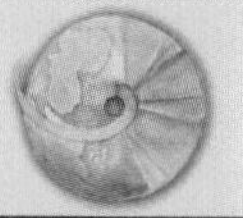

***Refer to the back of this chapter for a complete listing of multimedia learning materials available on the CD-ROM and the Web site.***

## Learning Objectives

After reading this chapter, you should be able to:

- **Explain how the aggregate demand curve differs from the *individual* demand curve.**
- **List and discuss two reasons why the aggregate demand curve slopes down.**
- **Define the aggregate supply curve.**
- **Explain why the aggregate supply curve slopes up.**

## THE CIRCULAR FLOW OF INCOME AND PRODUCT

In Chapter 10, you were introduced to the business cycle and business fluctuations. Business fluctuations—recessions and expansions—are an important aspect of macroeconomics. Indeed, much of macroeconomics is concerned with how to predict and prevent recessions. To make such predictions, economists and government policymakers have to use a model of the macroeconomy.

### THE TWO MODELS WE EXAMINE

In this chapter, we start off with the simplest model of the circular flow of income and product within our economy. Then we move on to an examination of how people's planned expenditures and businesses' planned production interact. By examining this interaction, we are better able to explain the root causes of the business cycle discussed in the last chapter. The simple model we present allows us to understand recessions and inflation.

As an individual, you have individual demands for goods and services. As an individual, you supply certain factors of production, from which goods and services are created. In this chapter, we add up the demands and supplies of everyone like you, your family, and friends into the total, or aggregate, demand and aggregate supply in the economy.

Before we do that, we look at the flow of income within our economy (leaving out for the moment government and the foreign sector).

> ***It is the flow of goods and services from businesses to consumers and payments from consumers to businesses that constitutes national economic activity.***

▸ Example 11-1 Many of your activities are part of national economic activity. When you work, you are providing labor services, from which you derive income. Then, when you spend that income on food, housing, movie tickets, and vacation travel, you are providing income to the sellers of those goods and services. ◂

### THE TWO PRINCIPLES OF THE CIRCULAR FLOW OF INCOME

**Circular flow of income**
*An economic model that pictures income as flowing continuously between businesses and consumers.*

The concept of a **circular flow of income** (ignoring taxes) involves two principles:

1. In every economic exchange, the seller receives exactly the same amount that the buyer spends.
2. Goods and services flow in one direction, and money payments flow in the other.

In the simple economy shown in Figure 11-1, there are only businesses and households. We assume that businesses sell their *entire* output *immediately* to households and that households spend their *entire* income *immediately* on consumer products. Households receive their income by selling the use of whatever factors of production they own, such as labor services.

An additional point should be made concerning the circular flow diagram in Figure 11-1. The inside flows represent the so-called real part of our economy. The outside flows represent the money values attached to the inside arrow real flows.

### DISTINGUISHING BETWEEN PRODUCT AND FACTOR MARKETS

You can see in Figure 11-1 that the top of the diagram refers to product markets and the bottom to factor markets.

Animated

**Figure 11-1 The Circular Flow of Income and Product**

Businesses provide final goods and services to households, represented by the upper clockwise arrow. Households pay for these goods and services with money income, represented by the upper counterclockwise arrow. Households provide factor services—labor, land, capital, and entrepreneurial activity—to businesses, represented by the bottom clockwise arrow. Total income is equal to the money income receipts of households for selling their labor services and other factors of production. The counterclockwise arrow of total income equaling wages, rents, interest, and profits represents this.

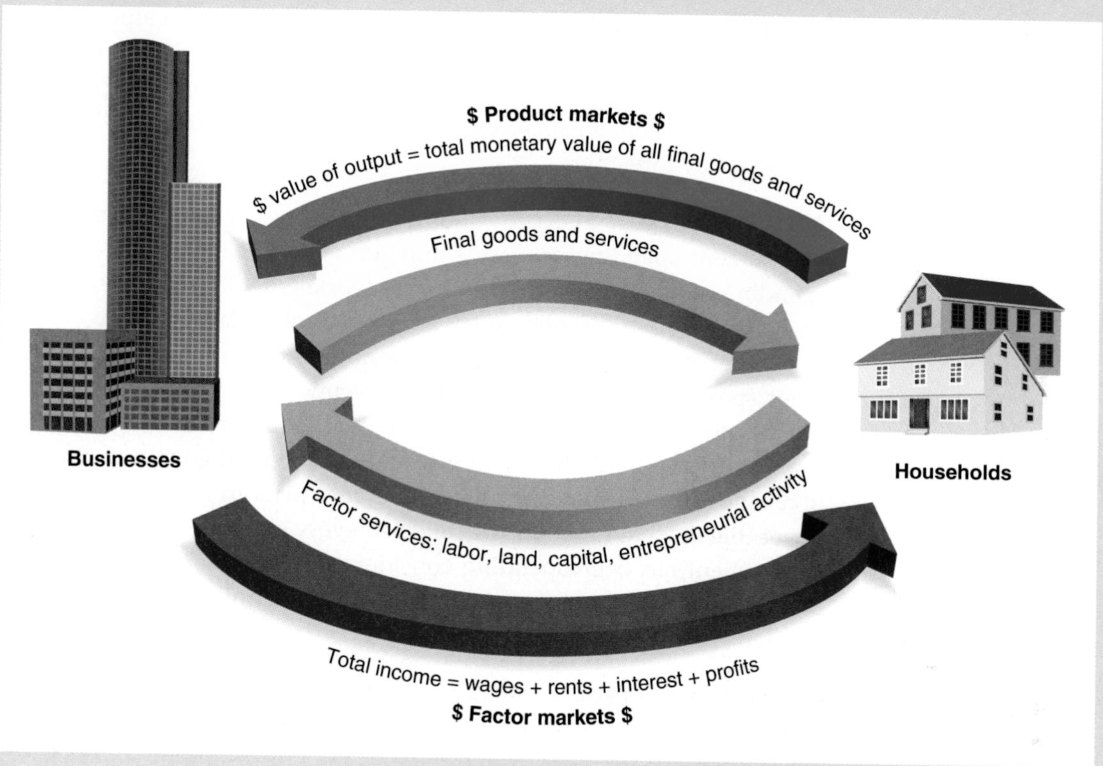


**Product Markets** Transactions in which households buy goods take place in the product markets—that's where households are the buyers and businesses are the sellers of consumer goods. *Product market* transactions are represented by the upper arrows in Figure 11-1. Note that final goods and services flow to household demanders, while money income flows in the opposite direction to business suppliers.

**Factor Markets** *Factor market* transactions are represented by the lower arrows in Figure 11-1. In the factor markets, households are the sellers; they sell resources such as labor, land, capital, and entrepreneurial ability. Businesses are the buyers in factor markets; business expenditures constitute income for households. In the lower arrows of Figure 11-1, factor services flow from households to businesses, while the money income paid for these services flows in the opposite direction from businesses to households.

Observe that, when we look at the top and bottom of the figure together, there is a continuous flow of money income (counterclockwise) from households to businesses and back again from businesses to households: it is an endless circular flow.

## Expanding the Circular Flow Model

If we add to the top of the circular flow model in Figure 11-1 the government and the foreign sector, that is, the net purchases of goods and services that foreigners make, then we come up with a more complete model of the economy.

***Indeed, we can think of the top part of the circular flow model with government and the foreign sector added as a representation of gross domestic product, or GDP, that you learned about in Chapter 2.***

Remember from that chapter that GDP is the current value of all *final* goods and services produced in our nation in one year. It includes all the goods and services that consumers buy, plus business spending on equipment and buildings, plus government spending. In addition, a small part of GDP includes the net purchases by foreigners.

**The Government Sector** The government sector of the circular flow involves government spending on goods and services, and it also includes government spending on wages and salaries for its workers and payments to welfare recipients and farm owners, plus many other types of outlays.

Of course, government collects revenues, too, from taxes. Whenever government spending exceeds government revenues, the government has to borrow. This is a topic we will look at more closely in Chapter 12.

▸ Example 11-2 From 1998 to 2001, the federal government collected more in revenues than it spent. For several decades prior to 1998, in contrast, the federal government spent more than it collected every single year. Since 2001, the federal government has been spending considerably more than it collects. The estimate for 2004 is a negative difference close to $400 billion! (You'll read more about this phenomenon in Chapter 12.) ◂

**Imports**
*The goods and services that we purchase from abroad.*

**Exports**
*The goods and services that foreigners purchase from the United States.*

**Net exports**
*The difference between exports and imports; can be (and has been) negative, meaning that we import more than we export.*

**The Foreign Sector** Americans purchase goods and services from foreigners, called **imports.** Foreigners purchase goods and services from us, called **exports.** When we purchase more from foreigners than they do from us, we have to talk in terms of *negative* **net exports,** where net exports equal the difference between exports and imports. We will be looking at the foreign sector in more detail in Chapters 16 and 17. ▸ International Example 11-3 Net exports as a part of GDP have been negative for decades. Indeed, imports of goods and services exceeded exports of goods and services by over $400 billion in 2003. ◂

**Putting It All Together** So, you now have all of the elements of gross domestic product, or

$$\text{GDP} = C + I + G + X$$

In this little formula, $C$ equals consumer spending; $I$ equals mainly business spending on investment; $G$ is government spending; and $X$ is net exports. Throughout the rest of this chapter, you will learn about the determination of total actual spending—GDP—each year.

**Mastering Concepts:** The Circular Flow of Income and Product

- **In the circular flow model of income and output, households sell factor services to businesses, which in their turn pay for those factor services. The receipt of payments is total income. Businesses sell goods and services to households, which in their turn use money income to pay for those goods and services.**

- **The dollar value of total output is equal to the total monetary value of all final goods and services produced.**
- **Actual annual spending is gross domestic product, or GDP. It consists of consumer spending, business investment, government spending, and net exports.**

## WATCH OUT! AGGREGATE DEMAND IS NOT THE SAME AS INDIVIDUAL DEMAND

You know how much you spend each year. Your spending constitutes part of total, or aggregate, spending. The dollar value of total expenditures in this country depends for the most part on what individuals, firms, and governments spend. ▸ **Example 11-4** Assume that during the summer months, you worked as a telemarketer for a local real estate developer. At the end of the summer, you decided to use your accumulated earnings as a down payment on a new car. Your decision to spend changed ever so slightly the actual dollar value of total expenditures in the economy. Had you decided to save that income, total expenditures in the economy would have been less. ◂

## ADDING IT ALL UP—THE AGGREGATE DEMAND CURVE

When you add up what you plan to spend, what your neighbors plan to spend, and what governments plan to spend (and even foreigners, too), you get what is called **aggregate demand.** The formal definition of aggregate demand is the total of all *planned* expenditures in the economy. As you learned earlier in this chapter, total expenditures in the economy consist of spending by consumers on goods and services, spending by businesses on investment, spending by the government, and net exports.

**Aggregate demand**
*The total dollar value of all planned expenditures in the economy.*

## GOING FROM AGGREGATE DEMAND TO THE AGGREGATE DEMAND CURVE

Go back and take a look at some of the demand curves in Chapter 3. They were all based on individuals' demands for specific goods and services. Now we are in the realm of aggregate demand, which is not the same thing.

If we have all of people's spending plans added up, these plans have to depend on or be a function of something. The individual demand curves in Chapter 3 were a function of the price of each good or service. For the economy as a whole, there is no one price of all goods and services. Rather, there is a price level, which is the average of all prices.

> ***When talking about aggregate demand, we examine the relationship between aggregate quantity demanded and the overall price level,* not *individual prices.***

### Graphing the Aggregate Demand Curve

The **aggregate demand curve** shows the total amount of output that will be purchased at each price level. This consists of the output of *final* goods and services in the economy—everything produced for final use by households, businesses, the government, and foreign residents. It includes stereos, socks, shoes, medical and legal services, computers, and millions of other goods and services that people buy each year.

**Aggregate demand curve**
*A graphed line showing the relationship between the aggregate quantity demanded and the average of all prices as measured by the overall price level, often the GDP price deflator.*

***Output, real income, and real GDP all represent* exactly *the same thing—the total output of final goods and services in an economy over a specific period, usually one year. These terms can be, and are, used interchangeably.***

You can see a graphical representation of the aggregate demand curve in Figure 11-2. On the horizontal axis is measured output, which is often formally referred to as real GDP, as mentioned above. For our measure of the price level, we use the GDP price deflator (discussed in Chapter 10) on the vertical axis. This is our price-level index. The aggregate demand curve is labeled *AD*. If the GDP deflator is 120, aggregate quantity demanded is $12 trillion of output per year (point *A*). At price level 140, it is $11 trillion of output per year (point *B*). At price level 160, it is $10 trillion per year (point C)

***The higher the overall price level, the lower the real GDP demanded by the economy, everything else remaining constant. Conversely, the lower the overall price level, the higher the real GDP demanded by the economy, everything else staying constant.***

## What Happens When the Price Level Rises?

Assume that the price level in the economy rises to 160 tomorrow. What will happen? You know what happens when the price of a good goes up, with all other prices remaining the same. The quantity demanded of that good falls. But now we are talking about the price level—the average price of *all* goods and services in the economy.

Well, the answer is still the same in the sense that when the price level rises, the total quantity of real goods and services demanded falls. The reasons are different, though. When the price of just one good or service goes up relative to the

*Animated*

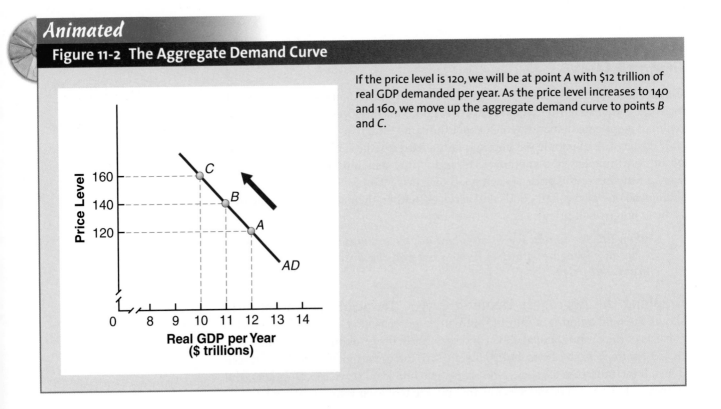

**Figure 11-2 The Aggregate Demand Curve**

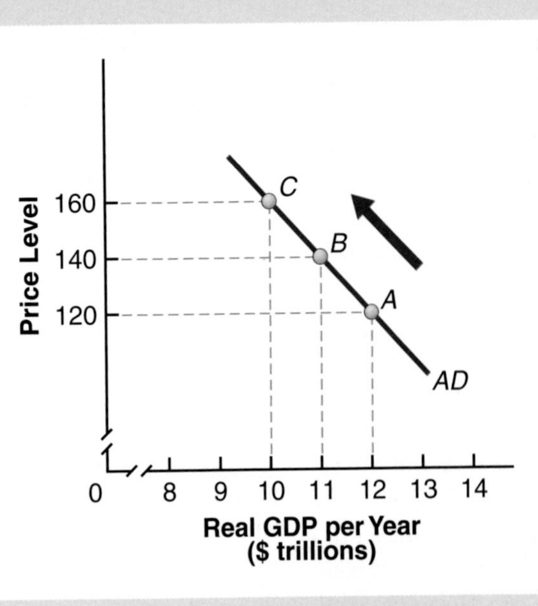


If the price level is 120, we will be at point *A* with $12 trillion of real GDP demanded per year. As the price level increases to 140 and 160, we move up the aggregate demand curve to points *B* and *C*.

prices of other goods and services, the consumer substitutes toward other goods and services.

***For the entire economy, when the price level goes up, the consumer does not simply substitute one good for another, because now we are dealing with the demand for* all *goods and services in a nation.***

**Yet Another Way of Examining the Downward Slope of the Aggregate Demand Curve** If you think of "aggregate demand" as simply another term for "planned expenditures," then you can get an intuitive feeling for why the aggregate demand curve slopes down. Aggregate demand is obviously some dollar-value amount. For a given level of planned expenditures, if the average price of goods and services is higher, then consumers *must* necessarily be buying fewer of these goods and services. Hence, the aggregate demand curve is downward sloping.

There are also *economy-wide* reasons why the aggregate demand curve slopes downward. They involve a variety of forces, the most important of which we discuss now.

**The Real-Balance Effect** Consider that individuals, firms, and governments carry out transactions using money. A portion of this money consists of the currency and coins that you have in your pocket or stashed away. Because people use money to purchase goods and services, the amount of money that people have influences the amount of goods and services they want to buy. ▸ Example 11-5 If your pocket is picked while you are shopping downtown, your desired spending will be affected. Assume that your wallet had $50 in it when it was stolen. The reduction in your **cash balances**—in this case, currency—would no doubt cause you to reduce your planned expenditures. You would ultimately buy fewer goods and services. ◂

This response is sometimes called the **real-balance effect** because it specifically concerns the real value of your cash balances.

***If the price level goes up while you hold cash, the real value of that cash goes down, just as if a pickpocket had stolen some cash out of your wallet.***

▸ Example 11-6 When you think of the real-balance effect, think of what happens to your real wealth if you have, say, a $100 bill hidden under your mattress. If the price level increases by 10 percent, the purchasing power of that $100 bill drops by 10 percent, so you have become less wealthy. This will reduce your desired spending on goods and services by some small amount. ◂

**Cash balances** *The amount of coins, currency, and readily available money that you normally have in a checking account.*

**Real-balance effect** *The change in planned expenditures resulting from the change in the real value of cash balances when the price level changes, all other things held constant; also called the wealth effect. A reason that the aggregate demand curve slopes downward.*

**The Open Economy Effect: The Substitution of Foreign Goods** There is another reason why the aggregate demand curve slopes down. It has to do with the foreign sector of our economy. Recall from the beginning of this chapter that GDP includes net exports—the difference between exports and imports.

In an open economy, we buy imports from other countries and ultimately pay for them through the *foreign exchange market* (a topic we treat in detail in Chapter 17). The same is true for foreign residents who purchase our goods (exports). Given any set of exchange rates between the U.S. dollar and other currencies, an increase in the price level in the United States makes U.S. goods more expensive for foreigners. Foreigners have downward-sloping demand curves for U.S. goods. When the relative price of U.S. goods goes up, foreign residents buy fewer U.S. goods and more of their own. At home, relatively cheaper prices for foreign goods cause U.S. residents to buy more foreign goods instead of domestically produced goods. Thus, when the domestic price level rises, the result is a fall in exports and a rise in imports. This is called the **open economy effect.**

**Open economy effect**
*The change in net exports resulting from a change in the price level, all other things held constant; one of the reasons that the aggregate demand curve slopes downward. A higher price level reduces net exports because foreign residents tend to buy fewer U.S.-made goods, while U.S. residents buy more foreign-made goods. These actions combine to yield a reduction in the amount of real goods and services purchased in the United States.*

***A price-level increase tends to reduce net exports, thereby reducing the amount of goods and services purchased in the United States. This is known as the open economy effect.***

▸ Example 11-7 Imagine that this year the price level jumped by 20 percent. If everything else stays the same, foreigners will have to pay 20 percent more for U.S. goods and services. At the same time, U.S. imports will be about 20 percent cheaper in relative terms, given the 20 percent increase in the U.S. overall price level. Consequently, U.S. residents will want to buy more foreign-produced goods and services. Fewer exports and more imports will lead to lower net exports. ◂

## Shifts in the Aggregate Demand Curve

Remember from Chapter 3 that whenever a relevant nonprice variable changes, the demand curve will shift outward or inward—to the right or to the left. The same analysis holds for the aggregate demand curve, except we are talking about relevant non-price-level variables that affect aggregate demand. So, when we ask, "What determines the position of the aggregate demand curve?" the fundamental proposition will be the following:

✦ **Remember!** *In Chapter 3, you learned to distinguish between a movement along a demand or supply curve and a shift of a curve. Here, a change in the price level will cause a movement along a given aggregate demand curve.*

***Any change in the economy that* increases *the amount of output people want to buy at a given price level is said to cause an* increase *in aggregate demand; graphically, this is shown as a shift of the aggregate demand curve to the* right.**

***Similarly, any change in the economy that* decreases *the amount of output people want to buy at a given price level is said to cause a* decrease *in aggregate demand; graphically, this is shown as a shift of the aggregate demand curve to the* left.**

The list of potential determinants of the position of the aggregate demand curve is long. Some of the most important "curve shifters" for aggregate demand are presented in Table 11-1.

The terrorists' action in September 2001 had an impact on the economy via a shift in the aggregate demand curve. Terrorism on such a large scale in the United

**Table 11-1 Determinants of Aggregate Demand**

Aggregate demand consists of the demand for domestically produced consumption goods, investment goods, government purchases, and net exports. Consequently, any change in the demand for any one of these components of real GDP will cause a change in aggregate demand. Some possibilities are listed here.

| Changes That Cause an Increase in Aggregate Demand | Changes That Cause a Decrease in Aggregate Demand |
|---|---|
| A drop in the foreign exchange value of the dollar | A rise in the foreign exchange value of the dollar |
| Increased security about jobs and future income | Decreased security about jobs and future income |
| Improvements in economic conditions in other countries | Declines in economic conditions in other countries |
| Tax decreases | Tax increases |

States caused business decision makers to change their view of the future, as you will read about in the next *Policy Application.*

## POLICY APPLICATION: The Importance of Planned Investment in Creating Recessions

### *Concepts Applied:* Components of Aggregate Demand, Shifts in Aggregate Demand

As you discovered earlier in Chapter 10, recessions are periods when the economy is not growing at all or is even declining in size. One such recession occurred in 2001–2002. Economists have attempted to understand why that recession occurred.

#### It Wasn't Because of a Loss of Output

After September 11, 2001, there was a loss of output. At least $70 billion in physical and human capital was lost as a result of the terrorist attacks. But that number, large though it may seem, represented about 0.4 percent of real GDP at the time.

#### Enter Abrupt Changes in Planned Investment

After September 11, 2001, in contrast, planned investment dropped dramatically. The uncertainty surrounding the future of U.S. business and even the U.S. political system in general caused numerous businesses to cut back drastically on their plans for expansion via additional investment.

Between the end of 2000 and the end of 2001, total U.S. investment spending declined by more than $200 billion, which was an amount equal to more than 1.2 percent of real GDP at the time.

Many economists believe that this abrupt drop in planned investment expenditures, which reduced aggregate demand, undoubtedly triggered the recession during that period.

**For Critical Analysis:**
*What factors do you think might have caused planned investment spending to start increasing again in 2003–2004?*

Most of the items in Table 11-1 on the previous page are straightforward. One that we have not yet touched on involves changes in taxes. The reasoning goes as follows: When consumers and businesses are taxed more, they spend less, thereby shifting the aggregate demand curve inward to the left. When consumers and businesses are taxed less, they spend more, thereby shifting the aggregate demand curve outward to the right.

## Mastering Concepts: Watch Out! Aggregate Demand Is Not the Same as Individual Demand

- **The aggregate demand curve can be thought of as a graphic representation of the relationship between total planned spending and the overall price level.**
- **There is an inverse relationship between the overall price level and planned expenditures (aggregate quantity demanded).**
- **One of the reasons the aggregate demand curve slopes down is the real-balance effect—as the price level goes up, the real value of your cash balances goes down, thereby making you poorer and causing you to demand less of all goods and services.**
- **Another reason the aggregate demand curve slopes down is the open economy effect—price-level increases reduce net exports, thereby reducing the demand for goods and services produced in the United States.**
- **Any change in the economy that affects aggregate demand will cause the aggregate demand curve to shift inward or outward.**

## WATCH OUT! AGGREGATE SUPPLY IS NOT THE SAME AS INDIVIDUAL SUPPLY

As always, no analysis is complete if it looks just at the demand side. We have to look at the supply side, too.

### ADDING EVERYBODY UP AGAIN

**Aggregate supply**
*Real domestic output of producers based on the rise and fall of the overall price level; total planned production.*

We define **aggregate supply** as the total of all planned production for the entire economy, usually over a year period. In the short run, there is a relationship between the overall price level and output of goods and services in the economy (real GDP).

As the price of a specific product goes up, relative to other prices, producers of that product find it profitable to produce more. A similar force is at work when we consider all producers in the economy over a short period of time. If the price level goes up and wages do not, overall profits will rise. Producers will want to supply more to the marketplace—they offer more output as the price level increases. The reverse is true as the overall price level falls. This positive relationship is called *aggregate supply.*

**Aggregate supply curve**
*A graphed line showing the relationship between the aggregate quantity supplied and the average of all prices as measured by the overall price level, often the GDP price deflator.*

Just as we created an aggregate demand curve, we can now create an **aggregate supply curve.** Examine Figure 11-3. There you see the positive relationship between the overall price level and the aggregate quantity supplied of output (real GDP). We label this curve *AS.*

### SHIFTS IN THE AGGREGATE SUPPLY CURVE

Remember from Chapter 3 that whenever a relevant nonprice variable changes, the supply curve shifts outward or inward—to the right or to the left. The same analysis holds for the aggregate supply curve, except we are talking about rele-

**Figure 11-3 The Aggregate Supply Curve in the Short Run**

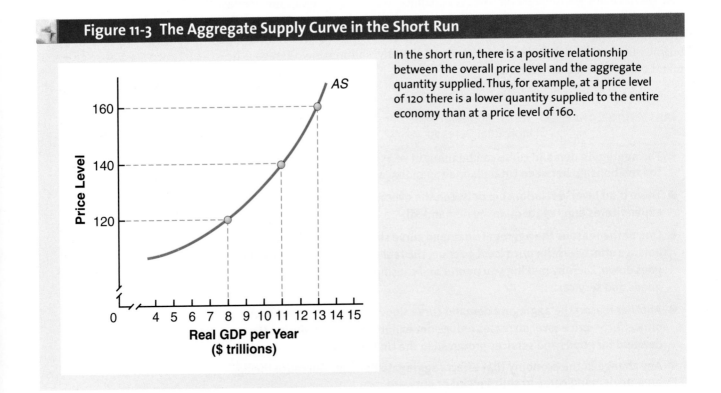

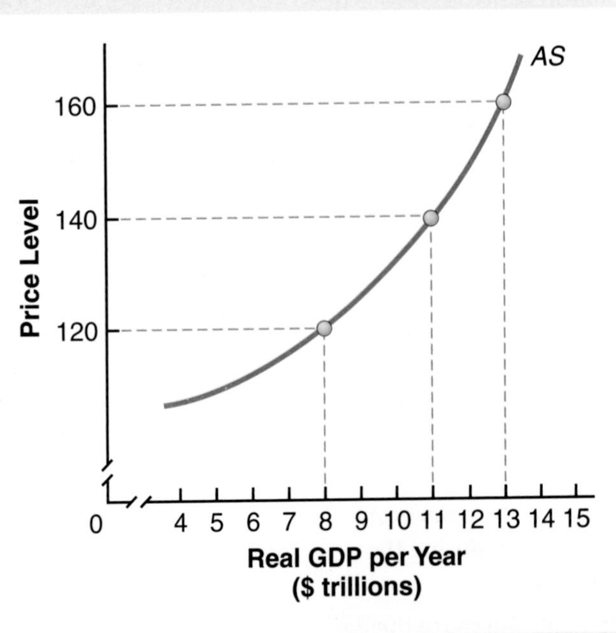


In the short run, there is a positive relationship between the overall price level and the aggregate quantity supplied. Thus, for example, at a price level of 120 there is a lower quantity supplied to the entire economy than at a price level of 160.

vant non-price-level variables that affect *aggregate* supply. So, when we ask, "What determines the position of the aggregate supply curve?" the fundamental proposition will be the following:

> ***Any change in the economy, other than the price level, that increases aggregate supply will shift the aggregate supply curve to the right. Conversely, any change in the economy that decreases aggregate supply will shift the aggregate supply curve to the left.***

▸ Example 11-8 One of the best examples of a change in the economy that decreases aggregate supply has occurred when various countries in the Middle East have restricted their oil exports to the United States. In other words, the supply of crude oil to this country has been restricted at times. These so-called oil **embargoes** have had an immediate impact on the price of oil and petroleum products, such as gasoline and heating oil. Higher petroleum prices raise the cost of production in many U.S. industries. The result is a shift to the left of the aggregate supply curve. ◂

**Embargo**
*A government prohibition (ban) on certain or all trade with one or more foreign nations.*

The information age has had a positive impact on the aggregate supply curve, but with a lag, as you will read about in the next *E-Commerce Application.*

## E-COMMERCE APPLICATION: Computers, the Information Age, and Increased Productivity in the United States

### *Concept Applied:* Shift in Aggregate Supply Curve

The United States has seen extraordinary productivity gains from 1999 to 2004. Labor productivity growth was higher than in any such period since World War II. In addition, from 1995 to 2004, labor productivity growth averaged 3 percent per year— twice the average rate over the previous two decades.

#### At First, Computers Made Little Difference in Productivity Growth

As one Nobel Prize–winning economist, Robert Solow, once said "You can see the computer age everywhere but in the productivity statistics." The widespread use of computers started in the 1980s. The Internet began to be used in the mid-1990s. E-commerce became part of the U.S. business landscape in the late 1990s. Nonetheless, the U.S. labor productivity growth rate actually stayed relatively the same from 1980 to 1995, even falling a bit in the middle of that period.

#### The Computer Age Finally Has a Payoff

Starting in the late 1990s, but more impressively since 2000, the information/computer/e-commerce age finally seems to be paying benefits. Why did it take so long?

The answer appears to be that productivity growth will not accelerate until years after the introduction of an important innovation, such as widespread computer use, the Internet, and e-commerce. It takes time for firms to figure out how to reorganize, particularly after an investment in information technology. Investing in computers and Internet communication does not automatically boost productivity growth. Firms need to change their business practices, too. A large manufacturing firm needs time to reorganize so that it can fully utilize its ability to purchase parts online, for example.

**For Critical Analysis:**
*How does increased labor productivity growth affect the aggregate supply curve?*

We summarize the possible determinants of the position of the aggregate supply curve in Table 11-2 on the following page.

**Table 11-2 Determinants of Aggregate Supply**

Some of the determinants of the position of the aggregate supply curve are listed here. Of course, all of those on the left side can be considered to have possible positive benefits for the economy as a whole.

| Changes That Cause an Increase in Aggregate Supply | Changes That Cause a Decrease in Aggregate Supply |
|---|---|
| Discoveries of new raw materials | Depletion of raw materials |
| A reduction in international trade barriers | An increase in international trade barriers |
| An increase in the supply of labor | A decrease in the supply of labor |
| Increased training and education | Decreased training and education |
| A decrease in marginal tax rates | An increase in marginal tax rates |

**Mastering Concepts:** Watch Out! Aggregate Supply Is Not the Same as Individual Supply

- **Aggregate supply is the total of all planned production for an economy over a specified time period, usually a year.**
- **The aggregate supply curve slopes up because as the price level goes up and wages do not, overall profits will rise, thereby inducing suppliers to produce more of everything.**
- **Any change in the economy other than the price level will shift the supply curve inward or outward.**

## DETERMINING THE PRICE LEVEL—PUTTING AGGREGATE DEMAND AND AGGREGATE SUPPLY TOGETHER

Just as we are able to combine demand and supply for a given product to find an equilibrium price and quantity, we can combine aggregate demand and aggregate supply. We do this in Figure 11-4.

✦ **Recall!** *Our analytical graphs show a tendency for variables to gravitate toward their equilibrium values, particularly where demand and supply curves intersect. But we live in a dynamic world, so such movements take time.*

The equilibrium price level is determined at the intersection of the aggregate demand curve and the aggregate supply curve, or *AD* and *AS*. In Figure 11-4 it is at a price level of 140. The equilibrium quantity demanded and supplied is $12 trillion per year of real GDP.

As long as nothing changes in this situation, the economy will produce that real GDP, and the price level will remain at 140. There will be neither inflation nor deflation.

Look at a price level above the equilibrium price level in Figure 11-4. At price level 160, planned expenditures, shown on the aggregate demand curve, *AD*, will be $10 trillion of real GDP per year, but planned production, shown on the aggregate supply curve, *AS*, will be about $13.5 trillion of real GDP per year. Producers will have larger-than-desired quantities of unsold goods. To get rid of those unsold goods, they will start offering them at lower prices, thereby causing the price level to fall to its equilibrium level of 140.

In contrast, if the price level is at 120, the situation is reversed. Planned expenditures are $14 trillion of real GDP, whereas planned production is only $10 tril-

**Figure 11-4 Putting Aggregate Demand and Supply Together—Equilibrium Price Level and Output**

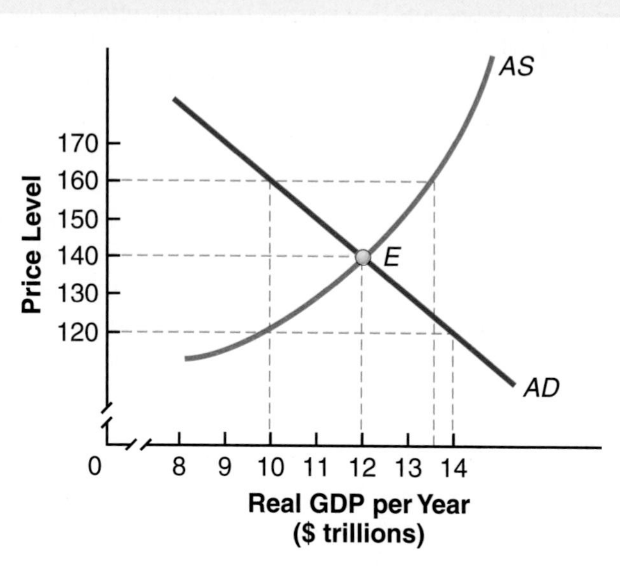


When we combine the aggregate demand curve, *AD*, with the aggregate supply curve, *AS*, we obtain equilibrium at point *E*. At that equilibrium, the price level will be 140 and real GDP per year will be $12 trillion. Without a shift in *AS* or *AD*, the economy will have a tendency to remain at that price level and at that real GDP (output) without changing.

lion of real GDP. Consumers and businesses will bid up the prices of goods, services, and investment goods so that the price level will rise to 140—equilibrium.

**Mastering Concepts:** Determining the Price Level—Putting Aggregate Demand and Aggregate Supply Together

- **When we combine the aggregate demand curve with the aggregate supply curve, we find equilibrium at their intersection.**
- **When the aggregate quantity demanded equals aggregate quantity supplied, the equilibrium price level is determined as well as the equilibrium level of real GDP per year.**

## LOOKING AT THE NATIONAL ECONOMY USING AGGREGATE DEMAND AND SUPPLY ANALYSIS

Now that we have developed this simple aggregate demand/aggregate supply model, represented succinctly in Figure 11-4, we can examine some forces that cause changes in aggregate demand and aggregate supply, thereby causing changes in the equilibrium price level and output.

### SHIFTS IN AGGREGATE DEMAND

Go back to Table 11-1 on page 232. There you see a list of some of the potential "shifters" of the aggregate demand curve. We will examine some of them now in more detail with real-world examples.

**Changes in Federal Taxes** In general, we predict that a decrease in taxes will cause the aggregate demand curve to shift outward to the right. An increase in taxes will cause the aggregate demand curve to shift inward to the left. Of course, other things happening in the economy may either amplify or decrease the effect of tax changes on the position of the aggregate demand curve.

In any event, consider the Bush tax cuts that started to go into effect in the early 2000s. ▸ **Example 11-9** Early in his administration, President Bush pushed for tax cuts, in particular reductions in marginal tax rates for individuals (see Chapter 2). Congress gave him those tax cuts, but spread them out over many years. After the recession of 2001–2002 and the slow pace of the expansion thereafter, Bush convinced Congress to put all of the tax cuts into effect in 2003. The result appeared to be an increase in the equilibrium level of real GDP. We can see this in Figure 11-5. $AD_1$ represents aggregate demand prior to the Bush tax cuts in 2003. At equilibrium, $AD_1$ intersects *AS* at a price level of 110 with equilibrium real GDP per year of $9 trillion. After the tax cuts take effect, the aggregate demand curve shifts to $AD_2$. Equilibrium real GDP per year increases to $10 trillion, and the price level rises to 112. ◂

**The War in Iraq—Effects on Aggregate Demand** War spending has often appeared to be the impetus for increases in aggregate demand. Again, other things may be happening in the economy that could counteract this positive impetus. Nonetheless, some argue that the war in Iraq in 2003, once it was certain we were going to win, caused the aggregate demand curve to shift outward to the right.

▸ **Example 11-10** You can see the effects of the 2003 war in Figure 11-6. The postwar aggregate demand curve has shifted outward to the right such that the equilibrium level of real GDP per year has increased. Of course, the price level has risen slightly, too. ◂

**Iraq War Uncertainty—A Horse of a Different Color** Sometimes, uncertainty about whether a country will go to war has negative effects on planned expenditures. In other words, it will cause the aggregate demand curve to shift inward to the left, thereby creating a recession or exacerbating an existing one. Some people argued that this happened in 2002 prior to the U.S. invasion of Iraq.

**Figure 11-5 The Effects of the Bush Tax Cuts in the Early 2000s**

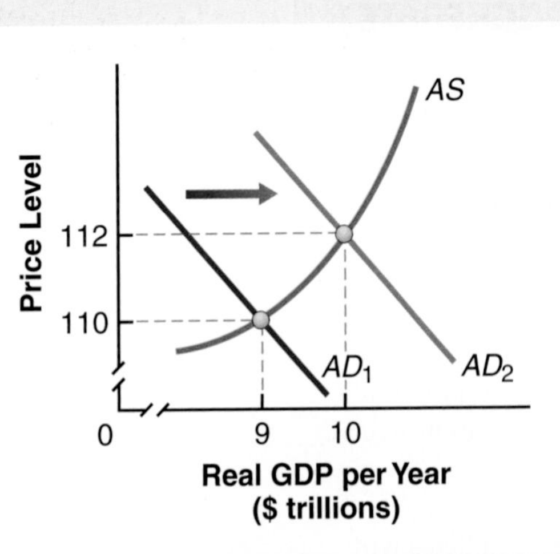


$AD_1$ represents aggregate demand prior to the Bush tax cuts in 2003. At equilibrium, $AD_1$ intersects *AS* at a price level of 110 with equilibrium real GDP per year of $9 trillion. After the tax cuts went into effect, the aggregate demand curve shifts to $AD_2$. Equilibrium real GDP per year increases to $10 trillion and the price level rises to 112.

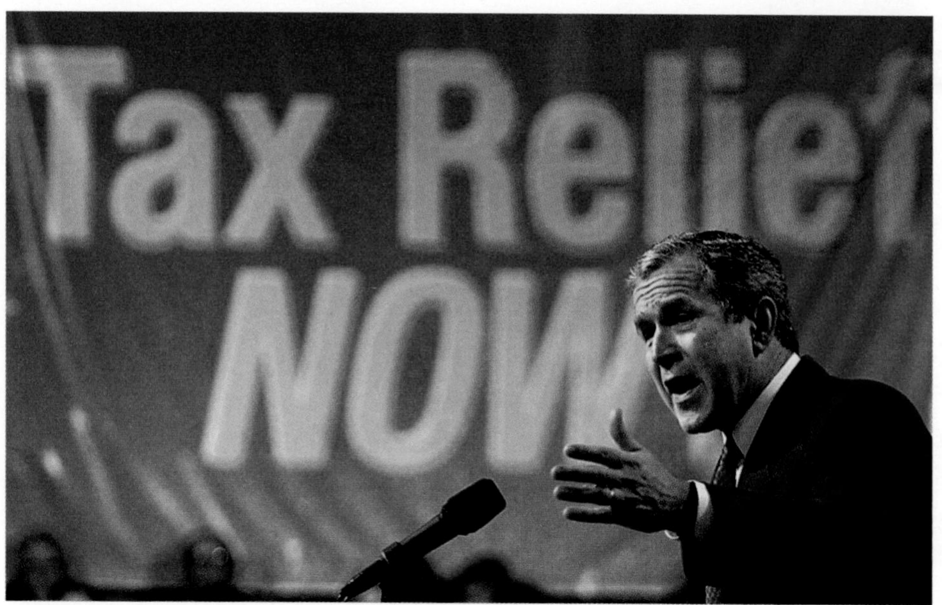


*President Bush campaigned throughout the nation for tax cuts to "get the economy going again." He succeeded in getting Congress to speed up already-legislated marginal tax rate decreases. What is the difference between such tax cuts and simple lumpsum tax rebates?*

▸ **Example 11-11** For a relatively long period prior to the invasion of Iraq in 2003, the United States faced tremendous uncertainty. For months, no one was certain whether we were going to war and, if we did, what such a war might entail. Many commentators questioned our ability to carry out a "quick and dirty" war in Iraq, especially since Iraq's leader, Saddam Hussein, might have chemical, biological, or nuclear weapons and be willing to use them. All of this uncertainty weighed heavily on the economy. Consider the graphic analysis of this example in Figure 11-7 on the following page. ◂

## Changes that Affect Aggregate Supply

Go back to Table 11-2 on page 236. There you see some of the potential "shifters" of the aggregate supply curve. In this section we examine some examples of these external shocks to our economic system.

### Figure 11-6 War Spending's Effect on Aggregate Demand

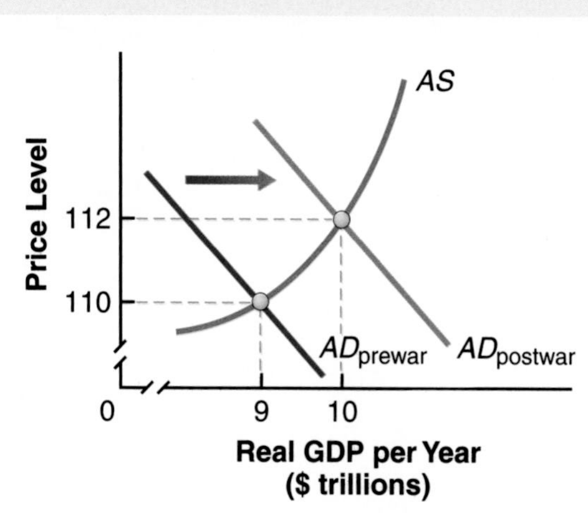


Because of increased government spending during the Iraq war in 2003, the aggregate demand curve shifted from $AD_{prewar}$ to $AD_{postwar}$. Equilibrium real GDP increased accordingly and so did the price level.

**Figure 11-7 The Negative Effect on Aggregate Demand of the Uncertainty Over War in Iraq**

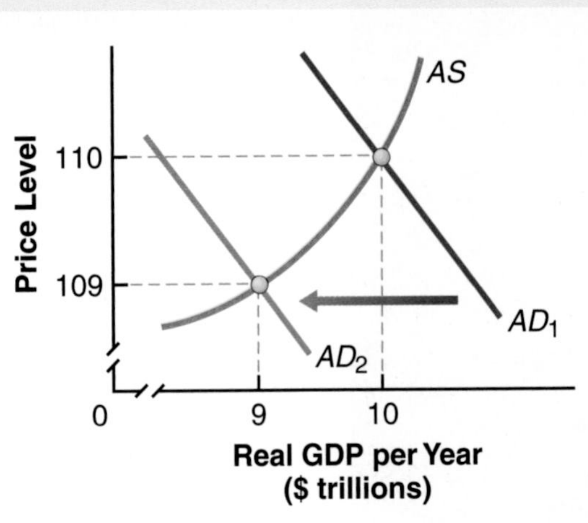


As uncertainty about the war in Iraq became prevalent, the aggregate demand curve shifted inward from $AD_1$ to $AD_2$. The equilibrium level of real GDP per year dropped from $10 trillion to $9 trillion.

**Immigration** Increased immigration over time leads to a larger supply of labor. Although many believe that immigration hurts the United States in the short run, certainly in the long run immigration causes the aggregate supply curve to shift outward to the right.

▸ **Example 11-12** Between 1900 and 1920, 14.6 million immigrants were officially welcomed to our shores. This dramatic increase in the supply of labor certainly shifted the aggregate supply curve outward to the right, as shown in Figure 11-8. All other things held constant, we would predict that during this time period

**Figure 11-8 The Effects of Immigration from 1900 to 1920**

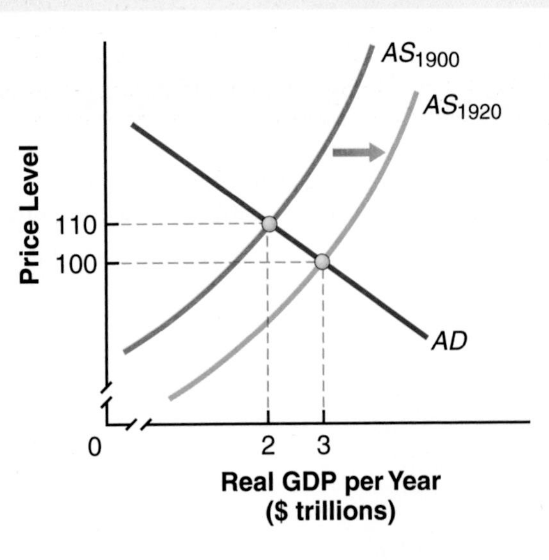

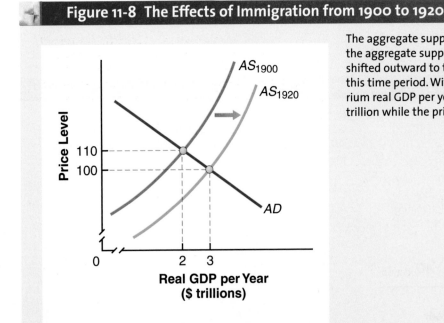

The aggregate supply curve in 1900 is shown as $AS_{1900}$, and the aggregate supply curve of 1920 is shown as $AS_{1920}$. It shifted outward to the right because of immigration during this time period. With a given demand curve, *AD*, the equilibrium real GDP per year would increase from $2 trillion to $3 trillion while the price level would fall from 110 to 100.

with an unchanged aggregate demand curve, *AD*, the equilibrium level of real GDP would increase while the equilibrium price level would fall. (Of course, other things did happen during this period, and the price level rose, rather than fall.) ◂

**The Potential Reduction in the Growth Rate of the Labor Supply** In spite of increased immigration, it is possible that the growth rate of the labor supply could slow in the United States. We know that this is possible if labor force participation rates fall, as was discussed in Chapter 10. But another possible factor is involved here—the aging of America.

▸ **Example 11-13** America is definitely getting older. The percentage of the U.S. population over 65 is increasing much faster than the percentage of the population under 20. What the aging of America means for the future can be examined using aggregate supply and aggregate demand analysis. As a larger percentage of the population leaves the labor force because of retirement or illness, all other things held constant, the aggregate supply curve will shift inward to the left.

We see this in Figure 11-9. There you see the aggregate demand curve as *AD*. The aggregate supply curve before the aging of America is shown as $AS_1$. The intersection of those two curves yields an equilibrium of $10 trillion of real GDP per year at a price level of 100. As the U.S. population grows older, the aggregate supply curve shifts to the left, creating an equilibrium real GDP of only $9 trillion per year at a higher price level, 120. ◂

In the following chapter, you will learn to use aggregate supply and demand analysis to analyze government attempts at "taming" business fluctuations. In this chapter you have already been introduced to one government stabilization action—tax changes.

**Figure 11-9 The Aging of America—Its Effect on Aggregate Supply**

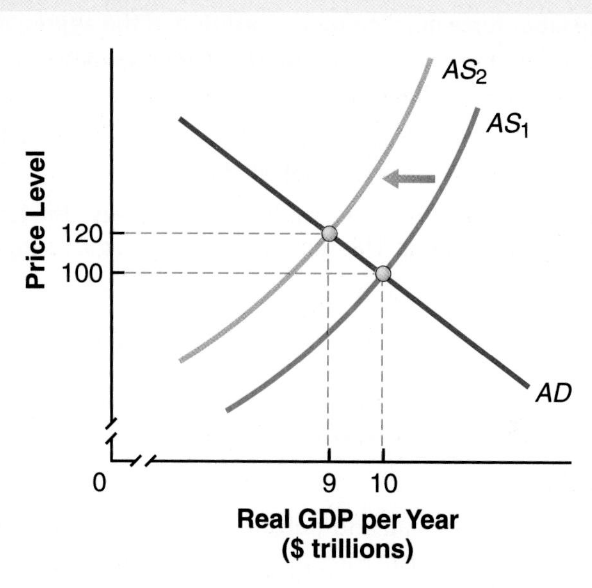


As America ages, all other things held constant, there will be fewer members of the labor force. Aggregate supply will decrease from $AS_1$ to $AS_2$, causing the equilibrium level of real GDP to drop from $10 trillion per year to $9 trillion per year and the price level to increase from 100 to 120.

## *Solving the Economic Problem:* What Are the Hidden Costs of Terrorism?

More people are now employed in helping secure the homeland against terrorists' attacks, and they benefit from this new employment. Nonetheless, there are both short- and long-run costs to the economy as a whole. In the short run, all of the resources going to protect our country cannot be used for other uses. Trucking, airplane travel, and electrical generation, to name only a few, are activities that now cost more than they did before September 11, 2001. As a consequence, both in the short and in the long run, the production possibilities curve for our nation will shift out more slowly than it would have otherwise. That is so say, the aggregate supply schedule will shift to the right at a slower rate because of the additional expenses associated with fighting terrorism at home (and abroad). So, the 2001 terrorists' attacks will lead to lower economic growth.

**Mastering Concepts:** Looking at the National Economy Using Aggregate Demand and Supply Analysis

- **A decrease in federal taxes normally will cause the aggregate demand curve to shift outward to the right. All other things held constant, a reduction in federal taxes will lead to an increase in the equilibrium level of real GDP and an increase in the price level.**
- **Wars have sometimes caused the aggregate demand curve to shift outward to the right, thereby causing an increase in the equilibrium level of real GDP per year and in the price level.**
- **Because the size of the labor force determines the position of the aggregate supply curve, higher-than-normal immigration rates will tend to move the aggregate supply curve outward to the right.**
- **With large amounts of immigration, other things held constant, the equilibrium level of real GDP will rise and the price level will fall.**
- **As our population ages, a larger percentage of individuals will leave the labor force because of retirement and illness. This will cause the aggregate supply curve to shift inward to the left.**

## SUMMING IT ALL UP

- In the circular flow model of income and output, households sell factor services to businesses, which in their turn pay for those factor services. The receipt of payments is total income. Businesses sell goods and services to households, which in their turn use money income to pay for those goods and services.

- The aggregate demand curve can be thought of as a graphic representation of the relationship between total planned spending and the overall price level.
- There is an inverse relationship between the overall price level and planned expenditures (aggregate quantity demanded).
- One of the reasons the aggregate demand curve slopes down is the real-balance effect—as the price level goes up, the real value of your cash balances goes down, thereby making you poorer and causing you to demand less of all goods and services.
- Another reason the aggregate demand curve slopes down is the open economy effect—price-level increases reduce net exports, thereby reducing the demand for goods and services produced in the United States.
- Aggregate supply is the total of all planned production for an economy over a specified time period, usually a year.
- The aggregate supply curve slopes up because as the price level goes up and wages do not, overall profits will rise, thereby inducing suppliers to produce more of everything.
- When the aggregate quantity demanded equals aggregate quantity supplied, the equilibrium price level is determined as well as the equilibrium level of real GDP per year.
- A decrease in federal taxes normally will cause the aggregate demand curve to shift outward to the right. All other things held constant, a reduction in federal taxes will lead to an increase in the equilibrium level of real GDP and an increase in the price level.
- Wars have sometimes caused the aggregate demand curve to shift outward to the right, thereby causing an increase in the equilibrium level of real GDP per year and in the price level.
- Because the size of the labor force determines the position of the aggregate supply curve, higher-than-normal immigration rates will tend to move the aggregate supply curve outward to the right.
- As our population ages, a larger percentage of individuals will leave the labor force because of retirement and illness. This will cause the aggregate supply curve to shift inward to the left.

## KEY TERMS AND CONCEPTS

aggregate demand **229**
aggregate demand curve **229**
aggregate supply **234**
aggregate supply curve **234**
cash balance **231**
circular flow of income **226**
embargo **235**
exports **228**
imports **228**
net exports **228**
open economy effect **232**
real-balance effect **231**

## MASTERING ECONOMIC CONCEPTS
## Questions and Problems

**11-1.** In the circular flow of income diagram depicted below, who is represented by the label A—the group that funnels funds into the product markets? Who is represented by the label B—the group that funnels funds into the factor markets?

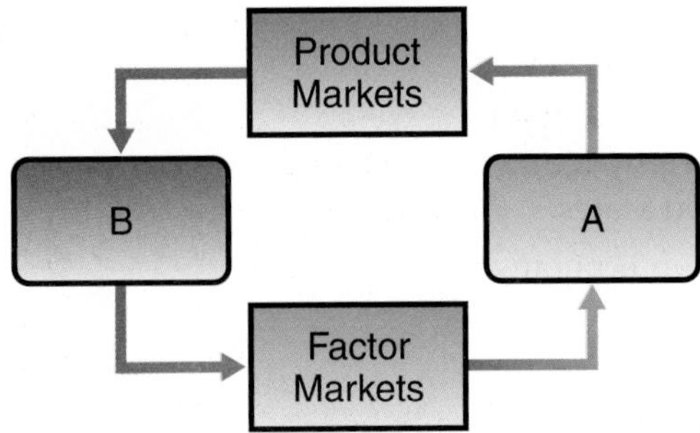


**11-2.** In the diagram in question 11-1, is the amount of funds that flows into the product market greater than, less than, or equal to the amount of funds that flows out of that market? Why? What is the measurement term that we use to describe this flow of funds into the product market?

**11-3.** State the expenditure formula for computing GDP based on four separate elements. In this formula, what does the variable *I* represent?

**11-4.** Based on the following graph, what amount of U.S. output would be demanded if the price level was 150? What amount of output would be demanded if the price level was 225?

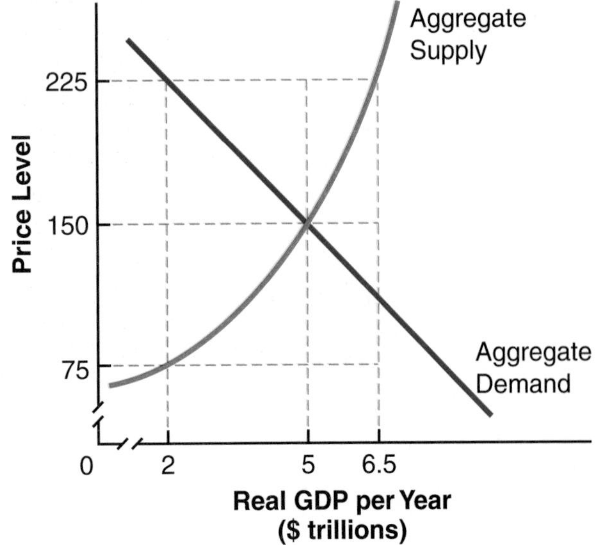


**11-5.** Recently, we have seen a situation in which the general price level might actually decrease. If this occurred, what would happen to the purchasing power of $1,000 sitting in your checking account? Would you be likely to plan to buy more goods or fewer goods as a result? What is this response known as in terms of aggregate demand?

**11-6.** Determine whether each of the following would cause an increase in aggregate demand, a decrease in aggregate demand, or no change in aggregate demand.

a. a decrease in the price level
b. reduced confidence in the job market and future earnings
c. a decrease in the tax rate

**11-7.** Assume that you own one of many manufacturing firms in the United States. In the short run, if the price level of all goods and services increases and wages remain constant, will you be more likely to increase or decrease the amount that you are producing? In the long run, will employers be forced to increase or decrease wages if the price level continues to increase? Why? If wages change when the price level changes, will manufacturers such as you experience a greater incentive to produce, less incentive to produce, or no change in their incentive to produce?

**11-8.** Determine whether each of the following would cause an increase in aggregate supply, a decrease in aggregate supply, or no change in aggregate supply.

a. a decrease in corporate tax rates
b. an increase in the amount of resources available for production
c. an increase in the price level

**11-9.** Based on the graph at the top of the following page, in the short run what amount of output would U.S. producers provide for sale if the price level was 160? What amount of output would they provide if the price level was 140?

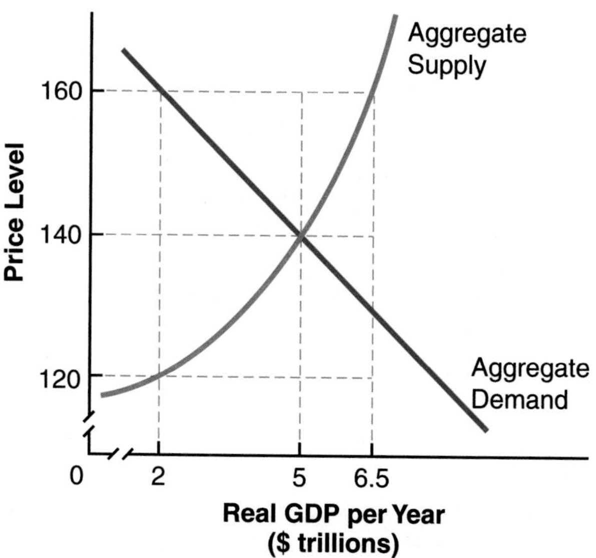


**11-10.** Holding all else constant, if the federal government increased corporate tax rates, would U.S. real GDP be more likely to increase or decrease? Would the U.S. price level be more likely to increase or decrease?

**11-11.** If the U.S. price level decreased while real GDP increased, which curve—aggregate supply or aggregate demand—shifted and in which direction?

**11-12.** For what reason could military conflict lead to an increase in aggregate demand? For what reason could such conflict lead to a decrease in aggregate demand?

**11-13.** Why does the aggregate demand curve slope downward?

**11-14.** Do lower interest rates generally cause consumers to buy more goods or fewer goods? As such, will lower interest rates increase or decrease aggregate demand? What impact will lower interest rates have on the price level and the level of real GDP in the United States?

**11-15.** If U.S. net exports are positive, which is greater—the amount that the United States exported or the amount that the United States imported?

## THINKING CRITICALLY

**11-1.** In the mid to late 1970s, the U.S. price level increased while real GDP decreased. This situation came to be known as "stagflation." In order for stagflation to take place, which curve—aggregate supply or aggregate demand—must have moved in which direction? What event from this time period would have increased resource prices and caused such a shift in the curve in question? What likely happened to the level of unemployment during this period?

**11-2.** Today, one U.S. dollar can be exchanged for approximately 0.6 British pounds sterling. If a British consumer wanted to purchase a U.S. product that cost $10, how many British pounds would he or she need? Assume that the exchange rate value of the dollar increased dramatically in relation to the pound so that one dollar could be exchanged for one pound. After this change, if the same British consumer wanted to purchase the same U.S. product for $10, how many British pounds would he or she need? Would the British consumer be more or less likely to purchase the U.S. good after the increase in the exchange rate value of the dollar? Based on this discussion, when the U.S. dollar increased in value in relation to the British pound in the early 1980s, what do you think happened to aggregate demand in the United States?

**11-3.** During 1990 and 1991, the United States experienced a significant recession. By 1994, however, conditions in the economy had improved significantly. Unemployment decreased from 7.7 percent in 1992 to 5.4 percent in 1994, and inflation fell from 6.1 percent per year in 1990 to 3.1 percent in 1991 and 2.7 percent by 1994. To better analyze these figures, we must discuss how unemployment and real GDP are related. Is there a direct relationship or an inverse relationship? Based on the situation described here and your answer to the previous question, which aggregate curve shifted and in which direction?

## LOGGING ON

1. For the latest U.S. economic data, go to http://research.stlouisfed.org/fred2/.
2. To view the latest economic data for nations around the world, go to http://www.imf.org, click on "Publications," click on the latest issue of "World Economic Outlook," and download the statistical appendix.
3. Take a look at the latest survey of professional forecasters' views about how the U.S. economy will respond to the most recent variations in aggregate demand and supply at http://www.phil.frb.org/econ/liv/.
4. To try your hand at conducting policies that affect aggregate demand or supply in a "virtual economy" for the United Kingdom, go to http://www.bized.ac.uk/virtual/economy/index.htm.

## USING THE INTERNET FOR ECONOMIC ANALYSIS

**Wages, Productivity, and Aggregate Supply** The amount firms pay their employees and the productivity of those employees influence firms' total planned production, so changes in these factors affect the position of the aggregate supply curve. This application gives you the opportunity to examine recent trends in measures of the overall wages and productivity of workers.

**Title:** Bureau of Labor Statistics: U.S. Economy at a Glance

**Navigation:** Go to http://www.bls.gov.

**Application** Perform the indicated operations, and answer the following questions.

1. Under "At a Glance Tables," click on "U.S. Economy at a Glance." Then click on the graph box next to "Employee Cost Index." What are the recent trends in wages and salaries and in benefits? How should these trends be related to movements in the overall price level? Why?
2. Back up to "U.S. Economy at a Glance," and now click on the graph box next to "Productivity." How has labor productivity behaved recently? What does this imply for the U.S. aggregate supply curve?
3. Back up to "U.S. Economy at a Glance," and now click on the graph box next to "Change in Payroll Employment." Does it appear that the U.S. economy is currently in a long-run growth equilibrium?

## MEDIA RESEARCH LIST

The following media resources are available with this Chapter:

- Load your CD-ROM to listen to the audio introduction to this chapter.
- Load your CD-ROM to access a Graph Animation of Figure 11-1, *The Circular Flow of Income and Product.*
- Load your CD-ROM to access a Graph Animation of Figure 11-2, *The Aggregate Demand Curve.*
- Load your CD-ROM to view the video on *Shifts in the Aggregate Demand Curve.*
- Load your CD-ROM to view the video on *Shifts in the Short-Run Aggregate Supply Curve.*
- Test your knowledge of chapter concepts with a quiz at www.miller-ume.com.
- Link to Web resources related to the text coverage at www.miller-ume.com.

## HOMEWORK SET

Go to the end of the this book to find the Homework Problems for this chapter.

# CHAPTER 12

# The Fiscal Policy Approach to Stabilization

## *Facing an Economic Problem:* What to Do When the Federal Government Hits the Federal Debt Ceiling

As you probably already know, your federal government often spends more than it receives in taxes. When it does, it usually makes up the difference by increasing its debt. The U.S. Congress, though, nominally controls this so-called public debt, currently at around $7 trillion. When the government has to borrow more funds, it faces a congressionally set maximum, called the **debt ceiling**.

Every couple of years, because of budget deficits, Congress must raise the debt ceiling. In 2003, the limit was increased a record $984 billion to $7.4 trillion, and it is rising. Do we have to worry about this huge number? What would happen if Congress refused to raise the debt ceiling? To answer these questions, you need to know more about how the government taxes and spends and how it uses these powers in its attempts to stabilize nationwide economic activity.

### Learning Objectives

After reading this chapter, you should be able to:

- **Describe the relationship between an individual's current disposable income and that individual's planned consumption.**
- **List three non-interest-rate variables whose changes might influence investment decisions.**
- **Describe two ways in which the government can engage in discretionary fiscal policy.**
- **Define an automatic stabilizer and give two examples.**

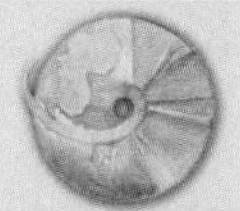

***Refer to the back of this chapter for a complete listing of multimedia learning materials available on the CD-ROM and the Web site.***

**Debt ceiling**
*The maximum size of the gross public debt.*

## IT SEEMS TO HAVE STARTED WITH A MAN NAMED KEYNES

In Chapter 10 you were introduced to the economy-wide phenomenon of the business cycle. During the business cycle, there are contractions, which may become recessions, and expansions, which may lead to "overheating" of the economy. The federal government has, by legislation, the job of trying to smooth out the ups and downs in national economic activity. One way it can do so is to use policies that shift the aggregate demand or aggregate supply curves that you learned about in Chapter 11. In so doing, it attempts to alter the equilibrium price level and the equilibrium level of real GDP. The government has several policy options. One is to change taxes or government spending. That is the subject matter of this chapter. The other possibility involves influencing interest rates and credit markets and the money side of the economy. That topic is the subject of Chapters 13 and 14.

Congress and the president are extremely interested in the growth in economy-wide economic activity. Incumbent presidents often find the road to reelection difficult if the economy is in a recession. Not surprisingly, federal government policymakers want to do "something" to either prevent recessions or pull us out of one. Sometimes, they rely on what is called **fiscal policy**. Fiscal policy involves either changing our tax structure or changing the rate of growth of government spending.

**Fiscal policy**
*The federal government's use of taxation and spending policies to affect overall business activity.*

***A fiscal policy approach to short-run stabilization is often associated with a twentieth-century economist named John Maynard Keynes.***

### THE LIFE AND TIMES OF MR. KEYNES

John Maynard Keynes (1883–1946) originated the school of economic thought referred to as **Keynesian economics,** which supports the use of government spending and taxing to help stabilize the economy. Keynes believed that there was a need for government intervention, in part because an economy may reach an equilibrium level of real GDP that generates less than **full employment.** Full employment is defined as that level of unemployment corresponding to normal frictional unemployment in the labor market. Also, remember that the equilibrium level of real GDP is found at the intersection of the aggregate demand and aggregate supply curves that you learned about in Chapter 11.

**Keynesian economics**
*A school of economic thought that tends to favor active federal government policymaking to stabilize economy-wide fluctuations, usually by implementing discretionary fiscal policy.*

**Full employment**
*An arbitrary level of unemployment that corresponds to "normal" friction in the labor market. In 1986, a 6.5 percent rate of unemployment was considered full employment. Today, it is assumed to be around 5 percent.*

Keynes developed his fiscal policy theories during the Great Depression in the 1930s. He observed that the forces of aggregate supply and aggregate demand operated too slowly on their own in such a serious recession. His idea was that government could step in to stimulate aggregate demand.

**Inflexible Prices—The Culprit** Keynes and his followers argued that prices, especially the price of labor (wages), were inflexible downward due to the existence of unions and long-term contracts between businesses and workers. That meant that prices were "sticky." Keynes argued that in such a world, when there are large amounts of **excess capacity** and unemployment, an increase in aggregate demand will not raise the price level. A decrease in aggregate demand will not cause a firm to lower prices either. You can see this in Figure 12-1.

**Excess capacity**
*That part of the economy's potential production capacity not being utilized.*

▸ **Example 12-1** From the early days of recovery from the Great Depression to the outbreak of World War II, real GDP increased with almost no increase in the price level. Hence, the most simplified Keynesian model in which the price level does not change is essentially an immediate post–Great Depression model. This model fits the data in the late 1930s very well, as you can see in Figure 12-2. ◂

**Figure 12-1 Changes in Aggregate Demand Do Not Alter the Price Level**

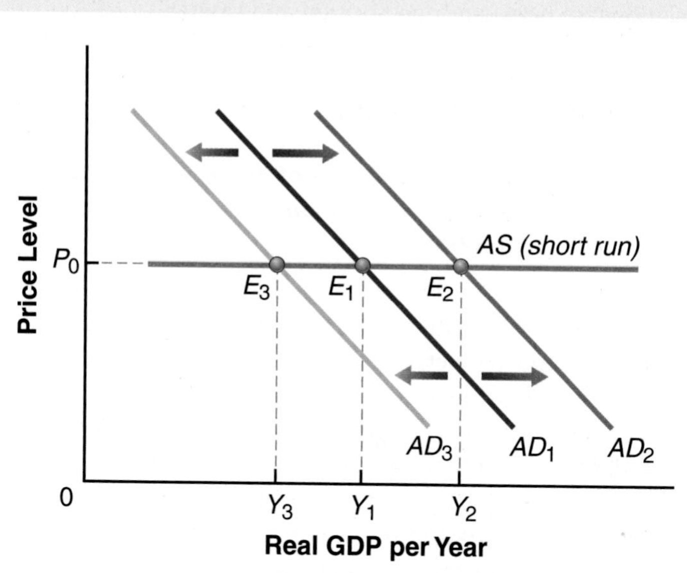


In a depression, the price level tends to stay the same (according to Keynes). Keynes assumed that when there is excess capacity, the price level would not rise when aggregate demand increases, as it does from $AD_1$ to $AD_2$. Keynes also believed that the price level would not fall when aggregate demand falls, as it does from $AD_1$ to $AD_3$.

## KEYNES SOUGHT TO UNDERSTAND WHY PEOPLE SPEND

Remember from Chapter 11 that aggregate demand consists of four components—consumer spending, business investment spending, government spending, and net exports. Consumer spending, called *consumption*, is therefore a key aspect of aggregate demand. Keynes focused much of his research on what determines how much you and I decide to spend each year. Specifically, he focused on

**Figure 12-2 Increasing Real GDP per Year and a Stable Price Level from 1934 to 1940**

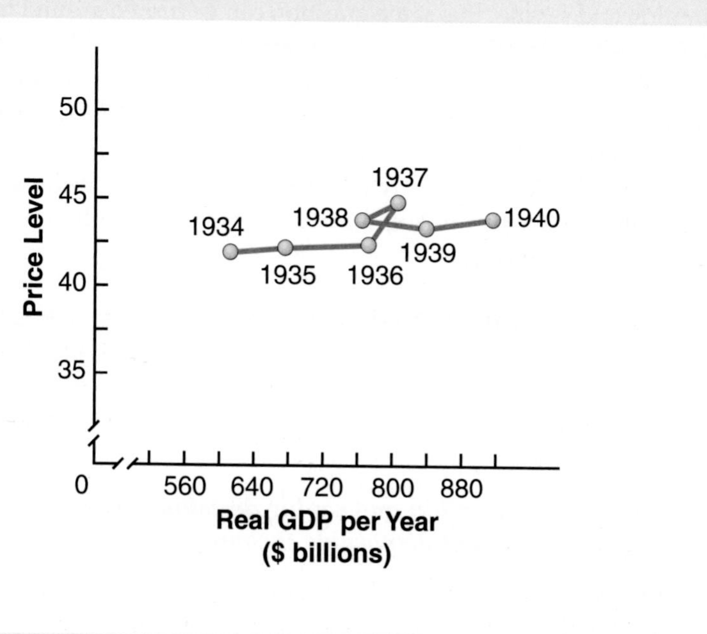

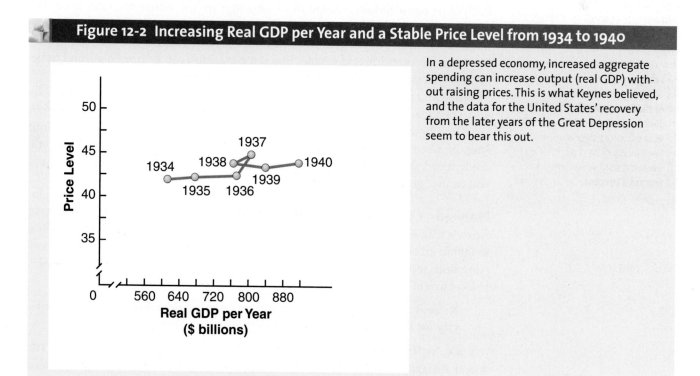

In a depressed economy, increased aggregate spending can increase output (real GDP) without raising prices. This is what Keynes believed, and the data for the United States' recovery from the later years of the Great Depression seem to bear this out.

**Personal consumption expenditures**
*Expenditures by individuals and households on consumption items such as restaurant meals and airline travel; sometimes just called consumption.*

**Disposable income**
*Income remaining for a person to spend or save after all taxes have been paid.*

**Consumption**
*Spending on new consumption goods and services out of a household's current income; includes such things as buying food and going to a concert. Whatever is not consumed is saved. Consumption can also be viewed as the use of goods and services for personal satisfaction.*

**Saving**
*Setting aside income for a period of time so that it can be used later.*

**Consumption goods**
*Goods and services bought by households to use up, such as food, clothing, and movies.*

the relationship between how much people earn and their willingness to engage in **personal consumption expenditures.** To understand his research, you need to learn about the relationship between consumption and saving.

## Relating Consumption to Saving

***You can do only two things with a dollar of* disposable income *(income net of taxes): either you can consume it or you can save it. If you consume it, it is gone forever.***

If you consume a dollar in disposable income, it is gone. If you save the entire dollar, however, you will be able to consume it (and perhaps more if it earns interest) at some future time. That is the distinction between **consumption** and **saving.**

Consumption is the act of using income for the purchase of **consumption goods.** Consumption goods are goods purchased by households for immediate satisfaction. ▸ Example 12-2 When you spend to watch a movie, eat a restaurant meal, or pay to play a video game, you are engaging in consumption. You have purchased consumption goods and services. ◂

Obviously, a dollar of take-home income can either be consumed or not be consumed. Realizing this, we can see the relationship between disposable income, saving, and consumption:

**Consumption + saving = disposable income**

The definition of saving now follows:

**Saving = disposable income − consumption**

## Planned Consumption and Planned Saving

Each of us has a certain amount of income that we can either spend or save. The question that Keynes and his followers examined was the following: What determines how much people plan to consume? Obviously, because of the relationship between consumption and saving, this same question can be turned around to become: What determines how much people plan to save?

When you think about it, there are probably hundreds of different reasons why you spend as much as you do. ▸ Example 12-3 You may increase your spending because you are confident about a future job. You may increase your spending because you are in love. You may decrease your spending because you are worried about threats of terrorism. You may decrease your spending because you cannot get rid of a nagging cold. ◂

✦ **Be Aware!** *When we refer to saving, we are referring to the act of saving over a specified period, such as a year. What you have saved is called your savings (with an "s" at the end of the word).*

### Planned Consumption and Actual Income—Keynes's Response

Keynes was as good a psychologist as anyone at the time. Nonetheless, he chose to ignore all of the psychological factors that might explain people's planned consumption and planned saving. Instead, he focused on a single important variable—current disposable income.

***Keynes argued that consumption and saving decisions depend primarily on an individual's current disposable income.***

▸ Example 12-4 Suppose you make $50,000 of after-tax income a year. You spend $45,000 and save $5,000. Someone else makes $100,000 of disposable income and plans to spend only $90,000, saving the rest—$10,000—for "a rainy day." ◂

## How Much Will You Consume Out of the Next Dollar of Income?

Keynes asked another question: What happens to your spending when you earn an extra dollar of income? Do you consume it all? Do you save it all? The answer is usually somewhere in between. Most people consume a relatively high percentage of any additional after-tax income that they earn. Although saving may be prudent, it requires people to wait to enjoy the fruits of their labor. Often, people do not want to wait to consume, so they don't save all, or even close to all, of any extra income that they earn.

**It's All on the Margin** You have already been introduced to the concept of *marginal* when you looked at marginal cost.

> ***The term* marginal *refers to a* small change *in something.***

What we are concerned about here is a household's **marginal propensity to consume (MPC).** You can understand the definition of this term if you think of the definitions of its parts. *Marginal* refers to a small incremental change, and *propensity* is simply a tendency to do something. So, your marginal propensity to consume is defined as:

$$\textbf{Marginal propensity to consume (MPC)} = \frac{\textbf{change in consumption}}{\textbf{change in disposable income}}$$

**Marginal propensity to consume (MPC)**
*The ratio of the change in consumption to the change in disposable income. A marginal propensity to consume of 0.8 indicates that an additional $100 in take-home pay will lead to an additional $80 consumed.*

Not surprisingly, the **marginal propensity to save (MPS)** can be defined similarly:

$$\textbf{Marginal propensity to save (MPS)} = \frac{\textbf{change in saving}}{\textbf{change in disposable income}}$$

**Marginal propensity to save (MPS)**
*The ratio of the change in saving to the change in disposable income. A marginal propensity to save of 0.2 indicates that out of an additional $100 in take-home pay, $20 will be saved. Whatever is not saved is consumed.*

**Adding MPC and MPS Together** Because you can take only two actions with any given disposable income—you can consume it or you can save it—necessarily there is an arithmetic restriction here. The marginal propensity to consume plus the marginal propensity to save must always add up to one, or 100 percent. There is a simple formula, therefore:

$$\textbf{MPC + MPS = 1}$$

### What Do the MPC and the MPS Tell You?

> ***The marginal propensities to consume and to save tell you what percentage of a given increase in income will go toward consumption and saving, respectively.***

In other words, the marginal propensity to consume indicates how much you will *change* your planned consumption if there is a *change* in your disposable income. Notice that the emphasis is on the word *change*. ▸ Example 12-5 If your marginal propensity to consume is 0.8, you will consume 80 percent of any increase in your disposable income. So, if your after-tax income rises by $1,000, you will spend 80 percent of that extra disposable income—$800—and save the other $200. If your MPC is 0.9, that means that you will consume 90 percent of any increase in your disposable income. ◂

**Mastering Concepts:** It Seems to Have Started with a Man Named Keynes

- **During periods of unemployment and inflexible prices, a change in aggregate demand will not affect the price level.**

- **Any dollar earned can be either spent or saved.**
- **Saving will always equal disposable income (income after taxes) minus consumption.**
- **Planned consumption and planned saving depend on an individual's current income.**
- **The marginal propensity to consume is the change in consumption divided by the change in disposable income.**
- **The marginal propensity to save is the change in saving divided by the change in disposable income.**

## INVESTMENT IS IMPORTANT, TOO

**Investment**
*Any use of today's resources to expand tomorrow's production; the portion of total output that will be used to produce goods in the future; can also be viewed as the spending by businesses on things, such as machines and buildings, that can be used to produce goods and services in the future.*

Keynes also believed that the equilibrium level of employment depends on the level of **investment,** which is a shorthand term for business investment spending. The term *investment* has a different meaning in economics than in common speech, where it often refers to putting funds into the stock market or real estate.

> ***In economic analysis, investment is defined as expenditures by firms on new machines and buildings that are expected to yield a future stream of income.***

In any event, Keynes argued that if the level of investment is low, full employment can't be achieved. So, what are the determinants of this very important variable called investment?

### INVESTMENT AND INTEREST RATES

We need to examine two aspects of investment: one relates to the price of borrowing funds for business investment spending, and the other relates to what might cause shifts in investment demand.

**Investment and Interest Rates** When a businessperson wants to invest, she or he normally has to borrow the funds. The cost of borrowing—the interest rate—is similar to the cost of any other aspect of doing business. That is to say, when the cost of borrowing falls, businesspeople can undertake more investment projects. When it rises, businesspeople tend to undertake fewer investment projects. Otherwise stated, if interest rates are low, businesspeople will want to borrow in order to invest more in new plant and machinery. If interest rates are high, businesspeople will probably borrow less and therefore will invest less. We can view this as a rule that:

> ***Planned investment rises as interest rates fall, all other things held constant. Planned investment falls as interest rates rise, all other things held constant.***

If we were to graph this relationship, the investment curve would look like any other demand curve, but price would become the interest rate.

▸ **Example 12-6** In the early 1980s, some nominal interest rates exceeded 20 percent. Consequently, businesspeople borrowed fewer funds for investing. We ended up in a recession. ◂

**What Causes All Planned Investment to Change No Matter What the Interest Rate?** Remember when we looked at individual demand curves in

Chapter 3? There you saw that quantity demanded was a function of price. If a variable other than the product's own price changed, the entire demand curve shifted. The same analysis can be applied to planned investment. You can look at planned investment as a demand for investment spending and the rate of interest as the price. Planned investment depends on the rate of interest. Hence, a change in any non-interest-rate variable can potentially change businesspersons' investment outlook. In other words, any change in a non-interest-rate variable can alter planned investment. Here are some possibilities:

✦ **Note!** *The planned investment curve is the investment demand curve and slopes downward if we place the interest rate on the vertical axis of a graph. Any change in the interest rate will cause a movement along a given investment demand curve.*

- ***Expectations of businesspeople are one possible variable.*** ▸ Example 12-7 If businesspeople expect higher future sales and hence higher profits, they will plan for more machines and bigger plants for the future. More investment will be undertaken because of the expectation of higher future profits. ◂
- ***Any change in productive technology can potentially shift businesspersons' investment plans.*** ▸ Example 12-8 Whenever there are breakthroughs in communications and computer networking technology, businesses find that they can better coordinate their diverse locations. Normally, this causes some of them to expand investment in plants and offices in places farther away from the central office. ◂
- ***Changes in business taxes can change businesspersons' investment plans.*** ▸ Example 12-9 When business taxes increase, planned investment at all rates of interest normally decreases. When business taxes decrease, planned investment at all rates of interest normally increases. ◂

**Using Aggregate Demand/Aggregate Supply Analysis** We can use the same aggregate demand/aggregate supply analysis that we developed in Chapter 11 to show how changes in planned investment affect the equilibrium price level and the equilibrium level of real GDP per year. Remember from Chapter 11 that when we drew aggregate supply and aggregate demand curves on the same graph, their intersection yielded an equilibrium price level and an equilibrium level of real GDP. This equilibrium will change when there is a change in investment spending brought about by a change in a non-interest-rate variable.

## More Bang for Your Buck—Changes in Investment Can Cause a Multiplier Effect

When a businessperson decides to spend more on an investment, that spending decision has ramifications throughout the economy. The extra income of the workers who are hired to build, say, a new plant, does not just sit around. This new income is spent. In fact, if the marginal propensity to consume is 80 percent, or 0.8, then all of those workers who get the extra income will spend 80¢ out of every extra dollar earned. Retailers and others will receive this 80¢ out of every dollar as income. They, in turn, will spend 80 percent of that additional income. This process goes on and on. It turns out that an increase in investment spending will lead to a multiple increase in the equilibrium level of real GDP. What is operating here is the **multiplier effect** of changes in investment spending.

**Multiplier effect**
*The effect of a permanent change in investment spending or government spending that goes beyond the initial change in those two variables; rather, the change in the equilibrium level of real GDP is a multiple of the change in investment or government spending.*

> ***The multiplier is the number by which a permanent change in investment spending is multiplied to get the change in the equilibrium level of real GDP.***

**Following the Rounds of Additional Spending** Let's take an example and put it into a table. Suppose that the marginal propensity to consume is 0.8, or $\frac{4}{5}$. Now let's run an experiment. Say that businesspeople decide to increase planned investment permanently by \$100 billion a year. In Table 12-1, we call this *Round 1* in column 1. The italicized letter *I* is an abbreviation for investment.

During Round 1, investment is increased by \$100 billion. This causes an initial increase of \$100 billion in the equilibrium level of real GDP as well. Column 3 shows the resulting increase in consumption by households that received this additional \$100 billion in income. We find this by multiplying the marginal propensity to consume, 0.8, by the increase in income. The result is \$80 billion. That is not the end of the story, however. This additional household consumption is also spending. It will provide \$80 billion of additional income for other individuals. Thus, during Round 2, you see an increase in the equilibrium level of real GDP of \$80 billion.

And so continues this multiplier process. The result? A permanent yearly \$100 billion increase in investment spending has induced an additional \$400 billion increase in consumption spending, for a *total* increase of real GDP of \$500 billion.

## Multiplier Formula

There is a relationship between the marginal propensity to consume and the size of the multiplier. In the example we just used, the marginal propensity to consume was 0.8 or $\frac{4}{5}$. A \$100 billion increase in planned investment led to a \$500 billion increase in the equilibrium level of real GDP. So, the multiplier turned out to be 5 when the marginal propensity to consume (MPC) was $\frac{4}{5}$. The formula then is the following:

$$\textbf{Multiplier} = \frac{\mathbf{1}}{\mathbf{(1 - MPC)}}$$

*Animated*

### Table 12-1 The Multiplier Process—An Example

We trace the effects of a permanent annual \$100 billion increase in investment spending on the equilibrium level of real GDP. If we assume a marginal propensity to consumer of 0.8, such an increase will eventually create a \$500 billion increase in the equilibrium level of real GDP per year.

**Assumption: MPC = 0.8, or $\frac{4}{5}$**

| (1) Round | (2) Annual increase in real GDP (\$ billions) | | (3) Annual Increase in Planned Consumption (\$ billions) |
|---|---|---|---|
| 1 (\$100 billion per year increase in *I*) | 100.00 | → | 80.000 |
| 2 | 80.00 | ↔ | 64.000 |
| 3 | 64.00 | ↔ | 51.200 |
| 4 | 51.20 | ↔ | 40.960 |
| 5 | 40.96 | ↔ | 32.768 |
| . | . | | . |
| . | . | | . |
| . | . | | . |
| All later rounds | 163.84 | | 131.072 |
| **Totals** | **500.00** | | **400.000** |

So, whenever you know the MPC, you can figure out the size of the multiplier. ▸ **Example 12-10** If the MPC is 0.75, or $\frac{3}{4}$, the multiplier is 4 because it is equal to $1/(1 - \text{MPC})$, or $1/(1 - \frac{3}{4}) = 1\frac{1}{4} = 4$. ◂

By working a few numerical examples, you can demonstrate to yourself an important property of the multiplier:

> ***The larger the marginal propensity to consume (MPC), the larger the multiplier. This fact has implications for the effectiveness of changes in government spending or taxes—what we call the realm of fiscal policy.***

**The Multiplier Formula Applies to Changes in Government Spending, Too** Although we developed the multiplier formula for changes in investment spending, it can be applied equally well to changes in government spending. ▸ **Example 12-11** If, as in the last example, the MPC is 0.75, or $\frac{3}{4}$, the multiplier is 4. That means that, other things held constant, an increase in yearly government spending of $100 billion could lead to a $400 billion increase in the equilibrium level of real GDP per year. ◂

**Mastering Concepts:** Investment Is Important, Too

- **In economic analysis, investment refers to expenditures by businesses on new machines and buildings.**
- **Because businesspeople borrow funds to invest, the quantity of investment spending demanded will fall as the rate of interest rises, and vice versa.**
- **Any change in (1) businesspersons' expectations, (2) productive technology, and (3) business taxes will change the quantity of investment spending demanded at each and every interest rate.**
- **Any permanent change in investment leads to a multiplier effect on the equilibrium level of real GDP, all other things held constant.**
- **The larger the marginal propensity to consume (MPC), the greater the multiplier.**

## USE AT YOUR DISCRETION—DISCRETIONARY FISCAL POLICY

When we talk about deliberate, discretionary—left to the judgment or discretion of a policymaker—changes in government spending or marginal tax rates (or both) to achieve certain national economic goals, we enter the realm of fiscal policy. Some national goals are high employment (i.e., low unemployment) and price-level stability.

> ***Fiscal policy can be thought of as a deliberate attempt via changes in government spending or taxes to cause the economy to move to full employment and price-level stability more quickly than it otherwise might.***

To John Maynard Keynes and his followers, during recessions and especially depressions, government has to step in to increase aggregate demand. In other words, expansionary fiscal policy—increases in government spending or tax reductions—initiated by the federal government is a way to ward off recessions.

According to Keynesian analysis, a decrease in taxes or an increase in government spending will have a multiplier effect, which you just learned about, on the equilibrium level of real GDP.

## Changing Taxes

For proponents of discretionary fiscal policy, if the government wants to stimulate aggregate demand growth, it should lower taxes. The way it lowers taxes is important, though. A once-and-for-all rebate does not have the same effect as a permanent reduction in tax rates. Once-and-for-all tax rebates don't really change people's expectations about their future after-tax income. Consequently, a tax change that is only temporary has relatively little effect on the equilibrium level of real GDP per year. ▸ **Example 12-12** In 2001, the federal government sent out a $300 tax rebate to every individual taxpayer and $600 to every couple filing federal tax returns. These tax rebates were considered temporary and had virtually no effect on bringing the U.S. economy out of the doldrums. ◂

Tax rate reductions that are known to be permanent tend to have an expansionary effect on national economic activity. ▸ **Example 12-13** During the early 1980s, the federal government significantly reduced marginal tax rates, particularly on those making high incomes. The result, according to some economists, was a surge in nationwide economic activity that lasted for many years. ◂

**Using Aggregate Demand/Aggregate Supply Analysis** We can use the same *AD/AS* curves that we developed in Chapter 11 to show how changes in taxes affect the equilibrium price level and the equilibrium level of real GDP per year.

Look at Figure 12-3. There you see the aggregate supply curve as *AS* and the aggregate demand curve before tax rates were reduced as $AD_{\text{pre-tax cuts}}$. After the

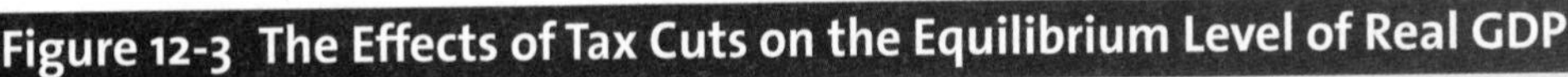

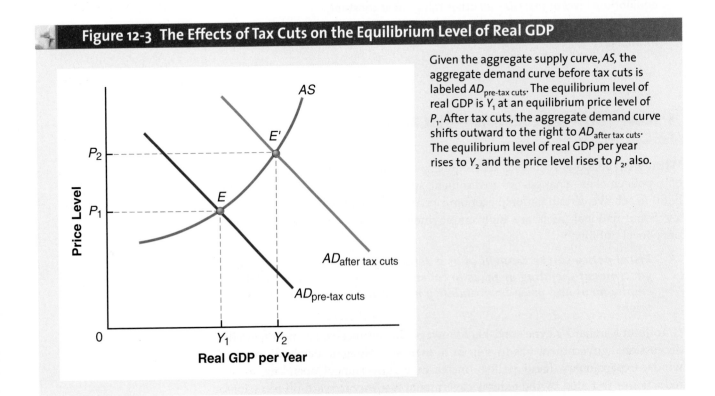

**Figure 12-3 The Effects of Tax Cuts on the Equilibrium Level of Real GDP**

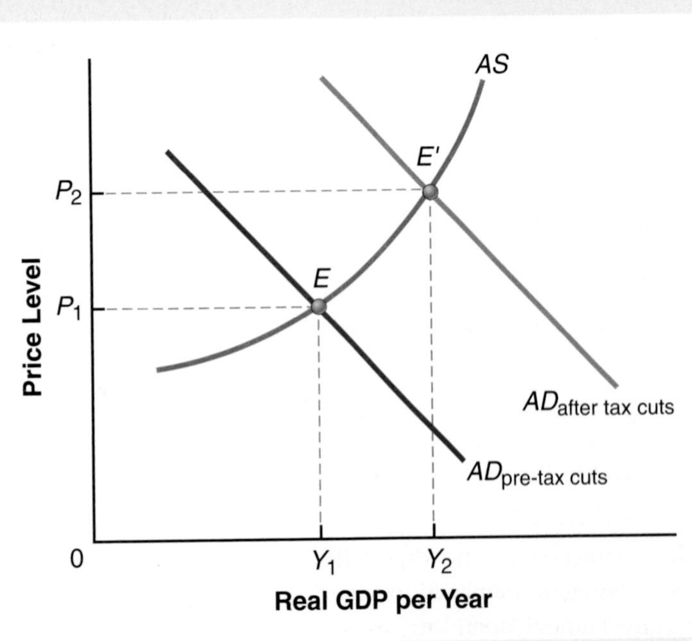


Given the aggregate supply curve, *AS*, the aggregate demand curve before tax cuts is labeled $AD_{\text{pre-tax cuts}}$. The equilibrium level of real GDP is $Y_1$ at an equilibrium price level of $P_1$. After tax cuts, the aggregate demand curve shifts outward to the right to $AD_{\text{after tax cuts}}$. The equilibrium level of real GDP per year rises to $Y_2$ and the price level rises to $P_2$, also.

tax rate cuts, the aggregate demand curve shifted outward to the right to $AD_{\text{after tax cuts}}$. Equilibrium moved from $E$ to $E'$. The equilibrium level of real GDP per year increased from $Y_1$ to $Y_2$. The equilibrium price level also increased from $P_1$ to $P_2$.

It may get harder in the future for Congress and the president to reduce tax rates, as you will read about in the next *Policy Application*.

## POLICY APPLICATION: The Disconnect Between Those Who Pay Taxes and Those Who Vote

***Concept Applied:***
**Federal Income Taxation**

A recent poll conducted by *USA Today*/CNN/Gallup asked a random sample of Americans whether their federal income taxes were too high. About 50 percent said no, they weren't. The same poll also asked a random sample whether federal income taxes on wealthy Americans were too high. Almost 40 percent actually responded that federal income taxes on the wealthy were too low.

### High-Income Earners Are the Ones Who Pay Most Federal Income Taxes

As it turns out, it is not surprising that half of Americans believe that federal income taxes are just about right. Because of tax exemptions, deductions, and credits, almost 35 million Americans who file tax returns pay *no* federal income taxes. Few of them probably believe that federal income taxes are too high. At the beginning of the 2000s, the top 5 percent of income earners paid 56 percent of total income taxes. The bottom 50 percent paid only 4 percent.

### The Policy Problem in Attempting to Reduce Federal Income Taxes

So, here is the dilemma that federal policymakers face: When they want to spur overall economic activity, they typically come up with a tax-cut plan. But any such plan is often attacked because it provides "too much" tax relief to the rich. Given, though, that higher-income earners pay most of federal income taxes, there is no possible way to have a *substantial* tax reduction that does not benefit the rich. Indeed, for many Americans, income taxes cannot be cut because these people are not paying income taxes to begin with!

The U.S. federal tax system was meant to be progressive. It has become increasingly so in the last few decades. Tax legislation over the last 20 years has greatly reduced (or eliminated) specific tax benefits that used to help the rich avoid taxes. In contrast, tax credits to the lower end of the income ladder have increased dramatically.

**For Critical Analysis:**
*Why do you think that policymakers believe that tax reductions will cause nationwide economic activity to increase?*

## Changing Government Spending

It seems simple, perhaps too simple. If the economy is in a recession, have the government spend more. This spending has an effect on real GDP just like an increase in planned investment spending. In other words, there will be a multiplier effect on the equilibrium level of real GDP. Indeed, Keynes argued that during the Great Depression, governments should have increased their spending to offset the dramatic reductions in private investment spending.

**Using Aggregate Demand/Aggregate Supply Analysis to Show the Effect of a Change in Government Spending** We can show the theoretical impact of increased government spending on the equilibrium price level and level of real GDP per year. Look at Figure 12-4 on the next page. There you see the short-run aggregate supply curve as *AS*. The aggregate demand curve is labeled

## Figure 12-4 The Effects of Increased Government Spending on Aggregate Demand

Assume the economy is in a recession shown by the intersection of $AS$ and $AD_{recession}$. The equilibrium level of real GDP is $Y_1$ with an equilibrium price level $P_1$. Then government spending increases. The aggregate demand curve shifts outward to the right to $AD_{with\ increased\ government\ spending}$. The equilibrium level of real GDP per year increases to $Y_2$.

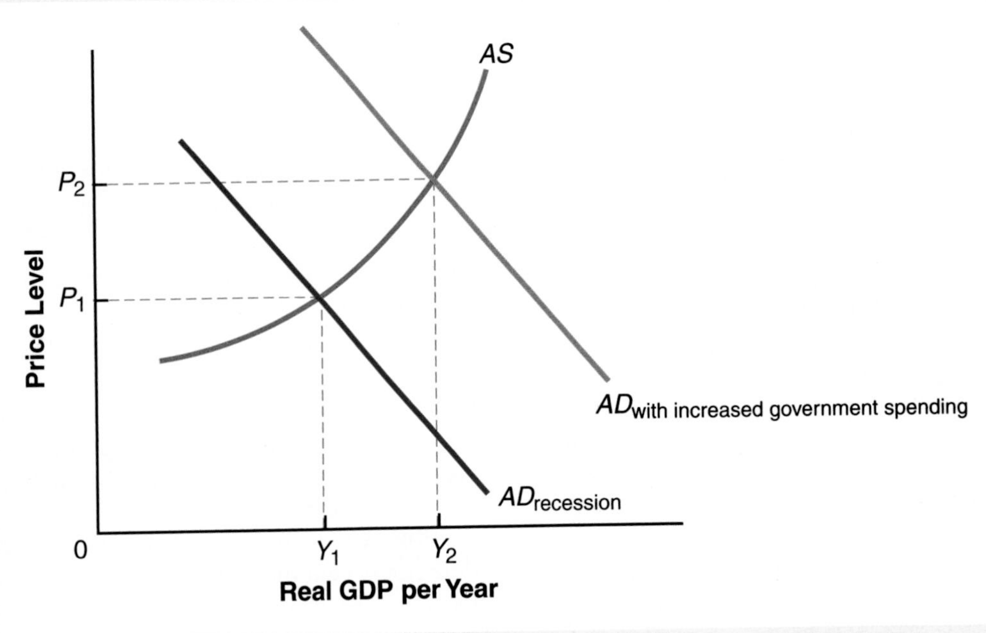


$AD_{recession}$, to indicate that a recession is occurring. The equilibrium level of real GDP per year is $Y_1$ with an equilibrium price level of $P_1$.

Now policymakers increase government spending as part of an active fiscal policy. A multiplier effect may be involved here, a topic we discussed earlier in this chapter. In any event, the aggregate demand curve shifts outward to the right to $AD_{with\ increased\ government\ spending}$. What has happened is that the equilibrium level of real GDP per year has increased from $Y_1$ to $Y_2$. In principle, this active fiscal policy of increased government spending has helped move the economy out of a recession.

### CONTRACTIONARY FISCAL POLICY

Policymakers can attempt to cool an overheated national economy by decreasing government spending. This is called contractionary fiscal policy because its goal is to contract the economy to reduce "overheating."

Look at Figure 12-5. As usual, aggregate supply is labeled $AS$. The overheated economy is shown by the aggregate demand curve labeled $AD_{overheated\ economy}$. The equilibrium price level is $P_1$, and the equilibrium level of real GDP per year is $Y_1$. The government decreases government spending (or, in a somewhat equivalent move, increases taxes) such that the aggregate demand curve shifts inward to the left to $AD_{with\ decreased\ government\ spending}$. The equilibrium price level drops to $P_2$ and the equilibrium level of real GDP per year drops to $Y_2$.

**Figure 12-5 Cooling Down an Overheated Economy with Contractionary Fiscal Policy**

A decrease in government spending causes the aggregate demand curve $AD_{\text{overheated economy}}$ to shift inward to the left to $AD_{\text{with decreased government spending}}$. The equilibrium price level drops from $P_1$ to $P_2$ and the equilibrium level of real GDP per year drops to $Y_2$.

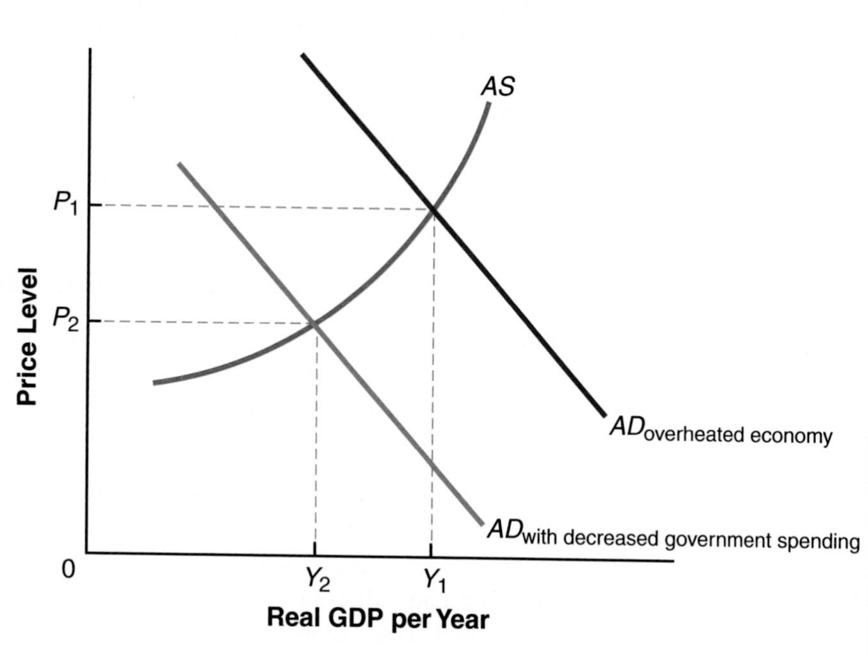


## The Way Increased Government Spending Is Financed Is Important

Government spending can be financed in a number of ways, including increasing taxes and borrowing. Tax reductions must be financed, too, either by borrowing or by reducing government expenditures.

> ***The effectiveness of increased government spending (or tax reductions) depends in large part on how such increased spending (or tax reductions) is financed.***

**Government Spending Matched by Increased Taxes** If the government simultaneously raises taxes to finance the increased spending, there will not be much *net* impact on the economy. ▸ Example 12-14 Suppose that the government decides to spend $50 billion more a year on terrorism prevention than it was previously spending. It simultaneously raises taxes by $50 billion to pay for this increased government spending. In the terrorism prevention industry, many individuals will receive higher incomes. At the same time, other (and perhaps some of the same) individuals will have reduced after-tax income because their taxes will have been raised by $50 billion. The reduction in possible spending by the latter group will more or less equal the increased spending by those in the terrorism prevention industry. ◂

**Government Spending Financed by Increased Borrowing—The Crowding Out Effect** If the government finances the increased spending by borrowing from the private sector, it may crowd out private investment. This is called the **crowding out effect**.

**Crowding out effect**
*The tendency of expansionary fiscal policy to cause a decrease in planned investment or planned consumption in the private sector; this decrease normally results from the rise in interest rates.*

Typically, when the government increases borrowing, it must offer higher interest rates to induce individuals and firms from the private sector (as well as from abroad) to lend it more funds. We already saw, though, that planned investment depends on the rate of interest. So, other things held constant, when increased borrowing by the federal government causes interest rates to rise, private investment spending will fall. That is the essence of the crowding out effect.

There is also another problem with raising government spending to fight recessions, which you will read about next.

## The Thorny Problem of Timing and Time Lags

As much as government policymakers would like to ignore the problem, the conduct of fiscal policy involves a variety of time lags. Policymakers must be concerned with time lags. At least three are important:

**Recognition time lag**
*The time required to gather information about the current state of the economy.*

**Action time lag**
*The time between the recognition of an economic problem and the implementation of policy to solve it. The action time lag is quite long for fiscal policy, which requires congressional approval.*

**Effect time lag**
*The time that elapses between the implementation of a policy and the results of that policy.*

1. **The Recognition Time Lag:** Quite apart from the fact that it is difficult to measure economic variables, it takes time to collect and assimilate such data. Policymakers must contend with the **recognition time lag,** which is the time that goes by before economic problems can be identified.
2. **The Action Time Lag:** After an economic problem is recognized, a solution must be formulated. Thus, there will be an **action time lag,** which is the period between the recognition of a problem and the implementation of policy to solve it. For fiscal policy, the action time lag can easily take a year or two.
3. **The Effect Time Lag:** After fiscal policy is enacted, it takes time for it to affect the economy. That is to say, there is an **effect time lag.** This means that the multiplier effect of increased government spending or reduced taxes may be much smaller in the short run than in the long run.

Because the fiscal policy time lags are long and variable, a policy designed to combat a recession may not produce results until the economy is already out of the recession.

**Mastering Concepts:** Use at Your Discretion—Discretionary Fiscal Policy

- **Fiscal policy is usually a deliberate attempt by the federal government to affect nationwide economic activity.**
- **Fiscal policy can consist of changing taxes or changing government spending, or both.**
- **Any effect on the nationwide economy due to increased government spending depends on how that spending is financed.**
- **The effectiveness of fiscal policy may be limited because of (1) the recognition time lag, (2) the action time lag, and (3) the effect time lag.**

## AUTOMATIC STABILIZERS

Not all changes in taxes or in government spending (including government transfers) constitute discretionary fiscal policy. There are several types of automatic (or nondiscretionary) fiscal policies. Such policies do not require new legislation on the part of Congress. Specific automatic fiscal policies—called **automatic**, or **built-in, stabilizers**—include the tax system itself and the government transfer system; the latter includes unemployment compensation and welfare spending.

**Automatic, or built-in, stabilizers** *Special provisions of certain federal programs that cause changes in desired aggregate expenditures without the action of Congress and the president. Examples are the federal progressive tax system, welfare benefits, and unemployment compensation.*

## The Tax System as an Automatic Stabilizer

You know that if you work less, you are paid less, and therefore you pay lower taxes. The amount of taxes that our government collects falls automatically during a recession. Incomes and profits fall when business production slows down, and the government's take drops, too. Some economists consider this an automatic tax cut. Like other tax cuts, it stimulates aggregate demand and therefore reduces the extent of recessions.

The progressive nature of both the federal personal and the corporate income tax system magnifies any automatic stabilization effect that may exist. ▸ Example 12-15 If your hours of work are reduced because of a recession, you still pay federal personal income taxes on what you earn. But because of our progressive system, you may drop into a lower tax bracket, thereby paying a lower marginal tax rate. As a result, your disposable income falls by a smaller percentage than your before-tax income falls. ◂

## Unemployment Compensation and Welfare Payments

Like our tax system, unemployment compensation payments may stabilize aggregate demand. Throughout the business cycle, unemployment compensation reduces *changes* in people's disposable income. When business activity drops, many laid-off workers automatically become eligible for unemployment compensation from their state governments. Their disposable income therefore remains positive, although certainly it is less than when they were employed.

During expansions, there is less unemployment, and consequently fewer unemployment payments are made to members of the labor force. Less purchasing power is being added to the economy because fewer unemployment checks are paid out. Historically, the relationship between the unemployment rate and unemployment compensation payments has been strongly positive.

Welfare payments act similarly as an automatic stabilizer. When a recession occurs, more people become eligible for welfare payments. Therefore, those people do not experience as dramatic a drop in disposable income as they would have otherwise. And, when the economy improves and some of these people get jobs, their incomes rise by less than their paychecks, because their welfare checks are cut.

✦ **Contrast!** *Congress doesn't have to do anything for an automatic stabilizer to come into play, whereas discretionary fiscal policy requires Congress to pass new legislation.*

## Stabilizing Impact

The key stabilizing impact of our tax system, unemployment compensation, and welfare payments is their ability to offset abrupt changes in disposable income, consumption, and the equilibrium level of national income. If disposable income is prevented from falling as much as it would have otherwise during a recession, the downturn will be moderated. In contrast, if disposable income is prevented from rising as rapidly as it would have during a boom, the boom is less likely to create an "overheated" economy. The progressive income tax and unemployment compensation thus provide automatic stabilization to the economy. We present this argument graphically in Figure 12-6 on the next page.

Some economists believe that Social Security payments have a stabilizing effect on the economy. This may or may not be true, but what is certain is that the Social Security system faces an uncertain future. You can read about this in the next *Policy Application*.

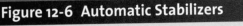

*Animated*

**Figure 12-6 Automatic Stabilizers**

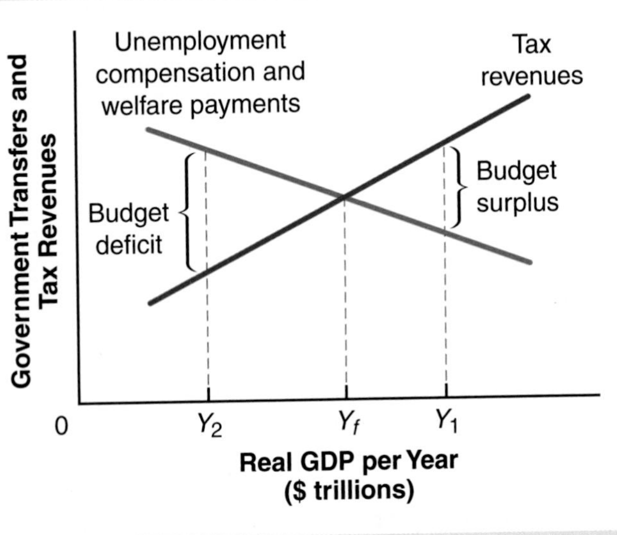

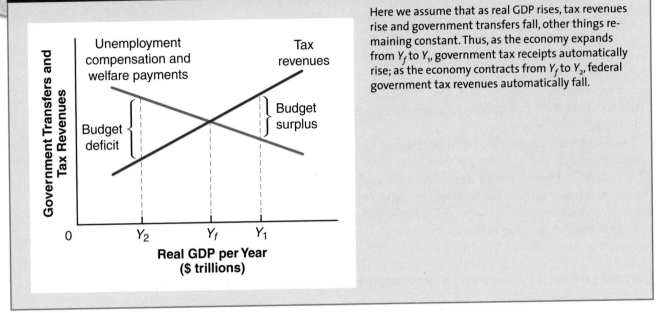

Here we assume that as real GDP rises, tax revenues rise and government transfers fall, other things remaining constant. Thus, as the economy expands from $Y_f$ to $Y_1$, government tax receipts automatically rise; as the economy contracts from $Y_f$ to $Y_2$, federal government tax revenues automatically fall.

## POLICY APPLICATION: The Necessity of Greater Taxes to Pay for Increasing Social Security and Medicare Benefits in the Future

***Concepts Applied:***
**Social Security, Medicare**

The fastest-growing demographic group in the United States consists of those over 80 years old. Improved diet and nutrition, a better understanding of the body, and, of course, modern medicine have contributed to the aging of America. We must remember, though, that those who retire start receiving from the federal government rather than giving. They receive Social Security retirement benefits, as well as Medicare benefits for health problems. These two programs are growing much more rapidly than the economy and faster than any other federal government spending programs.

### The Impact of Social Security and Medicare on the Federal Budget

At the beginning of the 2000s, Social Security and Medicare spending constituted about 6.5 percent of GDP. By 2040, this percentage will have almost doubled. Look at Figure 12-7.

The rise in Social Security and Medicare spending will be caused by two factors: (1) the increased number of retirees from the group of U.S. residents born right after World War II and (2) the aging of the population as a whole. By 2040, the life expectancy for those age 65 will be 17 percent longer than it is for that age group today.

### The Burden of Aging Falls on the Shoulders of the Young

At the beginning of the twenty-first century, there were 4.3 workers for every person aged 65 or older. In 2020, there will be only 2.6 workers for every retired person; in 2050, 2.4 workers, and by 2070, only 2.2 workers.

Look at this issue another way. By 2070, a working couple will have to provide almost all of the Social Security and Medicare support for a retired person. This same working couple will also have to support themselves and their children. So, you and those who are born after you are facing this reality: a larger and larger share of your paycheck will go for federal taxes.

*Continued on next page*

**Figure 12-7 Social Security and Medicare Spending as a Percentage of GDP**

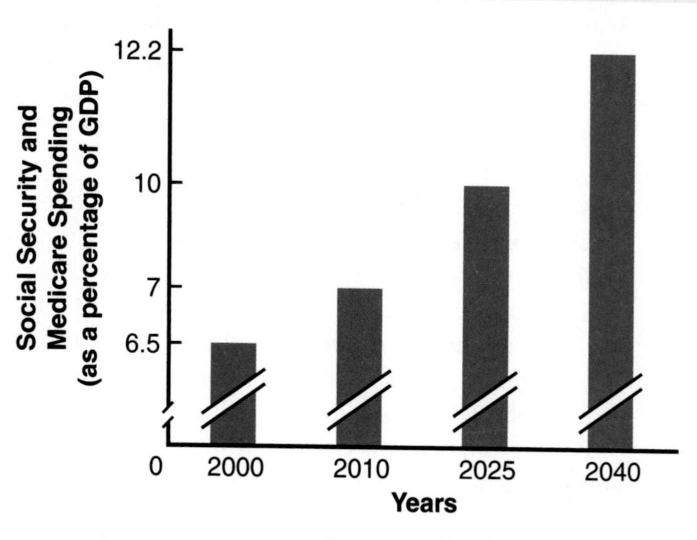


**For Critical Analysis:**
*Some argue that the way out of this dilemma is to allow younger, working-age immigrants into the United States. How would this help the situation?*

**Mastering Concepts:** Automatic Stabilizers

- **Our federal tax system may be an automatic stabilizer because when incomes fall, government taxes fall, too, thereby softening the reduction in nationwide economic activity.**
- **Unemployment compensation payments and welfare benefits may also act as automatic stabilizers.**

## DEFICIT SPENDING—FISCAL POLICY AT ITS FINEST

We have already talked about the major question associated with increased government spending or reduced taxes—how do you finance such actions? Government policymakers who contemplate raising government spending as part of a fiscal policy prescription also have to determine whether to ask Congress to raise taxes or increase government borrowing.

**Bonds**
*Legal claims against a business or government, usually entitling the owner of the bond to receive a fixed annual coupon payment, plus a lump-sum payment at the bond's maturity date. Bonds are issued in return for funds lent.*

**Public debt**
*The accumulation of all past federal government deficits; the total amount owed by the federal government to individuals, businesses, and foreigners.*

### GOVERNMENT BORROWING

Our governments—federal, state, and local—borrow funds all the time, just as households and businesses do. The federal government typically borrows by selling U.S. Treasury **bonds.** The sale of these federal government bonds to corporations, private individuals, pension plans, foreign governments, foreign businesses, and foreign individuals adds to this nation's **public debt.** ▸ International Example 12-16 In the last few years, foreigners have owned over 30 percent of the U.S. public debt. Two decades ago, foreign ownership of the U.S. public debt was only 15 percent. ◀

**The Public Debt in Perspective** Did you know that the federal government has accumulated trillions of dollars in debt? Does that scare you? It certainly would if you thought that we had to pay it back tomorrow. But we don't.

> ***The federal government refinances its debt all the time. That means that when one U.S. Treasury bond becomes due and payable, the Treasury simply sells another bond and uses the proceeds to pay off the old one.***

**Gross public debt**
*All federal government debt including federal government interagency borrowing.*

More importantly, though, there are two types of public debt—gross and net. The **gross public debt** includes all federal government interagency borrowings, which really do not matter. In other words, many agencies of the U.S. government borrow funds from other agencies of the U.S. government. This is similar to your taking an IOU out of your left pocket and putting it into your right pocket. ▶ Example 12-17 Currently, federal interagency borrowings account for close to $3 trillion of the gross public debt. That is the part of the public debt that you can ignore. ◀

**Net public debt**
*The gross public debt minus all government interagency borrowing.*

What is important is the **net public debt**—the public debt that nets out interagency borrowing, which you can see in Table 12-2.

**Table 12-2 Net Public Debt of the Federal Government**

| Year | Total (billions of current dollars) |
|---|---|
| 1940 | $ 42.7 |
| 1945 | 235.2 |
| 1950 | 219.0 |
| 1960 | 237.2 |
| 1970 | 284.9 |
| 1980 | 709.3 |
| 1990 | 2,410.1 |
| 1992 | 2,998.6 |
| 1993 | 3,247.5 |
| 1994 | 3,432.1 |
| 1995 | 3,603.4 |
| 1996 | 3,747.1 |
| 1997 | 3,900.0 |
| 1998 | 3,870.0 |
| 1999 | 3,632.9 |
| 2000 | 3,448.6 |
| 2001 | 3,200.3 |
| 2002 | 3,528.7 |
| 2003 | 3,714.8 |
| 2004 | 4,200.0* |
| 2005 | 4,500.0* |

**Estimate.*

Source: U.S. Office of Management and Budget.

## *Solving the Economic Problem:* What to Do When the Federal Government Hits the Federal Debt Ceiling

First, that $7 trillion mentioned at the beginning of this chapter is an exaggerated figure because it includes *interagency* borrowing. Interagency borrowing never has to be repaid because it simply constitutes changes in bookkeeping entries within the same entity—the federal government. From your perspective, what matters is the public debt net of interagency borrowing, called the net public debt. That number is much lower than $7 trillion.

Second, what really matters is the net public debt compared to the nation's capacity to produce, or to annual national output. From that perspective, the net public debt is only 35 percent of GDP. In many other countries, it sometimes reaches twice this percentage.

Finally, from a historical point of view, Congress has always increased the debt ceiling to allow the federal government to borrow when it needed to.

To get a real handle on the importance of the public debt, you need to compare it to a year's GDP. This is what we do in Figure 12-8. As you can see, since about 1960, the net public debt as a percentage of national output has ranged between 30 and 50 percent of national yearly output.

**Figure 12-8 Net U.S. Public Debt as a Percentage of GDP**

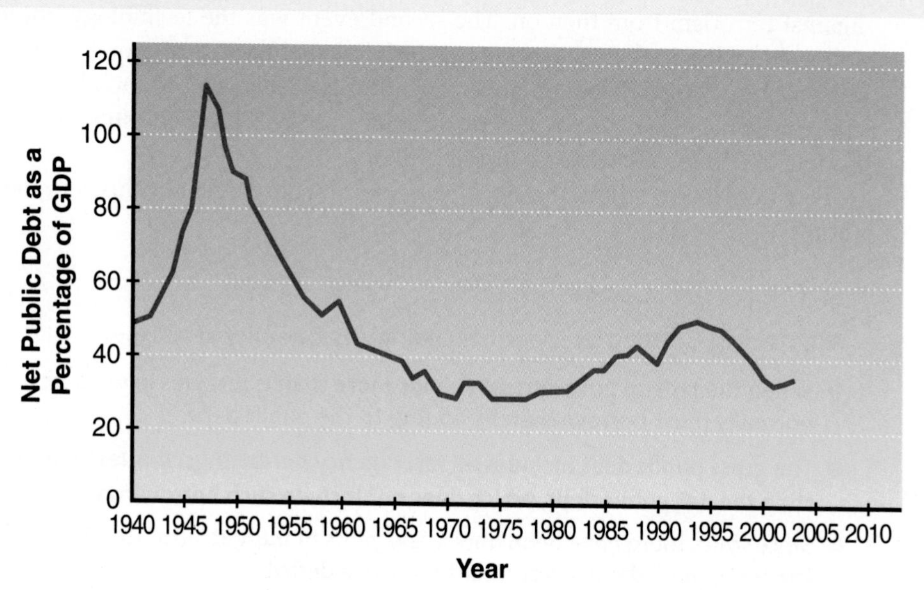


During World War II, the net public debt grew dramatically. It fell until the 1970s, rose again until the early 1990s, and declined until the early 2000s.

Cartoon by Clay Bennett, cartoonist for *The Christian Science Monitor*.

## Are We Always in Debt?

**Budget surplus**
*An excess of government receipts over expenditures during the fiscal year.*

The fact is that from 1960 until the last few years of the twentieth century, the federal government spent more than it received in all but two years. Starting in 1998, we had a **budget surplus** each year for four years. In other words, the federal government took in more than it spent. Some commentators predicted that we would be running federal government surpluses for years to come. All of those projections went by the wayside because of two events, one extraordinary, the other recurring.

The first event was September 11, 2001. Basically, as a result of the terrorist attacks, the federal government spent much more than it had planned in the period immediately after September 11 and continued spending on beefed-up security against terrorism from then on. The second event was the technology implosion followed by the 2001–2002 recession, which lowered the rate of growth of not only the economy, but also federal government tax receipts. And, to top all of that off, the government had to pay for the war in Iraq in 2003. The estimated federal budget deficit for 2004 is close to $400 billion.

Few people now think there will be government budget surpluses in the near future.

### Mastering Concepts: Deficit Spending—Fiscal Policy at Its Finest

- **When the federal government spends more than it receives in revenues, it normally must borrow, thereby adding to the public debt.**
- **The gross public debt includes all interagency borrowings. It is less important than the net public debt, which does not include such borrowings.**
- **Since 1960, there have been only a few years of budget surpluses. The rest of the time, the federal government has run a deficit.**

## SUMMING IT ALL UP

- During periods of unemployment and inflexible prices, a change in aggregate demand will not affect the price level.
- Saving will always equal disposable income (income after taxes) minus consumption.
- The marginal propensity to consume is the change in consumption divided by the change in disposable income, whereas the marginal propensity to save is the change in saving divided by the change in disposable income.
- In economic analysis, investment refers to expenditures by businesses on new machines and buildings.
- Because businesspeople borrow funds to invest, the quantity of investment spending demanded will fall as the rate of interest rises, and vice versa.
- Any change in (1) businesspersons' expectations, (2) productive technology, and (3) business taxes will change the quantity of investment spending demanded at each and every interest rate.
- Any permanent change in investment leads to a multiplier effect on the equilibrium level of real GDP, all other things held constant.
- The larger the marginal propensity to consume (MPC), the greater the multiplier.
- Fiscal policy can consist of changing taxes or changing government spending, or both.
- The effectiveness of fiscal policy may be limited because of (1) the recognition time lag, (2) the action time lag, and (3) the effect time lag.
- Our federal tax system may be an automatic stabilizer because when incomes fall, government taxes fall, too, thereby softening the reduction in nationwide economic activity. Unemployment compensation payments and welfare benefits may also act as automatic stabilizers.
- When the federal government spends more than it receives in revenues, it normally must borrow, thereby adding to the public debt.
- The gross public debt includes all interagency borrowings. It is less important than the net public debt, which does not include such borrowings.

## KEY TERMS AND CONCEPTS

action time lag **260**
automatic, or built-in, stabilizers **261**
bonds **263**
budget surplus **266**
consumption **250**
consumption goods **250**
crowding out effect **260**
debt ceiling **247**
disposable income **250**
effect time lag **260**
excess capacity **248**
fiscal policy **248**
full employment **248**
gross public debt **264**
investment **252**
Keynesian economics **248**
marginal propensity to consume (MPC) **251**
marginal propensity to save (MPS) **251**
multiplier effect **253**
net public debt **264**
personal consumption expenditures **250**
public debt **263**
recognition time lag **260**
saving **250**

## MASTERING ECONOMIC CONCEPTS Questions and Problems

**12-1.** What is the difference between the federal debt and the federal deficit?

**12-2.** Indicate whether each of the following is true or false.

a. Fiscal policy is short run in nature.
b. Keynes believed that fiscal policy was not needed because the economy corrects itself relatively quickly.
c. Keynes believed that current consumption decisions are based primarily on long-run anticipated income.
d. Fiscal policy decisions are finalized by the legislative branch of the federal government.

**12-3.** Does full employment imply that the unemployment rate equals zero? If so, how is this achieved? If not, what type or types of unemployment will still exist?

**12-4.** If the economy was growing too slowly (or not at all) and all workers agreed to accept lower wages, which curve—aggregate supply or aggregate demand—would increase? As a result, what would happen to the equilibrium level of real GDP per year? If workers were not so flexible about their wages, what curve must be shifted outward to accelerate the economy, according to Keynes?

**12-5.** Assume that the aggregate supply curve is shaped differently over different ranges as indicated in the diagram. With this being the case, assume that the government enacts fiscal policy that will expand the economy. For each of the situations below, indicate what the impact will be on real GDP and the price level.

a. at equilibrium *A* with $AD_1$
b. at equilibrium *B* with $AD_2$
c. at equilibrium *C* with $AD_3$

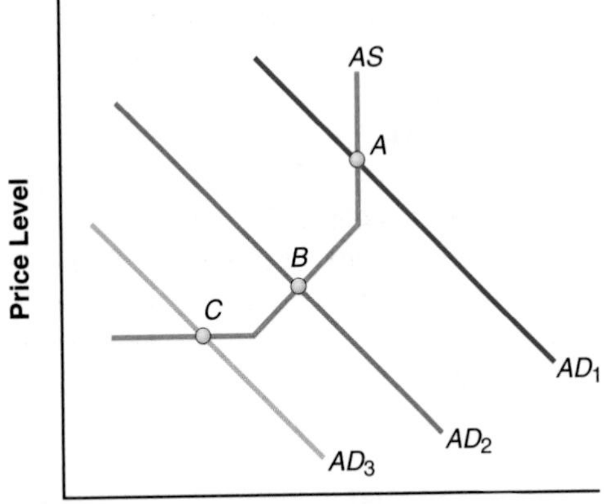


**12-6.** George's salary is $45,000 per year. He pays $11,000 in taxes to the federal government and $3,000 in taxes to the state government. What is his disposable income?

**12-7.** If you earn $70,000 in after-tax income in a year and save $6,000 of that income, by definition what does your consumption equal?

**12-8.** If, after completing your college degree, your annual after-tax income increases from $20,000 to $50,000 and your annual spending increases from $24,000 to $49,000, what is your marginal propensity to consume? What is your marginal propensity to save?

**12-9.** If your marginal propensity to consume is 0.9 and your after-tax earnings increase by $5,000, how much does your consumption increase?

**12-10.** Will planned investment, an important component of GDP, increase or decrease if interest rates increase?

**12-11.** Indicate whether each of the following will cause an increase (movement outward to the right) in the investment curve, a decrease (movement inward to the left) in the investment curve, or no change in the investment curve.

a. an improvement in productive technology
b. an increase in corporate taxes
c. a decrease in interest rates
d. an improvement in business expectations

**12-12.** If the government increases its spending by $30 billion, will the equilibrium level of GDP per year increase by more than $30 billion, less than $30 billion, or exactly $30 billion? Would the change in the equilibrium level of GDP per year have been greater or smaller if the initial increase had been in business spending as opposed to government spending?

**12-13.** If the marginal propensity to consume is 0.8, what does the multiplier equal? In this case, what impact would an additional $5 billion in investment have on the equilibrium level of GDP per year?

**12-14.** If the economy was suffering from significant inflation, which fiscal policy action would be more appropriate—an increase or a decrease in taxation? As a separate option, which would be more appropriate—an increase or a decrease in government spending?

**12-15.** Based on the following graph, should policymakers choose to increase or decrease taxation? In the same situation, should they choose to increase or decrease government spending? Does this graph depict a situation with high unemployment or high inflation?

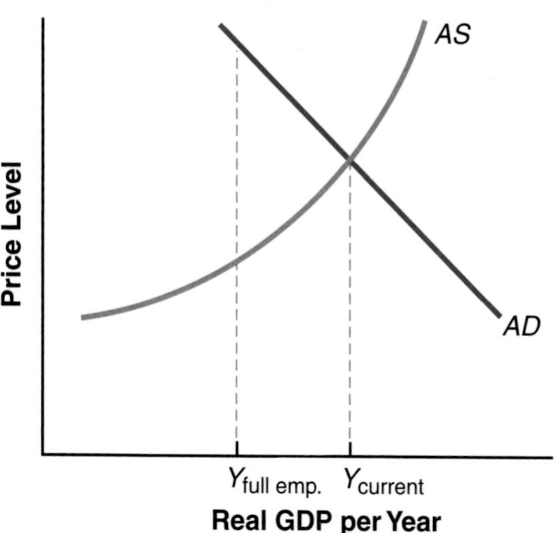


**12-16.** What symptom or economic problem is expansionary fiscal policy meant to address? What are the two tools that can be used for expansionary fiscal policy? If such an expansionary policy is effective, will this policy possibly lead to an increase or a decrease in the federal deficit?

## THINKING CRITICALLY

**12-1.** Assume that the average person in the United States saves approximately $50 out of every after-tax $1,000 she or he earns. Based on this figure, what is the marginal propensity to consume? What is the marginal propensity to save? What would the multiplier equal? In the case of a recession, should the federal government choose to increase or decrease government spending? If the federal government increased spending by $100 billion, by what amount would the equilibrium level of real GDP change? Which aggregate curve would shift as a result of this increased government spending? Holding all else constant, would the new government spending increase the price level? Is this a significant problem? Why or why not?

**12-2.** Assume that the graph alongside depicts the growth of real GDP over time. As we already know, GDP, our measure of national output, does not grow at a constant rate, but rather in patterns that sometimes vaguely resemble a cycle. At the point in time indicated by the arrow, is our economy more likely to be experiencing an expansion or a recession? Based on your previous answer, at that time should the government enact expansionary or contractionary fiscal policy? Assume that the recognition, action, and effect lags are represented by the spaces with the corresponding letters, that is, *R*, *A*, and *I*. Based on these lags, at what point in time will the discretionary fiscal policy that you suggested have an impact on the economy—during an expansion or a recession?

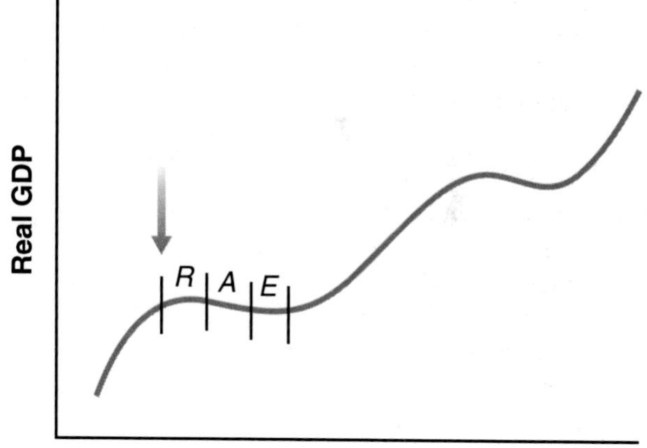


**12-3.** In the early 2000s, what percentage of GDP did the net U.S. public debt represent? Historically speaking, is this percentage relatively high or relatively low? If your personal debt represented a large percentage of your annual income, would it be tougher or easier for you to convince a bank to lend you funds for some worthwhile purpose? If the net public debt increased to a very large percentage of GDP, what might happen to the interest rate that the government was forced to pay on its borrowings?

## LOGGING ON

1. For an estimate of the current value of the U.S. gross public debt, go to the "U.S. National Debt Clock" at http://www.brillig.com/debt_clock/.
2. To see the distribution of federal income taxes paid across taxpayer incomes, go to http://www.ntu.org/links/FAQs/whopays incometaxes.php3.
3. To take a look at the latest U.S. federal budget, go to http://w3.access.gpo.gov/usbudget/.
4. For projections of future federal budget deficits, go to http://www.cbo.gov/byclasscat.cfm?cat=0.

## USING THE INTERNET FOR ECONOMIC ANALYSIS

**Exploring Social Security Privatization Possibilities** One proposal for reforming the Social Security system would allow people to direct at least a portion of their tax contributions to private investments. This application explores possible implications of privatization of Social Security.

**Title:** Social Security Choice

**Navigation:** Go to http://www.socialsecurity.org/.

**Application** Perform the indicated operations, and answer the following questions.

1. Click on each of the following and read the corresponding discussion: "African Americans," "Women," and "Low-Wage Workers." According to the perspectives offered at this Web site, what are the potential advantages of Social Security privatization for these groups?
2. Can you think of possible drawbacks of Social Security privatization not discussed at this Web site?

## MEDIA RESOURCE LIST

The following media resources are available with this chapter:

- Load your CD-ROM to listen to the audio introduction to this chapter.
- Load your CD-ROM to view the video on *Keynesian Economics and Changes in Aggregate Demand.*
- Load your CD-ROM to view the video on *Marginal Propensity to Consume and to Save.*
- Load your CD-ROM to view the video on *Determinants of Investment.*
- Load your CD-ROM to access a Graph Animation of Table 12-1, *The Multiplier Process—An Example.*
- Load your CD-ROM to view the video on *The Multiplier Formula.*
- Load your CD-ROM to view the video on *Coping with Time Lags.*
- Load your CD-ROM to access a Graph Animation of Figure 12-6, *Automatic Stabilizers.*
- Test your knowledge of chapter concepts with a quiz at www.miller-ume.com.
- Link to Web resources related to the text coverage at www.miller-ume.com.

## HOMEWORK SET

Go to the back of this book to find the Homework Problems for this chapter.

# CHAPTER 13

# Money and Our Banking System

## *Facing an Economic Problem:* Reverting to Barter in Modern Times—How Could It Happen?

Just about every transaction in which you engage involves an exchange of money for goods or services. An alternative to using money is *barter*—an exchange of goods or services for other goods or services. But barter virtually disappeared after nations discovered the benefits of using *money*. After all, barter requires a coincidence of wants—if you have a frying pan that you want to barter in exchange for a pair of shoes, I have to have a pair of shoes that fits you and also want the frying pan at the same time. Normally, the costs of finding a partner to a barter exchange are prohibitively high. Of course, that's why societies past and present eventually chose to use money. Today, though, the International Reciprocal Trade Association (IRTA) estimates that more than 350,000 companies actively participate in barter. The U.S. Department of Commerce estimates that about 20 percent of world trade is barter.

The question is, if barter is so expensive, why is it assuming such an important place in the U.S. and world economy? First, you should understand money and banking.

***Refer to the back of this chapter for a complete listing of multimedia learning materials available on the CD-ROM and the Web site.***

## Learning Objectives

After reading this chapter, you should be able to:

- **List the two functions of money.**
- **Explain the difference between the narrowest definition of money, M1, and the broader definition, M2.**
- **List four of the most important functions of the Federal Reserve System, our central bank.**
- **Explain in general terms how the Fed can increase the money supply.**
- **Explain the difference between an ordinary credit card and a smart card.**

# THE FUNCTIONS OF MONEY

In Chapter 12 you were introduced to one of the major policy tools of the federal government—fiscal policy. As you learned, fiscal policy involves the government's attempt at economy-wide stabilization via changes in its spending and taxing activities. The other way the government can engage in economy-wide stabilization is through the money side of our economy. To understand how the government can do this, you first have to learn about money and the U.S. banking system, the subject matter of this chapter.

## THE ORIGINS OF MONEY

Money did not just fall out of the sky, given from nature. Rather, money was invented or created by humans. ▸ International Example 13-1 Money has been around for at least 4,500 years. Wealthy citizens in Mesopotamia were flaunting money at least as early as 2500 B.C., and maybe hundreds of years before that. ◂

Notice here that *money* is not the same as *income*. Income is what you earn over a specified time period, such as a week, month, or year. Money is not wealth either, although it usually is part of your wealth. Wealth consists of those things that you own, such as houses, stocks, bonds, jewelry, fine art, and automobiles. Throughout this chapter, we will discuss money only in terms of the asset that we use to make exchanges.

In the U.S. economy, voluntary exchanges often involve money in return for goods or services. Many people think of money as bills, coins, and checks. In other countries and times, money has taken on numerous forms. ▸ International Example 13-2 The kinds and varieties of money that have been used throughout the world are surprising. They have included tortoise shells, porpoise teeth, whale teeth, boar tusks, large stones with centers removed, and cigarettes. Of course, gold and silver were used as money at one time in this country. Even today, gold is used as money in certain politically unstable parts of the world. ◂

***The fact is, money is whatever people accept as money.***

Today, we identify money by the functions that it fulfills. Money's principal functions are to serve as (1) a medium of exchange and (2) a unit of accounting.

## MONEY AS A MEDIUM OF EXCHANGE

**Medium of exchange**
*The function of money to serve as a means of payment for goods or services.*
**Barter**
*The exchange of goods and services for other goods and services.*

To say that money is a **medium of exchange** simply means that a seller will accept it in exchange for a good or service. Most people are paid for their work in money, which they then can use to buy whatever they need or want. Without money, people would have to **barter**—exchange goods and services for other goods and services. ▸ International Example 13-3 After the war in Iraq in 2003, many Iraqis had only the local currency, which many retailers refused to accept because they did not know whether the U.S. occupying authorities were going to honor that currency. As a result, many Iraqi residents had to barter what few goods they had for food and other necessities. ◂

**Barter in More Detail** Barter requires what economists call a *coincidence of wants*. Each party to a transaction must want exactly what the other person has to offer. This situation is rare. As a result, people in societies that barter for goods spend great amounts of time and effort making trades with one another. Until quite recently, bartering worked only in small societies with simple economic systems. Note, however, that barter may be used as a way to avoid paying income taxes. If barter transactions can be kept secret from the Internal Revenue Service, then the value of the bartered transaction is not considered income for tax purposes. Of course, in most circumstances, this tax evasion scheme is illegal.

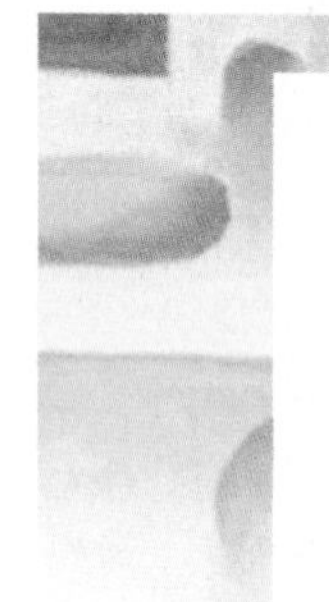

## *Solving the Economic Problem:* Reverting to Barter in Modern Times—How Could It Happen?

So, why is barter making a comeback in the United States and elsewhere? The answer—perhaps obvious to some—is that the Internet has reduced the cost of searching for a coincidence of wants. With the Internet and the modern computer, tracking barter transactions is a lot less costly than it used to be. In the past, bartered transactions were all recorded by hand. For example, in colonial times, John Hancock's uncle was one of those early bookkeepers who recorded commercial trades of rum and whale oil in exchange for wheat and furs on the early frontier.

Between 300,000 and 400,000 businesses today use some type of bartering arrangement, most often done via the Internet. At online barter exchanges, firms and individuals trade airline tickets for advertising space, surplus inventory for travel services, and so on.

The International Trade Exchange (ITEX) has 20,000 business members across North America. ITEX member companies trade all types of products and services, excess inventory, and production capacity in exchange for office products, car repairs, business meals, printing, and equipment.

There are also at least 400 regional barter exchanges. For example, JustBarter.com operates throughout the state of Massachusetts to help businesses find bartering partners. The Pennsylvania Barter Alliance claims it engages in bartering worldwide.

Barter is costly, but the costs of engaging in it are falling rapidly.

**Money and Transaction Costs** Money facilitates exchange by reducing the **transaction costs** associated with means-of-payment uncertainty. That is, with regard to goods that the partners in any exchange are willing to accept, the existence of money means that the individuals no longer have to hold a diverse collection of goods as an exchange inventory.

**Transaction costs**
*All of the costs associated with exchanging; the costs associated with making, reaching, and enforcing agreements, particularly for the exchange of goods and services.*

As a medium of exchange, money allows individuals to specialize in any area in which they have a competitive advantage and to receive money payments for

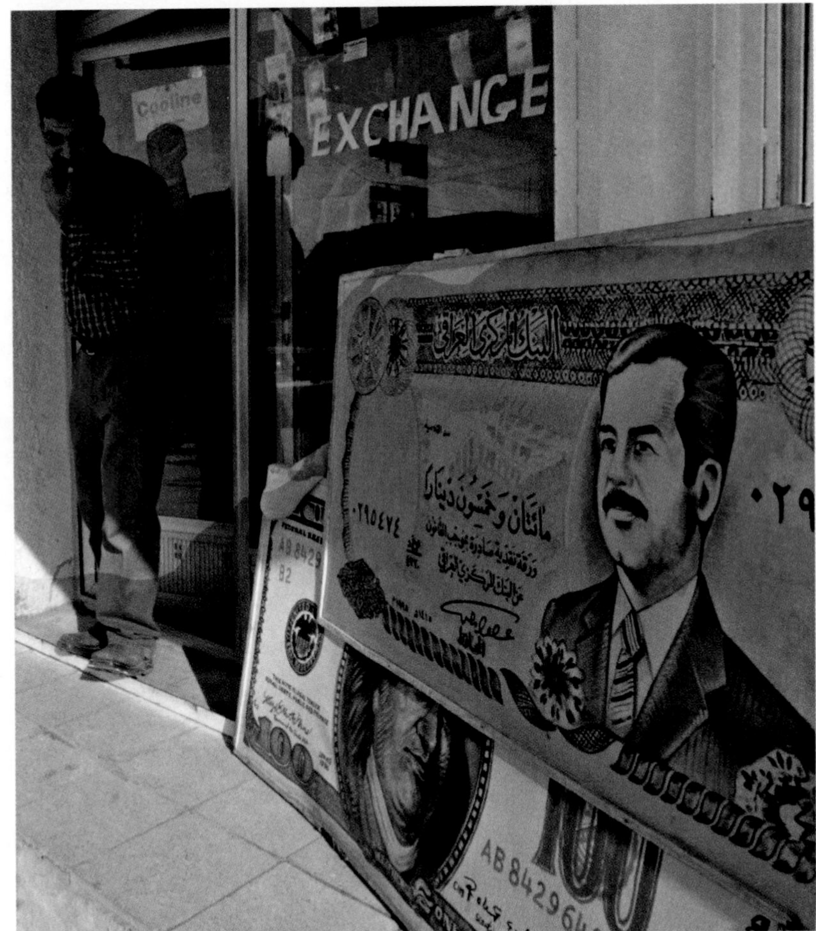


*This Iraqi is standing outside of a currency exchange shop in Baghdad a few months after a coalition of military forces outsted Saddam Hussein. Bank notes with Hussein's picture were still circulating as were U.S. dollars. Why don't we see two separate currencies in circulation in the United States?*

their labor. Money payments can then be exchanged for the fruits of other people's labor. The use of money as a medium of exchange permits more specialization and the inherent economic efficiencies that come with it (and hence greater economic growth).

## Money as a Unit of Accounting

**Unit of accounting**
*The function of money to serve as a yardstick for comparing the values of goods and services in relation to one another.*

Money is the yardstick that allows people to compare the values of goods and services in relation to one another. In this way, money functions as a **unit of accounting.** ▸ Example 13-4 Bill Gates, founder of Microsoft and one of the richest persons in the world, is probably worth around $50 billion. Nonetheless, he does not have much more money than most people do. His wealth, in contrast, exceeds most people's wealth by a dramatic amount. The dollar is the way we value his wealth. It is used as a unit of accounting. ◂

Each nation uses a basic unit to measure the value of goods, just as it uses the foot or meter to measure distance. ▸ International Example 13-5 In the United States, this basic unit of value is the dollar. In Japan, it is the yen; in much of Europe, the euro; and in Russia, the ruble. An item for sale is marked with a price that indicates its value in terms of the unit used in that country. ◂

***By using money prices as a factor in comparing goods, people can determine whether one item is a better bargain than another.***

Having a single unit of accounting also enables people to keep accurate financial records—records of debts owed, income saved, and so on.

## MORE THAN WATER IS LIQUID—THE CONCEPT OF LIQUIDITY

Money is an asset—something of value—that accounts for part of personal wealth. Wealth in the form of money can be exchanged later for other assets, goods, or services. Although it is not the only form of wealth that can be exchanged for goods and services, it is the most widely and most readily accepted one. This attribute of money is called **liquidity.**

**Liquidity**
*The degree to which an asset can be acquired or disposed of without much danger of any intervening loss in nominal value and with small transaction costs. Money is the most liquid asset.*

> ***We say that an asset is liquid when it can easily be acquired or disposed of without high transaction costs and with relative certainty as to its value. Money is the most liquid asset.***

People can easily convert money to other asset forms. Therefore, most individuals hold at least a part of their wealth in the form of the most liquid of assets, money. You can see how assets rank in liquidity relative to each other in Figure 13-1.

## WHAT BACKS MONEY?

If you look carefully at a dollar bill, you will find that it does not say that you can exchange it for anything. So, why are we willing to accept as payment something that, unlike gold or silver, has no intrinsic value? Checks are even worse—you probably could not even sell them for use as raw material for manufacturing.

### Fiduciary Monetary System

We accept currency and checks for payments because we have a **fiduciary monetary system.**

**Fiduciary monetary system**
*A system in which currency is issued by the government and its value is based solely on the public's faith that the currency can be exchanged for goods and services.*

> ***The value of payments in the form of currency and checks rests on the public's confidence that such payments can be exchanged for goods and services.***

*Fiduciary* comes from the Latin *fiducia,* which means "trust" or "confidence." In our fiduciary monetary system, money, in the form of currency or **checkable deposits** (accounts on which checks can be written), is not convertible to a fixed quantity of gold, silver, or some other precious commodity. The bills are just pieces of paper. Coins have a value stamped on them that today is much greater than the market value of the metal they contain. Nevertheless, currency and checkable deposits (checks) are money because of their acceptability and predictability of value.

**Checkable deposits**
*Any deposits in banks or banking-like institutions on which a check may be written.*

### Fiat Money

The currency that we use in the United States is considered a *fiat money.* This is any form of money that is not backed by anything other than faith

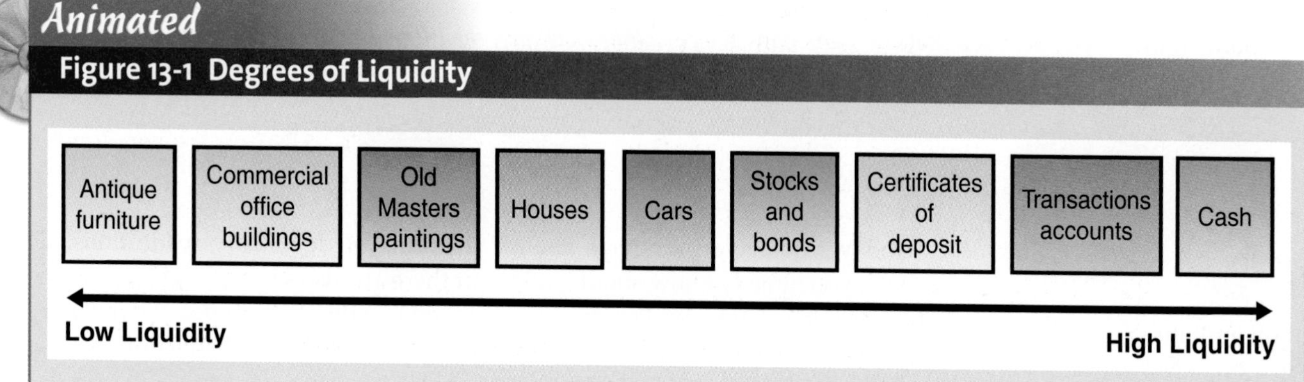


**Figure 13-1 Degrees of Liquidity**

in its universal acceptance in trade. As you will see later in this chapter, electronic money, or e-money, is also a type of fiat money. It is money that people can transfer directly via electronic impulses instead of paper currency, checks, and coins.

**Depository institutions**
*Financial institutions that accept deposits from savers and lend those deposits out at interest. Most allow for check writing, too.*

**Depository Institutions** Many banks and other **depository institutions**—financial institutions that accept money from savers, which is then lent out at interest—offer check-writing services for "free." Have bank managers gone crazy? No, as you will find out in the next *Policy Application*.

## POLICY APPLICATION: The Profits to Be Made in Offering Free Checking

### *Concepts Applied:* Implicit Interest Rate, Overdraft Charges

You cannot miss the offer. It is on TV, in newspaper ads, and in magazine ads. What is it? Every bank, savings and loan, and credit union seems to be offering you a free checking account. At times, you must have wondered how managers can offer a valuable service for free. After all, processing those checks clearly is *not* free. Banks incur costs when they provide you with checking accounts.

### It All Started a Few Years Ago

At first, only a few banks offered free checking, no required minimum balance, and no fees for interacting with live human tellers. Now, hundreds of major banks are even using billboards and posters to tell you all about their free services.

But how can they do this, given that such services, when provided, are not free to the banks? What has happened is that banks have figured out a way to earn revenues and thus make profits on so-called free checking accounts.

### It's All in the Overdraft Charges

If you read the fine print in your free checking account contract, you will see that the bank can charge you overdraft fees. These occur when you write a check or take cash from an automated teller machine (ATM) without having sufficient funds to cover those checks or cash withdrawals. A typical overdraft charge on a free checking account is $30. So, imagine that three to five times a year you step over the line with your checks and cash withdrawals—you don't have enough in your account to cover them. At $30 a pop, your bank will collect from $90 to $150 from you in fees. Although this amount may appear outrageous, it is in line with what most major banks are actually collecting.

### The Implied Interest Rate Is Astronomical

Consider a typical overdraft transaction. You have $30 in your bank account but you take $90 out of your local ATM in cash. You are in the hole for $60, which you normally have to pay back to the bank in a week. You are also socked with a $30 overdraft fee. Therefore, you have implicitly paid $30 in interest charges on a one-week loan of $60. That comes out to a 50 percent *weekly* interest rate ($30/$60). This in turn works out to an *annual* interest rate of 2,600 percent!

The moral of the story is that nothing is free.

**For Critical Analysis:**
*Which type of bank customer is most likely to be paying that 2,600 percent annual interest rate for his or her "free" checking account? Explain your answer.*

**Thrift institutions**
*Savings and loan associations, savings banks, and credit unions.*

Today, you have numerous choices in terms of depository institutions. Of course, you already know about banks. But there are also savings and loan associations, savings banks, and credit unions. Taken together these types of depository institutions are called **thrift institutions.** Here are some of the distinctions among these thrift institutions.

1. Savings and loan associations traditionally specialized in mortgage lending.
2. Savings banks are very similar to savings and loan associations, except that their ownership structure is different.
3. Credit unions accept deposits and make loans only to a group of individuals who are eligible for membership.

**Mastering Concepts:** The Functions of Money

- **The two functions of money are to serve as (1) a medium of exchange and (2) a unit of accounting.**
- **Money is the most liquid of assets in that it can be used to acquire goods and services under virtually all circumstances.**
- **Our monetary system is fiduciary, meaning that we place faith in our currency and checking accounts even though they have no intrinsic value.**
- **Our currency is fiat money because it has no intrinsic value.**
- **Besides banks, the main depository institutions are savings and loan associations, savings banks, and credit unions.**

## HOW WE DEFINE THE MONEY SUPPLY IN CIRCULATION

There are many ways to define the U.S. money supply in circulation. We start out with the narrowest official definition of the **money supply,** usually called M1.

**Money supply**
*The amount of money in circulation. The definition varies depending on how many near moneys are included.*

### Defining the Money Supply as M1

M1 is the narrowest definition of the money supply. M1 includes all currency (bills and coins), all checkable deposits, and traveler's checks.

**Checkable Deposits** We all know about paper currency, coins, and traveler's checks, but checkable deposits need a bit of explanation. Checks, as you know, are a way of transferring the ownership of deposits in financial institutions. They are normally acceptable as a medium of exchange. ▸ Example 13-6 Numerous financial institutions, including savings and loans, banks, savings banks, and credit unions, offer checkable deposits. In addition, many brokerage firms offer checkable deposits. For example, Merrill-Lynch offers its cash management account (CMA) for that purpose. ◂

**Why Credit Cards Are Not Part of the Money Supply** Often, students wonder why credit cards are not included in the definition of M1. After all, they seem to be very liquid. Actually, though, credit card accounts consist of short-term loans from credit card companies and banks to credit card users. When you use your credit card, you are borrowing funds from the credit card issuer for a period ranging from several days to several months, if you choose to maintain a credit card account balance on which you pay interest.

**The Importance of the Concept of Debt** Take out a dollar bill, which is a Federal Reserve note. This note is really an IOU—a type of debt. Indeed, in the past, dollar bills used to say that they were exchangeable for an equivalent amount of a precious metal. Not so today. If you take your dollar bill—which is an IOU—to a Federal Reserve bank and ask to collect on this debt, you will find that it is uncollectible (although they will give another dollar bill).

✦ **Note!** *The concept of debt cannot be divorced from the mirror concept of credit. That is to say, for every dollar in debt there must be a dollar in credit.*

All types of fiduciary money today are really forms of debt. We accept them because we know we can exchange them for goods and services—they are acceptable in exchange. For a checking account, you have a certain balance. This balance on your checking account is a debt of the bank.

## A Broader Definition of Money—M2

**Near moneys**
*Assets, such as savings account balances, that can be turned into money relatively easily and without the risk of loss of value.*

M1 includes liquid assets available to the general public. Nonetheless, other financial assets may be converted quickly into cash. These other financial assets are called **near moneys** because although they cannot be used in transactions, they are very liquid. Consequently, a broader definition of the money supply is M2, which is equal to M1 plus the following:

1. Savings deposits and money market deposit accounts at depository institutions.
2. Small-denomination time deposits at depository institutions.
3. Funds held by individuals in money market mutual funds.

**Savings deposits**
*Interest-bearing savings accounts without set maturities.*

**Money market deposit accounts**
*Savings accounts with limited check-writing privileges.*

**Small-denomination time deposits**
*Deposits with set maturities and denominations of less than $100,000.*

**Savings Deposits and Money Market Deposit Accounts** **Savings deposits** are interest-bearing deposits without set maturities. **Money market deposit accounts** are savings accounts that permit limited check-writing privileges.

**Small-Denomination Time Deposits** Time deposits have set maturities, meaning that the holder must keep the funds on deposit for a fixed length of time to be guaranteed a negotiated interest return. **Small-denomination time deposits** have denominations less than $100,000. A variety of small-denomination time deposits are available, including six-month money market certificates of deposit (CDs) and CDs with two to four years' maturity.

**Money market mutual funds**
*Pools of funds from savers that managing firms use to purchase short-term financial assets such as Treasury bills.*

**Money Market Mutual Funds** Many financial companies today offer **money market mutual funds**, which are pools of funds from savers that managing firms use to purchase short-term financial assets, such as Treasury bills and large CDs issued by depository financial institutions such as banks.

**Comparing the Growth of M1 and M2** M2 currently is about four times larger than M1. Indeed, savings and money market accounts together are twice as large as M1. You can see the growth of M1 and M2 compared in Figure 13-2.

**Mastering Concepts:** How We Define the Money Supply in Circulation

- **M1, the narrowest definition of the money supply, includes paper currency and coins, all checkable deposits, and traveler's checks.**
- **The broader definition of money, called M2, includes M1 plus numerous other types of account balances, such as savings and time deposits and money market mutual fund balances, plus other specialized accounts.**

## THE FEDERAL RESERVE SYSTEM—OUR CENTRAL BANK

**Fed**
*The Federal Reserve System created by Congress in 1913 as the nation's central banking organization.*

The Federal Reserve System, also known simply as the **Fed,** is the most important regulatory agency in the U.S. monetary system. The Fed is usually considered the monetary authority—our central bank. The Fed was established by the Federal Reserve Act, signed on December 23, 1913, by President Woodrow Wilson. The act

Figure 13-2 Comparing the Growth of M1 and M2

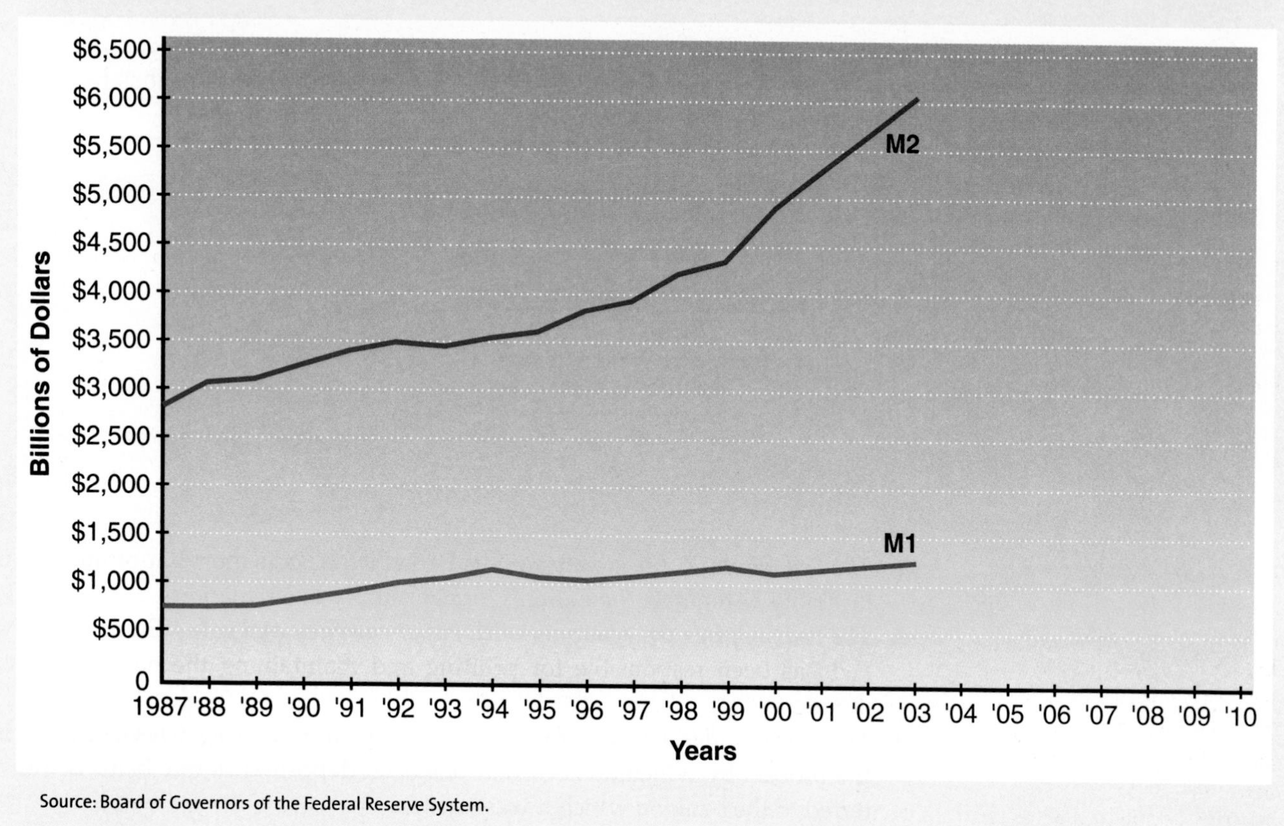


Source: Board of Governors of the Federal Reserve System.

was the outgrowth of recommendations from the National Monetary Commission. The commission had attempted to find a way to counter the periodic financial panics that had occurred in our country. Based on the commission's recommendations, which were developed after considerable study of the Bank of England and other central banks, Congress established the Federal Reserve System to aid and supervise banks and to provide banking services for the U.S. Treasury.

## Organization of the Federal Reserve System

Figure 13-3 on the next page shows how the Federal Reserve System is organized. The Board of Governors manages the Fed. This board is composed of seven full-time members appointed by the U.S. president with the approval of the Senate. The 12 Federal Reserve district banks have 25 branches. The boundaries of the 12 Federal Reserve districts and the cities in which Federal Reserve banks are located are shown in Figure 13-4 on page 280.

The Federal Open Market Committee (FOMC) determines the future growth of the money supply and other important economy-wide financial variables. This committee is composed of the members of the Board of Governors, the president of the New York Federal Reserve Bank, and presidents of four other Federal Reserve banks, rotated periodically.

✦ **Be Aware!** *The chairperson of the Fed is nominated by the president for a four-year term. By the time you read this, Alan Greenspan may be serving his fifth term.*

## The Federal Reserve System Has Many Functions

The Fed has a number of important functions. Without listing them all here, we present the most important.

## Figure 13-3 The Organization of the Federal Reserve System

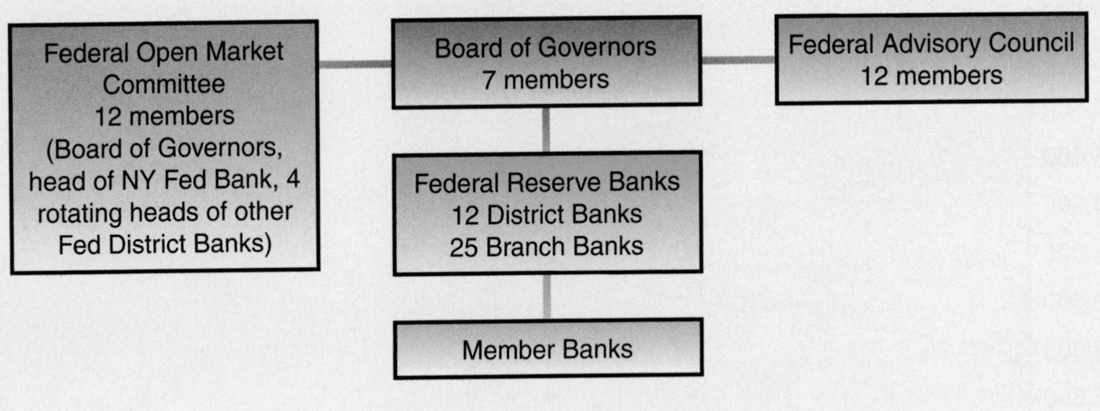


1. ***The Fed regulates the money supply.*** Perhaps the Fed's most important task is its ability to regulate the nation's money supply in circulation.
2. ***The Fed supplies the economy with paper currency and coins.*** Since 1914, the Fed has been responsible for printing and maintaining the nation's paper money.
3. ***The Fed provides a system for check collection and clearing.*** Check clearing is the process by which a check that has been deposited in one bank is transferred to the bank on which it was written.

## Figure 13-4 The Federal Reserve System

The Federal Reserve System is divided into 12 districts each served by one of the Federal Reserve district banks located in the cities indicated. The Board of Governors meets in Washington, D.C.

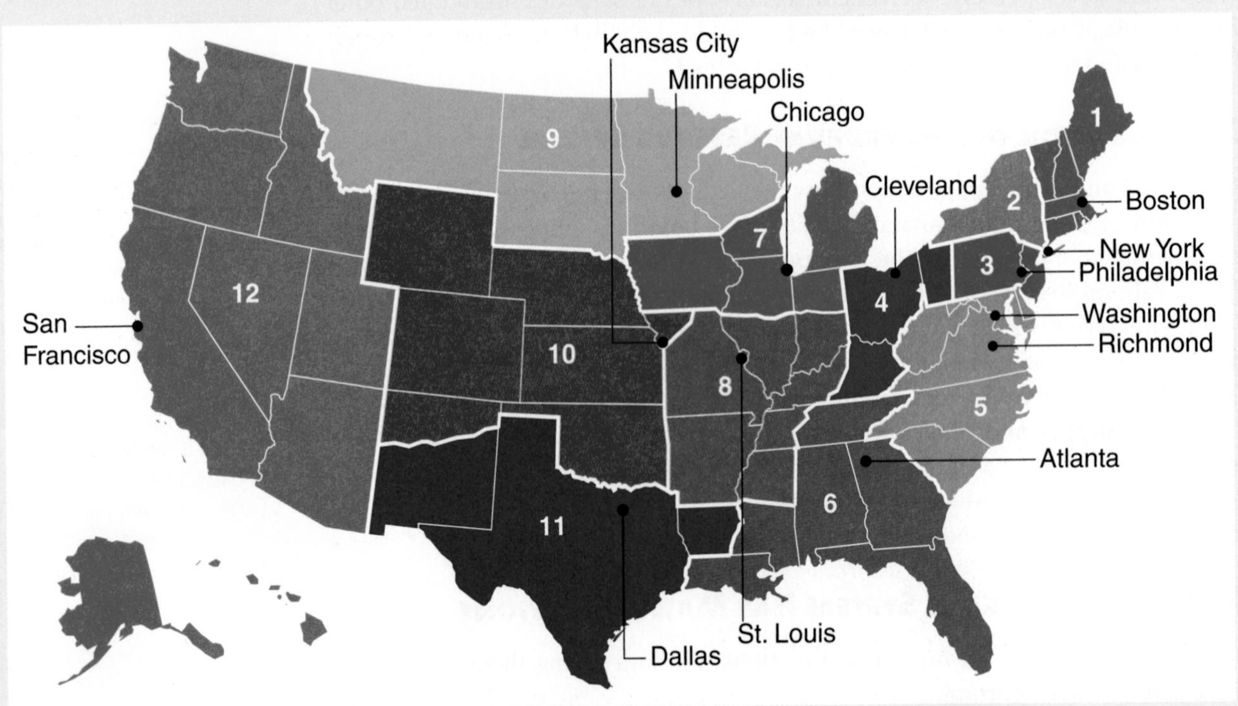

4. ***The Fed holds reserves for most of the nation's banks, savings and loans, savings banks, and credit unions.*** All depository institutions are required by law to keep a certain percentage of some of their deposits in reserve. They do so chiefly by keeping these **reserves** at the different Federal Reserve district banks. Reserves can be thought of as an IOU from the Federal Reserve bank to the depository institution that provides these reserves.

**Reserves**
*In the Federal Reserve System, deposits held by Federal Reserve district banks for depository institutions, plus depository institutions' vault cash.*

**Mastering Concepts:** The Federal Reserve System—Our Central Bank

- **Our monetary authority, or central bank, is the Federal Reserve System, often called the Fed.**
- **A Board of Governors manages the Fed. It consists of seven full-time members appointed by the president.**
- **The most important committee within the Fed is the Federal Open Market Committee (FOMC).**
- **Among its many functions, the Fed (1) regulates the money supply, (2) supplies the economy with paper currency and coins, (3) provides for check collection and clearing, and (4) holds reserves for the nation's depository institutions.**

## MONEY CREATION, RESERVES, AND THE MONEY MULTIPLIER

We just said that the most important function of the Federal Reserve System is to control the amount of money in circulation. Just how does it regulate the amount of money in circulation in our economy? That is what we explain now.

### FRACTIONAL RESERVE BANKING

Before you can understand how the Fed regulates the nation's money supply, you need to understand the basis of the U.S. banking system and the way money is created.

> ***The banking system is based on what is called* fractional reserve banking. *In other words, depository institutions do not keep 100 percent of their deposits on hand. Rather, they keep only a fraction of those deposits on hand as reserves.***

**Fractional reserve banking**
*A system in which a bank keeps only a fraction of its deposits on hand, or in reserve; the remainder is available to lend to borrowers or is otherwise invested.*

**Reserve requirements**
*Regulations set by the Fed requiring banks to keep a certain percentage of their deposits as cash in their own vaults or as deposits in their Federal Reserve district bank.*

Since 1913, the Fed has set specific **reserve requirements** for many banks. This means that they must hold a certain percentage of their total deposits either as cash in their own vaults or as deposits in their Federal Reserve district bank. Banks must hold these reserves by law. These are called *required reserves*. One of the reasons that banks are required to hold reserves is that this arrangement gives the Fed a way to control the money supply, as you will read shortly. Additionally, given that the Fed does not pay interest on required reserves, it is a way for the Fed to earn income. ▸ Example 13-7 Currently, most financial institutions in the United States must keep 10 percent of their checkable deposits as reserves with the Fed (but zero percent of other deposits). ◂

### THE EXPANSION OF THE MONEY SUPPLY

Currency is a small part of the money supply. A much larger portion consists of funds that the Fed and customers have deposited in banks. Because banks are not required to keep 100 percent of their deposits in reserve, they can use any newly created reserves to create what is, in effect, new money.

Assume that the Federal Reserve System—the Fed—wishes to increase the money supply in circulation. It typically does this by purchasing U.S. government securities in the open market. When it purchases them, the Fed simply writes a check on itself—it creates money that did not exist in the U.S. banking system prior to this purchase.

The U.S. securities dealer that receives the Federal Reserve check then deposits this check in a bank, which we will call Bank A. You can conceptualize the process now. Let's assume that the Fed purchased the U.S. government securities for $1,000. When the U.S. securities dealer deposits this Fed check with its bank—Bank A—that bank finds itself with a new deposit of $1,000. It has to keep legal reserves for only a portion of that, which we assume to be 20 percent. That means that Bank A has $800 in reserves that exceed its legal reserve requirement. It has $800 of what are called **excess reserves.** To understand how this sets off a chain reaction that ultimately increases the money supply by $5,000, carefully examine Figure 13-5.

**Excess reserves**
*Reserves held by a depository institution that exceed what is required by law; the difference between actual reserves and required reserves.*

## THE MONEY MULTIPLIER

In Figure 13-5, you saw that a $1,000 addition of new reserves into the banking system by the Fed led to a $5,000 increase in the money supply. This occurred because required reserves were only 20 percent of deposits. Also implicit was that

### Figure 13-5 Expanding the Money Supply

The chart shows how $1,000 in new reserves expands to $5,000 through simple loans.

In Round 1, the U.S. securities dealer deposits a check written on the Fed for $1,000 in Bank A. With a 20 percent reserve requirement, Bank A must hold $200 of the new deposit on reserve. This leaves the bank with $800 of excess reserves. Ms. Smith applies to Bank A for an $800 loan to buy a home cinema system. Bank A finds her creditworthy and credits her account with $800. Ms. Smith writes a check for $800 to Home Cinema.

In Round 2, Home Cinema deposits the check at Bank B. Bank B's reserves increase by $800. Of this amount, $160 (20 percent of $800) are required reserves, and the remaining $640 are excess reserves. Then, Bank B—to earn profits—loans its excess reserves to Ms. Wang, who wants to borrow $640. She, in turn, buys something from Mr. Portio, who does his banking at Bank C.

In Round 3, Mr. Portio deposits the check from Ms. Wang. Bank C now has $640 in new deposits, of which $128 are required reserves. Bank C now loans $512 of excess reserves to Mr. Rao, who buys something from Ms. Stevens, and so on.

| Round | Deposited by | Amount of Deposit | Required Reserves (20%) | Excess Reserves (80%) | Loaned to | Paid to |
|---|---|---|---|---|---|---|
| 1 | Dealer (Bank A) | $1,000.00 | $200.00 | $800.00 | Ms. Smith | Home Cinema |
| 2 | Home Cinema (Bank B) | $800.00 | $160.00 | $640.00 | Ms. Wang | Mr. Portio |
| 3 | Mr. Portio (Bank C) | $640.00 | $128.00 | $512.00 | Mr. Rao | Ms. Stevens |
| 4 | Ms. Stevens (Bank D) | $512.00 | $102.40 | $409.60 | Mr. Gibbs | Mr. Santana |
| 5 | Mr. Santana (Bank E) | $409.60 | $ 81.92 | $327.68 | | |
| | . | . | . | . | . | . |
| | . | . | . | . | . | . |
| | . | . | . | . | . | . |
| 6 | All others | $1,638.40 | $ 327.68 | | | |
| **Eventual totals** | | **$5,000.00** | **$1,000.00** | | | |

the $1,000 in new reserves created excess reserves that banks did not want to keep. Banks typically do not want to keep reserves over and above the legal requirement because banks earn no interest on reserves.

**The Money Multiplier Formula** We can now make a generalization about the extent to which the money supply will change when the banking system's reserves are increased or decreased by the Fed injecting new money into, or eliminating money (reserves) from, the banking system.

The **money multiplier** gives the change in the money supply due to a change in reserves brought about by the Fed's actions. If we assume that no excess reserves are kept and that all loan proceeds are deposited in depository institutions in the system, the following equation applies:

**Money multiplier**
*The reciprocal of the required reserve ratio, assuming no leakages into currency and no excess reserves. Its maximum value is equal to 1 divided by the required reserve ratio.*

$$\textbf{Potential money multiplier} = \frac{\textbf{1}}{\textbf{required reserve ratio}}$$

That is, the maximum possible value of the money multiplier is equal to 1 divided by the required reserve ratio for checkable deposits. ▸ **Example 13-8** In the example above, required reserves were 20 percent of deposits. Therefore, the required reserve ratio was 0.2. The maximum money supply multiplier equals $1 \div 0.2 = 5$. If the required reserve ratio fell to 0.1, the maximum money supply multiplier would increase to 10 (Why?). ◂

**Factors That Reduce the Actual Money Supply Multiplier** Two assumptions are implicit in the money supply multiplier presented above:

1. Banks do not keep any excess reserves.
2. There are no currency leakages out of the system. In other words, the entire loan (check) from one bank is always deposited in another bank. Nothing is taken out as currency.

**Mastering Concepts: Money Creation, Reserves, and the Money Multiplier**

- **With fractional reserve banking, depository institutions hold a small fraction of their total deposits as reserves in the form of vault cash or deposits in the Federal Reserve district bank.**
- **Currently, reserve requirements on checkable deposits are 10 percent for most banks.**
- **Because of fractional reserve banking, when the Fed adds to the money supply, there is a multiple increase in the total money supply.**

## E-MONEY EVENTUALLY WILL BE HERE TO STAY

When we discussed the money supply earlier in the chapter, we talked about various forms of money and near money ranging from currency and coins to money market mutual funds. Today, however, new forms of money are beginning to replace these traditional forms. We look at some of them here.

### SMART CARDS

**Smart cards**
*Cards with an embedded microchip that contains information that various machines can access and read; for example, European phone cards, which have a specific amount of phone-use units that are debited each time a phone call is made.*

One of the most important technological innovations in the banking system today is the development of **smart cards.** These are plastic cards containing minute computer microchips that can hold far more information than a magnetic stripe on normal credit cards.

Smart cards carry and process security programming. This makes them safer to use for both the issuers and the users. ▸ **International Example 13-9** Smart cards have been used throughout Europe for years. When you use a smart card, you have a personal code, usually four digits. When you make a purchase with the smart card, you put it into a machine that reads the computer chip. You then punch in your code. If the code does not match, the transaction is refused. (Only a few companies are starting to offer smart cards in the United States. American Express has its Blue Card, but very few merchants can use it as a veritable smart card.) ◂

In a smart-card-based system for e-money transfers, the user of a smart card can remain anonymous. There is also no need for online authorization using expensive telecommunication services. Each time a cardholder uses a smart card, the amount of a purchase is deducted automatically and credited to a retailer. The retailer, in turn, can store its electronic cash receipts in specially adapted point-of-sale terminals. At the end of each day, the retailer can transfer the accumulated balances to its bank via telephone links. This permits payments to be completed within seconds.

***Effectively, smart cards can do anything that paper currency and coins can do.***

## DIGITAL CASH

**Digital cash**
*Electronic money that exists on computer chips or other media.*

Today, the use of **digital cash,** sometimes called e-cash, which consists of funds contained on the computer software stored on microchips and other computer devices, promises to drastically reduce the nation's costs of transferring funds. It can do this because people can store and instantaneously transmit digital cash along preexisting electronic networks. People can keep digital cash on diskettes, compact discs, and hard drives. They can send digital cash payments along telephone lines, between cell phones, or over fiber-optic cables. Certainly, digital cash is still in the early stages of experimentation and adoption. Nevertheless, the use of digital cash promises to change the nature of money. It is just beginning to transform the world of banking.

Even though paper checks still dominate monetary transactions in the United States, things may be changing, as you will read in the following *E-Commerce Application*.

### E-COMMERCE APPLICATION: The Move Toward an Electronic Payment System

***Concepts Applied:*** **Currency, Debit Cards, E-Cash**

We do live in the electronic age. Internet use is growing rapidly worldwide. Strangely enough, though, much of the U.S. financial system still uses trucks and airplanes to move boxes of paper checks from bank to bank. In a world of electronic commerce, this is an anomaly, but it is changing.

#### Paper Check Use Already Peaked in the Late 1990s

The Federal Reserve reports that check use peaked sometime in the late 1990s. Credit and debit cards are now running a close second to check use. In 1979,

*Continued on next page*

these cards accounted for less than 10 percent of all transactions. Today, they account for well over a third.

Debit cards are a form of electronic money. When you use your debit card, all you receive is a statement. There are no canceled checks to hold. Everything consists of magnetic impulses or other types of records on electronic storage devices.

### Enter the World of Direct Deposit and Direct Payment

Various forms of electronic payment systems are also beginning to replace paper checks. Like smart cards, these systems were adopted faster in Europe than in the United States. Although direct deposit has been relatively well known throughout Europe for some time, Americans are only now getting used to electronic direct deposit of their Social Security benefits and payroll earnings. Little by little, U.S. consumers are paying certain routine bills, such as for electricity and telephone service, electronically, meaning that the customers' checking accounts are simply debited for the amounts. As these electronic payment systems become more widespread, the actual use of currency and checks will continue to fall.

### E-Cash on the Horizon

The use of currency and checks will decline even further when true e-cash becomes more popular. E-cash is simply the cash balances embedded in smart cards and computer hard drives that individuals eventually will be able to use. It will be particularly useful for payments for small items in retail outlets, such as drugstores and gas stations, and on the Internet.

**For Critical Analysis:**
*When you decide how much cash to hold relative to other assets, does it matter to you whether the cash is currency, in a checking account, or as a balance on a smart card or Internet-based cash account? Why or why not?*

## Mastering Concepts: E-Money Will Eventually Be Here to Stay

- **Smart cards differ from credit cards in that they contain a lot more information in a small computer chip.**
- **Smart cards can do anything that paper currency and coins can do.**
- **Digital cash consists of funds stored in computer devices and microchips.**

## SUMMING IT ALL UP

- The two functions of money are to serve as (1) a medium of exchange and (2) a unit of accounting.
- Money is the most liquid of assets in that it can be used to acquire goods and services under virtually all circumstances.
- Our monetary system is fiduciary, meaning that we place faith in our currency and checking accounts even though they have no intrinsic value.
- M1, the narrowest definition of the money supply, includes paper currency and coins, all checkable deposits, and traveler's checks.
- The broader definition of money, called M2, includes M1 plus numerous other types of account balances, such as savings and time deposits and money market mutual fund balances, plus other specialized accounts.
- Our monetary authority, or central bank, is the Federal Reserve System, often called the Fed.
- A Board of Governors manages the Fed. It consists of seven full-time members appointed by the president.

- The most important committee within the Fed is the Federal Open Market Committee (FOMC).
- Among its many functions, the Fed (1) regulates the money supply, (2) supplies the economy with paper currency and coins, (3) provides for check collection and clearing, and (4) holds reserves for the nation's depository institutions.
- With fractional reserve banking, depository institutions hold a small fraction of their total deposits as reserves in the form of vault cash or deposits in the Federal Reserve district bank.
- Currently, reserve requirements on checkable deposits are 10 percent for most banks.
- Because of fractional reserve banking, when the Fed adds to the money supply, there is a multiple increase in the total money supply.
- Smart cards differ from credit cards in that they contain a lot more information in a small computer chip.
- Digital cash consists of funds stored in computer devices and microchips.

## KEY TERMS AND CONCEPTS

barter **272**
checkable deposits **275**
depository institutions **276**
digital cash **284**
excess reserves **282**
Fed **278**
fiduciary monetary system **275**
fractional reserve banking **281**
liquidity **275**
medium of exchange **272**
money market deposit accounts **278**
money market mutual funds **278**
money multiplier **283**
money supply **277**
near moneys **278**
reserve requirements **281**
reserves **281**
savings deposits **278**
small-denomination time deposits **278**
smart cards **283**
thrift institutions **276**
transaction costs **273**
unit of accounting **274**

## MASTERING ECONOMIC CONCEPTS Questions and Problems

**13-1.** Name two functions of money.

**13-2.** Arrange the following items in order from most liquid to least liquid.

a. corporate stock
b. currency
c. automobiles
d. checking accounts
e. savings accounts

**13-3.** In a fiduciary monetary system such as ours, what backs the value of the U.S. dollar?

**13-4.** Name and briefly describe three types of thrift institutions.

**13-5.** Approximately what did M1 equal in 2003? Approximately what did M2 equal in 2003? Will M2 always be greater than M1? Why or why not?

**13-6.** How many people serve on the Federal Open Market Committee, and how are they selected? What are the responsibilities of the Federal Open Market Committee?

**13-7.** With fractional reserve banking, if the reserve requirement is 10 percent and a customer deposits $3,500, what amount of reserves is the depository institution required to hold? What amount of excess reserves is immediately created for that bank only?

**13-8.** If the reserve requirement is 12 percent, what is the maximum potential money multiplier?

**13-9.** If the money multiplier measures 8 and a foreign bank injects $4 billion into the U.S. banking system, what will be the total increase in the money supply including the initial $4 billion?

**13-10.** With a reserve requirement of 10 percent, by how much will the money supply increase if the Fed makes an initial deposit of $20,000 with a check written on itself?

**13-11.** Approximately what percentage of all transactions are currently completed using credit and debit cards? What percentage were completed using these means in 1979?

**13-12.** Do transactions conducted through a barter system require a coincidence of wants? Why or why not? Would a barter system likely increase or decrease the amount of tax revenues generated?

**13-13.** What are small-denomination time deposits? Are they included in M1? Are they included in M2?

**13-14.** Assume a reserve requirement of 15 percent. If George deposits $5,000 and the bank lends out $3,000 of this deposit, what amount of excess reserves remain in that bank only?

**13-15.** If a large amount of money is withdrawn from the U.S. banking system, will the money multiplier amplify this effect, or does the money multiplier apply only to *increases* in the money supply?

## THINKING CRITICALLY

**13-1.** The money multiplier is often referred to as a potential multiplier. That is, a money multiplier of 10 indicates that the money supply will increase or decrease by a *maximum* of 10 times the initial increase or decrease in reserves. In addition to excess reserves, what factor could cause the actual multiplier to be less than 10? Why would banks want to maintain excess reserves? What is their opportunity cost of maintaining excess reserves? Is the government spending or investment expenditure multiplier covered in Chapter 12 a *potential* multiplier or an *actual* multiplier?

**13-2.** Who appoints the seven full-time members of the Federal Reserve's Board of Governors? Who approves their appointment? These individuals serve 14-year terms. How does this compare to the terms for U.S. senators or for the president? The process of selecting Fed members is designed to ensure that the Fed remains independent of the political process in general. Why is this so important? What would happen to monetary policy if the Fed's Board of Governors were elected every two years in a general election?

**13-3.** When several bank customers rush to their bank at the same time to withdraw funds, the situation is known as a bank run, as depicted years ago in the Jimmy Stewart film, *It's a Wonderful Life*. Could such bank runs deplete the required reserves held by banking institutions? Would merely the threat of such a bank run pose a serious problem by itself? If we required that banks maintain reserves of 100 percent, would bank runs no longer be an issue? What new problem would a 100 percent reserve requirement create?

## LOGGING ON

1. To determine the latest trends in M1 and M2, go to http://www.federalreserve.gov/releases, and click on "Historical Data" next to "H.6: Money Stock Measures."
2. For more details about the structure, purposes, and functions of the Federal Reserve System, go to http://www.federalreserve.gov, and click on "About the Fed."
3. To learn more about network payment systems for transmitting digital cash, go to http://ganges.cs.tcd.ie/mepeirce/project.html.
4. For links to discussions of recent developments in smart card technology, go to http://www.smartcard.co.uk/.

## USING THE INTERNET FOR ECONOMIC ANALYSIS

**The Implications of Electronic Checking** In this chapter, you learned how policy actions of the Federal Reserve induce changes in total deposits in the banking system. Now let's think about Fed policymaking in a world with online checking.

**Title:** What is eCheck?

**Navigation:** Go to http://www.echeck.org/overview/what.html.

**Application** Read the discussion, and answer the following questions.

1. Are eChecks substitutes for currency and coins, or are they substitutes for traditional paper checks?
2. Does the answer to question 1 make a difference in how eChecks are likely to affect the manner in which an increase in reserves affects the total quantity of deposits in the banking system?

## MEDIA RESOURCE LIST

The following media resources are available with this chapter:

- Load your CD-ROM to listen to the audio introduction to this chapter.
- Load your CD-ROM to view the video on *Functions of Money*
- Load your CD-ROM to access a Graph Animation of Figure 13-1, *Degrees of Liquidity.*
- Load your CD-ROM to view the video on *Monetary Standards, or What Backs Money.*
- Load your CD-ROM to view the video on *Federal Reserve System.*
- Load your CD-ROM to view the video on *Depository Institution Reserves.*
- Load your CD-ROM to view the video on *Smart Cards and Digital Cash.*
- Test your knowledge of chapter concepts with a quiz at www.miller-ume.com.
- Link to Web resources related to the text coverage at www.miller-ume.com.

## HOMEWORK SET

Go to the back of this book to find the Homework Problems for this chapter.

# CHAPTER 14

# The Monetary Policy Approach to Stabilization

## *Facing an Economic Problem:* Why Do Interest Rates Sometimes Go Up During Periods of "Loose" Monetary Policy?

When the economy is slowing down or in a recession, the Fed (our monetary authority) engages in "loose" monetary policy by lowering "the" interest rate. Sometimes news reports say: "At its recent meeting, the Fed decided that the interest rate should be lowered by half a point."

In spite of such actions, at numerous times in this nation's history, the Fed has engaged in loose monetary policy, and the result has been higher, not lower, interest rates. This paradox is at first puzzling. After you learn more about monetary policy in this chapter, though, you will be able to understand this economic phenomenon.

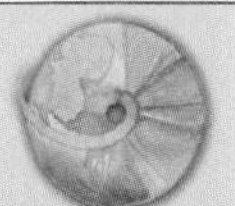

***Refer to the back of this chapter for a complete listing of multimedia learning materials available on the CD-ROM and the Web site.***

## Learning Objectives

After reading this chapter, you should be able to:

- **Explain how the Fed can create loose or tight monetary policies.**
- **List and explain the three traditional tools of monetary policy.**
- **Compare the direct versus the indirect effect of monetary policy on aggregate demand.**
- **Outline the relationship between the rate of growth of the money supply and the rate of inflation.**
- **Contrast the Keynesian and monetarist views of the transmission mechanism of monetary policy.**

## LOOSE AND TIGHT MONETARY POLICIES

In Chapter 12, you learned about one way for the federal government to stabilize nationwide economic activity—fiscal policy. In that chapter, you were able to use the tools of aggregate supply and aggregate demand to analyze fiscal policy. In Chapter 13, you learned about money and the banking system and how the Federal Reserve System can control the amount of money in circulation. In this chapter, you will examine the tools of monetary policy—the other type of stabilization policy available to the federal government. Again, you will examine some of these policies using aggregate supply and aggregate demand analysis.

You may have read a news report in which a business executive complained that money is "too tight." You may have run across a story about an economist warning that money is "too loose." In these instances, the terms *tight* and *loose* are referring to the monetary policy of the Fed.

> **Monetary policy** ***involves changing the amount of money in circulation in order to affect interest rates.***

Credit, like any good or service, has a cost. The nominal cost of credit is the nominal interest that must be paid to obtain it. As the cost of credit increases, the quantity demanded decreases. In contrast, if the cost of borrowing drops, the quantity of credit demanded rises.

**Loose monetary policy**
*Monetary policy that makes credit inexpensive and abundant, possibly leading to inflation.*

**Tight monetary policy**
*Monetary policy that makes credit expensive in an effort to slow the economy.*

Figure 14-1 shows the results of monetary policy decisions. If the Fed implements a **loose monetary policy** (often called "expansionary"), the supply of credit increases and its cost falls. If the Fed allows a **tight monetary policy** (often called "contractionary"), the supply of credit decreases and its cost increases.

A loose money policy is often implemented as an attempt to encourage economic growth. You may be wondering why any nation would want a tight money policy, however. The answer is to control inflation. As you will discover in this chapter, if money becomes too plentiful too quickly, prices and ultimately the price level increase—the purchasing power of the dollar decreases.

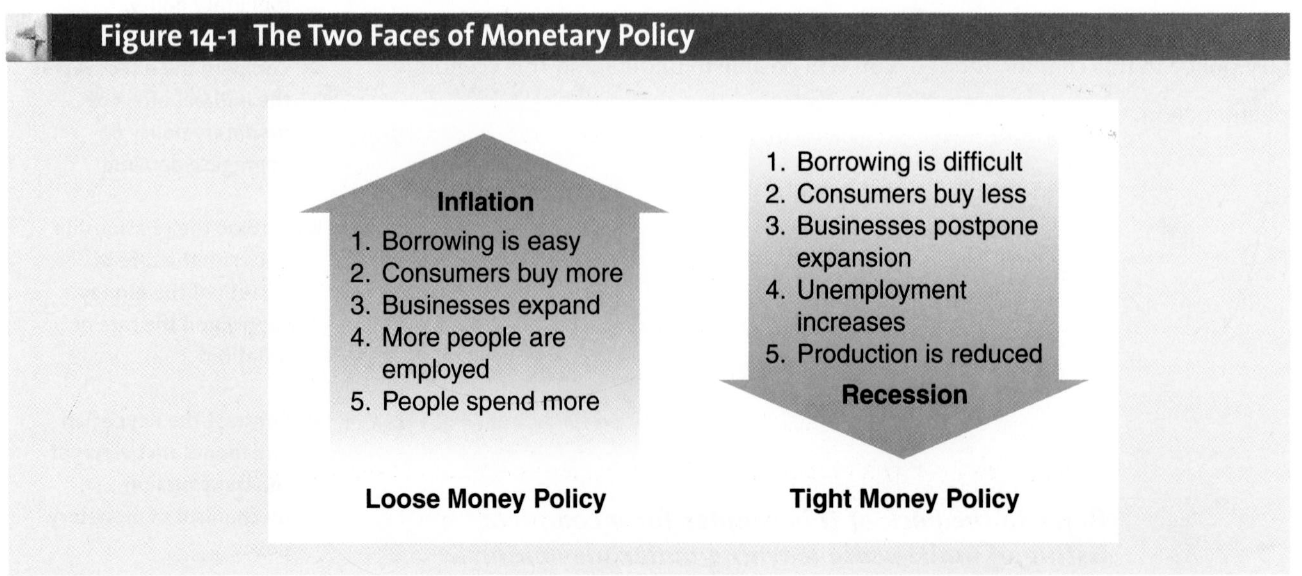

Figure 14-1 The Two Faces of Monetary Policy
Inflation
1. Borrowing is easy
2. Consumers buy more
3. Businesses expand
4. More people are employed
5. People spend more
Loose Money Policy
1. Borrowing is difficult
2. Consumers buy less
3. Businesses postpone expansion
4. Unemployment increases
5. Production is reduced
Recession
Tight Money Policy

"I told you the Fed should have tightened."

© Robert Mankoff. Reprinted by permission of Cartoonbank.com.

## *Solving the Economic Problem:* Why Do Interest Rates Sometimes Go Up During Periods of "Loose" Monetary Policy?

Whenever the Fed says that it is going to lower "the" interest rate because it wants to push the economy toward full employment, it is not really telling the whole truth. The only way the Fed can lower any interest rates is by expanding the money supply. In the short run, such expansion in the money supply can have the result of lowering interest rates.

In the long run, though, the story is quite different. Consistently increasing the money supply too much over a long period eventually leads to a higher rate of inflation. The interest rates that you see in the economy are *nominal* interest rates. They consist of two elements: the real interest rate plus the expected rate of inflation. If the Fed engages in loose monetary policy for a long enough period, the inflation rate will rise, and most people will come to anticipate this higher rate of inflation in the future. That means that nominal interest rates will rise. For example, during the early 1980s when the Fed was increasing the money supply very rapidly, nominal interest rates shot up to 20 percent for certain transactions. In the 2000s, with a low anticipated inflation rate, nominal interest rates remained relatively low.

**Mastering Concepts:** Loose and Tight Monetary Policies

- **When the Fed implements a loose, or expansionary, monetary policy, it creates a business environment in which the supply of credit increases and borrowing rates are low.**
- **When the Fed implements a tight, or contractionary, monetary policy, it creates an environment in which the supply of credit decreases and it is relatively expensive to borrow.**

## THE TRADITIONAL TOOLS OF MONETARY POLICY

The Fed has at its disposal a number of tools that it can use to engage in monetary policy. The most important tool is its ability to increase or decrease the money supply via **open market operations.**

**Open market operations**
*Buying and selling of U.S. Treasury securities by the Fed to affect the money supply.*

### CHANGING THE MONEY SUPPLY VIA OPEN MARKET OPERATIONS

Suppose that the Fed wants to change the supply of money in circulation. To do so, the Fed changes the amount of reserves in the banking system by its purchases and sales of government bonds issued by the U.S. Treasury. You learned about this process in Chapter 13 when we examined the money supply multiplier.

Briefly, the Fed can increase reserves in our banking system by writing a check on itself for purchases of government securities. Remember the example we used in Chapter 13 in which the Fed purchased $1,000 of U.S. securities from a U.S. securities dealer and paid for the securities with a check written on itself (i.e., new reserves were "created"—something only the Fed can do). The U.S. securities dealer deposited the check in Bank A, which then found itself with excess reserves.

> ***In a sense, the Fed can create new reserves (new money) out of "thin air." That is what gives it the power to change the money supply via open market operations.***

**Start Out in Equilibrium in the Bond Market** To understand how the Fed engages in open market operations, you must start out in an equilibrium in which everybody—including the holders of bonds—is satisfied with the current situation. There are therefore equilibrium levels of interest rates (and bond prices). Now, if the Fed wants to conduct open market operations, it must somehow induce individuals, businesses, and foreigners to hold more or fewer U.S. Treasury bonds. The inducement must be something that will make people better off.

> ***If the Fed wants to buy bonds, it is going to have to offer to buy them at a higher price than currently exists in the marketplace. If the Fed wants to sell bonds, it is going to have to offer them at a lower price than currently exists in the marketplace.***

Thus, an open market operation must cause a change in the price of bonds.

**Relationship Between the Price of Existing Bonds and the Rate of Interest** There is an *inverse* relationship between the price of *existing* bonds and the rate of interest. ▸ Example 14-1 Assume that the average yield on bonds is 5 percent. You decide to purchase a bond. A local corporation agrees to sell you a bond that will pay you $50 a year forever. What is the price you are willing to pay for the bond? It is $1,000—because $50 divided by $1,000 equals 5 percent, which is as good as the best return you can earn elsewhere. You purchase the bond. The next year something happens in the economy, and you can now buy similar bonds with an effective yield of 10 percent. (In other words, the prevailing interest rate in the economy is now 10 percent.) What has happened to the market price of the existing bond that you own, the one you purchased the year before? It will have fallen. If you try to sell the bond for $1,000, you will discover that no investors will buy it from you. Why should they when they can obtain the same $50-a-year yield from a bond that is selling for only $500 (i.e., a 10 percent yield)? Indeed, unless you offer your bond for sale at a price of $500, no buyers will be forthcoming. Hence, an increase in the prevailing interest rate in the economy has caused the market value of your existing bond to fall. ◂

The important point to understand is this:

> ***The market price of existing bonds is inversely related to the rate of interest prevailing in the economy.***

**Open Market Operations Again** What does all of the above explanation have to do with open market operations? When the Fed engages in open market operations, it goes into the open market for U.S. Treasury bonds. If it wants to buy some—expand the money supply—it has to offer a higher price. That means it bids up the price of all U.S. Treasury bonds, and hence the price of existing bonds in general. Because of the relationship just presented, this means that the prevailing interest rate in the economy will fall.

## Changing the Money Supply via Changes in the Discount Rate

When the Fed was founded in 1913, the most important tool in its monetary policy kit was the **discount rate,** which is the interest rate the Fed charges banks when they borrow reserves directly from the Fed. Occasionally, banks find that their reserve position falls below their required reserves. Consequently, they must borrow reserves (sometimes only for overnight). They can borrow the needed reserves directly from the Fed, and they then pay the Fed's discount rate. Alternatively, they can go to the **federal funds market,** which is a private market, made up of banks, in which banks can borrow reserves from other banks that want to lend them.

**Discount rate**
*The interest rate that the Fed charges on loans to member banks.*

**Federal funds market**
*A private market (made up of banks) in which banks can borrow reserves from other banks that want to lend them. Federal funds are usually lent for overnight use.*

**The Discount Rate Used to Be More Important** The Fed originally relied on the discount rate to carry out monetary policy because it had no power over reserve requirements. More importantly, its initial portfolio of government bonds was practically nonexistent and hence was insufficient to conduct open market sales. As the Fed has come increasingly to rely on open market operations, though, it has used the discount rate less frequently as a monetary policy tool—especially since the end of World War II.

**How Changes in the Discount Rate Affect Bank Behavior** An increase in the discount rate increases the cost of funds for depository institutions that seek loans from the Fed. That means that the price of one of their major lending inputs—the cost of money—has just gone up. Depository institutions pass at least part of this increased cost on to their borrowing customers by raising the interest rates they charge on loans.

Conversely, a reduction in the discount rate lowers depository institutions' cost of funds. Because of competition, they lower the rates they charge their customers for borrowing.

## Changing the Money Supply via Changes in Reserve Requirements

In the 1930s, Congress gave the Fed the authority to change reserve requirements. This was done to increase the Fed's ability to control the money supply. Nonetheless, the Fed rarely uses changes in reserve requirements as a form of monetary policy. Most recently it did so in 1992, when it decreased reserve requirements on checkable deposits to 10 percent. (At the same time, reserve requirements on noncheckable accounts—savings accounts, for example—were eliminated.) ▸ **International Example 14-2** Most countries in the European Union face reserve requirements of only 2 percent for both checkable accounts and savings accounts. In Japan, the requirement is even smaller—1.3 percent. In the United Kingdom, it is only 0.35 percent. Finally, depository institutions in Canada and New Zealand face no reserve requirements on checkable deposits. ◂

In any event, here is how changes in reserve requirements affect the economy.

**An Increase in Reserve Requirements** If the Fed increases reserve requirements, banks can now lend out less of every dollar of deposits. They must build up their reserves by reducing their lending. They induce potential borrowers to borrow less by raising the interest rates they charge on the loans they offer.

**A Decrease in Reserve Requirements** Conversely, when the Fed decreases reserve requirements, as it did in 1992, depository institutions will attempt to lend out their excess reserves. To induce customers to borrow more, depository institutions cut interest rates.

**Mastering Concepts:** The Traditional Tools of Monetary Policy

- **Monetary policy consists of open market operations, discount rate changes, and reserve requirement changes undertaken by the Fed.**
- **When the Fed sells bonds, it must offer them at a lower price. When the Fed buys bonds, it must pay a higher price.**
- **There is an inverse relationship between the prevailing rate of interest in the economy and the market price of existing bonds.**

## CHANGES IN THE MONEY SUPPLY MAY LEAD TO CHANGES IN AGGREGATE DEMAND

To show how monetary policy works in its simplest form, we are going to run an experiment in which you get to increase the money supply in a very direct way. Assume that the government has given you hundreds of millions of dollars in just-printed bills that you load into a helicopter. You then fly around the country, dropping the money out of the window. People pick it up and put it in their billfolds. Some deposit the money in their checking accounts. The first thing that happens is that people have too much money—not in the sense that they want to throw it away or burn it, but rather that they have too much money in relation to other things that they own. People can dispose of this "new" money, called cash, or money, balances, in a variety of ways.

## DIRECT EFFECT

The simplest thing that people can do when they have excess money balances is to go out and spend them on goods and services. Here we have a *direct* impact on aggregate demand. Aggregate demand rises because, with an increase in the money supply at any given price level, people now want to purchase more goods and services. In terms of the aggregate supply/aggregate demand analysis that you learned in Chapter 11, the aggregate demand curve shifts outward to the right.

## INDIRECT EFFECT

Not everybody will necessarily spend the newfound money on goods and services. Some people may wish to deposit some or all of this excess cash in banks. The recipient banks will now have higher reserves than they are required by law to hold. As you learned in Chapter 13, one thing that banks can do with excess reserves is to lend then out in order to earn interest.

✦ **Remember!** *Any change in a non-price-level variable in the economy will cause the aggregate demand curve to shift inward or outward. An increase in the growth rate of the supply of money in circulation will cause the aggregate demand curve to shift outward to the right.*

But banks cannot induce people to borrow more funds than they were borrowing before unless the banks lower the interest rate that they charge on loans. This lower interest rate encourages people to take out new loans. Businesses will engage in new investment with the borrowed funds. Individuals will purchase more durable goods such as housing, autos, and home entertainment centers. Either way, the increased loans will create a rise in aggregate demand. More people will be spending more, even those who did not pick up any of the money you originally dropped out of your helicopter.

The conclusion must be that an increase in the money supply can lead to an increase in aggregate demand in an *indirect* manner, as well as in the direct manner discussed above. (Beware, though, that excessively increasing the money supply in circulation can also lead to undesired rates of inflation, as you will read about next.)

## USING AGGREGATE SUPPLY/AGGREGATE DEMAND ANALYSIS

When the direct and indirect effects of changes in the money supply are combined, there will always be a change in aggregate demand and, consequently, a change in the equilibrium level of real GDP and the price level.

**Expansionary Monetary Policy** Look at Figure 14-2 on the next page. There you see the initial equilibrium of the economy at the intersection of $AS$ and $AD_1$. It is at price level $P_1$ and real GDP per year of $Y_1$. After expansionary monetary policy, the aggregate demand curve shifts outward to the right to $AD_{\text{expansionary monetary policy}}$. The equilibrium level of real GDP per year increases to $Y_2$. The price level also rises to $P_2$.

**Contractionary Monetary Policy** Obviously, the reverse situation occurs when the Fed engages in contractionary monetary policy. The Fed does this by taking money out of the banking system. The Fed sells U.S. government securities to the private sector. The funds that it receives stay within the Fed, so they are taken out of public circulation. There is a multiple reduction in the money supply in circulation as a consequence. The result is that aggregate demand is reduced.

**Figure 14-2 Graphing Expansionary Monetary Policy**

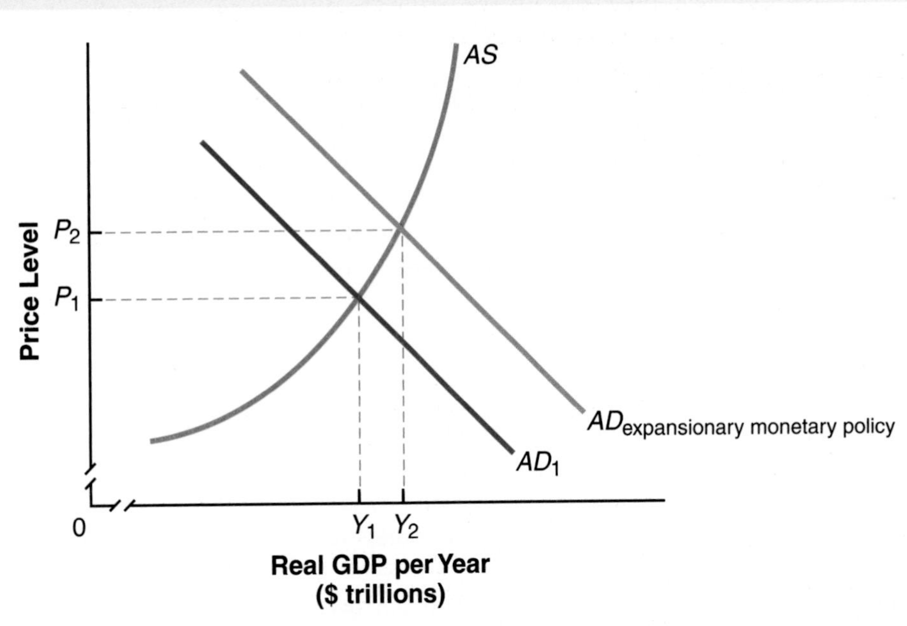


The initial equilibrium is at the intersection of $AD_1$ and $AS$, at an equilibrium level of real GDP of $Y_1$. After expansionary monetary policy, the aggregate demand curve shifts outward to $AD_{\text{expansionary monetary policy}}$, and the equilibrium level of real GDP rises to $Y_2$.

You can see this in Figure 14-3. There you see the initial equilibrium at the intersection of $AD_{\text{"overheated"}}$ and $AS$ at a real GDP per year of $Y_1$. Contractionary monetary policy shifts the aggregate demand curve leftward to $AD_{\text{contractionary monetary policy}}$. The equilibrium level of real GDP falls to $Y_2$ and the price level falls to $P_2$.

**Figure 14-3 Graphing Contractionary Monetary Policy**

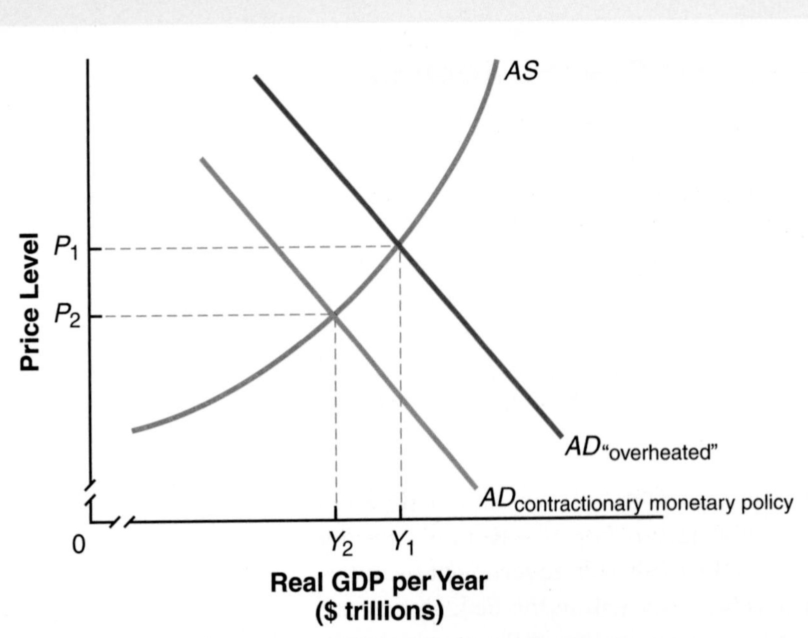

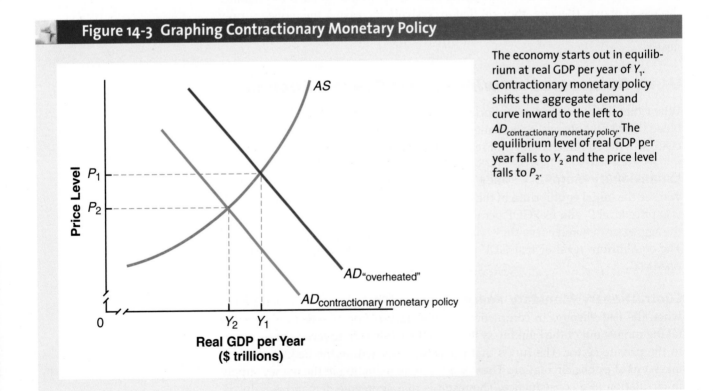

The economy starts out in equilibrium at real GDP per year of $Y_1$. Contractionary monetary policy shifts the aggregate demand curve inward to the left to $AD_{\text{contractionary monetary policy}}$. The equilibrium level of real GDP per year falls to $Y_2$ and the price level falls to $P_2$.

▸ **Example 14-3** The Great Depression during the 1930s was one of the most disastrous episodes in this nation's economic history. An examination of the money supply during that period reveals that the Federal Reserve System engaged, whether by design or not, in extremely contractionary monetary policy. During the Great Depression, the money supply in circulation dropped by fully one-third! This is probably the largest reduction in the money supply during a few-year period that has ever occurred in the United States. Certainly, the result was a decrease in aggregate demand. ◂

## Monetary Policy, Production, and Unemployment

You just saw in Figure 14-2 on page 296 that expansionary monetary policy could lead to an increase in the equilibrium level of real GDP per year. This has implications in the short run for the business cycle that you learned about in Chapter 10. During the trough of business cycles—recessions—the Federal Reserve System is expected to engage in expansionary monetary policy to shorten the length of the recession. In other words, politicians and the public often ask the Fed to "get us out of this mess." The "mess" typically means too much unemployment.

▸ **Example 14-4** The economy went into a recession at the beginning of the 2000s. When Alan Greenspan, the chair of the Federal Reserve System, testified before Congress, he was constantly grilled about what the Fed was "going to do" to help the economy reduce unemployment. In fact, the Fed did engage in "loose," or expansionary, monetary policy during the early 2000s. Apparently, though, the Fed was not as aggressive as the members of Congress wanted it to be. Moreover, the rate of unemployment remained above 6 percent even during the recovery phase of the business cycle in 2002 to 2004. ◂

In any event, as you will read later in this chapter, some economists believe that monetary policy can affect the equilibrium level of real GDP only in the short run, not in the long run. These economists believe that the Fed's monetary policy has its main impact on the rate of inflation.

**Mastering Concepts:** Changes in the Money Supply May Lead to Changes in Aggregate Demand

- **The direct effect of changes in the money supply is that people purchase more output because they have more money balances than they desire.**
- **The indirect effect of changes in the money supply occurs when monetary policy leads to changes in interest rates, which then lead to changes in desired borrowing by individuals and businesses.**

## MONETARY POLICY AND INFLATION

In the short run, many factors can affect inflation. The price index can fluctuate in the short run because of events such as abrupt oil price changes, labor union strikes, or discoveries of large amounts of new natural resources.

> ***In the long run, however, empirical studies show that "money matters." That is, in the long run, there is a relatively stable relationship between excess growth in the money supply and inflation.***

## Using Supply and Demand for Money Analysis

Supply and demand can explain why the price level rises when the money supply is increased. Consider what happens in general when the supply of something increases. Suppose that a major oil discovery is made, for example, and the supply of oil increases dramatically relative to the demand for oil. The relative price of oil will fall; that is, more units of oil will now be needed in exchange for specific quantities of non-oil products.

> ✦ **Recall!** *When demand is constant, but supply increases, the equilibrium price falls. Thus, when the demand for money remains the same while the supply of money increases, the price of money falls. The price of money is its purchasing power. So, an increase in the supply of money leads to a fall in purchasing power—inflation.*

Similarly, if the supply of money rises relative to the demand for money by the public—mainly households and businesses—it will take more units of money to purchase specific quantities of goods and services. That is merely another way of stating that the price level has increased or that the purchasing power of money has fallen. In fact, some economists in the past said that inflation was a consequence of more money chasing the same quantity of goods and services.

▸ **Example 14-5** Think of it this way. Assume that today the quantity of production is some level of real GDP and cannot be expanded—the economy is at its production limits. Assume further that there is a certain amount of money in circulation, say, $1 trillion. If all of a sudden the Federal Reserve System causes the amount of money in circulation to double to $2 trillion, an awful lot of people will find themselves with more money balances than they normally keep. They will start trying to buy things with those excess money balances. In our example, though, we assumed that the level of real GDP is fixed in the short run, so no more goods and services can be provided at this moment in time. The only thing that can happen is that people will bid up the prices of existing goods and services. The price level will have to rise. ◂

▸ **International Example 14-6** There is considerable evidence of the empirical validity of the relationship between high monetary growth and high rates of inflation. Figure 14-4 tracks the correspondence between money supply growth and the rates of inflation in various countries around the world. ◂

## Distinguishing Between the Long Run and the Short Run

Some of the above analysis has referred to the relationship between the rate of growth of the money supply and the rate of inflation in the long run. The distinction between the short run and the long run is important here. The short run may be considered a period of several months to a year or so. The price level may change up or down during the short run. In the long run—over several years—the price level may change quite differently than it does in the short run.

**Short-Run Inflation Rates Are Hard to Predict** In the short run, the relationship between the rate of growth of the money supply and the rate of inflation is much more tenuous. Specifically, you will not succeed very well in predicting what the price level will be next month by looking at the rate of growth of the money supply this month or even last month or even the month before that.

You may remember from Chapter 10 that any price index is made up of the prices of a variety of goods and services. That means that the measured rate of inflation can change if an important good or service experiences an abrupt change in its price. ▸ **Example 14-7** The Organization of Petroleum Exporting Countries (OPEC) decides to severely cut back the production of oil. Consequently, the prices of oil and oil products, such as gasoline, skyrocket in a short period. Quite naturally, the measured rate of inflation will experience a spike, because the price of oil and oil products is an important part of our economy and therefore an important part of the price indexes we use to measure inflation. ◂

## Figure 14-4 The Relationship Between Money Supply Growth Rates and Rates of Inflation

If we plot long-run rates of inflation and long-run rates of monetary growth for different countries, we come up with a scatter diagram that reveals an obvious direct relationship. If you were to draw a line through the "average" of the points in this figure, it would be upward sloping, showing that an increase in the rate of growth of the money supply leads to an increase in the rate of inflation.

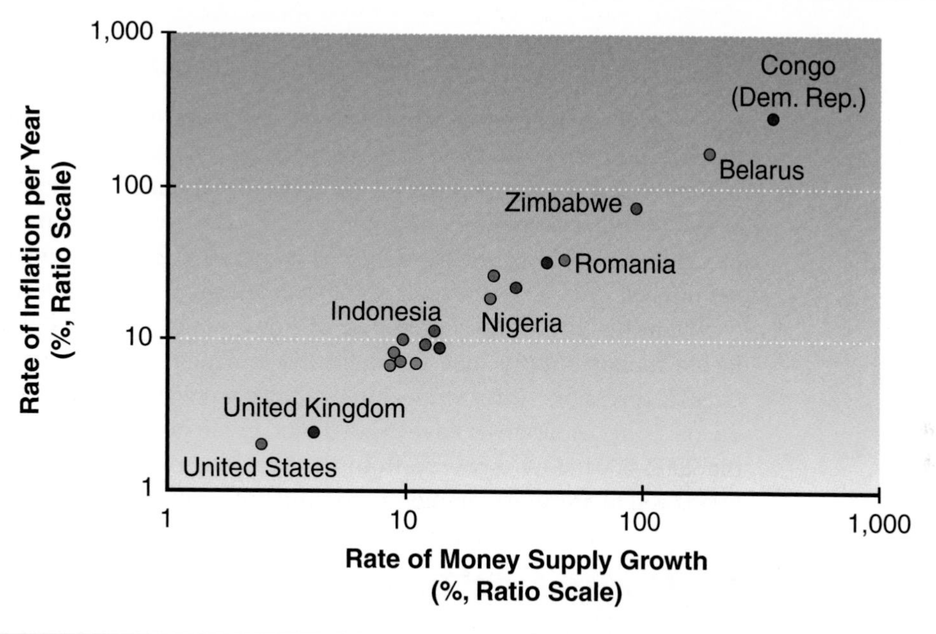


Sources: International Monetary Fund and national central banks. Data are for latest available periods.

**Examining Specific Price Changes Does Not Explain Inflation** Be careful, though. Simply observing that a few specific prices increased does not tell you much about the *causes* of long-term inflation. Moreover, inflation is always measured by changes in a set of properly weighted prices throughout the economy. Do not fall into the same trap as one less-than-astute U.S. president who said, "Inflation is caused by rising prices." That is equivalent to saying that a fever is caused by a high temperature—and is clearly not correct. Inflation is *measured* by the rate of change of some average of *all* prices. Ultimately in the long run, *inflation* is caused by excessive monetary growth.

**Mastering Concepts:** Monetary Policy and Inflation

- **In the long run, there appears to be a direct relationship between the rate of growth of the money supply and the rate of inflation.**
- **In the short run, many other factors besides monetary policy affect the rate of inflation.**

## MONETARY POLICY IN ACTION

Earlier in this chapter, we talked about the direct and indirect effects of monetary policy. The direct effect is simply that an increase in the money supply causes people to have excess money balances. To get rid of these excess money balances, people increase their expenditures. The indirect effect occurs because some people decide to purchase assets that earn interest, such as bonds, with their excess money balances. This causes the price of such assets—bonds—to go up. Because of the inverse relationship between the price of *existing* bonds and the interest rate, the interest rate in the economy falls. This lower interest rate induces people and businesses to spend more than they otherwise would have spent.

## The Keynesian Transmission Mechanism

One school of economists believes that the *indirect* effect of monetary policy is the more important of the two. These economists, typically called Keynesian because of their belief in Keynes's work, assert that the main effect of monetary policy occurs through changes in the interest rate. The Keynesian money transmission mechanism is shown in Figure 14-5. There you see that the money supply changes the interest rate, which in turn changes the desired rate of investment.

According to this interpretation of how monetary policy works, an increase in the money supply may be *in*effective during a severe recession, such as the Great Depression. At that time, interest rates were already quite low. ▸ **Example 14-8** Some economists have argued that, given how low interest rates fell during the 2002–2004 slow recovery from the previous recession, monetary policy may have been ineffective in increasing production and employment in the short run. ◂

## The Monetarists' Transmission Mechanism

**Monetarists**
*Supporters of the theory of monetarism, often linked with Milton Friedman.*

Another school of economists, the **monetarists,** contend that monetary policy works its way more directly into the economy. They believe that changes in the money supply lead to changes in equilibrium real GDP in the same direction in the short run.

The monetarist school of economic thought is usually associated with economist Milton Friedman, who wrote the book *A Monetary History of the United States* in 1963. In this book, he and his co-author, Anna Schwartz, showed how their research demonstrated the importance of money in the economy.

Their reasoning goes as follows: an increase in the money supply because of expansionary open market operations (purchases of bonds) by the Fed leads the public to have larger money holdings than desired. This excess quantity of money supplied induces the public to buy more of everything, especially more durable goods such as cars and houses.

If the economy is starting out at its long-run equilibrium rate of real GDP, there can be only a *short-run* increase in real GDP due to expansionary monetary policy.

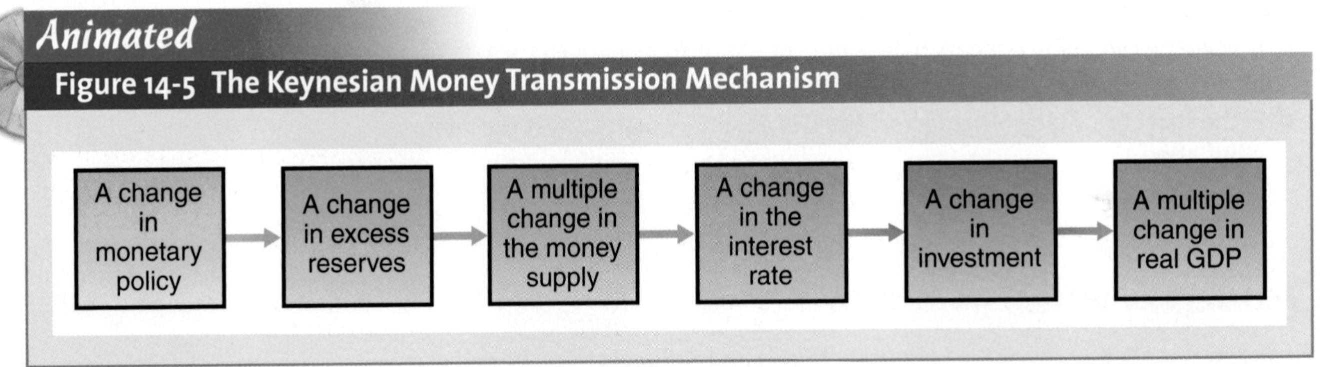


**Figure 14-5 The Keynesian Money Transmission Mechanism**

Ultimately, though, the public cannot buy more of everything; people simply bid up prices, so the price level rises.

## Criticism of Monetary Policy

The monetarists' belief that monetary policy works through changes in desired spending does not mean that they consider such policy an appropriate government stabilization tool. According to some monetarists, although monetary policy can affect output (and employment) in the short run, the length of time before money supply changes take effect is so long and variable that such policy is difficult to conduct.

**Time Lags Can Be the Real Killers** An expansionary monetary policy to counteract a recession may not take effect for a year and a half, and by that time inflation may be a problem. At that point, the expansionary monetary policy may end up making the then-current inflation worse. Some monetarists therefore see discretionary monetary policy as a possible *destabilizing* force in the economy. This may be borne out by the evidence until the 1990s, as you will read in the next *Policy Application.*

### POLICY APPLICATION: How Good Has the Fed Been at Countercyclical Monetary Policy Throughout Its History?

***Concept Applied:* Monetary Policy**

In the last half of the twentieth century and the beginning of the 2000s, the Fed has been viewed as the institution that makes monetary policy. Specifically, the Fed's job has been defined as smoothing out the ups and downs in nationwide business activity. That means that during recessions, the Fed is supposed to pump money into the economy, and during times of "overheating" and inflation, it is supposed to reduce the rate of growth of the money supply.

But how successful has the Fed been at its job? A look at the historical record tells the story.

#### The Fed's Historical Record Is Not a Pretty Picture

From the Fed's beginning in 1913 until the 1990s, the evidence is not too favorable. Researchers point out that on average the Fed's policies turned out to be procyclical rather than countercyclical. That is, by the time the Fed started pumping money into the economy, it was usually time to do the opposite. By the time the Fed started reducing the rate of growth of the money supply, it was usually time to start increasing it.

The Fed's biggest procyclical blunder occurred during the Great Depression in the 1930s. To be sure, a severe recession had begun, but many economists believe that the recession would not have become a depression had the Fed not acted so inappropriately. As mentioned before in this chapter, the Fed's policy actions at that time resulted in an almost one-third decrease in the amount of money in circulation, drastically reducing planned aggregate expenditures.

It has also been argued that the rapid inflation in the 1970s and early 1980s was largely the result of the Fed's increasing the money supply excessively fast.

#### The 1990s Were a Good Period for the Fed, Though

During the 1990s, the Fed's critics had to remain silent. They could not complain about monetary policy. Inflation had almost disappeared by the beginning of the 2000s. During the 1990s, the unemployment rate dropped to its lowest level in 40 years. That does not mean that all was rosy. Late in the decade, the Fed tightened monetary policy sharply, reducing monetary growth and thereby contributing to the recession that began in 2001.

So, will the Fed end up reverting to its procyclical ways, to the detriment of our economy? Only time will tell.

**For Critical Analysis:**
*Give some reasons why policymakers at the Fed might tend to make errors in monetary policy.*

**Time Lags for Short-Term Policies** Have you ever taken a shower, turned on the hot water, and had the water come out cold? Then, in frustration, you gave the hot water faucet another turn and were scalded? What happened was that there was a *lag* between the time you turned on the faucet and the time the hot water actually reached the showerhead. As Chapter 12 explained, policymakers concerned with short-run stabilization face several time lags:

1. **The Recognition Time Lag:** Before any policy can be made, policymakers need information on the *current* state of the economy—the rate of capital formation, the unemployment rate, changes in prices, and so on. Sometimes, however, accurate information about the *present* state of the entire economy is not available for months. In other words, due to the *recognition time lag,* we may not *recognize* that we are in a recession until, say, three to six months after it starts.

2. **The Action Time Lag:** Once it is discovered that the economy is indeed in a recession, time may elapse before any policy can be put into effect. But the action time lag for monetary policy is usually much shorter than for fiscal policy because the Federal Open Market Committee meets eight times a year and can relatively quickly put a policy into effect.

3. **The Effect Time Lag:** Even if there were no recognition or action time lags, there would still be an *effect time lag* because a change in an economic variable will not have an immediate impact upon the economy. A change in the rate of growth of the money supply may not have an effect for several months. Economists have spent considerable effort attempting to estimate the effect time lag. For monetary policy, the lag may range from only a few months to a year.

**Monetary rule**
*The monetarists' belief that the Fed should allow the money supply to grow at a smooth, consistent rate per year and not use discretionary monetary policy to stimulate or slow the economy.*

**One Alternative Monetary Policy—Following a Monetary Rule** According to some monetarists, policymakers should follow a **monetary rule:** Increase the money supply *smoothly* at a rate consistent with the economy's long-run potential growth rate. *Smoothly* is an important word here. Increasing the money supply at 20 percent per year half the time and decreasing it at 17 percent per year the other half of the time would average out to about a 3 percent annual increase, but the results would be disastrous, say the monetarists. Instead of permitting the Fed to use its discretion in setting monetary policy, monetarists would force it to follow a rule such as "Increase the money supply smoothly at 3.5 percent per year."

**Inflation targeting**
*Setting a specific annual rate of inflation that is desired. This rate is the only policy variable that the central bank has to worry about; the central bankers are then judged on how close they came to their target rate of inflation.*

**Another Alternative Monetary Policy—Inflation Targeting** Some countries have taken another policy route. They do not tell their central bankers to follow a monetary rule or to counter the business cycle. Rather, they tell their central bankers to engage in **inflation targeting,** which involves setting a goal, or target, for the measured rate of inflation. The target could be inflation of no more than 2 percent a year, for example. You will read about what some countries ask their central bankers to do in the following *Global Application.*

## GLOBAL APPLICATION: Inflation Targeting

***Concepts Applied:***
**Inflation, Central Banking**

While the Federal Reserve System has such vague goals as maintaining high employment, other nations' central banks have specific goals. Actually, they have one goal and one goal only—to target a specific inflation rate.

Australia, Canada, New Zealand, Sweden, and the United Kingdom have stopped attempting to engage in short-run efforts to stabilize economy-wide employment. Instead, these nations have adopted a policy approach called inflation targeting. The goal is to keep the actual rate of inflation very close to an announced target level.

### Two Success Stories—New Zealand and Canada

Before New Zealand adopted its inflation-targeting approach to monetary policy in 1990, its average annual inflation rate was more than 10 percent. Since then, the annual rate of inflation has been less than 2 percent.

In Canada, inflation rates reached as high as 14 percent in the early 1980s and hovered around 5 to 6 percent through the rest of that decade. Since Canada's central bank instituted inflation targeting, inflation rates have dropped to around 2 percent per year.

### The Policy Advantage of Inflation Targeting

One major advantage of inflation targeting is its transparency. That is to say, it is relatively easy to measure actual inflation rates and then compare them with the target rate specified by the central bank.

Moreover, inflation targeting—if successfully carried out—can provide a foundation for more consistent production and investment decisions by managers.

**For Critical Analysis:**
*Are there any benefits to you as a consumer to knowing that the inflation rate will remain stable?*

## THE WAY FEDERAL RESERVE POLICY IS CURRENTLY ANNOUNCED

No matter what the Fed has on its mind, the only way it signifies current monetary policy is by making announcements concerning an interest rate target. You should not be fooled, however. When the chair of the Fed states that the Fed is lowering "the" interest rate from, say, 3.75 percent to 3.25 percent, he really means something else. In the first place, the interest rate normally referred to is the **federal funds rate,** or the rate at which banks can borrow excess reserves from other banks. In the second place, even if the Fed talks about changing interest rates, it can do so only by actively entering the market for federal government securities (usually U.S. Treasury bills).

**Federal funds rate**
*The interest rate that depository institutions pay to borrow reserves in the interbank federal funds market.*

> ***If the Fed wants to lower "the" interest rate, it essentially must engage in expansionary open market operations. That is to say, it must buy more Treasury securities than it sells, thereby increasing the money supply. This tends to lower the rate of interest, at least in the short run.***

Conversely, when the Fed wants to increase "the" rate of interest, it engages in contractionary open market operations, thereby decreasing the money supply (or the rate of growth of the money supply).

**Mastering Concepts:** Monetary Policy in Action

- **The Keynesian monetary policy transmission mechanism involves the indirect effect of monetary policy. Monetary policy is transmitted through changes in interest rates, which change people's decisions about borrowing and spending.**
- **Monetarists believe most strongly that changes in the money supply have direct effects on planned aggregate demand.**
- **Like fiscal policy, monetary policy involves recognition, action, and effect time lags.**
- **An alternative to discretionary monetary policy is a monetary rule that allows the money supply to increase at a constant rate.**

## SUMMING IT ALL UP

- When the Fed implements a loose, or expansionary, monetary policy, it creates a business environment in which the supply of credit increases and borrowing rates are low.
- When the Fed implements a tight, or contractionary, monetary policy, it creates an environment in which the supply of credit decreases and it is relatively expensive to borrow.
- Monetary policy consists of open market operations, discount rate changes, and reserve requirement changes undertaken by the Fed.
- When the Fed sells bonds, it must offer them at a lower price. When the Fed buys bonds, it must pay a higher price.
- There is an inverse relationship between the prevailing rate of interest in the economy and the market price of existing bonds.
- The direct effect of changes in the money supply is that people purchase more output because they have more money balances than they desire.
- The indirect effect of changes in the money supply occurs when monetary policy leads to changes in interest rates, which then lead to changes in desired borrowing by individuals and businesses.
- In the long run, there appears to be a direct relationship between the rate of growth of the money supply and the rate of inflation.
- In the short run, many other factors besides monetary policy affect the rate of inflation.
- The Keynesian monetary policy transmission mechanism involves the indirect effect of monetary policy. Monetary policy is transmitted through changes in interest rates, which change people's decisions about borrowing and spending.
- Monetarists believe most strongly that changes in the money supply have direct effects on planned aggregate demand.
- Like fiscal policy, monetary policy involves recognition, action, and effect time lags.
- An alternative to discretionary monetary policy is a monetary rule that allows the money supply to increase at a constant rate.

## KEY TERMS AND CONCEPTS



## MASTERING ECONOMIC CONCEPTS
## Questions and Problems

**14-1.** If the Federal Reserve institutes a policy of "loose money," does this imply an increase or a decrease in the money supply? Does it imply an increase or a decrease in market interest rates in the short run?

**14-2.** Holding all else constant, if the money supply increases, what will happen to market interest rates in the short run? Why?

**14-3.** If the economy were experiencing severe inflation, would expansionary or contractionary monetary policy be more appropriate? Why?

**14-4.** What is a monetary rule, and how does it work?

**14-5.** What are open market operations? How would the Fed use open market operations to combat inflation? How would the Fed use open market operations to combat unemployment?

**14-6.** What is the discount rate? What is the federal funds rate?

**14-7.** At the point in time indicated on the graph below, what type of monetary policy should the Fed adopt if it wishes to counteract the change in the business cycle? What specific changes should be made in the three possible monetary policy tools?

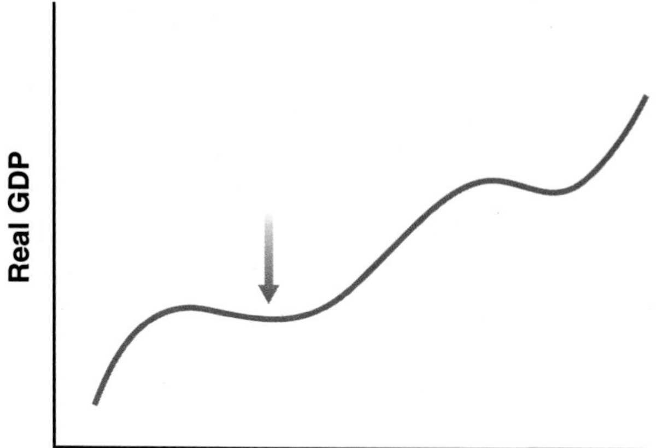


**14-8.** If the Fed wished to speed up the economy, would it increase or decrease reserve requirements? How would this action by the Fed serve to speed up the economy with respect to the money supply and interest rates?

**14-9.** Explain the difference between the direct and indirect effect of monetary policy.

**14-10.** If the Fed were to institute expansionary monetary policy by buying government securities and lowering the discount rate, what impact would these actions have on the equilibrium level of GDP? What would be the impact on unemployment? What would be the long-run impact on inflation?

**14-11.** Assuming that unemployment is the most significant problem in the economy, what should the Fed do with regard to each of the following policy tools?

a. open market operations
b. the discount rate
c. reserve requirements

**14-12.** If the economy is operating at $Y_A$ on the graph below, what general monetary policy action should the Fed take?

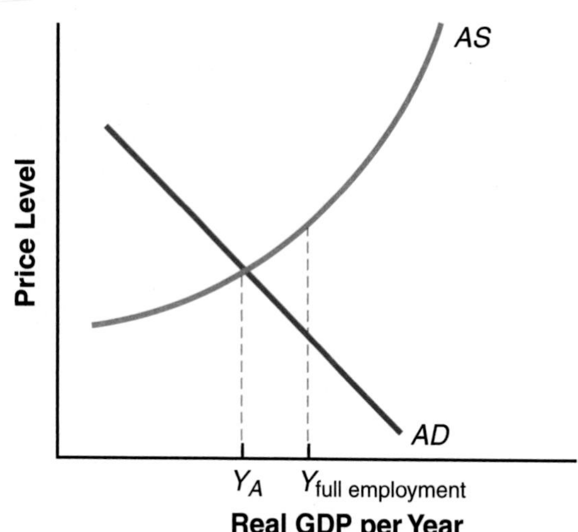


**14-13.** Would an increase or a decrease in the money supply cause inflation? Would an increase or a decrease in the demand for money cause inflation?

**14-14.** Based on changes in the money supply, which is easier to predict—short-run inflation or long-run inflation? Why?

**14-15.** What time lags exist with respect to monetary policy? How do these lags compare with the lags associated with fiscal policy? Are any of the monetary policy time lags shorter or longer than the corresponding lags for fiscal policy?

## THINKING CRITICALLY

**14-1.** The U.S. Treasury finances the federal debt by selling government securities such as U.S. Treasury bills at auction. The price is determined by a competitive bid method similar to other types of auctions. Assume that this year you buy a Treasury bill from the U.S. government for $900 that will pay you $1,000 in one year. The difference between the price and the repayment amount represents your interest for lending your money to the government. What interest rate does this arrangement imply? Assume that next year you buy a Treasury bill for $950 that also pays you $1,000 in one year. What interest rate is implied this time? Based on your previous answers, does a higher initial price imply a higher or a lower interest rate?

**14-2.** Generally, what must a bank do to earn money on its deposits? As you know from Chapter 13, banks are required to hold a portion of deposits on reserve. The difference between the actual reserves that a bank is holding and the required reserves is known as excess reserves. Why might a bank want to maintain at least some small amount of excess reserves? Banks do not frequently borrow money directly from the Fed, but they can use the Fed as a "lender of last resort." If the banks choose to do so, they will pay interest on any funds they borrow based on the discount rate. If the discount rate increases, would this make bank managers want to hold more excess reserves or less excess reserves?

**14-3.** Can the Fed change the discount rate simply by changing its policy, or does a change in the discount rate require that the Fed take action in the market for government securities? Can the Fed change the federal funds rate by a simple policy change, or would this change require that the Fed take action in the government securities market? In terms of open market operations, what should the Fed do if it wants to raise interest rates? What should the Fed do if it wants to lower interest rates?

## LOGGING ON

1. For a discussion of any of the Federal Reserve's primary tools of monetary policy, go to http://www.federalreserve.gov/policy.htm, and click on "Open market operations," "The discount rate," or "Reserve requirements."
2. To see a list of the main dealers with whom the Fed deals when it conducts open market operations, go to http://www.ny.fed.org, click on "News & Events," then click on "Open market Operations," and then click on "Latest."
3. To read the latest monetary policy testimony to Congress by the chair of the Federal Reserve's Board of Governors, go to http://federalreserve.gov/boarddocs/hh/.
4. For information about the current inflation target that the Reserve Bank of New Zealand is pursuing, go to http://www.rbnz.govt.nz/monpol/pta/index.html.

## USING THE INTERNET FOR ECONOMIC ANALYSIS

**Federal Reserve Policymaking** Central to the monetary policy approach to stabilization in the United States is the Federal Open Market Committee (FOMC), a policymaking body within the Federal Reserve System. This application focuses on factors that guide FOMC decisions.

**Title:** Minutes of the Federal Open Market Committee

**Navigation:** Go to http//federalreserve.gov, click on "Monetary Policy," and then click on "Federal Open Market Committee." Next, click on "Meetings calendar, statements, and minutes," and then click on "Minutes" for the most recent date.

**Application** Read the FOMC minutes, and answer the following questions.

1. What information does the FOMC consider when making its monetary policy decisions?
2. Based on the FOMC minutes, what, in your view, are the Fed's key monetary policy objectives?

## MEDIA RESOURCE LIST

The following media resources are available with this chapter.

- Load your CD-ROM to listen to the audio introduction to this chapter.
- Load your CD-ROM to access a Graph Animation of Figure 13-5, *The Keynesian Money Transmission Mechanism.*
- Load your CD-ROM to view the video on *Monetarists' Criticism of Monetary Policy.*
- Test your knowledge of chapter concepts with a quiz at www.miller-ume.com.
- Link to Web resources related to the text coverage at www.miller-ume.com.

## HOMEWORK SET

Go to the back of this book to find the Homework Problems for this chapter.

# CHAPTER 15

# How Economies Grow

## *Facing an Economic Problem:* Why Doesn't Foreign Aid Seem to Help Raise Living Standards?

You have just been put in charge of distributing foreign aid from the United States to various developing countries throughout the world. You decide to begin by looking at how past foreign aid grants have improved living standards in various countries. You are surprised to discover that there seems to be little relationship between foreign aid received by developing countries and the rate of improvement in living standards. Indeed, in one country living standards actually declined even though that country received more foreign aid per capita over a 20-year period than just about any other aid recipient. You cannot quite understand why foreign aid has not helped to improve the material way of life in certain developing countries. In this chapter, you will discover at least some of the reasons behind this anomaly.

## Learning Objectives

After reading this chapter, you should be able to:

- **Define economic growth.**
- **Explain why small differences in growth rates matter so much.**
- **Outline why saving is important for economic growth.**
- **Contrast inventions and innovations.**
- **Tell why improvement in secondary schooling is so important for developing nations.**

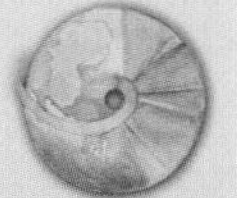

***Refer to the back of this chapter for a complete listing of multimedia learning materials available on the CD-ROM and the Web site.***

## HOW DO WE DEFINE ECONOMIC GROWTH?

In the previous chapters of this macroeconomic section of your text, you learned about the importance of aggregate demand and aggregate supply. In many chapters, you used *AD* and *AS* curves to examine the equilibrium level of real GDP per year. (Remember from Chapter 2 that real GDP is gross domestic product corrected for any price-level changes.) What happens over time to real GDP per year is as critical as what happens to it during the business cycle, which you learned about in Chapter 10. The growth in real GDP is often called economic growth.

You were already introduced to the concept of *economic growth* in Chapter 1. There you saw that economic growth could be represented by an outward shifting of the economy's production possibilities curve. Remember that the production possibilities curve represents the maximum output possible with a given amount of resources during a specified time. The speed at which the production possibilities curve shifts outward gives an indication of the rate of economic growth. That is a vague concept, though. We need to have some statistical measure that lets us know if a country's economy is growing.

### WE DO NOT JUST MEASURE GROWTH IN TOTAL OUTPUT

Most people have some idea of what economic growth means. When a nation grows economically, its citizens must be better off in at least some ways, usually in terms of their material well-being. We cannot measure the well-being of a nation, though, just in terms of *total* output of goods and services. We have to make some adjustments for the size of the population. ▸ **International Example 15-1** India's total national output is three times as large as that of Switzerland. India's population, though, is 125 times greater than that of Switzerland. Thus, when we take into account the amount of output that is available to the average person, we can conclude that India is a relatively poor country and Switzerland is a relatively rich country compared to each other. ◂

Clearly, we have to adjust our figures for population. We come up with a formal definition for economic growth.

> ***Economic growth occurs when there are increases in* per capita *output per unit time period, usually per year. Economic growth is measured by the annual rate of change in per capita real GDP.***

### THERE ARE PROBLEMS WITH OUR DEFINITION OF ECONOMIC GROWTH

**Distribution of income**
*The way income is allocated among the population.*

Our definition of economic growth does not say much about the **distribution of income** in a country. Some countries may grow very rapidly using our definition, but at the same time, the poor get poorer and the rich get richer. (Alternatively, a country may grow rapidly, and both the poor and the rich get richer—a scenario that has occurred in many countries, and certainly in the United States.)

Leisure is an important part of well-being, but our definition of economic growth does not take account of it. In other words, real living standards can go up even though economic growth remains zero. This can occur if we are enjoying more leisure by working fewer hours but producing as much as we did before. ▸ **Example 15-2** If per capita real GDP in the United States remained at $30,000 a year for a decade, we still might be better off. Assume that during that same ten-year period, we worked 33 hours a week instead of 40. That would mean the individuals in the labor force were consuming 7 hours more leisure a week. ◂

**Mastering Concepts:** How Do We Define Economic Growth?

- **Because some nations have larger populations than others and some nations' populations grow faster, we must correct increases in total national output by increases in population.**
- **Economic growth is measured by the rate of change in per capita real GDP.**
- **Sometimes a nation can grow economically even though the poor get poorer and the rich get richer at the same time. (But economic growth can also occur with both rich and poor getting richer.)**

## ECONOMIC GROWTH AND THE MAGIC OF COMPOUNDING

Some countries grow and others do not. You can see this in Table 15-1, which shows the annual average rate of economic growth in selected countries.

### SMALL DIFFERENCES MAKE FOR BIG CHANGES

The actual economic growth rates of the countries shown in Table 15-1 may not appear to be very different from each other. You may be asking yourself, what's the big deal? Why does it matter that the United States is growing at 2.4 percent and Germany is growing at 2.1 percent? We usually do not worry about such small differences in the real world, do we?

You are right. We usually do not care about such small differences—*if* they apply for only a brief period. But economic growth happens year in and year out.

> ***A small difference in the rate of economic growth may not matter for next year or the year after, but it surely does matter over longer periods.***

**Table 15-1 Per Capita Growth Rates in Various Countries**

| Country | Average Annual Rate of Growth of Income Per Capita, 1980–2003 (%) |
|---|---|
| Switzerland | 1.4 |
| Netherlands | 1.7 |
| France | 2.0 |
| Germany | 2.1 |
| Sweden | 2.2 |
| Canada | 2.2 |
| Italy | 2.4 |
| United States | 2.4 |
| Spain | 2.7 |
| United Kingdom | 2.9 |
| Turkey | 3.5 |
| Japan | 3.7 |
| China | 8.8 |

*Sources: World Bank; International Monetary Fund.*

**Compounding**
*Computing interest on the principal and accrued interest; in other words, earning interest on interest.*

It all has to do with the power of **compounding.** Compound interest is something to behold. ▸ Example 15-3 In 1626, Dutchman Peter Minuit arrived in Manhattan, charged by the West India Company with the task of administering the struggling colony. Minuit purchased Manhattan Island from Native Americans for the now legendary price of 60 guilders, or about $20. Some argue that he "stole" Manhattan because the price paid was so low. That $20 compounded at 6 percent would equal about $130 billion today, and at 7 percent it would be about $5.8 *trillion* today. ◂

## Putting It All in a Table

Look at Table 15-2. There you see $1 compounded annually at different interest rates. Although this table may seem a little abstract, it is a powerful tool for predicting what will happen in the future. ▸ Example 15-4 Let us see what happens with three different annual rates of growth: 3 percent, 4 percent, and 5 percent. We start with $1 trillion per year of U.S. GDP at some time in the past. We then compound this $1 trillion, or allow it to grow, into the future at these three different growth rates. The resulting difference is huge. In 50 years, $1 trillion per year becomes $4.38 trillion per year if compounded at 3 percent per year. Just one percentage point more in the growth rate, a move to 4 percent, results in a GDP of

**Table 15-2 One Dollar Compounded Annually at Different Interest Rates**

Here we show the value of a dollar at the end of a specified period during which it has been compounded annually at a specified interest rate. For example, if you took $1 today and invested it at 5 percent per year, it would yield $1.05 at the end of one year. At the end of 10 years, it would equal $1.63, and at the end of 50 years, it would equal $11.50.

| | Interest Rate | | | | | | |
|---|---|---|---|---|---|---|---|
| Number of Years | 3% | 4% | 5% | 6% | 8% | 10% | 20% |
| 1 | 1.03 | 1.04 | 1.05 | 1.06 | 1.08 | 1.10 | 1.20 |
| 2 | 1.06 | 1.08 | 1.10 | 1.12 | 1.17 | 1.21 | 1.44 |
| 3 | 1.09 | 1.12 | 1.16 | 1.19 | 1.26 | 1.33 | 1.73 |
| 4 | 1.13 | 1.17 | 1.22 | 1.26 | 1.36 | 1.46 | 2.07 |
| 5 | 1.16 | 1.22 | 1.28 | 1.34 | 1.47 | 1.61 | 2.49 |
| 6 | 1.19 | 1.27 | 1.34 | 1.41 | 1.59 | 1.77 | 2.99 |
| 7 | 1.23 | 1.32 | 1.41 | 1.50 | 1.71 | 1.94 | 3.58 |
| 8 | 1.27 | 1.37 | 1.48 | 1.59 | 1.85 | 2.14 | 4.30 |
| 9 | 1.30 | 1.42 | 1.55 | 1.68 | 2.00 | 2.35 | 5.16 |
| 10 | 1.34 | 1.48 | 1.63 | 1.79 | 2.16 | 2.59 | 6.19 |
| 20 | 1.81 | 2.19 | 2.65 | 3.20 | 4.66 | 6.72 | 38.30 |
| 30 | 2.43 | 3.24 | 4.32 | 5.74 | 10.00 | 17.40 | 237.00 |
| 40 | 3.26 | 4.80 | 7.04 | 10.30 | 21.70 | 45.30 | 1,470.00 |
| 50 | 4.38 | 7.11 | 11.50 | 18.40 | 46.90 | 117.00 | 9,100.00 |

$7.11 trillion per year in 50 years, almost double the previous amount. Two percentage points' difference in the growth rate—5 percent per year—results in a GDP of $11.5 trillion per year in 50 years, or nearly three times as much. ◂

As this example shows, very small differences in annual growth rates lead to great differences in economic growth. That is why countries are concerned if their growth rates fall even a little bit.

To make this clear, think again about economic growth rates. We are really talking about compounding. In Table 15-2, we show how $1 compounded annually grows at different interest rates. We see in the 3 percent column that $1 grows to $4.38 in 50 years. We merely multiplied $1 trillion times 4.38 to get the growth figure in our earlier example. In the 5 percent column, $1 grows to $11.50 after 50 years. Again, we multiplied $1 trillion times 11.50 to get the growth figure for 5 percent in the example.

▸ **Example 15-5** From 1872 to the present, the U.S. economy grew at an average annual rate of 1.75 percent. If the growth rate had been just one point higher—2.75 percent per year—each of us today would be earning about three times more than we actually do, or over $120,000 per year. ◂

**Mastering Concepts:** Economic Growth and the Magic of Compounding

- **Small differences in economic rates of growth over the long run create large differences in standards of living.**
- **The process of compounding is the reason that small differences in growth rates (or interest rates) matter.**
- **An increase of one percentage point in the rate of economic growth over this nation's history would have led to three times our current standard of living.**

## SAVING: AN IMPORTANT DETERMINANT OF ECONOMIC GROWTH

Economic growth does not occur in a vacuum. It is not some predetermined fate of a nation. Rather, economic growth depends on certain fundamental factors. One of the most important factors that affect the rate of economic growth and hence long-term living standards is the rate of saving.

### A Basic Economic Growth Proposition

A basic proposition in economics is that if you want more tomorrow, you have to consume less today.

> ***To have more consumption in the future, you have to consume less today and save the difference between your consumption and your after-tax income.***

On a national basis, this implies that higher saving rates eventually mean higher living standards in the long run, all other things held constant.

Concern has been growing that Americans are not saving enough; in other words, our rate of saving may be too low. Saving is important for economic growth because if all income is consumed each year, nothing is left over for saving, which could be used by business for investment. If there is no investment in our capital stock, we have little hope of economic growth.

✦ **Be Aware!** *Consumers are not the only ones who can add to a nation's saving activity. Governments that run surpluses add to saving activity, too, as can private companies.*

Remember from Chapter 11 that aggregate demand is the sum of consumption spending, spending by businesses on investment, government spending, and net exports. Investment spending is, therefore, an integral part of total planned expenditures in the economy. We saw in that chapter and in later chapters that changes in business investment spending can lead to a multiple change in the equilibrium level of real GDP per year. An increasing equilibrium level of real GDP per year is, of course, economic growth.

## Comparing Saving Rates and Growth Rates Worldwide

The relationship between the rate of saving and per capita real GDP is shown in Figure 15-1. Among the nations with the highest rates of saving are Japan and Germany. Until recently, they had relatively higher rates of growth than the United States.

**Mastering Concepts:** Saving: An Important Determinant of Economic Growth

- **Because investment requires saving, saving is an important determinant of economic growth.**
- **In general, nations that have had high rates of saving have experienced greater economic growth rates than those that have not.**

**Figure 15-1 Relationship Between Rate of Saving and Per Capita Real GDP**

This diagram shows the relationship between per capita real GDP and the rate of saving, expressed as the average share of annual real GDP saved.

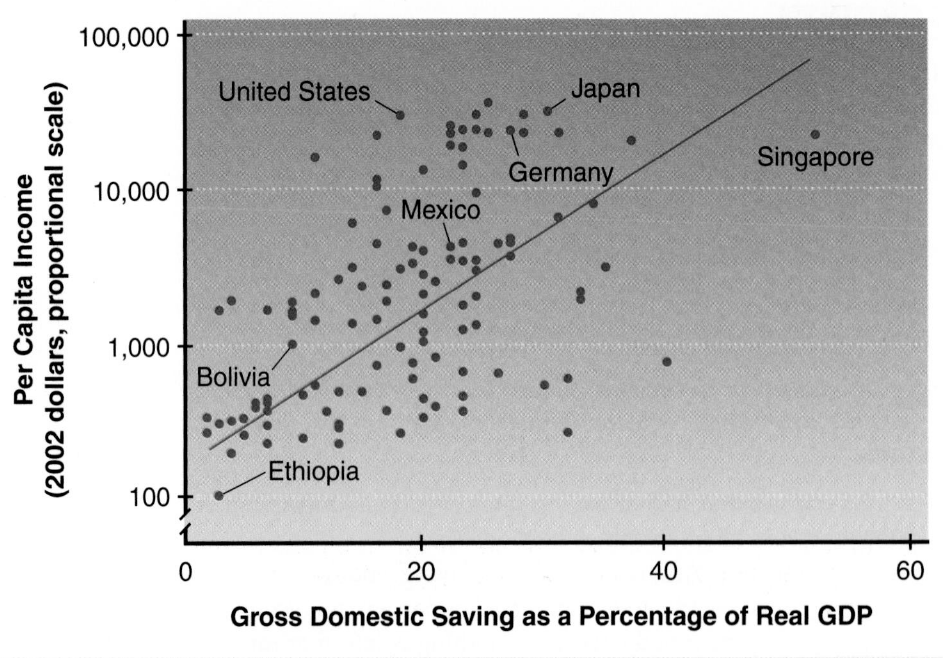

## PRODUCTIVITY INCREASES—THAT'S WHAT ECONOMIC GROWTH IS ALL ABOUT

Let's say that you are required to type ten term papers and homework assignments a year. You have a computer, but you do not know how to touch-type. You end up spending an average of two hours per typing job. The next summer, you buy a touch-typing tutorial to use on your computer. You spend a few minutes a day improving your typing speed. The following semester, you spend only one hour per typing assignment, thereby saving ten hours a semester. You have become more productive. This concept of productivity relates to your ability (and everyone else's) to produce the same output with fewer labor hours.

> ***Thus,* labor productivity *is normally measured by dividing real GDP by the number of workers or the number of labor hours.***

**Labor productivity**
*Total real GDP divided by the number of workers (output per worker).*

Labor productivity increases whenever average output produced per worker during a specified time period increases. Clearly, there is a relationship between economic growth and increases in labor productivity.

Of course, labor is not the only input, or factor of production. There is also capital. Consequently, we can also talk about **capital productivity.** We can define capital productivity similarly to the way we defined labor productivity. In other words, capital productivity is the average output produced per some common measure of machines during a specified time. Capital productivity increases whenever this measure of output per constant quality unit of machines increases during a specified time.

**Capital productivity**
*Average output produced per constant quality unit of machine (capital).*

### SEPARATING DIFFERENT RATES OF GROWTH OF PRODUCTION INPUTS

If you divide all resources into just capital and labor, economic growth can be defined as the cumulative contribution to per capita real GDP growth of three components:

- The rate of growth of capital.
- The rate of growth of labor.
- The rates of growth of capital and labor productivity.

If everything else remains constant, improvements in labor and capital productivity ultimately lead to economic growth and to higher living standards.

### THE GROWTH IN TECHNOLOGY—A KEY ELEMENT

Technology has grown erratically in the United States and elsewhere. Nonetheless, there are some startling statistics about the growth in technology. ▸ Example 15-6 Microprocessor speeds currently exceed 3,000 megahertz. By the year 2011, they will exceed 12,000 megahertz. During the same period, the size of the thinnest circuit line within a transistor will decrease by 80 percent. By 2011, microchip plants will produce 1,500 chips a week for every person on earth. ◂

We can actually consider technology a separate factor of production, even though it was not mentioned in Chapter 2. We also know that there is an important aspect of technology:

> ***The greater the reward to those who innovate, the more technological advances we will get.***

In other words, the higher the payoff to investing in technology, the more we will invest in technology. Of course, many factors affect technological development. Some people believe that the way governments tax the financial rewards earned by successful innovators is important. ▸ **International Example 15-7** A researcher once made a study of the disincentive effect of taxation on technological advances. He examined what Bill Gates would have kept for himself had he started Microsoft Corporation in France. The answer was only 20 percent of what he currently has as the president, entrepreneur, and founder of Microsoft Corporation in the United States. It is not surprising, therefore, that any way they are measured, fewer technological advances have taken place in France than in the United States. ◂

## Research and Development

**Research and development (R&D)**
*The exploration of new scientific concepts and systems, new production methods, new chemical compounds, and the like, coupled with the development of the research results so that they can later be used in actual production.*

A certain amount of technological advance results from **research and development (R&D)** activities that have as their goal the development of specific new materials, new products, and new machines.

***How much spending a nation devotes to R&D can have an impact on its long-term economic growth.***

**Patents**
*Government protection that gives an inventor the exclusive right to make, use, or sell an invention for a specified number of years.*

**Private R&D Spending** How much a nation spends on R&D depends in part on what businesses decide is worth spending. That in turn depends on the rewards they expect from successful R&D. If your company develops a new way to produce computer memory chips, how much will it be rewarded? The answer depends on whether others can freely copy the new technique.

To protect new techniques developed through R&D, we have a system of **patents:** the federal government gives the patent holder the exclusive right to

*Bill Gates is shown here before he became richer and older. Rumor has it that he sold his first computer operating system to IBM before he had even completed the purchase of the basis of that system from another small programming company. It's more than rumor that he worked 14-hour days with no vacations for two decades. Would he have worked so hard in a country with much higher tax rates than those that exist in the United States?*

make, use, and sell an invention for a period of 20 years. In essence, then, this exclusive right gives patent holders the possibility of making monopoly profits as a reward for innovation. One can argue that providing this special position to owners of patents increases expenditures on R&D and therefore adds to long-term economic growth.

**Government R&D Spending** In the United States, private spending by businesses is only part of R&D spending. Both the state and federal governments also often subsidize R&D or fund it directly. ▸ Example 15-8 The Internet had its origin in government-sponsored research. In 1957, when the Soviet Union launched the first satellite, called *Sputnik*, the United States responded by creating the Advanced Research Projects Agency (ARPA) within the Department of Defense, with an emphasis toward utilizing computers for communications. ARPA created ARPANET—the predecessor to today's Internet. By the late 1960s, various research institutes throughout universities were connected via ARPANET. The original ARPANET grew into the Internet. By the mid-1990s, the World Wide Web existed, allowing the transfer of text and media. Today, of course, the Internet is ubiquitous. ◂

## Innovation and Knowledge

We tend to think of technological progress as, say, the invention of the transistor. But invention means nothing by itself; **innovation** is also required.

**Innovation**
*The development of new products, systems, or processes that have wide-ranging effects.*

> ***Innovation involves the transformation of something new, such as an invention, into something that benefits the economy either by lowering production costs or by providing new goods and services.***

Indeed, many economic growth theorists believe that real wealth creation comes from innovation and that invention is but a small part of innovation.

Historically, technologies have moved relatively slowly from invention to innovation to widespread use. Today, the dispersion of new technology remains for the most part slow and uncertain. ▸ Example 15-9 The inventor of the transistor thought it might be used to make better hearing aids. At the time it was invented, the sole reference to it in the *New York Times* was in a small weekly column called "News of Radio." When the laser was invented, no one really knew what it could be used for. It was initially used to help in navigation, measurement, and chemical research. Today, it is used in the reproduction of music, printing, surgery, and telecommunications. Tomorrow, who knows? ◂

Figure 15-2 on the next page shows the process by which raw ideas turn into written ideas that are submitted for study in typical R&D laboratories. Businesses select a few of these for initial study and choose fewer still to evaluate in large research projects. Out of these full-scale research efforts, a few significant developments emerge and are launched as new products. If businesses are lucky, one or two of these product launches may ultimately pay off.

**Mastering Concepts:** Productivity Increases—That's What Economic Growth Is All About

- **Labor productivity is an important determinant of economic growth and is measured by dividing real domestic output by the number of workers or the number of labor hours.**

- **Economic growth can also be defined as the cumulative contribution of the rate of growth of capital, the rate of growth of labor, and the rates of growth of capital and labor productivity.**
- **The greater the rewards, the more technological advances we will observe.**
- **Research and development (R&D) often affects a nation's long-term economic growth prospects.**
- **While inventions are many, ultimately innovations are what drive economic growth rates, because they lower production costs or provide new goods and services.**

## INVESTING IN YOURSELF—THE IMPORTANCE OF HUMAN CAPITAL

Knowledge, ideas, and productivity are all tied together. One of the threads is the *quality* of the labor force. Increases in the productivity of the labor force depend on increases in human capital, the fourth factor of production discussed in Chapter 2. Recall that human capital is the knowledge and skills that people in the workforce acquire through education, on-the-job training, and self-teaching.

### How You Can Invest in Human Capital

To increase your own human capital, you have to invest by not working for pay while you attend school. Society also has to invest in the form of libraries and

**Figure 15-2 The Winnowing Process of Research and Development**

Only a portion of new ideas are actually submitted for formal study, and just a fraction of these become subjects of research projects. Very few ideas actually lead to the development of new products.

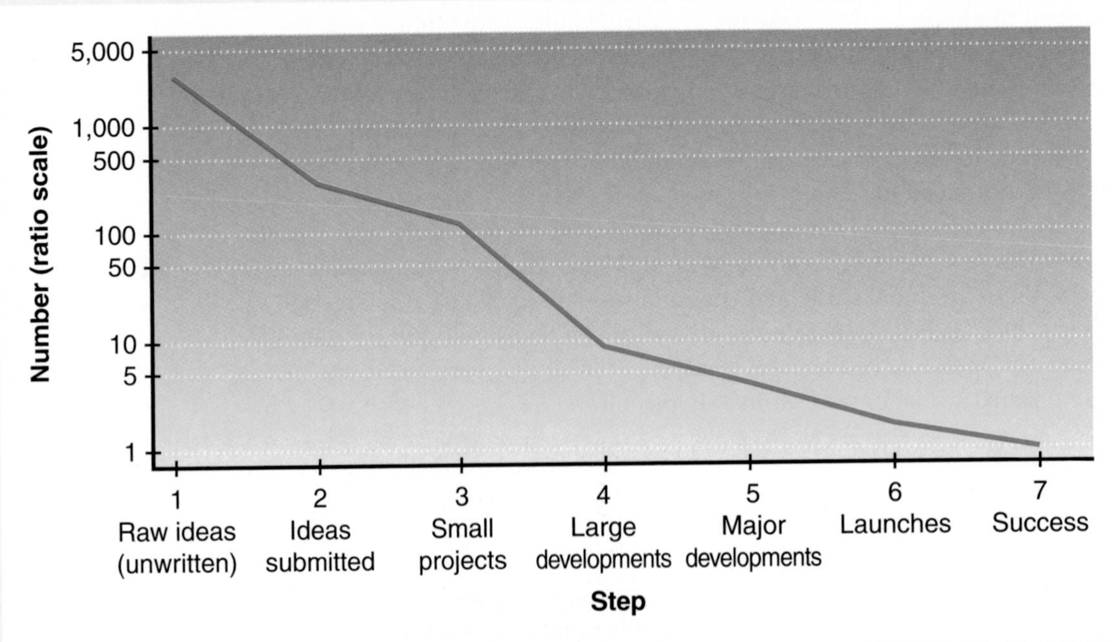

teachers. According to modern economic growth theorists, human capital is at least as important as physical capital, particularly when explaining international differences in living standards.

## Schooling Is Important

Researchers have found that one of the most effective ways that developing countries can become developed is by investing in secondary schooling. In other words, for a developing country, teaching more children ages 12 to 18 may be more important than having a large network of colleges and universities.

Some economists argue that policy changes that increase human capital will lead to more technological improvements. One of the reasons concerned citizens, policymakers, and politicians are trying to change the U.S. school system is that our primary and secondary education seems to be falling behind that of other countries. This lag is greatest in science and mathematics—precisely the areas that are required for technological advances.

Because historically there has been virtually no correlation between increased real spending per student and improvement in student achievement, this policy prescription does not involve increasing spending on education. Rather, it calls for more efficient delivery of educational services to students at all levels from grammar school through high school.

In some parts of the world, the AIDS epidemic is destroying much human capital, as you will read about in the next *Global Application*.

✦ **Note!** *Some of the school districts in the U.S. that have the highest per-student expenditures have relatively low student-achievement levels. In other words, spending more on primary and secondary schools does not guarantee better educational performance.*

### GLOBAL APPLICATION: What Happens When Human Capital Is Destroyed by an AIDS Epidemic?

***Concept Applied:* Human Capital**

Epidemics have been around since men and women first walked the earth. In the fourteenth century, the bubonic plague (Black Death) wiped out one-third of Europe's population. In 1918, a flu epidemic killed 40 million worldwide. Today, an AIDS epidemic is ravaging much of Africa.

#### The Effect of AIDS and Other Epidemics on Human Capital

As you have learned, human capital is the stock of knowledge and abilities that humans can use to fuel long-term economic growth. An epidemic such as AIDS tends to affect the stock of human capital in several ways. It kills society's most productive people—the young adults. It kills parents, thereby breaking the chain of knowledge transmission from generation to generation. In the process, it also reduces household incomes, with the result that young children do not go to school. Finally, these less-educated children have less knowledge to pass on.

#### The Long-Term Effects Can Be Devastating to an Economy

Researchers have examined the impact of AIDS on human capital and economic growth. They predict, for example, that if nothing is done to combat the AIDS epidemic in Africa, many countries will suffer complete economic collapse within only four generations. An already poor continent has an even bleaker future unless something is done to prevent the spread of AIDS.

**For Critical Analysis:**
*In countries where AIDS kills children, what do you think happens to the incentive for parents to invest in their children's education?*

**Mastering Concepts:** Investing in Yourself—The Importance of Human Capital

- **You can invest in your own human capital by going to school, obtaining on-the-job training, and teaching yourself new skills.**
- **Investment in secondary schooling is critical for the future economic growth of many developing countries.**

## PROPERTY RIGHTS AND ENTREPRENEURSHIP

**Property rights**
*The rights of an owner to use and to exchange property. When property rights are well defined, owners of property have an incentive to use their property efficiently. When property rights are ill defined, few owners of property are interested in making sure that what they own is used efficiently.*

If you were in a country where bank accounts and businesses were periodically confiscated by the government, how willing would you be to leave your money in a savings account or to invest in a business? Certainly, you would be less willing than if such things never occurred. You would be living in a political and economic system in which your **property rights** were not well defined and legally supported. ▸ **International Example 15-10** For several decades in Iraq before its government was ousted in 2003, entrepreneurs were never certain about the property rights in their investments. When a restaurant started doing well, one of dictator Saddam Hussein's sons might decide to buy it. He would offer a very low price, though. The restaurant owner had no option but to sell. This type of capital confiscation occurred with virtually all businesses. The result was that during the era of Saddam Hussein, Iraq experienced less investment than it would have otherwise and, therefore, less economic growth. ◂

***In general, the more certain private property rights are, the more capital accumulation there will be.***

### WELL-DEFINED PROPERTY RIGHTS ARE IMPORTANT

When property rights in people's wealth are sanctioned and enforced by the government, people will be willing to invest their savings in endeavors that will increase their wealth in future years.

In fact, some economic historians have attempted to show that it was the development of well-defined private property rights that allowed Western Europe to increase its growth rate after many centuries of stagnation.

▸ **International Example 15-11** Zimbabwe won its independence from Britain in 1980. At the time it was one of the richest nations in Africa. Its first and only president, Robert Mugabe, immediately started weakening the nation's rule of law. He reduced the security in property rights in land and eventually confiscated all such rights. Mugabe's government also confiscated large stocks of food. In effect, the government took virtually everything that had been produced or saved. Consequently, Zimbabweans had little incentive to save or to produce. Since 1980, the standard of living in that country has fallen by at least two-thirds, if not more. ◂

**Nationalization**
*The process of converting private property to government ownership and control of that property.*

The ability and certainty with which people can reap the gains from investing also determine the extent to which business owners in developed countries will invest capital in developing countries. The threat of **nationalization** that hangs over some developing nations probably discourages foreign businesses from injecting the massive amount of investment that might allow these nations to develop more rapidly. After all, private businesses from outside the country (and inside, too, for that matter) will be wary of investing large sums in the development of major projects if they believe that there is a distinct possibility that the government could take control of those projects once they are developed.

## A Nation's Legal Structure Affects Entrepreneurship

The degree to which individuals use their own entrepreneurial skills is intimately tied to any nation's legal structure, or system of property rights. In Chapter 2, we identified entrepreneurship as the fourth factor of production. Entrepreneurs are the risk takers who seek out new ways to do things and create new products. To the extent that entrepreneurs are allowed to capture the rewards from their entrepreneurial activities, they will seek to engage in those activities. In countries where such rewards cannot be captured because of a lack of property rights, there will be less entrepreneurship. Typically, this results in less investment and a lower rate of growth.

▸ **International Example 15-12** From 1964 to 1985, the African nation of Tanzania was ruled by Julius Nyerere. Under the economic system he imposed, the government owned much of the land and capital in the country. Entrepreneurs who were successful found that most, if not all, of their hard-earned rewards were confiscated in one way or another by Nyerere's government. Consequently, there was much less entrepreneurship in Tanzania during Nyerere's rule. Indeed, in spite of massive foreign aid inflows, the standard of living of Tanzanians fell dramatically under his rule. ◂

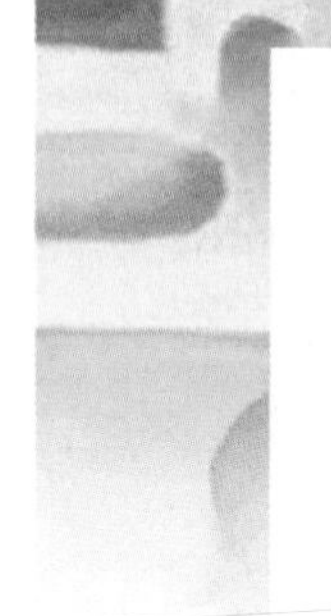

### *Solving the Economic Problem:* Why Doesn't Foreign Aid Seem to Help Raise Living Standards?

Upon closer inspection, you will find that the relationship between foreign aid and improved living standards is most tenuous (or even negative) in countries where private property rights are ill defined, not supported by the legal system, or nonexistent. In many of these countries, much, if not most, of the foreign aid went into the construction of projects owned and controlled by the government. In the period when the foreign aid was provided, very little was done to increase the percentage of residents receiving primary and secondary schooling. Those countries had something else in common—extensive graft and corruption among government officials, which are more likely in economic and political systems in which the private sector is small relative to the government-controlled sector of the economy.

After all is said and done, there are some straightforward rules that foster economic growth; you will read about them in the next *Global Application*.

## GLOBAL APPLICATION: The Formula for Economic Growth in Iraq and Afghanistan

### *Concept Applied:* Economic Growth

In both Iraq and Afghanistan, countries that were invaded by the United States in the early 2000s, the major issue is how to move those countries onto the path of stable economic growth. According to some economists (but certainly not all), there are some well-documented rules that should be followed.

#### Rules of the Road to Economic Growth

These rules of the road toward high economic growth can be summarized in five points;

1. **Keep taxes low and keep the tax code simple.** Hong Kong did this and grew from a poor country to a rich country. It was just a barren rock 150 years ago.
2. **Develop a stable money.** Countries that allow their currency's purchasing power to disintegrate rapidly rarely grow fast, if at all. The United States has rarely suffered long periods of rapid inflation or deflation.
3. **Make it easy to start businesses.** If entrepreneurs must contend with a huge bureaucracy, they will not start legal businesses. Instead, they will stay in an uncounted, illegal economy. Some poor countries, like Peru, require any prospective entrepreneur to jump through costly and lengthy bureaucratic hoops.
4. **Do not tax exports and keep import taxes low.** Chile did this with great success. The United States does not tax exports and in recent times has taxed imports very little. (You will learn more about exports and imports as well as restrictions on imports in Chapter 16.)
5. **Establish the rule of law.** Few countries can grow without a stable legal system. One problem in Russia and China today is that businesspeople must deal with an ever-changing legal landscape. Consequently, bribery is rampant.

#### Easier Said Than Done

The five keys to long-term economic growth are easy to understand, but putting them into practice may not be easy. Bureaucrats often create rules, regulations, roadblocks, and large government infrastructures. But look at it this way: the previous governments in Iraq and Afghanistan created environments in which there was no economic growth. Just about anything we do will be better than that.

**For Critical Analysis:**
*How hard is it to start a new business in the United States? Do you think this matters for economic growth in this country?*

### Mastering Concepts: Property Rights and Entrepreneurship

- **The more certain property rights are, the more capital accumulation there will be, and therefore the greater economic growth.**
- **Well-defined property rights have usually been necessary for economic growth to occur.**
- **Entrepreneurs will not take risks if they believe that their rewards from taking risks will be confiscated.**

## SUMMING IT ALL UP

- Because some nations have larger populations than others and some nations' populations grow faster, we must correct increases in total national output by increases in population.
- Economic growth is measured by the rate of change in per capita real GDP.

- Small differences in economic rates of growth over the long run create large differences in standards of living.
- The process of compounding is the reason that small differences in growth rates (or interest rates) matter.
- Because investment requires saving, saving is an important determinant of economic growth.
- In general, nations that have had high rates of saving have experienced greater economic growth rates than those that have not.
- Labor productivity is an important determinant of economic growth and is measured by dividing real domestic output by the number of workers or the number of labor hours.
- Economic growth can also be defined as the cumulative contribution of the rate of growth of capital, the rate of growth of labor, and the rates of growth of capital productivity and labor productivity.
- The greater the rewards, the more technological advances we will observe.
- Research and development (R&D) often affects a nation's long-term economic growth prospects.
- You can invest in your own human capital by going to school, obtaining on-the-job training, and teaching yourself new skills.
- The more certain property rights are, the more capital accumulation there will be, and therefore the greater economic growth.
- Entrepreneurs will not take risks if they believe that their rewards from taking risks will be confiscated.

## KEY TERMS AND CONCEPTS



## MASTERING ECONOMIC CONCEPTS Questions and Problems

**15-1.** Holding all else constant, would a 15 percent increase in real GDP over five years indicate that an economy was doing well? Over the same time period would the same 15 percent increase in real GDP coupled with a 20 percent increase in the population indicate that the economy was doing well?

**15-2.** Why is per capita real GDP possibly the single most important variable for measuring economic well-being?

**15-3.** The real GDP of Bermuda is approximately $2,145 million, and the real GDP of Aruba is approximately $2,548 million, if both figures are adjusted into U.S. dollars. If the population of Bermuda is 65,000 and the population of Aruba is 91,000, which country has a higher per capita real GDP?

**15-4.** Does per capita real GDP account for differences in the distribution of income? Would greater income equality in a nation likely lead to an increase or a decrease in total utility for the people of that nation? Would greater income equality in a nation likely lead to an increase or a decrease in incentives and the overall growth of GDP? Why?

**15-5.** Assume that the economy grew at a rate of 5 percent each year. With annual compounding, each dollar of income would increase to $1.28

in five years' time. If the growth rate had been 6 percent, how much would each dollar of economic activity have increased? Over a 50-year time period, what would be the difference in the total amount of growth with a 5 percent annual rate and a 6 percent annual rate?

**15-6.** If the rate of saving increases, what will be the impact on the consumption variable in the equation $Y = C + I + G + X$? What will be the impact on the investment variable?

**15-7.** If real GDP decreased by 0.5 percent while the length of the average workweek decreased by 2.0 percent, did worker productivity improve?

**15-8.** The total level of economic growth is equal to the sum of growth in what three areas?

**15-9.** Is technology a factor of production? What types of actions could the government take to give firms and individuals a greater incentive to develop new technologies?

**15-10.** Explain the difference between innovation and invention.

**15-11.** How will frequent military conflicts affect the security and stability of property rights in a developing economy? How will the growth rate of the developing economy likely be affected?

**15-12.** If a country's political structure changes such that it is less likely that the government will nationalize domestic businesses, will this cause an increase or a decrease in the amount of foreign investment? Why?

**15-13.** In two years, what will be the value of $100 invested at an interest rate of 3 percent compounded annually?

**15-14.** If a developing country wishes to spur economic growth, should this country establish high taxes on exports, high taxes on imports, or neither?

**15-15.** Assume that our economy is initially represented by curve *A* on the graph below. Which curve would we move to if our country experiences significant economic growth? If economic growth equals zero over a certain time period, which curve would we move to?

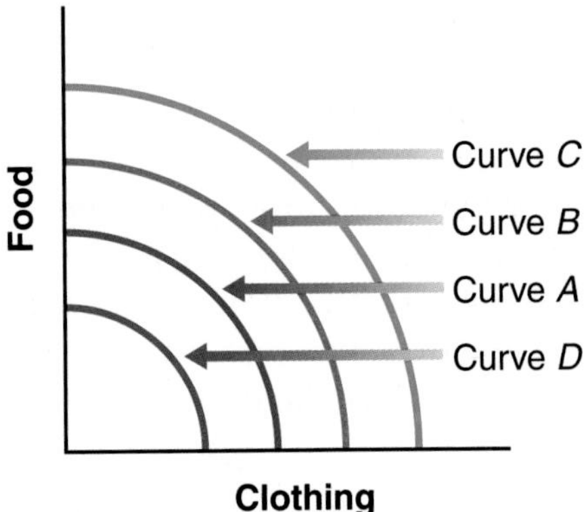


## THINKING CRITICALLY

**15-1.** From the 1960s to the late 1990s, Argentina and Venezuela experienced limited annual growth rates of 1.0 percent and 0.1 percent, respectively. In contrast, Hong Kong and Japan achieved significant annual growth rates of 6.0 percent and 4.7 percent, respectively. What factors might have led to this substantial growth? In 1960 both Argentina and Venezuela had per capita GDP much greater than that of either Hong Kong or Japan. Based on the growth rates mentioned above, which country or countries would you assume have the highest per capita GDP now? Use the following per capita GDP figures from 1960 to estimate the level of per capita GDP for each of these countries for the year 2000.

a. Argentina: $4,462
b. Venezuela: $6,338
c. Hong Kong: $2,247
d. Japan: $2,954

**15-2.** Would each of the following policies be more likely to increase or decrease the economic growth of a developing economy over time?

a. A national government significantly increases funding for basic education.
b. Because of a significant national debt, the government dramatically increases income taxes.
c. The military utilizes its personnel to maintain order and prevent looting.
d. The central bank establishes a monetary rule dictating that it will change the money supply only to keep inflation below 5 percent, in contrast to the average of 15 percent in the past.

**15-3.** Over the last 44 years, the United States has provided aid to the African nation of Zambia. In 2001 alone, the amount of assistance totaled $37 million. How does the U.S. government acquire the funds that it disburses in such programs? In Zambia, per capita real GDP has *decreased* a total of $275 over the past 40 years, economic output decreased an average of 2 percent each year in the 1990s, and the rate of inflation is currently 27.0 percent. Evaluate the economic situation in the country based on these figures. What would you suggest as a solution? Would eliminating the aid program be a good idea? If not, how would you suggest modifying the existing aid program?

## LOGGING ON

1. For a variety of Web links to sites relating to economic growth and development, go to http://www.nuff.ox.ac.uk/Economics/Growth/devel.htm.
2. To see how the U.S. Department of Commerce calculates the U.S. saving rate, go to http://www.bea.gov/briefrm/tables/ebr6.htm.
3. Take a look at measures of economic freedom and read about how they may relate to economic growth in a nation of your choice at http://www.heritage.org/research/features/index/.
4. For different views on possible relationships between inequality of incomes and economic growth, go to http://www.worldbank.org/poverty/inequal/econ/index.htm.

## USING THE INTERNET FOR ECONOMIC ANALYSIS

**Multifactor Productivity and Its Growth** As discussed in this chapter, growth in productivity is a key factor determining a nation's overall economic growth. This application helps you to perform your own evaluation of the factors contributing to U.S. growth.

**Title:** Bureau of Labor Statistics: Multifactor Productivity

**Navigation:** Begin at the home page of the Bureau of Labor Statistics, http://stats.bls.gov. Under "Productivity," click on "Multifactor Productivity."

**Application**

1. Under "People are asking, . . .," click on "How is MFP defined?" Read the full discussion of this and the other listed questions on the Web page that appears, and answer the following questions. Based on what you learned in this chapter, why do you suppose that economists find the multifactor productivity measure useful for predicting economic growth? Why is multifactor productivity for the "private business sector" most often used as an overall productivity measure?
2. Back up to the home page for multifactor productivity trends, and click on "Economic News Releases," and then click on either "HTML" or "PDF" next to "Multifactor Productivity Trends—Published Data for Major Sectors." Has productivity growth trended upward, trended downward, or remained relatively flat over the most recent period? How is this trend likely to affect U.S. economic growth?

## MEDIA RESOURCE LIST

The following media resources are available with this chapter.

- Load your CD-ROM to listen to the audio introduction to this chapter.
- Load your CD-ROM to view the video on *Importance of Growth Rates.*
- Load your CD-ROM to view the video on *Saving, a Fundamental Determinant of Growth.*

- Load your CD-ROM to view the video on *Importance of Human Capital.*
- Test your knowledge of chapter concepts with a quiz at www.miller-ume.com.
- Link to Web resources related to the text coverage at www.miller-ume.com.

## HOMEWORK SET

Go to the back of this book to find the Homework Problems for this chapter.

# PART 4

# International

# CHAPTER 16

# Trading with Other Nations

## *Facing an Economic Problem:* The Effect of Boycotting French Goods

After months of the U.S. military buildup in the Middle East, toppling the regime of Saddam Hussein in Iraq took just three weeks. Before and after the invasion of Iraq, however, the United States found itself diplomatically isolated from some of its most important European partners. After France and Germany publicly rebuked the Bush administration for pursuing a war with Iraq, anti-French and anti-German sentiment became national news in the United States. Most of the outrage, though, focused on France.

Along with a stream of anti-French jokes came a reduction in the demand for French-made products. Americans even started talking about boycotting all French goods.

Although U.S. residents buy millions of bottles of French wine a year, French-made products clearly represent only a small percentage of all of the goods purchased by U.S. residents. So, how effective could a boycott of French products be? In other words, could anti-French sentiment lead to a serious reduction in trade between France and the United States? If so, are there any consequences for U.S. industry in general? You will find out the answers as you read this chapter.

## Learning Objectives

After reading this chapter, you should be able to:

- **Distinguish between imports and exports and discuss the growth in world trade.**
- **State why comparative advantage is more important than absolute advantage.**
- **Explain the relationship between imports and exports.**
- **List and describe at least three arguments against free trade.**
- **Describe the two major ways of restricting imports.**

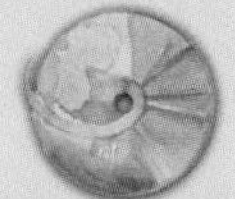

***Refer to the back of this chapter for a complete listing of multimedia learning materials available on the CD-ROM and the Web site.***

## THE IMPORTANCE OF WORLD TRADE

If we didn't trade with other nations, it would be more costly to buy coffee, chocolate, or pepper in the United States. Consider also that most of the consumer electronic goods you purchase—flat screen television sets, boom boxes, and digital cameras—are made in other countries. Many of the raw materials used in manufacturing in this country are also purchased abroad. For example, more than 90 percent of bauxite, from which aluminum is made, is brought in from other countries.

### IMPORTS—WHAT WE BUY FROM ABROAD

**Imports**
*Goods and services produced outside a country but sold within its borders.*

**Imports** are those goods (and services) that we purchase from outside the United States. Imports include not only goods we consume directly but also many of the parts that go into the manufacturing of U.S.-produced goods. ▸ Example 16-1 When you drink U.S.-branded orange juice, such as Tropicana or Minute Maid, look at the tiny print on the label. You will see that the juice was made from concentrate that came from Brazil or Mexico. If you buy a U.S.-branded computer, such as IBM, and take it apart, you will discover that many of the parts are imported. The same is true for U.S.-made Boeing 777s, Ford automobiles, and countless other "made in U.S.A." products. ◂

Today, about 14 percent of the value of all final goods and services produced in the United States (GDP) is made up of imports. This is an important share of the U.S. economy, but actually it is quite small in comparison to other countries. Look at Table 16-1, where you see the relative importance of imports in selected countries.

### EXPORTS—WHAT WE SELL TO OTHER COUNTRIES

**Exports**
*Goods and services produced domestically for sale abroad.*

International trade is a two-way street. Not only do we import goods and services from abroad, but we also sell goods and services abroad, called **exports.** Each year

**Table 16-1 The Importance of Imports in Selected Countries**

The United States is pretty far down the scale in terms of how important imports are to the total economy. Tiny Luxembourg has to import just about everything.

| Country | Imports as a Percentage of GDP |
|---|---|
| Luxembourg | 95.0 |
| Netherlands | 58.0 |
| Norway | 30.0 |
| Canada | 23.5 |
| Germany | 23.0 |
| United Kingdom | 21.0 |
| China | 19.0 |
| France | 18.4 |
| United States | 14.2 |
| Japan | 6.8 |

we export over $700 billion of goods. In addition, we export about $300 billion of services. These include computer software and, of course, travel and tourism. ▸ **Example 16-2** In any given year, the United States exports $60 billion of farm products, $2 billion of sporting goods and games, $9 billion of clothing, $45 billion of data processing equipment, and $28 billion of TVs, VCRs, and DVD players, plus many billions of dollars more in professional and scientific equipment, plastics and chemicals, and transportation equipment. ◂

The United States exports about 12 percent of GDP, which, like the import sector, is relatively small compared to other countries' exports. ▸ **International Example 16-3** Canada exports over 41 percent of GDP, Sweden almost 45 percent, Thailand almost 60 percent, and Belgium over 70 percent. ◂

## World Trade—It Just Keeps Growing

Back in the 1950s, imports and exports were only about 4 percent of annual GDP. As we pointed out already, today imports are over 14 percent of GDP, exports about 12 percent. In other words, international trade has become more important for the United States. This is also true for the world. Look at Figure 16-1. There you see that since the 1950s, world total annual output (world real GDP) has grown rather steadily. Using 1950 as a base year, world real GDP has grown almost eightfold. The real shocker, though, is what has happened to world trade. Again, using 1950 as a base, world trade has increased over 21 times its base level!

*Animated*

**Figure 16-1 World Trade Keeps Growing**

Here you can see the growth in world trade in relative terms. The volume of trade is represented by an index; the base year is 1950, meaning that the index is set equal to 100 for that year. World trade has increased much more than world output (world real GDP). Whereas world output has increased by about 8 times from 1950 to the present, world trade has increased by more than 21 times.

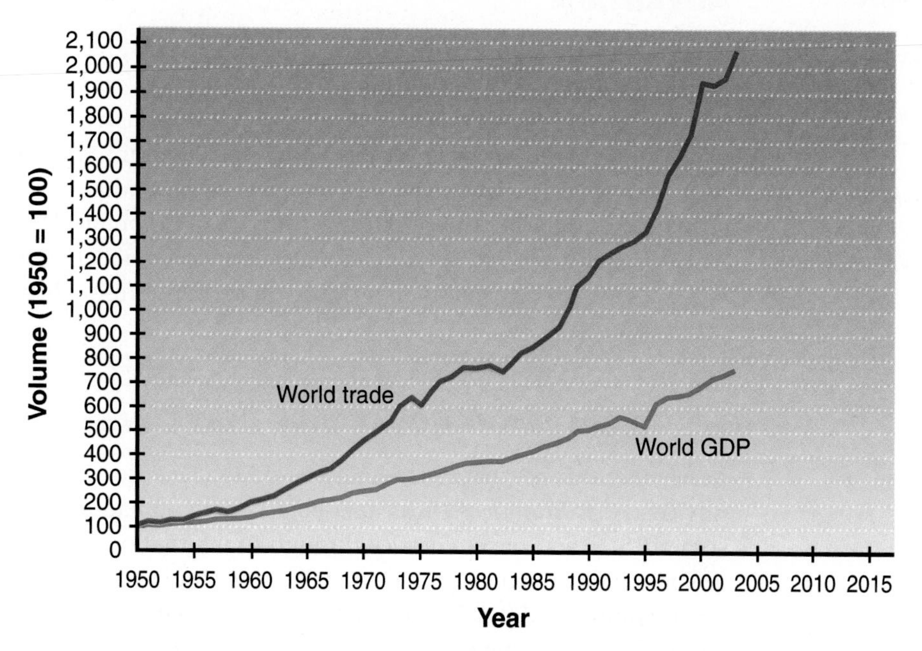

Trading among the peoples of different nations offers several benefits. It looks as though most of the world has figured that out.

**Mastering Concepts:** The Importance of World Trade

- **Imports are all of the goods and services that we buy from other countries for domestic consumption or use in the production of domestic goods and services.**
- **Exports are all of the goods and services that we sell to foreign countries.**
- **The growth in world trade since the 1950s has been much greater than the growth in world real GDP.**

## ABSOLUTE ADVANTAGE, COMPARATIVE ADVANTAGE, AND THE GAINS FROM SPECIALIZATION

Trade among the peoples of different nations occurs because the people of each nation have the ability to produce goods and services that residents of other nations find attractive in terms of price, quality, and special features. You might immediately think of tropical countries exporting bananas to countries that "can't" grow them. You might think the same for coffee. As you will see, though, international trade is not necessarily dependent on the particular climate of a country or its natural resources. ▸ **International Example 16-4** A hundred and fifty years ago, the island nation of Hong Kong was little more than a barren rock. Today, its residents have higher per capita incomes than the residents of France and Italy. Clearly, Hong Kong did not need natural resources to grow economically. ◂

### Doing It Better Than Everyone Else—Absolute Advantage

**Absolute advantage**
*The ability to produce more units of a good or service using a given quantity of labor or other resource inputs than other producers can; equivalently, the ability to produce the same quantity of a good or service using fewer units of labor or other resource inputs.*

A nation's particular distribution of resources often gives it an **absolute advantage** over another nation in the production of one or more goods. Obviously, Colombia's tropical climate and relatively inexpensive labor make it ideally suited for growing coffee. Even using the same amount of resources—land, labor, capital, and entrepreneurship—a country with a moderate climate, such as Belgium, would produce quite a bit less coffee than Colombia. We say that Colombia has an absolute advantage in coffee production over Belgium. Absolute advantage is defined as the ability to produce more output from given inputs than other producers can.

### It's Comparative Advantage That Counts

Remember that in Chapter 1 we discussed the key economic concept of opportunity cost. *Opportunity cost* was defined as what you had to give up in order to get something. This concept carries through to international trade. What really matters for trade is your (and a country's) opportunity cost in producing a good or service domestically rather than importing it. In other words, to understand international trade, we have to examine the opportunity cost of producing a particular good or service domestically versus simply importing it.

**Comparative Advantage—For the Individual and for the Nation** For the individual, **comparative advantage** is the ability to perform an activity at a lower opportunity cost. You have a comparative advantage in a particular activity whenever you have a lower opportunity cost of performing that activity. Comparative advantage is always a *relative* concept. ▸ Example 16-5 You may be able to change the oil in your car; you may even be able to change it faster than the local mechanic. But, if the opportunity cost you face by changing the oil exceeds the mechanic's opportunity cost, the mechanic has a comparative advantage in changing the oil. The mechanic faces a lower opportunity cost for that activity. ◂

**Comparative advantage**
*The ability to engage in an activity such as production at a lower opportunity cost than others who might engage in the same activity.*

Comparative advantage is an issue for managers of businesses and even sports teams, where coaches have to determine each player's comparative advantage. ▸ Example 16-6 Babe Ruth was one of the best pitchers in professional baseball when he played for the Boston Red Sox. After he was traded to the New York Yankees, the owner and the coach decided to make him an outfielder, even though he was a better pitcher than anyone else on the team roster. They wanted "The Babe" to concentrate on his hitting. Good pitchers do not bring in as many fans as home-run kings do. Babe Ruth's comparative advantage was clearly in hitting homers rather than in pitching. ◂

For a nation, comparative advantage is its ability to produce something at a lower opportunity cost than other nations. The best way to understand comparative advantages across nations is to look at a numerical example, which we do next.

**Comparing Costs of Production** Consider a hypothetical example in which we compare the cost of production of digital cameras and video game software. Our example involves two countries, the United States and Japan. Look at Table 16-2.

**Table 16-2 The Comparative Costs of Production**

| Product | United States (worker-days) | Japan (worker-days) |
|---|---|---|
| Digital cameras | 1 | 1 |
| Video games | 1 | 2 |

There you see that it takes one worker-day in the United States to produce a digital camera and one worker-day to produce software for a video game. In Japan, it also takes one worker-day to produce a digital camera, but it takes two worker-days to produce the software for a video game. Thus, the United States can produce both goods at least as cheaply—in terms of worker-days—as Japan. So, shouldn't we just produce both goods ourselves? The answer is no; if we do, we, and the world, will be worse off.

**Specialization Leads to World Output Increases** If we allow for international trade and *specialization*, then both Japan and the United States can be made better off. That is to say, they can both increase their total output without any additional resources, and hence they can increase the overall material welfare of their respective residents.

**Specialization**
*The division of productive activities among persons and regions so that no one individual or one area is totally self-sufficient. An individual may specialize, for example, in law or medicine. A nation may specialize in the production of coffee, computers, or cameras.*

**Specialization** involves working in a relatively well-defined, limited endeavor. For the individual, specialization means engaging in one particular occupation, rather than being "a jack-of-all-trades." For a nation, specialization means producing a limited number of goods and services, rather than all the goods and services that its residents consume.

In our example, Japan should produce only digital cameras because that is the product for which it has the lowest opportunity cost of production. In other words, Japan has a comparative advantage in producing digital cameras. Let's make things easy and say that there are 1,000 workers in each country and that each worker is capable of producing either digital cameras or video games according to the numbers shown in Table 16-2.

Look at Table 16-3. It shows the daily world output *before specialization* with 1,000 workers in each country, assuming that each country's workers are divided equally between the two goods' production. As you can see, world output is 1,000 digital cameras and 750 video games.

**Table 16-3 Daily World Output Before Specialization**

| | United States | | Japan | | |
|---|---|---|---|---|---|
| **Product** | **Workers** | **Output** | **Workers** | **Output** | **World Output** |
| Digital cameras | 500 | 500 | 500 | 500 | 1,000 |
| Video games | 500 | 500 | 500 | 250 | 750 |

## The Magic of Specialization and Trade—Increased World Output

Now assume that Japan produces only digital cameras, leaving the production of video games to the United States. Look at Table 16-4. Here you see that the world output of digital cameras stays the same at 1,000. But the world output of video games is now 1,000, instead of 750.

> ***There has been a gain to world production of 250 video games. These are essentially "free" because of a more efficient allocation of resources worldwide.***

✦ **Be Aware!** *While we talk about a nation specializing in production, it is individual producers who engage in the specialization and it is individual importers and exporters that create the trading that allows for the benefits of international trade.*

Moving digital camera production to Japan saves one-half of a video game for each camera. Why? Because it costs Japan only one-half of a video game to produce a digital camera, whereas it costs the United States an entire video game to produce a digital camera. In Table 16-4, we show the effects of moving the production of 500 digital cameras from the United States to Japan. Given the savings of 0.5 video games per digital camera, the result is 250 (= 500 × 0.5) extra video games for the world as a whole.

**Table 16-4 Daily World Output After Specialization**

| | United States | | Japan | | |
|---|---|---|---|---|---|
| **Product** | **Workers** | **Output** | **Workers** | **Output** | **World Output** |
| Digital cameras | 0 | 0 | 1,000 | 1,000 | 1,000 |
| Video games | 1,000 | 1,000 | 0 | 0 | 1,000 |

Of course, the gains from international trade occur through voluntary trade among individuals of different nations. This leads us to a general statement:

> ***Voluntary trade yields gains importantly because the traders in different countries reallocate production from high-cost locations to low-cost locations around the world.***

The reallocations are, of course, possible only if trade occurs. Farmers, for example, would hardly be willing to specialize in wheat production if they were forced to consume only what they produced and could not trade their wheat.

> ✦ **Note!** *There can be no gains from specialization unless there is trade. Thus, the benefits of specialization come from being able to engage in trade after the specialization takes place.*

**International Trade and the Production Possibilities Curve** Remember from Chapter 1 when you learned about the production possibilities curve. (See Figure 1-1 on page 7, which shows the production possibilities curve for digital camcorders and DVD recorders.) You can think about specialization and international trade as eventually having the effect of shifting the nation's production possibilities curve outward.

## International Trade Is Really a Choice Between Two Ways of Producing a Good or Service

International trade can be viewed in a simple fashion. We can say that world output is greater when countries specialize in producing the goods in which they have a comparative advantage and then engage in foreign trade. You can also think of it this way. Each country must choose between two ways of acquiring a good or service—produce it domestically or import it. Every firm or country will obviously want to utilize the *least* costly production process.

> ***It turns out that one way of "producing" a good or service is simply to import it. If the imported good is cheaper than the domestically produced equivalent good, a nation can in essence gain by "producing" the good by importing it.***

Not everyone, of course, is better off when free trade occurs. In our numerical example, U.S. digital camera producers and Japanese video game producers are worse off because these two *domestic* industries will have disappeared after complete specialization. Nevertheless, the nations as a whole are better off.

## Will the United States Ever Be Forced Out of All Export Markets?

Some people worry that the United States may someday be unable to export very much because foreign competition will have become so effective. The above analysis of comparative advantage tells us that this can never happen. No matter how much other countries compete for our business, the United States will always have a comparative advantage in *something* that it can produce and then export. Comparative advantages change over time, but they always exist *somewhere*.
▸ **Example 16-7** In the 1950s, the United States was a major exporter of toys, games, and sporting goods. Currently, as you learned earlier in this chapter, it exports about $2 billion of sporting goods and games. In contrast, the United States imports almost $20 billion of toys, games, and sporting goods—ten times more than it exports. Clearly, our comparative advantage has changed over time. ◂

## International Trade Leads to the Transmission of Ideas Among Nations

Beyond the overall increase in the output of goods and services as a result of comparative advantage and trading, there is another benefit from international trade. International trade bestows benefits on countries through the transmission of ideas. According to economic historians, international trade has been the principal means by which new goods, services, and processes have spread around the world.

▸ **International Example 16-8** Coffee was initially grown in Arabia near the Red Sea. Around 675 C.E., coffee began to be roasted and consumed as a beverage. Eventually, it was exported to other parts of the world; the Dutch started cultivating it in their colonies during the seventeenth century and the French in the eighteenth century. Consider also the lowly potato, which is native to the Peruvian Andes. In the sixteenth century, it was carried to Europe by Spanish explorers. Thereafter, its cultivation and consumption spread rapidly. In the early eighteenth century, it traveled back across the Atlantic and became part of the American agricultural scene. ◂

**Intellectual property**
*All of the fruits of humans' minds, including movies, computer games, software, music, and scientific discoveries.*

Today, we talk about international trade's role in spreading **intellectual property**—ideas, patents, inventions, software, movies, music, and the like. Virtually all of the intellectual property used throughout the world today has been transmitted through international trade.

Finally, production processes are transmitted through international trade. ▸ **International Example 16-9** An important Japanese manufacturing innovation emphasized redesigning the system rather than running the existing system in the best possible way. Inventories were reduced to just-in-time levels by reengineering machine setup methods. This production process, known as **just-in-time inventory control,** is now common in U.S. factories. Rather than having large stocks of parts for manufacturing cars and computers, firms that make these products (and others) have the necessary parts arrive just when they are needed. This reduces the cost of holding inventories. Just-in-time systems reduce manufacturing costs as a consequence. ◂

**Just-in-time inventory control**
*A manufacturing technique in which parts are supplied at the last minute, rather than being inventoried for a long time before they are needed in the production process.*

**Mastering Concepts:** Absolute Advantage, Comparative Advantage, and the Gains from Specialization

- **Absolute advantage refers to the ability to produce a unit of a good or service using fewer resources than another nation.**
- **Comparative advantage refers to the ability to produce a good at the lowest opportunity cost.**
- **When nations specialize in producing those goods and services in which they have a comparative advantage, total world production rises.**
- **One way of "producing" a good or service is simply to import it. If the imported good is cheaper than the domestically produced equivalent good, a nation can in essence gain by "producing" the good by importing it.**
- **International trade leads to the international transmission of ideas, otherwise called intellectual property.**

## THERE IS A RELATIONSHIP BETWEEN IMPORTS AND EXPORTS

In the chapter-opening economic problem, we asked whether there might be any consequences for the U.S. economy if U.S. residents boycotted French goods. In this section, you will find out that the answer is, indeed, yes.

### IMPORTS AND EXPORTS ARE RELATED

International trade is an economic activity just like any other. Thus, it is subject to the same economic principles. We can look at international trade as a kind of production process that transforms exports into imports. For you and everyone else in this country, the purpose of international trade is to obtain imports. What we gain as a country from international trade is the ability to *import* the things we want. We have to export other things to pay for those imports. A fundamental proposition for understanding all international trade is the following:

***In the long run, imports are paid for by exports.***

Exports ultimately pay for imports because people in other countries want something in exchange for the goods and services that they ship to the United States. For the most part, in the long run they want goods and services made in the United States—our exports.

Of course, in the short run, imports can also be paid for by the sale (or export) of U.S. assets, such as the title to land, stocks, and bonds, or through an extension of credit from other countries. Other nations, however, will not continue to give us credit forever for the goods and services that we import from them.

***The goal of production is indeed consumption. Foreigners wish to consume goods and services, not just send them to the United States for us to consume. They ultimately want goods and services in return.***

## The Impact of Restrictions on Imports

We can now add a corollary to the above basic propositions of international trade:

***Any restriction on imports ultimately reduces exports.***

That is to say, if we restrict the amount of imports coming from our trading partners, they will demand fewer exports in payment. Why? Because, as we pointed out above, ultimately the goal of international trade is to be able to consume more goods and services. If we restrict the ability of the rest of the world to sell goods and services to us, then the rest of the world will not have the ability to purchase all the goods and services that we want to sell as exports.

This revelation would surprise many people who want to restrict foreign competition to protect domestic jobs.

***Although it is possible to preserve jobs in narrow sectors of the economy by restricting foreign competition, it is impossible to preserve jobs throughout the economy by imposing import restrictions.***

In fact some evidence indicates that import restrictions actually *reduce* the total number of jobs in the economy. Why? Because ultimately such restrictions lead to a reduction in employment in export industries in any country that restricts imports.

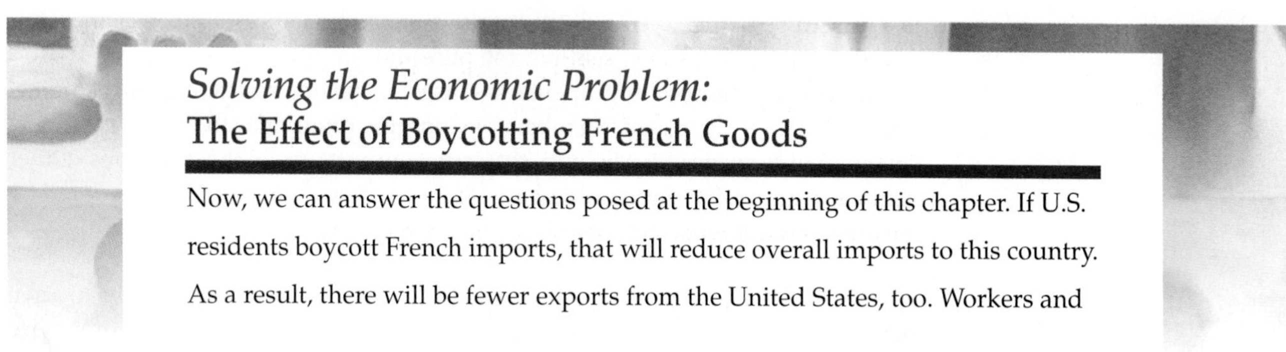

### *Solving the Economic Problem:* The Effect of Boycotting French Goods

Now, we can answer the questions posed at the beginning of this chapter. If U.S. residents boycott French imports, that will reduce overall imports to this country. As a result, there will be fewer exports from the United States, too. Workers and

*Continued on next page*

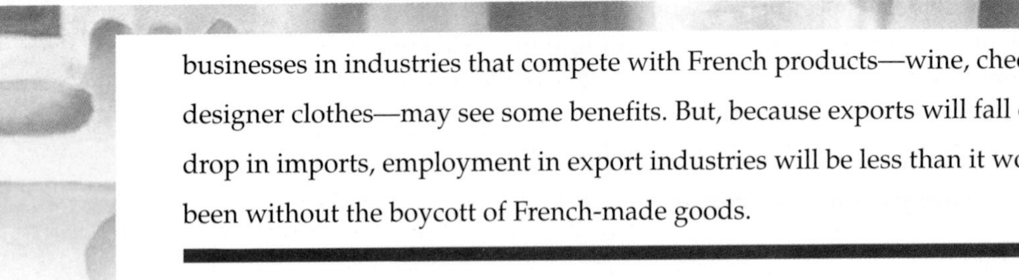

businesses in industries that compete with French products—wine, cheese, and designer clothes—may see some benefits. But, because exports will fall due to the drop in imports, employment in export industries will be less than it would have been without the boycott of French-made goods.

**Mastering Concepts:** There Is a Relationship Between Imports and Exports

- **Imports ultimately are paid for by exports.**
- **Any restriction on imports leads to a restriction on exports and therefore to lower employment in export industries.**
- **Although it is possible to preserve jobs in narrow sectors of the economy by restricting foreign competition, it is impossible to preserve jobs throughout the economy by imposing import restrictions.**

## THE ARGUMENTS AGAINST UNRESTRICTED INTERNATIONAL TRADE

When a company in one state competes directly with a company in another state, the more successful company may drive the other one out of business. Rarely, if ever, do we hear cries for preventing such competition. As soon as competition comes from other countries, though, cries for restrictions on international trade arise, and politicians often listen.

Of course, protecting U.S. jobs tops the list of reasons some people (and their elected representatives) give to support restrictions on international trade. There are other arguments, too. They involve so-called infant industries and countering foreign subsidies.

### PROTECTING AMERICAN JOBS

Let's face it, most people do not like competition—at least when they are the ones who have to compete. This is true for businesses and for workers, too. So, when domestic steelworkers making over $70,000 a year say that imports of foreign steel should be severely curtailed to save their jobs, what do they really mean? The workers mean that they want the company where they work to stay in business so that they can continue their present employment at the same or higher salaries. It is an argument based on their self-interest, pure and simple.

All sorts of patriotic arguments are used to justify restricting international trade in order to save jobs. Members of Congress often refer to "slave" wages in developing countries as a reason to restrict imports from those nations. Other politicians argue that we should restrict imports from countries that do not follow the same environmental standards as the United States.

**The Cost to Consumers** When imports are restricted supposedly to save jobs, the short-run effect is to reduce the supply of the particular good or service in question and thus to raise its price to consumers, as you can read in the following *Policy Application*.

## POLICY APPLICATION: The High Cost of Saving U.S. Jobs

### *Concept Applied:* Restricting Imports

One of the best examples of how import restrictions raise prices to consumers has been in the automobile industry, where "voluntary" restrictions on Japanese car imports were in place for more than a decade. Due in part to the enhanced quality of imported cars, sales of domestically produced automobiles fell from 9 million units in the late 1970s to an average of 6 million units per year between 1980 and 1982. As you can imagine, profits of U.S. automobile manufacturers fell as well. The U.S. automakers and the auto workers' unions demanded protection from import competition.

#### Politicians Responded with Trade Restrictions

Politicians from automobile-producing states were sympathetic to the "cause." The result was a "voluntary" agreement entered into by Japanese car companies. This agreement, which restricted U.S. sales of Japanese cars to 1.68 million units per year, began in April 1981 and continued into the 1990s in various forms.

#### The Cost per Job Saved

Economist Robert W. Crandall estimated how much this "voluntary" trade restriction cost U.S. consumers. According to his estimates, the reduced supply of Japanese cars pushed their prices up by over $1,500 apiece. The higher price of Japanese imports in turn enabled domestic producers to hike their prices an average of over $600 per car. The total tab in the first full year of the program was more than $6.5 billion (expressed in today's dollars). Crandall also estimated the number of jobs in automobile-related industries that were saved by the voluntary import restrictions; the total was about 26,000. Dividing $6.5 billion by 26,000 jobs yields a cost to consumers of more than $250,000 *every year* for each job saved in the automobile industry. U.S. consumers could have saved nearly $2 billion on their car purchases each year if, instead of implicitly agreeing to import restrictions, they had simply given $75,000 to every autoworker whose job was preserved by the voluntary import restraints.

**For Critical Analysis:**
*If it is so costly to save U.S. jobs via import restrictions, why do you think that politicians continue to pass import-restricting legislation?*

▸ Example 16-10 Restrictions on imports on clothing have cost the U.S. consumer $45,000 per year for each job saved. In the steel industry, the cost of preserving a job has been estimated at approximately $750,000 per year. ◂

## Remember That Imports and Exports Are Related

Earlier in this chapter you learned that we pay for imports by exports. Consequently, any restriction on imports leads to a reduction of exports. So, every attempt to save jobs in the United States by restricting imports results in a decline in export sales, at least in the long run. And that means a reduction in employment in export industries.

**The Long-Run Analysis—No Less Shocking** In the long run, the World Trade Organization (WTO) has discovered that attempts to save domestic jobs have been ineffective. The most protected industries in the world have been textiles, clothing, and iron and steel. In the long run, employment has fallen in these industries despite restrictions on imports. ▸ Example 16-11 The WTO estimated that during one long period of restrictions on imports of textiles, clothing, and iron and steel, U.S. employment fell 22 percent in textiles, 18 percent in the clothing industry, and 54 percent in the iron and steel industry. ◂

## Protecting the Infants

Another argument against free trade has to do with protecting so-called infant industries. These are industries that are just getting started. The argument goes as follows: if you protect the new industry from stiff competition from existing profitable companies in other nations, then it will grow to become a thriving industry that can compete with the "big boys" in other countries. At that point, you can lift the restrictions on competing imports.

**Infant industry argument**
*The contention that an industry that is just getting started should be protected from import competition. After the industry grows, the import restrictions can be lifted.*

### The Infant Industry Argument

Perhaps this **infant industry argument** has some merit in the short run. Such a policy is easily abused, however. Often the protectionist import restrictions remain in force long after the infant has "matured." If other countries can still produce more cheaply than our protected "infant," those who benefit from continued protection are the stockholders and workers in the protected industry. The people who lose out are, you guessed it, consumers. They must pay higher prices than the world price for the particular product or service in question.

### Additional Problems with the Infant Industry Argument

We do not know beforehand which "infant" industries will eventually survive. So, no one can really tell which "infant" industry should be protected. ▸ **Example 16-12** The infant industry argument was used to justify import restrictions on high-powered motorcycles in the 1980s. Strange as it may seem, politicians were able to argue that the Harley-Davidson Motor Company—founded in the early part of the twentieth century and the only U.S. company manufactur-

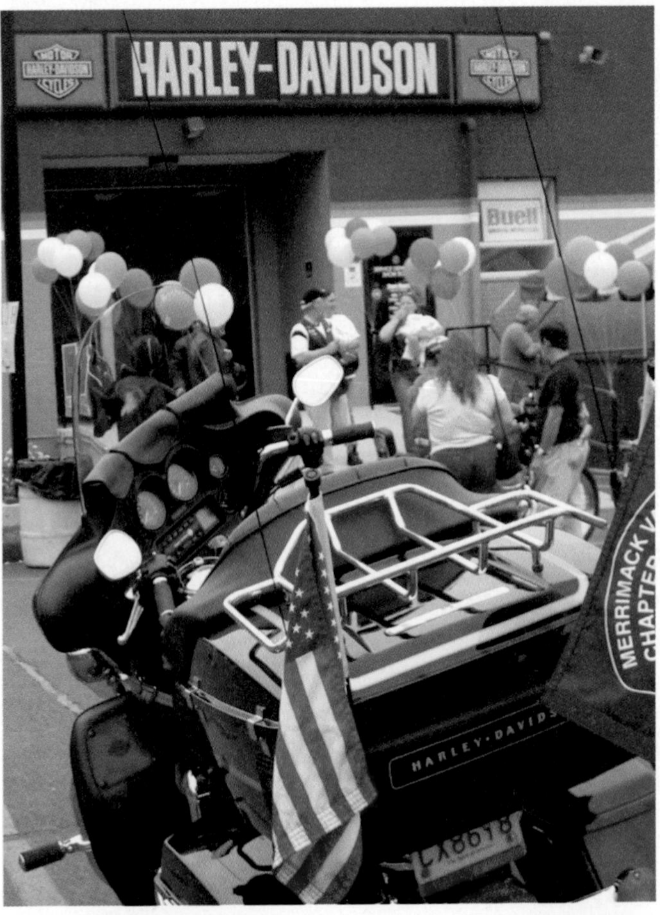


*This Harley-Davidson store has directly benefited from import restrictions on competing foreign-made motorcycles. Who, ultimately, paid for those restrictions?*

ing motorcycles at the time—should be treated as an "infant." Back in the early 1970s, Harley had 100 percent of the market for large motorcycles. A decade later, it had less than 15 percent. In the meantime, Honda, Yamaha, Suzuki, and Kawasaki became fierce competitors with serious product innovations and lower prices. Harley-Davidson was successful in getting import restrictions assessed against these competitors, perhaps so that it could have a second childhood. ◂

**The Ultimate Ulterior Motive** The infant industry argument in favor of restricting a specific imported good (or service) often masks the true reason why a particular industry believes it cannot compete. This true reason may be that the domestic industry has not been able to lower its costs sufficiently to be globally competitive. In other words, the infant industry argument in favor of international trade restrictions is used by those who will benefit most—workers and businesses in the particular industry—and, as always, consumers in general lose out.

Sometimes protecting an "infant industry" can have counterproductive effects, particularly from a government policy point of view, as you will discover in the following *Policy Application*.

## POLICY APPLICATION: Protecting an Undesirable Domestic Industry

### *Concept Applied:* Infant Industry Argument

After Prohibition ended in the 1930s, the head of the FBI convinced the federal government to make marijuana illegal. Nonetheless, the market for marijuana remained vigorous and growing.

#### Imports Were the Major Source of the Product

Before the 1930s, when marijuana was legal, most of it was imported, and it continued to come from abroad after it was made illegal. Indeed, until about 25 years ago virtually all of the marijuana consumed in the United States was imported. Since then, though, the domestic "infant" marijuana industry has thrived. Why? Because of import restrictions.

#### The War on Drugs Leads to Protection from Foreign Marijuana Imports

In the 1970s, President Richard Nixon declared a "war on drugs." Since then, large amounts of resources have gone into preventing the importation of marijuana from Mexico, Central America, South America, and Southeast Asia. In effect, the federal government has protected the domestic marijuana industry from imports. With virtually no foreign competition, the U.S. marijuana industry has expanded, and the producing participants have invested millions of dollars to develop more productive and more potent seeds as well as more efficient growing technologies.

Domestic marijuana growers now dominate the high end of the market where consumers pay from $300 to $700 per ounce for genetically modified homegrown product. This formerly "infant" industry has developed new growing technologies, such as high-intensity sodium lights, carbon-dioxide-enriched atmospheres, and genetically modified plants. The result: a kilogram of potent Sinsemilla marijuana can now be produced every two months in a space no bigger than a phone booth! The increasingly high-tech marijuana industry now generates $35 billion a year, and marijuana has become the nation's biggest cash crop.

**For Critical Analysis:**
*Why weren't domestic marijuana producers investing in new technologies before the 1970s?*

## The Foreign Subsidization Argument

Sometimes domestic producers argue that foreign producers are subsidized by their governments and therefore constitute "unfair" competitors. The domestic producers ask the U.S. government to protect them by imposing import restrictions on the supposedly subsidized foreign goods.

The amount of foreign producer subsidization is, of course, often exaggerated. Moreover, one might ask why foreign governments wish to subsidize U.S. consumers. And, if they want to give U.S. consumers free gifts, why shouldn't we take them?

### The Dumping Argument

**Dumping**
*Selling a good or a service abroad below the price charged in the home market or at a price below its cost of production.*

Some U.S. producers also argue that foreign producers sell their products in the United States at a price that is lower than the price at which they sell those same products in their own countries. This is called **dumping.** Dumping is defined as selling abroad at a lower price than at home or selling at a price that is below the marginal cost of production (defined in Chapter 5). Again, even though this phenomenon might exist, its effect is often exaggerated by proponents of so-called anti-dumping laws. Additionally, if a producer in another country wishes to sell its products to U.S. consumers at below marginal cost, this represents a gift. Why shouldn't U.S. consumers take such gifts?

**Mastering Concepts:** The Arguments Against Unrestricted International Trade

- **The most popular argument against free trade is that import restrictions save U.S. jobs. Given, though, that any restriction on imports reduces exports, restrictions on imports only benefit the protected industries; export industries lose out, as does the economy as a whole.**
- **Some argue that certain industries need to be protected during their early years because they are "infants." Once they grow up, according to this argument, trade restrictions can be lifted.**
- **Other arguments against free trade are that we must restrict trade from countries whose governments subsidize export industries or whose companies sell goods abroad for less than they sell them domestically.**

## QUOTAS, TARIFFS, AND FREE TRADE ZONES

The U.S. government uses two key tools to restrict foreign trade. They are *import quotas* and *tariffs.*

### Quotas

**Import quota**
*A restriction imposed on the value or number of units of a particular good that can be brought into a country. Foreign suppliers are unable to sell more than the amount specified in the import quota.*

An **import quota** is a restriction imposed on the value of or the number of units of a particular good that can be brought into the United States. The easiest way to understand the effects of a quota is to use a supply and demand analysis. We do this in Figure 16-2 for textiles.

Supply and demand are shown for textiles that are imported into the United States. In the absence of any restrictions, the equilibrium price is $1.00 per yard, and we import 900 million yards per year. Now the U.S. government imposes a quota of 800 million yards per year. That means that the supply curve can no longer extend outward and to the right, like a normal supply curve. Instead, it becomes a vertical line at 800 million yards of textiles imported per year. It intersects the demand curve at $1.50 per yard. The result is that U.S. consumers pay a higher price on imported textiles. In addition, they pay a higher price on substitute domestic textiles. This benefits domestic textile producers.

*Animated*

**Figure 16-2 The Effect of Quotas on Textile Imports**

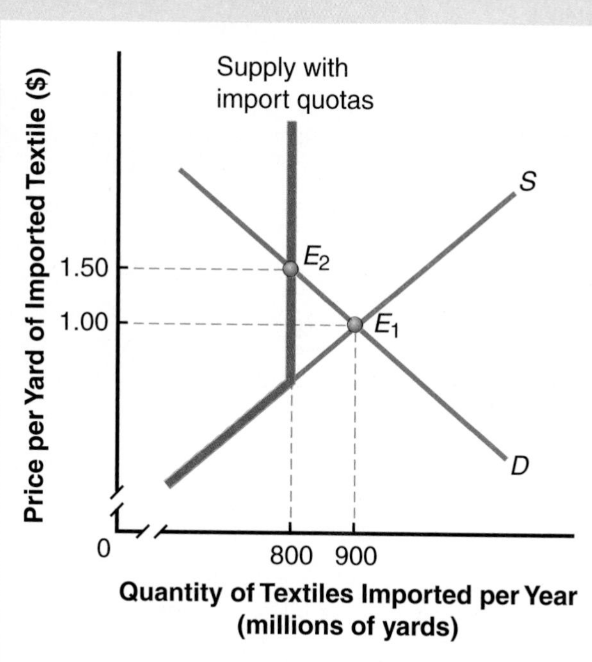


Without restrictions, at point $E_1$, 900 million yards of textiles would be imported each year into the United States at the world price of $1.00 per yard. If the federal government imposes a quota of only 800 billion yards, the effective supply curve becomes vertical at that quantity. It intersects the demand curve at point $E_2$, so the new equilibrium price is $1.50 per yard.

▸ **Example 16-13** Actually, the U.S. textile industry has its own import-restricting organization called the Committee for Implementation of Textile Agreements (CITA). The CITA holds no open meetings. At times, it has placed quotas on men's underwear from the Dominican Republic, cotton nightwear from Jamaica, and wool coats from Honduras. The benefit from CITA quotas for the U.S. textile industry has been estimated as high as $12 billion in additional profits each year. ◂

## Tariffs

**Tariffs** are taxes specifically on imports. They can be set as a particular dollar amount per unit, say, 10 cents per pound, or they can be set as a percentage of the value of the imported commodity.

**Tariffs**
*Taxes on imported goods.*

**Tariffs Have Been Around for a Long Time** Tariffs have been a part of the import landscape for 200 years. Look at Figure 16-3 on page 344, which shows tariff rates in the United States since 1820. ▸ **Example 16-14** One of the most famous examples of the use of tariffs was the Smoot-Hawley Tariff Act of 1930. It included tariff schedules for over 20,000 products, raising taxes on affected imports by an average of 52 percent. The Smoot-Hawley Tariff Act encouraged similar import-restricting policies by the rest of the world. The United Kingdom, France, the Netherlands, and Switzerland soon adopted high tariffs, too. The result was a massive reduction in international trade. According to many economists, this exacerbated the ongoing worldwide depression of the period. ◂

**Using Supply and Demand Analysis to Show the Effects of Tariffs** We can examine the effects of tariffs using supply and demand analysis, similar to the

## Figure 16-3 Tariff Rates in the United States Since 1820

Tariff rates in the United States have bounced around like a football; indeed, in Congress, tariffs are a political football. Import-competing industries prefer high tariffs. In the twentieth century, the highest tariff was the Smoot-Hawley Tariff of 1930, which was about as high as the tariff of "abominations" in 1828.

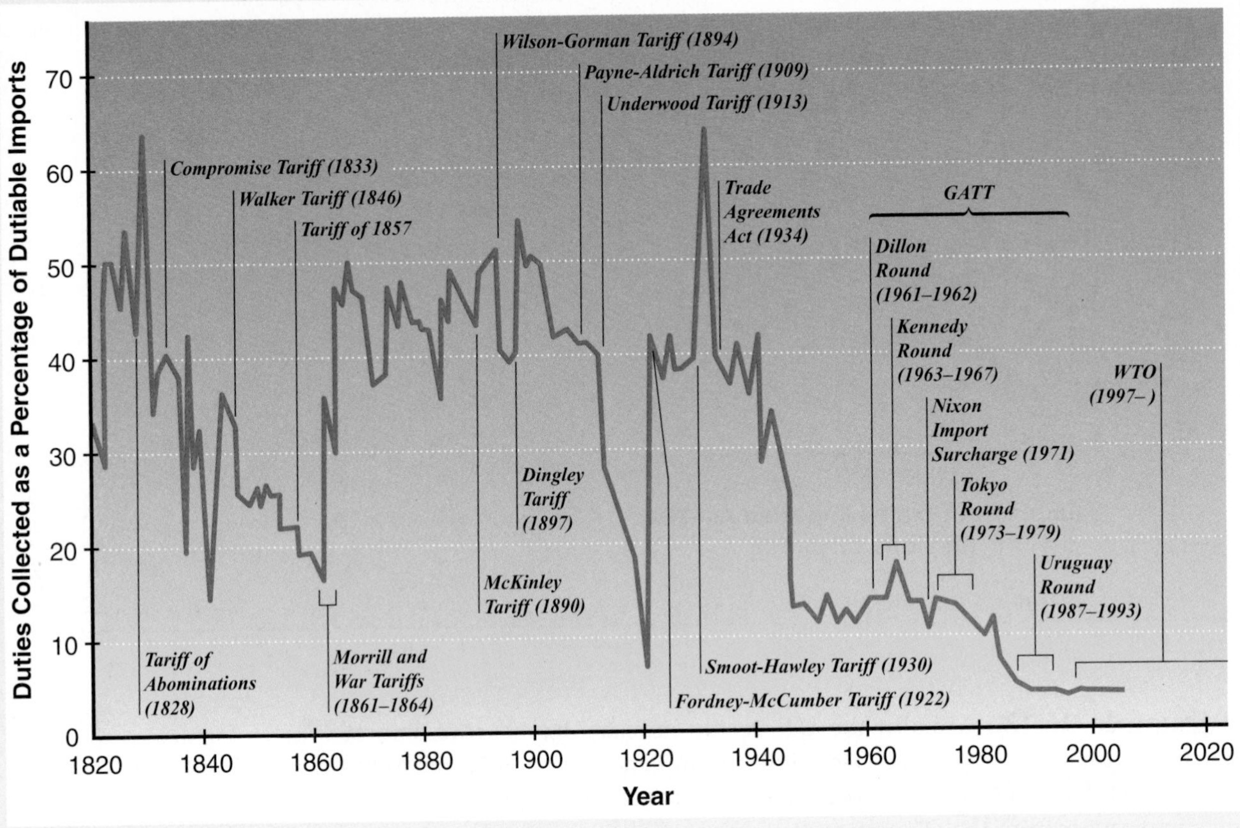


analysis we used in Figure 16-2. Look at the two panels of Figure 16-4. The good is a laptop computer, which in our example can be made in Japan and in the United States. In panel (a) of Figure 16-4, you see the demand for and supply of Japanese laptops. The equilibrium price is $1,000 per constant-quality unit, and the equilibrium quantity is 10 million per year. In panel (b), you see the same equilibrium price of $1,000; at this price, the *domestic* equilibrium quantity is 5 million units per year.

Now a tariff of $500 is imposed on all imported Japanese laptops. The supply curve shifts vertically by $500 to $S_2$. For purchasers of Japanese laptops, the price increases to $1,250. The quantity demanded falls to 8 million per year. In panel (b), you see that at the higher price of imported Japanese laptops, the demand curve for U.S.-made laptops shifts outward to the right to $D_2$. The equilibrium price increases to $1,250, and the equilibrium quantity also increases to 6.5 million units per year. Therefore, the tariff benefits domestic laptop producers because it increases the demand for their products due to the higher price of a close substitute, Japanese laptops. This causes a redistribution of income from Japanese producers and U.S. consumers of laptops to U.S. producers of laptops.

## Figure 16-4 The Effect of a Tariff on Japanese-Made Laptop Computers

Without a tariff, the United States buys 10 million Japanese laptops per year at an average price of $1,000, at point $E_1$ in panel (a). U.S. producers sell 5 million domestically made laptops, also at $1,000 each, at point $E_1$ in panel (b). A $500-per-laptop tariff shifts the Japanese import supply curve to $S_2$ in panel (a), so that the new equilibrium is at $E_2$. The price rises to $1,250, and the quantity sold declines to 8 million per year. The demand curve for U.S.-made laptops (which are not subject to the tariff) shifts to $D_2$, in panel (b). Domestic sales increase to 6.5 million per year, at point $E_2$.

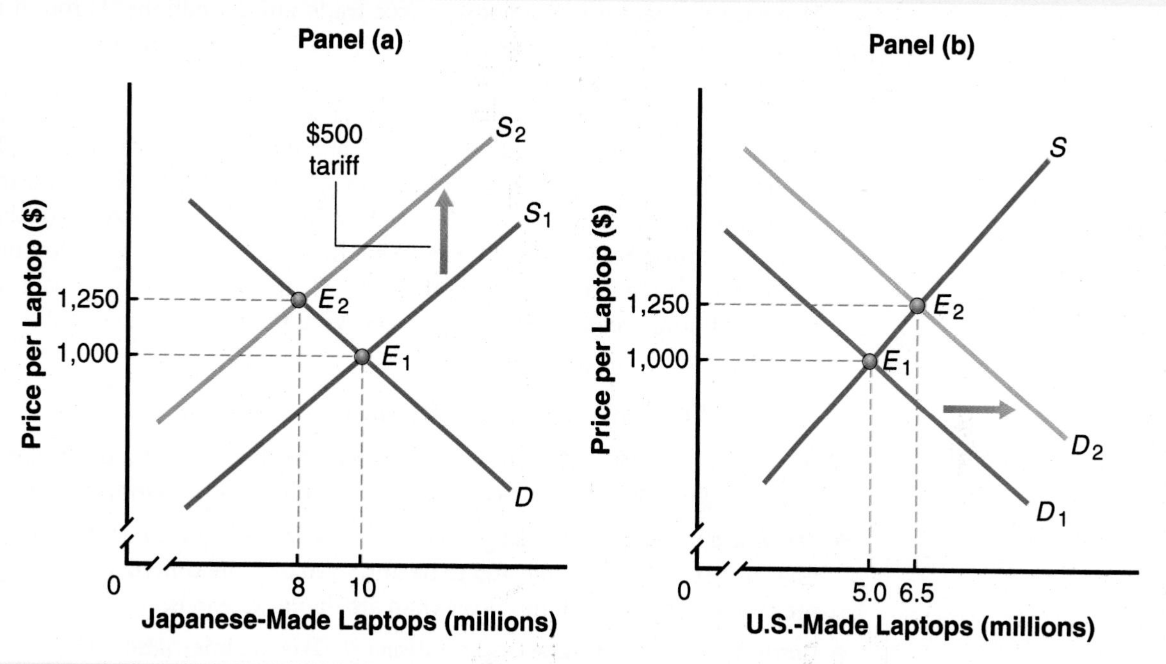


## THE WORLD TRADE ORGANIZATION (WTO)

Since 1997, the principal institution overseeing tariffs throughout the world has been the World Trade Organization (WTO). The goal of the nations that created the WTO was to lessen trade barriers throughout the world so that all nations can benefit from freer international trade.

The WTO's many tasks include administering trade agreements, acting as a forum for trade negotiations, settling trade disputes, and reviewing national trade policies. Today, the WTO has more than 140 members, accounting for over 97 percent of world trade. Another 30 countries are negotiating to obtain membership. Since the WTO came into being, it has settled many trade disputes between countries, sometimes involving the United States.

▸ **Example 16-15** A few years ago, the United States, backed by five Latin American banana-exporting nations, argued before the WTO that the banana import rules of the European Union (EU) favored former European colonies in Africa and the Caribbean at the expense of Latin American growers and U.S. marketing companies. Specifically, Chiquita Banana claimed that its earnings had fallen because its competitors' bananas received preferential treatment from the EU. Because the EU would not back down, the United States imposed a 100 percent tariff on almost $200 million worth of EU items in nine categories. The tariffs were backed by the WTO. Finally, the WTO brokered a deal between the United States and the EU. The EU agreed to dismantle its banana import policy that favored European multinationals and former European colonies. The United States agreed to drop the 100 percent tariff.

## Free Trade Areas and Common Markets—The Opposite of Restricting Trade

At least some politicians throughout the world understand the benefits of lowering or even eliminating restrictions on free trade among nations. Through their efforts, some nations and groups of nations have created free trade areas, sometimes called common markets.

The oldest and best-known common market is known today as the European Union (EU). As of 2004, the EU consists of 25 member nations, which have eliminated almost all restrictions on trade in both goods and services among themselves. On the other side of the Atlantic, the best-known free trade zone consists of Canada, the United States, and Mexico. This free trade zone was created by the North American Free Trade Agreement (NAFTA), approved by Congress in 1993. There are additional regional free trade areas within Latin America and Asia.

**Mastering Concepts:** Quotas, Tariffs, and Free Trade Zones

- **Import quotas limit either the value or the number of units of a particular imported good that can be brought into the United States during any period.**
- **Tariffs are taxes on imported goods. No restriction is imposed on the physical quantity of such goods allowed to be imported into the United States; they are simply subject to higher taxes than are domestic goods.**
- **Currently, the World Trade Organization (WTO) is the international body that acts as a forum for trade negotiations and attempts to reduce trade restrictions worldwide.**

## SUMMING IT ALL UP

- Imports are all of the goods and services that we buy from other countries for domestic consumption or use in the production of domestic goods and services.
- Exports are all of the goods and services that we sell to foreign countries.
- The growth in world trade since the 1950s has been much greater than the growth in world real GDP.
- Absolute advantage refers to the ability to produce a unit of a good or service using fewer resources than another nation.
- Comparative advantage refers to the ability to produce a good at the lowest opportunity cost.
- When nations specialize in producing those goods and services in which they have a comparative advantage, total world production rises.
- International trade leads to the international transmission of ideas, otherwise called intellectual property.
- Imports ultimately are paid for by exports.
- Any restriction on imports leads to a restriction on exports and therefore to lower employment in export industries.

- The most popular argument against free trade is that trade restrictions save U.S. jobs. Given, though, that any restriction on imports reduces exports, restrictions on imports only benefit the protected industries; export industries lose out, as does the economy as a whole.
- Some argue that certain industries need to be protected during their early years because they are "infants." Once they grow up, according to this argument, trade restrictions can be lifted.
- Other arguments against free trade are that we must restrict trade from countries whose governments subsidize export industries or whose companies sell goods abroad for less than they sell them domestically.
- Import quotas limit either the value or the number of units of a particular imported good that can be brought into the United States during any period.
- Tariffs are taxes on imported goods. No restriction is imposed on the physical quantity of such goods allowed to be imported into the United States; they are simply subject to higher taxes than are domestic goods.
- Currently, the World Trade Organization (WTO) is the international body that acts as a forum for trade negotiations and attempts to reduce trade restrictions worldwide.

## KEY TERMS AND CONCEPTS

absolute advantage **332**
comparative advantage **333**
dumping **342**
exports **330**
import quota **342**
imports **330**
infant industry argument **340**
intellectual property **336**
just-in-time inventory control **336**
specialization **333**
tariffs **343**

## MASTERING ECONOMIC CONCEPTS
## Questions and Problems

**16-1.** The table below lists the combinations of goods in millions of units that it is possible for each country to produce. Based on this table, determine which country has an absolute advantage in producing each good. Determine which country has a comparative advantage in producing each good.

| Ukraine | | Lithuania | |
|---|---|---|---|
| **Sugar Beets** | **Potatoes** | **Sugar Beets** | **Potatoes** |
| 0 | 12 | 0 | 20 |
| 1 | 9 | 2 | 15 |
| 2 | 6 | 4 | 10 |
| 3 | 3 | 6 | 5 |
| 4 | 0 | 8 | 0 |

**16-2.** Assume that it takes 40 worker-days to make a jet and 2 worker-days to make a car in the United States. In contrast, assume that it takes 30 worker-days to make a jet and 1 worker-day to make a car in Japan. Which country has a comparative advantage in producing jets? Which country has a comparative advantage in producing cars?

**16-3.** If the opportunity cost of producing a sweater in the United States is 3 shirts and the opportunity cost of producing a sweater in Canada is 4 shirts, which country should specialize in producing sweaters in order to expand the total production of both goods in the two countries?

**16-4.** What is an import quota? What is a tariff? In what ways are these policies different? In what ways are they similar?

**16-5.** Explain why imports are paid for by exports, at least in the long run.

**16-6.** If the United States establishes trade restrictions on foreign automobiles, what will be the short-run impact on employment in the U.S. auto industry? What will be the long-run impact on employment across all U.S. industries?

**16-7.** In the market for sugar in the United States, which curve—supply or demand—would be affected by an import quota? Would the quota cause an increase or a decrease in the price of sugar in the United States?

**16-8.** Explain the infant industry argument. Does this argument suggest that we should impose trade restrictions or not?

**16-9.** If a foreign government was subsidizing the operations of a foreign company that sold products in the United States, what effect would that government's actions have on the quantity of U.S. imports? In this situation, would U.S. trade restrictions be necessary or not? Why?

**16-10.** How would a 10 percent tariff on the sales price of a foreign good make product dumping more difficult for foreign manufacturers?

**16-11.** How does international trade serve as a means of spreading new ideas and new technology? Give examples.

**16-12.** In general, what effect will any type of trade restriction—an import quota or a tariff—have on the price and quantity of foreign goods sold in this country?

**16-13.** If the U.S. government establishes an import quota, how will this quota affect the price and quantity of imported goods? How will the import quota affect the price and quantity of U.S. substitute goods?

**16-14.** During what year in the 1900s, did the United States have the highest tariffs? What major event likely contributed to the government imposition of such high tariffs?

**16-15.** What is the WTO? Does this organization endeavor to increase or decrease the level of trade restrictions among countries across the world?

## THINKING CRITICALLY

**16-1.** Assume the following table indicates the ability of the United States and Brazil to produce both oranges and sugar, each using the same amount of existing labor over a one-year period.

| | United States | Brazil |
|---|---|---|
| Maximum sugar | 400,000 tons | 300,000 tons |
| Maximum oranges | 900,000 tons | 900,000 tons |

Based on these figures, which country has an absolute advantage in producing each good? Which country has a comparative advantage in producing each good? Of course, any industry would support any measure that gives that industry an advantage. In this particular case, however, which U.S. industry would be more likely to argue for trade restrictions against the corresponding good produced in Brazil?

**16-2.** In the United States, which of the following industries would politicians argue should have some form of protection through trade restrictions based on the infant industry argument?

a. computer software
b. airplanes
c. automobiles
d. soft drinks

Based on your answers, is the infant industry argument relevant in any situation? Would this argument be more likely to be relevant to an economy other than that of the United States? Why or why not? What potential problems might arise with respect to the appropriate time frame for establishing and maintaining trade barriers based on the infant industry argument?

**16-3.** If another nation imposed trade restrictions against the United States, would a similar response by the United States be appropriate? Would this situation with two sets of trade restrictions be beneficial to the production levels in both countries? Would this situation improve the average per capita levels of personal consumption in both countries? If the United States merely *threatened* to impose trade restrictions, how could this improve the situation? How would this threat change your answers to the previous two questions?

## LOGGING ON

1. To link to a variety of sources of information about U.S. and global anti-dumping policies, go to http://www.uoregon.edu/~bruceb/adpage.html.
2. To download PDF files for U.S. tariff rates on various categories of goods for the most recent year, go to http://www.usitc.gov/taffairs.htm.
3. For information about U.S. quotas on imports of textile products, go to http://www.customs.gov/xp/cgov/import/textiles_and_quotas/.
4. For more information about the World Trade Organization, go to http://www.wto.org.

## USING THE INTERNET FOR ECONOMIC ANALYSIS

**Taking a Look at U.S. International Trade** This application allows you to apply what you have learned in this chapter to actual U.S. international trade statistics.

**Title:** U.S. International Trade in Goods and Services

**Navigation:** Go to http://www.census.gov/foreign-trade/www/press.html.

**Application** Perform the indicated operations, and answer the accompanying questions.

1. Click on "Exhibit 15: Exports and Imports of Goods by Principal SITC Commodity Groupings" and examine the data. During the most recent months displayed in the report, for which goods did the United States export more units than it imported (a trade surplus)? For which goods did the United States import more than it exported (a trade deficit)? Are there any patterns among the types of goods within the surplus and deficit categories? If so, do these patterns provide any indication of whether the United States may have either an absolute or a comparative advantage?
2. Back up and click on "Exhibits 3 and 4: U.S. Services by Major Category—Exports and Imports," and examine the data in each exhibit. Does the United States tend to experience trade surpluses or deficits in services? Does this provide any indication of whether the United States may have either an absolute or a comparative advantage in services?

## MEDIA RESOURCE LIST

The following media resources are available with this chapter.

- Load your CD-ROM to listen to the audio introduction to this chapter.
- Load your CD-ROM to access a Graph Animation of Figure 16-1, *World Trade Keeps Growing.*
- Load your CD-ROM to view the video on *Output Gains from Specialization.*
- Load your CD-ROM to view the video on *Arguments Against Free Trade.*
- Load your CD-ROM to access a Graph Animation of Figure 16-2, *The Effect of Quotas on Textile Imports.*
- Test your knowledge of chapter concepts with a quiz at www.miller-ume.com.
- Link to Web resources related to the text coverage at www.miller-ume.com.

## HOMEWORK SET

Go to the end of this book to find the Homework Problems for this chapter.

# CHAPTER 17

# Financing World Trade

## *Facing an Economic Problem:* Do U.S. Residents Buy Too Many Goods and Services from Other Countries?

If you believe the popular press, you certainly must feel that the U.S. international trade situation is out of balance. After all, the value of what we purchase from abroad greatly exceeds the value of what the rest of the world buys from us. In other words, the United States suffers from a continuous trade deficit, which sometimes exceeds $400 billion a year.

Some see this huge trade deficit as an indication that the United States is no longer competitive in the global marketplace. Others claim that our "excessive" purchases of imports are unsustainable—they cannot go on year after year. Finally, yet others claim that the excess of imports over exports has actually reduced U.S. living standards.

You will find out in this chapter that we probably should not be too concerned that we are buying too many imports. You will also see that there is a flipside to this purported problem—foreigners have invested in the United States in record amounts.

## Learning Objectives

After reading this chapter, you should be able to:

- **Explain how foreign exchange rates are determined.**
- **Differentiate between floating and fixed exchange rate systems.**
- **Contrast the balance of trade and the balance of payments.**
- **Explain why a trade deficit is not necessarily detrimental to the U.S. economy.**

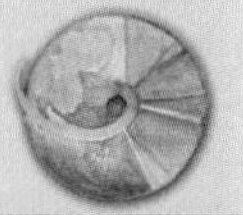

***Refer to the back of this chapter for a complete listing of multimedia learning materials available on the CD-ROM and the Web site.***

## TRADING CURRENCIES IN FOREIGN EXCHANGE MARKETS

You live in a nation where the U.S. dollar reigns supreme. It is the legal currency accepted in virtually all transactions in this country. Such is not the case elsewhere. ▸ Example 17-1 If you hop on a plane in San Francisco to visit a distant relative in Tokyo, you might be in for a rude awakening when you go to pay the taxi driver who picked you up at the airport. If you try to give him U.S. dollars, in most cases he will refuse them. Why? Because in Japan the national currency, or medium of exchange, is the yen, not the U.S. dollar. ◂

▸ Example 17-2 If you go on the Internet to purchase a case of Chardonnay white wine directly from a Chilean winery, you probably will not be able to send a check written on a U.S. bank. Why? Because the winery in Chile pays its workers in the local currency—the peso—not in U.S. dollars. Thus, the winery wants pesos from you. ◂

Currently, there are over 100 different national currencies in existence. When U.S. residents want to purchase goods or services in other countries, they typically have to exchange their U.S. dollars for the other countries' currencies. When foreigners wish to buy goods or invest in the United States, they have to do the reverse—exchange their local currency for U.S. dollars. Not surprisingly, a worldwide market exists for such exchanges. It is called the **foreign exchange market.** Like all markets, the worldwide foreign exchange market consists of the demand for, and the supply of, different currencies.

**Foreign exchange market**
*A worldwide market for buying and selling different currencies.*

### THE DEMAND FOR AND SUPPLY OF FOREIGN CURRENCIES

In general, people do not want to buy foreign currencies just for the fun of it. Of course, there are **speculators** who make their living betting on movements in the prices of foreign currencies. Let us ignore those speculative demands for foreign currency and focus on the demand by those who want to buy imports (or sell exports) of goods and services.

**Speculators**
*Those who assume a business risk in the hope of gains; those who buy and sell in expectation of profiting from market fluctuations.*

**The Demand for Foreign Exchange** To keep the analysis simple, we'll concentrate on the demand by U.S. residents for Japanese yen. Every time a U.S. resident wants to buy a Japanese laptop, a Japanese car, a Japanese-made MP3 player, or a Japanese-made DVD player/recorder, such decisions create a demand for Japanese yen.

In this sense, the demand for any foreign currency is a **derived demand;** that is, it is derived from the demand for the imported good or service desired. Derived demand is not a new concept—you already learned about it in Chapter 9 when you examined labor markets. There, you saw that the demand for labor is a derived demand in that it is derived from the demand for the final product.

**Derived demand**
*The demand for a currency that is derived from the demand for imports.*

The same analysis applies to foreign exchange.

> ***The more goods and services U.S. residents desire to purchase from Japanese companies, the greater the demand for Japanese yen. (This concept applies equally well to all countries and currencies.)***

**The Demand Curve for Foreign Exchange Slopes Downward** Paying an exchange rate, which is the price of one currency in terms of another currency, is no different from paying a certain price for anything else you want to buy. If you like hot tea, you know you have to pay about 75 cents a cup. If the price goes up to $2.50, you will probably buy fewer cups. If the price goes down to 25 cents, you will buy more. In other words, the demand curve for cups of tea, expressed in terms of dollars, slopes downward, following the law of demand. The demand curve for any foreign currency, such as Japanese yen, slopes downward, too.

**Appreciation and Depreciation** Let's think more closely about the demand schedule for yen. Let's say that it costs you 1 cent to purchase 1 yen; that is the exchange rate between dollars and yen. If tomorrow you had to pay $1\frac{1}{4}$ cents ($0.0125) for the same yen, the exchange rate would have changed. Looking at such a change, we would say that there has been an **appreciation** in the value of the yen in the foreign exchange market. But another way to view this increase in the value of the yen is to say that there has been a **depreciation** in the value of the dollar in the foreign exchange market. The dollar used to buy 100 yen; tomorrow, the dollar will be able to buy only 80 yen at a price of $1\frac{1}{4}$ cents per yen. If the dollar price of yen rises, you will demand fewer yen. Why? You can find the answer by looking at the reason you and others demand yen in the first place.

**Appreciation**
*An increase in the exchange value of one nation's currency in terms of the currency of another nation.*

**Depreciation**
*A decrease in the exchange value of one nation's currency in terms of the currency of another nation.*

**Appreciation and Depreciation of Japanese Yen** Recall that in our example you and others demand yen to buy Japanese-made laptops, cars, MP3 players, and DVD players/recorders. The demand curve for Japanese products, we will assume, follows the law of demand and therefore slopes downward. If it costs more U.S. dollars to buy the same quantity of Japanese products, presumably you and other U.S. residents will not buy the same quantity; your quantity demanded will be less. We say that:

> ***Your demand for Japanese yen is* derived from *your demand for Japanese products.***

Now let's look at the supply of Japanese yen.

**The Supply of Foreign Currency** Residents of Japan often wish to purchase goods and services from businesses located in the United States. Japanese residents may wish to purchase U.S.-made laptop computers from, for example, IBM. Certainly, Japanese residents buy lots of software from Seattle-based Microsoft Corporation. In any event, every time a Japanese resident desires to purchase a U.S. good or service, that resident must acquire dollars to make those purchases. The result is a supply of Japanese yen available in the marketplace, provided by Japanese residents who wish to purchase U.S.-made goods and services.

> ***The more U.S.-made goods and services Japanese residents desire, the greater the supply of Japanese yen. (This concept applies equally well to all countries and currencies.)***

**The Supply Curve for Japanese Yen Slopes Up** Assume that Japanese laptop manufacturers buy U.S. microprocessors. The supply of Japanese yen is a derived supply in that it is derived from the Japanese demand for U.S. microprocessors. We could go through an example similar to the one for laptop computers to come up with a supply schedule of Japanese yen in Japan. It slopes upward. Obviously, the Japanese want dollars to purchase U.S. goods. When the dollar price of yen goes up, Japanese residents will be willing to supply more yen because they can then buy more U.S. goods with the same quantity of yen. That is, the yen will be worth more in exchange for U.S. goods than when the dollar price of yen was lower.

▸ **Example 17-3** Suppose a U.S.-produced microprocessor costs $200. If the exchange rate is 1 cent per yen, a Japanese resident will have to come up with 20,000 yen (= $200 at $0.0100 per yen) to buy one microprocessor. If, however, the exchange rate goes up to $1\frac{1}{4}$ cents for yen, a Japanese resident must come up with only 16,000 yen (= $200 at $0.0125 per yen) to buy a U.S. microprocessor. At this lower price (in yen) of U.S. microprocessors, the Japanese will demand a larger quantity. In other words, as the price of yen goes up in terms of dollars, the quantity of U.S. microprocessors demanded will go up, and hence the quantity of yen supplied will go up. Therefore, the supply schedule of yen, which is derived from the Japanese demand for U.S. goods, will slope upward. ◂

**Equilibrium for Each Foreign Currency** Equilibrium is a condition in which the price of something has no further tendency to change, at least in the short run. Equilibrium in the market for a foreign currency is the result of the worldwide demand for and worldwide supply of that currency. We can depict equilibrium on a graph with which you are already familiar. We do this in Figure 17-1, which shows the equilibrium price of Japanese yen—the foreign exchange rate—at a point in time. The graph shows the demand for Japanese yen by U.S. residents and the supply of Japanese yen offered by Japanese residents. The result is a price of 1 cent per yen in terms of U.S. currency. The price of 1 cent per yen means that to purchase, say, a Japanese laptop computer that costs 200,000 yen in Japan, the U.S. resident would have to fork over 2,000 U.S. dollars.

▸ **Example 17-4** Of course, the equilibrium price of every foreign currency, including the Japanese yen, changes all of the time. Look, nonetheless, at Table 17-1. Here we show the value of the Japanese yen in terms of dollars at a recent date. We also show the dollar value of the euro, the British pound, the Russian ruble, and the Indian rupee. ◂

## SHIFTS IN THE DEMAND FOR FOREIGN CURRENCIES

You learned in Chapter 3 that a change, or a shift, in the demand for any good or service usually causes a change in the price of that good or service. The same is true for foreign currencies. ▸ **Example 17-5** Assume that the *New York Times* published an article demonstrating that Japanese laptop computers were more reliable

**Figure 17-1 Finding the Equilibrium Price of a Foreign Currency**

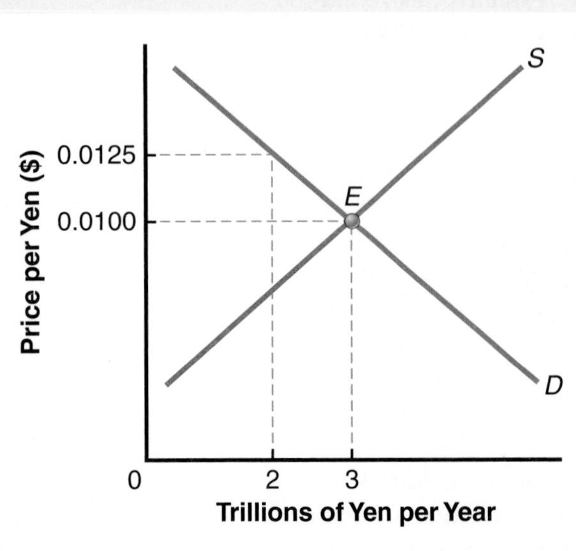


Equilibrium for any foreign currency is a result of the worldwide demand for and supply of that currency. That is what we show here. The equilibrium price, determined by the intersection of the demand and supply curves, is at *E*. The price is 1 cent per yen. At that price, U.S. residents demand 3 trillion yen per year in this hypothetical example. If the price increases to 1.25 cents per yen, U.S. residents will demand only 2 trillion yen per year.

## Table 17-1 Prices of Selected Foreign Currencies

Below you see foreign exchange rates (another way to say the price of foreign currencies) for Japan, Britain, Russia, India, and the European countries that use the common currency called the euro. If you needed 100 euros to pay for a taxi ride from the airport in Berlin to your hotel, how many U.S. dollars would you have to pay?

| Currency | Price in Terms of U.S. Dollars |
|---|---|
| Japanese yen | 0.009 |
| Euro | 1.211 |
| British pound | 1.731 |
| Russian ruble | 0.034 |
| Indian rupee | 0.022 |

than those made in the United States. That would probably cause an increase in the demand for Japanese laptops. Because the demand for Japanese yen is derived from the demand for Japanese goods and services, the result would be a rise in the demand for yen. The price per yen in dollars would then rise. ◂ Look at Table 17-1 to see some actual exchange rates.

**"Strong" versus "Weak" Currencies** Whenever a currency appreciates in value in the foreign exchange market, commentators talk about the currency "strengthening" or that it is a "strong" currency. Whenever a currency depreciates in value in the foreign exchange market, commentators refer to it as "weakening" or a "weak" currency. These casually used terms are simply a reflection of the value of a certain currency in the foreign exchange market relative to what it was

*"Good God! Has the dollar fallen that far?"*
© Sam Gross. Reprinted with the permission of the cartoonbank.com

*Animated*

**Figure 17-2 The Results of a Shift in the Demand for Japanese Yen**

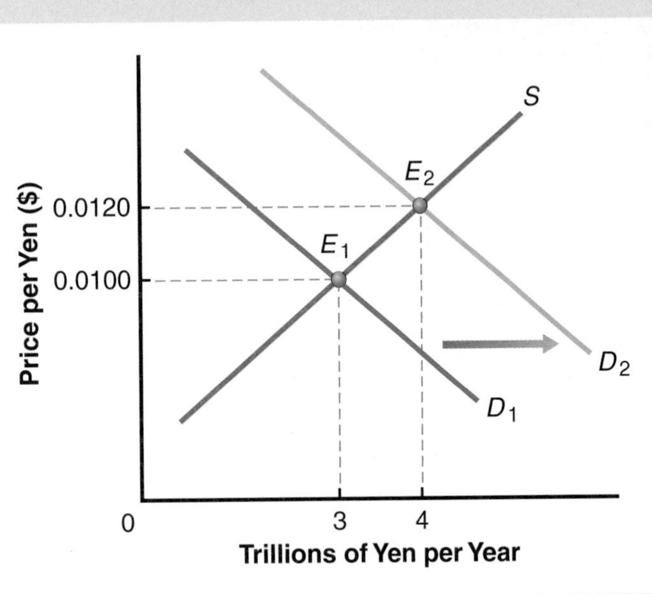


If U.S. residents demand more Japanese products, the derived demand curve for yen will shift outward to the right from $D_1$ to $D_2$. The equilibrium price will rise from 1.0 cent per yen to 1.2 cents per yen, and the equilibrium quantity will increase from 3 trillion to 4 trillion yen per year. Equilibrium changes from $E_1$ to $E_2$.

in the past. ▸ **Example 17-6** When the foreign exchange value of the dollar relative to the euro dropped by over 20 percent in the early 2000s, everyone talked about a "strong" euro and a "weak" dollar. The opposite was true when the dollar's value in the foreign exchange market rose relative to the euro in the late 1990s and 2000. ◂

**Graphing a Shift in the Demand for Japanese Yen** Look at Figure 17-2. There you see the original demand curve for Japanese yen labeled $D_1$. The original equilibrium price of Japanese yen is 1 cent per yen. If the demand for Japanese products in general increases, the derived demand curve for Japanese yen will shift outward to the right to $D_2$ in Figure 17-2. The new equilibrium will move from $E_1$ to $E_2$, and the new equilibrium price per yen will rise to 1.2 cents per yen, representing a "strengthening" of the yen against the dollar.

**Other Things Must Stay Constant** Remember, though, that when you look at a supply and demand graph such as the one in Figure 17-2, you are assuming that all other things do not change. In this case, the supply of Japanese yen has not changed while the demand has. Also, remember that:

> ***Supply and demand diagrams always show the* direction *of change. They do not necessarily show the* exact *magnitude.***

## Shifts in the Supply of Foreign Currencies

The supply of Japanese yen can also change. When that happens, the equilibrium price of yen is affected. ▸ **Example 17-7** Seattle-based Microsoft Corporation has just announced a revolutionary operating system that will make all existing computers run five times faster. It has announced that this new operating system will be sold in Japan this week. Consequently, Japanese computer users will demand more software products from Microsoft and, in the process, supply more yen to the foreign exchange market. ◀

**Graphing a Shift in the Supply of Japanese Yen** Look at Figure 17-3. There you see that the supply of Japanese yen has increased from $S$ to $S_1$. The equilibrium has changed from point $E$ to $E_1$. The equilibrium price of Japanese yen has dropped from 1.0 cent per yen to 0.5 cent per yen, representing a "weakening" of the yen in the foreign exchange market.

**Some Caveats** Just as for the demand for Japanese yen, remember that we are holding all other things constant when the supply of yen changes. We hold the demand for yen constant. In addition, we know that the movement from equilibrium point $E$ to $E_1$ may not last forever. Finally, we are looking only at bilateral trade between the United States and Japan. The market for yen, though, is worldwide because many countries trade with Japan. This means that there will be equilibrium exchange rates between the yen and all other internationally traded currencies, not just between the yen and the U.S. dollar.

## What Determines Exchange Rates?

There are numerous reasons why the demand and supply curves for foreign currencies change. That means that there are many reasons why the exchange rates you read about in the financial pages of local and national newspapers change constantly. Here are just some of the variables that may cause a change in exchange rates:

1. **Changes in Real Interest Rates:** If U.S. interest rates, corrected for people's expectations of inflation (that is, real interest rates), abruptly increase relative to interest rates in the rest of the world, international investors elsewhere will increase their demand for U.S. dollar–denominated assets, thereby increasing

*Animated*

**Figure 17-3 An Increase in the Supply of Japanese Yen**

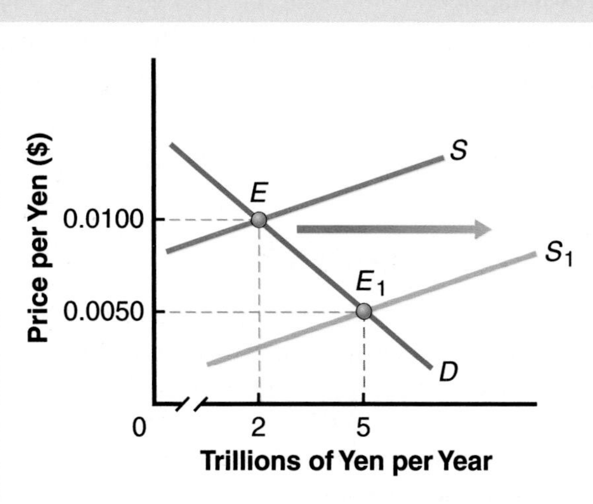


If the Japanese decide to buy more U.S. goods and services, that will be translated into an increase in the supply of Japanese yen from $S$ to $S_1$. Equilibrium will shift from $E$ to $E_1$. The U.S. price of Japanese yen will fall, in this case, from 1.0 cent per yen to 0.5 cents per yen.

the demand for dollars in foreign exchange markets. An increased demand for dollars in foreign exchange markets, other things held constant, will cause the dollar to go up in value—a "strengthening"—and other currencies to go down in value.

2. **Changes in Productivity:** Whenever one country's productivity (see Chapters 2 and 15) increases relative to another's, its products will become more price competitive in world markets. With lower prices in the country experiencing rapid productivity growth, the quantity of its exports demanded will increase. Thus, there will be an increase in the demand for its currency.
3. **Changes in Consumer Preferences:** If Germany's residents suddenly develop a taste for U.S.-made automobiles, this will increase the derived demand for U.S. dollars in foreign exchange markets. The dollar will "strengthen."
4. **Perceptions of Economic Stability:** If the United States looks economically and politically more stable relative to other countries, more foreign residents will want to put their savings into U.S. assets rather than in their own domestic assets. This will increase the demand for dollars. The converse is true, too.

✦ **Beware!** *Just because we can list some of the determinants of changes in exchange rates does not mean that, armed with this knowledge, we can make higher-than-competitive returns from engaging in foreign currency trading. The currencies markets are extremely competitive.*

▸ **Example 17-8** Shortly before the U.S. and British forces attacked Iraq in 2003, there was great uncertainty about whether the attack was going to happen. This uncertainty apparently created anxiety among foreign exchange traders. The value of the dollar relative to the euro fell over 3 percent in just a few days. Foreign exchange market participants must have believed that the political uncertainty created by this "waiting game" would reduce the attractiveness of future investment opportunities in the United States. Once the United States and Britain made it clear that they would not wait any longer to topple the Iraqi regime, the value of the dollar relative to the euro increased by about 3 percent in just a few days. ◂

**Mastering Concepts:** Trading Currencies in Foreign Exchange Markets

- **The demand for a foreign currency is a derived demand, derived from the demand for foreign-produced goods and services.**
- **The supply of a foreign currency is derived from the demand of foreign residents for U.S. goods and services.**
- **The intersection of the demand and supply curves for a foreign currency yields its equilibrium price—its foreign exchange rate.**
- **Any shift in the demand for or the supply of a foreign currency will change the equilibrium foreign exchange rate.**
- **Changes in foreign exchange rates are caused by changes in (1) real interest rates, (2) productivity, (3) consumer preferences, and (4) perceptions of economic stability.**

## FLOATING VERSUS FIXED EXCHANGE RATES

Throughout this text, you have been introduced to the theory and the application of supply and demand analysis as it applies to just about everything. In the previous section on exchange rates, you saw that supply and demand analysis applies equally well to the price of foreign currencies. The price of the yen in terms of dollars changed in response to changes in the supply of and the demand for yen and dollars. Without actually stating it in such terms, the analysis concerned a system of *floating* exchange rates.

## THE MEANING OF FLOATING EXCHANGE RATES

In a **floating (flexible) exchange rate system,** the value of a country's currency in terms of other currencies can change depending on world market conditions. In other words, under a floating exchange rate system, there is no government intervention to attempt to keep the exchange rate at a specific value.

**Floating (flexible) exchange rate system**
*A system in which exchange rates are allowed to fluctuate in the open market in response to changes in supply and demand.*

**Government Intervention in Foreign Exchange Markets** Today, most of the world uses a floating exchange rate system. Occasionally, however, governments do intervene to try to either alter the value of their own currency in the foreign exchange markets or help some other country do so. ▸ International Example 17-9 In the early spring of 2003, the Tokyo stock market hit a 20-year low. In an attempt to bolster its export sector, Japanese monetary officials hinted that they would engage in a massive currency intervention to weaken the yen. The goal of this intervention was to make Japanese exports relatively cheaper to the rest of the world. Within several months, U.S. Secretary of the Treasury John Snow appealed to Japan to stop trying to influence the value of the yen through currency intervention. He was reacting to the Japanese Central Bank's sale of about 630 billion yen in exchange for dollars. ◂

**Managed Exchange Rate Systems** When a government intervenes in an otherwise floating exchange rate system, the result is called a "managed" exchange rate system. In other words, when an exchange rate system is managed, some governments buy and sell currencies in the worldwide foreign exchange market in an attempt to either strengthen or weaken their own currency. Actually, on certain occasions, government leaders have decided to "help" a specific country by intervening in the foreign exchange market to strengthen or weaken the foreign exchange value of that particular currency.

## FIXING THE EXCHANGE RATE

In much of the world before the 1970s and in certain countries today, such as China, exchange rates have been or are fixed by various governments through intervention in the foreign exchange market. Because of this intervention, there are virtually no variations in the foreign exchange value of a domestic currency in a **fixed exchange rate system.**

**Fixed exchange rate system**
*A system in which a national government sets a price for its currency relative to some other currency or currencies.*

**How Does a Government Fix an Exchange Rate?** A good question to ask is, how does any government have the ability to fix the price of its currency in terms of other currencies? The answer relies on—you guessed it—supply and demand analysis.

At the beginning of this chapter, you saw how any change in supply and demand in the foreign exchange market changed the price of a currency—its foreign exchange rate. For our analysis, we will deal with the dollar and the euro. Assume that they are equal in value—one dollar equals one euro. If Americans suddenly want to buy more European products, they are going to flood the market with a larger supply of dollars. In the absence of any government intervention, an increased supply of dollars coupled with a stable demand for dollars from Europeans would lead to a reduction in the price of the dollar relative to the euro. It might fall to, say, 90 cents. ▸ International Example 17-10 So, if it originally took $200 to buy a 200-euro French Hermes silk scarf, and the foreign exchange value of the dollar fell to 90 cents per euro in foreign exchange markets, the scarf would now cost more. If you divide 0.90 into 200 euros, you get $222.22. You would have to pay $22.22 more to buy that same 200-euro French scarf. ◀

**Fixed Exchange Rates Require Government Intervention** In a fixed exchange rate system, if our government wanted to keep the value of a dollar equal to one euro, it would have to intervene in the foreign exchange market to increase the demand for the dollar relative to the euro. To do so, the U.S. government would have to have on hand a stock of euros (often called foreign exchange "reserves"). It would then go into the foreign exchange market with those euros and sell them in exchange for dollars. In this way, the increased *supply* of dollars would be met by an increased *demand* for dollars through the action of the U.S. government. The dollar could therefore remain fixed in value with respect to the euro.

## Currency Crises

As you can imagine, though, any government attempting to fix its own currency in terms of another currency has to have sufficient reserves to keep entering the foreign exchange market. In the example above, the U.S. government would have to continue to sell euros as long as Americans continued to want to buy more European products than in the past. Eventually, the U.S. government would run out of euro reserves, and a so-called *currency crisis* would occur. ▶ International Example 17-11 Before the 1970s, numerous countries on fixed exchange rates experienced recurrent "currency crises." These crises almost always happened because a government ran out of reserves in its attempt to prop up its own currency in the foreign exchange market. Britain faced currency crises in the 1970s. In other words, the British government often ran out of foreign currency reserves and was forced to lower the value of the pound (the British currency) in the foreign exchange market, that is, allow its price to fall to a new lower equilibrium level. ◀

## The Pros and Cons of a Fixed Exchange Rate System

Why might any nation, such as the People's Republic of China today, wish to keep the value of its currency from fluctuating? One reason is that changes in the exchange rate can affect the market values of assets that are denominated in foreign currencies. This can increase the financial risks that a nation's residents face, thereby forcing them to incur costs to avoid these risks.

**Foreign exchange risk**
*The possibility that changes in the value of a nation's currency will result in variations in market values of assets.*

**Foreign Exchange Risk** The possibility that variations in the market value of assets can take place because of changes in the value of a nation's currency is called the **foreign exchange risk** that residents of a country face because their nation's currency's value can fluctuate. ▶ International Example 17-12 Many companies in Thailand owe debts denominated in dollars, but they earn nearly all their revenues in the local currency, the baht, from sales within Thailand. Thus, a decline in the dollar value of the baht means that Thai companies have to allocate a larger portion of their earnings to make the same *dollar* loan payments as before. Thus, a fall in the baht's value increases the operating costs of these companies, thereby reducing their profitability and raising the likelihood of eventual bankruptcy. This happened in 1997–1998, when the dollar value of the baht fell dramatically. ◀

**Hedging to Avoid Foreign Exchange Risks** Limiting foreign exchange risk is a classic rationale for adopting a fixed exchange rate. A country's residents are not defenseless against foreign exchange risk in a floating rate system, though. They can **hedge** against such risk, meaning that they can adopt strategies intended to offset the risk arising from foreign exchange rate fluctuations. In these types of arrangements, the parties agree to the rates ahead of time so they no longer face the risk of price changes caused by fluctuations in currency values.

**Hedge**
*A financial strategy that shifts the risk of suffering losses arising from changes in foreign exchange values.*

▸ International Example 17-13 A company in Thailand has significant euro earnings from sales in Germany. At the same time, it has sizable loans from U.S. investors. It could arrange to convert its euro earnings into dollars via special types of foreign exchange contracts called *currency swaps*. Such currency swaps involve agreed-upon prices of currencies, thereby eliminating exchange rate risks. The Thai company could thereby avoid holding baht and shield itself—hedge—against fluctuations in the baht's value. ◂

**The Exchange Rate as a Shock Absorber** If fixing the exchange rate limits foreign exchange risk faced by individuals and businesses, why do so many nations allow their exchange rates to float? The answer must be that there are potential drawbacks associated with fixing exchange rates. One is that exchange rate variations can actually perform a valuable service for a nation's economy. Consider a situation in which residents of a nation speak only their own nation's language, which is so difficult that hardly anyone else in the world takes the trouble to learn it. As a result, the country's residents are very *immobile*: they cannot trade their labor skills outside their own nation's borders. Now consider two scenarios:

- **Increased Unemployment Under a Fixed Exchange Rate System:** Suppose this nation has chosen to fix its exchange rate. Now imagine that other countries begin to sell products that are *close* substitutes for the products this nation's people specialize in producing. The increased supply of substitutes will cause a sizable drop in demand for this nation's specialized goods. Over a short-run period in which prices and wages cannot adjust, the result will be a sharp decline in production of goods and services, a falloff in real GDP, and higher unemployment.
- **Less Unemployment Under Floating Exchange Rates:** Contrast this situation with one in which the exchange rate floats. In such a case, a sizable decline in outside demand for this nation's products will cause a significant drop in the demand for the nation's currency. As a result, the nation's currency will experience a sizable drop in value in foreign exchange markets, making the goods that this nation offers to sell abroad much less expensive in other countries. This will help offset the reduction in demand, implying that nationwide production will not fall as much and unemployment will not increase as much as under fixed exchange rates.

✦ **Note!** *There is no perfect foreign exchange rate system in which everyone is better off compared to alternative exchange rate systems. As always, different groups will be better off under different systems.*

This example illustrates how exchange rate variations can be beneficial, especially if a nation's residents are relatively immobile. ▸ International Example 17-14 Assume that there is a serious recession in Latvia but business is booming in Denmark. The Danish government allows Latvians to come to work in Denmark where Danish is the official language. Latvians who do not speak Danish can still move to Denmark in search of a better job. Once there, however, they will find that their labor services are not highly valued, despite their skills, because they cannot communicate in Danish. If most residents of Latvia face similar linguistic or cultural barriers, Latvia could be better off with a floating exchange rate system. The recession in Latvia would cause the Latvian currency to depreciate, thereby inducing greater exports while reducing imports. The Latvian economy might then pull itself out of its recession, causing unemployment to fall. ◂

**Mastering Concepts:** Floating versus Fixed Exchange Rates

- **In a floating (flexible) exchange rate system, supply and demand determine the foreign exchange value of a country's currency.**
- **In a fixed exchange rate system, a country's government attempts to keep its foreign exchange rate at some fixed level.**
- **Governments can fix exchange rates only to the extent that they hold sufficient reserves of other nations' currencies necessary to prop up the value of the domestic currency in foreign exchange markets.**
- **While a fixed exchange rate system reduces foreign exchange risk for private individuals and businesses, it eliminates the "shock absorber" function of flexible exchange rates and thereby may increase fluctuations in the unemployment rate.**

## THE BALANCE OF TRADE AND THE BALANCE OF PAYMENTS—THEY'RE MORE THAN JUST NUMBERS

Learning about foreign exchange systems helps in understanding something that is often in the news—changes in a country's international trade position.

### LOOKING AT THE BALANCE OF TRADE—IT NEVER SEEMS TO BALANCE

**Balance of trade**
*The difference between the value of a nation's exports of goods and its imports of goods.*

A currency's exchange rate can have an important effect on a nation's **balance of trade.** The balance of trade is the difference between the value of a nation's exports of goods and its imports of goods. If a nation's currency depreciates, or "weakens," the nation will likely export more goods because its products will become cheaper for other nations' residents to buy. At the same time, its residents will tend to import fewer goods because other nations' goods will become relatively more expensive. In contrast, if a nation's currency increases in value, or "strengthens," the amount of its exports will decline, and its imports will rise.

**Trade deficit**
*The negative difference between exports of goods and imports of goods.*

When the value of goods leaving a nation exceeds the value of those coming in, a positive balance of trade is said to exist. In this case, the nation is bringing in more funds as payments for goods than it is paying out. A negative balance of trade exists when the value of goods coming into a country is greater than the value of those going out. This situation is called a **trade deficit.** ▸ Example 17-15 Since the late 1970s, the United States has consistently had a trade deficit, as you can see in Figure 17-4 on page 364. ◂

As a country, we continue to have a trade deficit with the People's Republic of China, but that may be changing, as the next *Global Application* explains.

## GLOBAL APPLICATION: U.S. Trash Helps Our Trade Deficit with China

***Concepts Applied:***
**Imports, Exports, Trade Deficit**

The U.S. trade deficit with China has risen from about $50 billion in 1997 to over $200 billion today. The residents of China are not yet rich enough to buy much of what the United States produces. In one area, though, the Chinese have increased their purchases dramatically—U.S. scrap and waste.

### Good Old American Junk—There Is a Place for It

Because Americans consume so much, they throw out a lot, too. Our junk includes tons of metal from discarded cars and refrigerators, empty cardboard boxes, and plastic from soda bottles. Virtually every day of every week, U.S. junk is put into balers and crunchers to be stamped, processed, and then placed on ships. These ships often go to China. In fact, over a quarter of all U.S. junk ends up being exported to China. That makes U.S. junk the third largest export to that country, after airplanes and semiconductors.

### A Piece of Junk Here, a Piece of Junk There—It Adds Up

In 1997, we exported less than $200 million of junk to China. Today, that figure exceeds $1.4 billion. One California-based company alone, America Chung Man, Inc., sold U.S. scrap equal in weight to 17 aircraft carriers to China.

The more junk we send to China, the lower our trade deficit with that country. (Our current trade deficit with China exceeds $200 billion per year, so, of course, the current amount of junk exports to China will not change that very much.)

**For Critical Analysis:**
*Is it possible for every country in the world to simultaneously run a trade deficit with all other countries? Why or why not?*

**Trade in Goods versus Trade in Services** When international trade started, literally thousands of years ago, virtually all of it was in the form of trade in goods. Unfortunately, if we think today only in terms of trade in goods, we are actually missing a huge part of international trade. Why? Because today we trade in services, as well as goods. ▸ **Example 17-16** In a recent year, the United States sold $400 billion of services to other countries and purchased about $300 billion of services from other countries. This means that we had a services trade surplus of about $100 billion in that year. ◂

Even though our balance of trade in goods is regularly in deficit, our trade in services has not been for many years. A more logical way to look at trade would be to examine the trade among nations in goods *and* services. Look at Table 17-2 on page 365 to see a list of the major services that the United States trades today.

**Every Trade Deficit Means a Trade Surplus Somewhere Else** Unless you believe that we are trading with people on Mars, the world is a closed trading system. Therefore, when you read that the United States is "suffering" from a continuing trade deficit, you know that other countries are "enjoying" a trade surplus. In other words, world exports must equal world imports. Interestingly, most commentaries on our trade deficit conclude that somehow the United States is worse off because we have a trade deficit.

In reality, though, U.S. consumers are benefiting from all of the imported goods and services. If they were not benefiting, they would be buying domestically produced goods.

***Consumers are always better off if they are allowed to make purchases of any goods and services, no matter where they are produced.***

## Figure 17-4 The U.S. Balance of Trade Almost Always in Deficit

Since the late 1970s, the U.S. balance of trade has always been in deficit.

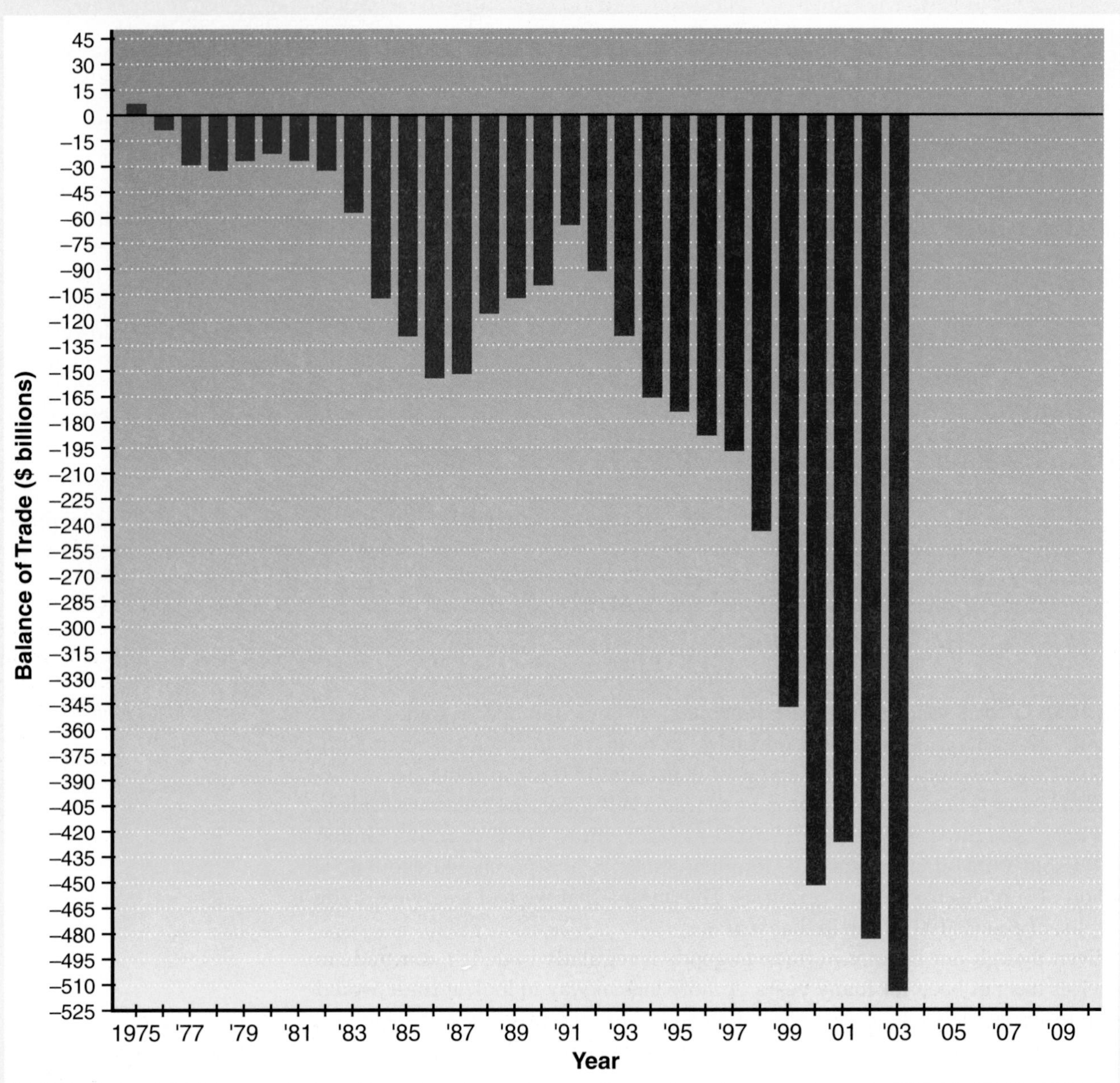


Businesses in competition with foreign producers do not, of course, like foreign competition. But that is true domestically, too. Competition among producers—regardless of where they are located—forces them to produce more efficiently and to create goods and services better suited for today's consumers.

## Now on to the Balance of Payments

The balance of trade refers to trade in physical goods. The balance of goods and services refers to physical goods, plus services, such as banking services. An even more general concept is the *balance of payments*.

**Table 17-2 List of Services That the United States Exports**

- Accounting (auditing, bookkeeping, and tax consulting)
- Advertising
- Business and management consulting
- Communications (including postal services and telecommunication services)
- Construction services (including architectural and engineering)
- Consulting
- Customized software creation
- Environmental technologies
- Financial services (including investment banking)
- Insurance
- Legal services
- Market research
- Personal, cultural, and recreational services (including audiovisual production)
- Public opinion polling services
- Public relation services
- Royalties and license fees (including franchise fees)
- Trade-related services (including merchandizing)
- Transportation (including passenger and freight on land, sea, and air)
- Travel

The **balance of payments** expresses the total of all economic transactions between a nation and the rest of the world, usually for a period of one year. Each country's balance of payments summarizes information about that country's exports, imports, earnings by domestic residents on assets located abroad, earnings on domestic assets owned by foreign residents, international capital movements, and other official transactions by central banks and government. In essence, then:

***The balance of payments is a record of all the transactions between households, firms, and the government of one country and the rest of the world.***

Any transaction that leads to a *payment* by a country's residents (or government) is a deficit item, identified by a negative sign (−) when we examine the actual numbers that might be in Table 17-3 on the next page. Any transaction that leads to a *receipt* by a country's residents (or government) is a surplus item and is identified by a plus sign (+) when actual numbers are considered. Table 17-3 gives a listing of the surplus and deficit items on international financial accounts.

**Balance of payments**
*A system of accounts that measures transactions of goods, services, income, and financial assets between domestic households, businesses, and governments and residents of the rest of the world during a specific time period.*

## Current Account versus Capital Account Transactions

While the minutia of the accounting that goes into the balance of payments can get pretty complicated, only two aspects of it are really important for your understanding of this subject. One is the **current account** and the other is the **capital account**.

**Current Account Transactions** You have already been introduced to the most important parts of current account transactions—the import and export of goods and services. The other part of current account transactions comprises what is called **unilateral transfers.** ▸ Example 17-17 You have an Irish cousin who is going to turn 16. You decide to be a good relative and send her a gift in

**Current account**
*A category of balance of payments transactions that measures the exchange of goods, services, and unilateral transfers.*

**Capital account**
*A category of balance of payments transactions that measures flows of real and financial assets among different coutries.*

**Unilateral transfers**
*One-way transfers that typically involve individuals in one country making gifts to other individuals residing in other countries. They are one-way transfers because those making the gifts receive nothing tangible in exchange.*

**Table 17-3 Surplus (+) and Deficit (−) Items on the International Financial Accounts**

Every international transaction listed on the left-hand side adds to a positive balance of payments, whereas every international transaction listed on the right-hand side subtracts from the balance of payments.

| Surplus Items (+) | Deficit Items (−) |
|---|---|
| Exports of merchandise | Imports of merchandise |
| Private and governmental gifts from foreigners | Private and governmental gifts to foreigners |
| Foreign use of domestically owned transportation | Use of foreign-owned transportation |
| Foreign tourists' expenditures in this country | Tourism expenditures abroad |
| Foreign military spending in this country | Military spending abroad |
| Interest and dividend receipts from foreign entities | Interest and dividends paid to foreigners |
| Sales of domestic assets to foreigners | Purchases of foreign assets |
| Funds deposited in this country by foreigners | Funds placed in foreign depository institutions |
| Sales of gold to foreigners | Purchases of gold from foreigners |
| Sales of domestic currency to foreigners | Purchases of foreign currency |

cash. To do so, you simply send a birthday card with a $100 check enclosed. The $100 is a unilateral (one-way) transfer. All such unilateral transfers involve a one-way transaction; funds, goods, or services are provided to someone in another country without receiving an equivalent payment or delivery of goods. ◂

**Balancing the Current Account** Like the balance of trade, the balance on the current account can be either negative or positive. For the last several decades, the current account balance generally has been in the red—negative. In other words, for most years since the 1970s, the balance in trading goods, plus the balance of trade in services, plus unilateral transfers has added up to a big negative number. In one recent year, it was over $400 billion.

**Capital Account Transactions** In world markets, it is possible to buy and sell not only goods and services but also real and financial assets. The international transactions involving these assets are what the capital accounts are concerned with. *Capital account transactions* occur because of foreign investments—either by foreign residents investing in the United States or by U.S. residents investing in other countries.

▸ **International Example 17-18** The purchase of shares of a British company's stock on the London stock market by a U.S. resident causes an outflow of funds from the United States to Britain. The building of a Japanese automobile factory in the United States causes an inflow of funds from Japan to the United States. Any time foreign residents buy U.S. government securities, there is an inflow of funds from other countries to the United States. Any time U.S. residents buy foreign government securities, there is an outflow of funds from the United States to other countries. Loans to and from foreign residents also cause outflows and inflows of funds. ◂

Like the current account, the capital account can be either in surplus or in deficit. Since the 1970s, the capital account has always been in surplus. What does this mean? Simply that more funds have flowed into the United States than have flowed out. In recent years, the capital account surplus has often been over $400 billion annually.

## The Relationship Between the Current Account and the Capital Account

As it turns out, any time you know the current account deficit, you also know approximately the capital account surplus. Indeed, look at Figure 17-5. There you

*Animated*

**Figure 17-5 If Non-U.S. Residents Invest in the United States, the Current Account Must Be in Deficit**

The capital account is largely the mirror image of the current account. We can see this in the years since 1970. When the current account has been in surplus, the capital account has been in deficit. When the current account has been in deficit, the capital account has been in surplus.

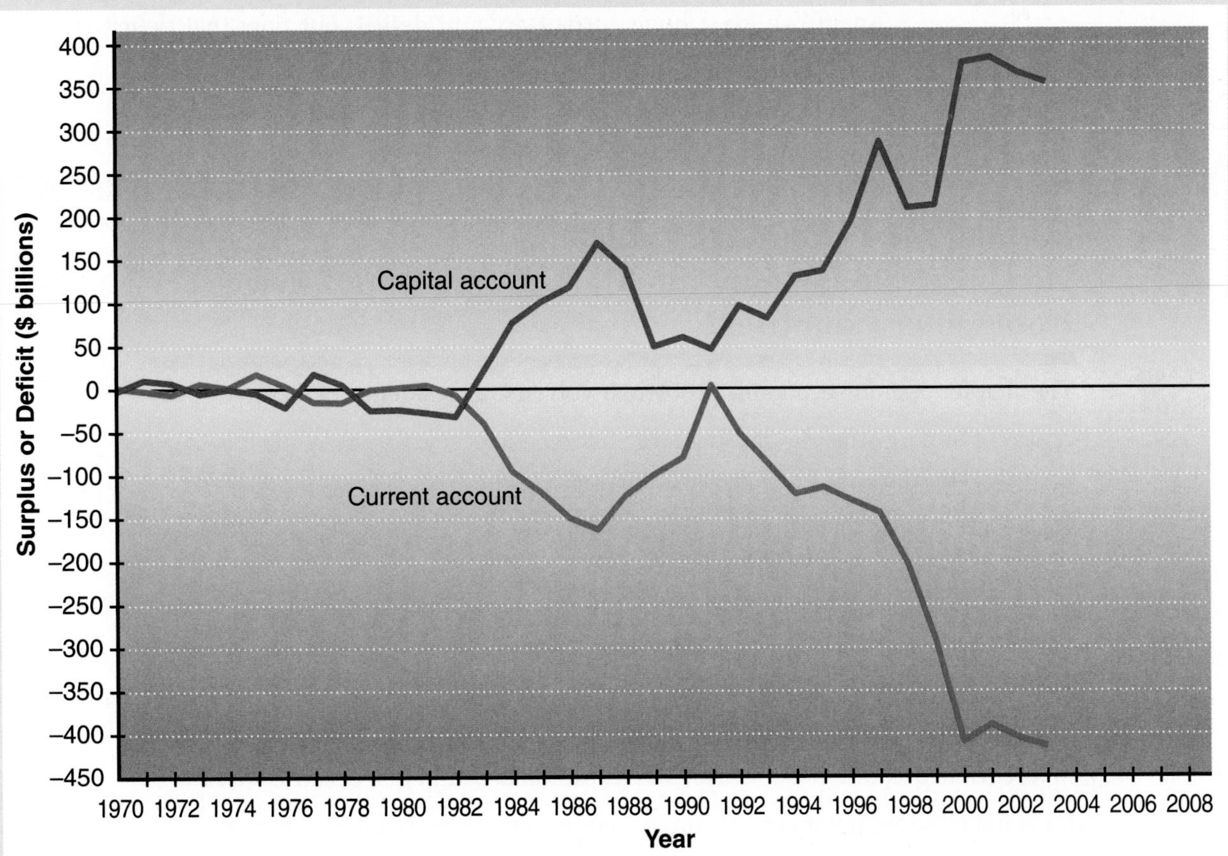

can see that the capital account is more or less the mirror image of the current account. This is not surprising. Remember the following:

> ***In the absence of interventions by finance ministries or central banks, the current account and the capital account must sum to zero. Stated differently, the current account deficit must equal the capital account surplus when governments or central banks do not engage in foreign exchange interventions. In this situation, any nation experiencing a current account deficit, such as the United States, must also be running a capital account surplus.***

## "Bad" versus "Good" Current Account Deficits

All transactors in the world economy face budget constraints. ▸ Example 17-19 Assume that U.S. residents decide to have an early tricentennial party and spend $20 billion on French champagne, financed by a loan from the French. U.S. residents then spend the next ten years or so paying off the debt and working off the hangover. In this case, the current account deficit is a clear signal that we are spending beyond our means, and it epitomizes the standard view of the current account deficit. ◂

Sometimes current account deficits can lead to a different outcome than the one just outlined in Example 17-19. ▸ Example 17-20 An American inventor creates a device that prevents pollution in air and water. Constructing the device requires a $20 billion investment, using parts imported from France and financed with a loan from France. But this investment will yield $10 billion a year in future profits and thus has a market value far in excess of the $20 billion investment. Again, we get a huge current account deficit, but now that deficit is a sign of higher wealth in the United States. ◂

## *Solving the Economic Problem:* Do U.S. Residents Buy Too Many Goods and Services from Other Countries?

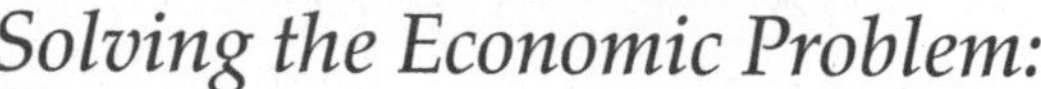

The chapter-opening economic problem involved U.S. residents' "excessive" purchases of imports, thereby causing large trade deficits every year. While it is true that the U.S. current account has been in deficit continuously since the early 1980s, this is not a new phenomenon. In the 1880s, the current account deficit was huge relative to the size of the economy. At that time, there was immense investment by the rest of the world in the United States to build railroads and other infrastructure here.

The fact is, as Figure 17-5 on page 367 shows, whenever any nation is in deficit in its current account, it is in surplus in its capital account. Just because we run trade deficits does not mean that our economy is weak and cannot compete in world markets. On the contrary, the bigger our trade deficit, the bigger our capi-

*Continued on next page*

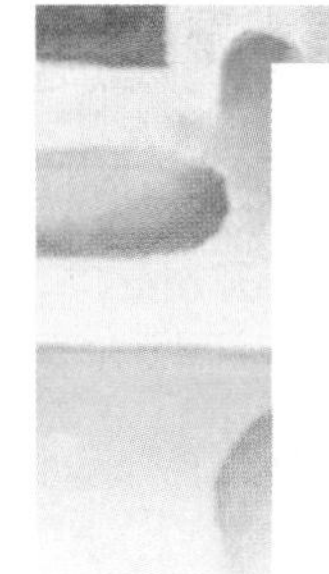

tal account surplus. This must mean that the United States remains a good place to invest capital because we have, relatively speaking, a more stable political environment and stronger prospects for growth than other countries. As long as foreign residents wish to invest more in the United States than U.S. residents wish to invest abroad, there *must* be a current account deficit. The United States is better off because of its large current account deficits, not worse off.

A lot can be learned from a close examination of a country's balance of payment statistics, as you will find out in the following *Global Application*.

## GLOBAL APPLICATION: The European Union's "Favorable" Balance of Trade Means Trouble on the Horizon

***Concept Applied:***
**Current Account, Surplus, Capital Account, Deficit**

Many European countries that are members of the European Union (EU) often brag about their positive balance of trade. In reality, they should not be so happy with those surpluses.

### Falling Imports May Not Be a Good Thing

Consider a recent year in which the EU's current account surplus doubled. This so-called improvement in the EU's balance of trade came about for the following reason: imports had dropped by 4 percent while exports rose by 1 percent. In other words, Europeans bought less from the rest of the world, particularly the United States, and sold a little bit more to the rest of the world. The reason for this drop in imports is not a good thing, though.

### Poor Economic Growth

Falling imports is usually a sign of falling economic growth. Indeed, during the same period, economic growth in Europe was only about 1 percent whereas in the United States it was over 3 percent.

### A Current Account Surplus Does Not Mean an Improvement in Standards of Living

As Europe buys less from the rest of the world while selling more to the rest of the world, its export industries thrive. But what happens to the standard of living of European residents? They are by no means better off. They have shipped more goods abroad than they purchased, thereby actually slightly lowering their real standard of living in the process. Countries such as the United States have been the beneficiaries. Remember: Imports of goods and services are the beneficial side of international trade; exports are the cost. Otherwise stated, imports are the object of international trade, while exports are the price we must pay because our trading partners insist upon being paid for their goods.

**For Critical Analysis:**
*How does importing benefit a country's residents?*

**Mastering Concepts:** The Balance of Trade and the Balance of Payments—They're More Than Just Numbers

- **Most statements about international statistics relate to the balance of trade in goods only. When the value of the goods we import is more than the value of the goods that we export, we incur a trade deficit.**

- **There is also international trade in services, in which the United States consistently runs a surplus.**
- **The balance of payments takes into account all international transactions and is therefore a summary of what firms, governments, and households of one country do with the rest of the world.**
- **Current account transactions involve trading goods, trading services, and unilateral transfers.**
- **Capital account transactions involve foreign investments, either those made by foreigners in the United States, or those made by U.S. residents in foreign countries.**
- **Whenever the current account is in deficit, the capital account is in surplus and vice versa.**

## SUMMING IT ALL UP

- The demand for a foreign currency is a derived demand, derived from the demand for foreign goods and services.
- The supply of a foreign currency is derived from the demand of foreign residents for U.S. goods and services.
- The intersection of the demand and supply curves for a foreign currency yields its equilibrium price—its foreign exchange rate.
- Any shift in the demand for or the supply of a foreign currency will change the equilibrium foreign exchange rate.
- Changes in foreign exchange rates are caused by changes in (1) real interest rates, (2) productivity, (3) consumer preferences, and (4) perceptions of economic stability.
- In a floating (flexible) exchange rate system, supply and demand determine the foreign exchange value of a country's currency.
- In a fixed exchange rate system, a country's government attempts to keep its foreign exchange rate at some fixed level.
- Governments can fix exchange rates only to the extent that they hold sufficient reserves of other nations' currencies necessary to prop up the value of the domestic currency in foreign exchange markets.
- While a fixed exchange rate system reduces foreign exchange risk for private individuals and businesses, it eliminates the "shock absorber" function of flexible exchange rates and thereby may increase fluctuations in the unemployment rate.
- Most statements about international statistics relate to the balance of trade in goods only. When the value of the goods we import is more than the value of the goods we export, we incur a trade deficit.
- There is also international trade in services, in which the United States consistently runs a surplus.
- The balance of payments takes into account all international transactions and is therefore a summary of what firms, governments, and households of one country do with the rest of the world.
- Current account transactions involve trading goods, trading services, and unilateral transfers.

- Capital account transactions involve foreign investments, either those made by foreigners in the United States, or those made by U.S. residents in foreign countries.
- Whenever the current account is in deficit, the capital account is in surplus and vice versa.

## KEY TERMS AND CONCEPTS



## MASTERING ECONOMIC CONCEPTS Questions and Problems

**17-1.** If an innovation in Great Britain makes British goods more popular, what will happen to the demand for the British pound, and why?

**17-2.** Based on the graph below, how many dollars would it take to acquire one Mexican peso? Approximately how many pesos would it take to acquire one U.S. dollar?

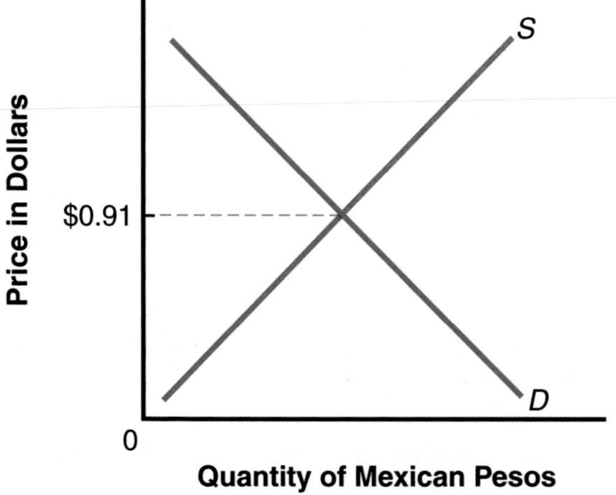


**17-3.** In 2003, one U.S. dollar could be exchanged for 112 Japanese yen. If the exchange rate changed so that one dollar could be exchanged for 120 Japanese yen, would we say that the dollar appreciated or depreciated? In this case, would we say that the yen appreciated or depreciated?

**17-4.** If there is a decrease in the demand for U.S. goods, what will happen to the exchange rate value of the U.S. dollar?

**17-5.** Assume that the U.S. government established a fixed exchange rate for the dollar in relation to the yen. If the value of the dollar began to increase relative to the yen, would the United States have to sell or purchase Japanese yen?

**17-6.** If one U.S. dollar is equal to 30.5 Russian rubles and a McDonald's "extra value" meal costs $3.69 in the United States, approximately how many rubles would you expect the same meal will cost in Russia?

**17-7.** Does the graph below depict an increase or a decrease in the demand for euros? Because the euro is the currency of France, holding all else constant, will the change depicted in this graph make French items more or less expensive to U.S. consumers? Will the change depicted make U.S. items more or less expensive to French consumers?

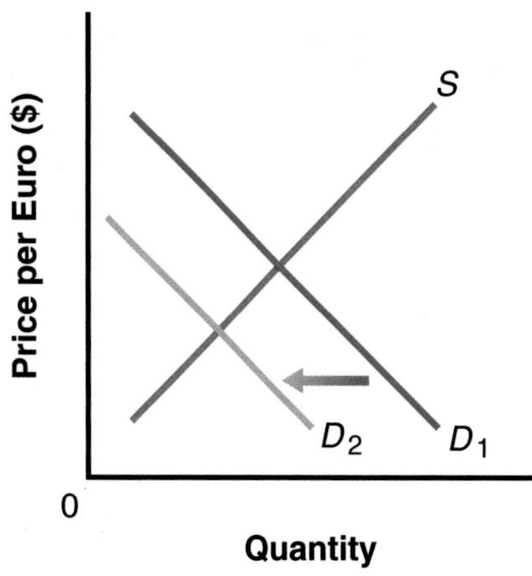

**17-8.** How would a decrease in real interest rates in the United States affect the exchange rate value of the dollar?

**17-9.** Holding all else constant, if productivity increased in Japan, what would happen to the exchange rate value of the dollar in relation to the Japanese yen?

**17-10.** What is a floating exchange rate system?

**17-11.** If a nation's government maintained a fixed exchange rate system and then began to sell units of a foreign currency held in reserve, would this increase or decrease the value of the domestic currency?

**17-12.** To maintain a fixed exchange rate system, does a country need to maintain reserves of foreign currency, its own currency, or both?

**17-13.** Would an increase or a decrease in the value of the peso be bad for Mexican companies that have borrowed dollars from U.S. banks?

**17-14.** In 2002, the United States imported roughly $1,218 billion worth of goods and exported $782 billion worth of goods. Based on these figures, what was the U.S. trade balance in 2002?

**17-15.** What would be the impact of a strong currency on a nation's balance of trade?

## THINKING CRITICALLY

**17-1.** In 2003, the exchange rate value of the dollar in relation to the euro was approximately one dollar to 0.87 euros. Give an example of an exchange rate that would indicate that the dollar appreciated in relation to the euro. Give an example of an exchange rate that would indicate that the euro depreciated in relation to the dollar. Are your answers to the two previous questions similar or different? Why?

**17-2.** A strong U.S. dollar will be beneficial for certain parties but will have an adverse impact on others. Of course, this is true internationally, but it is also true with respect to different interests in the United States as well. Within the United States, who will benefit, and who will be adversely affected? In other countries, who will benefit, and who will be adversely affected?

**17-3.** Because the United States is one country, we have only one currency. Assume, however, that the country split up into two regions, each with its own currency—east dollars and west dollars. If the economy in the western United States experienced a significant downturn, would inflation or unemployment be the greater problem in that area? If the economy in the eastern United States experienced a significant expansion, would inflation or unemployment be the greater problem in that region? Hypothetically, if we had two different currencies as indicated above, what would happen to the value of eastern dollars in relation to western dollars? How could this change in the exchange rate help to alleviate the economic problems that both regions face? Could our existing central bank use monetary policy to affect the economy in only one of these regions?

## LOGGING ON

1. To take a look at how exchange rates have varied in a recent year, go to http://research.stlouisfed.org/fred2/categories/13.
2. For market rates of exchange of the U.S. dollar for major world currencies at 10:00 a.m. each day, go to http://www.ny.frb.org/pihome/statistics/forex10.shtml.
3. For the latest U.S. balance of payments data, go to http://www.bea.doc.gov/bea/di/home/bop.htm.
4. To see recent trends in the U.S. balance of payments, go to http://research.stlouisfed.org/fred2/categories/14.

## USING THE INTERNET FOR ECONOMIC ANALYSIS

**Tracking Exchange Rates** This application gives you a chance to think about what exchange rates mean and the difficulties faced in trying to predict exchange rate movements.

**Title:** Federal Reserve Bank of New York: Foreign Exchange—12:00 Noon Rates

**Navigation:** Go to http://www.ny.frb.org/pihome/statistics/forex12.shtml.

**Application** Answer the following questions.

1. For each currency listed, how many dollars does it take to purchase a unit of the currency in the spot foreign exchange market?
2. Choose a currency from those listed, and for each day during a given week, keep track of its value relative to the dollar via this Web site. What factors might have caused the value of this currency to rise or fall relative to the U.S. dollar during the week?

## MEDIA RESOURCE LIST

The following media resources are available with this chapter:

- Load your CD-ROM to listen to the audio introduction to this chapter.
- Load your CD-ROM to access a Graph Animation of Figure 17-2, *The Results of a Shift in the Demand for Japanese Yen.*
- Load your CD-ROM to access a Graph Animation of Figure 17-3, *An Increase in the Supply of Japanese Yen.*
- Load your CD-ROM to view the video on the *Market Determinants of Exchange Rates.*
- Load your CD-ROM to view the video on *Fixed Exchange Rates.*
- Load your CD-ROM to access a Graph Animation of Figure 17-5, *If Non-U.S. Residents Invest in the United States, the Current Account Must Be in Deficit.*
- Test your knowledge of chapter concepts with a quiz at www.miller-ume.com.
- Link to Web resources related to the text coverage at www.miller-ume.com.

## HOMEWORK SET

Go to the back of this book to find the Homework Problems for this chapter.

# Mastering Economic Concepts: Answers to Odd-Numbered Problems

## Chapter 1

**1-1.** Economics is the study of decision making when faced with change. A student will decide to purchase a textbook for a class only if the benefit that he/she expects is greater than the cost. In the same way, a government will increase funding for mass transit if the benefits such as reduced traffic congestion are greater than the costs. Lastly, municipalities will use various tax structures to fund stadiums if they feel that the professional sports team will generate enough jobs, revenues, and possibly civic pride to outweigh the costs of the tax to area businesses.

**1-3.** All resources are scarce unless they are completely ubiquitous which is very rare. Seawater is a reasonable example of a resource that is ubiquitous. However, if we specify clean seawater, we could agree that the amount of clean seawater is not unlimited.

**1-5.** The cap would still be an economic good. As long as the item is scarce and someone will pay for it, it will be considered an economic good. This does not mean that you would be willing to pay your hard earned money for the item, but someone else would. Note that if you were given such an item for free, you would probably not throw it away because it has value to someone else. By selling the item on eBay, you could benefit from the transaction.

**1-7.** The opportunity cost of buying lunch at Wendy's would be the lunch that I did not get that day at Subway. If the Subway location was much closer, the opportunity cost would also include the travel and time involved in going to Wendy's which would be much greater than simply walking to Subway in the next building.

**1-9.** If you study enough to try to earn an "A" on your economics test, you are likely to earn a "D" on your accounting test. This result would be two letter grades lower than the "B" that you could possibly have earned on the accounting test. Thus your opportunity cost is the two letter grades that you lost on the accounting test.

**1-11.** The maximum amount of new homes is 14 million. The maximum amount of automobiles is 15 million.

**1-13.**

| Change | Opportunity Cost |
|---|---|
| zero to 5 million autos | 1 million new homes |
| 5 to 10 million autos | 3 million new homes |
| 10 to 15 million autos | 10 million new homes |

The opportunity costs are different for different points on the curve because resources are not equally well suited to all tasks. That is, when moving around the curve from bottom right to top left, we are devoting more and more of the country's resources to auto production. Some of these resources, some skilled laborers for example, were better suited to helping build new homes.

**1-15.** If the U.S. experienced economic growth, the production possibilities curve would shift outward toward curve C. Factors such as improved technology, an increased resource base, or greater investment levels would be likely to shift the PPC outward.

**1-17.** For most of us, these purchases and donation would be beyond our financial capabilities. As such they are unreasonable for us. However, this does not indicate in any way that these decisions were irrational for these individuals. In the case of Mr. Cuban, if he enjoys being the owner of an NBA franchise and all that goes with it more than the cost of buying the team, his decision was completely rational. In the same manner, if an individual purchased a rare item or donated millions or even billions to a charity, his/her actions would be rational if the benefits to that individual were greater than the cost.

## Chapter 2

**2-1.** Prices signal to producers what items they should produce. These items will be produced using the least cost combination of inputs. These items will be distributed to those consumers that have the ability and the willingness to purchase the items.

2-3. The other category of resources or factor of production is entrepreneurship. Examples of entrepreneurship include a willingness to take risk, an ability to create new products or services, and a talent to improve the production process.

2-5. The price of domestic goods purchased by U.S. consumers would increase because labor, a key factor of production, would become more scarce. Therefore the price of labor would increase which would lead to an increase in the cost of U.S. goods.

2-7. A CD player purchased by GM to be installed in a new Chevy Malibu would not be included in GDP because it is not a final good.

Lawn care service that I provide for free to my brother while visiting him would not be included in GDP because there is not market value assuming that I do not charge my brother.

A watch made in Switzerland sold in New York City would not be included in the U.S. GDP because it was not made in the U.S.

A 1998 Cadillac sold to a retired U.S. steel worker in 2004 would not be counted in the GDP for the year 2004, because it was not made in 2004.

2-9. If every couple had two children, then each person of an older generation would have one person in the next generation. There would be a one to one relationship. The fertility rate just over 2.0 allows for some couples who do not have children as well as deaths at younger ages.

2-11. The relatively high price indicated to DaimlerChrysler that the PT Cruiser was desirable to consumers.

2-13. The $30 commission would be included in GDP because this is a service that you consumed and it does have a market value. However, the $2,350 that you paid to acquire the shares of stock does not add to U.S. GDP because nothing is produced; this is simply a transfer of partial ownership.

2-15. Per capita real GDP increased because real GDP increased by 20% and the population increased by only 15%.

## Chapter 3

3-1. A decrease in the price of monthly cellular service would cause an increase in the demand for cell phones because these two goods are complements.

A decrease in the cost of the items used to make cell phones would not cause a change in the demand for cell phones. Instead this would cause an increase in the supply of cell phones because this event impacts the producers directly.

An increase in income levels across the population would cause an increase in the demand for cell phones being that consumers would have more purchasing power.

A decrease in the price of personal pagers would lead to a decrease in the demand for cell phones because pagers are a substitute providing another means of communication. Note that these two goods are by no means perfect substitutes but they are substitutes to some degree.

3-3. Inventory levels will indicate if retailers are charging an inappropriate price. If inventories continuously increase, retailers would realize that they are charging a price that is too high. That is, at this price level the quantity they are willing to supply is greater than the quantity demanded by consumers.

3-5. Supply must have increased. To confirm this compare the equilibria on the graph below.

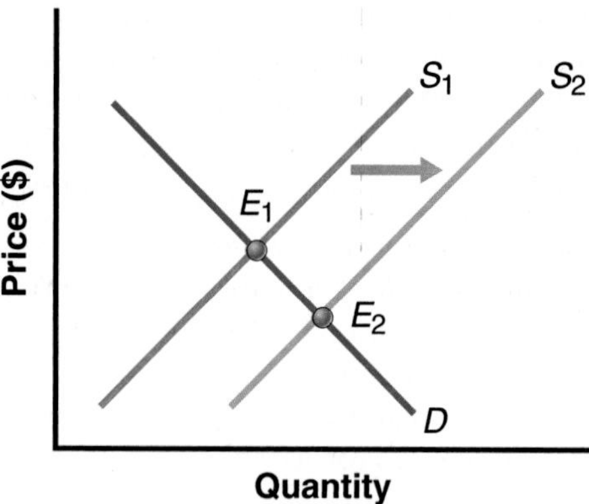


3-7. Since some level of electricity consumption is a necessity, an increase in the price of electricity will impact most everyone. As a result, consumers will have less income remaining to spend on all other items, so they are likely to purchase lesser quantities of all other items. In terms of the substitution effect, over time consumers are likely to purchase items for their homes such as appliances that are more energy efficient.

3-9.

**Market**

| Price | Quantity |
|---|---|
| $10 | 20 |
| $15 | 10 |
| $20 | 3 |

**3-11.**

| Price | Quantity Demanded | Quantity Supplied | |
|---|---|---|---|
| $10.00 | 50 | 250 | 200 unit surplus |
| $9.00 | 100 | 200 | 100 unit surplus |
| $8.00 | 150 | 150 | equilibrium |
| $7.00 | 200 | 100 | 100 unit shortage |
| $6.00 | 250 | 50 | 200 unit shortage |
| $5.00 | 300 | 0 | 300 unit shortage |

**3-13.** a. A decrease in the interest rates for auto loans would cause no change in the supply of automobiles. Since loan rates directly impact consumers, this would cause an increase in the demand.

b. A decrease in taxes on automakers would lead to an increase in supply because automakers would be able to keep more of the profits they generated.

c. A decrease in the number of firms making new cars would lead to a decrease in supply.

d. A decrease in the price of aluminum and steel used in auto production would lead to an increase in supply of new autos because these items are resources.

**3-15.** A decrease in supply will increase the equilibrium price and decrease the equilibrium quantity. See graph below.

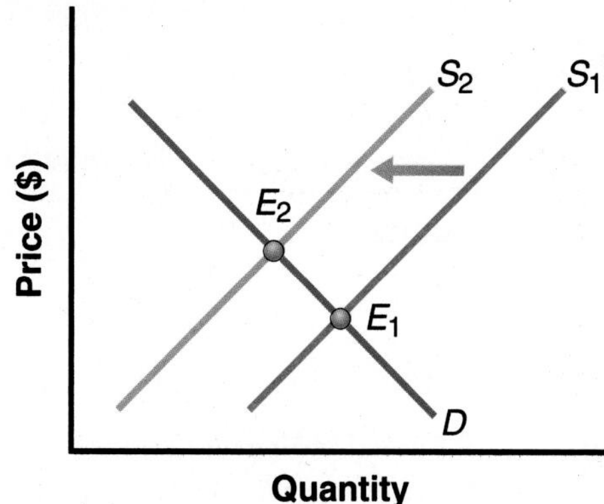


**3-17.** A lower price of processor chips would lead to an increase in the supply of personal computers. This would lead to a decrease in the equilibrium price and an increase in the equilibrium quantity as indicated by the graph below.

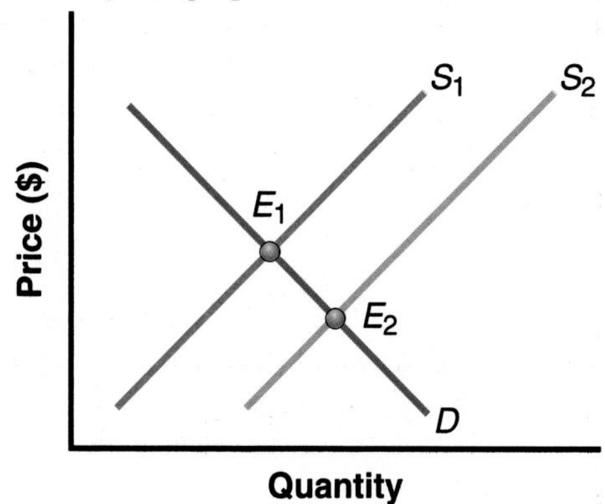


**3-19.**

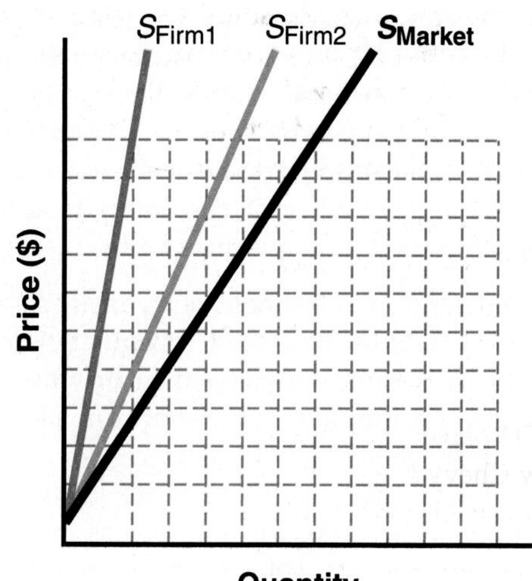


## Chapter 4

**4-1.**

| Slices of Pizza | | | Soft Drinks | | |
|---|---|---|---|---|---|
| Number of Slices | Total Utility | Marginal Utility | Number of Drinks | Total Utility | Marginal Utility |
| 0 | 0 | n/a | 0 | 0 | n/a |
| 1 | 40 | **40** | 1 | **30** | 30 |
| 2 | 55 | **15** | 2 | 45 | **15** |
| 3 | 65 | **10** | 3 | 50 | **5** |
| 4 | **70** | 5 | 4 | 50 | **0** |

**4-3.** Earle should buy another video game since he obtains more marginal utility per dollar from video games at his current level of consumption. This could be computed as follows: $MU_{DVD}/cost_{DVD} = 10/\$20 = 0.5/\$$; $MU_{games}/cost_{games} = 30/\$50 = 0.6/\$$.

**4-5.** a. Heart surgery would be relatively inelastic because it is necessary and there are few if any alternatives.

b. Old Navy T-shirts would be relatively elastic because there are several substitutes from various brands and other stores.

c. A DVD recorder would be relatively elastic because it is something of a luxury item and a VCR would be a substitute of almost comparable features.

d. Public transportation would be relatively inelastic; if you are using public transportation it is unlikely that you have other means of transportation such as your own car. Therefore you don't have much choice even if prices increase.

**4-7.** The price elasticity of demand would be −2.50 and demand would be relatively elastic. This price reduction would cause an increase in total revenues because the number of sales would increase 2.5 times as much as the price was decreased.

**4-9.** Total revenues will decrease. The price elasticity of demand of −3.2 for this restaurant indicates that for every 1% increase in price the number of customers will decrease by 3.2%. This being the case, if the owner increases prices he or she will cause a relatively large number of customers to dine elsewhere lowering total revenues for the restaurant.

**4-11.** The demand for gasoline is fairly inelastic with respect to price because most consumers would not be able to significantly alter their driving patterns and gas consumption in the short run. However, if consumers faced higher gas prices for months or even years, they would be more likely to make changes in their travel habits such as purchasing a more fuel efficient vehicle and moving closer to work or mass transit.

**4-13.** Since the price of the item increased and total revenues also increased, demand for the item must be inelastic. In this case even though the seller increased the price, total revenues increased which indicates that only a relatively small number of customers stopped buying this item.

**4-15.** The price elasticity would be −1.0 which represents unitary price elasticity of demand. In this case the total revenues would not change; the increase in quantity exactly offsets the decrease in price.

**4-17.** The price elasticity of demand would equal −2.0.

## Chapter 5

**5-1.** The greatest advantage of ownership by means of a corporation is that the liability of any shareholders is limited to the value of their shares. The chief disadvantage of ownership by means of a corporation is that the profits of the firm are subject to corporate taxes and the dividends distributed to shareholders are also subject to taxation. In contrast a sole proprietorship is not subject to this form of double taxation.

**5-3.** Complete the following table by calculating average product and marginal product.

| Machines | Total Output | Average Product | Marginal Product |
|---|---|---|---|
| 3 | 300 | **100** | **n/a** |
| 4 | 425 | **106.25** | **125** |
| 5 | 575 | **115** | **150** |
| 6 | 700 | **116.67** | **125** |
| 7 | 750 | **107.14** | **50** |

**5-5.** The $1,200 should not play a role in your decision making process because it is a sunk cost and as such cannot be recovered. The only factors that you should analyze are the costs and future benefits of the computer being considered.

**5-7.** Based on the information in the table below, compute total cost, average variable cost, average fixed cost, and average total costs at each level of output.

| Quantity | Fixed Cost | Variable Cost | Total Cost | Average Fixed Cost | Average Variable Cost | Average Total Cost |
|---|---|---|---|---|---|---|
| 13 | 400 | 100 | **500** | **30.77** | **7.69** | **38.46** |
| 14 | 400 | 105 | **505** | **28.57** | **7.50** | **36.07** |
| 15 | 400 | 109 | **509** | **26.67** | **7.27** | **33.93** |
| 16 | 400 | 112 | **512** | **25.00** | **7.00** | **32.00** |
| 17 | 400 | 117 | **517** | **23.53** | **6.88** | **30.41** |

**5-9.** The ATC would be $3.33.

**5-11.** Curve B depicted below is the average total cost curve.

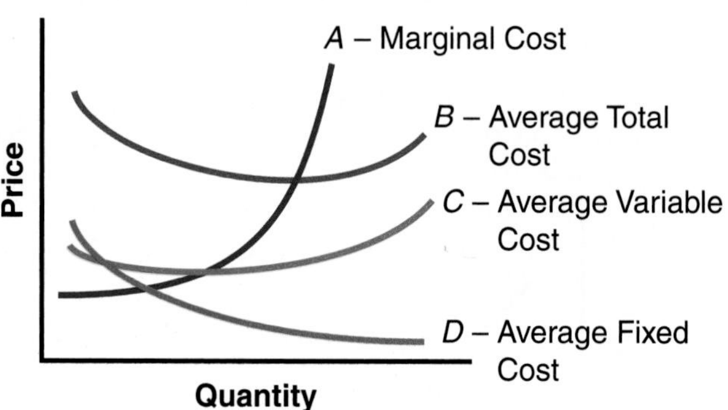


**5-13.** His economic profit would be $10,000.

**5-15.** Marginal cost equals $50 at a quantity of 90 units. Average total cost equals $32 at a quantity of 82 units. Average variable cost equals $20 at a quantity of 60 units.

**5-17.** AFC = $6.00; AVC = $2.00; ATC = $8.00

## Chapter 6

**6-1.**
a. perfect competition
b. perfect competition
c. monopoly or neither
d. neither

**6-3.** At a price of $3.30, the marginal revenue of any bushel sold is $3.30. If this farmer decided to sell wheat at a price of $4.00 per bushel he would not be able to sell any in a perfectly competitive market.

6-5. He should produce 24 hot dogs in order to maximize profits and his profits would equal $22.80.

| Q | TR | TC | MR | MC | Profit |
|---|---|---|---|---|---|
| 20 | **30.00** | 10.00 | - | - | **20.00** |
| 21 | **31.50** | 10.40 | **1.50** | **0.40** | **21.10** |
| 22 | **33.00** | 11.00 | **1.50** | **0.60** | **22.00** |
| 23 | **34.50** | 11.90 | **1.50** | **0.90** | **22.60** |
| 24 | **36.00** | 13.20 | **1.50** | **1.30** | **22.80** |
| 25 | **37.50** | 14.80 | **1.50** | **1.60** | **22.70** |

6-7. Quantity "C" would produce the highest level of profits and the firm would have to charge a price of "X".

6-9. In this case, you should shut down immediately since your revenues are not sufficient to cover your variable costs. You would be better off ceasing operations and paying the fixed costs out of your own pocket.

6-11.
a. This is true because the monopolistic firm is the industry. Consumers have no other choice.
b. This is false. For a monopolistic firm marginal revenue will always be less than price.
c. This statement is false; a perfectly competitive firm faces a perfectly elastic demand curve.

6-13. Use the following demand schedule for cable services to compute total revenue and marginal revenue at each level of output.

| Q | P | TR | MR |
|---|---|---|---|
| 100 | $45 | **$4,500** | – |
| 101 | $44 | **$4,444** | **−$56** |
| 102 | $43 | **$4,386** | **−$58** |
| 103 | $42 | **$4,326** | **−$60** |
| 104 | $41 | **$4,264** | **−$62** |
| 105 | $40 | **$4,200** | **−$64** |

6-15. The firm should produce "C" units of output. If the firm produced any more units the additional units would add more to costs than to revenues. If the firm produced any fewer, it would be missing an opportunity to increase profits being that all of the units up to "C" added more to revenues than to cost.

6-17. Economists expect each perfectly competitive firm to generate an economic break-even which is a satisfactory result because the firm's revenues must be sufficient to cover all explicit and implicit costs. In contrast, accounting profits of zero would suggest a very unsatisfactory result for the firm.

6-19. His total revenue for the week would be $1,440. His average revenue would be the same as the price of $40. Since this is a perfectly competitive industry, the marginal revenue would also equal $40.

6-21. If the costs for each firm were reduced, each firm would generate an economic profit in the short run. This would cause new firms to enter this industry.

## Chapter 7

7-1.
a. No, there are a large number of sellers.
b. No, each firm has some control over price in the market.
c. No, the firms sell differentiated goods.
d. Yes, there are limited barriers to entry.
e. Yes, we expect zero economic profit in the long run.

7-3. From most competitive to least: b, c, a, d

7-5. This firm will produce 40 units in order to maximize profits.

7-7. The company attempted to engage in signaling behavior by establishing a popular trademark or "mascot" in this case. The popularity of these ads would tend to indicate that the signaling has been effective.

7-9. This firm should produce 160 units in order to maximize profits or in this case to minimize its losses. Based on a loss of $28, existing firms would be likely to exit this industry.

7-11. We would expect Delta to set their prices to the height of the demand curve at the point where marginal revenue equals marginal cost. Other airlines might possibly set their prices at the same level as Delta's because Delta may be able to act as a price leader, coordinating the pricing efforts of other firms in a form of tacit collusion.

7-13. Long-run equilibrium for a monopolistically competitive firm

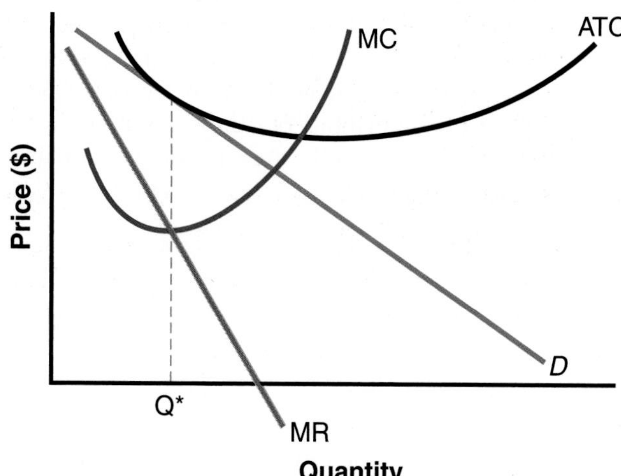


7-15. The economic argument that advertising is a signal of higher quality assumes that all else is held constant. Therefore, we are assuming that various

items such as the production quality and costs of the ads and the market area for the products are roughly equivalent. If we compare the advertising of a large national company to a small local company, we would expect to see substantial differences in quality. In addition, due to the lower cost to advertise on the local level, some firms selling goods of lower quality might choose to do so to get customers to try their product one time since they may be the only supplier in that area. In contrast, a national company would be very reluctant to advertise a product across several markets if the product quality was questionable.

## Chapter 8

**8-1.** An unregulated market will produce too much of a good with an external cost and the market price for the good will be too low.

**8-3.** This tax system would be proportional because both individuals are paying 20% of their income in taxes.

**8-5.** The Federal Trade Commission Act prohibited overly competitive behavior with respect to pricing. This act was intended to eliminate predatory pricing which is the practice by which a firm temporarily lowers its prices to force other firms out of business. After all other firms have been forced out, the remaining firm is free to charge almost any price at all.

**8-7.** Below the $87,000 income level the social security tax is proportional. Above $87,000, this tax becomes regressive.

**8-9.** Commercial fishers might choose to use larger fishing vessels or different equipment that would enable them to extract more fish from the area. By such means the commercial fishers would not be violating the regulations but they would be able to take more fish from the area, possibly over-fishing as before.

**8-11.** Based on these figures, we might prefer to use CMA to de-ice the roads because the total cost, including environmental damage, is lower. As such, the fact that state highway departments use salt does constitute government failure

**8-13.** These taxes have been eliminated because they are regressive. Although each customer pays the same percentage of the cost of the groceries in tax, this amount of tax will represent a smaller percentage of the income of a wealthy individual and food purchases are a necessity.

**8-15.** These two areas could be considered part of the same relevant product market because I drive in and through each of these areas most every day.

## Chapter 9

**9-1.** Your opportunity cost of spending the weekend watching television is the time you could have spent working and the wages that you would have been able to generate. Your opportunity cost of not working would increase significantly if you needed money for a Spring Break trip.

**9-3.** If the wage rate decreases, you are likely to substitute towards leisure. However, if you have pressing expenses, the income effect of the lower wages would make you increase the number of hours you work each week.

**9-5.** If the wage rate for these workers was $950 per week, the firm should employ five workers.

| Labor | Total Physical Product | Marginal Physical Product | Marginal Revenue |
|---|---|---|---|
| 2 | 100 | — | — |
| 3 | 200 | **100** | **$1,200** |
| 4 | 350 | **150** | **$1,800** |
| 5 | 450 | **100** | **$1,200** |
| 6 | 525 | **75** | **$900** |

**9-7.** If the marginal factor cost of labor is less than the marginal revenue product of labor a firm should employ more workers because currently the workers are adding more to the firm's revenues than to costs. The firm should continue to hire more workers until the marginal revenue product equals the marginal factor cost; the firm would not want to expand employment to the point where the marginal factor cost is greater than the marginal revenue product.

**9-9.** We would have to select $6.00 as our minimum wage to increase the compensation of these workers. This wage rate would create a 3,000 surplus of workers.

**9-11.** The potential benefits of the existence of labor unions include:

reduction of wage inequality

shifting wealth from shareholders to laborers

more enjoyable workplaces

increased productivity

political voice for laborers

increased stability of the workforce

**9-13.** 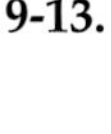

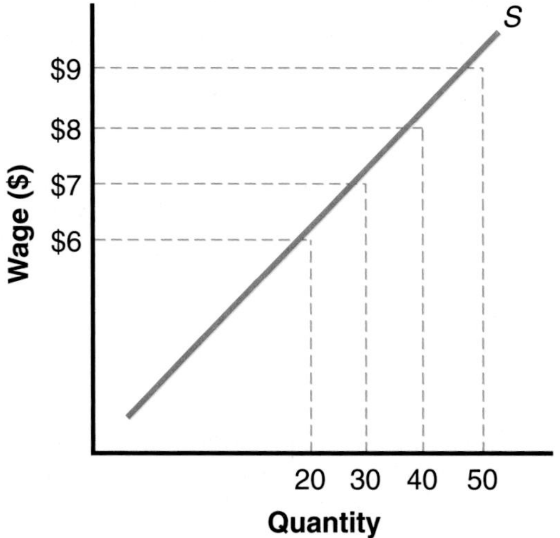


**9-15.** a. false
b. true
c. false
d. true

## Chapter 10

**10-1.** The search time needed to find a position would represent frictional unemployment.

**10-3.** a. not part of the labor force
b. employed
c. not part of the labor force
d. unemployed

**10-5.** The unemployment rate would be 6.25%.

**10-7.** 4 million people were classified as unemployed.

**10-9.** The CPI currently has base years of 1982–1984. The value of the CPI in these years is approximately 100; the value of any price index in its base year will be 100 or a value quite close to 100. If the CPI had increased to 180.9 at the end of 2005, this would indicate a price increase of 80.9%.

**10-11.** The market basket used in computing the GDP deflator represents a broader range of goods than the market basket used in computing the CPI. In addition, the CPI is based on a market basket of goods from several years ago which results in an overstatement of inflation since this static market basket cannot account for consumers' substitution of goods.

**10-13.** The lowest nominal interest rate you should charge is 8.0%.

**10-15.** The previous recession in the U.S took place in 1990–1991.

## Chapter 11

**11-1.** Households that funnel funds into the product market are represented by the label A and businesses that funnel funds into the factor market are represented by label B.

**11-3.** The expenditure formula for computing GDP is: $Y = C + I + G + X$. In this formula "$I$" represents investment which is business spending.

**11-5.** The purchasing power of $1,000 would increase and you would be likely to buy more goods as a result. This response is known as an increase in the quantity of aggregate demand.

**11-7.** If the price level of all goods increases and wages remained constant you would be more likely to increase the amount that you were producing. However, in the long-run, employers will be forced to increase wages if the price level increased because their employees' cost of living has increased. Based on such an increase in wages, manufacturers would experience no change in their incentive to produce.

**11-9.** U.S. producers would supply $6.5 trillion in output if the price level was 160. Producers would supply $5 trillion in output if the price level was 140.

**11-11.** If the price level in the U.S. decreases while real GDP increases, aggregate supply must have increased.

**11-13.** The aggregate demand curve slopes downward because of the real-balance effect and the open economy effect. The real-balance effect indicates that when the price level increases, the purchasing power of consumers' account balances decreases; as a result consumers will purchase a lesser quantity of goods and services. The open economy effect indicates that a higher price level in this country will cause consumers to purchase more goods and services from other countries and, as a result, fewer goods and services from the U.S.

**11-15.** If U.S. net exports are positive, the amount that the U.S. exported was greater than the amount that the U.S. imported.

## Chapter 12

**12-1.** The federal budget deficit is the annual measure of expenditures minus revenues. The federal debt is the cumulative measure of the budget deficits less budget surpluses from previous years.

**12-3.** Full employment does not imply that the unemployment rate equals zero. Frictional, structural, and seasonal unemployment will still exist.

**12-5.** a. increase the price level only
b. increase both real GDP and the price level
c. increase real GDP only

**12-7.** Your consumption would equal $64,000.

**12-9.** Your consumption would increase by $4,500.

**12-11.** a. an increase
b. a decrease
c. no change (change in the *quantity* of investment only)
d. an increase

**12-13.** If the marginal propensity to consume was 0.8, the multiplier would be 5. In this case, the impact of an additional $5 billion in investment would increase real GDP by $25 billion.

**12-15.** We should choose to increase taxation. In the same situation, we should choose to decrease government spending. This graph depicts a situation with high inflation.

## Chapter 13

**13-1.** Money is a medium of exchange and a unit of accounting.

**13-3.** In a fiduciary monetary system such as ours the value of the U.S. dollar is backed by our faith that the currency will be accepted as a means of payment based on our government's support of this currency.

**13-5.** In 2003, M1 and M2 equaled $1.3 trillion and $6.0 trillion, respectively. M2 will always be greater than M1 because M2 includes all of the items in M1 as well as savings accounts, small time deposits, and retail MMMFs.

**13-7.** The depository institution would be required to hold $350. This transaction would immediately create $3,150 in excess reserves.

**13-9.** The total increase in the money supply would be $32 billion.

**13-11.** Approximately 33% of all transactions are currently completed using credit and debit cards. Less than 20% of transactions were completed using these means in 1979.

**13-13.** Small-denomination time deposits are certificates of deposit under $100,000. These items are not included in M1 but they are included in M2.

**13-15.** If a large amount of money was withdrawn from the U.S. banking system, the money multiplier would amplify this effect.

## Chapter 14

**14-1.** If the Federal Reserve instituted a policy of 'loose money', this would imply an increase in the money supply and a decrease in interest rates.

**14-3.** If the economy were experiencing severe inflation, contractionary monetary policy would be more appropriate because the economy is essentially growing too fast with inflation as a likely consequence.

**14-5.** Open market operations refers to the Fed's purchase or sale of government securities. If inflation was a problem, the Fed would sell government securities in the open market and if unemployment was a problem the Fed would purchase government securities.

**14-7.** At the point in time indicated in the graph, the Fed should adopt expansionary monetary policy in order to counteract the situation in the business cycle. Specifically, the Fed could decrease reserve requirements, decrease the discount rate, or purchase government securities to lower the target fed funds rate.

**14-9.** The direct effect of monetary policy is that if people have greater money balances they are likely to spend these balances, increasing aggregate demand. In contrast, the indirect effect of monetary policy begins with greater balances in banking institutions. The banks wish to lend out these money balances to generate interest income. In order to do so, the banks must offer lower interest rates and these lower interest rates will cause an increase in aggregate demand.

**14-11.** a. purchase government securities
b. decrease the discount rate
c. decrease reserve requirements

**14-13.** An increase in the supply of money would cause inflation and a decrease in the demand for money could also cause inflation.

**14-15.** Recognition, action, and impact lags exist with respect to monetary policy. The recognition and impact lags are similar in length for both fiscal and monetary policy. However, the action lag is much shorter with regard to monetary policy than with regard to fiscal policy.

## Chapter 15

**15-1.** Holding all else constant, a 15% increase in real GDP over five years would indicate that an economy was doing well. However, a 15% increase in real GDP coupled with a 20% increase in the population would indicate a negative situation for the economy.

**15-3.** Bermuda has a higher per capita real GDP.

**15-5.** If the growth rate had been 6%, each dollar of income would increase to $1.34. Over a 50 year time period, the difference between a 5% and 6% annual rate would be $6.90 per dollar of original income.

**15-7.** Worker productivity did improve.

**15-9.** Technology is a factor of production. The government could establish a tax system that gives greater incentives to those who innovate and the government could also fund research and development outside of the private sector.

**15-11.** Military conflict will likely lead to a decline in the security and stability of property rights which will lead to a decrease in the growth rate of the developing economy.

**15-13.** In 2 years $100 invested at an interest rate of 3.0% compounded annually would be $106.09.

**15-15.** Curve C would indicate that our country experienced the most significant economic growth. If economic growth equaled zero, we would remain on curve A.

## Chapter 16

**16-1.** Based on these tables, Lithuania has the absolute advantage in producing each good. Lithuania has the comparative advantage in sugar beets and the Ukraine has the comparative advantage in potatoes.

**16-3.** The U.S. should specialize in producing sweaters in order to expand total production of both goods in both countries.

**16-5.** Exports ultimately pay for imports because people in other countries want to purchase goods made in the U.S. The sale of these goods gives us the purchasing power needed to import goods from other countries.

**16-7.** The supply curve would be impacted by an import quota. With a lesser supply curve, the quota would cause an increase in the price of sugar in the U.S.

**16-9.** If a foreign government was subsidizing the operations of a foreign company that sold products in the U.S., that government's actions would increase the quantity of U.S. imports. In this situation, U.S. trade restrictions might be necessary to 'level the playing field' and remove the artificial advantage that the foreign companies enjoy.

**16-11.** International trade provides a greater level of interaction through which ideas are also passed along to nations across the world. Examples include growing coffee, growing potatoes, and production processes such as just-in-time inventory.

**16-13.** If the U.S. government establishes an import quota, this quota will increase the price and decrease the quantity of imported goods. At the same time, both the price and quantity of U.S. substitute goods will increase.

**16-15.** The World Trade Organization is the principal institution that oversees tariffs throughout the world. The goal of this organization and the countries that created it is to decrease the level of trade restrictions between countries so that all countries are able to benefit from free trade.

## Chapter 17

**17-1.** The demand for the British pound will increase because it is the currency needed to purchase British goods.

**17-3.** We would say that the dollar appreciated and the yen depreciated.

**17-5.** If the value of the dollar began to increase in relation to the yen, the U.S. would need to purchase Japanese yen in order to maintain the fixed exchange rate.

**17-7.** The graph depicted a decrease in the demand for euros which would make French items less expensive to U.S. consumers. This change will also make U.S. items more expensive to French consumers.

**17-9.** If productivity increased in Japan, the exchange rate value of the dollar would decrease in relation to Japanese yen.

**17-11.** If a nation's government maintained a fixed exchange rate system and began to sell units of a foreign currency held in reserve, it would lead to an increase in the value of the domestic currency.

**17-13.** A decrease in the value of the peso would be bad for Mexican companies that have borrowed dollars from U.S. banks.

**17-15.** A strong domestic currency would lead to a decrease in a nation's balance of trade.

# Glossary

## A

**Absolute advantage** The ability to produce more units of a good or service using a given quantity of labor or other resource inputs than other producers can; equivalently, the ability to produce the same quantity of a good or service using fewer units of labor or other resource inputs.

**Accounting profits** Total revenues minus total explicit costs.

**Action time lag** The time between the recognition of an economic problem and the implementation of policy to solve it. The action time lag is quite long for fiscal policy, which requires congressional approval.

**Aggregate demand** The total dollar value of all planned expenditures in the economy.

**Aggregate demand curve** A graphed line showing the relationship between the aggregate quantity demanded and the average of all prices as measured by the overall price level, often the GDP price deflator.

**Aggregate supply** Real domestic output of producers based on the rise and fall of the overall price level; total planned production.

**Aggregate supply curve** A graphed line showing the relationship between the aggregate quantity supplied and the average of all prices as measured by the overall price level, often the GDP price deflator.

**Anticipated inflation** The inflation rate that we believe will occur; when it does, we are in a situation of fully anticipated inflation.

**Antitrust laws** Laws passed by federal and state governments to prevent new monopolies from forming and to break up those that already exist. Additionally, antitrust law attempts to prevent anticompetitive behavior, such as price fixing.

**Appreciation** An increase in the exchange value of one nation's currency in terms of the currency of another nation.

**Automatic, or built-in, stabilizers** Special provisions of certain federal programs that cause changes in desired aggregate expenditures without the action of Congress and the president. Examples are the federal progressive tax system, welfare benefits, and unemployment compensation.

**Average fixed costs** Total fixed costs divided by the number of units produced.

**Average physical product** Total product (output) divided by the number of units of the variable input.

**Average tax rate** The total tax payment divided by total income; the proportion of total income paid in taxes.

**Average total costs** Total costs divided by the number of units produced.

**Average variable costs** Total variable costs divided by the number of units produced.

## B

**Balance of payments** A system of accounts that measures transactions of goods, services, income, and financial assets between domestic households, businesses, and governments and residents of the rest of the world during a specific time period.

**Balance of trade** The difference between the value of a nation's exports of goods and its imports of goods.

**Barriers to entry** Obstacles to competition that prevent others from entering a market.

**Barter** The exchange of goods and services for other goods and services.

**Base year** The year used as a point of comparison for other years in a series of statistics.

**Bonds** Legal claims against a business or government, usually entitling the owner of the bond to receive a fixed annual coupon payment, plus a lump-sum payment at the bond's maturity date. Bonds are issued in return for funds lent.

**Boycott** Economic pressure exerted by unions urging the public not to purchase the goods or services produced by a company.

**Brand name** A word, picture, or logo on a product that helps consumers distinguish it from similar products. Brand names are used to create a reputation for products and services.

**Budget surplus** An excess of government receipts over expenditures during the fiscal year.

**Business fluctuations** Ups and downs in an economy.

## C

**Capital account** A category of balance of payments transactions that measures flows of real and financial assets among different countries.

**Capital productivity** Average output produced per constant quality unit of machine (capital).

**Capital** Previously manufactured goods used to make other goods and services.

**Cartel** An arrangement among groups of industrial businesses, often in different countries, to reduce international competition. This reduction in competition permits increased control over price, production, and distribution of goods.

**Cash balances** The amount of coins, currency, and readily available money that you normally have in a checking account.

**Checkable deposits** Any deposits in banks or banking-like institutions on which a check may be written.

**Circular flow of income** An economic model that pictures income as flowing continuously between businesses and consumers.

**Collective bargaining** The process by which unions and employers negotiate the conditions of employment.

**Collusion** A secret agreement among two or more parties to engage in some illegal activity, such as fixing prices or dividing up a specific market.

**Comparative advantage** The ability to engage in an activity such as production at a lower opportunity cost than others who might engage in the same activity.

**Complements** Two goods that are used together for consumption or enjoyment—for example, coffee and cream. The more you buy of one, the more you buy of the other. For complements, a change in the price of one causes an opposite shift in the demand for the other.

**Compounding** Computing interest on the principal and accrued interest; in other words, earning interest on interest.

**Constant-quality units** Items whose quality has been adjusted to make them comparable to one another.

**Consumer price index (CPI)** A measure of the change in price over time of a specific group of goods and services used by the average household.

**Consumption** Spending on new consumption goods and services out of a household's current income; includes such things as buying food and going to a concert. Whatever is not consumed is saved. Consumption can also be viewed as the use of goods and services for personal satisfaction.

**Consumption goods** Goods and services bought by households to use up, such as food, clothing, and movies.

**Contraction** The part of the business cycle during which economic activity is slowing down, leading to a trough.

**Corporation** A type of business organization owned by many people but treated by law as though it were a person; it can own property, pay taxes, make contracts, and so on.

**Cost-of-living adjustments (COLAs)** Clauses in contracts that allow for increases in specified nominal values to take account of changes in the cost of living.

**Craft union** A union made up of skilled workers in a specific trade or industry.

**Creative response** Behavior on the part of a firm that allows it to comply with the letter of the law but violate its spirit, significantly lessening the law's effect.

**Crowding out effect** The tendency of expansionary fiscal policy to cause a decrease in planned investment or planned consumption in the private sector; this decrease normally results from the rise in interest rates.

**Current account** A category of balance of payments transactions that measures the exchange of goods, services, and unilateral transfers.

**Cyclical unemployment** Unemployment resulting from recessions; unemployment that is associated with business cycles—hence, the word cyclical.

## D

**Debt ceiling** The maximum size of the gross public debt.

**Deflation** A sustained decline in the general price level of goods and services.

**Demand** The amount of a good or service that consumers are able and willing to buy at various possible prices during a specified time period.

**Demand curve** A downward-sloping line that graphically shows the quantities demanded at each possible price.

**Demand schedule** A table showing the quantities demanded at different possible prices.

**Depository institutions** Financial institutions that accept deposits from savers and lend those deposits out at interest. Most allow for check writing, too.

**Depreciation** A decrease in the exchange value of one nation's currency in terms of the currency of another nation.

**Depression** A major slowdown of economic activity during which millions are out of work, many businesses fail, and the economy operates at far below capacity.

**Derived demand** Demand for an input factor that is derived from the demand for the final product being produced; the demand for a currency that is derived from the demand of imports.

**Digital cash** Electronic money that exists on computer chips or other media.

**Disability payments** Government payments to individuals who satisfy a definition of being disabled.

**Discount rate** The interest rate that the Fed charges on loans to member banks.

**Discouraged workers** Individuals who have stopped looking for a job because they are convinced that they will not find a suitable one.

**Disposable income** Income remaining for a person to spend or save after all taxes have been paid.

**Distribution of income** The way income is allocated among the population.

**Dividends** The portion of a corporation's profits paid to its stockholders.

**Double taxation** Occurs with corporate profits because they are first taxed at the corporate level and then, if dividends are distributed to shareholders, taxed again at the shareholder level.

**Dumping** Selling a good or a service abroad below the price charged in the home market or at a price below its cost of production.

**Duopoly** A market structure in which there are only two sellers of a particular good or service for which there is no close substitute.

## E

**Economic growth** Expansion of the economy, allowing it to produce more goods, jobs, and wealth.

**Economic profits** Total revenues minus total opportunity costs of all inputs used, or the total of all implicit and explicit costs. Economic profits can also be viewed as the difference between total revenues and the opportunity cost of all factors of production.

**Economic regulation** Rules imposed by state and federal governments on the way businesses price their products, the way they market their goods and services, and how much they earn in profits.

**Economic system** The way in which a nation organizes its resources to satisfy its residents' wants.

**Economics** The study of how individuals and societies make choices about ways to use scarce resources.

**Economies of scale** Decreases in long-run average costs of producing that result from the large scale of output.

**Effect time lag** The time that elapses between the implementation of a policy and the results of that policy.

**Efficiency** The case in which a given level of inputs is used to produce the maximum possible output. Alternatively, the situation in which a given output is produced at minimum cost.

**Elastic demand** If a given change in price elicits a more-than-proportionate change in quantity demanded, demand is said to be elastic.

**Elasticity** A measure of how much consumers respond to a given change in the price of a particular good or service.

**Embargo** A government prohibition (ban) on certain or all trade with one or more foreign nations.

**Entrepreneurship** The ability of risk-taking individuals to develop new products and start new businesses in order to make profits.

**Equilibrium price** The price at which the quantity producers are willing to supply is equal to the amount consumers are willing to buy.

**Excess capacity** That part of the economy's potential production capacity not being utilized.

**Excess reserves** Reserves held by a depository institution that exceed what is required by law; the difference between actual reserves and required reserves.

**Expansion** The part of the business cycle in which economic activity increases.

**Explicit costs** Costs that business managers must take account of because they must overtly be paid; examples are wages, taxes, and rent.

**Exports** The goods and services that foreigners purchase from the United States.

**Externality** Economic side effects or by-products that affect an uninvolved third party; can be negative or positive.

## F

**Factors of production** The resources, or inputs, of land, labor, capital, and entrepreneurship that are used to produce goods and services.

**Fed** The Federal Reserve System created by Congress in 1913 as the nation's central banking organization.

**Federal funds market** A private market (made up of banks) in which banks can borrow reserves from other banks that want to lend them. Federal funds are usually lent for overnight use.

**Federal funds rate** The interest rate that depository institutions pay to borrow reserves in the interbank federal funds market.

**Feedback effect** The reaction of firms to government regulations; also the reaction of consumers to government regulations.

**Fertility rate** The average number of births per female of childbearing age in a given population.

**Fiduciary monetary system** A system in which currency is issued by the government and its value is based solely on the public's faith that the currency can be exchanged for goods and services.

**Fiscal policy** The federal government's use of taxation and spending policies to affect overall business activity.

**Fixed costs** Costs that do not vary with output.

**Fixed exchange rate system** A system in which a national government sets a price for its currency relative to some other currency or currencies.

**Floating (flexible) exchange rate system** A system in which exchange rates are allowed to fluctuate in the open market in response to changes in supply and demand.

**Foreign exchange market** A worldwide market for buying and selling different currencies.

**Foreign exchange risk** The possibility that changes in the value of a nation's currency will result in variations in market values of assets.

**Fractional reserve banking** A system in which a bank keeps only a fraction of its deposits on hand, or in reserve; the remainder is available to lend to borrowers or is otherwise invested.

**Frictional unemployment** Unemployment due to the fact that workers must search for appropriate job offers. This takes time, and so they remain temporarily unemployed.

**Full employment** An arbitrary level of unemployment that corresponds to "normal" friction in the labor market. In 1986, a 6.5 percent rate of unemployment was considered full employment. Today, it is assumed to be around 5 percent.

## G

**GDP deflator** A price index that measures the changes in prices of all new goods and services produced in the economy.

**Goods** Tangible objects that can satisfy people's wants.

**Government failure** Any situation in which the government intervenes in the economy with a negative result; that is, a situation in which government intervention reduces, rather than improves, the welfare of society.

**Government monopoly** A monopoly created and enforced by the government. In some countries, governments provide postal service and electricity and do not allow others to compete in those services.

**Gross domestic product (GDP)** The total dollar value of all final goods and services produced in a nation in a single year.

**Gross public debt** All federal government debt including federal government interagency borrowing.

## H

**Hedge** A financial strategy that shifts the risk of suffering losses arising from changes in foreign exchange values.

**Homogeneous** Uniform in structure or composition throughout; of the same or similar nature or kind.

**Human capital** The accumulated training and education of workers.

## I

**Imperfect competition** Any form of market structure in which the sellers have some control over price.

**Import quota** A restriction imposed on the value or number of units of a particular good that can be brought into a country. Foreign suppliers are unable to sell more than the amount specified in the import quota.

**Imports** Goods and services produced outside a country but sold within its borders.

**Incentive effect** The change in circumstances or a situation that causes humans to react by changing their behavior in response to the change in circumstances.

**Income distribution** The way in which income differences are distributed throughout society; for example, the percentage of "rich" versus the percentage of "poor" in a given economy.

**Income effect** The change in the quantity demanded of a good due to a change in real income.

**Industrial union** A union made up of all the workers in an industry, regardless of job or skill level.

**Industry concentration ratio** The percentage of all sales contributed by the leading four firms in an industry; sometimes called the concentration ratio.

**Inefficient point** Any point below the production possibilities curve at which resources are being used inefficiently.

**Inelastic demand** If a given change in price elicits a less-than-proportionate change in quantity demanded, demand is said to be inelastic.

**Infant industry argument** The contention that an industry that is just getting started should be protected from import competition. After the industry grows, the import restrictions can be lifted.

**Inflation** A sustained rise in the general price level of goods and services.

**Inflation targeting** Setting a specific annual rate of inflation that is desired. This rate is the only policy variable that the central bank has to worry about; the central bankers are then judged on how close they came to their target rate of inflation.

**Innovation** The development of new products, systems, or processes that have wide-ranging effects.

**Intellectual property** All of the fruits of humans' minds, including movies, computer games, software, music, and scientific discoveries.

**Interlocking directorates** A board of directors, the majority of whose members also serve as the board of directors of a competing corporation.

**Interstate trade** Trade between and among states within the United States. (Trade within a single state is called intrastate trade.)

**Investment** Any use of today's resources to expand tomorrow's production; the portion of total output that will be used to produce goods in the future; can also be viewed as the spending by businesses on things, such as machines and buildings, that can be used to produce goods and services in the future.

## J

**Just-in-time inventory control** A manufacturing technique in which parts are supplied at the last minute, rather than being inventoried for a long time before they are needed in the production process.

## K

**Keynesian economics** A school of economic thought that tends to favor active federal government policymaking to stabilize economy-wide fluctuations, usually by implementing discretionary fiscal policy.

## L

**Labor** Human effort directed toward producing goods and services.

**Labor force** All persons over 16 who are not in school or other institutions and are either working or actively looking for work.

**Labor force participation rate** The percentage of noninstitutionalized working-age individuals who are employed or seeking employment.

**Labor productivity** The amount of product that a worker can produce in a given time period; total real GDP divided by the number of workers (output per worker).

**Labor unions** Associations of workers organized to improve wages and working conditions for their members.

**Land** Natural resources plus surface land and water.

**Law of demand** An economic rule stating that the quantity demanded and price move in opposite directions.

**Law of diminishing returns** An economic rule that says as more units of a factor of production (such as labor) are added to a given amount of other factors of production (such as equipment), total output continues to increase but at a diminishing rate.

**Law of supply** An economic rule stating that price and quantity supplied move in the same direction.

**Limited liability** Limitation of an owner's responsibility for a company's debts to the size of the owner's investment in the firm.

**Limited liability company (LLC)** A hybrid form of business enterprise that offers the limited liability of the corporation but the tax advantages of a partnership.

**Liquidity** The degree to which an asset can be acquired or disposed of without much danger of any intervening loss in nominal value and with small transaction costs. Money is the most liquid asset.

**Lockout** A situation that occurs when management prevents workers from returning to work until they agree to a new contract.

**Loose monetary policy** Monetary policy that makes credit inexpensive and abundant, possibly leading to inflation.

## M

**Macroeconomics** The study of economy-wide phenomena such as unemployment, inflation, interest rates, and government stabilization policies.

**Macroeconomy** The economy as a whole.

**Marginal benefit** Additional benefit resulting from doing a small incremental amount of an activity, i.e., the extra revenue a firm gets when it sells one more unit of output.

**Marginal costs** The change in total costs due to a one-unit change in the production rate.

**Marginal factor cost (MFC)** The cost of using an additional unit of an input. For example, if a firm can hire all the workers it wants at the going wage rate, the MFC of labor is the wage rate.

**Marginal physical product** The change in output resulting from the addition of one more worker. The marginal physical product of the worker equals the change in total output accounted for by hiring the worker, holding all other factors of production constant.

**Marginal physical product (MPP) of labor** The change in output resulting from the addition of one more worker. The MPP of the worker equals the change in total output accounted for by hiring the worker, holding all other factors of production constant.

**Marginal propensity to consume (MPC)** The ratio of the change in consumption to the change in disposable income. A marginal propensity to consume of 0.8 indicates that an additional $100 in take-home pay will lead to an additional $80 consumed.

**Marginal propensity to save (MPS)** The ratio of the change in saving to the change in disposable income. A marginal propensity to save of 0.2 indicates that out of an additional $100 in take-home pay, $20 will be saved. Whatever is not saved is consumed.

**Marginal revenue** The change in total revenues due to a one-unit change in output or sales.

**Marginal revenue product (MRP)** The marginal physical product (MPP) times marginal revenue. The MRP gives the additional revenue obtained from a one-unit change in labor input.

**Marginal tax rate** The change in the tax payment divided by the change in income; the percentage of additional dollars that must be paid in taxes. The marginal tax rate is applied to the highest tax bracket of taxable income reached.

**Marginal utility** An additional amount of satisfaction.

**Market basket** A representative group of goods and services used to compile the consumer price index.

**Market clearing price** The price that clears the market, at which quantity demanded equals quantity supplied; the price where the demand curve intersects the supply curve.

**Market failures** Situations in which unrestrained market operations lead to either too few or too many resources going to a specific economic activity.

**Market share test** The percentage of a market that a particular firm supplies; used as the primary measure of market power.

**Market structure** The number, size, and interaction of firms in a given industry, or market.

**Median age** In a given population, the age at which there is an equal number of people who are younger and older than that particular age. Also, the midpoint in the age distribution in a nation.

**Medicare** A federal government program designed to help those over 65 pay for health care services.

**Medium of exchange** The function of money to serve as a means of payment for goods or services.

**Microeconomics** The study of decision making undertaken by individuals (or households) and by firms.

**Minimum wage** A wage floor, legislated by government, setting the lowest hourly rate that firms may legally pay workers.

**Monetarists** Supporters of the theory of monetarism, often linked with Milton Friedman.

**Monetary rule** The monetarists' belief that the Fed should allow the money supply to grow at a smooth, consistent rate per year and not use discretionary monetary policy to stimulate or slow the economy.

**Money market deposit accounts** Savings accounts with limited check-writing privileges.

**Money market mutual funds** Pools of funds from savers that managing firms use to purchase short-term financial assets such as Treasury bills.

**Money multiplier** The reciprocal of the required reserve ratio, assuming no leakages into currency and no excess reserves. Its maximum value is equal to 1 divided by the required reserve ratio.

**Money price** The price that we observe today, expressed in today's dollars. Also called the absolute or nominal price.

**Money supply** The amount of money in circulation. The definition varies depending on how many near moneys are included.

**Monopolistic competition** A market situation in which a large number of sellers offer similar but slightly different products and in which each has some control over price.

**Monopolization** The possession of monopoly power in the relevant market and the willful acquisition or maintenance of that power, as distinguished from growth or development as a consequence of a superior product, business acumen, or historical accident.

**Multiplier effect** The effect of a permanent change in investment spending or government spending that goes beyond the initial change in those two variables; rather, the change in the equilibrium level of real GDP is a multiple of the change in investment or government spending.

## N

**Nationalization** The process of converting private property to government ownership and control of that property.

**Natural monopoly** A monopoly that arises from the peculiar production characteristics in an industry. It usually arises when there are large economies of scale relative to the industry's demand, such that one firm can produce at a lower average cost than can be achieved by multiple firms.

**Near moneys** Assets, such as savings account balances, that can be turned into money relatively easily and without the risk of loss of value.

**Needs** The bare minimum for subsistence.

**Negative externalities** The results of a production or consumption activity that impose costs on third parties; for example, pollution from a factory and congestion from driving.

**Net exports** The difference between exports and imports; can be (and has been) negative, meaning that we import more than we export.

**Net public debt** The gross public debt minus all government interagency borrowing.

**Net worth** Usually defined as the difference between what you own and what you owe. Otherwise stated, the market value of stocks, bonds, houses, and the like minus all of your debts.

**Nominal price** The same as the money price of a good or service; the price you pay for anything in today's dollars.

**Nominal rate of interest** The market rate of interest at any point in time.

**Noncooperative behavior** Behavior among individuals or firms in which the parties attempt to maximize their own welfare at the expense of other parties. With noncooperative behavior, the parties neither negotiate nor cooperate in any way.

## O

**Oligopoly** A market structure in which the industry has a few sellers that supply a large percentage of the total output of the industry. Oligopolists have some control over price.

**Open economy effect** The change in net exports resulting from a change in the price level, all other things held constant; one of the reasons that the aggregate demand curve slopes downward. A higher price level reduces net exports because foreign residents tend to buy fewer U.S.-made goods, while U.S. residents buy more foreign-made goods. These actions combine to yield to a reduction in the amount of real goods and services purchased in the United States.

**Open market operations** Buying and selling of U.S. Treasury securities by the Fed to affect the money supply.

**Opportunistic behavior** Actions that ignore the possible long-run benefits of cooperation and focus solely on short-run gains.

**Opportunity cost** The value of the next-best alternative given up for the alternative that was chosen.

**Outsourcing** Assembling a product in a different country. With respect to services, the purchasing of services in another country that are then transferred back to the home country, often via the Internet.

## P

**Partnership** A noncorporate form of business owned and operated by two or more individuals.

**Patent** Government protection that gives an inventor the exclusive right to make, use, or sell an invention for a specified number of years.

**Per capita GDP** GDP divided by population.

**Per capita real GDP** Gross domestic product, corrected for inflation and then divided by the population for any given year.

**Perfect competition** A market situation in which there are numerous buyers and sellers, and no single buyer or seller can affect price.

**Personal consumption expenditures** Expenditures by individuals and households on consumption items such as restaurant meals and airline travel; sometimes just called consumption.

**Physical capital** Factories, equipment, and improvements to natural resources.

**Positive externality** A benefit from a production or consumption activity that is bestowed on third parties without them having to pay for this benefit; for example, you spend time to maintain a flower bed bordering your property with the result that all passersby benefit from its beauty, but do not have to pay for your time and expenses.

**Price discrimination** Selling a given product at more than one price, with the price difference being unrelated to differences in cost.

**Price elasticity of demand** The degree to which consumers respond to a given change in the price of a particular good or service; measured in terms of the relative change in quantity demanded compared to the relative in price.

**Price index** The cost of today's market basket of goods and services expressed as a percentage of the cost of the same market basket during a base year.

**Price leadership** A practice in many oligopolistic industries whereby the largest firm publishes its price list ahead of its competitors, which then match those announced prices.

**Price setter** A firm, other than a perfectly competitive one, that can control the price at which it sells its product. Price setters face downward-sloping demand curves.

**Price system** An economic system in which relative prices are constantly changing to reflect changes in the supply of and demand for different commodities. The prices of those commodities are signals to everyone within the system as to what is relatively scarce and what is relatively abundant.

**Price taker** A competitive firm that must take the price of its product as given because the firm cannot influence its price.

**Price war** A pricing campaign designed to capture additional market share by repeatedly cutting prices.

**Price-fixing agreement** An agreement between competitors to fix the prices of products or services at a certain level; prohibited by the Sherman Act.

**Principle of diminishing marginal utility** A principle, law, or rule that asserts that as consumers consume more of any given good or service, at a point in time, the additional (marginal) utility of even more units will continue to decline.

**Principle of rival consumption** The recognition that individuals are rivals in consuming private goods because one person's consumption reduces the amount available for others to consume.

**Private costs** Costs borne solely by the individuals who generate them; also called internal costs.

**Private goods** Goods that can be consumed by only one individual at a time. Private goods are subject to the principle of rival consumption.

**Production function** The relationship between inputs and maximum physical output.

**Production possibilities curve** A graph showing the maximal combinations of goods and services that can be produced from a fixed amount of resources in a given period of time.

**Productivity** The amount of output (goods and services) that results from a given level of inputs (land, labor, capital, and entrepreneurship); often measured in terms of how much output a given amount of labor input can produce.

**Profits** The differences between total revenues and total costs.

**Progressive taxation** A tax that takes a larger percentage of higher incomes than lower incomes.

**Property rights** The rights of an owner to use and to exchange property. When property rights are well defined, owners of property have an incentive to use their property efficiently. When property rights are ill defined, few owners of property are interested in making sure that what they own is used efficiently.

**Proportional taxation** A tax that takes the same percentage of all incomes. As income rises, the amount of tax paid also rises in proportion.

**Public debt** The accumulation of all past federal government deficits; the total amount owed by the federal government to individuals, businesses, and foreigners.

**Public goods** Goods for which the principle of rival consumption does not apply; they can be jointly consumed by many individuals simultaneously at no additional cost and with no reduction in quality or quantity. Also, non-payers cannot be excluded.

**Purchasing power** The value of money for buying goods and services. If your money income stays the same but the price of one good that you are buying goes up, your effective purchasing power falls, and vice versa.

**Pure monopoly** A market situation in which there is only one seller of a good or service with no close substitutes.

## R

**Rational self-interest** An assumption that we will never consciously choose an alternative that will make us worse off.

**Rationing function of prices** Because both consumers and producers respond to price changes, when prices go up, consumers wish to buy less and producers wish to produce more. Prices reflect relative scarcity and thereby ration available goods and services in our market economy.

**Real GDP** GDP corrected for inflation, or changes in the average of all prices over time.

**Real income effect** The change in people's purchasing power that occurs when, other things being constant, the price of one good that they purchase changes. When that price goes up, real income, or purchasing power, falls, and when that price goes down, real income increases.

**Real rate of interest** The nominal rate of interest minus the anticipated rate of inflation.

**Real-balance effect** The change in planned expenditures resulting from the change in the real value of cash balances when the price level changes, all other things held constant; also called the wealth effect. A reason that the aggregate demand curve slopes downward.

**Recession** A period of time during which the rate of growth of business activity is consistently less than its long-term trend. Another definition is when there is negative economic growth for at least two quarters (six months).

**Recognition time lag** The time required to gather information about the current state of the economy.

**Regressive taxation** A tax that takes a larger percentage of lower incomes than higher incomes.

**Regulation** A way in which government at all levels—federal, state, and local—imposes rules on business activities. These rules may take the form of economic regulation, in which prices or profits are regulated, or social regulation, in which the method of production or the way workers are treated is delineated by government.

**Relative price** The price of one commodity divided by the price of another commodity; the number of units of one commodity that must be sacrificed to purchase one unit of another commodity.

**Research and development (R&D)** The exploration of new scientific concepts and systems, new production methods, new chemical compounds, and the like, coupled with the development of the research results so that they can later be used in actual production.

**Reserve requirements** Regulations set by the Fed requiring banks to keep a certain percentage of their deposits as cash in their own vaults or as deposits in their Federal Reserve district bank.

**Reserves** In the Federal Reserve System, deposits held by Federal Reserve district banks for depository institutions, plus depository institutions' vault cash.

**Resources** Things used to produce other things to satisfy people's wants.

## S

**S corporation** A corporation in which the profits and losses pass directly through to the individual owners, who then pay federal personal income taxes on any profits. Similar to a corporation because of limited liability and to a partnership because only the individual pays the income taxes rather than the business entity.

**Saving** Setting aside income for a period of time so that it can be used later.

**Savings deposits** Interest-bearing savings accounts without set maturities.

**Scarcity** The condition of not being able to have all of the goods and services one wants, because wants exceed what can be made from all available resources at any given time.

**Seasonal unemployment** Unemployment resulting from the seasonal pattern of work in specific industries. It is usually due to seasonal fluctuations in demand or to changing weather conditions that render work difficult, if not impossible, as in the agricultural, construction, and tourist industries.

**Share of stock** A legal claim to a share of a corporation's future profits. If it is common stock, it incorporates certain voting rights regarding major policy decisions of the corporation.

**Short run** The time period when at least one input, such as plant size, cannot be changed.

**Shortage** The situation in which the quantity demanded is greater than the quantity supplied at a price below the market clearing price.

**Signal** A compact method of conveying to economic decision makers information needed to make decisions. A true signal not only conveys information but also provides the incentive to react appropriately. Economic profits and economic losses are such signals.

**Signaling behavior** Behavior that either implicitly or explicitly gives a signal to a third party about the intentions of the entity doing the signaling. Companies that invest large amounts in advertising give signals to consumers that the product and the company will be around for a long time.

**Small-denomination time deposits** Deposits with set maturities and denominations of less than $100,000.

**Smart cards** Cards with an embedded microchip that contains information that various machines can access and read; for example, European phone cards, which have a specific amount of phone-use units that are debited each time a phone call is made.

**Social regulation** Any method of government regulation that imposes rules on how a productive activity is undertaken; for example, environmental and worker safety regulations.

**Sole proprietorship** A noncorporate business owned and operated by one person.

**Specialization** The division of productive activities among persons and regions so that no one individual or one area is totally self-sufficient. An individual may specialize, for example, in law or medicine. A nation may specialize in the production of coffee, computers, or cameras.

**Speculators** Those who assume a business risk in the hope of gains; those who buy and sell in expectation of profiting from market fluctuations.

**Strategic dependence** A situation in which one firm's actions with respect to price, quality, advertising, and the like may be strategically countered by the reactions of one or more other firms in the industry. Such dependence can exist only when there are a limited number of major firms in an industry.

**Strike** Deliberate work stoppage by workers to force an employer to give in to their demands.

**Strikebreakers** Temporary or permanent workers hired by a company to replace union members who are striking.

**Structural unemployment** Unemployment resulting from a poor match of workers' abilities and skills with current requirements of employers.

**Subsidy** A negative tax; a payment to a producer from the government, usually in the form of a cash grant.

**Substitutes** Two goods that can be used for consumption to satisfy a similar want—for example, coffee and tea. For substitutes, a change in the price of one causes a shift in demand for the other in the same direction as the price change.

**Substitution effect** The change in the quantity demanded due to the substitution of a relatively cheaper good for a relatively more expensive good.

**Supply curve** A graphic representation of the supply schedule, showing the various quantities supplied associated with different prices.

**Supply schedule** A table showing the quantities supplied at different possible prices.

**Surplus** The situation in which quantity supplied is greater than quantity demanded at a particular price above the market clearing price.

## T

**Tacit collusion** Collusion among market participants—usually business firms—without those firms actually meeting and deciding on an explicit action such as fixing prices or dividing up a market.

**Tariffs** Taxes on imported goods.

**Tax bracket** A specified interval of income to which a specific and unique marginal tax rate is applied.

**Technological monopoly** A monopoly that usually arises from an invention that has been patented.

**Theory of contestable markets** A hypothesis concerning pricing behavior that holds that even though there are only a few firms in an industry, they are forced to price their products more or less competitively because of the ease of entry by outsiders. The key aspect of a contestable market is relatively cheap entry into and exit from the industry.

**Thrift institutions** Savings and loan associations, savings banks, and credit unions.

**Tight monetary policy** Monetary policy that makes credit expensive in an effort to slow the economy.

**Total costs** The sum of total fixed costs and total variable costs.

**Trade deficit** The negative difference between exports of goods and imports of goods.

**Trademark** A distinctive mark or motto that a manufacturer stamps, prints, or otherwise affixes to the goods it produces so that they may be identified on the market and their origins made known. Once a trademark is established, the owner is entitled to its exclusive use.

**Trade-off** Sacrificing one good or service to obtain or produce another.

**Transaction costs** All of the costs associated with exchanging; the costs associated with making, reaching, and enforcing agreements, particularly for the exchange of goods and services.

**Trust** In the business context, an arrangement in which owners of firms in the same industry temporarily pass the ownership of their business to a trustee who then runs all of the businesses for the benefit of their owners, usually in a manner more consistent with monopoly than with competition.

## U

**Unanticipated inflation** Inflation at a rate that comes as a surprise, either higher or lower than the rate anticipated.

**Unemployment** The inability of those who are in the labor force to find a job; sometimes referred to as the total number of those in the labor force actively looking for a job, but unable to find one.

**Unilateral transfers** One-way transfers that typically involve individuals in one country making gifts to other individuals residing in other countries. They are one-way transfers because those making the gifts receive nothing tangible in exchange.

**Unit of accounting** The function of money to serve as a yardstick for comparing the values of goods and services in relation to one another.

**Unit-elastic demand** If a given change in price leads to an exactly proportionate change in quantity demanded, this represents unit-elastic demand.

**Unlimited liability** The requirement that an owner is personally and fully responsible for all losses and debts of a business.

**Utility** The ability of any good or service to satisfy consumer wants; the amount of satisfaction one gets from a good or service.

**Utils** A hypothetical representative unit by which utility might be measured, even though we know that it cannot be measured. Thus, a util is an analytical construct only.

## V

**Variable costs** Costs that vary with the rate of production. They include wages paid to workers and purchases of materials.

## W

**Wants** What people would buy if their incomes were unlimited.

**Wealth** Those things of value owned by a person, household, firm, or nation. Household wealth usually consists of a house, cars, stocks and bonds, bank accounts, and personal belongings.

# Index

## A



## B

## C



## D

## G



## H



## I

## V



## W



## Y



## Z

Name Class Date

# CHAPTER 8
## HOMEWORK SET

**8-1.** In 1920, the Eighteenth Amendment to the U.S. Constitution, also known as the Volstead Act, prohibited the manufacture, sale, and transportation of alcohol throughout the United States. In response to the prohibition law, what actions were taken by individuals and organizations that fall under the heading of creative response?

**8-2.** What are the four areas in which the Environmental Protection Agency develops and enforces standards as part of its regulatory functions?

**8-3.** If each U.S. adult citizen were required to pay an equal income tax amount of $18,500, would this tax system be progressive, proportional, or regressive?

**8-4.** What are the two conditions that must be met in order for an imperfectly competitive market to be considered a contestable market?

**8-5.** What actions are specifically prohibited by the Clayton Act?

**8-6.** If I earn $50,000 and pay $12,000 in taxes and my brother earns $75,000 and pays $20,000 in taxes, is our tax system progressive, proportional, or regressive?

**8-7.** Assume that Danielle earns $55,000 and pays $13,500 in federal income taxes. What is her average tax rate? Using the average tax rate that you just computed, is it possible to determine how much Danielle will pay if she earns an additional $1,000 this year?

**8-8.** A flu shot is a good that implies an external benefit; those around you are less likely to become ill if you get a flu shot. Would an unregulated market produce too much of this good or too little? Would the market price for this good be too high or too low?

**8-9.** Some consider a highway to be a public good. However, do additional users ever take away from your benefits of using a highway? Is it possible to design a collection system for the use of a highway?

**8-10.** What external benefits are created when I buy and drive a gasoline-electric hybrid car? How could the government attempt to promote the use of such vehicles by means of the tax system?

Name Class Date

# CHAPTER 9
## HOMEWORK SET

**9-1.** If the equilibrium wage is $4.50 and the government sets a minimum wage of $5.25, would this lead to a shortage, a surplus, or neither?

**9-2.** Assuming that any union's primary goal is to increase wages for its members, state two reasons related to supply and demand for teachers' unions encouraging their members to obtain higher degrees.

**9-3.** What accounts for the spike in union membership around 1920? (Hint: Consider information from the previous chapter.)

**9-4.** If the demand for U.S. automobiles increases, what will happen to the demand for U.S. autoworkers? What will happen to the wages of these autoworkers? What will happen to the number of autoworkers employed?

**9-5.** If the productivity of your employees increases, will this increase or decrease your demand for labor?

**9-6.** Professional baseball players earn salaries that range up to $25 million per year. Describe the supply of and demand for labor in this field that create such immense salaries.

**9-7.** If the price of diesel fuel increases dramatically, what will this do to the demand for truck drivers? What will this do to truck drivers' wages and the number of truck drivers who have found work?

**9-8.** Use the daily information in the table below to compute marginal physical product, total revenue, and marginal revenue product.

| Workers | Total Output | Marginal Physical Product | Output Price | Total Revenue | Marginal Revenue Product |
|---|---|---|---|---|---|
| 6 | 1,000 | ___ | $2.00 | ___ | ___ |
| 7 | 1,250 | ___ | 1.90 | ___ | ___ |
| 8 | 1,450 | ___ | 1.80 | ___ | ___ |
| 9 | 1,625 | ___ | 1.70 | ___ | ___ |
| 10 | 1,775 | ___ | 1.60 | ___ | ___ |

**9-9.** Based on the table in problem 9-8, how many workers should this firm hire in order to maximize its profits if the wage per day is $120? Does this firm sell its product in a perfectly competitive market?

**9-10.** Compute marginal factor cost from the two tables below and use your results to answer the following questions. In a perfectly competitive labor market, how does the marginal factor cost of labor compare to the wage rate? In a labor market that is not perfectly competitive, how does the marginal factor cost compare to the wage rate?

Perfectly Competitive Labor Market

| Weekly Wage | Workers | Total Salary Expense | Marginal Factor Cost |
|---|---|---|---|
| $300 | 5 | $___ | $___ |
| 300 | 6 | ___ | ___ |
| 300 | 7 | ___ | ___ |
| 300 | 8 | ___ | ___ |

Imperfectly Competitive Labor Market

| Weekly Wage | Workers | Total Salary Expense | Marginal Factor Cost |
|---|---|---|---|
| $300 | 5 | $___ | $___ |
| 350 | 6 | ___ | ___ |
| 400 | 7 | ___ | ___ |
| 450 | 8 | ___ | ___ |

Name Class Date

# CHAPTER 10
## HOMEWORK SET

**10-1.** List the four categories of unemployment.

**10-2.** What measurement tool constructed by the Bureau of Labor Statistics is used to measure changes in the level of prices of goods and services?

**10-3.** Who would benefit from unanticipated inflation—lenders or borrowers? Why? Who would benefit from anticipated inflation—lenders, borrowers, or neither? Why?

**10-4.** If there were 1.5 million unemployed persons in Canada with 15.5 million employed and a population of 20 million, what would the unemployment rate equal? What would the labor force participation rate equal?

**10-5.** In 2000, a price index for medical care in the United States increased from 254 to 265. Based on these figures, compute the rate of inflation or percentage increase in prices for this industry. How does this price change compare to that across the economy that year?

**10-6.** If the nominal interest rate on my mortgage is 3.9 percent and the expected rate of inflation for next year is 0.5 percent, what real interest rate will my mortgage lender earn?

**10-7.** Holding everything else constant, if the government were to decrease welfare, unemployment, and Social Security disability payments, how would this action change the labor force participation rate? How would it change the unemployment rate? What would be the immediate impact of this action on the level of income inequality? In the short term, would this action likely cause an increase or decrease in the urban crime rate?

**10-8.** Assume that at some point in your life, you will maintain several bank accounts including a checking account and a money market account. You might pay a fee of $100 each year for your bank to sweep funds to and from your checking account depending on the balances. At the same time, you might have a job that provides for an increase in your salary based on changes in the rate of inflation. In this situation, does a loss in purchasing power represent a cost of inflation? Why or why not? Do your banking fees represent a cost of inflation? Why or why not?

**10-9.** Assume that you loaned me $1,000 at a very generous nominal interest rate of 3 percent to be paid back in one year. There is a sudden upturn in the economy, however, and inflation increases to 5 percent next year. As a result, when I repay you the $1,000 plus your $30 interest, has your purchasing power increased or decreased as a result of this loan and the interest that you received? What would your real rate of return equal? Based on your answers to the previous two questions and with the benefit of hindsight, what is the lowest nominal interest that you would be willing to accept in this situation?

**10-10.** If GDP and the rate of inflation increased and the unemployment rate decreased, what phase of the business cycle would we assume the economy is in?

Name Class Date

# CHAPTER 11
## HOMEWORK SET

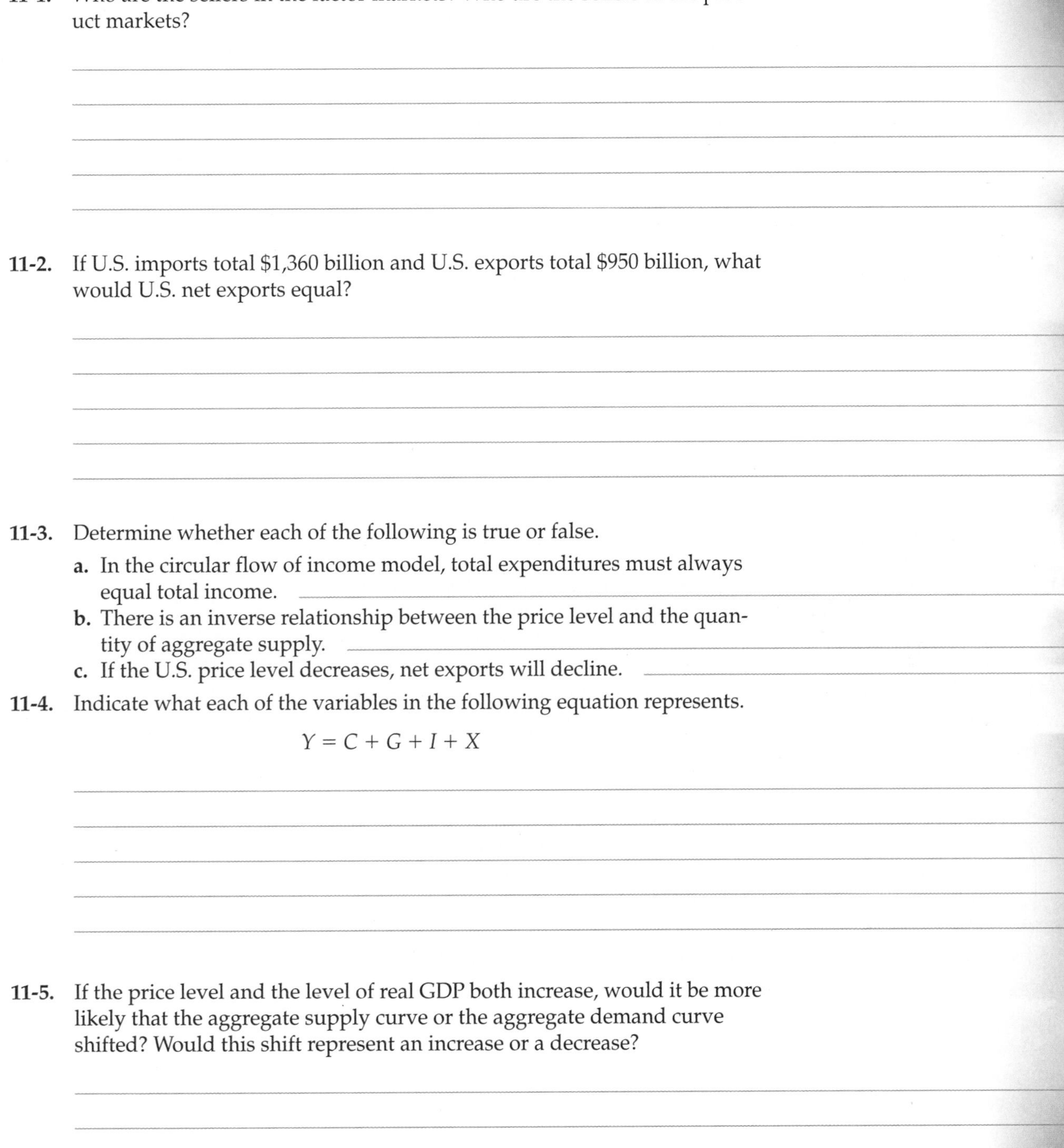

**11-1.** Who are the sellers in the factor markets? Who are the sellers in the product markets?

**11-2.** If U.S. imports total $1,360 billion and U.S. exports total $950 billion, what would U.S. net exports equal?

**11-3.** Determine whether each of the following is true or false.

**a.** In the circular flow of income model, total expenditures must always equal total income. ______

**b.** There is an inverse relationship between the price level and the quantity of aggregate supply. ______

**c.** If the U.S. price level decreases, net exports will decline. ______

**11-4.** Indicate what each of the variables in the following equation represents.

$$Y = C + G + I + X$$

**11-5.** If the price level and the level of real GDP both increase, would it be more likely that the aggregate supply curve or the aggregate demand curve shifted? Would this shift represent an increase or a decrease?

**11-6.** In terms of aggregate demand and aggregate supply, what does the graph below depict?

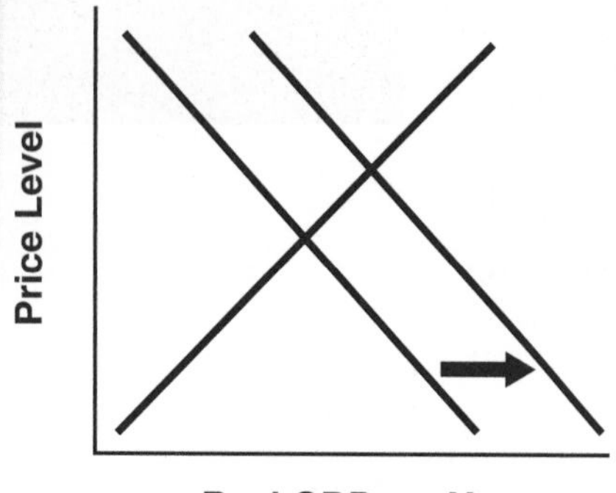


**11-7.** If the price of Pepsi increases, U.S. consumers can easily substitute to another brand of cola in the same stores. If the price level of all U.S. goods increases, to what type of goods would U.S. consumers have to substitute in order to avoid the higher prices? What would this do to the quantity demanded of all U.S. goods?

**11-8.** What would happen to the aggregate supply curve if worker productivity increased as a result of increased training and education?

**11-9.** Assume that you go on vacation to France. If the exchange rate value of the dollar increased in relation to the French currency, the euro, would the goods you purchase in France become more or less expensive to you? Would you be likely to buy more goods or fewer goods while in France?

**11-10.** Which of the following could lead to inflation? (More than one answer may be correct.)

**a.** an increase in aggregate supply ______

**b.** an increase in aggregate demand ______

**c.** a decrease in aggregate supply ______

**d.** a decrease in aggregate demand ______

Name Class Date

# CHAPTER 12
## HOMEWORK SET

**12-1.** If an increase in government expenditures is financed by an equal increase in taxation, what impact will these actions have on the economy? If the same increase in government expenditures is financed by additional borrowing by the federal government, what will the impact be?

**12-2.** Indicate whether each of the following would be considered an automatic stabilizer.

**a.** The president encourages Congress to decrease taxes prior to an election.

**b.** A higher level of jobless claims results in an increase in total disbursements of unemployment compensation.

**c.** An expansion in the economy increases the average person's income level, forcing some people into higher tax brackets.

**d.** The U.S. Congress increases highway spending programs in order to benefit local businesses.

**12-3.** If the marginal propensity to consume increases, what will happen to the expenditure multiplier? If the marginal propensity to save increases, what will happen to the expenditure multiplier?

**12-4.** If the average person spends \$90 out of every \$100 he or she earns, what does the multiplier equal?

**12-5.** Explain the difference between the gross public debt and the net public debt.

**12-6.** If the economy is moving too slowly, which economic problem is more likely to exist—high unemployment or high inflation? In this situation, should the federal government increase taxes or decrease taxes? Should the federal government increase or decrease government spending?

**12-7.** Indicate which fiscal policy time lag each of the following describes.

**a.** the time needed for policymakers to change the laws

**b.** the time needed for the change in policy to have an effect on the economy

**c.** the time needed for policymakers to realize that a problem exists

**12-8.** If my marginal propensity to save is 0.15, what is my marginal propensity to consume? What multiplier do these figures imply?

**12-9.** If the multiplier is 15 and the government increased government spending by $30 billion, holding all other factors constant, how much would real GDP increase? If the government decreased government spending by $30 billion, how much would real GDP decrease?

**12-10.** If unemployment is a significant problem, should the federal government take action that would increase or decrease the deficit? Why?

Name Class Date

# CHAPTER 13
## HOMEWORK SET

**13-1.** List all of the components of M1.

**13-2.** Indicate whether each of the following statements is true or false.

**a.** The U.S. Treasury is responsible for clearing all checks for credit unions.

**b.** A Federal Reserve district bank is located in Washington, D.C.

**c.** The Fed can be thought of as a "bank for banks."

**d.** The Fed's most important task is probably the regulation of the money supply.

**13-3.** How many Federal Reserve district banks are there? What is the function of the Federal Reserve district banks?

**13-4.** If the reserve requirement is 20 percent and Hanna deposits $1,000 into her checking account at Bank of America, how much of this deposit will this bank only be required to hold in reserves?

**13-5.** What potential money multiplier would result from a reserve requirement of only 5 percent?

**13-6.** If the reserve requirement is 12 percent and I deposit $800 in cash, what amount of excess reserves are immediately created at my bank only?

**13-7.** If the Fed injects $200 million of new money (reserves) into the banking system by purchasing a U.S. government security and the money multiplier is 10, by what maximum amount could the money supply increase?

**13-8.** If we did not have money to use as a medium of exchange, what type of transactions would we be limited to?

**13-9.** Will a larger reserve requirement increase or decrease the money multiplier? Why?

**13-10.** Why do banks want to loan out as much of their excess reserves as possible?

# CHAPTER 14
## Homework Set

**14-1.** If monetary policy decision makers believe that GDP is growing too slowly, will they increase or decrease the discount rate?

**14-2.** Will the aggregate supply curve or the aggregate demand curve shift as a result of expansionary monetary policy? In which direction will this curve shift? For what two reasons would we expect to see this curve shift?

**14-3.** To sell government securities, does the Fed have to offer a price lower or higher than the current market price? Based on your answer, will this price change lead to an increase or a decrease in interest rates?

**14-4.** If the Fed sold government securities as indicated in problem 14-3, holding all else constant, what impact would this action likely have on GDP, unemployment, and inflation?

**14-5.** If inflation is the most significant problem facing the U.S. economy, should the Fed buy or sell government securities? What impact will this action likely have on the money supply and interest rates?

**14-6.** Indicate whether each of the following statements is true or false.

**a.** Open market operations are the most frequently used monetary policy tool. ______

**b.** The Fed is a branch of the U.S. Treasury. ______

**c.** In the long run, an increase in the money supply will lead to an increase in inflation. ______

**d.** The recognition lag associated with monetary policy is much longer than the recognition lag associated with fiscal policy. ______

**14-7.** How successful was the Fed at counteracting the effects of the business cycle from the 1930s through the 1980s? How successful was the Fed during the 1990s?

**14-8.** Over an extended period of time, will an increase in the money supply cause an increase or a decrease in inflation? Why? What historical evidence from the chapter can be used to support your conclusion?

**14-9.** What school of economic thought believes that the direct effect of monetary policy is highly significant? What school of economic thought believes that the indirect effect of monetary policy is highly significant?

**14-10.** What are the macroeconomic goals of monetary policy? How are the goals of the central banks in other countries different from those of the U.S. central bank?

Name Class Date

# CHAPTER 15
## HOMEWORK SET

**15-1.** The real GDP of Nicaragua adjusted into U.S. dollars increased from approximately \$11.7 billion in 1999 to \$12.4 billion in 2000. The population increased from 4.7 million to 4.8 million over the same time period. Based on these figures, did per capita real GDP increase or not?

**15-2.** Compare the average annual growth rate of per capita income of the United States with the growth rates of other countries such as the United Kingdom, Germany, and Japan.

**15-3.** Is there a direct or an inverse relationship between the rate of saving and the growth rate of per capita real GDP? Why?

**15-4.** Based on the information in the table below, did labor productivity increase or decrease?

| Real GDP (in billions) | Number of Hours Worked per Week |
|---|---|
| \$3,000 | 40 |
| \$3,150 | 43 |

**15-5.** Determine whether each of the following statements is true or false.

**a.** Radical changes in the money supply will often lead to sustained economic growth. ______

**b.** The level of investment is directly correlated with the rate of saving. ______

**c.** If a production possibilities curve shifts outward to a minimal degree, this movement would indicate a limited degree of economic growth. ______

**d.** Substantial barriers to international trade are correlated with limited economic growth rates. ______

**15-6.** Holding all else constant, if the length of the average U.S. workweek increased from 35 hours to 39 hours, would U.S. workers be better off or worse off? How would this development affect per capita real GDP?

**15-7.** What type of investment in human capital will serve to increase the quality of the labor force?

**15-8.** Name three important rules for economic growth.

**15-9.** If people in general save a smaller percentage of their income, holding all else constant, what might be the impact on the growth rate of the economy? Why?

**15-10.** If the economy grew at an annual rate of 3 percent, by what percent would the economy expand within 10 years? Within 20 years? Within 50 years?

Name Class Date

# CHAPTER 16
## HOMEWORK SET

**16-1.** Which concept is more important with respect to specialization—comparative advantage or absolute advantage? Why?

______________________________

______________________________

**16-2.** Based on the graph below, if the United States established an import quota of 1 million 32-inch televisions, what would be the price of the imported TVs?

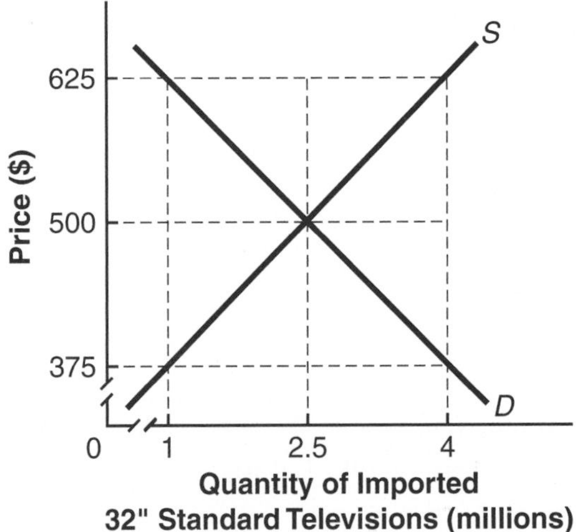


______________________________

______________________________

**16-3.** Based on the fact that the United States imports a much greater quantity of toys, games, and sporting goods than it exports, what, if anything, would you assume has happened to our comparative advantage in these areas? What, if anything, would you assume has happened to our absolute advantage in these areas? Briefly explain your answers.

______________________________

______________________________

**16-4.** Determine whether each of the following statements is true or false.

**a.** All the components of all products labeled "made in U.S.A." are made completely in the United States. ______________

**b.** Exports are more important to the U.S. economy than to the economy of other countries such as Belgium and Sweden. ______________

**c.** Currently, U.S. imports account for approximately 14 percent of GDP. ______________

**d.** Reducing inventory levels is an idea that spread to U.S. businesses as a result of international trade. ______________

**16-5.** If the U.S. government were to remove an existing tariff on steel, what would this do to the price of imported steel? What effect would the government's action have on the price of domestic steel? Why?

**16-6.** Describe the EU and NAFTA with as much detail as possible in terms of their roles as a common market or free trade zone.

**16-7.** Based on the table below indicating worker-hours needed for production of one unit of each good, which country has an absolute advantage for each of these goods? Which country has a comparative advantage for each of these goods?

| | United States | Costa Rica |
|---|---|---|
| Baseball | 0.25 | 1 |
| Computers | 6.00 | 16 |

**16-8.** Using the information provided in problem 16-7 and assuming that free trade will take place, should the United States produce baseballs, computers, or both? Why?

**16-9.** Define the terms *import* and *export*. Give examples of goods that are frequently exported by the United States. Give examples of goods that are frequently imported by the United States.

**16-10.** If the U.S. government imposes a tariff on imports, which of the following groups will be adversely affected?

**a.** foreign producers

**b.** domestic producers

**c.** the domestic government

**d.** domestic consumers

Name Class Date

# CHAPTER 17
## HOMEWORK SET

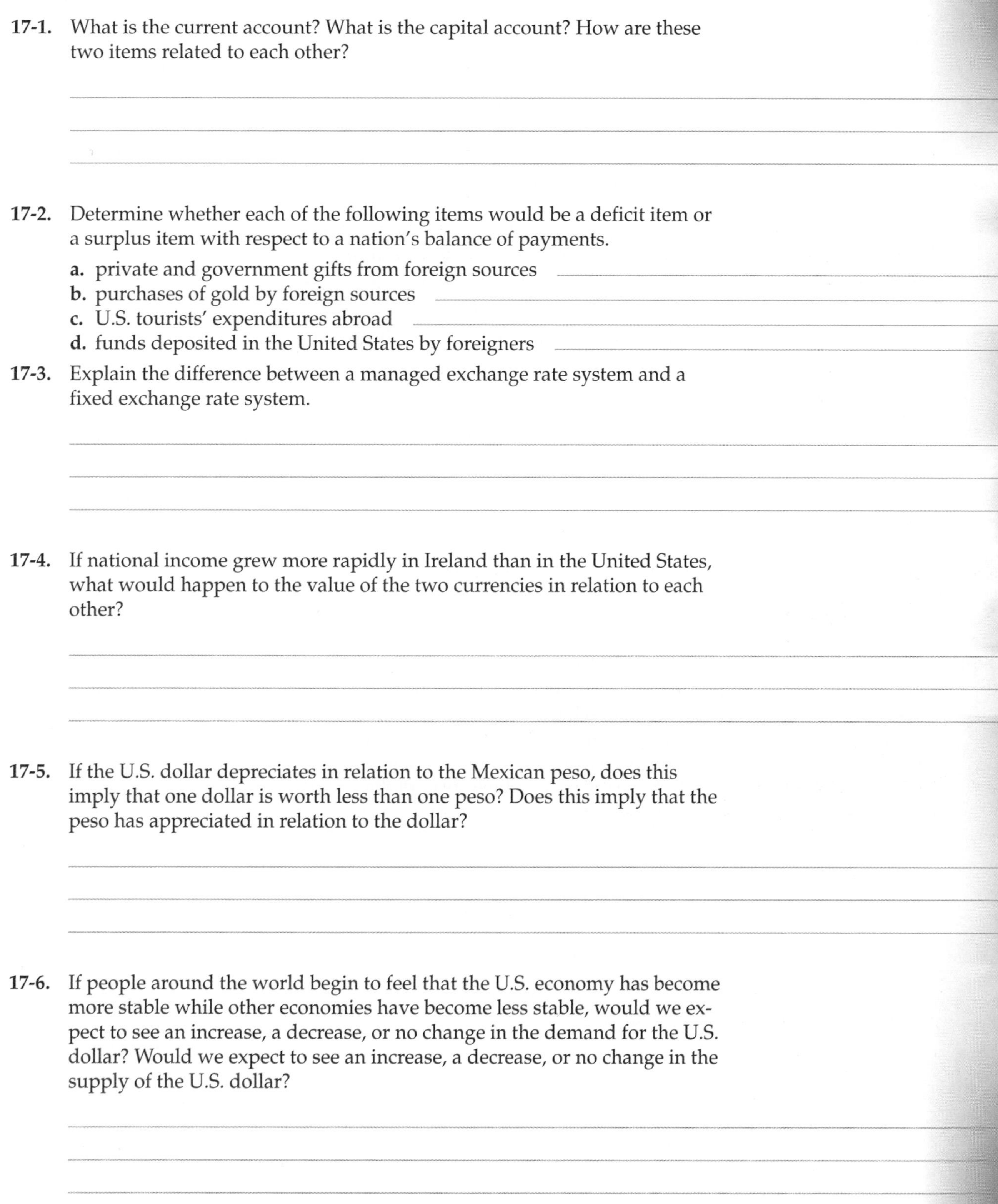

**17-1.** What is the current account? What is the capital account? How are these two items related to each other?

**17-2.** Determine whether each of the following items would be a deficit item or a surplus item with respect to a nation's balance of payments.

**a.** private and government gifts from foreign sources

**b.** purchases of gold by foreign sources

**c.** U.S. tourists' expenditures abroad

**d.** funds deposited in the United States by foreigners

**17-3.** Explain the difference between a managed exchange rate system and a fixed exchange rate system.

**17-4.** If national income grew more rapidly in Ireland than in the United States, what would happen to the value of the two currencies in relation to each other?

**17-5.** If the U.S. dollar depreciates in relation to the Mexican peso, does this imply that one dollar is worth less than one peso? Does this imply that the peso has appreciated in relation to the dollar?

**17-6.** If people around the world begin to feel that the U.S. economy has become more stable while other economies have become less stable, would we expect to see an increase, a decrease, or no change in the demand for the U.S. dollar? Would we expect to see an increase, a decrease, or no change in the supply of the U.S. dollar?

**17-7.** If the supply of the U.S. dollar decreases, what will happen to the exchange rate value of the dollar? What will happen to the quantity of U.S. dollars in the foreign exchange markets?

**17-8.** Determine whether each of the following statements is true or false.

**a.** Since 1977, the U.S. current account has always been in deficit. ______

**b.** If the United States exported more goods to Canada than it imported from Canada, we would say that the United States had a positive balance of trade. ______

**c.** The amount of services that the United States buys from other countries is greater than the amount of services that the United States sells to other countries. ______

**d.** Since 1977, the U.S. capital account has always been in deficit. ______

**17-9.** Holding all else constant, if the dollar depreciates in relation to the British pound, will U.S. goods become more expensive to the British, less expensive to the British, or not necessarily change in either direction? In the same situation, will U.S. goods become more expensive to the French, less expensive to the French, or not necessarily change in either direction?

**17-10.** Assume that the Canadian government decided to fix the exchange rate of the Canadian dollar in relation to the U.S. dollar. If the Bank of Canada, the central bank in that country, were to sell U.S. dollars, would this increase or decrease the exchange rate value of the Canadian dollar? Would this action increase or decrease the demand for Canadian goods? Would this action increase or decrease the purchasing power of the Canadian dollar?